WEAPONS *of* MASS DESTRUCTION

and TERRORISM

About the Authors

Brigadier General Russell D. Howard (Retired) was a career Special Forces officer and is now the director of the Jebsen Center for Counterterrorism Studies at the Fletcher School at Tufts University. His recent publications include *Terrorism and Counterterrorism: Understanding the New Security Environment—Readings and Interpretations,* 2nd ed. (McGraw-Hill, 2005), and *Defeating Terrorism: Shaping the New Security Environment* (McGraw-Hill, 2003), and *Homeland Security and Terrorism: Readings and Interpretations* (McGraw-Hill, 2005).

James J.F. Forest is director of terrorism studies and associate professor of political science at the U.S. Military Academy at West Point, where he teaches undergraduate courses on terrorism, counterterrorism, and information warfare, and directs research initiatives for the Combating Terrorism Center. His recent publications include *Teaching Terror: Strategic and Tactical Learning in the Terrorist World* (2006), *Homeland Security and Terrorism* (2005), and *The Making of a Terrorist: Recruitment, Training and Root Causes* (2005). His research has also appeared in the *Cambridge Review of International Affairs,* the *Journal of Political Science Education,* and *Democracy and Security.*

WEAPONS *of* MASS DESTRUCTION

---

and TERRORISM

Russell D Howard
Brigadier General USA (Ret)

James J. F. Forest
Combating Terrorism Center, West Point

With
Natasha Bajema

Foreword by
Ambassador Michael Sheehan

STAFF

Larry Loeppke   Managing Editor
Jill Peter   Senior Developmental Editor
Susan Brusch   Senior Developmental Editor
Lori Church   Permissions Coordinator
Beth Kundert   Production Manager
Jane Mohr   Project Manager
Maggie Lytle   Cover Designer

Cover: Corbis/Royalty Free

Compositor: Laserwords

The credit section for this book begins on page 596 and is considered an extension of the copyright page.

Library of Congress Control Number 1935-8431

MHID: 0-07-337970-0   ISBN: 978-0-07-337970-8

 Printed in the United States of America   123456789DOCDOC987

Brief Contents

Unit III

Responding to the Threat   331

Unit IV

Lessons Learned and Future Threats   459

Appendices   531

Contents

Unit III   Responding to the Threat 331

Unit IV   Lessons Learned and Future Threats 459

Foreword

The specter of terrorists using weapons of mass destruction (WMD) has dramatically shifted the way we think about our national security. The attacks of 11 September 2001 were the "wake-up call" to the threat of radical Islamic terrorism that had been brewing for many years. These attacks and the subsequent anthrax attacks via our postal system brought the discussion of terrorism and WMD to the forefront of the national security community and into the living rooms of everyday Americans. The relentless global pursuit of al Qaeda is meant not only to prevent them from attacking us again with conventional weapons, but also to prevent them from establishing the infrastructure to acquire or develop weapons of mass destruction. And of course, the war against Iraq was justified primarily on the notion that Americans cannot allow the chance of these weapons to fall into the hands of unrestrained terrorist organizations such as al Qaeda.

Five years after 9/11, it is appropriate to readdress the threat of WMD and terrorism. Conventional explosives, truck bombs, backpack bombs, and other improvised explosives have remained the weapon of choice for terrorist organizations around the world. These weapons are relatively easy to make and properly deployed can create significant damage and terrorize the intended target audience. However, there are limits as to what conventional explosives can accomplish for a terrorist organization. Most nations around the world that have been subjected to these explosive attacks have demonstrated a strong degree of resilience against this form of terror. For this reason, we know that a variety of terrorist organizations, including al Qaeda, have sought—and continue to seek—to acquire and use chemical, biological, radiological, or nuclear weapons to achieve their goals.

The United States and its allies are also concerned that rogue states such as North Korea and Iran continue to develop WMD capability, primarily nuclear. Pakistan has tested a nuclear weapon—and has been exposed for its role in proliferating nuclear technology. Scientific knowledge, including the information required to build improvised WMD systems, proliferates quickly and widely through the Internet. It is sobering to note that most of these weapons technologies are at least 50 years old. In a world of ever-accelerating technology transfer, the potential of these groups getting the knowledge and manufacturing capacity grows every year.

How serious is the threat today and over the next five to ten years? How can we prevent terrorists from developing these weapons from nations through intentional transfers or leaks within their national programs? And if we fail in our nonproliferation efforts, how can we protect ourselves or minimize the damage to our nation? These are the topics of this timely book, *Weapons of Mass Destruction and Terrorism.*

The book takes a balanced approach in terms of the threat perception, avoiding the pitfalls of WMD terrorism hype. Section I provides a detailed description of the security environment, the backdrop against which the growing threat of WMD terrorism takes place. Section II helps "deconstruct" the threat of WMD terrorism, illuminating its multidimensional nature, while Section III addresses the need to respond with a wide array of counterterrorism strategies and instruments depending on the specific type of CBRN weapon. Throughout the volume, chapters describe technical aspects of the threat, assess terrorist capabilities, describe possible scenarios, and make useful risk assessments that inform our strategic decisions and policymaking.

This is the fourth book in a series of terrorism-related texts coedited by Brigadier General (retired) Russell Howard for McGraw-Hill, and his second collaboration with Dr. James Forest. They are ideal coeditors of this book because collectively they have been researching, writing, and teaching on terrorism-related subjects for more than thirty years. They also personally know many of the world's best terrorism and WMD experts, many of whom are featured in this book. For my part, I appreciate their commitment and sustained contribution to the education of the next generation of security professionals, most of whom will someday find themselves working at the international, federal, state, and local level to design and implement effective measures against a determined enemy.

A book like this is long overdue. It would have been very useful in my offices both as the ambassador at large for counterterrorism at the State Department (1998 to 2000) and as the deputy commissioner for counterterrorism on the New York Police Department (2003 to 2006). In both positions, the threat of a terrorist equipped with weapons of mass destruction was constantly on my mind, yet the policy and academic literature on the subject was limited. As the chapters in this volume illustrate, there is much we still need to do in recognizing, understanding, and responding to the very real WMD terrorism threat in new and more informed ways. By bringing together long-standing voices in the fields of terrorism, counterterrorism, and WMD proliferation, the volume offers a unique collection of ideas, experiences, and opinions to bear on this important mission. In this respect, it will serve as an extraordinarily important contribution to the global dialogue on terrorism and national security for many years.

Michael A. Sheehan

Preface

Weapon of mass destruction (WMD) is a term describing munitions or other agents that have the capacity to kill and destroy on a massive scale. The phrase—first coined during the Spanish Civil War to characterize extensive German air raids—now generally refers to chemical, biological, radiological, and nuclear weapons.[1]

Relatively speaking, chemical and biological weapons are not new, but nuclear and radiological weapons are. Chemical "toxic fumes" were used in India as early as 2000 B.C. The first known use of biological warfare was in 1346 at Caffa (now Fedossia, Ukraine), where the bodies of Tartar soldiers who had succumbed to plague were catapulted over the walls of the besieged city.[2] The British were accused of distributing smallpox-infected blankets during the French and Indian War, waged from 1754 to1767. The use of mustard gas in World War I is well known. During World War II, the Japanese produced biological weapons and used them in 1942 at Congshan, China—the only confirmed air attack with biological weapons in modern history.[3] Iraq and Iran used chemical weapons during the Iran-Iraq war that stretched through the 1980s. For example, on March 16, 1988, approximately 5,000 civilians were killed and 10,000 injured when Iraqi air forces bombarded Halabja with mustard and other poison gases. Thirteen years after the attack, the people of Halabja still suffer from very high rates of cancer, neurological disorders, birth defects, and miscarriages.[4] More recently, when Bob Stevens, a tabloid photo editor in Boca Raton, Florida, died of anthrax poisoning in the months following the 9/11 attacks, he became the first U.S. casualty in a new era of bioterrorism threats. In the days and weeks to follow, four others succumbed to anthrax after handling tainted mail—two postal workers in Washington, DC, a New York City hospital stockroom employee, and an elderly Connecticut woman. At least 17 others fell ill but survived the still-unsolved post-9/11 bioterrorism attack.[5]

Radioactivity was discovered in the 1890s, but its potential danger was not fully recognized until much later. Brief contact with low-level radioactive material causes little harm; however, extended exposure increases the likelihood of cellular destruction and illness. To date, a radioactive device—a so-called "dirty bomb"—has not been used as a weapon. However, the materials necessary to build a radiological device are readily available at hospitals, research facilities, and industrial and construction sites. The dispersal of even modest quantities of radioactive materials by a conventional explosion in a populated area would have psychological consequences beyond the potential physical effects, potentially creating panic, overloaded hospitals, and rampant anxiety.

Nuclear weapons are recent phenomena, and their effects well known. In the history of warfare, nuclear weapons have only been used twice: on August 6, 1945, when an atom bomb was dropped on Hiroshima, Japan and the second on August 9, 1945, when another atom bomb destroyed Nagasaki, Japan. The estimated number of deaths resulting from the two detonations is not entirely clear, but most estimate the immediate effects of the blasts killed 70,000 in Hiroshima and 40,000 in Nagasaki. Countless others were sickened and later died due to after-effects of the explosions, including fires and radiation.[6]

Chemical and biological weapons are not always distinguished in popular discourse, but there are several important differences between them. Agents used in biological weapons are "living organisms or infective material derived from them, which are intended to cause disease or decay in man, animals, and plants, and which depend for their effects on their ability to multiply in the person, animal or plant."[7] Agents used in chemical weapons are gaseous, liquid, or solid chemical substances that cause death in humans, animals, or plants and depend on direct toxicity for their effect.[8]

Biological weapons are strategic. They can kill huge numbers of people if used properly, and their effects are not limited to one place or a small target.[9] By contrast, chemical weapons are tactical rather than strategic; they can be used for mass-casualty attacks in confined areas, but it is almost impossible to concentrate enough chemicals in the air to kill a great many people over a large territory. Biological weapons are more difficult to acquire and manufacture than chemical weapons, and chemical and biological attacks require different responses. An hour after a chemical attack, those who are going to survive do, and those who are not, do not. Once decontaminated and removed from the incident site, victims of chemical attacks can be dispersed to hospitals. Biological attacks are comparatively more difficult to manage. The victims must be immediately isolated and quarantined to prevent the agent from spreading. Unfortunately, given today's detection capabilities and the incubation period of biological agents, it is difficult to know who is—and who is not—contaminated. This possibility highlights the "diabolical genius" of biological attacks: targeted groups become the unwitting vehicles for further transmission.[10]

The differences between nuclear and radiological weapons are also often confused. Nuclear weapons use nuclear fission—the splitting of atomic nuclei—to produce enormous amounts of energy. The destructiveness of a nuclear weapon ranges from the equivalent of several thousand to several million tons of TNT,[11] an impact well documented in film footage of Hiroshima and Nagasaki. Radiological weapons—dirty bombs—use conventional explosives to scatter powdered radioactive material over the area surrounding the detonation point. Dirty bombs' immediate destructive power is not physical unless a victim is in the immediate vicinity of the detonation; the real impact of a dirty bomb is psychological. Nuclear weapons present considerable challenges to anyone trying to procure them without state support. They require fissile material in quantities that are beyond the reach of terrorists seeking to produce them from scratch.[12] Dirty bombs, properly called radiological dispersal devices, are conventional explosives wrapped in radioactive debris—debris that is unfortunately readily available in hospitals, research centers, and industrial sites, leading one website to comment, "The *really* shocking thing about dirty bombs is that no one has used one yet, considering how easy it is to get your hands on radioactive garbage."[13]

The use of WMD as a terrorist weapon is also a relatively new phenomenon. In the 1980s, when I first became engaged in counterterrorism efforts, the security community was primarily concerned with the proliferation of small arms, explosives (particularly plastique), rocket-propelled grenades, and the occasional, shoulder-fired anti-aircraft missile as terrorist weapons of choice. Today, the concern is about nuclear, radiological, chemical, and biological weapons—all dangerous and, with the possible exception of a low-yield radiological device, all potentially catastrophic and capable of massive casualties.

Still, there is a debate among analysts and scholars about the severity of the threat posed by WMD. Many, like Ambassador Robert A. Joseph, undersecretary of state for Arms Control and International Security, believe that "the spread of WMD by rogue states and terrorists is widely recognized as the greatest security threat that we face as a nation." Some, such as Steven Flynn, are even more fatalistic, believing it is a question of "when, not if" terrorists will attack the United States with WMD.[14] Many others, however, are not so sure. William Arkin believes the threat of WMD five years after 9/11 has diminished and the danger has declined.[15] Likewise, Shawn Choy believes it would be too difficult for terrorists to employ WMD:

> In reality, weapons of mass destruction present considerable challenges to anyone trying to procure them without state support. Nuclear weapons, which are the only type of WMD that can cause death on the scale of the September 2001 attacks, require fissile material in quantities that are beyond the reach of terrorists seeking to produce them from scratch. That leaves biological and chemical possibilities, whose manufacture and delivery demand technical savvy, abundant resources, and specialized facilities that non-state groups are not likely to possess.[16]

Others believe that "off the shelf" weaponry and conventional approaches will likely remain terrorist's primary means of attacking the United States and other Western targets.

My view is somewhat more pragmatic. The provable and strong interest among terrorist groups such as al Qaeda in acquiring WMD capabilities does not allow us the luxury to ignore the risks of WMD attack. While the risks may be low, the catastrophic consequences of a WMD attack (massive casualties, societal disruption, and financial losses) are so severe that even the slightest possibility that terrorists might acquire and use WMD warrants serious concern and preparation. To dismiss the risks of WMD use by terrorists seems simplistic and dangerous. Understanding the real threat of WMD requires in-depth and expert interdisciplinary analysis of terrorists' motivations and intentions, their technical capabilities, and anticipated means of attack. *Weapons of Mass Destruction and Terrorism*, the fourth terrorism-related book I have coedited for McGraw-Hill, does that but also—and equally important—it helps the reader understand the strengths and weaknesses in deterring, defeating, and, if necessary, managing a WMD attack.

Organization

Weapons of Mass Destruction and Terrorism is composed of four units. Unit I explains how the new forms of terrorism affect the post-9/11 security environment and introduce the notion that weapons of mass destruction could give terrorists short-term, asymmetric attack advantages over conventional military forces. Unit II is a detailed account of the characteristics, availability, and dangers of chemical, biological, radiological, and nuclear weapons. Six case studies complement this section by associating theory with practice— an important feature of this text. Unit III considers responses to WMD attacks and how to defeat terrorists who use WMD. Three case studies complete Unit III and provide the reader with "how to respond" guidance and policy advice. Learning from past events and mistakes and predicting future WMD threats are the substance of Unit IV.

References

1. Richard Pells, "Not With a Whimper: Visions of Mass Destruction in Fiction and Film," *E-Journal USA-Foreign Policy Agenda*, March 2005. Available at <http://usinfo.state.gov/journals/itps/0305/ijpe/pells.htm>.
2. Marc Wheelis, "Biological warfare at the 1346 siege of Caffa," *Emerging Infectious Diseases*, September 2002. Available at <www.cdc.gov/ncidod/EID/vol8no9/01-0536.htm>.
3. John Ellis van Courtland Moon, "Dubious Allegations," *Bulletin of The Atomic Scientists* (May/June 1999): 70.
4. Christine M. Gosden, "The 1988 Chemical Weapons Attack on Halabja, Iraq," *Super Terrorism: Biological, Chemical, and Nuclear*, by Yonah Alexander and Milton Hoenig, Editors. (Ardsley, NY: Transnational Publishers, Inc., 2001).
5. Peter Franceschina, "Anthrax Attacks Remain Unsolved," *Baltimore Sun*, October 15, 2006, p. 1.
6. Leonard A. Cole, "WMD and Lessons from the Anthrax Attacks," *The McGraw-Hill Homeland Security Handbook*, by David G. Kamien, Editor. (New York: McGraw-Hill, 2006): 159.
7. Jessica Stern, *The Ultimate Terrorists* (London: Harvard University Press, 1999) p. 21.
8. Ibid.
9. Richard Preston, "Annals of Warfare—the Bio Weaponeers," *The New Yorker*, March 9, 1998, p. 56.
10. Chris Seiple, "Consequence Management: Domestic Response to Weapons of Mass Destruction," *Parameters* (Autumn 1997), p. 120.
11. Bill Charlton, "Bill Charlton is a Nuclear Engineer, not a Diplomat," *Texas Engineer Research Magazine*, vol. 1, no. 1 (2006). Available at <http://engineering.tamu.edu/research/magazine/2006/policytech/>.
12. Shawn Choy, "No Apocalypse Now," *Columbia Political Review*, vol. 2, no. 1 (October 2001): 1.
13. See <www.rotten.com/library/crime/terrorism/terror-tactics/dirty-bomb>.
14. This is a catch phrase used—some may say abused—by several government officials, security experts, academics, and comedians to discuss the likelihood of the use of WMD against the United States. Stephen Flynn, in his book *America the Vulnerable* (HarperCollins: 2004) spoke of containers as "the poor man's missile" and implied that the question is "when, not if" such containers will be used to deliver WMD into the United States.
15. William Arkin, "The Continuing Misuse of Fear," *Bulletin of Atomic Scientists* vol. 62, no. 5 (September/October 2006): 45.
16. Shawn Choy, "No Apocalypse Now," *Columbia Political Review*, vol. 2, no. 1 (October 2001): 1.

Acknowledgments

This volume is the product of extensive collaboration between the Jebsen Center for Counter-Terrorism Studies at the Fletcher School of Law and Diplomacy, Tufts University, and the Combating Terrorism Center at West Point. At the Jebsen Center, Natasha Bajema played a critical role in helping identify and secure the most important research articles to include in the volume. Jan Henrik Jebsen provided moral and financial support, Miriam Seltzer provided invaluable research support, and Stacy Reiter Neal was the killer editor who saved our bacon in the final days. The faculty and staff of the Department of Social Sciences and the Combating Terrorism Center (CTC) at West Point have also been particularly important sources of support and encouragement, particularly General (R) Wayne Downing, Colonel Michael Meese, and Lieutenant Colonel Joe Felter. And of course, the CTC would not exist without the generous commitment, support, and vision of Mr. Vincent Viola, USMA Class of 1977.

New contributions to the study of weapons of mass destruction and counterterrorism have never been more urgently needed. Each of the chapters in this volume is the product of thoughtful research and analysis, and we offer our sincere thanks to the authors for their hard work and commitment to excellence. The insights and suggestions they have provided in these pages will undoubtedly inform discussions and debate in a variety of policymaking and academic settings for the foreseeable future. We would also like to thank Jill Peter at McGraw-Hill Contemporary Learning Series for her vision and encouragement throughout this effort. This is the fourth in a series of volumes we have published with McGraw-Hill, and Jill and her staff have been enormously professional and helpful collaborators for each one. Finally, we extend a sincere thank you to our families for their patience and tolerance throughout our respective scholarly adventures.

Russell D. Howard
James JF Forest

Unit I

Introduction

A terrorist attack using a weapon of mass destruction is one of the most acute threats to U.S. and international security. Thousands of chemical and biological weapons, huge quantities of weapon-related materials and expertise are scattered all across the globe, and substandard security at nuclear facilities in Europe, central Asia, Russia, and Pakistan increases the risk of terrorists seizing highly enriched uranium to make crude, but devastating, nuclear explosives. The possibility that a terrorist group or a rogue nation could acquire and use a weapon of mass destruction (WMD) to inflict unthinkable levels of death and injuries is more than a theoretical discussion, especially in the aftermath of the September 11 terrorist attacks. A number of intelligence sources in the United States, Europe, and elsewhere, as well as news media reports, have confirmed that terrorist groups like al Qaeda have attempted to seek WMD material and capabilities.

This volume provides a unique compilation of the enduring concepts and practical issues facing the United States when it contemplates WMD and working at the international, federal, state, and local level to design and implement effective measures against a determined enemy. We begin with four chapters that define key terms and address important strategic and policy debates. Authors explain how the new forms of terrorism affect the post-9/11 security environment and introduce the notion that weapons of mass destruction could give terrorists short-term, asymmetric attack advantages over conventional military forces. First, Brigadier General (retired) Russell Howard, director of the Jebsen Center for Counter-Terrorism Studies at the Fletcher School at Tufts University, describes eight distinguishing characteristics of a new type of terrorism, which has a much greater potential to cause harm to America, the West, and all secular countries, including those in the Muslim world. He notes how modern terrorist groups like al Qaeda and Hezbollah have developed a global reach, and how their networked, cellular structure facilitates multiple income streams and logistics support. Perhaps more worrisome are the strategic objectives of these modern terrorist groups, many of whom are determined to acquire chemical, biological, radiological, and nuclear (CBRN) weapons of mass destruction. He concludes

1

that the nexus of these elements creates an enemy that is difficult to find, difficult to defeat, and very dangerous, requiring a better understanding of how to address the problem in a comprehensive manner.

Next, Brian Jenkins—a senior advisor to the president of the RAND Corporation and director of the National Transportation Security Center at the Mineta Transportation Institute—considers how terrorism has changed over the past four decades. He describes how terrorists have developed new ways of funding themselves beyond state sponsorship, along with new models of organization, which enable them to more effectively evade intelligence and law enforcement efforts to disrupt their global campaigns of violence. However, despite these reflections of how terrorist organizations have evolved, and despite a number of acknowledged strategic results that some terrorists have achieved, Jenkins notes that to date, no terrorist organization has achieved its long-term objectives. This is a paradox of terrorism, he concludes. Terrorists often succeed tactically and thereby gain attention, cause alarm, and attract recruits. But their struggle has brought them no success measured against their own stated goals. In that sense, terrorism has failed, but the phenomenon of terrorism continues.

The next two chapters offer complementary views on the nature of the global WMD terrorism threat. First, Thomas Homer-Dixon, director of the Center for the Study of Peace and Conflict at the University of Toronto, examines various elements of "complex terrorism," including the potential linkages between transnational terrorist groups and international organized crime. He describes the steady increase in the destructive capacity of small groups and individuals as driven largely by three technological advances: more powerful weapons, the dramatic progress in communications and information processing, and more abundant opportunities to divert non-weapon technologies to destructive ends. Today's complex terrorism, he says, stems from an ability to exploit weaknesses in our globally interdependent economic and political networks—for example, attacking large gas and oil pipelines, contaminating the food system or disrupting modern communications networks. As a result, our capacity to defend ourselves depends on our ability to understand the complex systems that we depend on so critically. Further, governments are required to prepare for the unknown, an impossible task even for the most imaginative researchers and policymakers.

Next, Stewart Patrick, a research fellow at the Center for Global Development, provides a detailed analysis of the links between weak or failing states and terrorism, WMD proliferation, crime, disease, energy insecurity, and regional instability. He notes that policymakers and experts have presumed a blanket connection between weak governance and transnational threats and have begun to implement policy responses accordingly. Yet, they have rarely distinguished among categories of weak and failing states or asked whether (and how) certain types of developing countries are associated with particular threats. Thus, Patrick's chapter provides a useful framework for determining which states are associated with which dangers. For example, in the realm of WMD proliferation, he addresses specific concerns related to export controls, border security, and governance, which can facilitate the acquisition of CBRN materials by terrorists. Clearly, he concludes, crafting more effective security strategies will require a deep understanding of the underlying mechanisms linking poor governance and state incapacity in the developing world with the threat of global terrorism.

Both of these selections illustrate how globalization—in particular the technological and communications revolution—has changed the nature of terrorism, and thus make the threat of a WMD terror attack increasingly likely. However, the selections in the next chapter question whether the WMD threat has been overhyped. First, Andrew O'Neil, a senior lecturer in Political and International Studies at Flinders University in Adelaide, Australia, suggests that in some cases the attention given to WMD and terrorism is disproportionate to the real threat posed. Indeed, he notes, some analysts have tended to exaggerate the scope of the threat and assumed that large-scale terrorist acts involving WMD are only "a matter of time." O'Neil recognizes that the rise of a "new" brand of terrorism that operates across transnational networks and whose operations aim to inflict mass casualties, coupled with the destructive threshold crossed on September 11, 2001, mean that terrorist attacks using WMD will continue to be a realistic prospect in the future. However, he argues, although WMD terrorism remains a real prospect, the ease with which such attacks can be carried out has been exaggerated; acquiring WMD capabilities for delivery against targets is a lot more problematic for terrorists than is generally acknowledged in the literature.

Columbia University professor Richard Betts, the director of National Security Studies at the Council on Foreign Relations, also adopts a nuanced view of the threat. He notes that "the moment that WMD are used somewhere in a manner that produces tens of thousands of fatalities, there will be hysterical outbursts of all sorts." However, steps to deal with the potential capabilities and motivations for a terrorist attack against the United States are limited. There is surely a danger from religious or cultural groups that see the United States as an evil force blocking their legitimate aspirations—indeed, foreign resentment of the United States is a strong global phenomenon, and according to some polls anti-American sentiment is at its highest peak in history. Further, even if we were to see significant change in U.S. policies, foreign governments and non-state actors would continue to blame the United States for much that is currently wrong in the rest of the world. However, there are some things we could do to possibly reduce the threat that stems from this global animosity. At the very least, he argues, the pursuit of our broader interests of promoting democratic values, economic interdependence, and social Westernization may come into direct conflict with the core imperative of preventing mass destruction within America's borders.

Finally, Rutgers University adjunct professor Leonard Cole draws from the case of the 2001 anthrax attack in the United States to identify four lessons that form our national plans for counterterrorism, emergency preparedness, and response. First, the volume of a chemical or biological agent can be very small yet have an enormous impact; the ripple effect of even a small bioterrorism attack on a shopping mall in rural Ohio must therefore be anticipated, and coping with a collapse of public activity and services should be part of a national plan. Second, the effectiveness of the U.S. mail as a disseminator of anthrax was a surprise—we must analyze our current assumptions to identify and prevent other potential surprises of this type. Third, the first professional to see each anthrax victim was a primary care or emergency physician. This has implications for training and preparedness exercises that go beyond first responders, and include postal workers, teachers, store managers, bus drivers, train conductors, and others. And finally, the victims of the attack were from both urban and rural areas, thus demonstrating that preparedness must not be limited to heavily populated areas.

Together, the chapters of this introductory section provide a conceptual overview of themes and security challenges addressed more fully throughout the remainder of the volume. Certainly, understanding the threat from a macro-strategic perspective should be a high priority for policymakers, law enforcement and intelligence professionals, and local first responders. Nurturing this perspective must therefore be a primary goal of security-related education and training programs throughout the United States.

Chapter 1.1

Definitions, Trends, and the Concept of "New Terrorism"

Brigadier General (Retired) Russell D. Howard

The New Terrorism and Weapons of Mass Destruction

Bruce Hoffman, a professor at Georgetown University, a contributor to this book, and arguably one of the world's leading terrorism experts, put it this way: "I don't mean to sound perverse, but there is maybe certain nostalgia for the old style of terrorism, where there wasn't the threat of loss of life on a massive scale. It's a real commentary on how much the world has changed."[1] In much the same way that many Cold Warriors miss the predictability and transparency of the U.S.-Soviet confrontation, many intelligence professionals, military operators, pundits, and academics miss the familiar type of terrorism that, although quite dangerous, was in the end merely a nasty sideshow to the greater East-West conflict.[2] Much of this Cold War terrorism was inspired by Marxist-Leninist ideology; its perpetrators sought to draw attention to their cause and to gain political concessions. They were motivated by secular rather than apocalyptic ends and were quick to claim responsibility for their attacks.[3] The commando-style terrorism waged by the likes of Andreas Baader and Ulrike Meinhof of the German extreme left Rote Armee Fraktion (better known as the Baader Meinhof Gang) or by Abu Nidal of the Fatah National Council (who was killed in Baghdad in 2002) was ruthless, but it was not nearly as deadly as the threat the world faces today.[4] Now the old, predominantly state-sponsored terrorism has been supplanted by a religiously and ethnically motivated terrorism that "neither relies on the support of sovereign states nor is constrained by the limits on violence that state sponsors observed themselves or placed on their proxies."[5]

American security experts and intelligence analysts have not yet come to terms with the nature of al Qaeda and like-minded groups or with how they differ from the terrorist groups that operated during the Cold War. One difference is the alleged objective. While Cold War terrorist groups had goals that were theoretically attainable and mostly political in nature, "al Qaeda goes beyond the political into what Ralph Peters, military strategist and author, calls the transcendental—a vision formed by religion."[6]

Many new terrorist motives are also new. Terrorist groups such as al Qaeda have international objectives, and globalization has enabled and facilitated terrorists' world-wide goals. According to L. V. Gorka, terrorists no longer use terrorism for society or government-specific change; rather, "terrorism has gone international to support global causes, and the U.S. and the West have become primary targets."[7] Terrorist attacks have become increasingly sophisticated and designed to achieve mass casualties, a trend that is likely to continue. However, the difference is more than the increasing magnitude of deliberate mass-casualty attacks against civilians and non-combatants. These attacks are targeted against societies ever more vulnerable since they depend on openness and globalization for their existence.[8]

This new terrorism has a much greater potential to cause harm to America, the West, and all secular countries, including those in the Muslim world. Led by al Qaeda and Osama bin Laden, it "is built around loosely linked cells that do not rely on a single leader or state sponsor."[9] It is transnational, borderless, and prosecuted by non-state actors, and it is very, very dangerous.

The old and new styles of terrorism are distinguishable in at least eight different ways:

1. The September 11 attacks effectively shattered the illusion of an invulnerable U.S. homeland, protected by two oceans and bordered by friendly or weak neighbors. In the past, the nation was not vulnerable to terrorists, except for the homegrown, mostly right-wing variety such as the Oklahoma City bomber. Now, the American homeland is very much at risk. "When, not if" is how many terrorism experts regard the likelihood of another 9/11 type attack.

2. The new terrorism is more violent. Under the old paradigm, terrorists wanted attention, not mass casualties. Now they want both.

3. Unlike their Cold War counterparts, who were usually sub-state actors trying to affect change in local politics, today's terrorists are transnational, non-state actors who operate globally and want to destroy the West (the far enemy) and all secular states, including secular Muslim-majority states (the near enemy).

4. The new terrorists are much better financed than their predecessors, who relied mainly on crime or the largess of state sponsors. Today's terrorists have income streams from legal and illegal sources, and are not accountable to state sponsors—or anybody else.

5. Today's terrorists are better trained. This is evident from the materials captured in al Qaeda's training camps in Afghanistan and from the similar training materials of other Muslim extremist groups found in Europe and Central Asia.

6. This generation's terrorists are more difficult to infiltrate than terrorist organizations of previous generations. The networked, cellular structure used by al Qaeda and its allies is especially difficult for a hierarchical security apparatus like that of the United States to penetrate. Bribes and sting operations using sex or money as a lure could catch terrorists for prosecution and information in the old days; it is difficult to "turn" religious extremists with these methods. The $50 million reward on Osama bin Laden has yet to be collected, and it is unclear how successful other methods have been in getting bin Laden's followers to talk.

7. Most insidious, and the primary focus of this book, is the availability of weapons of mass destruction (WMD). In the 1980s, the security, military, and intelligence communities were concerned about small arms, explosives (particularly plastique), rocket-propelled grenades, and the occasional shoulder-fired anti-aircraft missile. Today, the concern is about nuclear, radiological, chemical, and biological weapons—all potentially catastrophic, with massive killing potential.

8. Victory will be elusive. More than likely, there will be no formal surrender by a defeated foe, no armistice ending combat on acceptable terms, no arrest and

incarceration of all the members of a terrorist organization. There will be no victory parade. At best, the U.S. and the West can probably return to a life of inconvenience with infrequent incidents. However, free societies will have to remain vigilant and permanently on alert. Not doing so will invite those who want to harm us to attack again, possibly with a nuclear, radiological, chemical, or biological weapon.

This article discusses these eight distinguishing characteristics of the new terrorism and argues that they must be understood and addressed if the United States and the West hope to prevail. Osama bin Laden's al Qaeda is the principal case study for this work because his ideology, organization, surrogates, and followers epitomize the new terrorism and are the number-one threat to America's security. Other terrorist groups, particularly Hezbollah, are also discussed. Aside from al Qaeda, no terrorist group has killed more Americans and none pose a more formidable threat than does Hezbollah.[10]

1. America at Risk

September 11 shattered the illusion that Americans are safe from troubles originating beyond our shores, which have traditionally been protected by geography and weak or friendly neighbors. The attacks forced American citizens and policymakers to learn how to fight a new kind of war. Some have compared September 11, 2001, to December 7, 1941, the only other occasion since the War of 1812 that American territory has been attacked.[11] There are many similarities. Both were surprise attacks, were probably predictable and possibly avoidable, were extraordinarily costly in life and national treasure, and were defining points in American history. However, as David Halberstam notes in *War in a Time of Peace*, there are also many differences. According to Halberstam, the historical demarcation point the U.S. crossed on September 11 is even greater than the one it crossed with the bombing of Pearl Harbor.[12] The post-Pearl Harbor war was easily understood: the enemy was a state, and interstate warfare was more traditional, definable, and susceptible to America's industrial and technological advantages. Today's enemy is not a state but a transnational, non-state actor. Its method of warfare is not traditional: it is more elusive, operates in the shadows—often at a great distance but sometimes right among us, through secret cells and aliases—and it exploits America's industrial and technological advantages.[13]

Different, too, seems the resolve of the American people to wage war. Throughout our nation's history, Americans have traditionally displayed an extraordinary degree of resourcefulness and self-sacrifice in times of war.[14] The best example of that tradition is World War II, when the war effort became an immediate extension of America's national will and purpose.[15] Today, says Stephen Flynn, "we are breaking with that tradition. Our nation faces grave peril, but we seem unwilling to mobilize at home to confront the threat before us."[16] For example, at the height of World War II, the United States committed roughly thirty-six percent of its gross domestic product (GDP) to the war effort, and when the Japanese surrendered on the battleship Missouri in 1945, America had more than twelve million men and women in uniform. Presently, less than four percent of U.S. GDP is committed to the campaign against terrorism and of the 2.6 million men and women presently in uniform, 1.4 million are in the National Guard and Reserve. Unlike the World War II era, when America's productive capacity was focused on the war effort, today there are no shortages and no rationing, and the production of goods and services for the consumer market runs unabated. Why are the American people unwilling to mobilize at home? Three reasons come to mind. First, they understand conventional war, but not the war on terror. Second, they fail to realize the security implications of globalization and information technology. Third, they are not affected by the war unless their children—less than one half of one percent of the U.S. population—are fighting it. Some, including this author, have said that it might take another catastrophic terrorist event in the U.S. before the nation wakes up to the security realities of this century.

The war on terror is not like engaging an enemy massed on a foreign battlefield. Destroying or confiscating the enemy's battlefield capabilities and dispersing its troops will not ensure victory.[17] Today, as Halberstam explains, "the more visible the enemy is, the further he is from the magnetic field of our intelligence operations and any potential military strike."[18] He continues,

> It is not that America, as it enters a very different kind of battle, lacks weaponry; it is that the particular kind of weaponry we specialize in lacks targets. This will be a difficult military-intelligence-security challenge: What we do best, they are not vulnerable to. What we do least well, they are vulnerable to. What they do best, we are—to a considerable degree—vulnerable to.[19]

Combating terrorism, particularly the Islamic extremist variety, is as much about fighting an international idea as an organized military force maneuvering within defined geographical boundaries. The danger posed by al Qaeda, its followers, its surrogates, and other Islamic extremists cannot be managed by relying primarily on overseas military campaigns. As Flynn puts it, "There are no fronts in the war on terrorism."[20] In fact, he says,

> The 9/11 attacks highlighted the fact that our borders offer no effective barrier to terrorists intent on bringing their war to our soil. Nor do their weapons have to be imported, since they have proven how easy it is to exploit the modern systems we rely upon in our daily lives and use them against us.[21]

These modern systems are the sophisticated networks that move people, goods, energy, money, and information at higher volumes and greater velocities[22]—the very systems that ensure America's competitive edge in the age of globalization. For years, our growing dependence on these networks has not been matched by a parallel focus on securing them.[23] Flynn continues,

> The architects of these networks have made efficiency and diminishing costs their highest priority. Security considerations have been widely perceived as annoying speed bumps in achieving their goals. As a result, the systems that underpin our prosperity are soft targets for those bent on challenging U.S. power.[24]

The attacks on the World Trade Center and the Pentagon ended a unique historical span for the U.S. as a great power. For nearly a century, America has been a major player in the world; but until 9/11, the homeland had escaped the ravages of modern warfare and weaponry because of its unique geographical position and unparalleled industrial technological base. When confronted with threats, the U.S. dealt with them on our adversaries' or allies' turf. Except for the occasional disaster or heinous crime, life in America had been terror-free. It has taken a group of rebels without a country—a ghost nation, as it were—to pose a threat to America and our way of life.[25]

2. More Violent

In the past, "terrorists wanted a lot of people watching, not a lot of people dead."[26] Unlike the terrorists of the 1960s through the 1990s, who generally avoided high-casualty attacks for fear of the negative publicity they would generate, al Qaeda is not in the least worried about that.[27] Terrorists in past decades did not want large body counts because they wanted converts; they also wanted a seat at the table. Today's terrorists are not particularly concerned about converts, and rather than wanting a seat at the table, "they want to destroy the table and everyone sitting at it."[28] Religious terrorists, and al Qaeda in particular, want casualties—lots of them.[29]

In the past, civilians usually became victims of terrorist operations either because they were captives of hostage-taking events or because they happened to be in the wrong place at the wrong time. Terrorists took hostages for three reasons: to gain attention for their cause, to secure the release of imprisoned comrades, or to collect ransom. The odds were—96 percent of the time in the 1980s—that hostages would survive the event. Victims were generally casualties because they happened to be in the proximity of an explosion, ambush, or bank robbery. However, the motive was to get attention or money, not cause the deaths of civilians. Today, however, mass casualties are a primary aspect of bin Laden's strategy:

> By causing mass casualties on a regular basis [bin Laden] could hope to persuade the Americans to keep clear of overseas conflicts. There was also a retributive element to the strategy . . . the militants of al-Qaeda and like-minded groups clearly wanted to punish the Americans for a whole range of policies, particularly for those it pursued in the Middle East, as well as for what they saw as its irreligious decadence.[30]

For example, nine months after the attack on New York, Osama bin Laden forwarded a chilling announcement on a now defunct al Qaeda-affiliated Web site, stating: "We have the right to kill four million Americans—two million of them children—and to exile twice as many and wound and cripple hundreds of thousands."[31]

Despite successes by coalition military forces success against al Qaeda in Afghanistan and in Iraq, and accomplishments by police agencies around the world, the frequency and reach of al Qaeda's attacks have continued to increase. Fortunately, despite continuing al Qaeda efforts to perpetuate mass casualty attacks—the foiled plot to hijack several U.S. airliners in the UK and continued efforts to acquire weapons of mass destruction, for example—the lethality of the 9/11 attack has not been eclipsed.[32]

3. Truly Global: Conducted by Transnational, Non-State Actors

In the 1970s and 1980s, terrorism was mostly local. The terrorists were usually state-sponsored, sub-state actors intent on affecting change in the political and/or economic systems. Today, there has been a shift away from localized terrorist groups, which were supported by states such as the Soviet Union, to loosely organized global networks. Presently, the new terrorists have global motives and capabilities. They are backed and financed by like-minded organizations throughout the world. In many respects, terrorist groups such as al Qaeda and Hezbollah have achieved *de facto* sovereign status by acquiring the means to conduct war—and have in fact declared war—posing significant military and security policy challenges for which the U.S. and the West had no preplanned response.[33] This parallels a change from primarily politically-motivated terrorism to a more religiously-motivated variety.[34]

Al Qaeda's global network consists of independently-operating permanent or semi-permanent cells of trained militants in more than seventy-six countries.[35] In fact, since September 11, more than 4,300 al Qaeda operatives hailing from forty-nine countries have been arrested in ninety-seven countries.[36] Moreover, the concept of global terrorism applies not just to al Qaeda but collectively to many terrorist organizations throughout the world. These organizations operate through an interconnected network that often provides mutual aid and support, making it difficult to isolate a particular group or faction.[37] There is also growing evidence that al Qaeda is now subcontracting work to like-minded terrorists. According to Jessica Stern:

> Bin Laden's organization has also nurtured ties with a variety of other groups around the world, including: Ansar al Islam, based mainly in Iraq and Europe, Jemaah Islamiyah in Southeast Asia, Abu Sayyaf and the Moro Islamic Liberation Front in the Philippines, and many Pakistani Jihadi groups.[38]

These affiliated or like-minded groups have the capacity to carry out attacks and inflict pain on the U.S. under al Qaeda's banner, says Hoffman. In fact, new revelations about the emerging al Qaeda network—the depth of its ranks and its ties to "franchise" terrorists in up to seventy countries—shows that the intent to attack America, the West, and secular states around the world has not diminished.[39] In fact, according to some, successes against al Qaeda in Afghanistan, Iraq, and elsewhere may have actually made defeating the organization more difficult. Since al Qaeda lost its sanctuary in Afghanistan, Jason Burke believes "there is no longer a central hub for Islamic militancy."[40] Instead, the al Qaeda worldview, or "al Qaedaism," is what sustains acts of terrorism against the West and the United States.[41]

This radical internationalist ideology—sustained by anti-Western, anti-Zionist, and anti-secular rhetoric—has adherents among many individuals and groups, few of whom are currently linked in any substantial way to bin Laden or those around him. They merely follow his precepts, models, and methods. They act in the style of al Qaeda, but they are only part of al Qaeda in the very loosest sense.[42] Perhaps most troubling is some evidence that al Qaeda—a Sunni organization—has limited connections with Hezbollah, a Shiite group considered by many to be the most sophisticated terrorist organization in the world.[43] Like al Qaeda, Hezbollah also has a worldwide network and has sleeper cells in Asia, Africa, Europe, North America, and South America.[44]

Al Qaeda's targets are global, another characteristic setting it apart from the local, tactical focus of earlier terrorist groups. Now, not only are targets selected to cause casualties without limit, they are selected to undermine the global economy; as Matthew Levitt explains, "the new terrorist tactics might be called strategic acts of destruction, rather than the tactical terrorist acts of the past."[45] According to Air Marshall Sir Timothy Garden, "it may have been possible for the international community to live with occasional acts of local terrorism around the world; it is much more difficult to live with non-state actors who have a mission to destroy a large part of the global system."[46]

In summary, recent years have seen the emergence of terrorism that is not ideological in a political sense but is inspired by religious extremists working in cells, small groups, and larger coalitions.[47] They do not answer to any government, they operate across national borders, and they have access to funding and advanced technology.[48] Such groups are not bound by the same constraints or motivated by the same goals as nation-states. And, unlike state-sponsored groups, religious extremist groups like al Qaeda are not susceptible to traditional diplomacy or military deterrence. There is no state with which to negotiate or against which to retaliate.

4. Well-Financed

Al Qaeda learned from the failings of previous terrorist groups, such as the Baader Meinhof, the Red Brigades, and the Abu Nidal group, all of which were perennially undercapitalized. According to Hoffman, al Qaeda under Osama bin Laden saw the need to be much more flexible and to maintain a steady supply of money, which is crucial to lubricate the wheels of terrorism.[49]

Estimates of Osama bin Laden's personal wealth range from $18 million to as high as $200 million, but "it is most commonly agreed that bin Laden inherited approximately $57 million at age sixteen."[50] Bin Laden has been able to leverage his millions into a global financial empire by investing in legitimate businesses, taking advantage of the globalized financial system, abusing the Islamic banking (*hawala*) system, and coercing an entire network of Islamic philanthropic and charitable institutions. The total net worth of the al Qaeda financial empire is unclear—perhaps in the hundreds of millions. Between September 11, 2001, and October 2002, more than 165 countries enacted blocking actions against terrorist assets, and approximately $112 million of these assets were frozen worldwide, including $34 million in the U.S. and $78 million overseas.[51] According to at least one report, international efforts to curtail terrorist fundraising, money laundering, and financing activities have resulted in a ninety percent reduction in al Qaeda's income, compared with the period before September 11, 2001.[52] However, most experts disagree, believing that al Qaeda and like-minded terrorist groups have moved out of normal channels into other sources of revenue that sustain operations at near pre-9/11 levels. For example, in a dissertation recently completed for the RAND Corporation's Ph.D. program, Steven Kiser concluded that al Qaeda's financial infrastructure has shown an impressive ability to adapt to adverse conditions, quickly take advantage of available opportunities, pursue creative, non-traditional, and unorthodox methods of money management, and geographically relocate operations to areas where laws are lax or non-existent. As Kiser explains, "this amoeba-like ability—to form oneself in whatever shape is necessary and still function effectively—has proven exceptionally useful."[53]

In fact, bin Laden's entrepreneurial skills are legendary. During his five-year stint in Sudan he cornered the market on gum Arabic, the basic ingredient in fruit juices produced in the United States.[54] According to Robin Wright, bin Laden "also started an Islamic bank, built a tannery, created an export company, launched construction projects, and developed agricultural schemes."[55] Other business ventures included a trading company in Kenya and a ceramic plant, publishing outlet, and appliance firm in Yemen.[56]

Al Qaeda's misuse of the ancient *hawala* underground banking system, which allows financial transfers without actual money movement, is particularly instructive.

Seemingly custom-made for al-Qaeda, the *hawala* is an ancient system that originated in South Asia and is still used worldwide to conduct legitimate business, as well as to illegally launder money. The components of *hawala* that distinguish it from other conventional remittance systems are trust and the extensive use of connections, such as family relation- ships or regional affiliations. Unlike traditional banking, *hawala* makes minimal use of any sort of negotiable instruments or documentation. Money transfers take place based on communications between members of a network of *hawaladars*, or *hawala* dealers.[57] A recent Council on Foreign Relations study illustrates how the *hawala* system works:

> Customers in one city hand their local *hawaladar* some money. That individual then contacts his counterpart across the world, who in turn distributes money out of his own resources to the intended recipient. The volume of transactions flowing through the system in both directions is such that the two *hawaladars* rarely have to worry about settlement.[58]

Hawaladars charge their customers a nominal cash transaction fee for the service. They are willing to carry debts for long periods of time because they are often related to their lending counterpart through familial, clan, or ethnic associations.[59]

Al Qaeda also uses other methods to move funds. Cash smuggling is one; moving assets in the form of precious metals and gemstones is another. The gold trade and the *ha- wala* are especially symbiotic: they flourish in the same locales and offer complementary services to those moving assets across borders. Al Qaeda also uses traditional smuggling routes and methods favored by international drug traffickers, arms dealers, and other orga- nized criminal groups.[60]

Charities and philanthropic organizations have also been sources of al Qaeda fund- ing. In 2003, the *New York Times* reported that since December 2001, the assets of more than a dozen Islamic charities worldwide have been frozen, three of them based in the United States."[61] For example, U.S. authorities have designated the U.S.-based Benevo- lence International Foundation (BIF) a terrorist financier with links to the al Qaeda net- work, and its assets have been frozen in the U.S., Canada, and Bosnia. But the bin Laden network is not the only terrorist group skimming funds from U.S.-based charities.[62] In fact, the U.S. Treasury Department found overwhelming evidence that the Holy Land Founda- tion for Relief and Development, the self-proclaimed largest Muslim charity in the United States, was an arm of Hamas, a radical Islamic organization that operates in the West Bank and Gaza strip.[63]

Al Qaeda-trained cells choose from a variety of methods to obtain local funding. Ac- cording to Kaiser, "credit card fraud, car theft, and document forgery are popular among Algerian cells in Europe. In North America, terrorist financiers practice cigarette smug- gling and coupon scams, both of which provide large profits but result in minor penalties if apprehended."[64]

More recently, evidence suggests that financial transactions are taking place between Islamist organizations—notably al Qaeda and affiliates—and criminal organizations. Ac- cording to Kiser:

> Al Qaeda appears to have a cooperative but limited relationship with some organized criminal networks, using these organizations to acquire materials they require for ter- rorist attacks, as well as aiding in the laundering of money. The biggest links are with

rebel groups that also served as diamond smuggling networks in western Africa. Al Qaeda's affiliates also are beginning to cooperate with organized crime. For example, Abu Sayyaf now raises funds through kidnapping ransoms, piracy, and gunrunning.[65]

Additionally, the terrorists responsible for the March 11, 2004 bombings in Madrid are believed to have funded their operation at least partially through the sale of narcotics.[66]

5. Well-Trained

Formalized terrorist training during the Cold War was generally conducted by the states sponsoring terrorist groups. For instance, the former Soviet Union ran terrorism training camps at Simferpol in the Crimea, Ostrova in Czechoslovakia, and Pankow in East Germany.[67] Captured PLO terrorist Adnan Jaber has given a comprehensive account of his Soviet training:

> [Jaber] did a six-month course there, during which Russian military and civilian instructors covered propaganda methods, political affairs, tactics, and weapons. Other such courses dealt with advanced explosives work, bomb-making, and training in biological and chemical warfare.[68]

However, it would be incorrect to assume that most Cold War-era terrorists went through such formal training. More than likely, many went into action without such instruction and simply learned by doing.[69] This is not at all the case today. In fact, graduating from training camp is the common denominator and rite of passage for both al Qaeda operatives and members of allied organizations.[70]

Al Qaeda manuals and records captured in Afghanistan training camps portray a comprehensive program that emphasizes paramilitary training, Islamic studies, and current politics. Common to all members of al Qaeda and its associated groups are the following personality traits and qualifications, which are required before one can become an Islamist military operative:

> Knowledge of Islam, ideological commitment, maturity, self-sacrifice, discipline, secrecy and concealment of information, good health, patience, unflappability, intelligence and insight, caution and prudence, truthfulness and wisdom, and the ability to observe and analyze, and the ability to act.[71]

Aspiring operatives are also taught forgery, assassination techniques, and the conducting of maritime or vehicular suicide attacks.[72] As a means of avoiding sophisticated National Security Administration signal intelligence capabilities, al Qaeda teaches its operatives how to use couriers and sophisticated telecommunications, the Internet, and encryption technologies to try to outfox U.S. surveillance.[73]

An al Qaeda manual, *Military Studies in the Jihad Against the Tyrants*, which was seized in Manchester, England at the home of a bin Laden follower, is a condensed version of thousands of pages of al Qaeda training materials seized in Afghanistan. An English translation of the 180-page Arabic document was placed in evidence during the recent Kenya and Tanzania bombing trials in New York City. The manual is extraordinarily comprehensive and instructs terrorist operatives in an array of techniques, including jihad (holy war), military organization, financial precautions and forged documents, security measures in public transportation, special operations and weapons, guidelines for beating and killing hostages, how to assassinate with poisons, spoiled food, and feces, and methods of physical and psychological torture.[74]

Al Qaeda's training is varied and comprehensive; its tacticians and trainers have taken much from the special operations forces of several nations, including the U.S., UK, and Russia. Indeed, al Qaeda fighters are as well or better trained than those of many national armies, as was the case in Afghanistan and in many cases in Iraq where al Qaeda tactics have been successful against new, American-trained Iraqi armed forces and police. What is even more startling is its intelligence and "black operations" acumen. Al Qaeda expert Rohan Gunaratna believes that "unlike the rag-tag terrorist groups of the Cold War period, sophisticated terrorist groups of the post-Cold War period, such as al Qaeda, have developed intelligence wings comparable to government intelligence agencies."[75]

6. Difficult to Penetrate

Another difference between old and new terrorism is that new-generation terrorists have adopted a networked and less hierarchical form. Unlike the anti-capitalist and national liberation operations of the 1970s and 1980s, which overwhelmingly employed hierarchical chains of command, terrorist groups like al Qaeda have adopted networked structural models in response to improved counter-terrorism capabilities and cooperation among governments.[76] Rapid advances in digital communication have also increased the viability of these networks, though they are not totally dependent on the latest information technology; for example, while cutting-edge technology "has made networks more effective, low-tech means such as couriers and landline telephones can enable networks in certain circumstances."[77]

Strict adherence to a flat, diffused, cellular, and networked structure has allowed al Qaeda to maintain a high degree of secrecy and security. "These cells are independent of other local groups al Qaeda may be aligned with and range in size from two to fifteen members."[78] Using code, targets are announced in the general media, and individuals or independent cells are expected to use initiative, stealth, and flexibility to destroy them. The network will obviously be more likely to achieve long-term effectiveness if its members share a unifying ideology, common goals, and mutual interests, as is the case with al Qaeda and its cells.[79] Networks are most effective when they distribute the responsibility for operations and provide redundancies for key functions; cells within the network "need not contact or coordinate with other cells except for those essential to a particular operation or function."[80] Avoiding unnecessary coordination or approval provides deniability to terrorist leaders and enhances the security of terrorist operations. Washington's predilection for technical means of intelligence collection at the expense of covert and clandestine operations with human sources, compounded by an acute lack of culturally attuned operatives, analysts, and linguists, has contributed greatly to the inability for U.S. operators to penetrate tightly knit cells of al Qaeda and other militant Islamic groups.[81]

Al Qaeda's loss of sanctuary in Afghanistan has forced it to disperse and go underground, thus making it even more difficult to penetrate. At the same time, like-minded terrorist organizations operating within their own affiliated groups—which "tend to be loosely organized, recruit their members from many different countries, and obtain support from an internal international network of like minded extremists"—have increased.[82] The new terrorism resembles a virus that morphs as its environment changes. Individual cells and nodes evolve their own strategy and, if hit, will adapt, regroup, generate new leadership, shift locations, adjust tactics, and evolve into a new set of cells and networks capable of reconstitution, dispersal, and innovation.[83] The resulting transnational and decentralized structure facilitates terrorists avoiding detection and penetration.[84]

Though weakened by the disruption of its finances and communications, the destruction of its base, and the flight of its leaders, al Qaeda is still dangerous and very difficult to penetrate.[85] Though they may share a common militant Islamic ideology, cells within the al Qaeda network have become a loose and "ever-shifting alliance of like-minded groups."[86] Instead of large, well-orchestrated attacks like those of September 11, al Qaeda operations are now smaller and less ambitious; yet, they remain extremely dangerous, and their "killer cells" seem to be growing and spawning imitations around the world.[87]

7. Access to Weapons of Mass Destruction

The seventh way new terrorists differ from the old is the most worrisome: they are determined to obtain and use nuclear, radiological, chemical, and biological weapons of mass destruction (WMD). According to Graham Allison's recent book *Nuclear Terrorism: The Ultimate Preventable Catastrophe*, polls taken in 2003 found that four out of every ten Americans worry about the chances of nuclear attack.[88] In the judgment of many experts, these fears are not exaggerated. For example, a study conducted in 2000 by Howard Baker and Lloyd Cutler determined that the most urgent unmet national security threat to the United States today is the danger that weapons of mass destruction or weapons-usable material in Russia could be stolen, sold to terrorists, and used against Americans abroad or at home.[89]

With a single act, terrorists using a weapon of mass destruction can cause the deaths of thousands, even millions.[90] Acquiring WMD has been made easier thanks to information age technologies and the availability of suppliers;[91] discoveries in Afghanistan have confirmed that al Qaeda and other terrorist groups are actively pursuing biological agents for use against the United States and its allies.[92] According to David Kay, this should not be a surprise:

> Only a blind, deaf, and dumb terrorist group could have survived the last five years and not been exposed at least to the possibility of the use of WMD, while the more discerning terrorists would have found some tactically brilliant possibilities already laid out on the public record.[93]

"We must be prepared for new types of attacks; anything could happen," says Koichi Oizumi, an international relations professor at Nihon University in Tokyo, the city where the Aum Shinrikio used saran nerve gas to kill twelve and injure 250 in the first major use of chemical agent in a terrorist attack.[94]

Steven Miller, director of the International Security Program at Harvard University's John F. Kennedy School of Government, says that policy-makers should be particularly concerned about terrorist access to nuclear weapons. Miller believes that there have been more than two dozen thefts of weapons-usable materials in the former Soviet Union in recent years. Although "several suspects have been arrested in undercover sting operations," he wonders about those who may have gotten away.[95] These thefts date from at least 1994, "when 350 grams of plutonium were smuggled on board a Lufthansa flight from Moscow to Munich. Fortunately, SWAT teams confiscated the material as soon as it arrived."[96]

In the past, any state that allowed a terrorist group it sponsored to use WMD against the United States knew it would be committing suicide, and the fear of nuclear retaliation was ample motivation for sponsors to keep the lid on. Today, any terrorist group with a known base of operations, even if it does not have a state sponsor, would similarly risk annihilation for waging a WMD terrorist attack. But al Qaeda's lack of a state sponsor and its loosely organized global network make retaliation much more problematic.

Furthermore, there is still considerable debate concerning the ability of jihadist groups like al Qaeda to acquire WMD and carry out an attack. Unfortunately, al Qaeda's record and its statements are very straightforward, confirming the notion that the organization would indeed use WMD to escalate its terrorist attacks on the United States and the West. Al Qaeda's view on WMD and its operational and symbolic importance is expressed by operational leader and ideologue Abu Musab al Suri in his open letter to the U.S. State Department:

> If I were consulted in the case of that operation I would advise the use of planes in flights from outside the U.S. that would carry WMD. Hitting the U.S. with WMD was and is still very complicated. Yet, it is possible after all, with Allah's help, and more important than being possible—it is vital.[97]

According to al Suri, WMD are the only means that would allow al Qaeda to alter the current balance of power in the organization's favor, and this explains why, in the aftermath of 9/11, al Qaeda's interest for WMD has increased exponentially.[98] The reciprocity argument, which is a second justification for using WMD, poses that al Qaeda has a right to use WMD and indiscriminately kill civilians in retaliation for the West's alleged crimes against Muslims all over the world.[99] Al Qaeda has also obtained religious justification to use WMD from radical Islamic scholars such as Saudi Islamist Shaykh Naser bin Hamad al-Fahd, who penned the first fatwa on the use of WMD on May 21, 2003.[100] When asked by an anonymous person about the permissibility of the use of WMD, and al-Fahd replied, "If the Muslims could defeat the infidels only by using these kinds of weapons, it is allowed to use them even if they kill them all, and destroy their crops and cattle."[101] He then wrote an additional memorandum elaborating upon the religious justification used to substantiate his conclusions, adding that, since the U.S. has killed about 10 million Muslims, the Muslim world was indeed allowed to retaliate and kill as many American citizens. This argument was also made in a 2002 statement by al-Qaeda leader Suleiman Abu Gheith, who had claimed that al Qaeda was allowed to kill at least four million Americans, including two million children.[102]

In past years, attempts to acquire, fabricate, and deploy WMD have been carried out by al Qaeda-affiliated organizations in Europe, the Caucasus, and in Central and Southeast Asia. In the Caucasus, Pankisi Gorge in Georgia has been identified as the past center of al Qaeda's biological and chemical weapons activity.[103] French judge Jean-Louis Bruguiére collected evidence showing that chemical-biological terrorists in Europe have "been trained in special camps in the zone [the Caucasus] in order to build biological and chemical systems and bombs."[104] Allegedly, al Qaeda scientist Abu Khatab operated in this area before his death in 2006, and was involved in Chechen cyanide plot against the Russian government.[105] The chemical and biological training camps in the Pankisi Gorge are particularly relevant because many of the mujahideen who complete their training there return to Europe, where they might try to use their knowledge and carry out local attacks.

In the past, Pakistan has been a strategic location for al Qaeda's WMD programs, and Pakistani scientists have been involved in attempts to support al Qaeda's efforts to acquire nuclear weapons. For example, nuclear scientist and atomic weapons expert Sultan Bashiruddin Mahmood has been accused of providing assistance to bin Laden to further his efforts to develop nuclear weapons. After retiring, Mahmood founded a charitable organization, Ummah Tameer E-Nau (UTN), whose real objective was: "to assist the Taliban, bin Laden, and his al Qaeda terrorist network in developing high-tech weapons."[106]

In Southeast Asia, the al-Qaeda affiliated Jemaah Islamiyah (JI) has been involved with several foiled plots to carry out local WMD attacks and to provide international assistance to develop WMD. *The 9/11 Commission Report* indicates that

> Atef Abu Hafs [a senior al Qaeda leader] turned to Hambali [Jeemah Islamiya leader] when al Qaeda needed a scientist to take over its biological weapons program. Hambali obliged by introducing a U.S.-educated JI member, Yazid Sufaat, to Ayman al Zawahiri in Kandahar. In 2001 Sufaat spent several months attempting to cultivate anthrax for al Qaeda in a laboratory he helped set up near the Kandahar airport."[107]

Moreover, JI has already attempted to carry out chemical or biological attacks. According to Gunaratna, there is a JI manual that explains how to carry out chemical attacks with chemical hydrogen cyanide. The manual said that "30ml of the agent can kill 60 million people, God willing," confirming the group's intention to cause the highest number of casualties possible.[108] Accordingly, says Gunaratna, JI was planning to use the chemical agents against western targets in May, 2006.[109]

In sum, there is ample evidence indicating al Qaeda's interest in developing, acquiring, and deploying WMD, and that if the group were to succeed in its efforts, it would not hesitate to use them against U.S. and Western targets. As President Bush correctly pointed out in the *2002 National Security Strategy*, "The gravest danger our nation faces lies at the crossroads of radicalism and technology. Our enemies have openly declared that they are seeking weapons of mass destruction, and evidence indicates that they are doing so with determination."[110]

8. Defining Victory and Defeat

Much has been written about winning the war on terrorism, defeating al Qaeda, and ending terrorism. In the 2004 presidential campaign, both candidates implied that the war on terror may not be winnable, and were criticized for saying so. However, there is ample reason to believe they were correct. Victory and defeat are elusive terms in a war on terrorism. Unlike World Wars I and II and the first Gulf War, when victory was sealed with an agreement, and the Vietnam War, when defeat was understood when Saigon fell, the war on terror will have no such defining moments. It is likely the war against terrorism will never be over, at least in the present generation. As James Fallows says, "There will always be a threat that someone will blow up an airplane or a building or a container ship."[111] The fact is, "one cannot defeat terrorism. Terrorism in one form or another has been around for centuries and will be around for many more."[112] Counter-terrorism is not about defeating terrorism as a tactic; it is about defeating terrorist groups, such as al Qaeda. The measures of success in a war against terror are different, too. Instead of body counts and casualty rates, success in the war on terror may be measured in numbers voting, schools opened, and women in the work force in places such as Afghanistan and Iraq.[113] Success against al Qaeda and like-minded terrorist groups will come when their operational, logistical, and financial activities are rendered too difficult to conduct and their freedom of movement to conduct operations is severely restricted.[114] The best we may be able to achieve is to understand that we live in danger, without living in fear.

Conclusion

One might say that America's war against the new terrorism is far colder than the Cold War—in terms of the cold-blooded murders in New York, Washington D.C., Bali, Madrid, and London. At least with the Soviets, the U.S. always knew who was in charge and that it couldn't be attacked without orders from the Soviet leadership. In fact, the U.S. president had a direct line to Soviet leaders and could work through difficult moments personally. By contrast, on September 11, 2001, the U.S. lost close to three thousand people; but although it is clear Osama bin Laden ordered the killings, there is no direct line to him or anyone else in the al Qaeda leadership. It is also clear that he and his followers will continue to hit the United States, its allies, and secular Muslim-majority states again and again until he and his network are stopped.

It has been said that generals always make the mistake of preparing for the last war instead of the next one. This article has emphasized changes in the terrorist threat from the Cold War decades so that today's generals and their civilian masters can understand how to fight and win the current war, and so that having won it, we will never have to fight a war like this again.

Notes

1. "Terror Cells of Today Hard to Combat." *The New York Times*, August 20, 2002. Available at: <www.nytimes.com/aponline/international/AP-Evolution-of-Terror.html>.
2. John Mearsheimer, "Why We Will Soon Miss the Cold War," *Atlantic Monthly*, August 1990. See also, Glenn Sacks, "Why I Miss the Cold War," available at <www.glennsacks.com>, published October 2, 2001.
3. Brian H. Hook, Margaret J. A. Peterlin, Peter L. Welsh, "Intelligence and the New Threat: The USA PATRIOT Act and Information Sharing Between the Intelligence and Law Enforcement Communities." (Chapter 25 in this volume). *Federalist Society for Law and Public Policy Studies*, December, 2001. p. 3
4. Brian Murphy, "The Shape of Terrorism Changes," *Fayetteville Observer*, Aug. 21, 2002, p. 9A.
5. Steven Simon and Daniel Benjamin, "America and the New Terrorism," *Survival*, vol. 42, no. 1, Spring 2000, p. 69.
6. Sebestyen L. V. Gorka, "Al Qaeda's Rhetoric and its Implications," *Jane's Terrorism and Security Monitor*, January 13, 2005, p. 1.
7. _____, "Combating Terrorism and its Implications for Intelligence," DCAF Internal Paper, June, 2004, p. 8.
8. "Combating Terrorism and its Implications for Intelligence," p. 8.
9. Ibid.
10. "Hezbollah in America," *The Washington Times*, May 20, 2005. Available at <www.washtimes.com/op-ed/20050519-092915-7312r.htm>.
11. Some in the Southwest may include Pancho Villa's excursion into New Mexico as an attack.
12. David Halberstam, *War in Time of Peace*. New York: Simon and Schuster, 2001, p. 498.
13. Ibid. p. 496–497.

14. Stephen Flynn, *America the Vulnerable*, New York: Harper Collins, 2004, p. x.
15. Halberstam, p. 496.
16. Flynn, p. x.
17. Hook et. al., p. 3.
18. Halberstam, p. 497.
19. Ibid.
20. Flynn, p. x.
21. Ibid.
22. Ibid. p. 5.
23. Ibid.
24. Ibid. p. 5.
25. Halberstam, p. 498.
26. Quote attributed to Brian Jenkins in 1974. See Jessica Stern, *Loose Nukes, Poisons, and Terrorism: The New Threats to International Security.*
27. Rohan Gunaratna, *Inside Al Qaeda—Global Network of Terror*, New York: Columbia Press, 2002, p. 91.
28. Quote attributed to James Woolsey, 1994.
29. Bruce Hoffman, *Inside Terrorism*, New York: Columbia University Press, 1998, p. 205.
30. Lawrence Freeman, "Out of Nowhere—Bin Laden's Grievances," *BBC News*. Available at <www.bbc.co.uk/history/war/sept_11/build_up_05.shtml>.
31. Graham Allison, *Nuclear Terrorism*, New York: Times Books, 2004, p. 13.
32. David Albright, "Al-Qaeda's Quixotic Quest to go Nuclear," *Asia Times*, Nov 22, 2002. Available at: <www.atimes.com/atimes/Middle_East/DK22Ak01>. See also Tina Tarvainen, "Al Qaeda and WMD, a Primer," *Terrorism Monitor*, Vol. 3, Issue 11 (June 2, 2005). Available at: <http://jamestown.org/terrorism/news/article.php?articleid52369714>.
33. Gorka, "Combating Terrorism and its Implications for Intelligence," p. 8. See also, Renee Montage, "Hezbollah's Role Unlikely to Change," *National Public Radio*, Interview, October 29, 2006. Available at <www.npr.org/templates/transcript/transcript.php?storyId=5662488>.
34. Michael Whine, "The New Terrorism." Available at <www.ict.org.il/articles/articledet.cfm?articleid=427>.
35. Jerrold M. Post, "Killing in the Name of God: Osama Bin Laden and Al Qaeda," from *Know Thy Enemy: Profiles of Adversary Leaders and Their Strategic Cultures*, ed. Barry R. Schneider and Jerrold M. Post, Maxwell Air Force Base: USAF Counterproliferation Center, p. 33.
36. Conversation with Dr. Rohan Gunaratna, November 15, 2002 in Garmisch, Germany.
37. Ibid, p. 9.
38. Jessica Stern, "The Protean Enemy," *Foreign Affairs*, July–August, 2003, p. 33.
39. See Ann Tyson, "Al Qaeda Broken, but Dangerous," *Christian Science Monitor*, Jun. 24, 2002. Available at <www.csmonitor.com/2002/0624/p01s02-usgn.htm>.
40. Jason Burke, "Al Qaeda," *Foreign Policy*, May/June 2004, p. 18.
41. Ibid.
42. Ibid.
43. Dan Eggen, "9/11 Panel Links Al Qaeda, Iran," The *Washington Post*, June 26, 2004, p. A12. See also Stern, "The Protean Enemy."
44. Matthew Levitt, "Islamic Extremism in Europe: Beyond al Qaeda, Hamas, and Hezbollah in Europe," testimony before the Joint Hearing of the House Committee on International Relations, Subcommittee on Europe and Emerging Threats, April 27, 2005. available at <www.washingoninstitute.org/teplateC07.php?CID-234>.
45. Ibid.
46. Timothy Garden, "Security and the War Against Terrorism," *Foreign and Security Policy* by Tim Garden. Available at <www.tgarden.demon.co.uk/writings/articles/2002/020320riia.html>.
47. Stephen A. Cambone, *A New Structure for National Security Policy Planning*, Washington, DC: Government Printing Office, 1996, p. 43.
48. Gideon Rose, "It Could Happen Here—Facing the New Terrorism," *Foreign Affairs*, March–April, 1999, p. 1.
49. Discussion with Bruce Hoffman.
50. Multiple conversations with John Dorschner. Also, see John Dorschner, "A Shadowy Empire of Hate was Born of a War in Afghanistan," Knight–Ridder Newspapers, September 24, 2001.

51. "CDI Primer: Terrorist Finances," Oct. 25, 2002. Available at <www.cdi.org/terrorism/finance_primer-pr.cfm>.
52. Rudner, p. 222. See also, "Al Qaeda Income Cut, Says Foreign Office," *Daily Telegraph* (London), April 7, 2003.
53. Steve Kiser, "Al Qaeda's Financial Empire," unpublished dissertation for RAND, March 2005, p. 45.
54. Robin Wright, *Sacred Rage*, New York: Simon and Schuster, 2001, p. 252.
55. Ibid.
56. Ibid.
57. Patrick M Yost and Harjit Singh Sandhu, "The *hawala* Alternative Remittance System and its Role in Money Laundering," Interpol General Secretariat, January 2002. Available at <www.interpol.int/Public/FinancialCrime/MoneyLaundering/hawala/default.asp>.
58. Maurice Greenberg, "Terrorist Financing," *Council on Foreign Relations Report*, 2002, p. 11.
59. Ibid.
60. Ibid.
61. Neil A. Lewis, "The Money Trail—Court Upholds Freeze on Assets of Muslim Group Based in U.S." The *New York Times*, June 21, 2003, p. A11.
62. "US Accuses Charity of Financing Terror," *BBC Online*, Nov. 20. 2002.
63. Lewis 2003, p. A11.
64. Ibid, p. 16.
65. Ibid, p. 19.
66. Ibid.
67. Christopher Dobson and Ronald Payne, *The Terrorists, Their Weapons, Leaders and Tactics*, (New York: Facts on File, 1982), p. 80.
68. Ibid.
69. Ibid.
70. Post p. 35.
71. Gunaratna, p. 73.
72. Ibid.
73. Rudner, p. 203. See also, Robert Fisk, "With Runners and Whispers, al Qaeda Outfoxes U.S. Forces," *The Independent* (London), December 6, 2002.
74. Abdullah Ali Al-Salama, *Military Espionage in Islam*. Available at <www.skfriends.com/bin-laden-terrorist-manual.htm>.
75. Gunaratna, p. 76.
76. Michael Whine, "The New Terrorism." Available at <www.ict.org.il/articles/articledet.cfm?articleid=427>.
77. *A Military Guide to Terrorism in the Twenty–First Century*, Version 1.0, May 13, 2003, p. 40.
78. Ibid. p. 33.
79. John Arqilla and David Ronfeldt, ie., *Networks and Netwars*, Santa Monica: RAND, 2001, p. 9.
80. *A Military Guide to Terrorism in the the Twenty–First Century*, p. 40.
81. Rudner, p. 216.
82. Gorka, "Combating Terrorism and its Implications for Intelligence," p. 9.
83. Ibid.
84. Ibid.
85. "Al-Qaeda, An Ever-Shifting Web," *The Economist*, October 19–25, 2002, p. 26.
86. Ibid.
87. Ibid.
88. Graham Allison, *Nuclear Terrorism: The Ultimate Preventable Catastrophe*, New York: Owl Books, 2005, p. 8.
89. Ibid, p. 9.
90. Richard B. Myers, "Fighting Terrorism in an Information Age," U.S. Department of State, International Information Programs, Aug. 19, 2002, p. 2. Available at <http://usinfo.state.gov/regional/nea/sasia/text/0819info.htm>.
91. Ibid.
92. Judith Miller, "Lab Suggests Qaeda Planned to Build Arms, Officials Say," *New York Times*, September 14, 2002, p. 1.

93. David Kay, "WMD Terrorism: Hype or Reality," from *The Terrorism Threat and US Government Response: Operational and Organizational Factors*, eds. James M. Smith and William C. Thomas, U.S. Air Force Academy: INSS Book Series, 2001, p. 12.
94. "Terror Cells of Today Hard to Combat." The *New York Times*, August 20, 2002. Available at: <www.nytimes.com/aponline/international/AP-Evolution-of-Terror.html>.
95. Ibid. p. 45.
96. Ibid, p. 48.
97. Reuven Paz, "Global Jihad and WMD: Between Martyrdom and Mass Destruction," Society for Internet Research, September 25, 2006. Available at <www.sofir.org/sarchives/005026. php>. Accessed September 30, 2006.
98. Ibid.
99. Hamid Mir, "Osama Claims he has Nukes: If U.S. uses N-arms it will get same response," *Dawn Internet Edition*. November 10, 2001. Available at <www.dawn.com/2001/11/10/top1. htm>. Accessed October 23, 2006.
100. Robert Wesley, "Al–Qaeda's WMD Strategy After the U.S. Intervention in Afghanistan," *Jamestown Foundation*, Terrorism Monitor Vol. 3 Issue 20, October 21, 2005. Available at <http:// jamestown.org/terrorism/news/article.php?issue_id=3502>. Accessed on October 23, 2006.
101. Paz.
102. Wesley.
103. Akaki Dvali, "Instability in Georgia: A New Proliferation Threat?" (October 23, 2006) *Center for Nonproliferation Studies*, Monterey Institute. Available at <www.nti.org/e_research/e3_ 31a.html#fn5>. Accessed October 23, 2006.
104. "Interview with Jean-Louis Bruguiére," PBS, January 25, 2005. Available at <www.pbs.org/ wgbh/pages/frontline/shows/front/map/bruguiere.html>. Accessed on September 30, 2006.
105. Dan Darling, "Al Qaeda's Mad Scientist. The significance of Abu Khabab's death," *The Weekly Standard*, January 19, 2006. Available at <www.weeklystandard.com/Content/Public/Articles/ 000/000/006/602zqghe.asp>. Accessed on September 30, 2006.
106. "Protecting Charitable Organizations," U.S. Department of Treasury, Office of Terrorism and Financial Intelligence. Available at <www.treasury.gov/offices/enforcement/key-issues/ protecting/charities_execorder_13224-p.shtml#u>. Accessed on September 30, 2006.
107. National Commission on Terrorist Attacks, *The 9/11 Commission Report: Final Report of the National Commission on Terrorist Attacks Upon the United States*, New York: W.W. Norton & Co., 2004, p. 150–52.
108. Natalie O'Brien, "JI planned Holocaust gas attack in buildings," *Weekend Australian*, May 27, 2006. Available at <http://lightonthings.blogspot.com/2006_06_01_lightonthings_archive. html>. Accessed on September 30, 2006.
109. Ibid.
110. The National Security Strategy of the United States of America, September 2002. Available at <www.whitehouse.gov/nsc/nss.pdf>. Accessed September 30, 2006.
111. James Fallows, "Success Without Victory," *The Atlantic Monthly*, January–February 2005.
112. Matthew Levitt, "Untangling the Terror Web: Identifying and counteracting the Phenomenon of Crossover Between Terrorist Groups," *SAIS Review*, Vol. 24, No. 1 (Winter–Spring 2004): p. 35.
113. Rowan Scarborough, "Metrics Help Guide the Pentagon." *The Washington Times*, April 5, 2005, p. 3.
114. Levitt, p. 35.

Brigadier General Russell D. Howard (Retired) was a career Special Forces officer and is now the director of the Jebsen Center for Counterterrorism Studies at the Fletcher School at Tufts University. His recent publications include *Terrorism and Counterterrorism: Understanding the New Security Environment—Readings and Interpretations,* 2nd ed. (McGraw-Hill, 2005), and *Defeating Terrorism: Shaping the New Security Environment* (McGraw-Hill, 2003), and *Homeland Security and Terrorism: Readings and Interpretations* (McGraw-Hill, 2005).

Brian Michael Jenkins

The New Age of Terrorism

The purpose of this chapter is to consider how terrorism has changed over the past four decades. The word *terrorism* dates from the eighteenth century, but as recently as 1971—when Rand published my essay "The Five Stages of Urban Guerrilla Warfare"—the term had not yet acquired its present currency. Nor did it then refer to a distinct mode of armed conflict. That meaning would be added subsequently, by terrorists themselves and by analysts of terrorism; and in my view the latter impart more coherence to the phenomenon than the former.

We should be careful not to think of terrorism or terrorists as monolithic. Terrorism is a generalized construct derived from our concepts of morality, law, and the rules of war, whereas actual terrorists are shaped by culture, ideology, and politics—specific, inchoate factors and notions that motivate diverse actions. But although terrorists are not monolithic, neither are they isolated. They innovate; exploit new technology; learn from one another; imitate successful tactics; produce manuals of instruction based on experience; debate tactics, targets, and limits on violence; and justify their actions with doctrines and theories.

Thus we can, cautiously, identify apparent trends:

- Terrorism has become bloodier.
- Terrorists have developed new financial resources, so that they are less dependent on state sponsors.
- Terrorists have evolved new models of organization.
- Terrorists can now wage global campaigns.
- Terrorists have effectively exploited new communications technologies.
- Some terrorists have moved beyond tactics to strategy, although none of them have achieved their stated long-range goals.

These trends do not allow prediction or extrapolation; analysis is not prophecy. Neither do they imply inexorable progress. Terrorists have not done many of the things we worried about 30 years ago—our worst fears have not been realized. On the other hand, no amount of analysis can cover every conceivable terrorist scenario, every form of attack, or every angle. The future, like the past 40 years, will probably bring surprises and shocks.

Terrorism has Become Bloodier

Perhaps the most striking development is that terrorism has become bloodier, in terms of what acts are committed and how many victims are involved. The order of magnitude has increased almost every decade. In the 1970s the bloodiest incidents caused fatalities in the tens. In the 1980s, fatalities from the worst incidents were in the hundreds; by the 1990s, attacks on this scale had become more frequent. On 9/11 there were thousands of fatalities, and there could have been far more. We now contemplate plausible scenarios in which tens of thousands might die.

At one time, I wrote that terrorists wanted a lot of people watching, not a lot of people dead. They were limited not only by access to weapons but by self-constraint. Mayhem as such was seldom an objective. Terrorists had a sense of morality, a self-image, operational codes, and practical concerns—they wanted to maintain group cohesion, avoid alienating perceived constituents, and avoid provoking public outrage, which could lead to crackdowns. But these constraints gave way to large-scale indiscriminate violence as terrorists engaged in protracted, brutal conflicts; as the more squeamish dropped out; as terrorism became commonplace and the need for headlines demanded higher body counts; and as ethnic hatred and religious fanaticism replaced political agendas.

Some terrorists still operate below their capacity. Even the most fanatic jihadists, who believe that God mandates the slaughter of infidels, debate, pragmatically, the acceptability of collateral Muslim casualties, whether Shiite Muslims are potential allies or apostates, and whether beheadings are counterproductive. Overall, though, jihadists seem ready to murder millions, if necessary. Many of today's terrorists want a lot of people watching and a lot of people dead.

To repeat, though, some fears about what terrorists might do have not been realized. In a poll conducted in 1985, most experts predicted chemical terrorism by the end of the twentieth century; but when nerve gas was released on the subway in Tokyo in 1995, the consequences were less severe than had been imagined. Biological warfare has taken place only on a small scale, as in the anthrax letters of 2001.

During the 1960s and 1970s there were fears of nuclear black markets and nuclear terrorism. This fear was heightened by the collapse of the Soviet Union and the exposure of its nuclear arsenal to corruption and organized crime. But although nuclear terrorism remains a concern, it has not yet happened, nor have cities been held hostage with weapons of mass destruction.

Although accurate surface-to-air missiles are widely available and have been in some terrorists' arsenals for years, they have not been used against commercial aircraft outside conflict zones. Terrorists, so far as we know, have not attacked agriculture. Terrorists have not attempted to seize or sabotage nuclear reactors.

Also, there are no more terrorist organizations today than 10 or 20 years ago; and the annual number of international incidents has remained in the hundreds, not the thousands.

What conclusion can we draw? Although not all our fears have been realized, some may materialize in the future. Scenarios that seemed far-fetched in the 1970s are now plausible; in fact, 9/11 redefined plausibility. In present attempts to anticipate and prepare for what terrorists might do next, virtually no scenario is dismissed. Analysts and the public seriously consider the possibility that terrorists may send waves of suicide bombers to America's shopping malls; wipe out Boston's waterfront with a hijacked liquid-natural-gas carrier; topple the George Washington Bridge in New York City; crash planes into the Houses of Parliament in London, the Capitol in Washington, or a nuclear reactor; spray anthrax over a city; sink tankers to block narrow straits; release hoof-and-mouth disease; sabotage the banking system; spread smallpox; or destroy Manhattan with a nuclear bomb.

Terrorists' own chatter, echoing this speculation, may be picked up by intelligence services and taken as confirmation.

These concerns are due partly to 9/11 and partly to a new basis for analysis. Whereas traditional threat-based analysis assessed an enemy's intentions and capabilities, today's vulnerability-based analysis identifies a weakness and hypothesizes a terrorist and a worst-case scenario. Vulnerability analysis is useful for assessing consequences and preparedness, but it relegates the terrorist to a secondary role: the scenario is driven by the vulnerability. Often, such a scenario is reified and becomes a threat: it is successively considered possible, probable, inevitable, and imminent. In vulnerability-based assessment, consequences trump likelihood. Terrorists' actual capabilities, ambitions, and fantasies blur with our own speculation and fears to create what the terrorists want: an atmosphere of alarm.

By contrast, "red team" exercises, in which analysts actually plan terrorist operations, put terrorists (or their red team surrogates) back in the main role. This approach narrows the spectrum of potential attacks. From a terrorist's assumed perspective, some operations appear less attractive, or planning them seems more challenging. This may indeed happen in real-life terrorist groups. Actual terrorists may contemplate many modes of attack but keep returning to common forms such as vehicle attacks.

Terrorists have Developed New Ways of Financing their Operations

Since terrorists are outlaws, unable to hold territory and openly collect taxes, their finances are necessarily clandestine and often depend on criminal activity. Terrorist organizations that have survived for long periods have developed various financial resources. In the 1960s, rival superpowers and their local allies were willing to finance terrorism; but this support (with some exceptions) declined at the end of the Cold War, and terrorists had to seek other means.

One innovation of South American urban guerrillas in the early 1990s was kidnapping for ransom. Terrorists had previously avoided such kidnapping because its criminal connotations might tarnish a group, but its use spread as it brought in tens of millions of dollars.

Some groups engaged in extortion and protection rackets, gradually adding fraud and even legitimate investments. Drug trafficking also offered large-scale returns that benefited groups in South America, central Asia, and the Middle East.

Ethnic diasporas, émigré communities, and coreligionists could also be a source of contributions, especially when charity was presumably ordered by a religion. Such groups may sometimes have been unwitting supporters. In some cases, they were duped; in other cases, their contributions were ostensibly meant for humanitarian efforts by the recipients—schools, medical supplies, assistance to widows and orphans. However, some private contributors knew that their money financed terrorist operations.

Collecting money from various foreign sources and disbursing it to scattered operational units and operatives require clandestine transfers of funds. Some terrorist organizations are skilled at moving money from charitable organizations and criminal operations through informal banking systems, money order and cash wire services, and regular banks. Some authorities have reduced high-volume transactions, but it is not clear that they have severely impeded terrorists' cash flows, which may simply move into less regulated areas. We know the sums that have been blocked, but it is difficult to estimate the amounts moving in ways governments cannot monitor.

Terrorists benefit from uneven enforcement. Many financial institutions and some countries remain reluctant to interfere with suspect transfers, not because they support terrorism but because strict controls could interfere with lucrative transactions deriving from tax evasion, white-collar crime, and political corruption.

Terrorists have become Less Dependent on State Sponsors

Even during the Cold War, there was less and less enthusiasm for backing guerrillas so as to wage surrogate warfare. The Soviet Union became disenchanted with national liberation movements and especially with the Palestinians: by the mid-1980s, Europe's colonial empires had been dismantled; the Americans had been driven from Indochina; Cuba was bankrupt; Marxist guerrillas in Latin America seemed stalled; and in 1985 Soviet diplomats were kidnapped in Lebanon. Similarly, in the United States support faded for clandestine projects to topple Fidel Castro in Cuba, an enterprise of the 1960s; and Congress restricted further funding for the contras in Nicaragua—although support continued for the mujahideen fighting against Soviet forces in Afghanistan. Also, both the United States and the Soviet Union were becoming increasingly concerned about terrorism.

With the departure of the Soviet Union from Afghanistan and the end of the Cold War, local conflicts no longer had strategic significance. This development facilitated the resolution of a few armed struggles—guerrillas and governments made peace. Others in the field were left to their own devices. Some, like the old Palestinian groups, became toothless; some, like those in Central America, turned to local banditry. But certain others, like the Afghan veterans, survived and created new, more autonomous enterprises.

The end of the Cold War also altered the calculations of the few nations identified by the United States as sponsors of terrorism. It reduced support from and protection by the Soviet Union—as in Syria, a patron of the Palestinians. Iraq, involved in a costly war with Iran, had sought assistance from the West, but that was ended when Iraq invaded Kuwait in 1990. Libya was bombed by the United States, and although it continued to support terrorist operations (notably sabotage of American and French airliners), it became more circumspect and eventually sought rapprochement with the West. Sanctions eventually had their effect. Gradually, therefore, state-sponsored terrorism became less of a problem.

However, state sponsorship had provided a means of monitoring terrorists, and its decline entailed less influence over terrorist movements and a loss of intelligence sources within them. With the severance of these links, we knew less. This was demonstrated on 9/11. Not only American intelligence but also other intelligence services had missed the preparations. They knew bits but lacked a complete picture.

Terrorists have Evolved New Models of Organization

Commenting on terrorists' organization requires distinguishing among groups that use terrorist tactics. Guerrilla groups, governments, and armies differ from urban guerrilla gangs and from groups like Germany's Red Army Faction, Italy's Red Brigades, or the Japanese Red Army for which terrorism was the primary (or only) activity. When we talk about the evolution of terrorist organization, we mean the latter—organizing to do terrorism. And even in this category, terrorist groups range from primitive gangs to sophisticated organizations.

The guiding principle of all terrorist organization is survival, which depends on maintaining secret membership and operational security, preventing infiltration, punishing betrayal, and limiting damage.

Larger organizations and more ambitious operations have functional specialization, with individuals devoted to recruiting, training, intelligence, reconnaissance, planning, logistics, finance, propaganda, and social services (e.g., support for widows, orphans, and families of suicide attackers). Functional specialization would normally lead to hierarchy and bureaucracy, as in al-Qaida before 9/11. Some groups are organized as miniature armies with general staffs, brigades, and battalions. But hierarchies are open to penetration and may stifle initiative.

Al-Qaida seems to be one of the first groups to pattern itself on a lean international business model: hierarchical but not pyramidal, loosely run, decentralized but linked, able to assemble and allocate resources and coordinate operations, but hard to depict organizationally or penetrate. Networks provide numerous operational benefits: they are quick to learn, adaptive, and resilient—hard to break. To work well, networks require strong shared beliefs, a collective vision, some original basis for trust, and excellent communications. Networks have become an object of intense analysis in the intelligence community. Whether the global jihadist network created by al-Qaida is unique or can be replicated by future groups remains a question.

The online monthly manuals to exhort and instruct would-be terrorists seem close to a concept suggested by Louis Beam—"leaderless resistance"—in which self-proclaimed combatants are linked by common beliefs and goals and wage a common terrorist war, but operate autonomously. This model may be possible for isolated actions, such as those by animal-rights activists and ecoguerrillas; but organizational continuity and major operations still require cooperation, coordination, and structure, which in turn require a basis for trust that is difficult to establish on the Internet.

Terrorists are Able to Mount Global Campaigns

Contemporary terrorism transcends national frontiers; in fact, this is what initially made it a subject of international concern. There are two ways in which terrorism can be international.

First, terrorists can attack foreign targets: foreign airliners, embassies, and local offices and employees of multinational corporations—a growing body of entities whose activities in a country, inadvertently or by design, make them participants (and thereby targets) in local conflicts. To draw international attention, embarrass, increase their leverage over local governments, or compel international intervention, terrorists have bombed embassies, assassinated or abducted diplomats, and held corporate executives for ransom. Most incidents of international terrorism fall into this first category.

Second, terrorists can cross national frontiers to carry out attacks abroad, again to gain international attention, or to isolate their foes from their hosts—or simply because distant targets are not as well guarded as targets at home. The Palestinians, inspired by the Algerian FLN's (Front de Libération Nationale) terrorist campaign in mainland France, were the first to systematically adopt this approach, but others soon followed.

Many terrorists have seen their struggles as global. Marxist revolutionaries are an example. In the late twentieth century, for instance, Marxist leaders considered themselves beyond borders and united in revolution. In 1966, the Tri-Continental Conference in Havana was intended to bring together the world's guerrilla movements. No coordinated revolutionary movement emerged, but some interesting alliances eventually evolved, such as that between the Japanese Red Army—rebels looking for a cause—and the Popular Front for the Liberation of Palestine (PFLP), which was both Palestinian and Marxist and cultivated foreign recruits and relationships. The brief coalescence of Europe's left-wing terrorist groups led to concerns about "Euroterrorism," and the Irish Republican Army (IRA) and Spain's Euskadi Ta Askatasuna (ETA) exchanged technical know-how.

The jihadists, inspired and guided by al-Qaida's ideology, represent a further and apparently more durable development. Historically, al-Qaida was never a centrally directed, disciplined organization, even when it operated training camps in Afghanistan. It remained a loose association, capable of centrally directed action and of assembling resources for specific operations, but always more of a network than a hierarchy. Its nature proved to be its strength at a time when survival required decentralization. Al-Qaida is truly a global enterprise, drawing recruits and funding from all over the world, maintaining connections in 60 countries, and carrying out operations in perhaps 20. It may properly be called a global insurgency—a phase that implies both scale and reach.

Lesser movements that are global in cause and ambition, though far below the jihadists in operational capabilities, include neo-Nazis, animal-rights extremists, and some segments of the disparate antiglobalization movement.

Terrorists have Effectively Exploited New Communications Technologies

For terrorists, the most significant technology is not weapons but direct communication with their multiple audiences. Terrorism, to repeat, was originally aimed at the people watching. Victims were threatened or killed to make a point, not only to the terrorists' foes but above all to the terrorists' own constituents. Technological developments in the 1960s and 1970s—the ubiquity of television, more portable television cameras, communications satellites, uplinks to remote news crews, global news networks—allowed terrorists to reach audiences worldwide almost instantaneously. By carrying out visually dramatic acts of violence, terrorists could virtually guarantee coverage, intensifying the terror and inflating their own importance.

It should be noted that terrorists have not always communicated effectively. For example, the dramas that draw the attention of the news media have often obscured the terrorists' political message: whatever they had to say was lost in the anguish caused by the attack itself. Moreover, terrorists' writings have frequently been incomprehensible to all but a few; and some terrorists have issued voluminous manifestos and strategic directives that mostly remain unread. Sometimes they have failed to use the media pragmatically, as when terrorists who had kidnapped a prominent figure released a photo of the victim holding a placard on which they had written not a short, bold slogan but a message of 50 words or more that was too small to be legible. Also, news editors, rather than the terrorists themselves, determine what will be covered on television. Images considered too gruesome may not be shown; and except for a sound bite, terrorists' messages may be omitted.

Videotape permitted terrorists to substitute motion pictures for still shots, so that they and their hostages could speak directly into the camera, but access to the media was still controlled by others. Not until the development of the Internet did terrorists have unmediated access to their audiences.

On the Internet, terrorist violence, performed on-camera, can be webcast directly and unedited. The Internet also allows direct communication between terrorists' public affairs departments and various audiences: recruits, sympathizers, broader constituencies, enemy states, and citizens who may disagree with their own governments' policies. A bombing no longer needs to be followed by a telephone call to a wire service. Today's terrorists have Web sites, publish online magazines, explain their causes, debate doctrine, and provide instruction in making explosives. They may use these same channels to clandestinely communicate with operatives through coded messages or, according to some reports, steganography.

Some of the jihadists' recruiting videos, emphasizing atrocities at the hands of infidels, are of high quality and probably appeal to potential adherents. And after a webcast of an execution appears on the Internet, mainstream media are more likely to show at least short edited segments. Such material may not spread significant alarm, but its appeal to violence-prone young men who harbor fantasies of revenge should not be underestimated. Iraq represents the latest phase in this evolution. Videos of beheadings of hostages circulate in Iraqi markets, and al-Qaida has reportedly compiled them in an exultant film.

This development suggests a democratization of extremism, whereby people can in a sense shop for belief systems and submerge themselves in "virtual groups" that encourage violence.

Terrorists have Achieved Strategic Results

Through dramatic acts of violence, terrorists have always attracted attention, evoked alarm, caused disruption, instigated crises, and obliged governments to divert resources to security and occasionally to make concessions. Strategically, though, they were less effective. They could sometimes upset negotiations and impede the resolution of conflicts. In fragile democracies they could sometimes provoke an overthrow of a government by those, usually the armed forces, who were determined to take a stronger line against terrorism. But terrorists rarely created powerful political movements. They were not able to fundamentally alter national policies, and they brought down no governments directly.

However, terrorists have gradually developed ways to achieve strategic results. Scale was one way. The best example is 9/11, which not only killed nearly 3,000 people, caused hundreds of billions of dollars in damage, and is still affecting the American economy but also has had a profound influence on U.S. policies. It made the "global war on terror" the framework for future policy, provoked two invasions, and led to some profound changes in government organization.

Another example of strategic effects is found in Iraq. In 2004, Iraqi insurgents kidnapped and beheaded or threatened to behead foreign nationals—aid officials, contract workers, journalists—and, despite the overall high level of violence in Iraq, were able to create political crises in countries participating in the multinational coalition, especially where there was strong domestic opposition to the war. In return for releasing the hostages, the kidnappers demanded, among other things, that governments withdraw forces or that companies cease operations. Only one government, the Philippines, pulled out; but, coming at a time when the United States was attempting to persuade additional countries to join the coalition, the kidnappings, more than the intensification of the conflict, persuaded others to stay away—not one new country joined. The kidnappings also forced aid organizations to suspend or reduce their activities, thereby slowing economic reconstruction and prolonging the misery that facilitated further recruiting by the insurgents.

Terrorist strategy is based not on achieving military superiority but rather on making the enemy's life unbearable by attacking incessantly (this contributed to Israel's decision to withdraw from Lebanon); by inflicting endless casualties (the strategy of the Palestinians' suicide bombings); by destroying tourism and discouraging investment, and thus inflicting economic pain; and by carrying out spectacular operations like 9/11.

Yet although terrorists have escalated their violence, developed new methods of financing their operations, exploited new communications technologies, created new organizational models, and undertaken global enterprises, they have yet to achieve their own stated long-range objectives.

Terrorists have not Accomplished their Long-Range Goals

The South American urban guerrilla groups that initiated the wave of kidnappings and bombings in the 1970s were wiped out in a few years, having achieved no political result except brutal repression. Their counterparts in Europe, Japan, and North America were also suppressed, although offspring of Italy's Red Brigades reemerge from time to time. The IRA has made peace; apart from a few diehards, it is no longer a fighting force—its contest has been resolved politically. In Europe, only Spain's ETA, now in its fourth decade, fights on for Basque independence.

The death of Yasir Arafat symbolized the end of an era in the Palestinians' struggle. If a viable, independent Palestinian state is ultimately formed, much credit will be given to him. It cannot be denied that terrorism kept the Palestinians' hopes alive when Arab governments were defeated on the battlefield, that terrorism galvanized the Palestinian population and contributed to the concept of the Palestinian state, and that terrorism compelled international intervention. But today, the violence continues. Different militants have taken the field. Suicide bombings have been elevated to a strategy. Walls have been erected. Peace initiatives are renewed. War-weary populations await some kind of resolution. What that will be remains uncertain.

Meanwhile, today's jihadists speak of driving the infidels out of the Middle East, of toppling the exposed apostate regimes that depend on their support, of then going on to destroy Israel and ultimately reestablishing the caliphate. They have proved to be dangerous terrorists, have achieved some strategic results, are determined to continue attacking, and are resilient survivors, capable of recruiting despite adversity. Destroying their terrorist enterprise will take years. And until that happens, they might prevail in Afghanistan or Pakistan and might make it too costly for the United States to remain in Iraq. But they have not yet achieved these successes, and the verdict on their movement must await the judgment of future historians.

This is a paradox of terrorism. Terrorists often succeed tactically and thereby gain attention, cause alarm, and attract recruits. But their struggle has brought them no success measured against their own stated goals. In that sense, terrorism has failed, but the phenomenon of terrorism continues.

Conclusion

The course of terrorism over the next few decades cannot be predicted, just as the actual evolution of terrorism over the last 30 years could probably not have been predicted.

Suppose that at the beginning of the 1970s, when contemporary terrorism was still in its early stages and formal research had just begun, I had, with remarkable prescience, outlined its future course. Take as the starting date President Nixon's creation of the Cabinet Committee to Combat Terrorism in October 1972.

It would have been easy to forecast hundreds of airline hijackings, since many had already occurred; but the screening of all passengers, let alone the elaborate security measures that have now become routine, would have been considered very unlikely. A terrorist attack had just occurred at the Munich Olympics; still, it would have been far-fetched to predict that in 2004, more than $1 billion would be spent on security at the games in Athens.

Suppose that I had predicted the terrorist assassinations of the former prime minister of Italy, the former president of Argentina, the presidents of Lebanon and Egypt, two prime ministers in India, and one in Israel; and the attempted assassinations of the pope and the heads of government of Pakistan, Egypt, and the United Kingdom.

Suppose that I had predicted hundreds of suicide bombings; the release of nerve gas on subways; a Senate office building shut down by letters containing anthrax spores; and the destruction of the World Trade Center (which was still being built in 1972). Suppose that, with regard to the United States, I had predicted its military retaliation against terrorism; a global war on terror as the framework for its foreign policy; its bombing of Libya; its invasions of Afghanistan and of Iraq; its creation of a new Department of Homeland Security; its detention of American citizens without trial; and its arguments supposedly justifying the use of torture.

Such predictions would have been dismissed as fiction, not sober analysis. Who, then, can say with confidence what will or will not happen over the next 30 years?

Brian Michael Jenkins is a senior advisor to the president of the RAND Corporation and director of the National Transportation Security Center at the Mineta Transportation Institute. A former Army captain who served with Special Forces in Vietnam, Jenkins has served on several national commissions and has provided testimony at numerous Congressional hearings on terrorism matters.

The Nature of the Post–9/11 WMD Terrorism Threat

Thomas Homer-Dixon

The Rise of Complex Terrorism

It's 4 a.m. on a sweltering summer night in July 2003. Across much of the United States, power plants are working full tilt to generate electricity for millions of air conditioners that are keeping a ferocious heat wave at bay. The electricity grid in California has repeatedly buckled under the strain, with rotating blackouts from San Diego to Santa Rosa.

In different parts of the state, half a dozen small groups of men and women gather. Each travels in a rented minivan to its prearranged destination—for some, a location outside one of the hundreds of electrical substations dotting the state; for others, a spot upwind from key, high-voltage transmission lines. The groups unload their equipment from the vans. Those outside the substations put together simple mortars made from materials bought at local hardware stores, while those near the transmission lines use helium to inflate weather balloons with long silvery tails. At a precisely coordinated moment, the homemade mortars are fired, sending showers of aluminum chaff over the substations. The balloons are released and drift into the transmission lines.

Simultaneously, other groups are doing the same thing along the Eastern Seaboard and in the South and Southwest. A national electrical system already under immense strain is massively short-circuited, causing a cascade of power failures across the country. Traffic lights shut off. Water and sewage systems are disabled. Communications systems break down. The financial system and national economy come screeching to a halt.

Sound far-fetched? Perhaps it would have before September 11, 2001, but certainly not now. We've realized, belatedly, that our societies are wide-open targets for terrorists. We're easy prey because of two key trends: First, the growing technological capacity of small groups and individuals to destroy things and people; and, second, the increasing vulnerability of our economic and technological systems to carefully aimed attacks. While commentators have devoted considerable ink and airtime to the first of these trends, they've paid far less attention to the second, and they've virtually ignored their combined effect. Together, these two trends facilitate a new and sinister kind of mass violence—a "complex terrorism" that threatens modern, high-tech societies in the world's most developed nations.

Our fevered, Hollywood-conditioned imaginations encourage us to focus on the sensational possibility of nuclear or biological attacks—attacks that might kill tens of thousands of people in a single strike. These threats certainly deserve attention, but not to the neglect of the likelier and ultimately deadlier disruptions that could result from the clever exploitation by terrorists of our societies' new and growing complexities.

Weapons of Mass Disruption

The steady increase in the destructive capacity of small groups and individuals is driven largely by three technological advances: more powerful weapons, the dramatic progress in communications and information processing, and more abundant opportunities to divert nonweapon technologies to destructive ends.

Consider first the advances in weapons technology. Over the last century, progress in materials engineering, the chemistry of explosives, and miniaturization of electronics has brought steady improvement in all key weapons characteristics, including accuracy, destructive power, range, portability, ruggedness, ease-of-use, and affordability. Improvements in light weapons are particularly relevant to trends in terrorism and violence by small groups, where the devices of choice include rocket-propelled grenade launchers, machine guns, light mortars, land mines, and cheap assault rifles such as the famed AK-47. The effects of improvements in these weapons are particularly noticeable in developing countries. A few decades ago, a small band of terrorists or insurgents attacking a rural village might have used bolt-action rifles, which take precious time to reload. Today, cheap assault rifles multiply the possible casualties resulting from such an attack. As technological change makes it easier to kill, societies are more likely to become locked into perpetual cycles of attack and counterattack that render any normal trajectory of political and economic development impossible.

Meanwhile, new communications technologies—from satellite phones to the Internet—allow violent groups to marshal resources and coordinate activities around the planet. Transnational terrorist organizations can use the Internet to share information on weapons and recruiting tactics, arrange surreptitious fund transfers across borders, and plan attacks. These new technologies can also dramatically enhance the reach and power of age-old procedures. Take the ancient *hawala* system of moving money between countries, widely used in Middle Eastern and Asian societies. The system, which relies on brokers linked together by clan-based networks of trust, has become faster and more effective through the use of the Internet.

Information-processing technologies have also boosted the power of terrorists by allowing them to hide or encrypt their messages. The power of a modern laptop computer today is comparable to the computational power available in the entire U.S. Defense Department in the mid-1960s. Terrorists can use this power to run widely available state-of-the-art encryption software. Sometimes less advanced computer technologies are just as effective. For instance, individuals can use a method called steganography ("hidden writing") to embed messages into digital photographs or music clips. Posted on publicly available Web sites, the photos or clips are downloaded by collaborators as necessary. (This technique was reportedly used by recently arrested terrorists when they planned to blow up the U.S. Embassy in Paris.) At latest count, 140 easy-to-use steganography tools were available on the Internet. Many other off-the-shelf technologies—such as "spread-spectrum" radios that randomly switch their broadcasting and receiving signals—allow terrorists to obscure their messages and make themselves invisible.

The Web also provides access to critical information. The September 11 terrorists could have found there all the details they needed about the floor plans and design characteristics of the World Trade Center and about how demolition experts use progressive collapse to destroy large buildings. The Web also makes available sets of instructions—or "technical ingenuity"—needed to combine readily available materials in destructive ways. Practically anything an extremist wants to know about kidnapping, bomb making, and assassination is now available online. One somewhat facetious example: It's possible to convert everyday materials into potentially destructive devices like the "potato cannon." With a barrel and combustion chamber fashioned from common plastic pipe, and with propane as an explosive propellant, a well-made cannon can hurl a homely spud hundreds of meters—or throw chaff onto electrical substations. A quick search of the Web reveals dozens of sites giving instructions on how to make one.

Finally, modern, high-tech societies are filled with supercharged devices packed with energy, combustibles, and poisons, giving terrorists ample opportunities to divert such non-weapon technologies to destructive ends. To cause horrendous damage, all terrorists must do is figure out how to release this power and let it run wild or, as they did on September 11, take control of this power and retarget it. Indeed, the assaults on New York City and the Pentagon were not low-tech affairs, as is often argued. True, the terrorists used simple box cutters to hijack the planes, but the box cutters were no more than the "keys" that allowed the terrorists to convert a high-tech means of transport into a high-tech weapon of mass destruction. Once the hijackers had used these keys to access and turn on their weapon, they were able to deliver a kiloton of explosive power into the World Trade Center with deadly accuracy.

High-Tech Hubris

The vulnerability of advanced nations stems not only from the greater destructive capacities of terrorists, but also from the increased vulnerability of the West's economic and technological systems. This additional vulnerability is the product of two key social and technological developments: first, the growing complexity and interconnectedness of our modern societies; and second, the increasing geographic concentration of wealth, human capital, knowledge, and communication links.

Consider the first of these developments. All human societies encompass a multitude of economic and technological systems. We can think of these systems as networks—that is, as sets of nodes and links among those nodes. The U.S. economy consists of numerous nodes, including corporations, factories, and urban centers; it also consists of links among these nodes, such as highways, rail lines, electrical grids, and fiber-optic cables. As societies modernize and become richer, their networks become more complex and interconnected. The number of nodes increases, as does the density of links among the nodes and the speed at which materials, energy, and information are pushed along these links. Moreover, the nodes themselves become more complex as the people who create, operate, and manage them strive for better performance. (For instance, a manufacturing company might improve efficiency by adopting more intricate inventory-control methods.)

Complex and interconnected networks sometimes have features that make their behavior unstable and unpredictable. In particular, they can have feedback loops that produce vicious cycles. A good example is a stock market crash, in which selling drives down prices, which begets more selling. Networks can also be tightly coupled, which means that links among the nodes are short, therefore making it more likely that problems with one node will spread to others. When drivers tailgate at high speeds on freeways, they create a tightly coupled system: A mistake by one driver, or a sudden shock coming from outside the system, such as a deer running across the road, can cause a chain reaction of cars piling onto each other. We've seen such knock-on effects in the U.S. electrical, telephone, and air traffic systems, when a failure in one part of the network has sometimes produced a cascade of failures across the country. Finally, in part because of feedbacks and tight coupling, networks often exhibit nonlinear behavior, meaning that a small shock or perturbation to the network produces a disproportionately large disruption.

Terrorists and other malicious individuals can magnify their own disruptive power by exploiting these features of complex and interconnected networks. Consider the archetypal lone, nerdy high-school kid hacking away at his computer in his parents' basement who can create a computer virus that produces chaos in global communications and data systems. But there's much more to worry about than just the proliferation of computer viruses. A special investigative commission set up in 1997 by then U.S. President Bill Clinton reported that "growing complexity and interdependence, especially in the energy and communications infrastructures, create an increased possibility that a rather minor and routine disturbance can cascade into a regional outage." The commission continued: "We are convinced that our vulnerabilities are increasing steadily, that the means to exploit those weaknesses are readily available and that the costs [of launching an attack] continue to drop."

Terrorists must be clever to exploit these weaknesses. They must attack the right nodes in the right networks. If they don't, the damage will remain isolated and the overall network will be resilient. Much depends upon the network's level of redundancy—that is, on the degree to which the damaged node's functions can be offloaded to undamaged nodes. As terrorists come to recognize the importance of redundancy, their ability to disable complex networks will improve. Langdon Winner, a theorist of politics and technology, provides the first rule of modern terrorism: "Find the critical but nonredundant parts of the system and sabotage . . . them according to your purposes." Winner concludes that "the science of complexity awaits a Machiavelli or Clausewitz to make the full range of possibilities clear."

The range of possible terrorist attacks has expanded due to a second source of organizational vulnerability in modern economies—the rising concentration of high-value assets in geographically small locations. Advanced societies concentrate valuable things and people in order to achieve economies of scale. Companies in capital-intensive industries can usually reduce the per-unit cost of their goods by building larger production facilities. Moreover, placing expensive equipment and highly skilled people in a single location provides easier access, more efficiencies, and synergies that constitute an important source of wealth. That is why we build places like the World Trade Center.

In so doing, however, we also create extraordinarily attractive targets for terrorists, who realize they can cause a huge amount of damage in a single strike. On September 11, a building complex that took seven years to construct collapsed in 90 minutes, obliterating 10 million square feet of office space and exacting at least $30 billion in direct costs. A major telephone switching office was destroyed, another heavily damaged, and important cellular antennas on top of the towers were lost. Key transit lines through southern Manhattan were buried under rubble. Ironically, even a secret office of the U.S. Central Intelligence Agency was destroyed in the attack, temporarily disrupting normal intelligence operations.

Yet despite the horrific damage to the area's infrastructure and New York City's economy, the attack did not cause catastrophic failures in U.S. financial, economic, or communications networks. As it turned out, the World Trade Center was not a critical, nonredundant node. At least it wasn't critical in the way most people (including, probably, the terrorists) would have thought. Many of the financial firms in the destroyed buildings had made contingency plans for disaster by setting up alternate facilities for data, information, and computer equipment in remote locations. Though the NASDAQ headquarters was demolished, for instance, the exchange's data centers in Connecticut and Maryland remained linked to trading companies through two separate connections that passed through 20 switching centers. NASDAQ officials later claimed that their system was so robust that they could have restarted trading only a few hours after the attack. Some World Trade Center firms had made advanced arrangements with companies specializing in providing emergency relocation facilities in New Jersey and elsewhere. Because of all this proactive planning—and the network redundancy it produced—the September 11 attacks caused remarkably little direct disruption to the U.S. financial system (despite the unprecedented closure of the stock market for several days).

But when we look back years from now, we may recognize that the attacks had a critical effect on another kind of network that we've created among ourselves: a tightly coupled, very unstable, and highly nonlinear psychological network. We're all nodes in this particular network, and the links among us consist of Internet connections, satellite signals, fiber-optic cables, talk radio, and 24-hour television news. In the minutes following the attack, coverage of the story flashed across this network. People then stayed in front of their televisions for hours on end; they viewed and reviewed the awful video clips on the CNN Web site; they plugged phone lines checking on friends and relatives; and they sent each other millions upon millions of e-mail messages—so many, in fact, that the Internet was noticeably slower for days afterwards.

Along these links, from TV and radio stations to their audiences, and especially from person to person through the Internet, flowed raw emotion: grief, anger, horror, disbelief, fear, and hatred. It was as if we'd all been wired into one immense, convulsing, and reverberating neural network. Indeed, the biggest impact of the September 11 attacks wasn't the direct disruption of financial, economic, communications, or transportation networks—physical stuff, all. Rather, by working through the network we've created within and among our heads, the attacks had their biggest impact on our collective psychology and our subjective feelings of security and safety. This network acts like a huge megaphone, vastly amplifying the emotional impact of terrorism.

To maximize this impact, the perpetrators of complex terrorism will carry out their attacks in audacious, unexpected, and even bizarre manners—using methods that are, ideally, unimaginably cruel. By so doing, they will create the impression that anything is possible, which further magnifies fear. From this perspective, the World Trade Center represented an ideal target, because the Twin Towers were an icon of the magnificence and boldness of American capitalism. When they collapsed like a house of cards, in about 15 seconds each, it suggested that American capitalism was a house of cards, too. How could anything so solid and powerful and so much a part of American identity vanish so quickly? And the use of passenger airplanes made matters worse by exploiting our worst fears of flying.

Unfortunately, this emotional response has had huge, real-world consequences. Scared, insecure, grief-stricken people aren't ebullient consumers. They behave cautiously and save more. Consumer demand drops, corporate investment falls, and economic growth slows. In the end, via the multiplier effect of our technology-amplified emotional response, the September 11 terrorists may have achieved an economic impact far greater than they ever dreamed possible. The total cost of lost economic growth and decreased equity value around the world could exceed a trillion dollars. Since the cost of carrying out the attack itself was probably only a few hundred thousand dollars, we're looking at an economic multiplier of over a millionfold.

The Weakest Links

Complex terrorism operates like jujitsu—it redirects the energies of our intricate societies against us. Once the basic logic of complex terrorism is understood (and the events of September 11 prove that terrorists are beginning to understand it), we can quickly identify dozens of relatively simple ways to bring modern, high-tech societies to their knees.

How would a Clausewitz of terrorism proceed? He would pinpoint the critical complex networks upon which modern societies depend. They include networks for producing and distributing energy, information, water, and food; the highways, railways, and airports that make up our transportation grid; and our healthcare system. Of these, the vulnerability of the food system is particularly alarming [see sidebar on opposite page]. However, terrorism experts have paid the most attention to the energy and information networks, mainly because they so clearly underpin the vitality of modern economies.

The energy system—which comprises everything from the national network of gas pipelines to the electricity grid—is replete with high-value nodes like oil refineries, tank farms, and electrical substations. At times of peak energy demand, this network (and in particular, the electricity grid) is very tightly coupled. The loss of one link in the grid means that the electricity it carries must be offloaded to other links. If other links are already operating near capacity, the additional load can cause them to fail, too, thus displacing their energy to yet other links. We saw this kind of breakdown in August 1996, when the failure of the Big Eddy transmission line in northern Oregon caused overloading on a string of transmission lines down the West Coast of the United States, triggering blackouts that affected 4 million people in nine states.

Substations are clear targets because they represent key nodes linked to many other parts of the electrical network. Substations and high-voltage transmission lines are also "soft" targets, since they can be fairly easily disabled or destroyed. Tens of thousands of miles of transmission lines are strung across North America, often in locations so remote that the lines are almost impossible to protect, but they are nonetheless accessible by four-wheel drive. Transmission towers can be brought down with well-placed explosive charges. Imagine a carefully planned sequence of attacks on these lines, with emergency crews and investigators dashing from one remote attack site to another, constantly off-balance and unable to regain control. Detailed maps of locations of substations and transmission lines for much of North America are easily available on the Web. Not even all the police and military personnel in the United States would suffice to provide even rudimentary protection to this immense network.

The energy system also provides countless opportunities for turning supposedly benign technology to destructive ends. For instance, large gas pipelines, many of which run near or even through urban areas, have huge explosive potential; attacks on them could

Feeding Frenzies

Shorting out electrical grids or causing train derailments would be small-scale sabotage compared with terrorist attacks that intentionally exploit psychological vulnerabilities. One key vulnerability is our fear for our health—an attack that exploits this fear would foster widespread panic. Probably the easiest way to strike at the health of an industrialized nation is through its food-supply system.

Modern food-supply systems display many key features that a prospective terrorist would seek in a complex network and are thus highly vulnerable to attack. Such systems are tightly coupled, and they have many nodes—including huge factory farms and food-processing plants—with multiple connections to other nodes.

The recent foot-and-mouth disease crisis in the United Kingdom provided dramatic evidence of these characteristics. By the time veterinarians found the disease, it had already spread throughout Great Britain. As in the United States, the drive for economic efficiencies in the British farming sector has produced a highly integrated system in which foods move briskly from farm to table. It has also led to economic concentration, with a few immense abattoirs scattered across the land replacing the country's many small slaughterhouses. Foot-and-mouth disease spread rapidly in large part because infected animals were shipped from farms to these distant abattoirs.

Given these characteristics, foot-and-mouth disease seems a useful vector for a terrorist attack. The virus is endemic in much of the world and thus easy to obtain. Terrorists could contaminate 20 or 30 large livestock farms or ranches across the United States, allowing the disease to spread through the network, as it did in Great Britain. Such an attack would probably bring the U.S. cattle, sheep, and pig industries to a halt in a matter of weeks, costing the economy tens of billions of dollars.

Despite the potential economic impact of such an attack, however, it wouldn't have the huge psychological effect that terrorists value, because foot-and-mouth disease rarely affects humans. Far more dramatic would be the poisoning of our food supply. Here the possibilities are legion. For instance, grain storage and transportation networks in the United States are easily accessible; unprotected grain silos dot the countryside and railway cars filled with grain often sit for long periods on railway sidings. Attackers could break into these silos and grain cars to deposit small amounts of contaminants, which would then diffuse through the food system.

Polychlorinated biphenyls (PCBs)—easily found in the oil in old electrical transformers—are a particularly potent group of contaminants, in part because they contain trace amounts of dioxins. These chemicals are both carcinogenic and neurotoxic; they also disrupt the human endocrine system. Children in particular are vulnerable. Imagine the public hysteria if, several weeks after grain silos and railway cars had been laced with PCBs and the poison had spread throughout the food network, terrorists publicly suggested that health authorities test food products for PCB contamination (U.S. federal food inspectors might detect the PCBS on their own, but the inspection system is stretched very thin and contamination could easily be missed.) At that point, millions of people could have already eaten the products.

> Such a contamination scenario is not in the realm of science fiction or conspiracy theories. In January 1999, 500 tons of animal feed in Belgium were accidentally contaminated with approximately 50 kilograms of PCBs from transformer oil. Some 10 million people in Belgium, the Netherlands, France, and Germany subsequently ate the contaminated food products. This single incident may in time cause up to 8,000 cases of cancer.
>
> *—T.H.D.*

have the twin effect of producing great local damage and wider disruptions in energy supply. And the radioactive waste pools associated with most nuclear reactors are perhaps the most lethal targets in the national energy-supply system. If the waste in these facilities were dispersed into the environment, the results could be catastrophic. Fortunately, such attacks would be technically difficult.

Even beyond energy networks, opportunities to release the destructive power of benign technologies abound. Chemical plants are especially tempting targets, because they are packed with toxins and flammable, even explosive, materials. Security at such facilities is often lax: An April 1999 study of chemical plants in Nevada and West Virginia by the U.S. Agency for Toxic Substances and Disease Registry concluded that security ranged from "fair to very poor" and that oversights were linked to "complacency and lack of awareness of the threat." And every day, trains carrying tens of thousands of tons of toxic material course along transport corridors throughout the United States. All a terrorist needs is inside knowledge that a chemical-laden train is traveling through an urban area at a specific time, and a well-placed object (like a piece of rail) on the track could cause a wreck, a chemical release, and a mass evacuation. A derailment of such a train at a nonredundant link in the transport system—such as an important tunnel or bridge—could be particularly potent. (In fact, when the U.S. bombing campaign in Afghanistan began on October 7, 2001, the U.S. railroad industry declared a three-day moratorium on transporting dangerous chemicals.) Recent accidents in Switzerland and Baltimore, Maryland, make clear that rail and highway tunnels are vulnerable because they are choke points for transportation networks and because it's extraordinarily hard to extinguish explosions and fires inside them.

Modern communications networks also are susceptible to terrorist attacks. Although the Internet was originally designed to keep working even if large chunks of the network were lost (as might happen in a nuclear war, for instance), today's Internet displays some striking vulnerabilities. One of the most significant is the system of computers—called "routers" and "root servers"—that directs traffic around the Net. Routers represent critical nodes in the network and depend on each other for details on where to send packets of information. A software error in one router, or its malicious reprogramming by a hacker, can lead to errors throughout the Internet. Hackers could also exploit new peer-to-peer software (such as the information-transfer tool Gnutella) to distribute throughout the Internet millions of "sleeper" viruses programmed to attack specific machines or the network itself at a predetermined date.

The U.S. government is aware of many of these threats and of the specific vulnerability of complex networks, especially information networks. President George W. Bush has appointed Richard Clarke, a career civil servant and senior advisor to the National Security

Council on counterterrorism, as his cyberspace security czar, reporting both to Director of Homeland Security Tom Ridge and National Security Advisor Condoleezza Rice. In addition, the U.S. Senate recently considered new legislation (the Critical Infrastructure Information Security Act) addressing a major obstacle to improved security of critical networks: the understandable reluctance of firms to share proprietary information about networks they have built or manage. The act would enable the sharing of sensitive infrastructure information between the federal government and private sector and within the private sector itself. In his opening remarks to introduce the act on September 25, 2001, Republican Sen. Bob Bennett of Utah clearly recognized that we face a new kind of threat. "The American economy is a highly interdependent system of systems, with physical and cyber components," he declared. "Security in a networked world must be a shared responsibility."

Preparing for the Unknown

Shortly following the September 11 attacks, the U.S. Army enlisted the help of some of Hollywood's top action screenwriters and directors—including the writers of *Die Hard* and *McGyver*—to conjure up possible scenarios for future terrorist attacks. Yet no one can possibly imagine in advance all the novel opportunities for terrorism provided by our technological and economic systems. We've made these critical systems so complex that they are replete with vulnerabilities that are very hard to anticipate, because we don't even know how to ask the right questions. We can think of these possibilities as "exploitable unknown unknowns." Terrorists can make connections between components of complex systems—such as between passenger airliners and skyscrapers—that few, if any, people have anticipated. Complex terrorism is particularly effective if its goal is not a specific strategic or political end, but simply the creation of widespread fear, panic, and economic disruption. This more general objective grants terrorists much more latitude in their choice of targets. More likely than not, the next major attack will come in a form as unexpected as we witnessed on September 11.

What should we do to lessen the risk of complex terrorism, beyond the conventional counterterrorism strategies already being implemented by the United States and other nations? First, we must acknowledge our own limitations. Little can be done, for instance, about terrorists' inexorably rising capacity for violence. This trend results from deep technological forces that can't be stopped without producing major disruptions elsewhere in our economies and societies. However, we can take steps to reduce the vulnerabilities related to our complex economies and technologies. We can do so by loosening the couplings in our economic and technological networks, building into these networks various buffering capacities, introducing "circuit breakers" that interrupt dangerous feedbacks, and dispersing high-value assets so that they are less concentrated and thus less inviting targets.

These prescriptions will mean different things for different networks. In the energy sector, loosening coupling might mean greater use of decentralized, local energy production and alternative energy sources (like small-scale solar power) that make individual users more independent of the electricity grid. Similarly, in food production, loosening coupling could entail increased autonomy of local and regional food-production networks so that when one network is attacked the damage doesn't cascade into others. In many industries, increasing buffering would involve moving away from just-in-time production processes. Firms would need to increase inventories of feedstocks and parts so production can continue even when the supply of these essential inputs is interrupted. Clearly this policy would reduce economic efficiency, but the extra security of more stable and resilient production networks could far outweigh this cost.

Circuit breakers would prove particularly useful in situations where crowd behavior and panic can get out of control. They have already been implemented on the New York Stock Exchange: Trading halts if the market plunges more than a certain percentage in a particular period of time. In the case of terrorism, one of the factors heightening public anxiety is the incessant barrage of sensational reporting and commentary by 24-hour news TV. As is true for the stock exchange, there might be a role for an independent, industry-based monitoring body here, a body that could intervene with broadcasters at critical moments, or at least provide vital counsel, to manage the flow and content of information. In an emergency, for instance, all broadcasters might present exactly the same information (vetted by the monitoring body and stated deliberately and calmly) so that competition among broadcasters doesn't encourage sensationalized treatment. If the monitoring body were under the strict authority of the broadcasters themselves, the broadcasters would—collectively—retain complete control over the content of the message, and the procedure would not involve government encroachment on freedom of speech.

If terrorist attacks continue, economic forces alone will likely encourage the dispersal of high-value assets. Insurance costs could become unsupportable for businesses and industries located in vulnerable zones. In 20 to 30 years, we may be astonished at the folly of housing so much value in the exquisitely fragile buildings of the World Trade Center. Again, dispersal may entail substantial economic costs, because we'll lose economies of scale and opportunities for synergy.

Yet we have to recognize that we face new circumstances. Past policies are inadequate. The advantage in this war has shifted toward terrorists. Our increased vulnerability—and our newfound recognition of that vulnerability—makes us more risk-averse, while terrorists have become more powerful and more tolerant of risk. (The September 11 attackers, for instance, had an extremely high tolerance for risk, because they were ready and willing to die.) As a result, terrorists have significant leverage to hurt us. Their capacity to exploit this leverage depends on their ability to understand the complex systems that we depend on so critically. Our capacity to defend ourselves depends on that same understanding.

Thomas Homer-Dixon is associate professor of political science and director of the Center for the Study of Peace and Conflict at the University of Toronto. His most recent publication is *The Ingenuity Gap: How Can We Solve the Problems of the Future?*

Stewart Patrick

Weak States and Global Threats: Fact or Fiction?

It has become a common claim that the gravest dangers to U.S. and world security are no longer military threats from rival great powers, but rather transnational threats emanating from the world's most poorly governed countries. Poorly performing developing countries are linked to humanitarian catastrophes; mass migration; environmental degradation; regional instability; energy insecurity; global pandemics; international crime; the proliferation of weapons of mass destruction (WMD); and, of course, transnational terrorism. Leading thinkers such as Francis Fukuyama have said that, "[s]ince the end of the Cold War, weak and failing states have arguably become the single-most important problem for international order."[1] Official Washington agrees. Secretary of State Condoleezza Rice declares that nations incapable of exercising "responsible sovereignty" have a "spillover effect" in the form of terrorism, weapons proliferation, and other dangers.[2] This new focus on weak and failing states represents an important shift in U.S. threat perceptions. Before the September 11 attacks, U.S. policymakers viewed states with sovereignty deficits exclusively through a humanitarian lens; they piqued the moral conscience but possessed little strategic significance. Al Qaeda's ability to act with impunity from Afghanistan changed this calculus, convincing President George W. Bush and his administration that "America is now threatened less by conquering states than we are by failing ones."[3]

This new strategic orientation has already had policy and institutional consequences, informing recent U.S. defense, intelligence, diplomatic, development, and even trade initiatives. The U.S. government's latest *National Defense Strategy* calls on the U.S. military to strengthen the sovereign capacities of weak states to combat internal threats of terrorism, insurgency, and organized crime. Beyond expanding its training of foreign security forces, the Pentagon is seeking interagency buy-in for a U.S. strategy to address the world's "ungoverned spaces."[4] The Central Intelligence Agency (CIA), which has identified 50 such zones globally, is devoting new collection assets to long-neglected parts of the world.[5] The National Intelligence Council is assisting the Department of State's new Office of the Coordinator for Reconstruction and Stabilization in identifying states at risk of collapse so that the office can launch conflict prevention and mitigation efforts. Not to be outdone, the U.S. Agency for International Development (USAID) has formulated its own "Fragile States Strategy" to bolster countries that could breed terror, crime, instability, and disease. The Bush administration has even justified the Central American Free Trade Area as a means to prevent state failure and its associated spillovers.[6]

This new preoccupation with weak states is not limited to the United States. In the United Kingdom, the Prime Minister's Strategy Unit has advocated a government-wide approach to stabilizing fragile countries,[7] and Canada and Australia are following suit. The

United Nations has been similarly engaged; the unifying theme of last year's proposals for UN reform was the need for effective sovereign states to deal with today's global security agenda. Kofi Annan remarked before the Council on Foreign Relations in New York in 2004 that, "[w]hether the threat is terror or AIDS, a threat to one is a threat to all. . . . Our defenses are only as strong as their weakest link."[8] In September 2005, the UN endorsed the creation of a new Peacebuilding Commission to help war-torn states recover. The Development Assistance Committee (DAC) of the Organization for Economic Cooperation and Development (OECD) in January 2005 also launched a "Fragile States" initiative in partnership with the World Bank's Low-Income Countries Under Stress (LICUS) program.[9]

It is striking, however, how little empirical evidence underpins these sweeping assertions and policy developments. Policymakers and experts have presumed a blanket connection between weak governance and transnational threats and have begun to implement policy responses accordingly. Yet, they have rarely distinguished among categories of weak and failing states or asked whether (and how) certain types of developing countries are associated with particular threats. Too often, it appears that the entire range of Western policies is animated by anecdotal evidence or isolated examples, such as Al Qaeda's operations in Afghanistan or cocaine trafficking in Colombia. The risk in this approach is that the United States will squander energy and resources in a diffuse, unfocused effort to attack state weakness wherever it arises, without appropriate attention to setting priorities and tailoring responses to poor governance and its specific, attendant spillovers.

Before embracing a new strategic vision and investing in new initiatives, conventional wisdom should be replaced by sober, detailed analysis. The ultimate goal of this fine-grained approach should be to determine which states are associated with which dangers. Weak states do often incubate global threats, but this correlation is far from universal. Crafting a more effective U.S. strategy will depend on a deeper understanding of the underlying mechanisms linking poor governance and state incapacity in the developing world with cross-border spillovers.

Defining Weak and Failing States

There is no consensus on the precise number of weak and failing states. The Commission on Weak States and U.S. National Security estimates that there are between 50 and 60; the United Kingdom's Department for International Development classifies 46 nations with 870 million inhabitants as "fragile"; and the World Bank treats 30 countries as LICUS.[10] These divergent estimates reflect differences in the criteria used to define state weakness, the indicators used to gauge it, and the relative weighting of various aspects of governance.

State strength is relative and can be measured by the state's ability and willingness to provide the fundamental political goods associated with state-hood: physical security, legitimate political institutions, economic management, and social welfare. Many countries have critical gaps in one or more of these four areas of governance. In effect, they possess legal but not actual sovereignty. In the security realm, they struggle to maintain a monopoly on the use of force, control borders and territory, ensure public order, and provide safety from crime. In the political sphere, they lack legitimate governing institutions that provide effective administration, ensure checks on power, protect basic rights and freedoms, hold leaders accountable, deliver impartial justice, and permit broad citizen participation. In the economic arena, they strain to carry out basic macroeconomic and fiscal policies or establish a legal and regulatory climate conducive to entrepreneurship, private enterprise, open trade, natural resource management, foreign investment, and economic growth. Finally, in the social domain, they fail to meet the basic needs of their populations by making even minimal investments in health, education, and other social services.

Yet, not all weak states look alike. They range in a spectrum from collapsed states, such as Somalia, that have gaps in all four capacities to fragile "good performers," such as Senegal, that are making some progress in most or all areas. In between, most weak states struggle on many fronts or muddle through. Not by coincidence, weak and failing states tend to be ineligible for the Millennium Challenge Account (MCA), an innovative aid window announced by Bush in March 2002 to reward countries that have a demonstrated commitment to "ruling justly," "investing in their people," and "promoting economic freedom."[11]

State weakness is not just a question of capacity but also of will. History provides repeated examples of corrupt, incompetent, or venal regimes—Zimbabwe today under President Robert Mugabe, for example—that have driven promising countries into the ground.[12] By distinguishing between capacity and will, four categories of weak states can be differentiated: relatively good performers, states that are weak but willing, states that have the means but not the will, and those with neither the will nor the way to fulfill the basic functions of statehood (see table 1). Such analytical distinctions have policy utility, informing the mix of incentives external actors might deploy in engaging poor performers. The goal is to move weak states toward the upper left quadrant of table 1 by filling capacity gaps, persuading unre-constructed states to mend their ways, or both.

Compared to other developing countries, weak and failing states are more likely to suffer from low or no growth and to be furthest away from reaching the Millennium Development Goals, a set of commitments made by UN member states in 2000 to make concrete progress by 2015 in critical development objectives, such as eradicating extreme poverty and hunger, achieving universal primary education, and reducing child mortality. The inhabitants of these weak and failing states are likely to be poor and malnourished, live with chronic illness and die young, go without education and basic health care, suffer gender discrimination, and lack access to modern technology. Compared to OECD, or developed, countries, fragile states are 15 times more prone to civil war, with such violence both more extreme and longer lasting than even in other developing countries. Such states are the overwhelming source of the world's refugees and internally displaced peoples. Many are also among the world's worst abusers of human rights.[13]

Table 1

Capacity and Will as Dimensions of State Weakness

	Strong Will	**Low Will**
High Capacity	**Relatively Good Performers**	**Unresponsive/Corrupt/Repressive**
	(e.g., Senegal, Honduras)	(e.g., Burma, Zimbabwe)
Low Capacity	**Weak but Willing**	**Weak and Not Willing**
	(e.g., Mozambique, East Timor)	(e.g., Haiti, Sudan)

The most comprehensive and well-respected system for evaluating state performance is the World Bank's "Governance Matters" data set. The most recent installment, in 2005, ranks 209 countries and territories along six dimensions: voice and accountability, political instability and violence, government effectiveness, regulatory burden, rule of law, and control of corruption.[14] Table 2 lists the 44 countries that rest in the bottom quintile, ranked from weakest (Somalia) to strongest (Algeria).

Three observations can be drawn from this data. First, the weakest states are not necessarily the poorest. Accordingly, the fifth quintile includes several lower-middle-income countries, such as Venezuela, and excludes a few very poor countries, such as Gambia and Niger. This definition of state weakness differs from that adopted by the World Bank and OECD/DAC donors, which restrict the category "fragile state" to very poor countries that are eligible for the bank's concessional (International Development Association) window and that score lowest on the bank's Country Policy and Institutional Assessment indicators. That approach, although consistent with the poverty reduction mandate of aid agencies, is overly restrictive for policy analysts and officials interested in the security implications of weak governance across the entire range of developing countries.

Second, the list of weak and failing states in table 2 captures a diverse collection of countries that pose a similarly diverse array of potential challenges to U.S. foreign and national security policy. Most of these countries are either in conflict or recovering from it, have experienced recurrent bouts of political instability, or rank very low in terms of

Table 2

Bottom Quintile of Aggregate Governance Rankings

Somalia (weakest)	Cote d'Ivoire	Venezuela
Iraq	Nigeria	Guinea
Myanmar	Laos	Togo
Democratic Republic of Congo	Angola	Azerbaijan
	Equatorial Guinea	Bangladesh
Afghanistan	Tajikistan	Cuba
Liberia	Republic of Congo	Iran
Haiti	Belarus	Nepal
Zimbabwe	Chad	Libya
Turkmenistan	Yemen	Syria
Sudan	Solomon Islands	Sierra Leone
North Korea	West Bank/Gaza	Guinea-Bissau
Uzbekistan	Pakistan	Cameroon
Burundi	Ethiopia	Comoros
Central African Republic	Eritrea	Algeria (strongest)

Source: Kaufmann, Kray, and Mastruzzi, *Governance Matters IV*, 2005.

"human security," as measured by risk of violent death and abuses to core human rights.[15] Several are "outposts of tyranny," in the Bush administration's parlance (e.g., North Korea, Belarus, Cuba, Zimbabwe), authoritarian states that may appear superficially strong but rest on a brittle foundation. Others are sites of ongoing U.S. combat and reconstruction efforts (Iraq, Afghanistan); active or potential WMD proliferators (North Korea, Iran, Pakistan); past or present safe havens for terrorism (Afghanistan, Yemen); anchors of regional stability or instability (Nigeria, Pakistan); bases for narcotics trafficking and crime (Burma); potential sources of uncontrolled migration (Haiti); critical energy suppliers (Venezuela, Nigeria); locations of epidemic disease (Angola, Democratic Republic of Congo [DRC]); or settings for recent atrocities and humanitarian crises (Sudan, Liberia, Burundi, Sierra Leone). Needless to say, a single state frequently falls into more than one of these categories of concern.

Third, the relationship between state weakness and spillovers is not linear. It varies by threat. Some salient transnational dangers to U.S. and global security come not from states at the bottom quintile of the Governance Matters rankings but from the next tier up, countries such as Colombia, the world's leading producer of cocaine; Saudi Arabia, home to a majority of the September 11 hijackers; Russia, a host of numerous transnational criminal enterprises; and China, the main source both of SARS and avian flu. These states tend to be better run and more capable of delivering political goods; nearly half are eligible or on the threshold of eligibility for the MCA in 2006. Nevertheless, even these middling performers may suffer from critical gaps in capacity or political will that enable spillovers.

How do these sets of states correlate with significant transnational threats to the United States and the international community? The answer depends in part on which threat you are talking about.

Transnational Threats and U.S. National Security

The growing concern with weak and failing states is really based on two separate propositions: first, that traditional concepts of security such as interstate violence should expand to encompass cross-border threats driven by nonstate actors (such as terrorism), activities (crime), or forces (pandemics); and second, that such threats have their origins in large measure in weak governance in the developing world.

Since the Reagan administration, successive versions of the *National Security Strategy* have incorporated nonmilitary concerns such as terrorism, organized crime, infectious disease, energy security, and environmental degradation. The common thread linking these challenges is that they originate primarily in sovereign jurisdictions abroad but have the potential to harm U.S. citizens. Some national security traditionalists resist this definitional expansion on the grounds that such concerns pose at best an indirect rather than existential threat to U.S. national interests or even human life. Proponents of a wider view respond that unconventional threats may contribute to violence by destabilizing states and regions. More fundamentally, they argue that the traditional "violence paradigm" for national security must adapt to accommodate other threats to the safety, well-being, and way of life of U.S. citizens. Such threats include not only malevolent, purposive ones such as transnational terrorism, something many traditionalists now accept, but also "threats without a threatener"—malignant forces that emerge from nature, such as global pandemics, or as by-products of human activity, such as climate change.[16]

Traditionalists may similarly be dubious that weak and failing states in general endanger U.S. national security.[17] More relevant, they contend, are a handful of pivotal weak states, such as nuclear-armed Pakistan or North Korea, whose fortunes may affect regional balances of power or prospects for large-scale destruction.[18] Yet, it is not always easy to predict where threats may emerge. In the 1990s, few anticipated that remote, poor, and war-ravaged Afghanistan would be the launching pad for the most devastating attack on the United States in the nation's history.

The challenge for policy analysts is to discern more carefully which states are likely to present which baskets of transnational problems. Such distinctions will allow them to direct limited resources to address the priority challenges in critical countries and tailor responses to the key incentive structures in those countries accordingly. A start here is to look more closely at the potential links of weak and failing states to terrorism, WMD proliferation, crime, disease, energy insecurity, and regional instability.

Hotbeds of Terrorism?

Both the Bush administration and outside commentators frequently contend that countries with weak or nonexistent governance are greater risks to generate and serve as hosts of transnational terrorist organizations. As the *New York Times* argued in July 2005, "Failed states that cannot provide jobs and food for their people, that have lost chunks of territory to war-lords, and that can no longer track or control their borders, send an invitation to terrorists."[19]

Such claims have some justification. Data on global terrorist attacks from the University of Maryland show that, from 1991 to 2001, most individual terrorists came from low-income authoritarian countries in conflict, such as Sudan, Algeria, and Afghanistan.[20] Similarly, data compiled annually by the State Department reveals that for 2003–2005 most U.S.-designated Foreign Terrorist Organizations use weak and failing states as their primary bases of operations.[21] Weak and failing states appeal to transnational terrorist organizations for the multiple benefits they offer: safe havens, conflict experience, settings for training and indoctrination, access to weapons and equipment, financial resources, staging grounds and transit zones, targets for operations, and pools of recruits. Al Qaeda, for example, enjoyed the hospitality of Sudan and Afghanistan, where it built training camps and enlisted new members; exploited Kenya and Yemen to launch attacks on U.S. embassies in Nairobi and Dar es Salaam as well as on the USS *Cole*; and financed its operations through illicit trade in gemstones, including diamonds and tanzanite, from African conflict zones.[22]

Accordingly, the United States is seeking to deny terrorists access to weak states. Africa has emerged as a primary arena of concern. An analysis of the 9/11 Commission report by the Congressional Research Service warns that "the international terror threat against the [United States] and local interests is likely to continue to grow in several parts of Africa because of porous borders, lax security, political instability, and a lack of state resources and capacities."[23] The Department of Defense is responding by training African security forces in a dozen countries in the Sahel to control their borders and territories more effectively.[24] More comprehensively, the *National Strategy for Combating Terrorism* commits the United States to "diminishing the underlying conditions that terrorists seek to exploit"[25] by bolstering state capacities, alleviating poverty, and promoting good governance. Bush echoed this theme in his September 2005 speech at the UN High-Level Plenary Meeting, declaring, "We must help raise up the failing states and stagnant societies that provide fertile ground for terrorists."[26]

A closer look suggests that the connection between state weakness and transnational terrorism is more complicated and tenuous than often assumed. First, obviously not all weak and failed states are afflicted by terrorism. As historian Walter Laqueur points out, "In the 49 countries currently designated by the United Nations as the least developed hardly any terrorist activity occurs."[27] Weak capacity per se cannot explain why terrorist activity is concentrated in particular regions, particularly the Middle East and broader Muslim world, rather than others such as Central Africa. Other variables and dynamics, including political, religious, cultural, and geographical factors, clearly shape its global distribution.

Similarly, not all terrorism that occurs in weak and failing states is transnational. Much is self-contained action by insurgents motivated by local political grievances, such as the Revolutionary Armed Forces of Colombia (FARC), or national liberation struggles, such as the Liberation Tigers of Tamil Eelam (LTTE) in Sri Lanka. It is thus only tangentially related to the "global war on terrorism," which, as defined by the Bush administration, focuses on terrorists with global reach, particularly those motivated by an extreme Salafist strand of Wahhabi Islam.

Third, not all weak and failing states are equal. Conventional wisdom holds that terrorists are particularly attracted to collapsed, lawless polities such as Somalia or Liberia, or what the Pentagon terms "ungoverned spaces." In fact, as Davidson College professor Ken Menkhaus and others note, terrorists are more likely to find weak but functioning states, such as Pakistan or Kenya, congenial bases of operations. Such badly governed states are not only fragile and susceptible to corruption, but they also provide easy access to the financial and logistical infrastructure of the global economy, including communications technology, transportation, and banking services.[28]

Fourth, transnational terrorists are only partially and perhaps decreasingly reliant on weak and failing states. For one, the Al Qaeda threat has evolved from a centrally directed network, dependent on a "base," into a much more diffuse global movement consisting of autonomous cells in dozens of countries, poor and wealthy alike. Moreover, the source of radical Islamic terrorism may reside less in state weakness in the Middle East than in the alienation of de-territorialized Muslims in Europe. The "safe havens" of global terrorists are as likely to be the *banlieues* of Paris as the wastes of the Sahara or the slums of Karachi.[29]

In other words, weak and failing states can provide useful assets to transnational terrorists, but they may be less central to their operations than widely believed. If there is one failed state today that is important to transnational terrorism, it is probably Iraq. As CIA director Porter Goss testified in early 2005, the U.S.-led invasion and occupation transformed a brutal but secular authoritarian state into a symbol and magnet for the global jihadi movement.[30]

Although all four governance gaps associated with weak and failing states may contribute to transnational terrorism, political and security gaps are the most important. In the absence of peaceful outlets for political expression, frustrated groups are more likely to adopt violence against repressive regimes and their perceived foreign sponsors. Similarly, states that do not control borders or territory facilitate terrorist infiltration and operations. Two other gaps may play supporting roles. When states do not meet basic social needs, they provide openings for charitable organizations or educational systems linked to radical networks. Similarly, states lacking effective economic institutions are more likely to suffer from stagnant growth, breed political extremism, and be unable to regulate terrorist financing.

In seeking to bolster weak states against transnational terrorism, policymakers must distinguish between capacity and will. The U.S. Anti-Terrorist Assistance program is predicated on the belief that well-intentioned but poor governments, in the Sahel or East Africa, for example, simply lack the tools to do the job. Yet, the cases of Pakistan and Saudi Arabia suggest a more serious impediment: a lack of determination by governing regimes, worried about alienating an already radicalized population, to take forceful steps such as cracking down on jihadi groups or imposing central authority over restive regions.[31]

Weapons Proliferation Risks?

Fears that weak and failing states may incubate transnational terrorism merge with a related concern: that poorly governed countries may be unable or disinclined to control stocks of nuclear, biological, or chemical weapons or prevent the onward spread or leakage of WMD-related technology. This is not an idle worry. According to the British government, of the 17 states that have current or suspended WMD programs beyond the five permanent members of the UN Security Council, 13 are "countries at risk of instability."[32] The most frightening prospect is that a nuclear-armed state such as Pakistan or North Korea might lose control of its nuclear weapons through collapse or theft, placing the weapons into the hands of a successor regime or nonstate actors with little compunction about their use. A more likely scenario might involve the transfer of biological weapons, which are easier to make and transport but difficult to track.

Direct transfer of functioning WMD should not be the only concern. Revelations about the extensive international nuclear arms bazaar of Abdul Qadeer Khan suggest that poor governance may be the Achilles' heel of global nonproliferation efforts. For more than two decades, Khan, Pakistan's leading nuclear scientist, orchestrated a clandestine operation to sell sensitive expertise and technology, including the means to produce fissile material and to design and fabricate nuclear weapons, to Iran, Libya, and North Korea. As David Albright and Corey Hinderson stated, "The Khan network could not have evolved into such a dangerous supplier without the utter corruption and dishonesty of successive Pakistani governments, which, for almost two decades, were quick to deny any involvement of its scientists in illicit procurement."[33] Furthermore, it could not have gone global without institutional weaknesses in more advanced middle-income countries, including Malaysia, South Africa, and Turkey, that possessed manufacturing capabilities but lacked the knowledge, capacity, or will to implement relevant export control and non-proliferation laws.

Although U.S. officials are understandably preoccupied with the dangers of WMD proliferation, for most of the world the spread of more mundane but still deadly conventional weapons poses the greatest threat to human security and civil peace. There is clear evidence that weak, failing, and postconflict states play a critical role in the global proliferation of small arms and light weapons. According to the Geneva-based *Small Arms Survey*, more than 640 million such weapons circulate globally, many among private hands and for illicit purposes.[34] Weak states are often the source, transit, and destination countries for the illegal arms trade. On the borderlands of the former Soviet Union, for example, vast stockpiles of weapons remain in ill-secured depots, providing tempting targets for rebel groups, terrorists, and international criminal organizations. Such matériel frequently surfaces on the global black or grey markets, as corrupt officials manipulate legitimate export licenses to obscure the military purpose or ultimate recipient of the shipment. In one notable instance in 1999, Ukraine's export agency transferred 68 tons of munitions to Burkina Faso. The weapons were then shipped to Liberia and ultimately to Sierra Leone, landing in the hands of Foday Sankoh's Revolutionary United Front.[35]

The availability of conventional weapons further weakens state capacity by fueling civil wars and insurgencies, fostering a culture of criminality and impunity. As the experiences of Afghanistan, Haiti, and the DRC, among others, show, easy access to instruments of violence complicates efforts by governments and international partners to establish public order and the rule of law, provide relief, and pursue more ambitious development goals.

As with terrorism, the risk of proliferation from weak states is often more a matter of will than of objective capacity. This is particularly true for WMD proliferation. The technological sophistication and secure facilities needed to construct such weapons would seem to require access to and some acquiescence from the highest levels of the state apparatus. This may be less true for small arms proliferation. Some weak states simply lack the capacity to police the grey or black market and to control flows of such weapons across their borders.

Of the four governance gaps, WMD proliferation is most likely to be correlated with security and political shortcomings, particularly poor civilian oversight of the defense establishment and the presence of an authoritarian and corrupt regime. In the case of small arms, weak economic institutions may also create incentives and opportunities for proliferation.

Dens of Thieves?

Beyond posing terrorist or proliferation risks, weak and failing states are said to provide ideal bases for transnational criminal enterprises involved in the production, transit, or trafficking of drugs, weapons, people, and other illicit commodities and in the laundering of the profits from such activities. The surging scope and scale of global organized crime underpins these concerns. The worldwide narcotics trade alone is now estimated to be a $300–500 billion business, on a par with at least the global automobile industry or at most the global oil industry. Former International Monetary Fund managing director Michel Camdessus estimates that money laundering accounts for 2–5 percent of world gross domestic product, or between $800 billion and $2 trillion.[36]

The rise in organized crime is being driven by the dynamics of globalization. Recent advances in communications and transportation, the removal of commercial barriers, and the deregulation of financial services have created unprecedented opportunities for illicit activity, from money laundering to trafficking in drugs, arms, and people. National authorities, particularly in weak states, strain to encourage legitimate commerce while curbing illicit trade.[37]

The relationship between transnational organized crime and weak states is parasitic. All things being equal, criminal networks are drawn to environments where the rule of law is absent or imperfectly applied, law enforcement and border controls are lax, regulatory systems are weak, contracts go unenforced, public services are unreliable, corruption is rife, and the state itself may be subject to capture. As University of Pittsburgh professor

Phil Williams said, such capacity gaps provide "functional holes" that criminal enterprises can exploit. Poor governance has made Africa, in the words of the UN Office on Drugs and Crime, "an ideal conduit through which to extract and/or transship a range of illicit commodities, such as drugs, firearms, minerals and oil, timber, wildlife, and human beings."[38] Transnational organized crime further reduces weak-state capacity, as criminals manipulate corruption to gain protection for themselves and their activities and to open new avenues for profit. Criminal groups have become adept at exploiting weak-state capacity in conflict zones, such as Colombia or the DRC, where political authority is contested or formal institutions have collapsed, and in fluid postconflict settings, such as Bosnia or Kosovo, where they have not yet been firmly reestablished.

Yet, if state weakness is often a necessary condition for the influx of organized crime, it is not a sufficient one. Even more than a low-risk operating environment, criminals seek profits. In a global economy, realizing high returns depends on tapping into a worldwide market to sell illicit commodities and launder the proceeds, which in turn depends on access to financial services, modern telecommunications, and transportation infrastructure. Such considerations help explain why South Africa and Nigeria have become magnets for transnational and domestic organized crime and why Togo has not.[39] Criminals will accept the higher risks of operating in states with stronger capacity in return for greater rewards.

In addition, the link between global crime and state weakness varies by sector. The category "transnational crime" encompasses a vast array of activities, not limited to narcotics trafficking, alien smuggling, piracy, environmental crime, sanctions violations, contraband smuggling, counterfeiting, financial fraud, high-technology crime, and money laundering. Some of these activities, such as narcotics trafficking, are closely linked to state weakness. Poorly governed states dominate the annual list of countries Washington designates as "major" drug-producing and -transiting nations. Nearly 90 percent of global heroin, for example, comes from Afghanistan and is trafficked to Europe via poorly governed states in Central Asia or along the "Balkan route." Burma is the second-largest producer of opium and a key source of methamphetamine. Weak states similarly dominate the list of countries designated as the worst offenders in human trafficking, a $7–8 billion business that sends an estimated 800,000 women and children across borders annually for purposes of forced labor or sexual slavery.[40]

Other criminal sectors such as money laundering, financial fraud, cyber crime, intellectual property theft, and environmental crime are less obviously correlated with state weakness. With few exceptions, for example, money laundering occurs primarily in small offshore financial centers, wealthy nations, or middle-income countries. The reason is straightforward: most weak and failing states lack the requisite banking systems. On the other hand, many of the profits being laundered come from activities that emanate from or transit through weak states.

Among the four governance gaps, the rise of transnational organized crime in weak states appears to be most closely correlated with poor economic and political institutions. Poor regulatory environments and unaccountable political systems constrain the growth of the licit economy and create opportunities for corruption, both grand and petty. Inadequate public security and social welfare may play a secondary role by fostering a culture of lawlessness and permitting criminals to win support by meeting basic needs of a beleaguered population. Finally, the relative role of capacity versus will in facilitating transnational organized crime in weak states tends to vary. As crime becomes more entrenched, a compromised political elite is less likely to deploy the capacities at its disposal to fight it.

Plague and Pestilence?

The threat of the rapid spread of avian influenza, which could conceivably kill tens of millions of people, has placed infectious disease into the first tier of national security issues. There is growing concern that weak and failing states may serve as important breeding grounds for new pandemics and, lacking adequate capacity to respond to these diseases, endanger global health. As development economists Clive Bell and Maureen Lewis said, "Failed or faltering states cannot or will not perform basic public health functions . . . placing the rest of the world at risk."[41]

Since 1973, more than 30 previously unknown disease agents, including HIV/AIDS, Ebola, and the West Nile virus, have emerged for which no cures are available. Most have originated in developing countries. During the same time span, more than 20 well-known pathogens, including tuberculosis, malaria, and cholera, have reemerged or spread, often in more virulent and drug-resistant forms.[42] In an age of mass travel and global commerce, when more than 2 million people cross international borders a day and air freight exceeds 100 billion ton-kilometers a year, inadequate capacity or insufficient will to respond with vigorous public health measures can quickly threaten lives across the globe. National security and public health experts worry that weak and failed states, which invest little in epidemiological surveillance, health information and reporting systems, primary health care delivery, preventive measures, or response capacity, will lack the means to detect and contain outbreaks of deadly disease.

These worries are well founded. Although there is little solid data on the link between state capacity and epidemic patterns, it is known that the global infectious disease burden falls overwhelmingly (90 percent) on low- and middle-income countries that account for only 11 percent of global health spending. The Armed Forces Medical Intelligence Center has devised a typology of countries by health care status, ranking nations into five categories on the basis of resources and priority devoted to public health, quality of health care, access to drugs, and capacity for surveillance and response. States in the bottom two quintiles are the main victims of the world's seven deadliest infectious diseases: respiratory infections, HIV/AIDS, diarrheal diseases, tuberculosis, malaria, hepatitis B, and measles. SubSaharan Africa is the hardest hit, with just 10 percent of the world's population but 90 percent of its malaria and 75 percent of its HIV/AIDS cases.[43]

The spread of infectious disease is being driven partly by breakdowns in public health, especially during periods of political turmoil and war. HIV/AIDS is a case in point. Nearly all instances of the disease in South and Southeast Asia can be traced to strains that evolved in northern Burma, an ungoverned warren of drug gangs, irregular militias, and human traffickers. Similarly, the collapse of the DRC made it a petri dish for the evolution of numerous strains of HIV. Nor does peace always improve matters, at least initially. In Ethiopia and several other African countries, rising HIV/AIDS prevalence has paralleled the return and demobilization of ex-combatants and their reintegration into society, exposing the wider citizenry to disease contracted during military deployments.[44]

Beyond countries in conflict, many developing and transitional states possess decrepit and decaying public health systems that can easily be overwhelmed. Following the end of the Cold War, the states of the former Soviet Union all experienced spikes in the incidence of measles, tuberculosis, and HIV. In the spring of 2005, weak health infrastructure in Angola amplified an outbreak of the hemorrhagic fever Marburg. The same year, the government of Nigeria failed to enforce a national immunization program, allowing polio, a disease on the brink of eradication, to spread across a broad swath of Africa and beyond to Yemen, Saudi Arabia, and Indonesia.

Diseases incubated in weak and failing states pose both direct and indirect threats to the United States. Significant numbers of U.S. citizens may become infected and die. Even if they do not, such epidemics may impose high economic costs and undermine key countries or regions. The World Bank estimates that SARS cost the East Asian regional economy some $20–25 billion, despite killing only 912 people.[45] The political costs of disease are more nuanced but no less real. In the most heavily affected African countries, HIV/AIDS has decimated human capital and fiscal systems, undermining the already limited capacity of states to deliver basic services, control territory, and manage the economy. It has strained health and education systems, eroded social cohesion, undermined agriculture and economic growth, and weakened armies. The pandemic is spreading rapidly into Eurasia and could surge to 110 million cases by 2010, with dramatic increases in countries of strategic significance such as India, China, and Russia.[46]

In the growing transnational threat posed by epidemics, the weak-state problem tends to be one of capacity more than will. Although there have been prominent cases of official denial and foot-dragging (e.g., over HIV/AIDS in Russia or SARS in China), the greater problem is a genuine inability to prevent and respond adequately to disease outbreaks. The most salient governance gap in the case of epidemics is in providing social welfare, notably underdeveloped public health infrastructure.

Energy Insecurity?

The doubling of world oil prices in 2005 exposed strains and volatility in the global energy market at a time of surging global demand, intensifying competition over dwindling reserves, and instability in key producer countries from Iraq to Nigeria to Venezuela. To some, these trends suggest that reliance on oil and gas from weak and failing states may endanger U.S. and global energy security by increasing the volatility, costs, and risk of interruption of supplies. Beyond requiring the United States to pay an "insecurity premium," such dependence may complicate the pursuit of broader U.S. national security and foreign policy objectives.

Anxiety about U.S. energy security is nothing new. Much hand-wringing accompanied the oil crisis of the mid-1970s, when domestic U.S. production peaked and the country confronted an Arab oil embargo. Despite temporary shortages and an oil price shock, the Nixon-era United States managed to find alternate sources of supply. Most economists are confident that today's markets are similarly capable of absorbing temporary interruptions, albeit at a price.

Nevertheless, some new dynamics deserve consideration. First, the U.S. quest for energy security is occurring at a time of increased global competition for limited supplies. Since 2000, the world's consumption of fossil fuels has risen much faster than most analysts had predicted, driven not only by sustained U.S. demand but also by China's seemingly unquenchable thirst for energy. During 2004 alone, Chinese oil imports surged by 40 percent, making China the world's second-largest oil importing country.[47] The removal of excess production and refining capacity has resulted in a dramatic tightening of the global energy market and has left prices vulnerable to sudden spikes in the event of disturbances in producer countries.

Second, price shocks are increasingly likely, given the world's growing reliance on energy supplies from weak states, as proven reserves in stable countries peak or become depleted. As Hampshire College professor of security studies Michael Klare said, the geographic concentration of exploitable fossil fuels means that the availability of energy is "closely tied to political and socioeconomic conditions within a relatively small group of countries."[48] Significantly, many of the world's main oil exporters, including Iraq, Nigeria, Russia, Saudi Arabia, and Venezuela, are less stable today than in 2000. The United Kingdom calculates that some 60 percent of global oil reserves are located in countries "facing stability challenges," such as Azerbaijan, where untapped reserves could generate $124 billion in revenue by 2024. Complicating matters, a large percentage of the world's oil and gas transits unstable regions, such as Transcaucasia, and vulnerable choke points, such as the Straits of Hormuz and Malacca, via pipeline or tanker.[49]

The U.S. exposure to volatility and interruption of energy supplies has grown markedly since 1973, when it imported only 34 percent of its crude oil. By 2005 this figure was 58 percent, with fully one-third coming from Venezuela, Nigeria, Iraq, and Angola. Increasingly, U.S. energy security is hostage to foreign political developments.[50] During the past several years, oil markets have tightened in response to strikes in Venezuela, violence in Nigeria, and insurgency in Iraq. This dependence on weak states will only increase. By 2015 the United States is forecast to be importing 68 percent of its oil, a quarter of it from the Gulf of Guinea, up from today's 15 percent. All of the countries in that region—Angola, Cameroon, Congo-Brazzaville, Gabon, Equatorial Guinea, and Nigeria—face tremendous governance challenges.[51] Nigeria, a fragile democracy that Washington hopes will become an anchor of stability in the region, is beset by rampant corruption and crime, simmering ethnic tensions, and grinding poverty. During the past three years, rebels in the Niger Delta have repeatedly disrupted Nigeria's oil flow.

Rising dependence on energy from weak and failing states promises to have unpleasant ramifications for wider U.S. foreign policy objectives. It will surely complicate U.S. democracy promotion by encouraging Washington to cozy up to authoritarian dictators or to intervene to shore up unstable regimes in regions such as the Caucasus or Central Asia. Even where the United States sticks to its principles, it may find good governance elusive in countries awash in petrodollars. For such "trust fund states," as Fareed Zakaria terms them, it is all too easy to rely on easy natural resource revenue rather than to do the hard work of building the economic and political institutions necessary to create enduring wealth and foster human liberty.[52]

By definition, the transnational threat of energy insecurity is peculiar to a subset of weak states that either possess large energy resources or sit astride transit routes. The nature of this threat varies according to whether state weakness is a function of insufficient will, inadequate capacity, or both. For Venezuela or Iran, for example, the main risk of interrupted supplies comes from the unpredictability of autocratic regimes. For Nigeria or post–Saddam Hussein Iraq, in contrast, the risk is that weak elected governments will be unable to ensure oil flows in the face of domestic instability. In either case, the governance gaps most closely correlated with energy insecurity tend to be political and economic, reflecting the tendency of natural resource riches to produce endemic corruption, abusive state power, and long-term stagnation.

Bad Neighbors?

Experience since the end of the Cold War has shown that conflict in developing countries can have critical transnational dimensions.[53] A common contention is that violent conflict and complex emergencies often spill over the porous borders of weak and failing states, destabilizing regions. Such claims have merit. As state structures collapse and borders become more porous, these countries often export violence as well as refugees, political instability, and economic dislocation to states in their vicinity. This risk is compounded when weak, vulnerable, or collapsed states are adjacent to countries with similar characteristics that possess few defenses against spillovers. Weaknesses in one state can thus encourage the rise of an entire bad neighborhood. Such a pattern emerged in West Africa during the 1990s, as the conflict in Liberia under Charles Taylor poured across national borders in the form of people, guns, and conflict diamonds, undermining neighboring Sierra Leone, Guinea, and Cote d'Ivoire.[54]

In reciprocal fashion, bad neighborhoods can undermine governance and encourage violence in already weak states. Many recent internal conflicts, from that of Burundi in the Great Lakes Region of Africa to that of Tajikistan in Central Asia, have been embedded in such regional conflict formations. In some cases, contiguous countries have fomented civil war by supporting armed groups across borders that share their political goals. In other cases, transnational networks, whether based on ethnic identity, political affinity, or economic interest, have undermined the central government and fueled violent conflict by facilitating illicit traffic in small arms, drugs, people, or lootable commodities. Where regional conflict formations are present, sustainable peace may depend on successful peacebuilding in the larger region.[55]

Given their propensity to descend into violence and embroil neighboring countries, weak and failing states are disproportionately at risk of external military intervention. State failure preceded virtually every case of the 30-odd instances of U.S. military intervention between 1960 and 2005.[56] Failed and failing states have also been the overwhelming focus of the 55 UN peacekeeping operations over the same period.[57]

Even in the absence of violence, failing states impose significant economic hardship on their regions, undoing years of development efforts. Recent analysis by the World Bank suggests that the average total cost of a failed state to itself and its neighbors amounts to a staggering $82.4 billion, or more than the total global foreign aid budget of $79 billion. In other words, the collapse of a single state can effectively erase an entire year's worth of worldwide official development assistance.[58]

The link here between state failure or weakness and regional instability is not universal but obvious: when weak or failed states are contiguous, the risk of regional instability is higher. The spillover of violent conflict itself may reflect a lack of capacity or will. Some governments are unable to control cross-border activities of rebel groups operating from their territory. The most salient governance gap here is inability to provide public security. Other governments adopt a conscious policy of destabilizing their neighbors. In this case, internal weakness and external aggression tend to reflect authoritarian political institutions.

A Road Map for Policy

Although more research is clearly warranted, it is not too soon to offer some recommendations for a more effective U.S. strategy toward weak and failing states. In developing this new strategy, policymakers must be better equipped with the tools to calculate what countries are at risk from which particular threats when determining when and how the United States should become involved. The strategy should have at least three components lacking in current U.S. policy: deeper intelligence collection and analysis on the links between state weakness and transnational threats; improved policy coherence to integrate all instruments of U.S. national influence in crisis countries; and robust international engagement to leverage efforts of partners and allies who share Washington's interest in stemming the negative spillovers of state weakness in the developing world.

To determine where U.S. involvement is warranted and to tailor state-building efforts in a manner that mitigates the most salient dangers, policymakers must first be able to anticipate which threats are likely to arise from particular countries. For one, they should recall the distinction between state capacity and will as determinants of good governance and state functionality. One testable hypothesis is that a weak state's propensity to generate spillovers, as well as the nature of these threats, will vary according to whether that weakness is a function of capacity, will, or both. The initial analysis above suggests that weak capacity is especially conducive to health epidemics and small arms proliferation, that inadequate will is often central to terrorism and WMD proliferation, and that both play roles in transnational organized crime, energy insecurity, and regional instability (see table 3). All things being equal, it is reasonable to predict that countries lacking both capacity and will for good governance should generate the most transnational threats. Accordingly, it should be expected that the six categories of spillovers—terrorism, proliferation, crime, health, energy, and regional instability—will cluster around such states. A related hypothesis is that states that are irresponsible as well as or instead of being powerless should be more likely to generate transnational threats that are not merely malignant, such as epidemics, but also malevolent, such as terrorism and weapons proliferation.

Table 3

Tentative Links between Capacity/Will and Transnational Threats

	Capacity	Will
Terrorism		X
WMD Proliferation		X
Small Arms Proliferation	X	
Crime	X	X
Disease	X	
Energy Insecurity	X	X
Regional Instability	X	X

A second set of hypotheses links particular transnational threats to specific short-comings in state performance. Weak states suffer from one or more of four functional gaps, in their ability to provide physical security, legitimate political institutions, effective economic management, or basic social welfare. Although any such hypotheses would need to be refined, it seems reasonable to predict that those states most associated either with transnational terrorism, proliferation risks, or regional instability would have shortcomings in security and political capacities; that infectious disease would rank low on social welfare, particularly health investments; and that transnational-crime as well as energy-insecurity candidates would lack stable political and economic institutions (see table 4). Assessing these hypotheses will require breaking state strength down into its component parts and testing whether gaps in these areas correlate with the relevant threats.

A third testable hypothesis would be that some categories of threats are more closely correlated with the weakest quintile of states, whereas others are more typical of the next higher tier. The concept of spillover, after all, implies a transnational connection. In some cases, such as violent conflicts or epidemics, spillovers can travel fairly easily from the weakest states. In other cases, including WMD proliferation and some forms of crime, the transnational diffusion of threats is more likely to come from states that are superficially strong but possess critical "sovereignty holes" and that provide easy access to the transportation, communications, and financial infrastructure of the global economy. If this hypothesis is borne out in empirical analysis, the implication is profound. A state need not possess capacity or commitment gaps across the board to pose a major risk of spillovers. A few critical gaps can make all the difference and should be targeted by external actors.

Working from these hypotheses, policymakers can begin to assemble a more effective strategy to address the specific threats presented by different characteristics of weak and failing states. Since late 2004, the National Intelligence Council has prepared a semiannual "Instability Watch List" that identifies countries at risk of state failure within two years. Although this development is welcome, busy policymakers find only marginal utility in periodic warning products that resemble the "conventional wisdom watch," with the requisite up and down arrows, that appears in *U.S. News and World Report* or *Newsweek*. To be

Table 4

Tentative Links between Governance Gaps and Transnational Threats

	Political	Security	Economic	Social
Terrorism	X	X		
Weapons Proliferation	X	X		
Crime	X		X	
Disease				X
Energy Insecurity	X		X	
Regional Instability	X	X		

useful, such a list should also be accompanied by a consequences matrix that outlines not only the potential negative developments within each country but also the implications of such turmoil for transnational threats such as disruption of oil supplies, regional instability, or WMD proliferation likely to affect U.S. national security interests. A sophisticated early-warning system could help policymakers determine where to devote U.S. efforts and help them build the political will for effective preventive action.

In addition, the U.S. government must replace its current fragmented approach to weak and failing states with a truly integrated strategy that allows it to bring all relevant tools of national power to bear in the service of coherent country plans. The State Department and Pentagon have made recent, modest progress in creating standing capacities to stabilize and rebuild war-torn societies, and they are beginning to coordinate the civilian and military sides of these undertakings. There has been no similar effort to define a unified interagency strategy to prevent states from sliding into failure and violence in the first place. Too often, Washington's engagement with weak states is in practice little more than a collection of independent bilateral diplomatic, military, aid, trade, and financial relationships, influenced by the institutional mandates and bureaucratic hobbyhorses of respective agencies. What is missing is a coordinated approach uniting the three Ds of U.S. foreign policy—defense, development, and diplomacy—as well as intelligence, financial, and trade policies. Integration must occur not only in Washington but also at U.S. embassies, within country teams under the direction of the ambassador. The precise country strategy will vary according to the perceived root causes of weakness. Where capacity is lacking, the United States should enable states to fill the gaps. Where will is lacking, the United States should deploy incentives to persuade or compel a stronger commitment. Where both are absent, the United States must try to change the attitudes of the country's leadership while working with civil society to build basic capacities and empower agents of reform.

Finally, the United States must spearhead a more coherent multilateral response to the linked challenges of state weakness and global threats. National governments and intergovernmental organizations are groping for new mechanisms and instruments to prevent and respond to state failure, but similar to internal U.S. efforts, progress has been hampered by fragmented institutional mandates. The United States should advance common approaches to state-building and transnational threats within the G-8, the UN, NATO, the Organization of American States, the OECD, and the World Bank and within regional bodies to which it does not belong, such as the European Union, the African Union, and the Association of Southeast Asian Nations. Such leadership would provide a tangible expression of the administration's espoused commitment to effective multilateral cooperation and of its willingness to help faltering states offer better futures to their citizens. This mission can unite developed and developing countries. Although transnational dangers are reshaping the rich world's security agenda, the poor countries nevertheless remain the main victims of global dangers such as crime, disease, and terrorism.

Weak and failing states can and do generate transnational spillovers such as terrorism, weapons proliferation, crime, disease, energy insecurity, and regional instability that endanger U.S. national interests and international security. At the same time, the blanket equation of weak states and global threats provides only modest analytic insights and even less practical guidance for policymakers. Each poorly performing country suffers from a distinctive set of pathologies and generates a unique mixture of challenges, of varying gravity.[59] There can be no one-size-fits-all response to addressing either the sources or consequences of these weaknesses. At a practical level, neither the United States nor its allies have the unlimited resources or attention spans required to launch ambitious state-building exercises in all corners of the world. U.S. officials will thus need to investigate the sources and consequences of transnational threats better and subsequently be able to set priorities and make tough choices about where, when, and how to engage weak and failing states to improve U.S. and international security.

Notes

1. Francis Fukuyama, *State-Building: Governance and World Order in the 21st Century* (Ithaca, N.Y.: Cornell University Press, 2004), p. 92. See John J. Hamre and Gordon R. Sullivan, "Toward Postconflict Reconstruction," *The Washington Quarterly* 25, no. 4 (Autumn 2002): 85–96; Susan E. Rice, "The New National Security Strategy: Focus on Failed States," *Brookings Policy Brief*, no. 116 (February 2003); Chester A. Crocker, "Engaging Failing States," *Foreign Affairs* 82, no. 5 (September/October 2003): 32–44; "Grappling With State Failure," *Washington Post*, June 9, 2004, =. A20; Mark Turner and Martin Wolf, "The Dilemma of Fragile States," *Financial Times*, February 18, 2005; Lee Hamilton, "The Dangerous Connection—Failed and Failing States, WMD, and Terrorism" (webcast, Woodrow Wilson International Center for Scholars, Washington, D.C., April 25, 2005), http://www.wilsoncenter.org/index.cfm?fuseaction=events.event&event_id=116497.
2. Adam Garfinkle, "A Conversation With Condoleezza Rice," *American Interest* 1, no. 1 (Autumn 2005): 47–50. See Richard Haass, "Sovereignty: Existing Rights, Evolving Responsibilities" (speech, Georgetown University, Washington, D.C., January 14, 2003), http://www.state.gov/s/p/rem/2003/16648.htm; U.S. Agency for International Development (USAID), *Foreign Aid in the National Interest: Promoting Freedom, Security and Opportunity* (Washington, D.C.: USAID, 2003), p. 1; Caroline Daniel, "U.S. in Final Stage of National Security Revamp," *Financial Times*, January 5, 2006.
3. *National Security Strategy of the United States of America* (September 2002), p. 1, http://www.whitehouse.gov/nsc/nss.html.
4. *National Defense Strategy of the United States of America* (March 2005), http://www.defenselink.mil/news/Mar2005/d20050318nds1.pdf. See Bradley Graham, "Pentagon Strategy Aims to Block Internal Threats to Foreign Forces," *Washington Post*, March 19, 2005, p. A2; Jim Garamone, "Rumsfeld Describes Changing Face of War," Armed Forces Press Service, May 25, 2005.
5. George Tenet, "The World Wide Threat in 2003: Evolving Dangers in a Complex World," testimony before the Senate Select Committee on Intelligence, February 12, 2003; "Possible Remote Havens for Terrorists and Other Illicit Activity," May 2003 (unclassified Central Intelligence Agency [CIA] map).
6. Stephen D. Krasner and Carlos Pascual, "Addressing State Failure," *Foreign Affairs* 84, no. 4 (July/August 2005): 153–163; USAID, *Fragile States Strategy* (Washington, D.C.: USAID, February 2005); Robert Zoellick, "CAFTA Is a Win-Win," *Washington Post*, May 24, 2005, p. A17.
7. Prime Minister's Strategy Unit (PMSU), *Investing in Prevention: An International Strategy to Manage Risks of Instability and Improve Crisis Response* (London: PMSU, February 2005).
8. Kofi Annan (speech, Council on Foreign Relations, New York, December 16, 2004). See High-Level Panel on Threats, Challenges and Change, "A More Secure World: Our Shared Responsibility," 2004, p. 9.
9. "Development Effectiveness in Fragile States," http://www.oecd.org/department/0,2688,en_2649_33693550_1_1_1_1_1,00.html.
10. Commission on Weak States and U.S. National Security, *On the Brink: Weak States and U.S. National Security* (Washington, D.C.: Center for Global Development, 2004); British Department for International Development (DFID), *Why We Need to Work More Effectively in Fragile States* (London: DFID, January 2005), pp. 27–28; "World Bank Group Work in

Low-Income Countries Under Stress: A Task Force Report," September 2002. See "The Failed States Index," *Foreign Policy*, no. 149 (July/August 2005): 56–65 (developed by the Fund for Peace and *Foreign Policy*, focusing on susceptibility to instability and conflict as opposed to broader state capacities); Robert Rotberg, "Strengthening Governance: Ranking States Would Help," *The Washington Quarterly* 28, no. 1 (Winter 2004–05): 71–81; Ashraf Ghani, Clare Lockhart, and Michael Carnahan, "Closing the Sovereignty Gap: An Approach to State-Building," *Overseas Development Institute Working Paper*, no. 253, September 2005.

11. Office of the Press Secretary, The White House, "President Proposes $5 Billion Plan to Help Developing Nations," March 14, 2002, http://www.whitehouse.gov/news/releases/2002/03/20020314-7.html.

12. Michael Clemens and Todd Moss, "Costs and Causes of Zimbabwe's Crisis," *CGD Notes*, July 2005, http://www.cgdev.org/content/publications/detail/2918/.

13. DFID, *Why We Need to Work More Effectively in Fragile States*, p. 9; United Nations High Commission for Refugees, "2004 Global Refugee Trends," June 17, 2005, http://www.unhcr.org/cgi-bin/texis/vtx/events/opendoc.pdf?tbl=STATISTICS&id=42b283744; Paul Collier and Anke Hoeffler, "The Challenge of Reducing the Global Incidence of War," *Copenhagen Consensus Challenge Paper*, March 26, 2004, http://www.copenhagenconsensus.com/Files/Filer/CC/Papers/Conflicts_230404.pdf; Freedom House, *The Worst of the Worst: The World's Most Repressive Societies* (Washington, D.C.: Freedom House, 2004).

14. Daniel Kauffmann, Aart Kray, and Massimo Mastruzzi, *Governance Matters IV: Governance Indicators for 1996–2004* (Washington, D.C.: World Bank, 2005).

15. Center for Human Security, *Human Security Report 2005*, p. 92.

16. Gregory F. Treverton, "Enhancing Security Through Development: Probing the Connections" (Annual Bank Conference on Development Economics, Amsterdam, May 23–24, 2005), http://siteresources.worldbank.org/INTAMSTERDAM/Resources/GregTreverton.pdf; Peter Bergen and Laurie Garrett, "Report of the Working Group on State Security and Transnational Threats," Princeton Project on U.S. National Security, September 2005.

17. Justin Logan and Christopher Preble, "Failed States and Flawed Logic: The Case Against a Standing Nation-Building Office," *Policy Analysis*, no. 560 (January 11, 2006), http://www.cato.org/pubs/pas/pa560.pdf.

18. John Mearshimer, *The Tragedy of Great Power Politics* (New York: W.W. Norton, 2001); Gary T. Dempsey, "Old Folly in a New Disguise: Nation Building to Combat Terrorism," *Policy Analysis*, no. 429 (March 21, 2002), http://www.cato.org/pubs/pas/pa429.pdf.

19. "Fighting Terrorism at Gleneagles," *New York Times*, July 5, 2005, p. A22.

20. Monty G. Marshall, "Global Terrorism: An Overview and Analysis," September 12, 2002, p. 25, http://www.cidcm.umd.edu/inscr/papers/GlobalTerrorismmgm.pdf (report from the Center for International Development and Conflict Management, University of Maryland).

21. *Patterns of Global Terrorism* (Washington, D.C.: U.S. Department of State, 2003); *Country Reports on Terrorism* (Washington, D.C.: U.S. Department of State, 2005).

22. Ray Takeyh and Nicholas Gvosdev, "Do Terrorist Networks Need a Home?" *The Washington Quarterly* 25, no. 3 (Summer 2002): 97–108; Sebastian Mallaby, "The Reluctant Imperialist: Terrorism, Failed States and the Case for American Empire," *Foreign Affairs* 81, no. 2 (March/April 2002): 2–7.

23. Francis T. Miko, "Removing Terrorist Sanctuaries: The 9/11 Commission Recommendations and U.S. Policy," *CRS Report for Congress*, RL32518, August 10, 2004, http://www.maxwell.af.mil/au/awc/awcgate/crs/rl32518.pdf. See Princeton N. Lyman and J. Stephen Morrison, "The Terrorist Threat in Africa," *Foreign Affairs* 83, no. 1 (January/February 2004): 75–86.

24. Eric Schmitt, "As Africans Join Iraqi Insurgency, U.S. Counters With Military Training in Their Lands," *New York Times*, June 10, 2005, p. A11.

25. *National Strategy for Combating Terrorism* (February 2003), p. 22, http://www.whitehouse.gov/news/releases/2003/02/counter_terrorism/counter_terrorism_strategy.pdf.

26. Office of the Press Secretary, The White House, "President Addresses United Nations High-Level Plenary Meeting," September 14, 2005, http://www.whitehouse.gov/news/releases/2005/09/20050914.html.

27. Walter Laqueur, *No End to War: Terrorism in the Twenty-First Century* (New York: Continuum, 2003), p. 11.

28. Ken Menkhaus, "Somalia: State Collapse and the Threat of Terrorism," *Adelphi Paper* no. 364 (2004). See Greg Mills, "Africa's New Strategic Significance," *The Washington Quarterly* 27, no. 4 (Autumn 2004): 157–169.

29. Olivier Roy, *Globalized Islam: The Search for a New Ummah* (London: Hurst, 2004); Timothy M. Savage, "Europe and Islam: Crescent Waxing, Cultures Clashing," *The Washington Quarterly* 27, no. 3 (Summer 2004): 25–50.

30. Dana Priest, "Iraq New Terror Breeding Ground; War Created Haven, CIA Advisers Report," *Washington Post*, January 14, 2005, p. A1.

31. Daniel Byman, "Passive Sponsors of Terrorism," *Survival* 47, no. 4 (Winter 2005–06): 117–144.

32. PMSU, *Investing in Prevention*, p. 12. See *Deadly Arsenals* (Washington, D.C.: Carnegie Endowment for International Peace, 2005).

33. David Albright and Corey Hinderson, "Unraveling the A.Q. Khan and Future Proliferation Networks," *The Washington Quarterly* 28, no. 2 (Spring 2005): 111–128.

34. Graduate Institute of International Studies, *Small Arms Survey 2003: Development Denied* (Oxford: Oxford University Press, 2003), p. 57.

35. C. J. Chivers, "Ill-Secured Soviet Arms Depots Tempting Rebels and Terrorists," *New York Times*, July 16, 2005, p. A1.

36. *International Crime Threat Assessment* (Washington, D.C.: December 2000), p. 18, http://www.fas.org/irp/threat/pub45270index.html; *Moises Naim, Illicit: How Smugglers, Copycats and Traffickers Are Hijacking the Global Economy* (New York: Doubleday, 2005).

37. Peter Andreas, "Transnational Crime and Economic Globalization," in *Transnational Organized Crime and International Security: Business as Usual?*, eds. Mats Berdal and Monica Serrano (Boulder, Colo.: Lynne Rienner, 2002).

38. Phil Williams, "Transnational Criminal Enterprises, Conflict, and Instability," in *Turbulent Peace: The Challenges of Managing International Conflict*, eds. Chester Crocker, Fen Osler Hampson, and Pamela Aall (Washington, D.C.: United States Institute of Peace, 2001), pp. 97–112; UN Office on Drugs and Crime (UNODC), *Why Fighting Crime Can Assist Development in Africa: Rule of Law and Protection of the Most Vulnerable* (Vienna: UNODC, May 2005).

39. Williams, "Transnational Criminal Enterprises, Conflict, and Instability," p. 100.

40. U.S. Department of State, "Presidential Determination on Major Drug Transit or Major Illicit Drug Producing Countries for Fiscal Year 2006," *International Country Narcotics Strategy Reports*, September 15, 2005; UNODC, *2005 World Drug Report*; U.S. Department of State, "Trafficking in Persons Report," March 2005.

41. Clive Bell and Maureen Lewis, "The Economic Implications of Epidemics Old and New," *Center for Global Development Working Paper* no. 54, p. 31. See Allen Sipress, "Indonesia Stretched to the Limit in Battle Against Two Diseases," *Washington Post*, November 6, 2005, p. A19.

42. National Intelligence Council (NIC), *The Global Infectious Disease Threat and Its Implications for the United States* (Washington, D.C.: NIC, 2000).

43. Dennis Pirages, "Containing Infectious Disease," in *State of the World 2005: Redefining Global Security* (New York: W.W. Norton, 2005), p. 46; NIC, *Global Infectious Disease Threat*, fig. 9, http://www.cia.gov/cia/reports/nie/report/752049.gif.

44. Laurie Garrett, "HIV and National Security: Where Are the Links?" *Council on Foreign Relations Report*, 2005; Paul Collier et. al., *Breaking the Conflict Trap: Civil War and Development Policy* (Washington, D.C.: The World Bank and Oxford University Press, 2003); NIC, *Global Infectious Disease Threat*, p. 37.

45. World Bank, "The World Bank Responds to SARS," June 4, 2003, http://web.worldbank.org/WBSITE/EXTERNAL/NEWS/0,,contentMDK:20114259~menuPK:34457~pagePK:34370~piPK:34424~theSitePK:4607,00.html.

46. NIC, *The Next Wave of HIV/AIDS: Nigeria, Ethiopia, Russia, India and China* (Washington, D.C.: NIC, 2002).

47. "China Reports Soaring Oil Imports," BBC News, September 14, 2004, http://news.bbc.co.uk/1/hi/business/3654060.stm.

48. Michael Klare, *Resource Wars: The New Landscape of Global Conflict* (New York: Henry Holt, 2001), p. 44.

49. PMSU, *Investing in Prevention*, p. 11; U.S. Department of Energy, "World Oil Transit Chokepoints," August 1999.

50. John Mintz, "Outcome Grim at Oil War Game," *Washington Post*, June 24, 2005, p. A19.

51. David L. Goldwyn and J. Stephen Morrison, "A Strategic Approach to U.S. Governance and Security in the Gulf of Guinea," July 2005 (report of the CSIS task force on Gulf of Guinea Security).

52. Fareed Zakaria, *The Future of Freedom: Illiberal Democracy at Home and Abroad* (New York: W.W. Norton, 2003), p. 75.

53. Michael E. Brown, ed., *The International Dimensions of Internal Conflict* (Cambridge, Mass.: MIT Press, 1996).

54. Myron Weiner, "Bad Neighbors, Bad Neighborhoods: An Inquiry Into the Causes of Refugee Flows," *International Security* 21, no. 1 (Summer 1996): 5–42.

55. Barnett Rubin, *Blood on the Doorstep: The Politics of Preventive Action* (New York: Century Foundation/Council on Foreign Relations, 2002), pp. 134–137.

56. Jeffrey D. Sachs, "The Strategic Significance of Global Inequality," *The Washington Quarterly* 24, no. 3 (Summer 2001): 187–198.

57. UN Department of Peacekeeping Operations, "Operations Timeline," http://www.un.org/Depts/dpko/dpko/timeline/pages/timeline.html.

58. Paul Collier and L. Chauvet, "Presentation to the DAC Learning and Advisory Process on Difficult Partnerships," November 5, 2004.

59. Simon Chesterman, Michael Ignatieff, and Ramesh Thakur, eds., *Making States Work: State Failure and the Crisis of Governance* (Tokyo: United Nations University, 2005), p. 359.

Stewart Patrick is a research fellow at the Center for Global Development in Washington, D.C. Patrick earned his D.Phil. and M.Phil in International Relations and his M.St. in European history from Oxford University, where he was a Rhodes Scholar. He earned his bachelor's degree in human biology from Stanford University.

Chapter 1.3

The WMD Terrorism Hype

Andrew O'Neil

Terrorist Use of Weapons of Mass Destruction: How Serious Is the Threat?

This article examines the extent to which terrorist use of nuclear, chemical, and biological weapons poses a tangible threat to international security. In the literature on terrorism and weapons of mass destruction (WMD) some analysts have tended to exaggerate the scope of the threat and assumed that large-scale terrorist acts involving WMD are only 'a matter of time'. In short, there is a tendency among observers to converge on analogous assessments at the higher end of the threat spectrum. In this article I argue that although WMD terrorism remains a real prospect, the ease with which such attacks can be carried out has been exaggerated; acquiring WMD capabilities for delivery against targets is a lot more problematic for terrorists than is generally acknowledged in the literature. However, this is not to say that the possibility of such attacks can (or should) be ruled out. The rise of a 'new' brand of terrorism that operates across transnational networks and whose operations aim to inflict mass casualties, coupled with the destructive threshold crossed on 11 September 2001, mean that terrorist attacks using WMD will continue to be a realistic prospect in the future.

Introduction

Accurately assessing threats is a notoriously problematic undertaking for states. The challenge of itemising and attaching specific priority to tangible and potential threats to national security in a way that is readily accessible for policy makers remains especially difficult. Even generously funded and highly capable intelligence agencies struggle to formulate coherent and timely threat assessments across the security spectrum. Terrorism is a particularly difficult threat to assess. Usually comprised of amorphous associations of highly mobile individuals whose intentions are virtually impossible to gauge without access to reliable (and timely) human intelligence, terrorist groups remain elusive (Hoffman 1996). Nevertheless, in recent years assessing terrorist threats has become the single most salient preoccupation for Western national security agencies. Faced with the most destructive phase of international terrorism in the modern era, critically evaluating the nature and scope of the threat in order to select the most appropriate countermeasures to safeguard the state and its interests has become a fixation for most Western political leaders.

Of the manifold threats posed by terrorist organisations, attacks using nuclear, chemical, or biological weapons against state assets loom especially large. The fear that terrorists will resort to using Weapons of Mass Destruction (WMD) is nothing new. The spectre of terrorist attacks involving WMD has preoccupied security analysts both within and outside official government circles since at least the early 1970s.[1] However, the perceived threat of

WMD use by terrorist groups has been magnified dramatically since the end of the Cold War. This can be attributed to three main factors.

The first is the collapse of the USSR in 1991 and attendant concerns about the physical security of WMD assets in the territories of the former Soviet Union (FSU). The primary concern has been that lax security practices in the FSU have made it easier for terrorist organisations to access WMD technologies, either via covert purchasing arrangements or theft. The phenomenon of 'loose nukes' in the FSU has received wide publicity, but less acknowledged are the enormous stocks of unsecured biological and chemical weapons stemming from the massive Soviet Cold War inventory. One authoritative source has identified several dozen repositories in Russia housing BW stocks from the former Soviet program that lack adequate security and tracking arrangements (Cirincione, Wolfsthal, and Rajkumar 2002: 125). The second factor has been the rise of what is generally regarded as a new breed of terrorism worldwide. Prone to using far more lethal and indiscriminate forms of violence than older, more established, terrorist groups, the new terrorist groups are said to covet those weapons that can do the maximum damage to their target set: WMD. The third factor contributing to increased anxiety over the threat of WMD terrorism has been a gradual realisation that, in contrast to the Cold War period when worldwide terrorist attacks were concentrated largely in Europe and the Middle East, terrorism now poses a distinctive security threat to the United States mainland as well as other parts of the globe traditionally regarded as relatively safe. The 1993 attacks on the World Trade Centre, the 1995 Oklahoma City bombing, and the 11 September 2001 attacks each had the effect of dramatically illustrating America's vulnerability to terrorism. While none of these attacks involved the use of WMD, they nevertheless raised fears about the possibility of such an attack on American territory. As a general rule, when the world's sole remaining superpower becomes the target of a specific security danger, this invariably raises the profile of such threats internationally—and so it has been with WMD terrorism.

Over the past decade there has been a surge in the academic literature on the subject of WMD terrorism. Yet, as Amy Sands (2002) has noted, in dealing with this issue much of the literature has been marred by a tendency to 'comfortably reiterate the same threat mantra without examining more closely certain underlying assumptions'. A particularly salient feature has been an assumption that if terrorist groups are able to get their hands on WMD *materials*, they will, as a matter of course, be capable of fabricating a viable *weapon* to use against a target set (for instance, see Laqueur 1996; Falkenrath 1998; and Hoffman 1998: 196–97). One of the unfortunate by-products of this analytical trend among security specialists has been that 'a great deal of reporting on the subject has been careless and exaggerated, creating a mood of political paranoia' (Stern 1998–99: 176). This has been further fuelled by a prevailing view among policy elites and much of the academic community that large-scale terrorist acts using WMD are only 'a matter of time'.

Part of the problem is that insufficient attention has been devoted to assessing dispassionately whether hypothetical scenarios are likely to be transformed into reality. This article is concerned with addressing this issue, along with the broader question of whether the WMD threat has been exaggerated. I address three inter-related propositions that I maintain are central to understanding the degree to which WMD terrorism should be categorised as a security threat: can terrorists acquire WMD; what is the likelihood that terrorists will actually use WMD; has the threat increased since 11 September 2001?

My argument is essentially twofold. First, while terrorist attacks involving WMD remain a real prospect, the ease with which such attacks can be executed has been exaggerated. In particular, the inherent difficulties of weaponising a WMD capability (as distinct from merely having access to WMD materials) has often been underestimated. To achieve a realistic understanding of the scope of the threat it is necessary to draw a clear distinction between nuclear, biological, and chemical weapons. Second, although it is important to temper assumptions about the 'inevitability' of WMD terrorism, it is equally important not to let the pendulum swing too far in the other direction.[2] There is abundant evidence that a wide range of terrorist outfits have actively sought WMD materials, and it is very likely that some have obtained them. While the challenges of weaponising WMD capabilities remain formidable, groups which invest enormous amounts of time, energy, and resources in endeavouring to acquire these capabilities have a very strong incentive to succeed, which itself should not be underestimated as a factor. On balance, there can be little doubt that once terrorist groups who are intent on acquiring a WMD capability gain that capability, they will seek to use it.

Can Terrorists Acquire WMD?

Starting from Scratch

Accounts vary over the ease with which terrorist groups could acquire nuclear, chemical, and biological weapons. Nuclear weapons clearly remain the most powerful of the WMD triad in terms of the sheer destruction they can wreak. The demonstrated blast, heat and longer-term radiation effects of fission and fusion weapons mark them out as unrivalled in the history of warfare. Because of this, they are no doubt attractive from a terrorist standpoint: but how easy are they to acquire?

Those who maintain that nuclear weapons are accessible for terrorist groups point out that knowledge on 'how to build a bomb' is now freely available to anyone who has Internet access. They also point to documented lapses in Russia's nuclear system during the 1990s that indicated a leakage of weapons-grade fissile material on to the black market and a striking level of vulnerability in Russia to theft of tactical nuclear warheads and smaller atomic demolition munitions (Collina and Wolfsthal 2002). However, there is general consensus that nuclear weapons are more difficult to obtain than their chemical and biological counterparts. Despite some claims to the contrary, the core ingredients of weapons grade fissile material—highly enriched uranium and plutonium—are scarce internationally and very expensive to produce in sufficient quantities to manufacture even the crudest of nuclear devices. Moreover, since the mid-1980s, tight export controls have been observed by the small group of countries able to supply nuclear materials and equipment worldwide (Milhollin 2002). Even assuming that a terrorist organisation was able to amass enough fissile material to fabricate a nuclear device, the challenges of secure storage prior to use, the risks of being discovered transporting the device to the target area, and effective delivery would be prohibitive for all but the most sophisticated terrorist group.

A more readily attainable option would be acquiring the requisite materials to fabricate a radiological weapon, or 'dirty bomb' (i.e. conventional explosives laced with radioactive material aimed at propelling the latter across a wide area). There is some indication that elements of the Al Qaeda network have exhibited an interest in obtaining radioactive materials on the Russian black market for possible use in a 'dirty bomb', although it remains unclear whether their quest has been successful (see Warrick 2002; and Stout 2002).

While yielding nowhere near the destructive effects of nuclear weapons, terrorist use of a radiological weapon could induce considerable panic among a target population by exploiting fears of radioactive poisoning. And unlike nuclear weapons, the materials required for a radiological weapon are widely used in 'unsecured' civilian applications such as medical imaging equipment. Although not usually included in the WMD threat template, radiological weapons could impose significant financial costs on the target state and would be an ideal terrorist weapon in severely disrupting public health and safety among a target population (Levi and Kelly 2002). As in the case of a complete nuclear warhead, however, terrorist groups would still confront significant challenges in transporting a radiological device over land, sea, or air and delivering that device against an assigned target.

The requisite technologies for manufacturing viable biological warfare (BW) agents and chemical warfare (CW) agents are widely available.[3] The inherent dual-use nature of these technologies means that many of the key ingredients comprising chemical and biological weapons can also be found in perfectly legitimate biotechnology and chemical industry sectors in any number of states around the world.[4] Indeed, it is generally agreed that if a country possesses a functioning civilian chemical or biotechnology industry then it is in a position to acquire the necessary materials to manufacture CW and BW agents. Certainly when compared with the difficulty of obtaining fissile material for manufacturing nuclear weapons, acquiring the requisite materials for constructing chemical and biological weapons is much less challenging for states and non-state entities alike. In many respects, a greater challenge for a terrorist organisation would be choosing the most appropriate CW or BW agent to weaponise for use against their designated target. As one authoritative US report has concluded, 'the ease or difficulty with which terrorists could cause mass casualties with an improvised chemical or biological weapon or device depends on the chemical or biological agent selected' (US General Accounting Office 1999: 10).

The use of CW agents by terrorist groups has provoked serious concern among observers, particularly since the 1995 sarin gas attack by the Aum Shinrikyo sect on the Tokyo subway which killed twelve and injured in excess of five thousand people. If the operation had not been botched, it is estimated that the attack could have killed thousands given the acutely lethal nature of the nerve agent used (Stern 1999: 64). Yet while a terrorist attack using chemical weapons cannot be ruled out, the prospect of terrorists employing biological weapons against population centres is now regarded as the most likely scenario across the entire WMD threat spectrum. Biological weapons are judged to be the ideal terrorist WMD instrument for three key reasons.

First, BW agents are far easier to acquire than nuclear weapons and it takes considerably less BW agent to produce the same killing impact as chemical weapons. Quantum leaps in biotechnology applications may mean revolutionary advances in drug discovery for treatment, but the very same quantum leaps can be used to broaden horizons for acquiring new, and refining existing, BW agents (Wheelis 2002). Moreover, on a pound for pound basis, BW agents are far more potent than any of the most deadly CW agents which must be 'delivered in massive quantities to inflict lethal concentrations over large areas' (Tucker 2000: 5). As Tucker (2000: 5) observes:

> [A] chemical attack that caused 50 per cent casualties over a square kilometre would require about a metric ton of sarin. In contrast, microorganisms infect people in minute doses and then multiply within the host to cause disease. For example, a mere 8,000 anthrax bacteria—an amount smaller than a speck of dust—are sufficient to infect a

human being. As a result, a biological attack with a few kilograms of anthrax could inflict the same level of casualties over a square kilometer as a metric ton of sarin—provided that the anthrax was effectively disseminated.

Second, the effects of biological weapons on a target population would be extremely hard to counter. Administering vaccines and rendering more general medical assistance to a widely affected population would place unprecedented strains on emergency authorities (Katz 2002). This is assuming that an attack using BW agents could be detected in a timely fashion. Indeed, one of the major obstacles for state authorities would be detecting that a covert attack using BW agents had actually taken place. For instance, vaccination against the most contagious BW agent, smallpox, is only effective if administered within seven days of exposure to the virus. Yet during the early stages of contracting the virus, individuals merely exhibit flu-like symptoms making prompt diagnosis problematic. Left undetected for even a few days, smallpox has the potential to spread rapidly among the target population, creating an epidemic that could be impossible to contain (Chyba 2002: 134).

Third, the insidious nature of BW agents—composed as they are of living microorganisms with the capacity to reproduce and mutate—has the potential to psychologically 'unhinge' target populations. As one analyst has put it, 'because they are silent, stealthy, invisible, and slow acting, germs are capable of inducing levels of anxiety approaching hysteria (Regis 2001: 12). One only has to look at the American public's angst-ridden reaction to the tightly targeted anthrax attacks in October 2001 to appreciate the potential panic induced by a widespread terrorist attack involving BW agents. The fact that these attacks used small, though highly lethal, quantities of anthrax and were carried out by using a highly novel dissemination route (the postal service) merely served to accentuate the sense of vulnerability among the US public.

Although the necessary materials for manufacturing BW agents are relatively easy to acquire, it would be a mistake to assume that these materials can be easily weaponised for use against a target population. In order to ensure effective delivery to inflict mass casualties, a terrorist group would need to develop a powder or aerosol that could be disseminated over a wide geographical radius.[5] This requires considerable scientific skill and expertise that, most analysts agree, is still beyond the reach of most terrorist organisations (see Falkenrath 1998: 47; Chyba 2002: 127; and Parachini 2001: 4). One of the main reasons why the Aum Shinrikyo sect used the CW agent sarin in its 1995 Tokyo subway attack was that it had previously failed to develop sufficiently virulent BW strains of anthrax and botulinum toxin. This was despite the group being generously financed and its employment of some two dozen professionally trained microbiologists working in well-equipped scientific laboratories (Mangold and Goldberg 1999: 335–51).

Alternative Avenues?

Given the intrinsic difficulties associated with manufacturing a viable WMD device from scratch, would terrorist groups have alternative avenues for acquiring such a capability? One possible scenario would be the theft of complete or partially complete devices from established state inventories. As noted earlier, the security and tracking systems for all categories of WMD remains woefully underdeveloped in the FSU, especially Russia. But this is not to say that the latter would be the only target for terrorist groups intent on pilfering a WMD device. The 2001 anthrax attacks in the US were carried out with material that appears to have come from the US defence establishment, an establishment that has maintained some of the tightest security and tracking systems in the world (Cirincione, Wolfsthal, and Rajkumar 2002: 181–84).

Another scenario is that a nuclear, biological or chemical weapon could be provided to a terrorist organisation by a state that remains sympathetic to the terrorists' motives and aims. This threat has gained increased currency in US policy-making circles, with the Bush administration linking international terrorist networks with individual states it alleges are actively seeking WMD capabilities—Iran, Iraq, and North Korea (*The Economist* 2002). Yet despite these states having demonstrated a willingness to sponsor terrorist activities in the past, it is doubtful whether any state would transfer WMD to a non-state entity, assuming they were in a position to do so. It is difficult to imagine any state that would be willing to risk being discovered as having links with a terrorist group that had attacked US targets (for instance) with WMD, let alone one that would be willing to furnish such a group with a WMD capability. For as long as regime preservation remains the paramount credo in Iran, Iraq, and North Korea, it is highly improbable that ruling elites would risk certain US retaliation (probably with nuclear weapons) in the wake of a WMD attack on American territory.

However, this cautious approach could be revised if a leadership elite found itself in mortal peril. While regime preservation may be the overriding priority in Baghdad, if the regime judged that its demise was imminent in the latter stages of a war with the United States, then it is entirely plausible that it would attempt to use all the WMD assets at its disposal. This could well include nuclear, biological, or chemical weapons supplied to terrorist groups for use against targets on the American mainland or targets in Israel. With the regime's demise imminent, there would be little, if any, incentive to exercise restraint and no fear of retaliation from the United States and its allies (O'Neil 2002: 14–15). Other countries for whom 'contracting out' WMD terrorism may be an option are US adversaries (possibly including China) who fear the longer term strategic implications of National Missile Defence (NMD). If Washington successfully deploys NMD, these states may be more inclined to consider using terrorists as 'delivery systems' if the option of delivering their WMD payloads against US targets with long range missiles has been effectively nullified (Glaser and Fetter 2001: 54–57). In such a scenario these states may well calculate that they would not be identified as the source of an attack.

What is the Likelihood of Terrorists Using WMD?

Norms and Strategic Value

Just as the issue of WMD accessibility for terrorist groups is contested, so too is the question of whether such groups would actually use WMD in certain circumstances. Scepticism towards the notion that terrorists will seek to use WMD is largely predicated on accepting the much-quoted observation of US terrorist expert Brian Jenkins that 'terrorists want a lot of people watching and a lot of people listening, not a lot of people dead' (quoted in Hoffman 1998: 198). Traditionalists like Jenkins, who maintain that the WMD threat is exaggerated, point to the fact that historically few terrorist groups have shown an active interest in acquiring a capability to inflict mass casualties in the thousands or tens of thousands. According to this line of thinking, the best assurance we have that a mass casualty terrorist attack involving WMD will not happen is that it hasn't happened yet. While terrorist groups by their very nature aim to effect radical political and social change, an attack on this scale could not be vindicated by any conceivable ideology (see Kamp 1998–99: 170). No terrorist group, so the argument goes, would risk attracting the international opprobrium such a mass casualty attack would provoke. From this perspective, although terrorists may be violent, they are also rational and calculating; they understand that a mass casualty attack using WMD would serve no instrumental purpose in propagating their ideology and objectives.

However, this traditionalist argument overlooks several important variables which suggest that, far from being remote, the likelihood of terrorist groups that have acquired nuclear, chemical, or biological weapons using these weapons is increasingly plausible. The most conspicuous of these variables is that non-state actors in international relations do not, as a general rule, operate according to the same normative constraints as sovereign states (Starr 1995: 306). While there is strong circumstantial evidence to support the claim that a norm of WMD non-use has evolved over time among states, there are few grounds for assuming that terrorist organisations will necessarily adhere to this norm. Indeed, the inherent shock value of terrorism is essentially based on the willingness of terrorist groups to flout generally accepted international norms of behaviour. Moreover, the perceived strategic merits of WMD are likely to outweigh any normative considerations for most terrorists. Due to the unprecedented mass casualties that they can cause, nuclear, biological, and chemical weapons are optimal instruments for achieving the asymmetric warfare strategy that lies at the heart of terrorist operations (Lesser 1999: 94–96; for broader discussion of asymmetric warfare strategies, see Arreguin-Toft 2001). Avoiding confrontation with a target state where it is strongest (in conventional military terms), the modus operandi of terrorist groups has been to strike states where they are most vulnerable to attack (in densely populated cities). From a terrorist perspective, using WMD would graphically illustrate a capacity to inflict maximum damage against a stronger power at a time and place of the terrorist group's own choosing.

The Rise of 'New' Terrorism

But the single most important variable that makes terrorist use of WMD increasingly credible is the changing nature of the underlying philosophy of terrorist groups themselves. International terrorism has, over time, become a more complex phenomenon. Long gone are the days when terrorism was exemplified by the gun-toting anarchist seeking to overturn a corrupt political order within the strict confines of state borders. The terrorist of the twenty-first century is exemplified by the operative who is part of a loose, yet sophisticated, transnational network whose goal is to overturn *global* trends that are deemed to be in profound conflict with their core religious or political beliefs (see Chalk 1999). Throughout the last decade of the twentieth century, the capacity of terrorist groups to organise themselves into transnational networks for the purpose of coordinating operations across different continents was significantly enhanced by the rapid globalisation of information technologies. The most well-known of these groups, Al Qaeda, used coded e-mail communications and posted encrypted messages on various Internet web sites to coordinate several high profile attacks during the 1990s as well as the 11 September attacks on the American mainland (Brownfeld 2001; and Risen and Engelberg 2001).

In the mid to late 1990s, official and non-official analysts began distinguishing between the ideology of 'old' terrorism and 'new' terrorism. Encompassing groups such as

ETA, the IRA, and the various 'Red' terrorist cells operating in Western Europe during the Cold War, the 'old' paradigm of terrorism was characterised by a calculation that indiscriminate or excessive violence would have the effect of undermining claims of legitimacy among domestic constituencies and international public opinion more generally. In eschewing mass casualty attacks of the type carried out by Aum Shinrikyo and Al Qaeda, old-style terrorist groups sought to preserve their eligibility for a seat at the post-conflict negotiating table. In short, these groups regarded themselves as fundamentally part of the political process, not separate from it (Stevenson 2001: 153–54).

Examples of the new terrorism include extremist fundamentalist organisations, millenarian and apocalyptic-inspired sects, and radical anti-government 'hate' groups. In marked contrast to the old terrorist groups, who invariably rationalised violence as an instrument for achieving a clear-cut political strategy, the violence employed by new terrorist groups is far less discriminating and far more lethal as a consequence. As evidenced over the last decade, the terrorist operations performed by these groups have frequently (and deliberately) failed to distinguish between 'legitimate' targets symbolising 'corrupt' state authority (such as military installations and police barracks) and civilian sectors of the population. The single most influential element uniting new terrorist groups has been hard-core religious dogma. Groups such as Al Qaeda, Aum Shinrikyo, and the various Christian Identity organisations active in the West are each inspired by the doctrine of 'cosmic war', in which violence is seen as the only means to achieve 'moral restoration' (Juergensmeyer 2001: 145–63). According to this mindset, violent acts 'are 'sanitised' because they are symbolic, enacted on a cosmic stage' (Simon and Benjamin 2000: 66). Engaged in a cosmic struggle where 'a satanic enemy cannot be transformed, only destroyed', the intensity of the violence used in specific terrorist acts is unconstrained by 'worldly' ethical considerations (Juergensmeyer 2001: 217). As Peter Chalk has observed:

> The prevalence of radical religious imperatives [. . .] has significant implications for the lethality of terrorism. For the religious zealot, there is essentially no reason to show restraint in the perpetration of violence. The main objective is to inflict as much pain and suffering as possible, with the enemy typically denigrated as fundamentally evil and beyond all redemption.

In sum, terrorist groups subscribing to this form of ideology are much more likely to be attracted to the mass destructive properties of WMD than terrorist organisations have been in the past.

Has the WMD Terrorist Threat Increased since 11 September 2001?

Would a terrorist group actively attempt to acquire and use WMD when the events of 11 September 2001 showed that spectacular attacks can be staged using fully fuel-laden hijacked civilian airliners? The short answer is that a successful large-scale use of nuclear, chemical, or biological weapons would make the events of 11 September pale in comparison. The mass casualties resulting from a large-scale WMD attack against US urban centres has been the most important issue exercising the collective minds of American national security agencies post-11 September. A leaked US intelligence report in March 2002 estimated that a ten kiloton nuclear device (of similar yield to the Hiroshima bomb) detonated in lower Manhattan would kill over one hundred thousand people instantly, poison several hundred thousand people with radiation sickness, and level all infrastructure standing within one kilometre of the blast's epicentre (Gellman 2002). An extensive attack against an urban centre with an acutely lethal chemical weapon such as the nerve agent sarin could potentially kill thousands and render the surrounding area a heavily contaminated zone for an extended period of time. While slower in its impact, a successful large-scale attempt to target densely populated centres with a highly contagious BW agent such as smallpox would trigger an epidemic of unparalleled scope in the modern era.

On balance, the likelihood of a terrorist organisation using WMD has increased in the wake of the 11 September attacks for two reasons. First, the events of 11 September exposed—much more dramatically than did the 1993 World Trade Centre attack and the 1995 Oklahoma City bombing—the vulnerability of open societies like the United States to large-scale terrorist strikes. The Al Qaeda operatives who carried out the 11 September attacks were inserted into the US, received flight school training in the US, coordinated their pre-attack planning in the US, hijacked the airliners from US airports, and successfully struck high value targets on American soil without warning. To be sure, any terrorist group with a serious grudge against the United States and its democratic allies will take heart from the events of 11 September. While the United States and allies including Australia have taken some significant steps to bolster early warning and crisis response capabilities (see, for example, Gellman 2002; Connolly 2002; and Hill 2002), their cities will continue to remain extremely vulnerable to terrorist attacks involving WMD.[6]

Second, the events of 11 September set an entirely new benchmark, or threshold, for future terrorist attacks. There can be little doubt that the motivation to 'surpass 11 September' will be a strong incentive for future terrorist groups contemplating the use of WMD. Never before had thousands been killed in a single terrorist attack. That the most powerful country in the international system was the target merely added potency to its psychological impact. As Jenkins (2001: 4) has argued, the events of 11 September created 'a new level of destruction toward which other terrorists will strive'. Rather than being cowed by the 2001 attacks, the Bush administration responded forcefully by declaring a 'War on Terrorism' and expelling Al Qaeda from its home base in Afghanistan. Yet, it is far less certain whether the United States would be able to cope with a massive WMD strike against a key urban centre such as Los Angeles, with fatalities ranging in the tens of thousands. Would the US public be willing to maintain its support for America's global strategic commitments following such an attack? The US public may well conclude that the benefits flowing from American global hegemony are far outweighed by the costs of being a terrorist target. In this scenario, it is certainly conceivable that public pressure for the United States to return to its pre-1941 isolationalist policy would be too intense for any administration to resist. The subsequent unravelling of America's strategic alliances in the Asia-Pacific, Europe, and the Middle East would inject a degree of instability into international relations not witnessed since the end of the Cold War. Some terrorist groups could well judge that this possibility more than justifies any endeavour to launch a large-scale WMD assault along the lines sketched above.

Conclusion

Given the high stakes involved, it is all too easy to exaggerate possible scenarios involving terrorists using WMD. Yet it is equally easy to dismiss possible threat scenarios as being unduly alarmist. As the head of the United Nation's Terrorism Prevention Branch has remarked, the greatest challenge in evaluating the WMD terrorist threat is 'walking the fine line between fear and paranoia on the one hand, and prudence and disbelief on the other' (Schmid 2000: 108).

One of the most prevalent features in mainstream discussions of WMD terrorism has been the conflation of motive and capability. All too often observers assume that simply because terrorist groups are motivated to acquire WMD they will be successful in doing so. A related assumption is that once terrorists gain access to WMD materials they will, ipso facto, be able to build a weapon and deliver it against assigned targets. The prevalence of this approach has meant that insufficient attention has been paid to addressing the key issue of accessibility to nuclear, chemical, and biological weapons on the part of terrorist groups and the likelihood of such groups actually using WMD. Consequently, the challenging nature of assessing the threat of WMD terrorism has frequently been overlooked in much of the academic literature. Simply accepting at face value the hypothesis that WMD terrorism is only 'a matter of time' is no substitute for detailed and measured threat assessment. As I have argued, the issue is complex and not one that lends itself to hard and fast conclusions.

On the one hand, I demonstrated that it remains very difficult for all but the most technologically advanced terrorist organisations to successfully weaponise nuclear material and CW and BW agents for delivery against targets. This is particularly the case with respect to nuclear weapons, but also holds true for chemical and biological weapons. In the case of biological weapons—which have become the most feared category of WMD in terms of likely terrorist use—although the requisite material for devising BW agents is widely available, the skill and expertise for effectively weaponising a BW agent is still seemingly beyond terrorist groups. Overall, acquiring WMD capabilities for delivery against targets is a lot harder for terrorists than is generally acknowledged in the literature.

On the other hand, however, it is clear that contemporary terrorists have fewer moral scruples about initiating mass casualty attacks targeting civilian populations than the terrorists of yesteryear. Since the end of the Cold War, terrorism has become far more lethal in its scope due to the increasingly indiscriminate violence sanctioned by new terrorist groups such as Al Qaeda. In short, contrary to the view held in some quarters, terrorists of today are far more likely to use WMD (assuming they can weaponise capabilities) than those in the past. As I have argued, this trend will only be strengthened in the wake of the 11 September 2001 attacks which graphically underscored the vulnerability of open societies like the United States to mass casualty attacks, while setting a new threshold for future terrorist attacks worldwide.

Notes

1. Nuclear terrorism was the primary concern during the Cold War period. The United States devoted considerable resources to putting in place contingency plans specifically designed to counter this threat. Between 1975 and 1981 alone it is estimated that the US Nuclear Emergency Search Team (a specialist unit attached to the Department of Energy) was tasked with investigating *plausible* threats involving nuclear devices in no less than eight separate major urban centres. See Richelson (2002).
2. Existing examples of exaggerated scepticism about the WMD terrorist threat range from dismissing the threat as 'somewhat fanciful' (Spear 1997: 114–15) to overlooking it through omission (see, for instance, Butfoy 2001; and Martin 2002).
3. CW agents rely on the toxic properties of chemical substances, rather than explosive properties, to inflict physical and physiological effects on an enemy. Similarly, BW agents rely on their

innate properties rather than any explosive power to cause casualties. But unlike CW agents, BW agents exploit naturally occurring and genetically modified infectious diseases by spreading them among the target population.

4. For instance, one of the most basic CW choking agents, phosgene, is widely used in the international chemical industry as a chlorinating substance.

5. This is not to say that much cruder systems of delivery could not be effective in causing significant casualties among a target population. One possible 'delivery system' that has been canvassed in sections of the literature is the 'suicide sneezer' who is deliberately infected with a lethal and highly contagious BW agent and charged with the mission of circulating among the target population. See Zilinskas (2001: 441).

6. A recent study commissioned by the Council on Foreign Relations and chaired by former US Senators Gary Hart and Warren Rudman concluded that 'A year after [11 September], America remains dangerously unprepared to prevent and respond to a catastrophic terrorist attack on US soil'. See Mintz (2002).

References

Arreguin-Toft, A., 2001. 'How the Weak Win Wars: A Theory of Asymmetric Conflict', *International Security*, 26, 1: 93–128.

Brownfeld, A, 2001. 'Bin Ladin's Activities Exposed in New York Trial', *Jane's Terrorism & Security Monitor*, 14 March, http://janes.com/security/international_security/news/jtsm/jtsm010314_1_n.shtml

Butfoy, A., 2001. 'Controlling the Spread of Weapons of Mass Destruction', in M. Hanson and W. Tow (eds), *International Relations in the New Century: An Australian Perspective* (South Melbourne: Oxford University Press): 38–54.

Chalk, P., 1999. 'The Evolving Dynamic of Terrorism in the 1990s', *Australian Journal of International Affairs*, 53, 2: 151–67.

Chyba, C., 2002. 'Toward Biological Security', *Foreign Affairs*, 81, 3: 122–36.

Cirincione, J., J. Wolfsthal, and M. Rajkumar, 2002. *Deadly Arsenals: Tracking Weapons of Mass Destruction* (Washington DC: Carnegie Endowment for International Peace).

Collina, T. and J. Wolfsthal, 2002. 'Nuclear Terrorism and Warhead Control in Russia', *Arms Control Today*, April, http://www.armscontrol.org/act/2002_04/colwolfapril02.asp

Connolly, C., 2002. 'Smallpox Vaccine Program Readied', *Washington Post*, 8 July.

Falkenrath, R., 1998. 'Confronting Nuclear, Biological and Chemical Terrorism', *Survival*, 40, 3: 43–65.

Gellman, B., 2002. 'Fears Prompt US to Beef Up Nuclear Terror Detection', *Washington Post*, 3 March.

Glaser, C. and S. Fetter, 2001. 'National Missile Defence and the Future of US Nuclear Weapons Policy', *International Security*, 26, 1: 40–92.

Hill, R., 2002. 'Defence Recruiting New Scientists to Combat Terrorism', *Media Release, Senator the Hon. Robert Hill, Minister for Defence*, MIN 431/02, 28 August.

Hoffman, B., 1996. 'Intelligence and Terrorism: Emerging Threats and New Security Challenges in the Post-Cold War Era', *Intelligence and National Security*, 11, 2: 207–223.

———— 1998. *Inside Terrorism* (New York: Columbia University Press).

Jenkins, B., 2001. *Statement of Brian Michael Jenkins, Senior Adviser to the President of the RAND Corporation Before the Senate Armed Services Subcommittee on Emerging Threats, 15 November 2001*.

Juergensmeyer, M., 2001. *Terror in the Mind of God: The Global Rise of Religious Violence* (Berkeley and Los Angeles: University of California Press).

Kamp, K., 1998–99. 'Nuclear Terrorism is Not the Core Problem', *Survival*, 40, 4: 168–71.

Katz, R., 2002. 'Public Health Preparedness: The Best Defence Against Biological Weapons', *The Washington Quarterly*, 25, 3: 69–82.

Laqueur, W., 1996. 'Postmodern Terrorism', *Foreign Affairs*, 75, 5: 24–37.

Lesser, I., 1999. 'Countering the New Terrorism: Implications for Strategy', in I. Lesser et al. (eds), *Countering the New Terrorism* (Santa Monica: Rand Corporation): 85–144.

Levi, M. and H. Kelly, 2002. 'Weapons of Mass Disruption', *Scientific American*, November: 77–81.

Mangold, T. and J. Goldberg, 1999. *Plague Wars: A True Story of Biological Warfare* (London: Macmillan).

Martin, S., 2002. 'The Role of Biological Weapons in International Politics: The Real Military Revolution', *The Journal of Strategic Studies*, 25, 1: 63–98.

Milhollin, G., 2002. 'Can Terrorists Get the Bomb?', *Commentary*, 113, 2: 45–49.

Mintz, J., 2002. 'Report: US Still Vulnerable', *Washington Post*, 25 October.

O'Neil, A., 2002. 'Waging War Against Iraq: Rationale, Possibilities, and Risks', *AQ: Journal of Contemporary Analysis*, 74, 4: 12–15.

Parachini, J., 2001. *Combating Terrorism: Assessing the Threat of Biological Terrorism—Testimony Before the Subcommittee on National Security, Veteran's Affairs, and International Relations, Committee on Government Reform, US House of Representatives, 12 October 2001.*

Regis, E. 2001. 'Does Mass Biopanic Portend Mass Destruction?', *Scientific American*, December: 11–13.

Richelson, J., 2002. 'Defusing Nuclear Terror', *Bulletin of the Atomic Scientists*, March-April, http://www.thebulletin.org/issues/2002/ma02/ma02richelson.html

Risen, J. and S. Engelberg, 2001. 'Failure to Heed Signs of Change in Terror Goals', *New York Times*, 14 October.

Sands, A., 2002. 'Deconstructing the Chem-Bio Threat: Testimony for the United States Senate Foreign Relations Committee, 19 March 2002', *CNS Report*, Monterey Institute of International Studies, http://www.cns.miis.edu/pubs/reports/asands.htm

Schmid, A., 2000. 'Terrorism and the Use of Weapons of Mass Destruction: From Where the Risk?', in M. Taylor and J. Horgan (eds), *The Future of Terrorism* (London: Frank Cass): 106–32.

Simon, S. and D. Benjamin, 2000. 'America and the New Terrorism', *Survival*, 42, 1: 59–75.

Spear, J., 1997. 'Arms and Arms Control', in B. White, R. Little and M. Smith (eds), *Issues in World Politics* (London: Macmillan Press): 111–133.

Starr, H., 1995. 'International Law and International Order', in C. Kegley (ed.), *Controversies in International Relations Theory: Realism and the Neoliberal Challenge* (St Martin's Press: New York): 299–315.

Stern, J., 1998–99. 'Apocalypse Never, But the Threat is Real', *Survival*, 40, 4: 176–79.

_____1999. *The Ultimate Terrorists* (Cambridge: Harvard University Press).

Stevenson, J., 2001. 'Terrorism: New Meets Old', *Survival*, 43, 2: 153–57.

Stout, D., 2002. 'US Arrests American Accused of Planning "Dirty Bomb" Attack', *New York Times*, 10 June.

The Economist, 2002. 'George Bush and the Axis of Evil', 2 February: 13–14.

Tucker, J., 2000. 'Introduction', in J. Tucker (ed.), *Toxic Terror: Assessing Terrorist Use of Chemical and Biological Weapons* (Boston: MIT Press): 1–14.

US General Accounting Office, 1999. *Combating Terrorism: Need for Comprehensive Threat and Risk Assessments of Chemical and Biological Attacks* (Washington DC: US General Accounting Office).

Warrick, J., 2002. 'Hunting a Deadly Soviet Legacy', *Washington Post*, 11 November.

Wheelis, M., 2002. 'Biotechnology and Biochemical Weapons', *The Nonproliferation Review*, 9, 1: 48–53.

Zilinskas, R., 2001. 'Rethinking Bioterrorism', *Current History*, 100, 650: 438–42.

Andrew O'Neil is a senior lecturer in political and international studies at Flinders University in Adelaide, Australia. Dr. O'Neil received his bachelors, masters, and Ph.D. in international relations from Flinders University.

Richard K. Betts

The New Threat of Mass Destruction

What if McVeigh had used Anthrax?

During the Cold War, weapons of mass destruction were the centerpiece of foreign policy. Nuclear arms hovered in the background of every major issue in East-West competition and alliance relations. The highest priorities of U.S. policy could almost all be linked in some way to the danger of World War III and the fear of millions of casualties in the American homeland.

Since the Cold War, other matters have displaced strategic concerns on the foreign policy agenda, and that agenda itself is now barely on the public's radar screen. Apart from defense policy professionals, few Americans still lose sleep over weapons of mass destruction (WMD). After all, what do normal people feel is the main relief provided by the end of the Cold War? It is that the danger of nuclear war is off their backs.

Yet today, WMD present more and different things to worry about than during the Cold War. For one, nuclear arms are no longer the only concern, as chemical and biological weapons have come to the fore. For another, there is less danger of complete annihilation, but more danger of mass destruction. Since the Cold War is over and American and Russian nuclear inventories are much smaller, there is less chance of an apocalyptic exchange of many thousands of weapons. But the probability that some smaller number of WMD will be used is growing. Many of the standard strategies and ideas for coping with WMD threats are no longer as relevant as they were when Moscow was the main adversary. But new thinking has not yet congealed in as clear a form as the Cold War concepts of nuclear deterrence theory.

The new dangers have not been ignored inside the Beltway. "Counterproliferation" has become a cottage industry in the Pentagon and the intelligence community, and many worthwhile initiatives to cope with threats are under way. Some of the most important implications of the new era, however, have not yet registered on the public agenda. This in turn limits the inclination of politicians to push some appropriate programs. Even the defense establishment has directed its attention mainly toward countering threats WMD pose to U.S. military forces operating abroad rather than to the more worrisome danger that mass destruction will occur in the United States, killing large numbers of civilians.

The points to keep in mind about the new world of mass destruction are the following. First, the roles such weapons play in international conflict are changing. They no longer represent the technological frontier of warfare. Increasingly, they will be weapons of the weak—states or groups that militarily are at best second-class. The importance of the different types among them has also shifted. Biological weapons should now be the most serious concern, with nuclear weapons second and chemicals a distant third.

Second, the mainstays of Cold War security policy—deterrence and arms control— are not what they used to be. Some new threats may not be deterrable, and the role of arms control in dealing with WMD has been marginalized. In a few instances, continuing devotion to deterrence and arms control may have side effects that offset the benefits.

Third, some of the responses most likely to cope with the threats in novel ways will not find a warm welcome. The response that should now be the highest priority is one long ignored, opposed, or ridiculed: a serious civil defense program to blunt the effects of WMD if they are unleashed within the United States. Some of the most effective measures to prevent attacks within the United States may also challenge traditional civil liberties if pursued to the maximum. And the most troubling conclusion for foreign policy as a whole is that reducing the odds of attacks in the United States might require pulling back from involvement in some foreign conflicts. American activism to guarantee international stability is, paradoxically, the prime source of American vulnerability.

This was partly true in the Cold War, when the main danger that nuclear weapons might detonate on U.S. soil sprang from strategic engagement in Europe, Asia, and the Middle East to deter attacks on U.S. allies. But engagement then assumed a direct link between regional stability and U.S. survival. The connection is less evident today, when there is no globally threatening superpower or transnational ideology to be contained—only an array of serious but entirely local disruptions. Today, as the only nation acting to police areas outside its own region, the United States makes itself a target for states or groups whose aspirations are frustrated by U.S. power.

From Modern to Primitive

When Nuclear weapons were born, they represented the most advanced military applications of science, technology, and engineering. None but the great powers could hope to obtain them. By now, however, nuclear arms have been around for more than half a century, and chemical and biological weapons even longer. They are not just getting old. In the strategic terms most relevant to American security, they have become primitive. Once the military cutting edge of the strong, they have become the only hope for so-called rogue states or terrorists who want to contest American power. Why? Because the United States has developed overwhelming superiority in conventional military force—something it never thought it had against the Soviet Union.

The Persian Gulf War of 1991 demonstrated the American advantage in a manner that stunned many abroad. Although the U.S. defense budget has plunged, other countries are not closing the gap. U.S. military spending remains more than triple that of any potentially hostile power and higher than the combined defense budgets of Russia, China, Iran, Iraq, North Korea, and Cuba.

More to the point, there is no evidence that those countries' level of military professionalism is rising at a rate that would make them competitive even if they were to spend far more on their forces. Rolling along in what some see as a revolution in military affairs, American forces continue to make unmatched use of state-of-the-art weapons, surveillance and information systems, and the organizational and doctrinal flexibility for managing the integration of these complex innovations into "systems of systems" that is the key to modern military effectiveness. More than ever in military history, brains are brawn. Even if hostile countries somehow catch up in an arms race, their military organizations and cultures are unlikely to catch up in the competence race for management, technology assimilation, and combat command skills.

If it is infeasible for hostile states to counter the United States in conventional combat, it is even more daunting for smaller groups such as terrorists. If the United States is lucky, the various violent groups with grievances against the American government and society will continue to think up schemes using conventional explosives. Few terrorist groups have shown an interest in inflicting true mass destruction. Bombings or hostage seizures have generally threatened no more than a few hundred lives. Let us hope that this limitation has been due to a powerful underlying reason, rather than a simple lack of capability, and that the few exceptions do not become more typical.

There is no sure reason to bet on such restraint. Indeed, some have tried to use WMD, only to see them fizzle. The Japanese Aum Shinrikyo cult released sarin nerve gas in Tokyo in 1995 but killed only a few people, and some analysts believe that those who attacked the World Trade Center in 1993 laced their bomb with cyanide, which burned up in the explosion (this was not confirmed, but a large amount of cyanide was found in the perpetrators' possession). Eventually such a group will prove less incompetent. If terrorists decide that they want to stun American policymakers by inflicting enormous damage, WMD become more attractive at the same time that they are becoming more accessible.

Finally, unchallenged military superiority has shifted the attention of the U.S. military establishment away from WMD. During the Cold War, nuclear weapons were the bedrock of American war capabilities. They were the linchpin of defense debate, procurement programs, and arms control because the United States faced another superpower—one that conventional wisdom feared could best it in conventional warfare. Today, no one cares about the MX missile or B-1 bomber, and hardly anyone really cares about the Strategic Arms Reduction Treaty. In a manner that could only have seemed ludicrous during the Cold War, proponents now rationalize the $2 billion B-2 as a weapon for conventional war. Hardly anyone in the Pentagon is still interested in how the United States could use WMD for its own strategic purposes.

What military planners are interested in is how to keep adversaries from using WMD as an "asymmetric" means to counter U.S. conventional power, and how to protect U.S. ground and naval forces abroad from WMD attacks. This concern is all well and good, but it abets a drift of attention away from the main danger. The primary risk is not that enemies might lob some nuclear or chemical weapons at U.S. armored battalions or ships, awful as that would be. Rather, it is that they might attempt to punish the United States by triggering catastrophes in American cities.

Choose Your Weapons Well

Until the past decade, the issue was nuclear arms, period. Chemical weapons received some attention from specialists, but never made the priority list of presidents and cabinets. Biological weapons were almost forgotten after they were banned by the 1972 Biological Weapons Convention. Chemical and biological arms have received more attention in the 1990s. The issues posed by the trio lumped under the umbrella of mass destruction differ, however. Most significantly, biological weapons have received less attention than the others but probably represent the greatest danger.

Chemical weapons have been noticed more in the past decade, especially since they were used by Iraq against Iranian troops in the 1980–88 Iran-Iraq War and against Kurdish civilians in 1988. Chemicals are far more widely available than nuclear weapons because the technology required to produce them is far simpler, and large numbers of countries have undertaken chemical weapons programs. But chemical weapons are not really in the same class as other weapons of mass destruction, in the sense of ability to inflict a huge number of civilian casualties in a single strike. For the tens of thousands of fatalities as in, say, the biggest strategic bombing raids of World War II, it would be very difficult logistically and operationally to deliver chemical weapons in necessary quantities over wide areas.

Nevertheless, much attention and effort have been lavished on a campaign to eradicate chemical weapons. This may be a good thing, but the side effects are not entirely benign. For one, banning chemicals means that for deterrence, nuclear weapons become even more important than they used to be. That is because a treaty cannot assuredly prevent hostile nations from deploying chemical weapons, while the United States has forsworn the option to retaliate in kind.

In the past, the United States had a no-first-use policy for chemical weapons but reserved the right to strike back with them if an enemy used them first. The 1993 Chemical Weapons Convention (CWC), which entered into force last April, requires the United States to destroy its stockpile, thus ending this option. The United States did the same with biological arms long ago, during the Nixon administration. Eliminating its own chemical and biological weapons practically precludes a no-first-use policy for nuclear weapons, since they become the only WMD available for retaliation.

Would the United States follow through and use nuclear weapons against a country or group that had killed several thousand Americans with deadly chemicals? It is hard to imagine breaking the post-Nagasaki taboo in that situation. But schemes for conventional military retaliation would not suffice without detracting from the force of American deterrent threats. There would be a risk for the United States in setting a precedent that someone could use WMD against Americans without suffering similar destruction in return. Limiting the range of deterrent alternatives available to U.S. strategy will not necessarily cause deterrence to fail, but it will certainly not strengthen it.

The ostensible benefit of the CWC is that it will make chemical arms harder to acquire and every bit as illegal and stigmatized as biological weapons have been for a quarter-century. If it has that benefit, what effect will the ban have on the choices of countries or groups who want some kind of WMD in any case, whether for purposes of deterrence, aggression, or revenge? At the margin, the ban will reduce the disincentives to acquiring biological weapons, since they will be no less illegal, no harder to obtain or conceal, and far more damaging than chemical weapons. If major reductions in the chemical threat produce even minor increases in the biological threat, it will be a bad trade.

One simple fact should worry Americans more about biological than about nuclear or chemical arms: unlike either of the other two, biological weapons combine maximum destructiveness and easy availability. Nuclear arms have great killing capacity but are hard to get; chemical weapons are easy to get but lack such killing capacity; biological agents have both qualities. A 1993 study by the Office of Technology Assessment concluded that a single airplane delivering 100 kilograms of anthrax spores—a dormant phase of a bacillus that multiplies rapidly in the body, producing toxins and rapid hemorrhaging—by aerosol on a clear, calm night over the Washington, D.C., area could kill between one million and three million people, 300 times as many fatalities as if the plane had delivered sarin gas in amounts ten times larger.[1]

Like chemical weapons but unlike nuclear weapons, biologicals are relatively easy to make. Innovations in biotechnology have obviated many of the old problems in handling and preserving biological agents, and many have been freely available for scientific research. Nuclear weapons are not likely to be the WMD of choice for non-state terrorist groups. They require huge investments and targetable infrastructure, and are subject to credible threats by the United States. An aggrieved group that decides it wants to kill huge numbers of Americans will find the mission easier to accomplish with anthrax than with a nuclear explosion.

Inside the Pentagon, concern about biological weapons has picked up tremendously in the past couple of years, but there is little serious attention to the problem elsewhere. This could be a good thing if nothing much can be done, since publicity might only give enemies ideas. But it is a bad thing if it impedes efforts to take steps—such as civil defense—that could blunt nuclear, chemical, or biological attacks.

Deterrence and Arms Control in Decline

An old vocabulary still dominates policy discussion of WMD. Rhetoric in the defense establishment falls back on the all-purpose strategic buzzword of the Cold War: deterrence. But deterrence now covers fewer of the threats the United States faces than it did during the Cold War.

The logic of deterrence is clearest when the issue is preventing unprovoked and unambiguous aggression, when the aggressor recognizes that it is the aggressor rather than the defender. Deterrence is less reliable when both sides in a conflict see each other as the aggressor. When the United States intervenes in messy Third World conflicts, the latter is often true. In such cases, the side that the United States wants to deter may see itself as trying to deter the United States. Such situations are ripe for miscalculation.

For the country that used to be the object of U.S. deterrence—Russia—the strategic burden has been reversed. Based on assumptions of Soviet conventional military superiority, U.S. strategy used to rely on the threat to escalate—to be the first to use nuclear weapons during a war—to deter attack by Soviet armored divisions. Today the tables have turned. There is no Warsaw Pact, Russia has half or less of the military potential of the Soviet Union, and its current conventional forces are in disarray, while NATO is expanding eastward. It is now Moscow that has the incentive to compensate for conventional weakness by placing heavier reliance on nuclear capabilities. The Russians adopted a nuclear no-first-use policy in the early 1980s, but renounced it after their precipitous post–Cold War decline.

Today Russia needs to be reassured, not deterred. The main danger from Russian WMD is leakage from vast stockpiles to anti-American groups elsewhere—the "loose nukes" problem. So long as the United States has no intention of attacking the Russians, their greater reliance on nuclear forces is not a problem. If the United States has an interest in reducing nuclear stockpiles, however, it is. The traditional American approach—thinking in terms of its own deterrence strategies—provides no guidance. Indeed, noises some Americans still make about deterring the Russians compound the problem by reinforcing Moscow's alarm.

Similarly, U.S. conventional military superiority gives China an incentive to consider more reliance on an escalation strategy. The Chinese have a long-standing no-first-use policy but adopted it when their strategic doctrine was that of "people's war," which relied on mass mobilization and low-tech weaponry. Faith in that doctrine was severely shaken by the American performance in the Persian Gulf War. Again, the United States might assume that there is no problem as long as Beijing only wants to deter and the United States does not want to attack. But how do these assumptions relate to the prospect of a war over Taiwan? That is a conflict that no one wants but that can hardly be ruled out in light of evolving tensions. If the United States decides openly to deter Beijing from attacking Taiwan, the old lore from the Cold War may be relevant. But if Washington continues to leave policy ambiguous, who will know who is deterring whom? Ambiguity is a recipe for confusion and miscalculation in a time of crisis. For all the upsurge of attention in the national security establishment to the prospect of conflict with China, there has been remarkably little discussion of the role of nuclear weapons in a Sino-American collision.

The main problem for deterrence, however, is that it still relies on the corpus of theory that undergirded Cold War policy, dominated by reliance on the threat of second-strike retaliation. But retaliation requires knowledge of who has launched an attack and the address at which they reside. These requirements are not a problem when the threat comes from a government, but they are if the enemy is anonymous. Today some groups may wish to punish the United States without taking credit for the action—a mass killing equivalent to the 1988 bombing of Pan Am Flight 103 over Lockerbie, Scotland. Moreover, the options the defense establishment favors have shifted over entirely from deterrence to preemption. The majority of those who dealt with nuclear weapons policy during the Cold War adamantly opposed developing first-strike options. Today, scarcely anyone looks to that old logic when thinking about rogues or terrorists, and most hope to be able to mount a disarming action against any group with WMD.

Finally, eliminating chemical weapons trims some options for deterrence. Arms control restrictions on the instruments that can be used for deterrent threats are not necessarily the wrong policy, but they do work against maximizing deterrence. Overall, however, the problem with arms control is not that it does too much but that it now does relatively little.

From the Limited Test Ban negotiations in the 1960s through the Strategic Arms Limitation Talks, Strategic Arms Reduction Talks, and Intermediate-range Nuclear Forces negotiations in the 1970s and 1980s, arms control treaties were central to managing WMD threats. Debates about whether particular agreements with Moscow were in the United States' interest were bitter because everyone believed that the results mattered. Today there is no consensus that treaties regulating armaments matter much. Among national security experts, the corps that pays close attention to START and Conventional Forces in Europe negotiations has shrunk. With the exception of the Chemical Weapons Convention, efforts to control WMD by treaty have become small potatoes. The biggest recent news in arms control has not been any negotiation to regulate WMD, but a campaign to ban land mines.

The United States' Cold War partner in arms control, Russia, has disarmed a great deal voluntarily. But despite standard rhetoric, the United States has not placed a high priority on convincing Moscow to divest itself of more of its nuclear weapons; the Clinton administration has chosen to promote NATO expansion, which pushes the Russians in the opposite direction.

The 1968 Nuclear Nonproliferation Treaty remains a hallowed institution, but it has nowhere new to go. It will not convert the problem countries that want to obtain

WMD—unless, like Iraq and North Korea in the 1980s, they sign and accept the legal obligation and then simply cheat. The NPT regime will continue to impede access to fissile materials on the open market, but it will not do so in novel or more effective ways. And it does not address the problem of Russian "loose nukes" any better than the Russian and American governments do on their own.

Civil Defense

Despite all the new limitations, deterrence remains an important aspect of strategy. There is not much the United States needs to do to keep up its deterrence capability, however, given the thousands of nuclear weapons and the conventional military superiority it has. Where capabilities are grossly underdeveloped, however, is the area of responses for coping should deterrence fail.

Enthusiasts for defensive capability, mostly proponents of the Strategic Defense Initiative from the Reagan years, remain fixated on the least relevant form of it: high-tech active defenses to intercept ballistic missiles. There is still scant interest in what should now be the first priority: civil defense preparations to cope with uses of WMD within the United States. Active defenses against missiles would be expensive investments that might or might not work against a threat the United States probably will not face for years, but would do nothing against the threat it already faces. Civil defense measures are extremely cheap and could prove far more effective than they would have against a large-scale Soviet attack.

During the Cold War, debate about antimissile defense concerned whether it was technologically feasible or cost-effective and whether it would threaten the Soviets and ignite a spiraling arms race between offensive and defensive weapons. One need not refight the battles over SDI to see that the relevance to current WMD threats is tenuous. Iraq, Iran, or North Korea will not be able to deploy intercontinental missiles for years. Nor, if they are strategically cunning, should they want to. For the limited number of nuclear warheads these countries are likely to have, and especially for biological weapons, other means of delivery are more easily available. Alternatives to ballistic missiles include aircraft, ship-launched cruise missiles, and unconventional means, such as smuggling, at which the intelligence agencies of these countries have excelled. Non-state perpetrators like those who bombed the World Trade Center will choose clandestine means of necessity.

A ballistic missile defense system, whether it costs more or less than the $60 billion the Congressional Budget Office recently estimated would be required for one limited option, will not counter these modes of attack. Indeed, if a larger part of the worry about WMD these days is about their use by terrorist states or groups, the odds are higher that sometime, somewhere in the country, some of these weapons will go off, despite the best efforts to stop them. If that happens, the United States should have in place whatever measures can mitigate the consequences.

By the later phases of the Cold War it was hard to get people interested in civil defense against an all-out Soviet attack that could detonate thousands of high-yield nuclear weapons in U.S. population centers. To many, the lives that would have been saved seemed less salient than the many millions that would still have been lost. It should be easier to see the value of civil defense, however, in the context of more limited attacks, perhaps with only a few low-yield weapons. A host of minor measures can increase protection or recovery from biological, nuclear, or chemical effects. Examples are stockpiling or distribution of protective masks; equipment and training for decontamination; standby programs for mass vaccinations and emergency treatment with antibiotics; wider and deeper planning of emergency response procedures; and public education about hasty sheltering and emergency actions to reduce individual vulnerability.

Such programs would not make absorbing a WMD attack tolerable. But inadequacy is no excuse for neglecting actions that could reduce death and suffering, even if the difference in casualties is small. Civil defenses are especially worthwhile considering that they are extraordinarily cheap compared with regular military programs or active defense systems. Yet until recently, only half a billion dollars—less than two-tenths of one percent of the defense budget and less than $2 a head for every American—went to chemical and biological defense, while nearly $4 billion was spent annually on ballistic missile defense.[2] Why haven't policymakers attended to first things first—cheap programs that can cushion the effects of a disaster—before undertaking expensive programs that provide no assurance they will be able to prevent it?

One problem is conceptual inertia. The Cold War accustomed strategists to worrying about an enemy with thousands of WMD, rather than foes with a handful. For decades the question of strategic defense was also posed as a debate between those who saw no alternative to relying on deterrence and those who hoped that an astrodome over the United States could replace deterrence with invulnerability. None of these hoary fixations address the most probable WMD threats in the post–Cold War world.

Opposition to Cold War civil defense programs underlies psychological aversion to them now. Opponents used to argue that civil defense was a dangerous illusion because it could do nothing significant to reduce the horror of an attack that would obliterate hundreds of cities, because it would promote a false sense of security, and because it could even be destabilizing and provoke attack in a crisis. Whether or not such arguments were valid then, they are not now. But both then and now, there has been a powerful reason that civil defense efforts have been unpopular: they alarm people. They remind them that their vulnerability to mass destruction is not a bad dream, not something that strategic schemes for deterrence, preemption, or interception are sure to solve.

Civil defense can limit damage but not minimize it. For example, some opponents may be able to develop biological agents that circumvent available vaccines and antibiotics. (Those with marginal technical capabilities, however, might be stopped by blocking the easier options.) Which is worse—the limitations of defenses, or having to answer for failure to try? The moment that WMD are used somewhere in a manner that produces tens of thousands of fatalities, there will be hysterical outbursts of all sorts. One of them will surely be, "Why didn't the government prepare us for this?" It is not in the long-term interest of political leaders to indulge popular aversion. If public resistance under current circumstances prevents widespread distribution, stockpiling, and instruction in the use of defensive equipment or medical services, the least that should be done is to optimize plans and preparations to rapidly implement such activities when the first crisis ignites demand.

As threats of terrorism using WMD are taken more seriously, interest will grow in preemptive defense measures—the most obvious of which is intensified intelligence collection. Where this involves targeting groups within the United States that might seem to be potential breeding grounds for terrorists (for example, supporters of Palestinian militants, home-grown militias or cults, or radicals with ties to Iran, Iraq, or Libya), controversies will arise over constitutional limits on invasion of privacy or search and seizure. So long as the WMD danger remains hypothetical, such controversies will not be easily resolved. They have not come to the fore so far because U.S. law enforcement has been unbelievably lucky in apprehending terrorists. The group arrested in 1993 for planning to bomb the Lincoln Tunnel happened to be infiltrated by an informer, and Timothy McVeigh happened to be picked up in 1995 for driving without a license plate. Those who fear compromising civil liberties with permissive standards for government snooping should consider what is likely to happen once such luck runs out and it proves impossible to identify perpetrators. Suppose a secretive radical Islamic group launches a biological attack, kills 100,000 people, and announces that it will do the same thing again if its terms are not met. (The probability of such a scenario may not be high, but it can no longer be consigned to science fiction.) In that case, it is hardly unthinkable that a panicked legal system would roll over and treat Arab-Americans as it did the Japanese-Americans who were herded into concentration camps after Pearl Harbor. Stretching limits on domestic surveillance to reduce the chances of facing such choices could be the lesser evil.

Is Retreat the Best Defense?

No programs aimed at controlling adversaries' capabilities can eliminate the dangers. One risk is that in the more fluid politics of the post–Cold War world, the United States could stumble into an unanticipated crisis with Russia or China. There are no well-established rules of the game to brake a spiraling conflict over the Baltic states or Taiwan, as there were in the superpower competition after the Cuban missile crisis. The second danger is that some angry group that blames the United States for its problems may decide to coerce Americans, or simply exact vengeance, by inflicting devastation on them where they live.

If steps to deal with the problem in terms of capabilities are limited, can anything be done to address intentions—the incentives of any foreign power or group to lash out at the United States? There are few answers to this question that do not compromise the fundamental strategic activism and internationalist thrust of U.S. foreign policy over the past half-century. That is because the best way to keep people from believing that the United States is responsible for their problems is to avoid involvement in their conflicts.

Ever since the Munich agreement and Pearl Harbor, with only a brief interruption during the decade after the Tet offensive, there has been a consensus that if Americans did not draw their defense perimeter far forward and confront foreign troubles in their early stages, those troubles would come to them at home. But because the United States is now the only superpower and weapons of mass destruction have become more accessible, American intervention in troubled areas is not so much a way to fend off such threats as it is what stirs them up.

Will U.S. involvement in unstable situations around the former U.S.S.R. head off conflict with Moscow or generate it? Will making NATO bigger and moving it to Russia's doorstep deter Russian pressure on Ukraine and the Baltics or provoke it? With Russia and China, there is less chance that either will set out to conquer Europe or Asia than that they will try to restore old sovereignties and security zones by reincorporating new states of the former Soviet Union or the province of Taiwan. None of this means that NATO expansion or support for Taiwan's autonomy will cause nuclear war. It does mean that to whatever extent American activism increases those countries' incentives to rely on WMD while intensifying political friction between them and Washington, it is counterproductive.

The other main danger is the ire of smaller states or religious and cultural groups that see the United States as an evil force blocking their legitimate aspirations. It is hardly likely that Middle Eastern radicals would be hatching schemes like the destruction of the World Trade Center if the United States had not been identified for so long as the mainstay of Israel, the shah of Iran, and conservative Arab regimes and the source of a cultural assault on Islam. Cold War triumph magnified the problem. U.S. military and cultural hegemony—the basic threats to radicals seeking to challenge the status quo—are directly linked to the imputation of American responsibility for maintaining world order. Playing Globocop feeds the urge of aggrieved groups to strike back.

Is this a brief for isolationism? No. It is too late to turn off foreign resentments by retreating, even if that were an acceptable course. Alienated groups and governments would not stop blaming Washington for their problems. In addition, there is more to foreign policy than dampening incentives to hurt the United States. It is not automatically sensible to stop pursuing other interests for the sake of uncertain reductions in a threat of uncertain probability. Security is not all of a piece, and survival is only part of security.

But it is no longer prudent to assume that important security interests complement each other as they did during the Cold War. The interest at the very core—protecting the American homeland from attack—may now often be in conflict with security more broadly conceived and with the interests that mandate promoting American political values, economic interdependence, social Westernization, and stability in regions beyond Western Europe and the Americas. The United States should not give up all its broader political interests, but it should tread cautiously in areas—especially the Middle East—where broader interests grate against the core imperative of preventing mass destruction within America's borders.

Notes

1. U.S. Congress, Office of Technology Assessment, *Proliferation of Weapons of Mass Destruction: Assessing the Risks*, Washington: Government Printing Office, 1993, p. 54.
2. John F. Sopko, "The Changing Proliferation Threat," *Foreign Policy*, Spring 1997, pp. 3–20.

Richard K. Betts is director of National Security Studies at the Council on Foreign Relations and professor of political science and director of the Institute for War and Peace Studies at Columbia University.

Chapter 1.4

The Terrorist WMD
of Choice

Leonard A. Cole

WMD and Lessons from
the Anthrax Attacks

The anthrax mailings in the aftermath of 9/11 demonstrated how varied a terrorist's arsenal can be and increased Americans' anxiety about terrorism. Especially worrisome are weapons of mass destruction (WMD), which include biological agents like anthrax, as well as chemical, radiological, and nuclear weapons. Any of these materials can cause extensive damage and widespread fear. But while they are commonly lumped together as WMD, each is distinct. Differences among them include the nature of the materials, the difficulty and cost of production, potential effectiveness, and means of protection. Still, although germ weapons are distinct from other WMD, some aspects of bioterrorism are also relevant to other forms of terrorism involving WMD. After summarizing various weapons, this chapter reviews the biological attack of 2001 and the lessons it has taught.

The Specter of Terrorism

An ironic aspect of 9/11 and the anthrax mailings is that although anthrax is commonly deemed a WMD and an airliner is not, the letters resulted in only five deaths whereas 9/11 resulted in some 3,000. But the small number of casualties from anthrax in this particular case does not diminish the catastrophic potential of bioterrorism. Many additional deaths were avoided by appropriate health-care responses and simply by good luck: relatively few anthrax letters were mailed, and the organism was responsive to antibiotics. Even so, the mailings caused serious disruptions, including the closing of government buildings and the quarantine of tens of thousands of pieces of mail. Attacks with other WMD are likely to be no less disruptive.

Obviously, 9/11 made a deeper impact on the national consciousness than the anthrax mailings. In fact, few people now recall the specific dates of the anthrax attack: 18 September, when the earliest recovered anthrax letters were postmarked; 4 October, when the first case of anthrax was diagnosed; and 21 November, when the last case was diagnosed.

Thus far, apart from turning airliners into missiles, al-Qaida apparently has used only conventional munitions, even for suicide bombings, but it is seeking biological and other nonconventional weapons. In 2002, George Tenet, director of Central Intelligence, cited a declaration by bin Ladin that acquiring weapons of mass destruction was "a religious duty."[1] Two years later the staff of the federal commission investigating 9/11 reported that al-Qaida "remains extremely interested in conducting chemical, biological, radiological, or nuclear attacks" against the United States.[2]

In June 2004 Deputy Attorney General James Comey declared that Jose Padilla and other al-Qaida operatives had revealed to U.S. authorities their intention to detonate a radiological device in the United States.[3] It was not clear whether they had come close to realizing the plan.

Palestinian groups that have dispatched suicide bombers against Israel have also sought biological and chemical weapons. One of these organizations, HAMAS, acknowledged experimenting with chemical weapons for attacks against Israel. Israeli officials contend that HAMAS may have already tried to use cyanide and rat poison in suicide bombings.[4]

Keeping these weapons out of the hands of Palestinian terrorists, bin Ladin's minions, and other rogue groups should be a preeminent goal of the United States and its allies. But it is clear that despite dedicated efforts, unsavory groups might well acquire WMD. An essential requirement of preparedness is to understand the nature of these different weapons and the challenges they pose.

Nuclear Weapons

Nuclear arms, unlike other weapons, originated on a precise date: 16 July 1945, when the first atomic bomb was detonated at a desert site in Alamogordo, New Mexico. This event was the culmination of three years of secret work by 130,000 American-led scientists and other workers. The Manhattan Project, as the program was called, arose from fear that Nazi Germany would try to develop an atomic bomb. In 1938, scientists in Germany had bombarded a uranium atom with neutrons that split its nucleus, releasing energy. It was then understood that splitting numerous nuclei of uranium atoms could release an immense amount of energy. The challenge was to harness that division, or fission, into a controlled blast. Only after the war did the United States and its allies learn that Germany had failed to embark on a similar effort. German scientists apparently considered the technical challenge too formidable.[5]

By the time the atom bomb was developed, Germany had surrendered. But Japan had not yet capitulated, and military planners estimated that invading Japan would cost tens of thousands of American lives. In hopes of ending the war quickly, President Harry Truman ordered the use of the two available atomic bombs. One was dropped on 6 August over Hiroshima, and the other on 9 August over Nagasaki. Both cities were leveled. Some 70,000 people in Hiroshima and 40,000 in Nagasaki were killed instantly. Many more died later from effects of the blasts, the resulting fires, and the radiation released by the explosions. The Japanese sued for peace, and the war ended on 3 September.

The destructive force of the atom bomb is produced by a chain reaction within a mass of uranium 235, a scarce isotope of the element. Bombarding the uranium with neutrons causes nuclei to split and release more neutrons, which cause more nuclei to split, and so on. The amount of energy released depends on the mass of uranium and the frequency of neutron bombardment. At predictable levels, the nuclear energy transforms into heat, which can generate electricity. But with enough uranium and neutron bombardments, the energy can cause a huge explosion. The explosive force of each bomb dropped on Japan was about 15 kilotons (15,000 tons) of TNT. After World War II, far more powerful nuclear arms were developed, including hydrogen bombs whose force could exceed 1 million tons of TNT.

The number of countries with nuclear weapons has been limited by the technical challenges of development and by international agreements aimed at curbing nuclear proliferation. Nine countries are now believed to have nuclear arms—China, France, India,

Israel, North Korea, Pakistan, Russia, the United Kingdom, and the United States.[6] Others, especially Iran, are suspected of trying to develop them.

Developing even a low-level atomic bomb requires sophisticated technology and materials not readily available. Expertise from several disciplines is necessary: nuclear physics, nuclear chemistry, materials chemistry, mathematics, and mechanical and electrical engineering. But developing a bomb is not the only way to acquire one. Although guarded by the countries that have them, nuclear arms ultimately might be acquired by theft or illicit purchase. Especially troubling in this regard are recent disclosures that Pakistani scientists sold nuclear know-how and materials to Libya and possibly to North Korea and others.[7]

Radiological Weapons

A complicating feature of nuclear reactions is that they are radioactive: they release radiation, which itself can be harmful. Although radioactivity was discovered in the 1890s, the potential danger was not initially appreciated. In time, it was understood that radiation can destroy human cells, and exposure to very high levels can kill a person quickly. But lower levels also affect the DNA in cells and make them prone to cancer. Only uranium and a few other elements, notably plutonium, can be turned into explosive weapons, but many more elements emit radiation.

Several radioactive materials are used in legitimate biological and medical work. Others are unwelcome by-products of nuclear power reactors. Radioactive carbon and potassium, for example, are used routinely as markers in biological laboratory research. Radioactive iodine is used to treat certain thyroid conditions. Radiation is also integral to some medical equipment, notably X-ray machines. The waste from nuclear power plants includes highly radioactive cesium, tritium, and strontium. In short, radioactive materials are plentiful. They are in hospitals, research institutions, universities, and other locations throughout the country. Even if radioactive items are monitored, their sheer quantity increases the chance that a terrorist could acquire them.

This possibility raises the specter of a "dirty bomb" in which radioactive material is mixed with conventional explosives. A detonation could release radiation over large areas. According to one study, if a casket of spent fuel from a nuclear power plant was exploded in downtown Manhattan, more than 2,000 people might die quickly and thousands more would suffer from radiation poisoning.[8]

Although brief contact with low-level radioactive material causes little harm, extended exposure increases the likelihood of cellular destruction and illness. The dispersal of even modest quantities of radioactive materials in a populated area could cause panic. Droves of fearful people might try to flee. Many might seek medical attention and overload hospitals and other health-care facilities. Anxiety would be rampant. The challenge to the medical responders would be to differentiate people most at risk from those least at risk. One approach would be to quickly develop a grid to help establish who had been closest to the point of release and for how long.

Chemical Weapons

Unlike nuclear and radiological weapons, chemical and biological weapons extend back thousands of years. Until the nineteenth century, when microorganisms were found to be the cause of disease, little distinction was made between toxic chemical and biological materials. The ancients understood that arsenic—just like water polluted by animal carcasses—could cause illness and death. No matter how a poison was made up, it could be used to kill and debilitate. But by the early twentieth century, chemical and biological warfare agents were recognized as being in different categories.

The first large-scale use of chemical weapons was in World War I. Germany introduced chlorine on the battlefield in 1915; it was followed later in the war by other agents, including mustard gas. By the end of the war all the major powers had used chemicals, resulting in more than 1 million casualties. These agents caused painful blisters, blindness, burned lungs, and tortured deaths. The horrible effects prompted the Geneva Protocol of 1925, an international agreement prohibiting chemical weapons in war. Beyond chemicals, which are inanimate, the protocol also prohibited "bacteriological" agents.[9]

Despite the prohibition, countries continued to develop and stockpile chemical arms. In the 1930s, the Germans developed nerve agents, including sarin. A small drop of sarin absorbed by the skin, or a whiff of its vapor, can impair the nervous system and cause death in minutes. In the 1950s, the United States and the United Kingdom developed an even more potent nerve agent, VX. Still, after World War I chemicals were rarely used as battlefield weapons. The major exception was Iraq's extended use of chemicals against Iran in the 1980s. Inspectors under the auspices of the United Nations Security Council repeatedly reported between 1983 and 1988 that Iraq was attacking with mustard and possibly nerve agents, though neither the Security Council nor individual nations offered vigorous protests.[10]

A spectacular terror attack with chemicals occurred in 1995, when the Japanese cult Aum Shinrikyo released a nerve agent in the subway in Tokyo. On 20 March, using sharp umbrella tips, cult members punctured 11 plastic pouches filled with sarin. As the liquid and its vapor leaked out, people began to suffocate and collapse. Twelve people died, and more than 1,000 became ill. An investigation by the staff of a U.S. Senate committee found that the sarin had been impure and was poorly disseminated. If not for these mistakes, "tens of thousands could have easily been killed," the committee's report concluded.[11]

Several countries are in the process of destroying their chemical arsenals in accordance with the Chemical Weapons Convention of 1933, which bans the development or possession of these weapons.[12] Still, at least three countries—Iran, Syria, and North Korea—maintain chemical arsenals, and more than a dozen others are suspected of continuing their chemical programs.[13]

A chemical poison is far easier to produce than a nuclear bomb. For some agents, advanced knowledge of chemistry would be required; but the equipment and ingredients are readily available since precursor chemicals are often used for commercial purposes. Mustard agent, for example, can be made by combining hydrochloric acid with thiodiglycol, a chemical used in the manufacture of dyes and inks. Sarin, like other nerve agents, is an organophosphate. Its chemical structure resembles that of insecticides which kill by breaking down an insect's nervous system. Production requires special apparatus, and dispersing an agent with, say, a low-explosive grenade, would need additional expertise. But as Aum Shinrikyo demonstrated in Tokyo, releasing a chemical in a populated area can also be very simple.

Biological Weapons

Biological weapons—bacteria, viruses, and other microorganisms that cause disease and death—pose a unique threat. Unlike any other category of weapons, most biological agents can reproduce and make an environment more dangerous over time. Among the biological agents deemed likely weapons, some, like anthrax and botulinum toxin (a poisonous bacterial product), are not transmitted from person to person. But others, including plague bacteria and smallpox viruses, are highly contagious. People infected with a contagious agent can spread the disease, in effect themselves becoming biological bombs. Further, the potential to genetically engineer an organism toward greater virulence and resistance to drug treatment creates additional concern.

Still, biological agents as weapons of war or terror have been even rarer than chemical agents. In the twentieth century, the only known biowarfare against humans occurred in the late 1930s and early 1940s, when Japanese aircraft dropped porcelain bombs filled with plague-infected fleas. The germs reportedly caused epidemics that killed thousands.[14]

Various groups, including American right-wing extremists, have sought biological poisons. In 1991, members of the Minnesota Patriots Council produced the toxin ricin from castor beans, but were arrested before using it.[15] In fact, until the anthrax attacks in 2001, the only large-scale bioterrorism incident in the United States took place in 1984 in Oregon. Members of the Rajneesh cult poured a liquid containing salmonella bacteria onto salad bars and into coffee creamers in several restaurants. At least 750 people became ill, though none died.[16]

The salmonella incident demonstrated how easily and unobtrusively a biological attack could be launched. But the Rajneeshees had also released bacteria on earlier occasions, with no apparent effect. Similarly, in the early 1990s Aum Shinrikyo tried to infect people with anthrax but did not succeed. These unsuccessful efforts underscore the variables that can affect the outcome of a biological attack: type of organism, susceptibility of targeted victims, weather and other environmental conditions, and availability of appropriate antibiotics and vaccines.

The variability extends as well to the nature of the particular agent species. In a natural habitat, anthrax spores may lie dormant under the soil indefinitely. But in the human lungs they can transform to an active state in which they reproduce and release a lethal toxin. Unless the victim is treated promptly with appropriate antibiotics, death can follow in days.

The smallpox virus poses a different kind of biological threat. Smallpox was eradicated in the 1970s after a global public health campaign. Samples of the virus are now legitimately preserved at only two locations: one in the United States and the other in Russia. But analysts believe that rogue states or terrorists are interested in acquiring the virus and that some may have already succeeded. Concern that Iraq might have developed smallpox as a weapon prompted the vaccination of American troops on the eve of the invasion in March 2003. (After Iraq was occupied, neither smallpox nor other WMD were found there.) Since the terror attacks in 2001, the United States has acquired a stockpile of 300 million doses of smallpox vaccine and has developed plans for quick distribution.

Other possible biological weapons, such as the Ebola virus, offer their own variations. A cause of hemorrhagic fever, Ebola is contagious, untreatable, and deadly. Yet Ebola does not survive long outside a living host; thus storing and disseminating it are especially challenging.

Despite the Biological Weapons Convention, a treaty that bans germ weapons,[17] perhaps a dozen countries are suspected of maintaining illegal biological programs. Among the most worrisome are some that have chemical weapons programs, including, again, Iran, Syria, and North Korea.[18]

Moreover, a formidable biological weapon might be developed through genetic engineering. The result could be a drug-resistant hybrid that is as hardy as an anthrax spore, as contagious as a flu virus, and as deadly as a virulent plague bacterium. According to scientists who worked in the biological weapons program of the former Soviet Union, efforts there included trying to produce such nightmarish concoctions.[19]

Comparative Effectiveness of WMD

The distinctive qualities of weapons of mass destruction—biological, chemical, radiological, nuclear—bear on their comparative effectiveness and likelihood of use. Figure 1 makes comparisons in six categories: (1) complexity of production, (2) difficulty of acquisition, (3) cost of production, (4) difficulty of delivery or dispersal, (5) likelihood of effectiveness, and (6) worst-case consequences. For each category, 1 denotes "lowest or least," and 5 "highest or most." These rankings are partially subjective because some categories encompass a range of agents. This is especially true of biological and chemical agents. For example, the smallpox virus and the anthrax bacterium are both potential bioweapons, but they differ in accessibility, the symptoms they produce, and the anticipated manner of delivery. Still, as a group, biological agents are typically distinct from any other agent, as their numerical ranking suggests.

Similarly, the complexity of producing a chemical weapon varies from one chemical to another. Making VX nerve agent is more complicated than, say, making hydrogen cyanide or chlorine gas. Thus a chemical weapon is given a 3 for complexity—somewhere between rather simple and somewhat complicated. In contrast, producing a nuclear weapon, which is indisputably complicated, warrants a 5.

The designations are based on literature that has compared various WMD as well as information relevant to the individual agents.[20] As Figure 1 indicates, the weapon most likely to be effective (in general) and most devastating (in a worst-case scenario) is a nuclear bomb. But it is also very costly, complicated to produce and handle, and difficult to acquire. Radiological and chemical weapons are less likely to cause mass destruction, though in worst-case scenarios they certainly would cause many illnesses and deaths.

Figure 1

Characteristics of weapons of mass destruction

	Biological	Chemical	Radiological	Nuclear
Complexity of production	2	3	1	5
Cost of production	2	3	3	5
Difficulty of acquisition	2	2	2	5
Difficulty of delivery or dispersal	1	2	1	4
Likelihood of effectiveness	3	3	3	5
Worst-case consequences	5	4	4	5

Note: 1 = lowest or least; 5 = highest or most.

Of all WMD, biological agents are the most problematic. As with chemical weapons, their effectiveness varies markedly. Virulence varies not only between species but also within species. Thus certain strains of anthrax kill quickly whereas others are quite harmless. Growing any of the organisms, whether virulent or not, is easy and inexpensive, but transforming them into optimal weapons may be more complicated. The anthrax spores sent in the mail were dried and manipulated to reduce clumping. This enhanced their danger because individual organisms are more likely than larger clumps to reach deep into the lungs, where they can be lethal. Even the more easily produced moist spores, though, could be sprayed from an atomizer and pose a deadly danger to anyone who inhaled them.

The release of a biological agent is less certain to produce an effect than the detonation of a nuclear weapon. But in worst-case scenarios, some biological agents could be devastating. A virulent strain of smallpox or flu virus, both highly contagious, could cause widespread illness and death.[21] Finally, biological weapons evoke a particular horror for many people. The Biological Weapons Convention of 1972, which prohibits their development or production, describes the use of biological weapons as "repugnant to the conscience of mankind." As the episode with the anthrax letters demonstrates, a small volume of spores can cause widespread fear and anxiety.

Mailed Anthrax[22]

The anthrax attack in 2001 was the only known deliberate bioattack in the United States that resulted in loss of life. The powdered anthrax spores sent through the mail infected 22 people, five of them fatally. The experience moved fears and expectations about an intentional germ assault from theory to reality. It upset many earlier assumptions and has left a trail of uncertainties. Indeed, as of the summer of 2005 the mailer or mailers had still not been identified and it remained unclear whether there was any connection to the 9/11 terrorists.

The first victim, Bob Stevens, age 63, was a tabloid photograph editor in Florida. A presumptive diagnosis of anthrax was confirmed on 4 October, and he died the next day. The last victim was Ottilie Lundgren, age 94, who had been active in her Connecticut community until her death on 21 November. All 11 who contracted the skin form of the disease survived, as did six of those who became ill from inhaling the germs.

Although the death toll was only five, the letters and their trail of contamination terrorized much of the nation. During the anthrax scare, congressional sessions were suspended, buildings on Capitol Hill were closed, the U.S. Supreme Court was evacuated, media studios were sealed off, the postal system was disrupted, and many people were afraid to open mail.

An estimated six or seven threatening letters, each containing 1 or 2 grams of powdered anthrax, had been mailed. Four letters were later found. The recovered letters were addressed to media and political figures, including NBC's anchorman Tom Brokaw and the Senate majority leader, Tom Daschle. The postmarks, "Trenton NJ," meant that the letters had been mailed in the Princeton-Trenton area and processed at the postal sorting facility in Hamilton Township. Two of the recovered letters were processed on 18 September and two on 9 October.

Not until the third week of October did anyone realize that anthrax had been leaking from the sealed envelopes. By then, some 85 million pieces of mail had been processed at the sorting center in New Jersey and another sorting center in Washington, D.C. Perhaps millions of letters carried some spores after having been contaminated in those anthrax-infected facilities. Subsequently at least 30,000 people who were considered at risk of exposure took Cipro or other appropriate antibiotics, an action that doubtless saved lives.

The anthrax bacterium exists in two forms. In spore form, the bacterium is a durable kernel so tiny that 1,000 spores side by side would hardly reach across the thin edge of a dime. In warm, moist environments like the human lungs, the bacterium can transform into an active state, reproduce, and release toxin that may kill untreated victims. A single spore is about 1 micron wide. Only in hindsight was it realized that spores apparently were leaking through envelope paper whose pores, though microscopic, were 20 times larger than the width of a spore.

The effectiveness of the mail as a bioterror vehicle was a surprise to security experts, although many other delivery scenarios had been devised by weapons planners through the years. During the 1950s and 1960s, the U.S. Army conducted hundreds of germ warfare tests in populated areas throughout the United States. Mock biowarfare agents were released from boats, slow-flying airplanes, automobiles, germ-packed lightbulbs, perforated suitcases, and wind-generating machines. The test agents included the bacteria *Serratia marcescens* and *Bacillus subtilitis,* and the chemical zinc cadmium sulfide. (Although less dangerous than real warfare agents, the test bacteria and chemicals did pose risks.) Cities and states including San Francisco, Minneapolis, St. Louis, and parts of Illinois, Ohio, and Hawaii were blanketed with these agents. Some attacks were more focused, such as those in which bacteria were released in the New York subway and on the Pennsylvania Turnpike. In each instance, the spread and survivability of the bacteria were measured to assess the country's vulnerability to a germ attack.[23] But apparently the testers never considered the U.S. mail as a possible vehicle.

Inhalation anthrax is so rare that proposed treatment protocols were in part speculative. Only 18 cases of anthrax from inhaled spores in the United States were recorded in the twentieth century. Until the attack in 2001, the supposition was that if antibiotics were not administered before symptoms (such as a headache and difficulty breathing) appeared, almost all victims would die. The reality proved less grim. All six survivors received antibiotics only after they became ill. However, three years later, only one victim had fully recovered and returned to work—Ernesto Blanco, a mail room clerk at American Media in Boca Raton, where Bob Stevens worked. At 73, Blanco was also the oldest of the survivors. The other five continued to tire easily and suffered from memory loss.

National Preparedness and Lessons from the Anthrax Attack

Is the United States better prepared now than in 2001 for an attack with biological or other weapons of mass destruction? Yes and no. The nation now could surely deal better with another attack by mail. In September 2003, postal officials announced the successful testing of a system that sets off an alarm if anthrax spores are detected near mail-handling equipment.[24] And officials would doubtless act more quickly to close facilities now than they did in 2001. The medical community is also more alert to threats from biological and chemical agents. Physicians are more aware of symptoms caused by anthrax, smallpox, sarin, and other prospective killer agents.

Of course, if a drug-resistant strain of a lethal bacterium or virus was mailed or otherwise dispersed, it could cause havoc. Nor can protection ever be guaranteed against terrorism from any possible weapon. But advances have been made in both detection and response capabilities. Radiation monitors, including Geiger counters, can indicate the presence of radioactive material. Spectrophotometers, which measure the wavelength of molecular structures, can identify particular chemical or biological agents. None of these methods is foolproof, but research is under way to improve the speed and accuracy of the devices as well as other means of coping with terrorist threats.

In the area of biodefense alone, government spending on preparedness has risen more than tenfold since the attacks in 2001. Civilian biodefense funding was $414 million in fiscal year 2001 and $5.5 billion in 2004. The largest share went to the Department of Health and Human Services, which in 2004 received $3.5 billion, while the Department of Homeland Security (DHS) received $1.6 billion.[25] Money was being spent on a variety of projects to enhance preparedness, including improving detection capabilities; developing more effective antibiotics, antidotes, and vaccines; enhancing strategic stockpiles of medical supplies; strengthening the public health system; and enhancing coordination and education among responders. Instruction has also included understanding the different responses required for a biological, chemical, radiological, or nuclear attack.

The increased budget for bioterrorism preparedness may be better appreciated by relating it to the dollar cost of an actual attack. Figure 2 shows estimated costs for several activities associated with the anthrax attack in 2001. The overall total, which probably exceeds $6 billion, would be greater than the annual total now being spent on biopreparedness.

Conclusion

Four salient lessons from the experience with anthrax bear on terrorism preparedness in general and should inform the nation's counterterrorism and response plans. First, the volume of agent can be very small and still have an enormous effect. Even if a material was not as broadly dispersed as the anthrax, anxiety might still be widespread. If a shopping mall in, say, Ohio was the target of sarin or low-level radiation, exposure would be limited to people in the area. But anxiety could spread from coast to coast and affect the daily routines of millions. Reluctance to travel and to visit malls and other public locations might well be the result. Coping with such a collapse of public activity and services should be part of a national plan.

Second, the effectiveness of the U.S. mail as a disseminator of anthrax was a surprise. Initially, testing for the presence of the bacteria in postal and other facilities was not a consideration, because no one understood that the germ could leak from sealed envelopes. The applicable lesson here is to be wary of conventional assumptions. Most colleagues of Dr. Larry Bush, the physician who first suspected that Bob Stevens had anthrax, were dubious. Had Bush not ignored the skeptics and pushed for more tests, confirmation of Stevens's anthrax might have come later, if at all. The lesson: remain open to seemingly far-fetched possibilities and be prepared for the unexpected.

Third, in almost every instance, the first professional to see each anthrax victim was a primary care or emergency room physician. Understandably, the anthrax attack initially eluded officials who are thought likely to address a terrorist incident, such as police, fire, hazmat, FBI, or military personnel. The lesson, again, is to prepare for likely scenarios, but also be open to the possibility of the unlikely. Rehearsing for terrorist incidents by law enforcement and emergency responders is a must. But many others in public roles should receive instruction about WMD terrorism. Besides health care workers, they should, for example, include postal workers, teachers, store managers, bus drivers, and train conductors.

Figure 2

Estimated costs associated with the anthrax attack in 2001

Source of Cost	Basis of Calculation	Total
Tests by laboratories associated with Centers for Disease Control and Prevention (CDC) on 125,000 clinical specimens and 1 million environmental specimens[a]	$25–$30 per test	$30 million
CDC personnel[b]	5,000 individuals at $800 per week for 6 weeks	$24 million
Prophylactic antibiotics and associated medical care[c]	30,000 individuals, $10 each per day for 60 days	$18 million
Federal Bureau of Investigation (FBI) personnel[d]	251,000 person-hours (through January 2004) at $25 per hour	$6 million
Decontamination of Hart Senate Office Building[e]	Publicly reported	$42 million
Decontamination of U.S. postal facilities plus preparedness measures[f]	Publicly reported	$1.7 billion
Reduced mail revenue[g]	October 2001–June 2002 compared with equivalent period 1 year later	$2.7 billion
Additional costs.[h] State and local health and law enforcement Clinical and environmental tests at military laboratories Medical and hospital care for victims and the "worried well" Lost work time and relocations associated with affected facilities Lawsuits by victims and families Ongoing FBI investigation		$1–$2 billion (?)
Grand Total (likely): >$6 billion		

Note: Estimates are based on personal communications with officials from CDC, the FBI, the U.S. Postal Service, and the following references.

[a] James M. Hughes and Julie Louise Gerberding, "Anthrax Bioterrorism: Lessons Learned and Future Directions." *Emerging Infectious Diseases* 8:10 (October 2002): 1013.

[b] Personal communications with CDC officials. The figure of 5,000 personnel is somewhat arbitrary. One official told me that at times all 8,000 CDC personnel were working on anthrax-related matters.

[c] Judith Miller and David Johnston, "Investigators Liken Anthrax in Leahy Letter to That Sent to Daschle," New York Times (21 November 2001).

[d] Michael D. Lemonick, "Homegrown Terror," Time (16 February 2004): 41.

[e] Scott Shane, "Cleanup of Anthrax Will Cost Hundreds of Millions of Dollars," Baltimore Sun (18 December 2002).

[f] John E. Potter, Postmaster General, U.S. Postal Service Emergency Preparedness Plan for Protecting Postal Employees and Postal Customers from Exposure to Biohazardous Material... (6 March 2002), http://www.usps.com/news/2002/epp/emerprepplan.pdf. David Firn, "U.S. Spends $800 Million on Clean-Up after Anthrax Scare," *Financial Times* (22 April 2004).

[g] U.S. Postal Service, Financial Operating Statements (by Month), http://www.usps.com/financials/fos/welcome.htm.

[h] Reference sources unavailable.

Fourth, the anthrax attack victimized people not only in large cities but also in remote communities. People became infected in New York City and Washington, D.C., but also in Boca Raton, Florida; Hamilton Township, New Jersey; and Oxford, Connecticut. Responsible preparedness must not be limited to heavily populated areas. A similar lesson was taught in 1984 when the Rajneeshees disseminated salmonella bacteria. The germs had been placed in restaurants in a small Oregon town called The Dalles. The lesson is clear: the target of a terrorist attack, whether with conventional or nonconventional weapons, can be anywhere.

In sum, recognizing the differences among WMD is essential to preparing for an attack with each weapon. Such recognition will indicate the appropriate techniques for protection and response. Some weapons, such as a nuclear bomb, could be so devastating that any response plan would scarcely be effective. But proper plans to address most types of WMD attacks could lessen their threat and severity. Still, the unanticipated effectiveness of the anthrax letters stands as a reminder that however prepared we think we are, surprises are always possible.

Notes

1. Worldwide Threat—Converging Dangers in a Post 9/11 World, testimony of Director of Central Intelligence George J. Tenet, before the Senate Armed Services Committee, 19 March 2002.
2. National Commission on Terrorist Attacks Upon the United States, Overview of the Enemy, Staff Statement No. 15, presented at public hearing, May 18, 2004, http://www.9–11commission.gov/hearings/hearing12/staff_statement_15.pdf. Also see Joshua Sinai, "How to Forecast and Preempt al-Qaeda's Catastrophic Terrorist Warfare," *Journal of Homeland Security* (August 2003), http://www.homelanddefense.org/journal/Articles/sinaiforecast.htm.
3. Remarks of Deputy Attorney General James Comey Regarding Jose Padilla, June 1, 2004, http://www.usdoj.gov/dag/speech/2004/dag6104.htm.
4. World Tribune.com, "HAMAS Threatens to Use Chemical Weapons Against Israel," (June 17, 2002), http://216.26.163.62/2002/me_palestinians_06_17.html.
5. For discussion of possible reasons that the Germans did not try to develop an atomic bomb see Stanley Goldberg and Thomas Powers, "Declassified Files Reopen 'Nazi Bomb' Debate," *The Bulletin of the Atomic Scientist* (September 1992).
6. Federation of American Scientists, accessed June 11, 2004 at http:www.fas.org/irp/threat/wind_state.htm.
7. Raymond Bonner and Craig S. Smith, "Pakistani Said to Have Given Libya Uranium," *The New York Times* (February 21, 2004): A–1.
8. Center for Defense Information, accessed April 6, 2004 at www.cdi.org/terrorism/nuclear-pr.cfm.
9. Protocol for the Prohibition of the Use in War of Asphyxiating. Poisonous or Other Gases, and of Bacteriological Methods of Warfare (signed at Geneva 17 June 1925), United Nations Department for Disarmament Affairs, *Status of Multilateral Arms Regulation and Disarmament Agreements*, (2nd ed.) (New York: United Nations, 1983).
10. Leonard A. Cole, *The Eleventh Plague: The Politics of Biological and Chemical Weapons* (New York: W.H. Freeman, 1998). pp. 87–91.
11. U.S. Senate Permanent Subcommittee on Investigations, Minority Staff Statement, "A Case Study on the Aum Shinrikyo," Washington, D.C., October 31, 1995, p. 52.
12. Convention on the Prohibition of the Development, Production, Stockpiling and Use of Chemical Weapons and on Their Destruction. Signed in 1993, entered into force in 1997. Accessed June 28, 2004 at www.opcw.org/html/db/cwc/eng/cwc_frameset.html.
13. Monterey Institute of International Studies, "Chemical and Biological Weapons: Possession and Programs Past and Present," accessed June 25, 2004 at http://cns.miis.edu/research/cbw/possess.htm.

14. Wendy Orent, *Plague: The Mysterious Past and Terrifying Future of the World's Most Dangerous Disease* (New York: Free Press, 2004), p. 213.

15. Jonathan B. Tucker and Jason Pate, "The Minnesota Patriots Council (1991)," in Jonathan B. Tucker, ed., *Toxic Terror: Assessing Terrorist Use of Chemical and Biological Weapons* (Cambridge, Mass: MIT Press, 2000), pp. 159–83.

16. W. Seth Carus, "The Rajneeshees (1984)," in Tucker, ibid., pp. 115–37.

17. Convention on the Prohibition of the Development, Production and Stockpiling of Bacteriological (Biological) and Toxin Weapons and on Their Destruction. Signed in 1972, entered into force in 1975. Accessed June 28, 2004 at www.state.gov/t/ac/trt/4718.htm.

18. "Chemical and Biological Weapons: Possession and Programs Past and Present," op cit.

19. Ken Alibek, *Biohazard: The Chilling Story of the Largest Covert Biological Weapons Program in the World* (New York: Random House, 1999), pp. 258–62.

20. U.S. Congress, Office of Technology Assessment, *Proliferation of Weapons of Mass Destruction: Assessing the Risks* (Washington, D.C.: Government Printing Office, August 1993); U.S. Congress, Office of Technology Assessment, *Technologies Underlying Weapons of Mass Destruction* (Washington, D.C.: Government Printing Office, December 1993); Richard A. Falkenrath, Robert D. Newman, and Bradley A. Thayer, *America's Achilles' Heel: Nuclear, Biological, and Chemical Terrorism and Covert Attack* (Cambridge, Mass: MIT Press, 2001).

21. A mock bioterrorism exercise in 2002, titled "Dark Winter," created a scenario in which a smallpox attack resulted in thousands of deaths, www.homelandsecurity.org/darkwinter/index. cfm. The naturally occurring flu pandemic in 1918 killed an estimated 40 million people worldwide. See Gina Kolata, *Flu: The Story of the Great Influenza Pandemic of 1918 and the Search for the Virus That Caused It* (New York: Touchstone Books, 2001).

22. This section is largely drawn from Leonard A. Cole, *The Anthrax Letters: A Medical Detective Story* (Washington, D.C.: Joseph Henry Press/National Academies Press, 2003), http://www. anthraxletters.com.

23. Leonard A. Cole, *Clouds of Secrecy: The Army's Germ Warfare Tests Over Populated Areas* (Lanham, Md.: Rowman and Littlefield, 1990).

24. "Postal Service Completes Test of New Anthrax Detection System." *Global Security Newswire* (September 9, 2003), accessed October 10, 2003 at www.govexec.com/dailyfed/0903/090903gsnl.htm.

25. Ari Schuler, "Billions for Biodefense: Federal Agency Biodefense Funding, FY2001–FY2005," *Biosecurity and Bioterrorism: Biodefense Strategy, Practice, and Science*, 2:2 (2004): 87.

Leonard A. Cole is an adjunct professor of political science at Rutgers University, Newark, New Jersey, where he teaches science and public policy. He is an expert on bioterrorism. Trained in the health sciences and public policy, he holds a Ph.D. in political science from Columbia University.

Unit II

Understanding
the Threat

Our understanding of the WMD terrorism threat requires a recognition of how different types of chemical, biological, radiological and nuclear (CBRN) weapons have different levels of appeal to terrorist groups as well as different levels of difficulty in cost and production, potential effectiveness, and means of protection. This section thus offers detailed accounts of the characteristics, availability, and dangers of CBRN weapons, along with six case studies that associate theory with practice—an important feature of this volume. The first chapter provides two selections that explore the complex threat of nuclear terrorism. The first of these is authored by Morten Bremer Maerli of the Norwegian Institute of International Affairs, Annette Schaper of the Peace Research Institute Frankfurt, and Frank Barnaby of the Oxford Research Group, who write that the risk of nuclear terrorism may be low, but the possible level of physical destruction, fatalities, and injuries is so great that the potential for terrorist acquisition and use of nuclear devices warrants serious consideration. Their analysis provides some observations on the likelihood of nuclear terrorism and on the technical feasibility of crude nuclear weapons production. Of particular importance, they illustrate how the production obstacles may be lower than anticipated and that technical barriers should not be regarded as sufficient to avoid nuclear terrorism in the future. They conclude that preventing any extremist group from achieving their goals of large-scale nuclear violence can best be done by denying them access to highly enriched uranium or plutonium, the essential ingredients of any nuclear device, and that adequate protection and control of such materials is thus vital.

Next, Matthew Bunn and Anthony Wier of the Managing the Atom Project at Harvard University identify seven myths about the threat of nuclear terrorism. First, they argue that despite a longstanding observation that "terrorists want a lot of people watching, not a lot of people dead," many terrorist groups are indeed interested in staging a nuclear catastrophe. A second myth, apparently believed by many officials, is that the nuclear materials required to make a bomb are nearly impossible for terrorists to obtain. A related third myth is that the difficulties of constructing or stealing a nuclear bomb are unlikely to be overcome by a terrorist group. A fourth myth is that the only plausible way that terrorists could acquire a nuclear bomb (or the ability to make one) is from a state. A fifth mistaken belief is that it is possible to put in place around the United States and other major countries a security cordon that can reduce to a low level the risk that nuclear weapons and materials might be smuggled in. Sixth, they argue, the notion that an offensive security posture alone will mitigate the threat of nuclear terrorism is another myth. And finally, the seventh myth they identify applies to states, rather than terrorist groups: A number of analysts argue that states would not be especially interested in a stolen nuclear weapon or stolen material to make one, because what they want is an indigenous capability to produce the material for as many nuclear weapons as they think they need. Like the other myths, this view leads those who believe it to downplay the importance of securing nuclear weapons and materials so that they cannot be stolen. Overall, this analysis should guide our understanding of the threat and how best to prevent and respond to nuclear terrorism in new and more sophisticated ways.

The next chapter of the volume—by Charles Ferguson and Joel Lubenau of the Center for Nonproliferation Studies—illustrates the need to secure the sources of radiation that could be used to develop a radiological dispersal devise (RDD, or "dirty bomb"). They note that even a very powerful RDD would cause far less damage than a nuclear weapon, and would likely cause few deaths from the direct effects of exposure to the radiation. Nevertheless, the costs of decontamination and, if necessary, rebuilding could soar into the billions of dollars, especially if the attack took place in an urban center. They argue that although the U.S. government has stepped up efforts to prevent acts of radiological terrorism, significant gaps in security remain to be filled. For example, they point to several vulnerabilities in radioactive source security—vulnerabilities which are not solely the responsibility of the government. Instead, they call for a new approach which incorporates a high level of cooperation and shared responsibility among government agencies, suppliers and licensees of radioactive sources.

The next three chapters examine the potential terrorist threat to nuclear facilities and related forms of critical infrastructure. First, Gavin Cameron, a Fellow of the Center for Military and Strategic Studies in Canada, assesses the threat of terrorist attacks on nuclear reactors or attacks using radiological materials. He begins by examining the danger posed by aircraft being crashed into a reactor, and compares that threat with the more familiar one posed by terrorists using truck bombs against reactors. The chapter then examines the history of terrorism directed against nuclear facilities; the problems posed by insiders, both as potential saboteurs and thieves of nuclear material; the risk to parts of the nuclear fuel cycle other than reactors; and finally, the threat of radiological terrorism. Cameron concludes that although the ramifications for the nuclear industry of the attacks on 11 September remain unclear, better protection of facilities and materials is clearly justified.

This is followed by another examination of the threat to nuclear power and research reactors, authored by George Bunn and Chaim Braun of the Center for International Security and Cooperation at Stanford University. They begin by suggesting that if terrorists could steal 25kg to 50kg of highly enriched uranium fuel (meant for use at one or more large research reactors), they might be able to make a nuclear weapon from it. The same is not true of unburned fuel from power reactors, because the uranium is not highly enriched and therefore not useful for making such weapons without a difficult uranium enrichment process. If terrorists could steal radioactive fuel that has been burned in either kind of reactor, they could probably make a radioactive dispersal device or "dirty bomb." If terrorists could use an airplane or truck bomb to crash through walls and fences protecting either kind of reactor and penetrate the reactor's containment, or blow up in the pond where irradiated spent nuclear fuel is stored, they might be able to disperse radioactivity over an area the shape and size of which would depend not only on the effect of the crash or explosion but also on the direction and speed of the wind. The amount and degree of radioactivity of irradiated fuel is likely to be much greater in power reactors, but the vulnerability of irradiated fuel is likely to be greater in research reactors. Their analysis has implications for where the Department of Homeland Security and the Nuclear Regulatory Commission should focus more attention and resources.

Next, Doug Chapin and a group of senior scientific colleagues provide a brief overview of the physical safety features and multiple layers of security at nuclear power plants. They note that the probability of a plant meltdown is quite low. For example, despite many dramatic news stories, tests have shown that it is impossible to penetrate the 1.5 meter thick walls surrounding a nuclear reactor by crashing a commercial airplane into it. In sum, these three selections enhance our understanding of the true realities of nuclear terror threats.

In the next chapter, Dave Franz—Vice President and Senior Biological Scientist at the Midwest Research Institute, Director of the National Agricultural Biosecurity Center and Kansas State University, and a Senior Fellow with the Combating Terrorism Center at West Point—examines the potential threat of terrorists weaponizing biotechnology. Although the risk of a biological terrorism attack is still probably quite low, he argues, the potential impact is just too great to ignore. Technical barriers to the use of biology as a weapon are falling, he notes, and we can do little to control the growing population worldwide, in academe and industry, that will understand the technology necessary to manipulate things biological. However, we must understand how to prepare, respond, recover and reduce the number of (or limit the technical capabilities of) those individuals or groups with the intent to harm our citizens or our economy with traditional microbial weapons or products of the biotechnology revolution. He concludes that while we cannot afford to impede the progress of biotechnology used for good, we must do everything we can to control and eliminate the potential for using these advances to cause harm.

This is followed by additional analysis on biotechnology and bioterrorism in a selection by Christopher Chyba and Alex Greninger of the Center for International Security and Cooperation at Stanford University. They suggest that biotechnology capacity is increasing and spreading rapidly, a trend which seems unstoppable since the economic, medical and food-security benefits of genetic manipulation are considerable. As a result, they argue, thresholds for the artificial enhancement or creation of dangerous pathogens—disease causing organisms—will steadily drop, which will almost inevitably place greater destructive power in the hands of small groups with technically competent, ideologically-motivated members. Thus, legitimate private and academic research has important global security implications in the 21st century. In addition to self-monitoring among members of the biotechnology community, the authors also call for global cooperation to circumvent, or at least mitigate, an otherwise endless biological arms race.

In the next chapter, Jonathan Tucker—a Senior Fellow at the Washington, D. C. office of the Center for Non-Proliferation Studies—assesses the threat of chemical terrorism and examines strategies for prevention and response. [Several case studies provided later in this section also address various dimensions of the chemical terrorism threat.] Tucker identifies four primary types of threat: release of a military-grade chemical warfare agent against a civilian target; sabotage of a chemical manufacturing plant or storage facility; contamination of public water or food supplies; and targeted use of a chemical agent to assassinate specific individuals. He notes that most incidents of chemical terrorism have involved the use of household or industrial chemicals, but that the sabotage of a commercial chemical plant or a series of railroad tank cars could be catastrophic and more likely than the large-scale release of a military nerve agent. Thus, he calls for improving the security of chemical plants and the transportation infrastructure, which will require greater cooperation between government and the private sector.

The next two chapters also examine specific areas of homeland security and critical infrastructure that could be targeted in a catastrophic terrorism attack. First, the threat of agricultural terrorism is examined by Mark Wheelis, a microbiologist at UC Davis, Rocco Casagrande, the Director of the Homeland Security program for ABT in Cambridge,

Massachusetts, and Laurence V. Madden, a Professor with the Department of Plant Pathology at Ohio State University. Their analysis reveals that the U.S. is vulnerable to a deliberate introduction of exotic plant and animal diseases by terrorist groups with an ideological agenda or by governments, corporations, or individuals with a profit motive. The vulnerability to an agricultural bioterrorist attack is a consequence of the low security of agricultural targets, the technical ease of introducing consequential diseases, and the large economic repercussions of even small outbreaks. It is exacerbated by structural features of U.S. agriculture that are unlikely to change without forceful government intervention: low genetic diversity of plants and animals, extensive monoculture, and highly concentrated animal husbandry. While our vulnerabilities cannot be eliminated, effective response can minimize the damage from both intentionally and naturally introduced disease. They suggest an aggressive scientific agenda, to include continuing education programs for farmers, veterinarians, and extension specialists; development of new diagnostics, vaccines, and pesticides; development of new sensing technologies for early identification of plant disease outbreaks; development of plant varieties resistant to diseases not yet endemic; and an increase in the number of outbreak control specialists assigned to international disease control efforts.

Their analysis is complemented by a selection authored by Gavin Cameron, Jason Pate and Kathleen Vogel of the Center for Nonproliferation Studies at the Monterey Institute of International Studies. Based on an examination of open-source historical and technical information, they suggest that the threat of agricultural bioterrorism has been exaggerated. However, in an increasingly globalized society, the potential for damaging outbreaks can grow, and given their potential impact, more efforts should be directed at disease prevention and response. Thus, they recommend several specific steps that should be taken, such as identifying and changing agricultural practices which increase U.S. vulnerability to disease outbreaks; providing increased funding for work related to foreign animal and plant diseases; equipping local and state public health and veterinary laboratory systems to allow rapid diagnosis of animal samples in emergency situations; extending national and international disease surveillance networks to include individual farms and facilities; increasing communication among scientists concerned with animal, human, and plant diseases; and expanding our surveillance of disease outbreaks among wildlife populations.

The next chapter, by James Lewis, Senior Fellow and Director for Technology and Public Policy at the Center for Strategic and International Studies, examines the relationship between cybersecurity and critical infrastructure protection. Lewis begins by describing cybersecurity as the safeguarding of computer networks and the information they contain from penetration and from malicious damage or disruption. Since the use of computer networks has become a major element in governmental and business activities, he notes, tampering with these networks can have serious consequences for agencies, firms and individuals. The question is to what degree these individual-level consequences translate into risk for critical infrastructure. While some have overstated the threat, he argues, cybersecurity cannot be entirely ignored in planning for critical infrastructure protection. However, from his analysis of the threat, he concludes that the best path to better cybersecurity may lay outside of critical infrastructure protection. It is hard to motivate people to defend when risks are obscure or appear exaggerated. However, the risks of espionage (including economic espionage) and cybercrime are very real for individuals, firms and agencies. A security agenda that focused on measures to respond to cybercrime and espionage would produce tangible benefits, win greater support, and reduce many vulnerabilities in computer networks used by critical infrastructure.

The remainder of this section provides several recent case studies which enhance our understanding of the WMD terrorism threat. First, Bruce Hoffman—a professor at Georgetown University and a Senior Fellow at the Combating Terrorism Center at West Point—examines the WMD threat post-9/11, especially from al Qaeda and associated jihadis. His chapter outlines how we face a two-fold threat: one from al Qaeda itself, given the grandiose ambitions spanning chemical, biological, radiological and nuclear weapons—evidence of which was uncovered by our forces in Afghanistan. But we also face a threat from associated jihadis who are attracted to these weapons not for their putative killing potential, but because of the profoundly corrosive and unsettling psychological effects even a limited attack can have on a targeted society. From this perspective, Hoffman then focuses on the case of Kamal Bourgass, an Algerian who trained in al Qaeda camps, and plotted to stage an attack in Britain using ricin (a poison that can be made from the waste left over from processing castor beans). He notes that Bourgass' intent was not to kill—as one would assume about a terrorist using biological weapons—but rather, for the psychological blow it would deal to British society, causing fear and panic and undermining confidence in government and the authorities. Clearly, understanding the motivations and strategic intentions of terrorists is a critical component of comprehending the true nature of the WMD terror threat.

Next, Adam Dolnik (Director of Research Development at the Center for Transnational Crime Prevention at the University of Wollongong, Australia) and Rohan Gunaratna (Head of the International Center for Terrorism and Political Violence Research at the Nanyang Technological University, Singapore) analyze the threat of chemical and biological terrorism posed by Jemaah Islamiya (JI), the most important terrorist organization operating in Southeast Asia. They describe the ideological and motivational progression of the group's radical wing toward the goal of achieving mass casualties, and assess the group's capability to acquire and weaponize the necessary agents. The main focus of the chapter is then devoted to an analysis of a chemical and biological weapons manual discovered in the apartment of a top JI operative in Cotabato City in the southern Philippines, which provides unique insights into the current capabilities of the organization. The individual agents considered by JI are reviewed, followed by an assessment of the group's knowledge level with respect to those agents. The authors conclude that the likelihood of a mass casualty chemical or biological attack being carried out by the group in the near future is low.

This is followed by a case study by Lewis Dunn, a Senior Vice President at Science Applications International Corporation, on al Qaeda's interest in nuclear weapons. Today, it is very widely assumed that acquisition of CBRN by al Qaeda would be rapidly followed by the use of those weapons—that is, employment via the release of a biological or chemical agent, the dispersal of radiological materials, or the detonation of a nuclear explosive. Dunn's chapter examines this proposition, and in so doing, illuminates the conditions and calculations that could shape al Qaeda's posture regarding the employment of CBRN. His analysis then highlights the possible contribution of deterrence to the overall U.S.-led war on terrorism.

And in the final chapter of this section, David Albright and Cory Hinderstein of the Institute for Science and International Security examine the development and implications of the A. Q. Khan clandestine network. Khan, with the help of associates on four continents, managed to buy and sell key nuclear weapons capabilities for more than two decades while eluding the world's best intelligence agencies and nonproliferation institutions and organizations. They created a network of suppliers, manufacturers, and shippers that provided secret nuclear technology to Iran, Libya, North Korea, and perhaps others. Over the course of several years, U.S. intelligence agents were able to penetrate the network's operations, leading to many revelations and ultimately, in October 2003, the dramatic seizure of uranium-enrichment gas-centrifuge components bound for Libya's secret nuclear weapons program aboard the German-owned ship *BBC China*, followed by the eventual arrest of Khan and his colleagues. The Khan network caused enormous damage to efforts aimed at stopping the spread of nuclear weapons, to U.S. national security, and to international peace and stability. After describing the problems in the current global system of export controls, Albright and Hinderstein argue for a treaty-based system of export controls and verification that would impose new requirements on all states, making it significantly more difficult for nuclear smuggling to occur.

In sum, there are obviously a host of ways in which terrorist organizations could expand their powers of destruction. Together, these chapters highlight the clear and present danger to America posed by terrorist organizations seeking WMD capabilities. The challenges and questions raised by these authors frame the importance of the remaining sections in this volume. The threat we face is not insurmountable, but we must work to counter the rapid change of techniques and procedures used by the terrorists. Clearly, we must develop better tools for understanding and managing the threat, if we are to have any hope of preventing WMD terrorism.

Chapter 2.1

Different "Faces" of Nuclear Terrorism

Morten Bremer Maerli, Annette Schaper, and Frank Barnaby

The Characteristics of Nuclear Terrorist Weapons

No terrorist group has ever fielded or deployed a nuclear device. The deadly cocktail of terrorists and nuclear weapons thus remains a fiction, despite a transpiring quantity of alerts and speculations of mean substate characters with nuclear capabilities. Only weeks after the devastating terrorist attacks on September 11, 2001, a secret intelligence alert went out, for instance, to a small number of U.S. government agencies. According to the alert, terrorists were thought to have obtained a nuclear weapon from the Russian arsenal and planned to smuggle it into New York City. In response to the threat, the Federal Bureau of Investigation (FBI) alerted a number of other federal agencies, including the Nuclear Emergency Search Team (NEST).

In the days after September 11, 2001, doomsday scenarios like a terrorist nuclear attack suddenly seemed plausible. But in the end, and probably as was to be expected, the investigators found nothing and concluded that the information was false. The yield of the alleged nuclear weapon was equivalent to 10 kilotons of TNT, 1,000 times higher than the biggest conventional bomb ever exploded. Detonated in lower Manhattan, the effects would have been devastating.

Opinions about the threat of nuclear terrorism differ among scholars and security experts. One recent assessment (M. Bunn, Holdren, & Wier, 2002) concludes that "the possibility that terrorists could acquire a nuclear weapon and explode it in a U.S. city is real" and that the absence of nuclear terrorism so far is "due to lack of means rather than lack of motivation." According to others, however, nuclear terrorism is "an overrated nightmare" (Kamp, 1996), and whereas "chemical, biological, or radiological is likely to occur (in the U.S.), nuclear terrorism is unlikely to do so, as it is too difficult" (Cameron, 2000b). Others dismiss the risk of large-scale nuclear terrorist violence in their country on the grounds of internal factors such as geography, politics, and security policy (Anet, n.d.).

Indeed, conventional means are likely to remain the weaponry of choice for most terrorists (Rapoport, 2002). Conventional weaponry, as painfully evidenced September 11, 2001, could still more than effectively serve their goals, and there will be both practical, strategic, and perhaps even moral constraints against uses of so-called weapons of mass effect (WMEs).[2] The constraints against the use of weapons of mass destruction are particularly severe for terrorists who are concerned with their fellow citizens (like social revolutionary and national separatist terrorists) (Post, 2001). Conventional off-the-shelf weaponry and well-known approaches are thus likely to remain the major tools for the bulk part of terrorist groups.

However, because the world will experience new acts of terror, provable and strong interest among some high-profile terrorist groups in acquiring nuclear weapon capabilities does not allow us to ignore the risk of nuclear terrorism.[3] The risk may still be low, but the possible level of physical destruction, fatalities, and injuries is so great in and of itself that the potential for terrorist acquisition and use of nuclear devices warrants serious consideration.

To dismiss the risks of nuclear terrorism therefore seems to us not only to be an overly simplified but possibly also a dangerous approach. Not only could this make us less prepared but, more disturbingly, it could make us less willing to try to mitigate the risks. By denying terrorists access to nuclear weapons or highly enriched uranium (HEU) and plutonium—the essential ingredient of any nuclear device—the risk of nuclear terrorism can be drastically reduced. In this sense, we may have a comparative advantage to combating biological and chemical terrorism. Such acts of terrorist violence could be harder to interdict as they may be performed with a wide range of fairly accessible materials that are much harder to protect than fissile materials.

Understanding the real threat of nuclear terrorism requires in-depth and probably interdisciplinary analysis of both possible terrorist motivations and intentions, and of their potential technical capabilities. To help come to grips with some of the aspects of the potential risk of nuclear terrorism, we will present some possible characteristics of terrorist nuclear weapons.[4] We will do so by discussing the general steps toward nuclear weaponization, the differing requirements between crude terrorist nuclear devices and traditional military nuclear weapons, and moreover, by looking into the technical feasibility of manufacturing crude nuclear devices.

The article concludes that the most formidable barriers against nuclear terrorism may in fact not be technical obstacles but getting access to sufficient quantities of high-quality fissile materials. Prevention of any of the terrorist cells from obtaining weapons or materials of mass destruction is therefore paramount. However, whereas the potential proliferation threats and the consequences of such chilling scenarios are fairly easy to understand, the problems of fissile weapons–usable material management have proven anything but simple to solve (Daughtry & Wehling 2000). The gap between the threat and the appurtenant international response seems to be widening.

Nuclear Explosives as a Terrorist Tool

Although any terrorist attack involving weapons of mass effect potentially could inflict serious damages and wide-ranging consequences (massive casualties, societal disruption, and financial losses), nuclear weapons could be the ultimate terrorist weapon. The immense destructive power and the definitive "shock value" of nuclear weapons will immediately create a manifest confirmation of an attack and, of course, widespread and direct attention. As clearly evidenced in Manhattan on September 11, 2001, terrorist incidents are often high-profile events. Terrorism may be regarded as a way of communicating. The news media tend to focus on spectacular and negative events (Galtung & Ruge, 1965), and to get attention, most terrorists traditionally want showy attacks that produce a great deal of noise (e.g., Laqueur, 1999).[5]

As seen from the media hullabaloo when an American citizen with alleged ties to the Al Qaeda terror network was arrested on suspicion of plotting to build and detonate a radioactive "dirty bomb" in the United States, the psychological impact of any form of "nuclear terrorism" may be strong.[6] Strong emotional reactions were as well seen in March 2001. In the wake of the rumors about Al Qaeda's alleged progress toward obtaining a nuclear or radiological weapon in Afghanistan, hundreds of new and sophisticated radiation detection sensors were then deployed to U.S. borders, overseas facilities, and points around Washington, D.C. The ability of the sensors to detect nuclear materials, however, may be limited (Glanz, 2002).

Generally, the public has greater fear of events and consequences that are confirmed, catastrophic, and not well understood, common features of a nuclear threat (Tønnessen, 2002). Past nuclear explosions and nuclear accidents, limited public understanding, and knowledge of radiation and the human inability to sense potential exposures may have cultivated (disproportionate) negative perceptions of radiation. Nuclear detonations could therefore inflict a radius of psychological damage far exceeding that of injury and death. Terrorists who capitalize on these factors are likely to have a strong impact.

By far, the effects of a nuclear explosion are likely to surpass those of any previous terrorist action. An actual detonation of a nuclear device could set a terrorist organization apart from any other group and could compel governments to take them seriously (Cameron, 2000b). Even a credible hoax, for example, where terrorists provide workable weapon designs together with samples of high-quality fissile material to blackmail authorities, could challenge proper governmental responses.

Terrorist groups are clearly running a definitive risk of strong retaliatory actions after any large-scale nuclear violence. But terrorists operate outside traditional patterns of deterrence and the cellular and often transnational structure of contemporary terrorist organizations could make effective reprisals hard to accomplish. Where states, with their defined geographical boundaries open to potential retaliation, could renounce any nuclear use, terrorists may operate more freely in a substate context. This also could make a "war on terrorism" based primarily on military power projections and traditional armed state-to-state interaction a dubious path for defeating future terrorism.[7]

Terrorists' Steps Toward Nuclear Capabilities

One route to terrorist acquisition of a nuclear weapon explosive is through theft or purchase of an intact weapon from the stockpiles of any state possessing such weapons. Another option, which will be emphasized throughout this text, is fabricating a bomb based on available (and/or purchasable) resources.

Presumably it is easier to get a hold of fissile materials than of a complete nuclear weapon. Although over the past decade there have been several confirmed cases of the theft of kilogram quantities of weapons-usable materials, no diversion of intact nuclear weapons has been proven so far (M. Bunn et al., 2002). Moreover, any unauthorized use of nuclear weapons could make it necessary to circumvent the protective systems of the warheads (so-called permissive action links [PALs]) and to reconfigure weapon electronics.

In September 1997, General Alexander Lebed caused a stir when he claimed that the Soviet Union created and probably lost 100 atomic demolition munitions (ADMs) ("Ongoing Speculation About Missing Russian 'Suitcase Nukes,'" 1997; Parrish & Lepingwell, 1997). Allegedly, these low-yield (1 kiloton) devices were to be used by special forces for wartime sabotage and thus were small, portable, and not equipped with standard security devices against unauthorized use. Several of these weapons were located in states of the former Soviet Union and might not have been returned to Russia. Russian officials, however, have disputed these claims. Moreover, it is questionable whether the nuclear material that is contained in the warhead is still suitable for use in a weapon. As a rule, nuclear weapon plutonium has to be replaced every 5 to 10 years. The material in the "forgotten" Russian warheads has certainly not been replaced.

As a result, fabricating its own nuclear device, even with the challenges involved, could be a more viable path for a terrorist group with nuclear ambitions.

Any actor seeking to develop a nuclear device must deal with a number of design options and must complete a number of essential steps. The aspiring nuclear actor must (Carnegie Analysis, 2001) (a) develop a design for its nuclear device or obtain such a design from a weapon-holding state; (b) produce the fissile material for the core of the device or obtain it from an external source and then machine the fissile material to fabricate the nuclear parts of the weapon; (c) fabricate, or obtain from outside, the nonnuclear parts of the device, including the high-explosive elements and triggering components that will detonate the nuclear core; (d) verify the reliability of these various elements individually and as a system; and (e) assemble all of these elements into a deliverable nuclear armament, commonly referred to as "weaponization."

Each of these steps represents particular challenges. Unsuccessful state nuclear weapon programs (e.g., the Iraqi) are often taken as evidence of the infeasibility of establishing nuclear weapon capabilities. This is probably why some scholars uncritically choose to dismiss the risk of nuclear terrorism. According to such analysts, "Significant technical hurdles stand in the way of practicing nuclear terrorism in any form" (Cameron, 2000a). And indeed, all demonstrably successful efforts by states to develop nuclear weapons have to date been major enterprises, involving several years of work, with large design teams and recourses devoted to the development of nuclear devices. But most of the resources have been put on the production of fissile materials (MacKenzie & Sinardi, 1995).

Moreover, all of the well-documented efforts since 1945 seem to have been created as a step-stone to an eventually more sophisticated arsenal. Even the Iraqi nuclear weapon program was overdimensioned from the point of view of simply producing a crude nuclear weapon (MacKenzie & Sinardi, 1995). A modest program aiming simply at producing crude nuclear weapons may thus circumvent the need for extensive know-how.

The Differing State and Terrorist Nuclear Weapon Requirements

A "homemade" nuclear device, although cruder and less efficient than a state military weapon, could very well serve the needs of a terrorist group. The highly differing requirements for performance and delivery could make weapons designed to meet the "terrorist nuclear weapon standards" less technically challenging than traditional state nuclear weapons. Terrorist groups are likely to be satisfied with a nuclear explosive device that is far less sophisticated than the types of nuclear weapons required by the military.

First, a state would be at least as concerned with the nuclear device not going off during storage and transportation as with optimizing the yield and detonation of the weapon. One example is the so-called one-point safety requirements of the United States to prevent accidental detonations of nuclear weapons. This set of strict requirements is designed to ensure that a nuclear explosion will not result if the conventional explosive that surrounds the fissile material were accidentally detonated. Although safety is a must for states, such concerns could be given less consideration by terrorists, especially groups with strong affection to martyrdom.

Second, the reliability concerns may be equivalently low among terrorists. Although an ignition failure or a fizzle yield would be unfortunate from the viewpoint of terrorists, it could, potentially, have profound impact on the security of a state, for example, in a nuclear offensive mode. To predict the damages, to perform nuclear planning, and to estimate the number of warheads needed, states are looking for fairly predicable and accurate yields. For this, the technical sophistication of the military nuclear devices is again likely to increase. For terrorists, however, any explosion in the lower kiloton range represents an unprecedented yield. Moreover, as seen below, fizzling plutonium weapons may very well serve as effective radiological dispersion devices.

Third, weapons for military uses are normally required in fairly large numbers, and they must be delivered by conventional military means (missiles, mortars, etc.). Terrorists, on the other hand, will aim at a limited arsenal. Moreover, the most important constraining factors for state nuclear weapons are often the weight capacity of the delivery vehicle and the space available to carry the weapon (e.g., the diameter and length of a nosecone or the length and width of a bomb bay). Developing reliable delivery systems and slender nuclear explosives is technically challenging and expensive, even for states. Crude terrorist nuclear devices, however, will easily fit into a van, or even automobiles, for subsequent detonation, possibly in densely populated areas. Other nonmilitary means of delivery could involve trucks, hot-air balloons, ships, or simply a complete assembling of the nuclear device inside a garage or an out-of-the-way residence.

Crude Terrorist Nuclear Weapons

Two basic designs of crude nuclear explosives are likely to be adequate for most purposes of a terrorist group intent on nuclear terrorism. Both designs were used in the first generation of nuclear weapons produced. One design is a so-called gun-type nuclear explosive device, similar to the nuclear weapon that destroyed Hiroshima. It can only use HEU as the fissile material, not plutonium. This is the simplest crude device to design and construct and the most likely one to produce a powerful nuclear explosion.

The second design is an implosion type of nuclear explosive device using a solid sphere of plutonium metal or, possibly, a spherical vessel filled with plutonium dioxide. This would require the dioxide to be quite close to its critical mass before the compression. However, using dioxide, it is likely that only a fizzle yield or a very moderate yield will result. But even such limited yields could be adequate for terrorist purposes.[8] The implosion design is essentially a crude version of the nuclear weapon that destroyed Nagasaki. Both plutonium and HEU can be used in an implosion device. Whether terrorists will go for a uranium or a plutonium device depends on range of practical considerations, especially the (potential) availability of material and their technical skills.

Primitive Nuclear Explosives Using HEU

Generally, it is considerably simpler to make a bomb using enriched uranium than to make one using plutonium, but the critical mass is larger (Bodansky, 1996).[9] Moreover, the low radioactivity levels of fresh uranium makes it easier to handle, without the need for protective shielding and any problem of self-heating of the device.

Luis Alvarez (1987), a prominent nuclear-weapon physicist, has emphasized the ease of constructing a nuclear explosive with HEU:

> With modern weapons-grade uranium, the background neutron rate is so low that terrorists, if they have such material, would have a good chance of setting off a high-yield explosion simply by dropping one half of the material onto the other half. Most people seem unaware that if separated highly-enriched uranium is at hand it's a trivial job to set off a nuclear explosion . . . even a high school kid could make a bomb in short order.

However, if the two halves of HEU are just dropped onto each other, the probability is high that a neutron from spontaneous fission causes preignition. A much lower yield would result. Ideally, therefore, the two pieces of uranium should be fired on each other.[10] Terrorists could possibly do this by using a thick-walled cylindrical barrel to force two subcritical masses of HEU together with the use of high explosives surrounding the fissile material at the top of the barrel. This mass would then be propelled into a larger mass of uranium placed at the bottom of the barrel, with a hollowed out cylinder of the same size as the smaller uranium mass. The total length of the nuclear explosive device is likely to be no more than about 1 m and about 25 cm in diameter. It should weigh no more than 300kg or so, and it could easily be transported by, and (remotely) detonated in, an ordinary van.

It is probably quite easy to produce or get a hold of all the necessary weapon components, with the exception of the HEU, and to perform the fabrication and the assembly operations without attracting too much attention. Past experience suggests that crude HEU nuclear weapons will function without prior testing due to the low neutron background, and thus a limited risk of preignition. Its possessors could thus have reasonable confidence in the performance of those weapons.

The disadvantages of uranium devices are similarly obvious. Military HEU weapons are bulky with large weights and a large amount of HEU needed. The device is also inherently inefficient. Only some 700 g of the total of 60 kg of uranium fissioned in the bomb that was dropped on Hiroshima, indicating an efficiency of a little more than 1%.

However, even a crude nuclear weapon using HEU could explode with an explosive power equivalent to that of a few hundred to a few thousand tons TNT. To put this in context, the nuclear weapon that destroyed Hiroshima, which was a gun-type weapon, exploded with an explosive power equivalent to that of 12,500 tons of TNT. The largest conventional bomb used in World War II, however, contained "only" about 10 tons of TNT; it was christened "the earthquake bomb." And the terrorist bomb that destroyed the federal building in Oklahoma City had a yield of about 3 tons of TNT.

Primitive Nuclear Explosives Using Plutonium

In contrast to a HEU device, plutonium devices need to have a fast compression (in the order of microseconds) due to the higher fraction of spontaneous neutrons. The need for a rapid and simultaneous compression of the fissile material requires the much more challenging implosion design and, desirably but not necessarily, advanced computerized analysis to optimize the yield. If the assembly were to be compressed too slowly, it could be blown apart before many nuclei would have been fissioned, with a significantly reduced yield as the result.

For well-functioning plutonium weapons, high densities can be achieved in the fissile material. This reduces the quantities of material needed. The efficiency of the Trinity bomb, the first nuclear device ever deployed,[11] was about 20% and thus significantly higher than the HEU bomb (Serber, 1992). The plutonium device could have a limited size. A bare sphere of reactor-grade plutonium dioxide having a critical mass would be about 18 cm in diameter. Depending of the chemical form and size of the plutonium sphere, the radius of the total device could be in the range of 40 cm, including high explosives.

Fairly large amounts of different explosives, shaped around the reflector/tamper placed around the sphere of plutonium, are needed to create a roughly symmetrical shock wave to sufficiently compress the plutonium. The high explosive suppressing the fissile material could be TNT[12] or preferably a plastic explosive, such as Semtex. A plastic explosive is easier to handle and can be molded into the special shapes, called "explosive lenses," that are arranged around the plutonium sphere ensuring a more even compression of the plutonium.

Detonators could be inserted into each of the symmetrically arranged explosive lenses so that the distance between each detonator and the surface of the plutonium sphere is constant. The need for a simultaneous detonation of all explosive triggers surrounding the sphere of plastic explosives could be a challenge but most likely achievable. It must occur within microseconds. Any delay would cause a nonuniform compression of the device, and thus a nonsymmetric compression and a (highly) reduced yield.

The explosive yield of the device will also depend on how close to critical the mass of the plutonium sphere was before the conventional explosion and then how effectively the conventional high explosives compressed it. Some of the energy released by the conventional explosion will enter the plutonium sphere, the rest going in other directions. Of the energy entering the plutonium, some will compress the sphere and the rest will heat it up. The more energy that goes into compression, the more powerful the nuclear explosion is likely to be. Also, the more symmetrical the compression, the more sustained the nuclear explosion will be.

Potentially, civilian plutonium from nuclear power plants also could be used in nuclear devices. Declassified U.S. documents reveal that a significant nuclear yield can be accomplished by utilizing reactor-grade plutonium in the nuclear explosive.[13] In reactor-grade plutonium, there will be an increased presence of the isotopes Pu-238 and Pu-240, causing the spontaneous neutron emission rate to increase (as will the thermal output). This could cause preignition concerns and self-heating concerns and complicates the weapon design. However, it is also possible that the higher neutron flux could ease the detonation of a crude plutonium device, thereby making reactor-grade a more feasible terrorist option than readily more well-protected weapons-grade plutonium.[14] Reactor-grade plutonium is considered by the International Atomic Energy Agency (IAEA) as direct-use, that is, weapons-usable materials (National Academy of Sciences, 1994).

The exact size of the nuclear explosion from such a crude plutonium device is impossible to predict. To reduce the risk of preignition to close to zero in an implosion assembly, an implosion velocity of about 1,000 m per second is required. A terrorist group is most unlikely to achieve this. The explosive yield of a terrorist nuclear device using implosion is, therefore, unlikely to exceed 1,000 tons of TNT equivalent. However, even if it were only equivalent to the explosion of a few tens of tons of TNT, it would completely devastate the center of a large city.

Radiological Dispersion Devices

Even if the plutonium device, when detonated, did not produce a significant nuclear explosion, the explosion of the chemical high explosives would disperse the plutonium widely, especially if in the form of powder. If an incendiary material, such as an aluminum-iron oxide (thermite), were mixed with the high explosives, the explosion would be accompanied by a fierce fire. A high proportion of the plutonium is likely to remain unfissioned and would be dispersed by the explosion or volatilized by the fierce heat. Much of the plutonium is likely to be dispersed in this way as small particles of plutonium dioxide taken up into the atmosphere in the fireball and scattered far and wide downwind. Radioactive contamination locally, exposures, and strong psychological may result.

A large fraction of the particles are likely to be smaller than 3 microns in diameter and would, therefore, be able to be breathed into, and retained by, the lung. Here they could cause lung cancer by irradiating the surrounding tissue with alpha particles. Once dispersed into the environment, plutonium dioxide is insoluble in rainwater and would remain in surface dusts and soils for a protracted period. The half-life of the plutonium isotope plutonium-239, for example, is 24,400 years.

These factors would combine to render a large part of an affected city uninhabitable until decontaminated, an extremely costly procedure that could take many months or years. The (additional) threat of dispersion of many kilograms of plutonium could make a crude nuclear explosive device a particularly attractive weapon for a terrorist group, the threat being enhanced by the general population's fear of radioactivity.

The Amount of Material Needed

For any of the two designs, the first thing a terrorist group would need to do is to acquire sufficient fissile material—HEU or plutonium—to produce a nuclear explosion. The task would then be to assemble the fissile material in a fast way to produce a critical mass.

The critical mass of plutonium of a type suitable to manufacture a nuclear explosive is about 13 kg for a bare metal sphere. The critical mass of uranium enriched to 93% in uranium-235 is about 52 kg (Mark, 1991). However, quantities above this may be needed to produce a workable device because the chain reaction in an assembly that is just critical would not release enough energy. Moreover, the fabrication of a nuclear explosive inevitably produces material losses due to the machining of its special shape, which implies that initially more material is needed.

The performance of the weapon could be improved and the critical mass reduced, however, by fairly simple measures. A reflector that returns escaping neutrons back into the fissioning assembly could, for example, surround the nuclear device. As a consequence, more neutrons become available to produce fissions and less material is needed. The reduction can be considerable. As an example, the reduction when a beryllium reflector is placed around a mass of uranium containing 93% of uranium-235 is shown in Table 1 (from Mark, 1991).

To assure high neutron flux the very moment the system goes critical, a strong neutron source that becomes active as soon as the pieces come into position can be introduced. The bust of neutrons will then boost the fissioning of uranium atoms and thus increase the weapon yield.

For an implosion device, a shell of material, such as beryllium or uranium, could surround the plutonium sphere to reflect back neutrons. A thick reflector could reduce the critical plutonium mass by a factor of two or more. Because the shell of reflecting material is heavy, it also acts as a tamper. When the high explosives are detonated, the shock wave causes the tamper to collapse inward. Its inertia helps hold together the plutonium during the explosion to prevent the premature disintegration of the fissioning material and thereby to obtain a larger explosion.

Table 1

Critical (minimum) Masses to Be Assembled as a Function of Reflector (Beryllium) Thickness

Beryllium Reflector Thickness (cm)	Mass to be Assembled (kg)
None	52
2	33
9	16
15	12

Source: Mark (1991).

The amounts needed to produce a workable nuclear terrorist weapon thus depend on the design, technical weapon sophistication, and material applied. Advanced nuclear weapon states would need far less material than inexperienced small beginner groups. As a very rough estimate, a terrorist group would need about 30 kg to 80 kg HEU for a gun-type device, or 8 kg to 20 kg HEU or 2 kg to 5 kg plutonium for an implosion device (Schaper, 1999).

Access to Fissile Material

A majority of the nuclear weapon states have been reluctant to engage in any transparency exercises with regard to their nuclear capabilities or holdings of fissile materials. In most states, this information remains classified. Thus, to a large extent, the quantities of plutonium and HEU stocks are unknown. Estimates normally are based on unofficial figures. There is estimated to be about 450 tons of separated military and civil plutonium and more than 1,700 tons of HEU (Albright, Berkhout, & Walker, 1997).[15] Much of this material is in the hands of the five officially recognized nuclear weapon states, but 1,306 kg of civil HEU is spread among a further 27 countries, some of which harbor quantities sufficient to produce a warhead (IAEA, 2000).

A sophisticated terrorist group should have little difficulty in building a primitive nuclear explosive device using HEU. Now and in the near future, a terrorist group may, however, find it easier to acquire civil plutonium than HEU. The stocks of highly enriched uranium and plutonium are under national physical protection. In non-nuclear-weapon states, they also are subject to international safeguards that aim at controlling that none of this material might be diverted for undeclared purposes. Safeguards are carried out by the IAEA in non-nuclear-weapon states under the Non-Proliferation Treaty (NPT), in accordance with their treaty obligations.

The amount of plutonium available from civil reprocessing plants, however, will rapidly increase, particularly as more reprocessing capacity becomes operational. It will be stored in a number of countries, and if it is not properly protected, it might become easier to obtain plutonium illegally. Despite the technical challenges, the risk that a terrorist group may acquire plutonium and fabricate a nuclear device should therefore be taken seriously.

Despite the technical challenges, the risk that a terrorist group may acquire plutonium and fabricate a nuclear device should therefore be taken seriously. These states are the nuclear weapon states under the NPT[16] and India, Pakistan, and Israel. The states of the former Soviet Union have been the subject of great concern for many years, with regard to the security of nuclear material. It seems that an exact overview of stocks has been lost or never existed in a sufficiently accurate form. Moreover, many plants and deposits are not sufficiently secure.

According to the U.S. Department of Energy (DOE), more than 600 metric tons of weapons-grade nuclear material, HEU and plutonium, is at risk of theft in Russia. This material would be highly attractive to nuclear thieves because (a) it can be directly used in nuclear devices without further enrichment or processing, (b) it is not extremely radioactive and can be handled by thieves, and (c) it can be transported easily in a variety of ways. International programs are underway to upgrade security at Russian nuclear sites, but progress has been slow, particularly at the most proliferation attractive material (U.S. General Accounting Office, 2001). Today, after nearly a decade of cooperation, only some 40% of the facilities housing nuclear materials in Russia have received security improvements through U.S. assistance. Estimates indicate that if current rates are not accelerated, Russia's nuclear material will not be completely secure until 2029 (Lugar, 2002).

However, the problem of insecure nuclear material may not only be confined to the former Soviet Union, or in the nuclear weapon states outside the Non-Proliferation Treaty. Even in the United States, complaints about the limited security surrounding weapon-ready material have repeatedly been filed, even though much stricter and more modern regulations concerning the physical protection of nuclear material are in place (President's Foreign Intelligence Advisory Board, 1999). In the first decades after the invention of nuclear weapons, the recording of nuclear materials was still very incomplete.

The U.S. DOE (1996) published a detailed account of the history of American plutonium production. It was demonstrated that the stocks taken by measurement and the number calculated from historical documents differ by 2.8 tons. This material has not necessarily been lost or stolen; this number could just signify the extent to which the early recording of material was inexact. However, what becomes clear is that it is not possible to determine whether material has been taken away in the past. It can be assumed that such inaccuracies are even worse in Russia.

International Efforts to Stem Proliferation

Strategies must be devised that would reduce the risk of nuclear terrorism. First and foremost, international cooperation to improve the security of nuclear material in Russia must be enhanced. At many Russian nuclear installations, physical protection and nuclear material accountancy fall below defined Western standards.

Over the past decade, a lot of international efforts have been initiated to improve the material protection, control, and accountancy in Russia and to stem proliferation of knowledge and materials. Among them are the U.S. Cooperative Threat Reduction efforts, the establishment of the International Science and Technology Centers in Russia and Ukraine that provide civil projects for former nuclear weapon scientists and that are funded by the United States, the European Union (EU), Japan, and other Western countries. The EU runs the Tacis program that assists the Commonwealth of Independent States (CIS) countries in various fields. However, the priorities of the latter lay still in other fields; nuclear disarmament and nonproliferation is only a small part. On December 17, 1999, the EU Council adopted a Joint Action for Nonproliferation and Disarmament in the Russian Federation, using the Cooperative Threat Reduction Program of the United States as model (EU, 1999). However, its funding is still modest.

At the June 2002 G8 summit, leaders agreed to spend U.S. $20 billion over the next decade in further securing nuclear materials in Russia, citing the attacks of September 11, 2001, as evidence of the need for what is called the G8 global partnership against the spread of weapons and material of mass destruction (G8, 2002). Under this initiative, specific cooperation projects to address nonproliferation, disarmament, counterterrorism, and nuclear safety issues will be supported.

These initiatives, that all point in the right direction, are, however, not enough. More has to be done. Assigning a higher priority to such initiatives would be an important step in reducing the probability of nuclear terrorism. Moreover, much remains to be done to improve international nuclear nonproliferation standards.

For instance, the physical protection and security of nuclear installations varies considerably from one country to the next, as do the lists of scenarios against which plants have to be protected. In some countries, such lists do not even consider the possibility of terrorism or sabotage (G. Bunn, 2000). Despite the increasing threat, there is no international treaty committing states to protect their weapon-ready material from theft or their nuclear plants from sabotage. The only relevant treaty is the 1980 Convention on the Physical Protection of Nuclear Material that lays down rules for material that is to be transported internationally. Currently, however, the treaty does not apply to material or plants that are used, stored, or transported nationally.

Conclusion

Technical barriers to crude nuclear weapon production may be lower than perceived. Dismissing the risk of nuclear terrorism on technical grounds may be an overly simplified—and possibly dangerous—approach for understanding the threat.

Although conventional weaponry remains the weapon of choice for most terrorists, some groups could use weapons of mass effect, hereunder nuclear weapons, if allowed the opportunity. Denying terrorists access to HEU or plutonium, the essential components of any nuclear device, is therefore of indispensable importance.

Acquisition of fissile material of sufficient qualities and quantities remains the most formidable obstacle to (crude) nuclear terrorist capabilities. Depending on the technical weapon sophistication, design, and material applied, quantities in the kilo range of weapons-usable material may be sufficient to produce a workable nuclear device. It is therefore imperative that preventing terrorists from gaining access to fissile materials be a high priority in the new global battle against terrorism. This can only be done by establishing stringent domestic and international standards of protection, control, and accounting.[17]

Such standards and norms, however, require political leadership not only to secure the financial resources urgently needed but also to make sure states invest politically in the long-term sustainability of the international nonproliferation regime.

Notes

1. Traditionally, biological, chemical, and nuclear weapons are collectively grouped in the weapons of mass destruction (WMDs) category. However, the destructive powers of the weapons differ significantly and the term *weapons of mass effect* may be more appropriate. Moreover, such a term may better cover the likely psychological consequences of their uses.
2. Both the Aum Shinrikyo, the Japanese cult that released sarin on the Tokyo metro, and bin Laden's Al Qaeda have had provable nuclear ambitions.
3. Other, and somewhat related, forms of nuclear terrorism are radiological terrorism and attacks on nuclear power plants. This will be outside the scope of this article. Moreover, in an article like this, there will always be a balance of how much to publish without actually assisting potential nuclear terrorists in their weaponization attempts. We have attempted to perform this act of balance by providing only basic—and widely available—technical background information. Moreover, the assessment is of a highly qualitative character, with far less quantitative information that is in fact available in the open (technical) literature (see also Kelle & Schaper, 2001).
4. Several terrorist researchers have observed this. The renowned phrase "terrorists want a lot of people watching, not a lot of people dead" was earlier coined by Jenkins (1977).
5. For more on this arrest, see Eggen (2002).
6. Bush's first-strike policy on terror cells may therefore be in vain. For more on this policy, see Allen and DeYoung (2002).
7. A nuclear device could be constructed using either plutonium dioxide, perhaps sintered into solid form, or plutonium in metal form. But the critical mass of plutonium dioxide is considerably greater than that of the metal. The critical mass of reactor-grade plutonium in the form of plutonium dioxide crystals is about 35 kg, if in spherical shape, whereas that of plutonium metal using the plutonium normally produced in a civil nuclear-power reactor (called reactor-grade plutonium) is about 13 kg (from Lovins, 1990). A terrorist group prepared to convert the dioxide to the metal would, therefore, need to acquire significantly less plutonium dioxide.
8. If the neutrons from the fission of a nucleus cause the fission of at least one other nucleus, a fission chain reaction is produced. This leads to a nuclear explosion. The minimum mass that can sustain a nuclear fission chain reaction is called the critical mass. The fission cross-section and the average number of neutrons per fission are somewhat smaller for U-235 than they are for Pu-239, making the critical mass larger. However, with uranium, there is essentially no problem of premature detonation due to neutrons from spontaneous fission.
9. A very rough assessment of the time we need to assemble a critical mass is the following: The neutrons per kg and second originating from spontaneous fission are 0.2 for U-235, 17 for U-238, 30 for Pu-239, and 100000 for Pu-240. Assuming that a very simple gun-type nuclear explosion device needs roughly about 50 kg HEU that is 93% enriched, then this mass produces almost 70 neutrons per second. As long as the assembly time is above a few milliseconds, there is still a rather high preignition probability. If you just drop the masses on each other, the assembly time is much too long, and the preignition probability is very high.
10. This device, which was a blue copy of the bomb dropped on Nagasaki, was tested in the New Mexico desert July 16, 1945.
11. A mixture of different explosives such as TNT and RDX or HMX also could be used.
12. The test was carried out with reactor plutonium provided by the United Kingdom. The isotopic composition of the material is classified but may have had some weapons-grade qualities. Generally, reactor-grade plutonium is significantly more radioactive than weapons-grade plutonium. This complicates the design, manufacture, and stockpiling of weapons. Moreover, due to the high neutron-background in reactor-grade plutonium, the material is less controllable. An increased risk of preignitions and fizzle yields will be the result. On the weapons usability of low-grade plutonium, see Kankeleit, Küppers, and Imkeller (1989), which has been translated by the Livermore Laboratory under the title "Report on the weapon usability of reactor-grade plutonium," and Mark (1993).

13. Alternatively, a neutron source could be added to the weapons-grade material to boost the neutron flux.
14. The figures are brought up-to-date with the Web page of the Institute of Science and International Security (ISIS): www.isis-online.org.
15. The United States of America, Russia, China, Great Britain, and France are all nuclear weapon states according to the Non-Proliferation Treaty (NPT).
16. For a comprehensive overview of political and technical challenges and possible policy options, see M. Bunn, Holdren, & Wier (2002).

References

Albright, D., Berkhout, F., & Walker, W. (1997). *Plutonium and highly enriched uranium 1996: World inventories, capabilities and policies, SIPRI.* Stockholm: Oxford University Press.

Allen, M., & DeYoung, K. (2002, June 3). Bush charts first-strike policy on terror cells. *The Washington Post.* Retrieved from http://tm0.com/IHT/sbct.cgi?s=205739983&i=555200&m=1&d=2724784

Alvarez, L. W. (1987). *The adventures of a physicist.* New York: Basic Books.

Anet, B. (n.d.). *Nuclear terrorism: How serious a threat to Switzerland?* Fact Sheet, Spiez Laboratory, Defense Procurement Agency. Retrieved from http://www.vbs.admin.ch/acls/e/current/fact_sheet/nuklearterrorismus/pronto

Bodansky, D. (1996). *Nuclear energy: Principles, practices and prospects.* New York: Woodbury.

Bunn, G. (2000, Summer). Raising international standards for protecting nuclear materials from theft and sabotage. *Nonproliferation Review.*

Bunn, M., Holdren, J. P., & Wier, A. (2002). *Securing nuclear weapons and materials: Seven steps for immediate action.* Report of the Project Managing the Atom, Belfer Center for Science and International Affairs, John F. Kennedy School of Government, Harvard University. Retrieved from http://ksgnotes1.harvard.edu/BCSIA/MTA.nsf/www/N-Terror

Cameron, G. (2000a, April). Nuclear terrorism reconsidered. *Current History.*

Cameron, G. (2000b, Spring). WMD terrorism in the United States: The threat and possible countermeasures. *Nonproliferation Review.*

Carnegie Analysis. (2001, November). Going nuclear: What it takes to build a bomb. Based on R. W. Jones, M. G. McDonough, T. Dalton, & G. Koblentz, *Tracking nuclear proliferation: A guide in maps and charts.* Washington, DC: Carnegie Endowment for International Peace.

Daughtry, E. E., & Wehling, F. (2000, Spring). Cooperative efforts to secure fissile materials in the NIS: Shortcomings, successes, and recommendations. *Nonproliferation Review.*

Eggen, D. (2002, June 11). "Dirty bomb" plot uncovered in U.S. *The Washington Post.* Retrieved from http://www.iht.com/articles/60917.html

European Union. (EU). (1999). *Council Joint Action of 17 December 1999 establishing a European Union Cooperation Programme for non-proliferation and disarmament in the Russian Federation.* Retrieved from http://www.eur.ru/eng/neweur/user_eng.php?func=rae_disarmament

G8. (2002, June 27). *Statement by the G8 leaders: The G8 global partnership against the spread of weapons and materials of mass destruction.* Kananaskis, Canada.

Galtung, J., & Ruge, H. M. (1965). The structure of foreign news. *Journal of International Peace Research, 1.*

Glanz, J. (2002, March 18). Despite new tools, detecting nuclear material is doubtful. *New York Times.*

International Atomic Energy Agency. (IAEA). (2000, September). *Nuclear research reactors in the world* (IAEA-RDS-3).

Jenkins, B. (1977). *The potential for nuclear terrorism* (Paper P-5876). Santa Monica, CA: RAND.

Kamp, K. H. (1996, July/August). An overrated nightmare. *Bulletin of the Atomic Scientists, 52*(4).

Kankeleit, E., Küppers, C., & Imkeller, U. (1989). *Bericht zur Waffentauglichkeit von Reaktor-plutonium* [Report on the weapon usability of reactor-grade plutonium] (Report IANUS-1/1989).

Kelle, A., & Schaper, A. (2001). *Bio- und Nuklearterrorismus—Eine kritische Analyse der Risiken nach dem 11. September 2001* [Bio- and nuclear terrorism: A critical analysis of the risks after 11 September 2001] (HSFK-Report). Frankfurt, Germany.

Laqueur, W. (1999). *The new terrorism: Fanaticism and the arms of mass destruction.* New York: Oxford University Press.

Lovins, A. B. (1990). Nuclear weapons and power-reactor plutonium. *Nature, 283,* 190, 284, 817–823.

Lugar, D. (2002, May 27). *Reducing the threats from weapons of mass destruction and building a global coalition against catastrophic terrorism.* Nuclear Threat Initiative Conference, Moscow.

MacKenzie, D., & Sinardi, G. (1995, July). Tacit knowledge, weapons design and the uninvention of nuclear weapons. *American Journal of Sociology, 101*(1).

Mark, C. J. (1991). *Some remarks on Iraq's possible nuclear weapon capability in light of some of the known facts concerning nuclear weapons.* Washington, DC: Nuclear Control Institute.

Mark, C. J. (1993). Explosive properties of reactor-grade plutonium. *Science & Global Security,* 4.

National Academy of Sciences. (1994). *Management and disposition of excess weapons plutonium.* Washington, DC: National Academy Press.

Ongoing speculation about missing Russian "suitcase nukes." (1997, October). *Disarmament Diplomacy,* 19. Retrieved from www.acronym.org.uk/19nukes.htm

Parrish. S., & Lepingwell, J. (1997, November). Are suitcase nukes on the loose? The story behind the controversy. *Center for Nonproliferation Studies Report.* Retrieved from www.cns.miis.edu/pubs/reports/lebedst. htm

Post, J. M. (2001, October 29–November 1). *Differentiating the threat of radiological/nuclear terrorism: Motivations and constraints.* Paper presented at the International Atomic Energy Agency (IAEA) Symposium on International Safeguards: Verification and Nuclear Material Security, Vienna, Austria.

President's Foreign Intelligence Advisory Board. (1999, June). *Science at its best, security at its worst: A report on security problems at the Department of Energy (the Rudman Report).* Washington, DC. Retrieved from www.fas.org/sgp/library/pfiab

Rapoport, D. C. (2002). Then and now: What have we learned? *Terrorism and Political Violence, 13*(3).

Schaper, A. (1999, March 5). *Zur Waffentauglichkeit verschiedener Uranbrennstoff.* Working paper for the expert commission of the German Ministry for Education and Research on the Research Reactor Garching.

Serber, R. (1992). *The Los Alamos primer: The first lectures on how to build an atomic bomb.* Berkeley: University of California Press.

Tønnessen, A. (2002). *Psychological reactions to nuclear threats: Information, coping and the uncertainties of outcome at the individual level.* Doctor of Philosophy Faculty of Medicine dissertation, University of Oslo, Sweden.

U.S. Department of Energy (U.S. DOE). (1996, February). *Plutonium: The first 50 years. United States plutonium production, acquisition, and utilization from 1944 to 1994.* Washington, DC.

U.S. General Accounting Office. (2001, February). *Nuclear nonproliferation: Security of Russia's nuclear material improving; further enhancements needed* (GAO-01-312).

Morten Bremer Maerli is a researcher and Ph.D. candidate at the Norwegian Institute of International Affairs, working on nuclear nonproliferation and prevention of nuclear terrorism. A physicist by training, from 1995 to 2000 he served as a senior executive officer at the Nuclear Safety Department of the Norwegian Radiation Protection Authority, with prime responsibility for control and protection of nuclear materials, gaining extensive experience concerning nuclear materials in northwest Russia.

Annette Schaper is senior research associate at the Peace Research Institute Frankfurt (PRIF). Her publications include the report *Bio- and Nuclear Terrorism* (co-author, in German, 2001), *Principles of the Verification for a Future Fissile Material Cutoff Treaty* (2001), *Tactical Nuclear Weapons: Options for Control* (co-author, 2000), *Emerging Nuclear Energy Systems: Their Possible Safety and Proliferation Risks* (co-author, 1999), and *A Nuclear Weapon Free World—Can It Be Verified?* (co-author, 1999).

Frank Barnaby is nuclear issues consultant to Oxford Research Group (ORG), and has been on ORG's Council of Advisers since its inception. He is a nuclear physicist by training and worked at the Atomic Weapons Research Establishment, Aldermaston between 1951 and 1957. He was on the senior scientific staff of the Medical Research Council when a university lecturer at University College London (1957–67). He was executive secretary of the Pugwash Conferences on Science and World Affaires in the late 1960s and director of the Stockholm International Peace Research Institute (SIPRI) from 1971 to 1981.

Matthew Bunn and Anthony Wier

The Seven Myths of
Nuclear Terrorism

In early 2003, Osama bin Laden sought and received from a radical Saudi cleric a religious ruling, or *fatwa*, that the use of a nuclear bomb against US civilians would be permissible under Islamic law—indeed mandatory—if it were the only means to stop US actions against Muslims. "If a bomb that killed 10 million of them and burned as much of their land as they have burned Muslims' land were dropped on them, it would be permissible," the ruling held. Also in 2003, proceedings in a Russian criminal case revealed that a Russian businessman had been offering $750,000 for stolen weapon-grade plutonium and had made contact with residents of the closed city of Sarov, home of one of Russia's premier nuclear weapons laboratories, to try to arrange a deal.

The terrorists are racing to get a nuclear bomb—and the removal of their sanctuary in Afghanistan has not stopped their efforts. What is needed now is a fast-paced global effort to lock down every nuclear weapon and every kilogram of plutonium and highly enriched uranium (HEU) before terrorists and criminals can get to them. The agreement on securing nuclear stockpiles reached at the Bush-Putin summit in February 2005 represents a promising first step—but sustained and energetic follow-through from the highest levels will be needed for President George W. Bush and Russian President Vladimir Putin to seize the opportunity to leave, as a lasting legacy, a world with a greatly reduced danger of nuclear terrorism.

The use of an actual nuclear bomb would be among the most difficult types of attack for terrorists to accomplish. Getting a nuclear bomb or the nuclear material to make one—particularly making the connection with people with access to such material and the ability to steal it—is difficult. Even after acquiring nuclear material, building a nuclear bomb, or setting off a stolen bomb, would be a great challenge.

Many policy makers and analysts appear to believe that these difficulties are so great that the danger of terrorists carrying out a nuclear attack is vanishingly small—unless, perhaps, they were sponsored by a state with nuclear capabilities. As Karl-Heinz Kamp, a noted European security analyst put it, "religious zealots or political extremists may present many dangers, but wielding nuclear bombs and killing hundreds of thousands of innocent people is not one of them."

Unfortunately, this view is profoundly wrong. While a nuclear attack would by no means be easy for terrorists to carry out, the probability that terrorists could succeed in doing so is large enough to justify doing "everything in our power," in President Bush's words, to prevent it.

If world leaders were convinced that the risk of a terrorist nuclear attack on a major city is substantial, and that there are actions they could take that would dramatically reduce that risk, they presumably would act, and act swiftly, to diminish this deadly threat. Therefore, dispelling the key myths that lead officials and policy elites to downplay the danger is crucial to building momentum for an effective response. Each of these myths, like all myths, contains an element of truth, but each is a dangerously weak proposition on which to rest the world's security against nuclear attack.

What Terrorists Want

The first myth is that terrorists are not especially interested in staging a nuclear catastrophe. Before the 9-11 attacks, it was often said that "terrorists want a lot of people watching, but not a lot of people dead." Many argued that terrorists would remain focused on violence at relatively modest scales, and would be highly unlikely to pursue the incineration of an entire city in a nuclear blast. A large number of security experts outside the United States still appear to believe that a serious terrorist effort to inflict destruction far beyond the scale of the World Trade Center or Pentagon attacks is highly unlikely.

This conclusion is correct for the vast majority of the world's terrorist groups. But Al Qaeda and the global jihadist network it has spawned are different. They are focused on a global struggle, for which the immense power of nuclear weapons might be seen as necessary, not a local battle for which such weapons are unneeded. They have gone to considerable lengths to justify to their supporters and audiences the use of mass violence, including the mass killing of innocent civilians. And they have explicitly set inflicting the maximum possible damage on the United States and its allies as one of their organizational goals.

Al Qaeda's followers believe that they, in effect, brought down the Soviet Union—that the mujahideen's success in forcing the Soviet Union from Afghanistan was a key factor leading to the Soviet collapse. And they appear to believe that the United States, too, is a "paper tiger" that can be driven to collapse—that the 9-11 attacks inflicted grievous damage on US economic power, and that still larger blows are needed to bring the United States down. As bin Laden put it in a message to his followers in December 2001, "America is in retreat by the grace of God Almighty and economic attrition is continuing up to today. But it needs further blows. The young men need to seek out the nodes of the American economy and strike the enemy's nodes." The notion that major blows could cause the collapse of the United States is, in essence, Al Qaeda's idea of how it will achieve victory. A nuclear blast incinerating an American city would be exactly the kind of blow Al Qaeda wants.

From long before the 2003 *fatwa,* bin Laden and the global jihadist network have made their desire for nuclear weapons for use against the United States and its allies explicit, by both word and deed. Bin Laden has called the acquisition of weapons of mass destruction (WMD) a "religious duty." Intercepted Al Qaeda communications reportedly have referred to inflicting a "Hiroshima" on the United States. Al Qaeda operatives have made repeated attempts to buy stolen nuclear material from which to make a nuclear bomb. They have tried to recruit nuclear weapon scientists to help them. The extensive downloaded materials on nuclear weapons (and crude bomb design drawings) found in Al Qaeda camps in Afghanistan make clear the group's continuing desire for a nuclear capability.

Getting the Bomb

A second myth, apparently believed by many officials, is that the nuclear materials required to make a bomb are nearly impossible for terrorists to obtain. Former Undersecretary of State John Bolton, for example, told the *Washington Post* that there had been no "significant risk of a Russian nuclear weapon getting into terrorist hands" for "some number of years," because of both Russia's own efforts to upgrade nuclear security and US assistance. Similarly, in December 2003, Russian Deputy Minister of Atomic Energy Sergei Antipov argued that "the nuclear thief does not stand a chance in Russia: it is nearly impossible to steal nuclear materials, let alone of weapons grade, such as plutonium or enriched uranium."

The reality, however, is that not only do nuclear thieves stand a chance in Russia (and elsewhere), they have repeatedly been successful, stealing weapons-usable nuclear material without setting off any alarm or detector. The International Atomic Energy Agency database of illicit trafficking incidents includes 18 cases of seizure of stolen HEU or plutonium confirmed by the states involved, and more cases are known to have occurred that the relevant states have not been willing to confirm. In one case in 1992, for example, a worker at a facility manufacturing fuel from 90 percent-enriched uranium exploited an accounting system designed to write off missing material as normal waste, stealing 1.5 kilograms (3.3 pounds) of HEU in a series of small, unnoticed thefts.

Unfortunately, around the world stocks of potential bomb material are dangerously insecure. In Russia, security for the many thousands of nuclear weapons and hundreds of tons of potential bomb material left over from the cold war has improved significantly, but tight budgets still mean broken alarms that do not get fixed and security forces without adequate body armor and communications equipment. Security culture remains a difficult problem, not only in Russia but around the world, with employees propping open security doors for convenience, and guards patrolling without ammunition in their guns to avoid accidental firing incidents. Yet these systems must defeat outsider and insider threats that are frighteningly high.

Elsewhere, some 130 civilian research reactors in more than 40 countries still use HEU as their fuel. Many have no more security than a night watch-man and a chain-link fence. The nuclear stockpile in Pakistan is heavily guarded, but faces deadly threats from armed remnants of Al Qaeda in the country and senior nuclear insiders who have marketed nuclear bomb technology around the globe. In short, the problem of insecure nuclear stockpiles is not just a Russia problem, it is a global problem.

Making connections between the terrorists or hostile states that might want stolen nuclear materials and the insiders in a position to steal them—or to provide information that would help outsiders steal them—seems to have been difficult in the past. Thieves who have stolen nuclear material have often had no particular buyer in mind, and have been caught as a result of their clumsy efforts to find a buyer. But the world cannot rely on criminals and terrorists failing to figure out how to make these connections. Given the case of the Russian businessman offering hundreds of thousands of dollars to anyone who could steal weapons-grade plutonium for sale to a foreign client, as well as cases of terrorist scouts succeeding in finding out where Russian nuclear warhead storage sites were and where and when nuclear warhead transport trains were moving, critical linkages already appear to be occurring.

Moreover, substantial smuggling networks are shipping a wide variety of contraband back and forth across Russia's borders to the Central Asian states and beyond; for example, much of the burgeoning Afghan heroin crop is believed to be shipped through Central Asia and Russia to markets in Europe. If even one of the cross-border criminal connections made by such means were successfully used to market stolen nuclear material to the terrorists seeking to get it, the world could face a devastating catastrophe.

Making the Bomb

Kamp, the European security analyst, has argued that "actually building [a crude nuclear weapon] is extremely difficult. A number of countries with vast resources and expertise, such as Iraq, have struggled unsuccessfully to produce one. It is difficult to imagine that a small terrorist group would find bomb-building any easier." This third myth about nuclear terrorism conflates the difficulty of producing the nuclear material needed for a bomb—the key area on which Iraq spent billions of dollars—with the difficulty of making a bomb once the material is in hand. (The CIA, for example, has estimated that obtaining stolen nuclear material from abroad would have cut the time Iraq required to make a bomb from years to months.)

The argument also misses the crucial distinction between making a safe, reliable, and efficient nuclear weapon suitable for delivery by a missile or a fighter aircraft—that is, the kind of nuclear weapon that a typical state would want for its arsenal, the design and construction of which would require substantial scientific and technical expertise—and the far simpler task of making a crude, unsafe, unreliable terrorist nuclear explosive that might be delivered by truck or boat.

If enough HEU is gathered in the same place at the same time, a nuclear chain reaction will occur. Indeed, considerable care has to be taken to prevent this from happening accidentally. The only trick to making this nuclear chain reaction a nuclear explosion is getting the material together fast enough. The atomic bomb that obliterated the Japanese city of Hiroshima at the end of World War II was a cannon that fired a projectile of HEU into rings of HEU—a "gun-type" bomb. The basic principles that need to be understood to make this kind of bomb are widely available in the open literature.

It is impossible to make an effective gun-type bomb with plutonium. Hence, if the terrorists had plutonium, or if the amount of HEU they had available was too small for a gun-type weapon, they would have to build an "implosion type" weapon. An implosion weapon uses a set of precisely shaped explosives arranged around a less-than-critical mass of HEU or plutonium to crush the atoms of material closer together, thereby setting off the nuclear chain reaction.

Designing and building an implosion bomb would be a significantly greater challenge for a terrorist group. But the possibility that terrorists could make at least a crude implosion bomb is very real—particularly if they obtained knowledgeable help, which they have been actively trying to do.

Repeated examinations of the question, "Could resourceful terrorists design and build a crude nuclear bomb if they had the needed nuclear material?" by nuclear weapons experts in the United States and elsewhere have concluded that the answer is "yes"—for either type of nuclear bomb. These conclusions were drawn before the 9-11 attacks demonstrated the sophistication and careful planning and intelligence gathering of which Al Qaeda is capable.

A detailed examination in 1977 by the US Office of Technology Assessment, drawing on all the relevant classified information, summed up the situation: "A small group of people, none of whom have ever had access to the classified literature, could possibly design and build a crude nuclear explosive device. They would not necessarily require a great deal of technological equipment or have to undertake any experiments. Only modest machine-shop facilities that could be contracted for without arousing suspicion would be required. The financial resources for the acquisition of necessary equipment on open markets need not exceed a fraction of a million dollars. The group would have to include, at a minimum, a person capable of researching and understanding the literature in several fields and a jack-of-all trades technician."

Given the importance of the question of whether terrorists could design and make a nuclear explosive, the answer has not been left to analysis alone, but has been subjected to "experiment" as well. In the 1960s, in an experiment sponsored by the Atomic Energy Commission, three recent physics graduates with no prior knowledge of nuclear weapons, nuclear materials, or explosives, and no access to classified information, successfully designed a workable implosion bomb. More recently, Senator Joseph Biden (D-DE), when serving as chairman of the Senate Foreign Relations Committee, asked the three US nuclear weapons laboratories whether terrorists, if they had the nuclear material, could make a crude but workable nuclear bomb. They answered "yes." Senator Biden reports that within a few months after he asked the question, the laboratories had actually built a gun-type device, using only components that, except for the nuclear material itself, were off the shelf and commercially available without breaking any laws. The device was brought into a secure Senate hearing room to demonstrate the gravity of the threat.

Having help from someone familiar with nuclear weapon design and construction would certainly be useful to terrorists trying to build a bomb—as would having actual bomb blueprints—though neither would be essential. Al Qaeda and its allies have actively attempted to recruit such help. For example, bin Laden and his deputy, Ayman al-Zawahiri, met at length with two senior Pakistani nuclear weapons experts, Sultan Bashiruddin Mahmood and Chaudari Abdul Majeed—both Taliban sympathizers with extreme Islamic views—and pressed them for information on making nuclear weapons. Similarly, in 2000, an official of Russia's National Security Council reported that the Taliban regime had attempted to recruit a nuclear expert from a Russian facility.

The world has also seen confirmed an extraordinary leakage of nuclear technology from Pakistan, including designs for uranium-enrichment centrifuges, components for such centrifuges, complete centrifuges apparently taken from Pakistan's own enrichment plant, consulting services for any problems the buyers might have, and even actual nuclear weapon blueprints. The leakers were apparently motivated both by money and by Islamic fervor.

Extreme Islamic views, including sympathy for Al Qaeda and the Taliban, appear to be commonplace in Pakistan's military and nuclear establishment, as they are in broader Pakistani society. Abdul Qadeer Khan, the former head of Pakistan's nuclear weapons program who confessed to leading this clandestine nuclear network, is a strident nationalist prone to harsh Islamic rhetoric. In 1984, Khan spoke of his opposition to "all the Western countries" as "enemies of Islam." He discussed the possibility that nuclear technology might be shared among Islamic countries, specifically mentioning Iraq, Libya, and Iran.

The possibility that Al Qaeda has access to complete blueprints for an implosion-type nuclear explosive—or may soon obtain such access—is very real. Of course, even with a working design, and even if the nuclear material could be acquired, manufacturing a weapon to the specifications called for in the design would not be a trivial task. But the potential availability of a nuclear bomb recipe reinforces the urgency of keeping the ingredients needed to make that recipe out of terrorist hands.

Stealing the Bomb

A terrorist group that gained receipt of a stolen nuclear weapon would face somewhat different challenges. The difficulty of setting off a stolen weapon would depend substantially on the specifics of the weapon's design. Many US nuclear weapons are equipped with "permissive action links" (PALs), which are effectively electronic locks, intended to make it difficult to detonate the weapon without first inserting an authorized code. Modern versions also have "limited try" features that will permanently disable the weapon if the wrong code is entered too many times, or if attempts are made to tamper with or bypass the lock. Older versions do not have all of these features, and therefore would provide somewhat less of an obstacle to a terrorist group attempting to detonate a stolen weapon it had acquired.

Unfortunately, what little information is publicly available suggests that earlier Soviet -designed weapons, especially older tactical weapons, may not be equipped with modern versions of safeguards against unauthorized use. In both the United States and Russia, thousands of nuclear weapons, particularly older varieties, have been dismantled in recent years, and it is likely that the bulk of the most dangerous weapons lacking modern safeguards have been destroyed. But neither country has made any commitment to destroy all of these weapons. Nuclear powers such as Pakistan, India, and China are not believed to incorporate equivalents to modern PALs in their weapons, although many of these weapons are probably stored in partly disassembled form.

Perhaps even more than in building a crude nuclear device of their own, terrorists seeking to detonate a stolen weapon would benefit greatly from the help of a knowledgeable insider, if such help could be procured. It may well be that an insider willing to help in stealing a weapon in the first place might also be willing to help in providing important information related to setting the weapon off. In the case of a weapon equipped with a modern PAL, without the actual use codes most insiders, too, would not be able to provide ready means to overcome the lock and use the weapon.

But if they could not figure out how to detonate a stolen weapon, terrorists might still remove the nuclear material from it and seek to fashion it into a bomb. If the weapon were a modern, highly efficient design using a modest amount of nuclear material, the material contained in it might not be enough for a crude, inefficient terrorist bomb. In any case, terrorists who had a stolen nuclear weapon would be in a position to make fearsome threats—for no one would know for sure whether they could set it off or not. The bottom line is that if a sophisticated terrorist group gained control of a stolen nuclear bomb or enough nuclear material to make one, there would be little grounds for confidence that they would be unable to use it.

The Search for Sponsors

A fourth myth is that the only plausible way that terrorists could get a nuclear bomb or the ability to make one is from a state. Richard Butler, the Australian diplomat who once headed the United Nations inspectors in Iraq, put this belief simply: "It is virtually certain that any acquisition by a terrorist group of nuclear explosive capability could be achieved only through the assistance of a state in possession of that capability—either given directly or provided by individuals within that state who have slipped out of its legal control."

This belief appears to be widespread within the Bush administration, and it determines the policy prescription: if the principal danger of terrorists' acquiring weapons of mass destruction is that hostile states might provide them, then the key element of the solution is to take on those hostile states and make sure that they do not provide them. This is the idea that animates the preemptive doctrine laid out in the administration's *National Security Strategy,* and it was fundamental to the argument for going to war with Iraq.

Indeed, although the president has warned again and again of the danger that terrorists might get weapons of mass destruction, the key policy prescription he draws in speech after speech is that the United States must take on hostile states before they provide such weapons to terrorists. It is this myth—the supposed need of state sponsorship—that above all others has led many of the most senior officials of the US government to place only modest priority on securing the world's stockpiles of nuclear weapons and materials.

In fact, the belief that terrorists would need the help of a state to gain a nuclear capability is simply wrong. As has been shown, even without any help from a state, without access to the classified literature, and potentially without any detailed knowledge of the relevant technical fields before they began their research, a small but dedicated and resourceful terrorist group could very plausibly design and build at least a crude nuclear bomb. And the danger that they could get the nuclear material needed to do so is very real.

Whatever measures are taken to reduce the already low chance that hostile states will actively decide to give nuclear weapons or the materials and expertise to make them to terrorists, such steps will do nothing to address the dozens of other terrorist pathways to the bomb around the world. These other pathways are opened by inadvertence rather than by conscious hostile acts by foreign powers—and they can only be successfully addressed by cooperation on a global scale. Wherever there is a cache of unsecured nuclear material, there is a vulnerability that an effective war on catastrophic terrorism must address—and quickly.

The Defense of Borders

A fifth mistaken belief is that it is possible to put in place around the United States and other major countries a security cordon that can reduce to a low level the risk that nuclear weapons and materials might be smuggled in. Customs and Border Protection Commissioner Robert C. Bonner, for example, was already arguing in mid-2002 that the measures the US Customs Service had taken since the 9-11 attacks had made it "much, much, much less likely" that "an international terrorist organization could smuggle in … any kind of radiological material or any kind of nuclear device."

Putting radiation detectors in place at US ports and airports, and at facilities that ship to the United States, has been the subject of substantial investment since 9-11 (though far less investment than would be needed to have a good chance of detecting even those things brought in by the most obvious routes). The millions of cargo containers that carry a large fraction of US imports every year have been a particular focus of such efforts.

While some investment in improving border detection capabilities is certainly worthwhile, this last line of defense will always be a very porous one. The physics of nuclear materials and nuclear weapons, the geography of the huge and complex American borders, and the economics of the global flow of people and goods conspire to make the terrorists' job easy and the defenders' job very difficult. Once stolen, the nuclear material for a bomb could be anywhere, and it is very difficult to detect, especially if shielding is used to limit radiation emissions.

Typical nuclear weapons are not large, and could readily be smuggled across America's or other nations' borders. The nuclear material needed for a bomb could easily fit in a suitcase. Even an assembled bomb could fit in a van, a cargo container, or a yacht sailed into a US harbor. Or the materials could be smuggled in and the bomb built at the site of its intended use. Terrorists have routinely used truck bombs that were physically larger than even a crude terrorist nuclear bomb would need to be.

America's borders stretch for thousands of miles, and millions of trucks, trains, ships, and airplanes in which nuclear material might be hidden cross them every year. Hundreds of thousands of illegal immigrants and thousands of tons of illegal drugs cross US borders every year, despite billions of dollars of investment in trying to stop them. (Some have said that the easiest way to bring nuclear material into the United States would be to hide it in a bale of marijuana.) Every nation's border is vulnerable to various types of illicit movement, be it drugs, terrorists, or the material needed to unleash nuclear terror.

The radiation from plutonium, and especially from HEU, is weak and difficult to detect at any significant distance, particularly if the material is surrounded with shielding. Technology does exist, and is being further developed, to make it possible to detect HEU or plutonium in objects right in front of the detectors (as might be possible at controlled border crossings), including finding hidden nuclear material in everything from airline baggage to cargo containers. Programs are now under way to put these kinds of detection capabilities into place at an increasing number of sites.

But these capabilities should not be exaggerated. While US Customs officers have been equipped with "radiation pagers," these would have essentially no chance of detecting HEU with even minor shielding, even if it were in a bag directly in front of the inspector. More sophisticated equipment that can detect both HEU and plutonium is being purchased—but it will be years before such equipment is installed and in use at all the major ports and border crossings into the United States.

Two points are crucial to understand. First, inspecting cargo as it arrives in the United States is not good enough: if a bomb were on a boat sailing into a major US harbor, it could wreak horrible devastation before the ship ever pulled up to the dock to be inspected. That is why many of the new initiatives after the 9-11 attacks involve putting detectors in place at foreign ports that ship to the United States. But it will take an immense and continuing effort to ensure that detection at these ports is effective, that there are no ready possibilities for bribing a customs official to let a container through uninspected and that already inspected containers cannot be tampered with.

Second, and more fundamentally, the number of possible pathways to smuggle a nuclear bomb or its ingredients into the United States is immense, and intelligent adversaries will choose whichever pathway remains undefended. If an effective system were put in place to make it very difficult to get nuclear material into the country in a cargo container without detection—and the country is a long way from that point today—then terrorists would bring their bomb in on a yacht, a fishing boat, or by some other means.

None of this is to say that the United States and other countries should not invest in attempting to make the nuclear smuggler's job as difficult as possible; they should. But it will never be possible to be confident in this last-ditch line of defense: the length of borders, the diversity of means of transport, and the ease of shielding radiation from plutonium or HEU all improve the odds too much for the terrorists. All that realistically can be hoped for is to make the easiest paths for terrorists more difficult. Primary reliance will still have to be placed on the first line of defense: keeping nuclear weapons and materials from being stolen in the first place.

The Military Option

President Bush and the senior officials of his administration repeatedly focus on maintaining the offensive against terrorist groups with global reach as the key to preventing catastrophic terrorism. As the president put it in his 2004 State of the Union address: "America is on the offensive against the terrorists. … As part of the offensive against terror, we are also confronting the regimes that harbor and support terrorists, and could supply them with nuclear, chemical, or biological weapons. The United States and our allies are determined: We refuse to live in the shadow of this ultimate danger."

The notion that such an offensive alone will be able to dispel this shadow of danger is the sixth myth of nuclear terrorism. Certainly it is crucial for the United States and its allies to do everything they can to destroy terrorist groups that have nuclear ambitions. A successful offensive, keeping these groups constantly on the run and off balance, can greatly reduce the likelihood that they would succeed in carrying out a nuclear attack. Indeed, the war on these groups launched since 9-11 has undoubtedly led to substantial disruptions in their ability to manage and carry out large and complex operations.

But as attack after attack around the world has demonstrated, Al Qaeda and a range of loosely affiliated groups retain the ability to carry out deadly strikes. There is little prospect that US intelligence on terrorist cells and their operations will ever be good enough to be confident that the terrorist operation required to assemble a crude nuclear device— perhaps only a cell of a few resourceful people, a machine shop, and off-the-shelf parts, other than the nuclear material itself—would be detected and destroyed before it could finish its deadly work.

A strong offense against terrorist groups with nuclear ambitions must be a critical part of the world's toolbox in reducing the danger of nuclear terrorism. But without a greatly increased effort to keep nuclear weapons and materials out of terrorists' hands in the first place, offensive action cannot reduce the threat to an acceptable level.

What States Want

The seventh myth applies to states, rather than terrorist groups. A number of analysts argue that states would not be especially interested in a stolen nuclear weapon or stolen material to make one, because what they want is an indigenous capability to produce the material for as many nuclear weapons as they think they need. Like the other myths, this myth leads those who believe it to downplay the importance of securing nuclear weapons and materials so that they cannot be stolen.

There is little doubt that states would *prefer* to have indigenous nuclear material production capabilities. But such capabilities are expensive and difficult to acquire. History demonstrates that states do indeed consider buying a bomb or the materials to make one if they believe they can avoid the cost and difficulty of putting together their own nuclear material production facilities; if they see an urgent need to establish a nuclear deterrent before their own nuclear material production succeeds; or if they face an international nonproliferation effort that is making it very difficult to establish their own production facilities.

The case of Iraq is illustrative. Baghdad repeatedly sought to purchase weapons-usable nuclear material from sources with connections in the former Soviet Union. When Iraq realized, after its invasion of Kuwait, that the United States and an international coalition would respond, it launched a "crash program" to build one bomb quickly, using the HEU it already had from its research reactors; it certainly would have been desperately eager to receive stolen HEU at that time.

Iran, too, has sought to purchase nuclear material. Iran put together a substantial procurement network to acquire a wide range of technologies and materials related to weapons of mass destruction, including from the former Soviet Union. Unclassified US intelligence assessments have repeatedly reported that Iran was also seeking to purchase stolen fissile material for a nuclear bomb.

Nor were these unique cases. Australia wanted to purchase a nuclear bomb when it was considering the nuclear weapons option. Egypt explored the possibility of a purchase when it was pursuing a nuclear weapons program. Libya, realizing the weakness of its own indigenous science and technology base, reportedly made repeated attempts to buy a nuclear weapon, including an unsuccessful approach to China. The more that nonproliferation efforts focus on limiting states' ability to build their own enrichment and reprocessing facilities, the more likely it is that additional states will pursue the purchase alternative.

Ultimately, if worldwide efforts to secure nuclear weapons and the materials needed to make them fail—creating a situation in which any dictator or terrorist who wanted a nuclear bomb could buy its essential ingredients on a nuclear black market— nothing else the world does to stem the spread of nuclear weapons is likely to work.

Reducing the Threat

The good news is that nuclear terrorism is a largely solvable problem. Plutonium and HEU—the essential ingredients of nuclear bombs—do not exist in nature, and are too difficult for terrorist groups to plausibly produce themselves. Hence, if nuclear bombs and bomb materials can be kept out of terrorist hands, nuclear terrorism can be reliably prevented: no material, no bomb.

A comprehensive, multifaceted approach is needed to block the terrorist pathway to the bomb. Offensive action against terrorist groups and defensive steps such as nuclear material detection at borders have their place in such an effort, but because nuclear materials and the activities needed to turn them into a bomb may be difficult to detect, both are weak reeds to rely on. The greatest leverage in reducing this threat is in preventing nuclear material from leaving the sites where it is supposed to be in the first place. Once it is out the door, the difficulty of finding and recovering it increases enormously.

The United States, other countries, and the International Atomic Energy Agency have a wide range of efforts under way to secure, monitor, and reduce stockpiles of nuclear weapons and materials in the former Soviet Union and around the world. These efforts have had real, demonstrable successes, representing an excellent investment in American and world security. Enough material for thousands of nuclear weapons has been permanently destroyed. Security for scores of vulnerable nuclear sites has been demonstrably improved. At least temporary civilian employment has been provided for thousands of nuclear weapons scientists and workers who might otherwise have been driven by desperation to seek to sell their knowledge or the materials to which they had access.

Yet, in virtually every aspect of these efforts, much more remains to be done. While US-funded security upgrades have been completed at some 70 percent of the sites where potential nuclear bomb material is located in the former Soviet Union, most of that material is in the remaining buildings where even the first round of initial upgrades has not yet been completed. Less than a fifth of Russia's stockpile of bomb uranium has been destroyed, and the process of destroying excess bomb plutonium has not even begun. Only a tiny fraction of Russia's excess nuclear weapons experts have yet received self-supporting civilian jobs (as opposed to short-term subsidized grants). Beyond the former Soviet Union, cooperative security upgrades are only just beginning, leaving many sites dangerously vulnerable.

Current US spending on all cooperative programs to secure and dismantle stockpiles of weapons of mass destruction around the world is in the range of $1 billion per year, supplemented to some degree by contributions from Europe and Japan. While that amounts to less than one-quarter of one percent of the US defense budget, the current obstacles to faster progress are more political and bureaucratic than budgetary. Disputes over access to sensitive sites, tax exemptions for threat reduction assistance, who pays in the event of an accident, and a number of other issues have been allowed to fester unresolved. As a result, dozens of sets of equipment for a "quick fix" of security at Russia's nuclear warhead bunkers are still sitting in warehouses, uninstalled, more than four years after the United States delivered them.

At their February 2005 summit, Presidents Bush and Putin issued a promising statement calling for expanded and accelerated cooperation to secure nuclear stockpiles, warning that nuclear terrorism was "one of the gravest threats our two countries face." As the leaders of the two countries that possess the vast majority of the world's nuclear weapons and weapons-usable nuclear material, Bush and Putin have a historic opportunity, building on the February 2005 accord, to lead a global partnership to lock down the world's nuclear stock-piles, a step that would dramatically reduce the danger of nuclear terrorism. But because the summit statement did not resolve any of the key impediments to progress, sustained and energetic presidential leadership on both sides will be needed to translate the statement's words into effective action. Many of the needed programs are already in place, and the necessary technology largely already exists. The key is mustering the political will to overcome the obstacles to progress.

Three steps are urgently needed if the world is to win the race to lock down these stockpiles before the terrorists and criminals get to them. First, the administration's new Global Threat Reduction Initiative (GTRI), focused on removing potential bomb material entirely from facilities around the world, must be implemented as quickly, flexibly, and comprehensively as possible. It should have as its target the removal of potential bomb material from the world's highest-risk facilities within four years. In the fall of 2004, the US Congress gave the administration both explicit, flexible authority and some additional funding for the GTRI to offer targeted incentives to convince facilities around the world to give up their weapons-usable material. The administration must now apply these tools quickly and creatively. At the same time, Congress should act to broaden the authority provided in 2004, and further boost the available funds.

Second, the United States and Russia must accelerate and strengthen their efforts to secure Russia's stockpiles. Putin should offer expanded access to all but the most sensitive areas of nuclear facilities to allow this cooperation to proceed, and Bush should offer reciprocal access to comparable areas of US facilities, as he pledged to do in his end-of-year press conference in 2004. The two sides should also quickly agree on approaches to carry out needed security upgrades for those areas that genuinely are too sensitive for either side to allow the other's experts to visit, such as using photographs and videotapes to confirm that work has been done as agreed. The two countries need to compromise on the problem of liability in the event of an accident (the United States has been insisting that Russia accept 100 percent of the liability even in the event of intentional sabotage by US personnel). The liability issue has already delayed efforts to destroy thousands of bombs' worth of plutonium by several years, and could bring the entire edifice of cooperation to secure and dismantle cold war stockpiles crashing down if not resolved soon: the overall agreement that governs this work expires in June 2006, and will not be extended unless a compromise is reached.

Putin needs to allocate the necessary resources to ensure strong security for Russia's nuclear stockpiles; give his nuclear agencies the mission, authority, and resources to set and enforce effective nuclear security rules; direct that nuclear weapons and materials be consolidated in far fewer buildings and sites, which will achieve more security at lower cost; and pledge to sustain effective security and accounting for all of Russia's nuclear stockpiles after international assistance comes to an end. The high-level US-Russian group established at the February 2005 summit should provide a venue for pursuing all these critical steps.

Third, the United States, Russia, and other countries must lead a global effort to lock down all the vulnerable nuclear caches worldwide that cannot simply be removed or eliminated, as quickly as possible—and to secure it to standards that ensure that these caches are safeguarded against the threats that terrorists and criminals have demonstrated they can pose. Considerable creativity and perseverance will be required to ensure that effective security measures are taken in countries such as Pakistan, India, Israel, or even China, where it is not likely that foreign experts will be allowed to visit the key facilities to review security or help to improve it.

Making all this happen will require sustained White House leadership. A full-time senior official is needed, with the president's ear, to lead the myriad efforts in the many agencies that are working on pieces of the job of blocking the terrorist pathway to the bomb, and to keep this issue on the front burner at the White House day-in and day-out.

The Day After

In hearings held after a terrorist nuclear attack to determine who was responsible for allowing this event to occur and what should be done to prevent it from happening again, what would government officials and policy makers want to be able to say they had done to forestall such a horrible catastrophe?

The terrorists have made clear that they want nuclear weapons, and are working to get them. A continuing stream of attacks and intelligence analyses makes clear that Al Qaeda is regrouping, recruiting and training new operatives, and still seeking to carry out catastrophic attacks on the United States and other countries. President Bush has eloquently warned that "history will judge harshly those who saw this coming danger but failed to act." The question remains: on the day after a terrorist nuclear attack, what will we wish we had done to prevent it? And why are we not doing that now?

Matthew Bunn is a senior research associate in the Project on Managing the Atom in the Belfer Center for Science and International Affairs at Harvard University's John F. Kennedy School of Government. Bunn received his bachelors' and masters' degrees in political science, specializing in defense and arms control, from the Massachusetts Institute of Technology in 1985.

Anthony Wier is a research associate with the Project on Managing the Atom at Harvard University. He has a master of public affairs and a master of arts in Russian, East European, and Eurasian Studies from the LBJ School of Public Affairs at the University of Texas at Austin, and a bachelor of arts summa cum laude from Trinity University in San Antonio.

Chapter 2.2

Radiological Dispersal Devices

Charles D. Ferguson and Joel O. Lubenau

Securing U.S. Radioactive Sources

The catastrophic attacks of September 11, 2001, and the anthrax mailings that took place shortly thereafter highlighted the nation's vulnerability to unconventional forms of terrorism. One type of threat that has recently received close attention from policymakers and the news media is the potential for attacks with radiological dispersal devices (RDDs). Such weapons, which include so-called dirty bombs, are designed to spread radioactive contamination, causing panic and disruption over a wide area. The number and diversity of radioactive sources pose a serious security challenge, and the United States has yet to take all the necessary steps to strengthen controls to match the heightened terrorist threat.

Most people are aware of the danger of radioactive material associated with nuclear power, but the potential sources of material for an RDD include a large class of commercial radioactive sources used in medicine, industry, and scientific research. Of the millions of sources in use worldwide, only a small fraction, if maliciously employed in an RDD, are powerful enough to cause serious harm to human health. Yet this fraction still includes tens of thousands of sources of the type and quantity useful for a potent RDD. (See the sidebar for information on the types of potentially high-risk sources within the United States.)

Although an RDD uses radioactive materials, even a very powerful RDD would cause far less damage than a nuclear weapon. The difference between a dirty bomb and a nuclear bomb is, as Graham Allison of Harvard University so eloquently put it, "the difference between a lightning bug and lightning." Unlike a nuclear weapon, an RDD would likely cause few deaths from the direct effects of exposure to ionizing radiation. Nevertheless, many people could develop cancer over years or decades. And the costs of decontamination and, if necessary, rebuilding could soar into the billions of dollars, especially if an RDD attack occurred in a high-value urban setting. Moreover, terrorists detonating RDDs would try to sow panic by preying on people's fears of radioactivity.

Although there have been no actual RDD detonations, two case studies involving radioactive sources point to the psychological, social, and economic damage that could result from an RDD. First, in 1987 in Goiania, Brazil, scavengers stole a powerful radioactive source (containing about 1,375 curies of radioactivity) from an abandoned medical clinic. Not realizing what it was, they broke the source open. Four people died, more than 100,000 others had to be monitored for contamination, and cleanup costs amounted to tens of millions of dollars. The second case study concerns the U.S. steel industry. Radioactive sources that found their way into scrap yards have accidentally been melted in steel mills 21 times, most recently in July 2001. Those contamination incidents have cost the steel industry an estimated quarter billion dollars. In response, the industry has installed radiation detectors in scrap yards, as well as at the entrances of and throughout mills. Such "defense in depth" appears to have reduced the frequency of incidents.

The sources that fall outside regulatory controls are not limited to those that show up in scrap yards. In the United States, a radioactive source is lost, stolen, or missing about once a day. Although most of those "orphan" sources are relatively weak, they could still cause panic and disruption if detonated in an RDD.

Federal agencies are now reviewing and revising their programs and policies to improve the security of radioactive sources against theft, diversion, and use in radiological terrorism. It is a challenging assignment: Regulatory responsibilities were fragmented enough before the new Department of Homeland Security was added to the mix. This is an appropriate time to review the origins of security practices and past problems with the security of radioactive sources in order to gain insights into whether current efforts to improve security are soundly based and properly directed. It is also essential to examine whether the United States has a well-developed, coordinated national plan for managing the risks of radiological terrorism.

Even before the terrorist attack of September 11, 2001, the Nuclear Regulatory Commission (NRC) had begun action to tighten controls on general-licensed radioactive sources, in particular those used in manufacturing and other settings, because disused sources were sometimes being found mixed with scrap metal. After September 11, the NRC requested that licensees undertake more stringent interim security measures. Although the details of the measures are sensitive information not intended to be published openly, we know that these security improvements were meant to increase security mainly at locations containing very highly radioactive material. The enhanced security entails, among other efforts, restricting access to radioactive material and coordinating the security efforts of licensees with local and federal law enforcement. The NRC's security plans use as a starting point the results of a joint Department of Energy and NRC study identifying radioactive sources in the highest risk categories based on potential health effects resulting from radiation exposure. As we will explain, to realize maximum effectiveness the plans should incorporate a multifaceted approach that also includes cooperation and shared responsibility among government agencies, suppliers, and licensees.

Life Cycle of Radioactive Sources

Developing a systematic plan requires understanding the stages of a source's life cycle and the security measures in place at each stage. The first stage is the production of the radioisotopes that power radioactive sources. Such radioisotopes are made either in nuclear reactors or in particle accelerators. Reactor-produced radioisotopes present a greater security risk because they typically have longer half-lives and are generated in larger quantities. Government-required security standards are typically in place at the reactor sites, but the United States is not a leading producer of commercial radioisotopes at reactors.

The next stage involves placing radioisotopes into radioactive sources and manufacturing the equipment that will contain the sources. Major U.S. equipment manufacturers import most of their radioisotopes from foreign reactors. These companies are believed to protect their materials using the same industrial security measures that are applied to other high-value goods. After September 11, the NRC advised manufacturers to step up security. Sources are shipped to hospitals, universities, food irradiation facilities, oil well drilling sites, industrial radiography facilities, and other venues. Security practices vary according to the type of facility and activity. Food irradiation plants, which employ highly radioactive materials, probably have tighter security than hospitals, for example.

Security is of particular concern in the oil industry, which often transports radioactive sources across borders. Recently, a high-risk radioactive source was stolen from a major oil company in Nigeria. Of the more than 22,000 portable radioactive gauges in use, about 50 are reported stolen each year, according to the NRC. To prevent such thefts, the NRC announced in July 2003 that it is considering a new rule that would require portable gauges to be secured with at least two independent physical controls whenever they are left unattended.

Some radioactive sources pass through yet another phase if they are shipped overseas. Current U.S. regulations allow the import and export (except to the embargoed countries of Cuba, Iran, Iraq, Libya, North Korea, and Sudan) of most high-risk radioactive sources under a general license, meaning that the government is not required to conduct a detailed review of the credentials of the sender and recipient. The NRC is reportedly considering a proposed rule change to remedy this problem and has already instituted interim security measures. In March, during Operation Liberty Shield, licensees were requested to give the NRC at least 10 days' notice of any shipment of highly radioactive sources. The commission is also working closely with U.S. Customs to develop a source-tracking database. Monitoring began in earnest in April, and preliminary data suggest that a few hundred shipments of highly radioactive sources enter or leave the United States every year.

A radioactive source eventually becomes ineffective as its potency declines, but the "disused" source might still contain potent amounts of radioactivity. Ideally, users would dispose of or recycle such sources quickly, but because disposal is expensive and proper facilities are few, users often hold on to their sources. The risk of loss, theft, or seizure by terrorists goes up accordingly. Not all source manufacturers provide disposal or recycling services, so the government also must provide safe and secure disposal sites. As we explain below, the current disposal system in the United States is in dire need of repair.

Other issues attend the shipment of sources between stages of their life cycle. The U.S. Department of Transportation (DOT) regulates shipments within the United States, adjusting security measures according to the size of the shipment. Labeling and packaging requirements provide for the protection of transportation workers and bystanders both in routine transit and under accident conditions. DOT sets packaging specifications for small quantities of radioactive material, and the NRC is responsible for large quantities. Although the security measures for large, highly radioactive shipments are reportedly stringent, both industry and parts of the government have resisted implementing improved security efforts such as background checks of drivers and adequate arming of guards.

Alternative Technologies

The International Commission on Radiological Protection and the congressionally chartered National Council on Radiation Protection and Measurements (NCRP) hold as a pillar of radiation protection the principle of justification. This principle calls for evaluating the risks and benefits of using a radioactive source for a particular application. Users are supposed to opt for a nonradioactive alternative if there is one that provides comparable benefit and less risk, including the risk associated with waste management.

The NRC has taken the position that advocating alternative technologies is not part of its mission. The commission's reasons, which have not been explained, might be that it believes it is only in the business of regulating the radioactive sources that licensees choose to use, not the business of overseeing licensees' decisions to use them. Nonetheless, it can be argued that the NRC's charge from Congress—to protect public health, safety, and property as well as provide for the common defense and security—is sufficient to require the commission to adopt the principle of justification and, at least in principle, to encourage the consideration of alternative technologies. This is not to suggest that the NRC should second-guess licensees' decisions to use radioactive sources, simply that the commission should ensure that licensees are making informed decisions that take into account justification and technological alternatives. Applying the principle of justification would reduce the number of radioactive sources in use and thus cut the risk of an RDD event occurring.

Radioactive Sources in the United States

Because the United States lacks a comprehensive national inventory of radioactive sources, their exact number is unknown. In 1998, Joel O. Lubenau and James G. Yusko estimated that some 2 million U.S. devices contained licensed radioactive sources. Some devices, such as radiography cameras and teletherapy units, contain a single source; others, such as large irradiators for sterilization and food preservation, some medical devices, and certain nuclear gauges, contain multiple sources. About a quarter of the devices, including those containing the largest sources, are used under a specific license, the rest under a general license. The absence of a national inventory also hinders reporting the number of radioactive devices or sources by category of use. The following table lists many of the more common practices using larger radioactive sources. The data are derived from IAEA-TECDOC-1344.

Practice	Typical Radioisotopes	Typical Radioactivity Amounts (Curies)
Radioisotope thermoelectric generators	Strontium-90	20,000
	Plutonium-238	280
Sterilization & food irradiators	Cobalt-60	4,000,000
	Casium-137	3,000,000
Self-contained & blood Irradiators	Cobalt-60	2,400–25,000
	Cesium-137	7,000–15,000
Single-beam teletherapy	Cobalt-60	4,000
	Cesium-137	500
Multibeam teletherapy	Cobalt-60	7,000
Industrial radiography	Cobalt-60	60
	Iridium-192	100
Calibration	Cobalt-60	20
	Cesium-137	60
	Americium-241	10
High and medium dose rate brachytherapy	Cobalt-60	10
	Cesium-137	3
	Iridium-192	6
Well logging	Cesium-137	2
	Americium-241/beryllium	20
	Californium-252	0.03
Level & conveyor gauges	Cobalt-60	5
	Cesium-137	3–5

The National Academy of Sciences, the International Atomic Energy Agency (IAEA), the NCRP, and the Health Physics Society have all recommended that users consider alternative technologies.

One U.S. industry that is adopting alternative technologies is steel, itself no stranger to the risks and costs of radioactive contamination. Steel mills use nuclear gauges to monitor the level of molten steel in continuous casters. If molten steel breaks through the casting system and strikes a gauge, the gauge housing and even the source could melt, causing contamination. Accordingly, mill operators are replacing nuclear gauges on continuous casters with eddy current and thermal systems, even though they are more expensive. The tradeoff—the cost of alternative technology versus the cost of contamination—makes the new systems a smart choice.

Some of the national laboratories are performing R&D to replace the most dangerous radioactive sources (those containing very dispersible radioactive compounds) with sources that pose less of a security hazard. Unfortunately, technology developed at the national labs is not readily available to the marketplace. At an IAEA conference on the radioactive source industry in April 2003, major source producers reportedly expressed interest in forming public-private partnerships to bring these alternative technologies to market. In the United States, such partnerships are sorely needed.

Licensing Fraud

A major vulnerability of the process for licensing radioactive sources is its susceptibility to fraud. The first noteworthy U.S. case became public in 1996, when Stuart Lee Adelman pled guilty to fraudulently obtaining radioactive material and was sentenced to a five-year prison term. Adelman, also known as Stuart von Adelman, posed as a visiting professor at the University of Rochester and, illicitly using university resources, obtained licensed materials from suppliers. That was not his first such crime. In 1992, he was arrested in Toronto on a U.S. fugitive warrant and was found to have illegally obtained radioactive material and stashed it in a public storage locker.

Although no definite evidence points to terrorism in the Adelman case, an assistant U.S. District Attorney remarked that the radioactive material found in Canada may have been part of a scam to obtain money from terrorists. Adelman, who reportedly possessed a graduate degree in nuclear physics, had been employed by a state licensing agency and had worked as a radiation safety officer at two universities, illustrating the alarming potential for insider crime.

Fraudulent licenses might also be used to import radioactive sources into the United States. In May 2003, Argentina's nuclear regulatory agency red-flagged a request from a party in Texas for a teletherapy-sized shipment of radioactive cobalt. That quantity could provide enough radioactivity for a potent RDD. When the "license" presented to the supplier proved to be nothing more than a dental x-ray registration certificate, a concerned Argentine official contacted the Texas radiation control program. The FBI is investigating to determine whether the incident was a serious attempt to fraudulently import radioactive material, a hoax, or a test of the regulatory system.

Such incidents teach many lessons. First, fraud is not hypothetical; it is happening. Second, creation of a master list on the Web of regulatory authorities worldwide would facilitate communication among officials (in the Argentine case, the official had to search the Internet to find the relevant agency in Texas). The IAEA could host such a list. Third, regulatory agencies should exchange information about possible fraud and do so expeditiously. In the United States, information needs to flow more freely between the NRC, the Agreement States (33 U.S. states that regulate certain radioactive materials under NRC agreements), and other federal agencies. Internationally, such communication could be encouraged by the IAEA. Finally, suppliers should routinely verify requests for the purchase of large quantities of radioactive material.

Disposal

One of the most worrisome unresolved problems concerning the safety and security of radioactive sources in the United States is providing for adequate end-of-life cycle management. In principle, users can return their disused sources to manufacturers, transfer them to other users, store them, or ship them to government disposal sites. However, none of those methods is foolproof.

The option to return radioactive sources to the manufacturer is an acceptable disposal method to list on an application for a license, but manufacturers can and do go out of business. That has happened in the case of some teletherapy sources, which usually contain cobalt-60 in kilocurie quantities and hence meet NRC criteria for high security concerns. Owners of General Electric or Westinghouse teletherapy machines cannot return sources to the manufacturer, because neither company makes the machines any longer.

In the United States, the use of teletherapy units has declined as accelerators, which generate cancer-treating radiation without using a radioactive source, have replaced them. Some units have been abandoned or are in the possession of clinics that have gone bankrupt. In other cases, former users have exported their sources to countries that still use the technology. Many of the recipient countries are in the developing world, which taps into this secondhand market. As the IAEA has emphasized, more than half of the world's nations, including most of the developing world, have inadequate regulatory controls. Thus, the secondhand market could pose increasing security risks.

Thousands of high-risk disused radioactive sources throughout the United States have no clear disposal pathway and could therefore fall into the hands of terrorists. Only three disposal sites for low-level waste—a classification that includes most disused radioactive sources—operate in the United States. These sites are located in Barnwell, South Carolina; Hanford, Washington; and Clive, Utah. The Clive disposal site can accept waste from all states, but it handles only the lowest-level waste. The other two sites are available only to certain states. Starting in 2008, when restrictions on access to the Barnwell site take effect, most states will have no disposal site for the bulk of their low-level radioactive waste. Unwanted radioactive materials will accumulate at hospitals, universities, and other facilities where they are vulnerable to loss, theft, or seizure by terrorists. Even when a disposal site is available, disused sources are often kept at relatively unsecured facilities for long periods because of high disposal costs. An estimated half million radioactive sources in the United States belong to this category, but only a small fraction of these sources could fuel potent RDDs.

Why does the country face this problem? In 1986, Congress passed the Low Level Radioactive Waste Policy Amendments Act, which placed responsibility for most low-level waste disposal on the states and gave the federal government responsibility for disposal of the higher-level waste. But because of strong resistance to siting low-level disposal facilities on states' land, fewer commercial disposal sites are operating today than when Congress enacted the legislation. Another problem is that after 17 years, the federal government has yet to provide a permanent repository for the higher-activity waste. Indeed, it has only begun to make progress toward securing some of this radioactive material in temporary storage.

Although the federal effort got off to a slow start, the Off-Site Source Recovery (OSR) Project of the U. S. Department of Energy (DOE) has in recent years rounded up more than 7,000 disused sources, most of them radioactive enough to pose a security concern. Thousands more sources that remain to be secured are now registered on the OSR database. Despite the project's relative success, a recent U.S. General Accounting Office audit found that the OSR suffers from a lack of DOE management support and that the project has not identified a pathway toward final disposal of the higher-activity waste. The project also faces an impending funding shortage: The supplemental support issued by Congress in October 2002 is slated to run out next year.

The United States lacks a comprehensive functioning national program for managing the radioactive waste generated from disused sources. As a step toward a solution, regional repositories could be established to securely store unwanted sources until their final disposal. Existing secure federal sites could be used for interim storage as a way to cut through the roadblocks that have stalled the states from siting disposal facilities. In parallel, the federal government can move toward a decision on final disposal. The states still have a crucial role to play by pressing the federal government to use its resources to correct the problem. New legislation must establish clear requirements for DOE to set up, without delay, safe and secure federal regional storage facilities for unwanted radioactive sources.

Managing the Risks

Clearly, other measures are needed to close the gaps in the security of radioactive sources. The priority that the NRC assigns to the security requirements for different radioactive sources should take into account the kind of damage they would inflict if they were used in an RDD. The commission's current priority system is based on preventing radiation injuries and deaths, which, in the case of a terrorist act using an RDD, are likely to be limited. The major consequences of an RDD would be psychosocial and economic, and the NRC's system for prioritizing sources does not reflect that.

Although psychosocial effects can be difficult to quantify, there is an ample body of data on the economic effects. The cost for contaminated steel mills to shut down and clean up and dispose of radioactive waste averaged $12 million per event. Most of the sources that caused that damage would not have met NRC criteria for high priority. But radioactive sources that are less likely to cause radiation injuries or deaths are still quite capable of causing significant economic damage. The U.S. priority system for radioactive sources needs to be refined to account for such consequences.

Of course, the responsibility for improving radioactive source security does not fall solely on the U.S. government. Suppliers, users, and the states have a fundamental interest in closing gaps and, equally important, can contribute ideas to improve safety and security. Fostering partnerships that facilitate information exchange and cooperation among federal agencies, state regulators, suppliers, and states would do much to reduce the risk of radioactive sources going astray. Indeed, given the number and diversity of radioactive sources, cooperation and shared responsibility are the only way to achieve the highest level of security.

Recommended Reading

Committee on Science and Technology for Countering Terrorism, National Research Council, "Nuclear and Radiological Threats," chapter 2 in *Making the Nation Safer: The Role of Science and Technology in Countering Terrorism* (Washington, D.C.: National Academy Press, 2002) (available at http://www.nap.edu/html/stct/39-64.pdf).

DOE/NRC Interagency Working Group on Radiological Dispersal Devices, *Radiological Dispersal Devices: An Initial Study to Identify Radioactive Materials of Greatest Concern and Approaches to Their Tracking, Tagging, and Disposition*, Report to the Nuclear Regulatory Commission and the Secretary of Energy, May 2003.

Charles D. Ferguson, Tahseen Kazi, and Judith Perera, *Commercial Radioactive Sources: Surveying the Security Risks*, Occasional Paper No. 11 (Center for Nonproliferation Studies, January 2003) (available at http://cns.miis.edu/pubs/opapers/op11/index.htm).

Charles D. Ferguson, "Reducing the Threat of RDDs," *IAEA Bulletin*, 45, no. 1 (2003) (available at http://www.iaea.or.at/worldatom/Periodicals/Bulletin/Bull451/article3.pdf).

General Accounting Office, *Nuclear Nonproliferation: DOE Action Needed to Ensure Continued Recovery of Unwanted Sealed Radioactive Sources* (Washington, D.C.: GAO-03-483, April 2003).

Health Physics Society, "State and Federal Action is Needed for Better Control of Orphan Sources" (HPS Position Statement, April 2002) (available at http://hps.org/documents/orphansourcesposition.pdf).

International Atomic Energy Agency, *Categorization of Radioactive Sources*, (IAEA-TECDOC-1344, June 2003, Vienna, Austria).

Michael A. Levi and Henry C. Kelly, "Weapons of Mass Disruption," *Scientific American* (November 2002).

Joel O. Lubenau and Daniel J. Strom, "Safety and Security of Radiation Sources in the Aftermath of 11 September 2001," *Health Physics* 88, no. 2 (August 2002): pp. 155–164.

Joel O. Lubenau and James G. Yusko, "Radioactive Material in Recycled Metals—An Update," *Health Physics* 74, no. 3 (March 1998): pp. 293–299.

National Council on Radiation Protection and Measurements, *Management of Terrorist Events Involving Radioactive Material* (NCRP Report No. 138, October 2001).

Charles Ferguson is a fellow for Science and Technology at the Council on Foreign Relations and an assistant professor at Georgetown University. He recently served as scientist-in-residence at the Center for Nonproliferation Studies of the Monterey Institute of International Studies, and co-directed a project that systemically assessed how to prevent and respond to nuclear and radiological terrorism. This project's major findings were published in *The Four Faces of Nuclear Terrorism* (2005).

Joel Lubenau is a senior advisor to the Center for Nonproliferation Studies' Washington Office. He is an associate editor of *Operational Radiation Safety,* editorial reviewer for *Health Physics,* adjunct member of the National Council on Radiation Protection and Measurements, and a fellow member of the Health Physics Society.

Chapter 2.3

Sabotage of Nuclear Facilities and Other Critical Infrastructure

Gavin Cameron

Nuclear Terrorism: Reactors & Radiological Attacks After September 11

Attacks on Reactors

Introduction

Reactors, with their nuclear component, are potentially attractive targets for terrorists, in large part because they offer a means for the group to achieve a spectacular attack that sets them apart from other groups and ensures that they are noticed as an organization. There are a variety of possible motivations that might lead terrorists to consider such an attack, varying from an attempt to create a barricade-and-hostage situation for the purposes of blackmail; to steal strategic nuclear material, either as a prelude to a radiological attack or as part of an effort to develop a nuclear capability of their own; or, finally, to destroy the reactor itself.[1] These various types of incidents are of variable probabilities. Terrorism is surprisingly derivative and certain tactics rise and fall in use amongst groups. For example, barricade-and-hostage attacks were, relatively, very common in the 1970s and early 1980s with the spate of embassy sieges and aircraft hijackings. However, as an increasing number of states developed their own special police or military units to deal with the threat and security at vulnerable sites was improved, the dangers of such an action rose for the terrorist and their likelihood of success and escape afterwards fell. Consequently, so did the popularity of the tactic. However, as the potential dangers of any incident at a reactor are so great, all threats or attacks have to be treated extremely seriously. This is particularly so since the terrorist attacks of 11 September, 2001 on the World Trade Center and Pentagon. The airline hijackings on this date were unlike their predecessors in the 1970s: the terrorists were not intent on escaping after the attack. The hijacking was not the principal aspect of the terrorists' action, merely a means to the greater act of violence: crashing the planes and the passengers aboard into World Trade Center and Pentagon. The attacks appeared to usher in a new era of high casualty and high consequence terrorism, unmatched even by previous incidents such as Aum Shinrikyo's release of sarin in the Tokyo subway in March 1995.

This paper will assess the threat of terrorist attacks on nuclear reactors or attacks using radiological materials. It will begin by examining the danger posed by aircraft being crashed into a reactor and compare that threat with the more familiar one posed by terrorists using truck bombs against reactors. The paper will then assess the history of terrorism directed against nuclear facilities; the problems posed by insiders, both as potential saboteurs and thieves of nuclear material; the risk to parts of the nuclear fuel cycle other than reactors; and finally, the threat of radiological terrorism. The paper concludes that although the ramifications for the nuclear industry of the attacks on 11 September remain unclear, better protection of facilities and materials is clearly justified.

11 September

Even before 11 September, such an event was not as far-fetched as it at appeared. In November 1972, three criminals hijacked a Southern Airways flight between Birmingham and Memphis and threatened to crash the plane into AEC's research facility at Oak Ridge, Tennessee, unless they were flown to Havana, Cuba.[2] In December 1994, members of the Armed Islamic Group (GIA) hijacked an Air France plane and planned to blow it up over Paris in a suicide mission.[3]

Most of the world's 440 nuclear power reactors would be highly vulnerable to a similar attack to those launched on 11 September: a passenger aircraft laden with fuel being crashed into the building. The impact and fire caused by such an attack would likely compromise the containment system that surrounds reactors, increasing the risk of a radioactive leak. Many containment facilities are designed to withstand the impact of a small plane: the concrete dome may be 3 feet thick and heavily reinforced by steel, with a 1inch to 4 inch lining, also made of steel. There may be a further two concrete walls near the reactor vessel, each one foot thick and reinforced with steel bars. The reactor vessel itself is made of high-carbon steel, about 4 inches to 6 inches thick.[4] In the United States, reactors are designed to withstand both earthquakes and hurricanes.[5] This might or might not be enough to prevent the reactor vessel itself being broken open by a plane crashing into the facility. The exact nature of the damage caused by such an attack would depend on the size of plane, amount of fuel it carried, speed and angle of impact. Although the emergency coolant systems would ordinarily prevent an explosion, it is possible that both primary and back up systems could also be severely compromised by such an attack, possibly leading to a steam explosion at the reactor.[6] It is unlikely to be feasible for existing reactors to be engineered to withstand the impact of such a plane, although new reactors might be planned with this as one criterion.

There are suggestions also that the 11 September terrorists considered attacks on US nuclear facilities: Mohammed Atta, leader of the cell responsible for the attacks last month, sought information at Tennessee's Martin Campbell airport last Spring about local landmarks, including a nuclear reactor, a chemical plant and a dam.[7] More ominous still, United Airlines 93, travelling between Newark, New Jersey, and San Francisco on 11 September, but which crashed in rural Pennsylvania, may have been targeted at nuclear reactors in the south of the state. The plane was hijacked in the area of Cleveland or Pittsburgh and then did a sharp turn and rapidly lost height. It crashed when passengers attempted to regain control of the plane. Original analysis suggested that the hijackers intended to fly the plane into Camp David, the Presidential retreat in northern Maryland, or into a target in Washington DC. However, it now appears that one of three nuclear reactors in southern Pennsylvania, Three Mile Island, Peach Bottom or Hope Creek, Salem, may have been the real target. The intended target may be essentially unknowable, but the rapid descent of the plane (which occurred before the passengers attempted to regain control) appears to suggest a location closer to Pittsburgh than to Washington DC. The suggestion is supported by claims that the FBI had sent a report to the British domestic intelligence service, MI5 and to several other European governmental agencies, citing a "credible source" that the hijackers had planned to hit a nuclear plant. The report alleged that Three Mile Island had been under surveillance from the hijackers and their associates in the months leading up to 11 September. In response to this threat, security at reactors in the UK and US has been significantly tightened. At the end of October, warned about further imminent terrorist attacks, the US Federal Aviation Authority placed a week-long ban on any aircraft movements within 20 kilometres of over 80 nuclear facilities. Aircraft could pass over those facilities only at heights above 5,500 metres, limiting the effect of commercial airlines but offering some degree of security to the nuclear sites.[8] Concern was fuelled by the escape of six men of Middle Eastern appearance, with Israeli passports, who were carrying detailed plans of a Florida nuclear power plant and box-cutters, the weapons used in the 11 September hijackings. The men had been detained in the Midwest and then inadvertently released.[9] French authorities suggested that airliners threatening reactors might be shot down and had installed an anti-aircraft missile system around the reprocessing facility near Le Havre.[10] In Canada too, security at nuclear facilities was tightened after a detained Kuwaiti man was found to be carrying sensitive documents on Canadian nuclear energy. Canada has 22 reactors, and radioactive material is regularly shipped by truck across the country.[11]

The threat to reactors, posed by the terrorists responsible for the attacks of 11 September, was credible because it appeared to fit a pattern consistent with the organisation's other activities. The attacks on the World Trade Center and the Pentagon were high casualty events, directed at highly symbolic and visible targets. An attack on a reactor or other nuclear facility with a potentially effective weapon such as a plane or truck bomb would clearly have possessed many of the same characteristics.

Truck Bombs

However, there is a risk in focusing too heavily on the specific events of 11 September, horrific as it was. It would be dangerous to assume that the next threat to nuclear facilities or the next major terrorist attack will be similar to those events. Given that access to flights may become increasingly difficult for hijackers, a more realistic long-term threat is likely to come from the more familiar issue of truck bombs. Trucks have been familiar weapons of organisations such as al-Qaida: attacks such as the 1993 bombing of the World Trade Center, the 1996 Khober towers bombings, the 1998 Embassy bombings in Tanzania and Kenya, all relied on such means. However, other relatively recent terrorist attacks, such as the 1996 Murrah Building bombing in Oklahoma City or that on Colombo's central business district on January 31 1996 (an attack that killed nearly a hundred people and injured 1,400 others), also relied on truck bombs. It may even be that associates of the 11 September hijackers acquired licences to transport hazardous materials around the United States in trucks, hinting at the possible strategy for a new assault.[12]

Such a threat has, historically, caused widespread concern, particularly in the United States. Other forms of frontal assault on reactors by terrorists have a low probability of success, particularly of creating a radiation release, largely because reactors are not only well defended but can also be shut down from several different locations. It is hard to envisage a scenario in which terrorists were able to capture an entire reactor before the process was shut down. If terrorists were to succeed in destroying or disabling both the backup and the primary coolant systems at a reactor, they might manage to cause a core meltdown, even if the reactor was shut down. This is because the decay heat generated by a reactor is so intense that cooling has to continue for days after the reactor has been shut down. Reactors are designed to withstand the failure of its primary coolant systems and have backup systems to cope with this problem: this is a design basis accident. However, the simultaneous failure of both its primary and auxiliary systems has potentially disastrous consequences. To ensure a radiological dispersal, the terrorists would also have to engineer the failure of the reactor's containment system. Although this can occur naturally, once the core melts, containment vessels are built with safety devices that hopefully ensure that its integrity is maintained for as long as possible, to minimize the consequences of such an incident. If terrorists were able to damage the containment system severely, particularly in the early stages of an attack, then that would greatly increase their chances of achieving an off-site radiological dispersal.[13]

However, since truck bombs have a more immediate effect, the threat is more pertinent. Such devices continue to be one of the most favored, and successful, tactics employed by terrorists. Its effectiveness on non-nuclear sites needs little reiteration. A similar attack on a nuclear facility would cause extensive damage and might, at worst, lead to a release of radiological material. In August 1994, the Nuclear Regulatory Commission (NRC) approved a series of measures to improve security at US nuclear power plants. However, these measures were designed to protect primarily against either a vehicle intrusion (in which a vehicle is used to crash through the perimeter fences enabling the driver to gain access to the plant) or a vehicle bomb (which would be parked outside the security fence), rather than against a moving suicide truck bomb, which was not regarded as a plausible threat in the United States. The design-basis threat (DBT) was therefore intended to protect against a relatively small suicide truck bomb.[14] Despite the concerns of some experts,[15] the DBT has not been increased to reflect the increasing lethality and violence of terrorism. This is because the DBT is not intended to protect against a worst-case scenario, but "to provide a reasonable enumeration of adversary characteristics for use in the design of protection systems."[16] This decision was a compromise between the needs to maximize security at nuclear facilities and the requirement not to burden the nuclear industry with excessive costs and hindrances to their processes. However, a 1999 US Department of Energy report noted that the barrier and vault system used by the Department was not as robust in offering protection as had been believed, but that "Although many approaches have been investigated, a promising technological alternative has not yet been identified."[17] Although, in the US, there is some protection for reactors against vehicle bombs, and employees are subject to security clearance background checks, limiting the scope for insider sabotage, even here it is clearly only a partial solution.[18]

Terrorism Directed Against Nuclear Reactors

Historically, relatively few groups have sought to cause a radiological release from a nuclear facility and such an attack provides an unlikely means of seeking to cause casualties. Where groups have actively sought to cause widespread casualties from their actions, they have attacked people directly. Crashing passenger-filled planes into the World Trade Center towers would certainly qualify as such an example. An attack on a reactor would be an indirect attack on people, one that sought to maximise the political, social and economic consequences of the attack without necessarily causing widespread casualties. Although the potential for inflicting such injuries is clearly present, the certainty is not. Any subsequent attack on nuclear facilities is therefore likely to continue this trend: its primary purpose will be to create terror and strike at an important symbolic target, rather than to cause casualties per se.

To date, threats against nuclear reactors can be readily divided into three motivations: those with an overtly anti-nuclear motivation; those that chose to attack a reactor because it was a high profile target; and those that chose a reactor because it was the most convenient target. Historically, particularly in the West, most actions directed against reactors could be classified in either the first or the second categories. Incidents of the third variety include lone lunatics such as Pierce Hye, who in February 1993, recently released from the mental ward of a community hospital in Ephrata (Pennsylvania), drove through the main gate at the Three Mile Island nuclear plant, and crashed through two closely spaced chain-link fences into the "protected area" of the plant, where he hid for four hours but caused no damage. Hye's motive was unclear, but he had no obvious anti-nuclear agenda.[19] However, it is attacks in the second category, assaults on a reactor because it is a high profile target, that have been most often caused by the groups most traditionally considered terrorist. Moreover, it is this type of attack, particularly combined with a desire to cause massive disruption or even extensive casualties, that is most worrying.

Anti-nuclear actions have been characterised by a preference for attacking property rather than people, a tendency common in single-issue terrorism. Examples of anti-nuclear violence include: a bomb planted outside the Lawrence Livermore Laboratory on 28 November 1987. It detonated just after midnight and destroyed dozens of windows and a car, damaged three other cars and scattered debris over a wide area. However, it injured no-one. Responsibility was claimed by the Nuclear Liberation Front.[20] Attacks on reactors include: five anti-tank rockets were fired at the Creys-Malville Superphoenix full-scale breeder reactor, near Lyon, France in January 1982. The reactor was still under construction and, apart from damaging the outer shell of the building, little damage was done by the attack. A previously unknown group, the Pacifist and Ecologist Committee, claimed responsibility for the attack.[21] The connection between anti-nuclear and environmental attacks tends to be a close one. The Evan Mecham Eco-Terrorist International Conspiracy conducted actions against nuclear facilities as part of wider, environmentally-driven, campaigns. The Evan Mecham Eco-Terrorist International Conspiracy (EMETIC) grew out of the most radical elements of Earth First!, a radical environmental group. EMETIC was led by Dave Forman who formed it in October 1987 with four others who had grown disillusioned by Earth First!'s increased dedication to civil disobedience as a tactic. Members of the nascent organization were probably responsible for the May 1986 attack on power lines at Palo Verde Nuclear Generating Station, although they never claimed responsibility. The group was formed to conduct sabotage against nuclear power plants in the southwestern US. On 26 September 1988, the group destroyed power lines feeding uranium mines around the Grand Canyon. Thirty-four power poles were damaged, restricting power supplies to two mines owned by Energy Fuels Nuclear. EMETIC claimed responsibility two days after the attack. On 30 May 1989, three members of the group were arrested near Wendon, Arizona, attempting to cut through a support tower that delivered power to a local substation. The attack was intended as a dry-run before simultaneously attacking the electricity transmission cables at three nuclear facilities in Colorado, California and Arizona.[22] It is worth noting that the majority of anti-nuclear campaigns are intrinsically demonstration actions, aimed at displaying the ineffective safety and security of nuclear installations and materials. Their purpose is thus to highlight the danger and interfere with the plant's operations. Consequently, such attacks are extremely unlikely to seek to threaten the integrity of the reactor, for fear of sparking the type of incident that anti-nuclear activists most fear. Groups whose primary motivation is environmental are also extremely unlikely to seek any results that would threaten the environment.[23]

Attacks in the second category, directed against a high profile target, have been motivated by both political and economic considerations. There are examples of incidents, both of attempts to extort financial gain from the threat and, alternatively, political gain: on 15 August 1975, two bombs exploded at the Mt. D'Arree Nuclear Power Plant in Brennilis, Brittany, causing minor damage. The chief suspects were Breton separatists.[24] In May of the same year, two bombs were detonated at the partially constructed Fessenheim power station, also in France, causing a fire but no casualties. The Meinhof-Puig-Antich Group claimed responsibility.[25] In 1973, a group of ERP terrorists attacked a nuclear power plant, which was not yet operational, near Buenos Aires, Argentina. ETA, perhaps more than any other politically-motivated terrorist group, has also targeted reactors. In part, this was a reaction against the imposition of two facilities, Ea and Lemoniz, on the Basque homeland by Iberduero SA (the electricity company) and the Spanish central government without widespread consultation. Although mostly nationalist-separatist in its motivation, ETA also came to subsume and dominate the anti-nuclear aspects of the fight against the two reactors. Their campaign was wide-ranging, encompassing repeated bombings of the facilities from 1977 onwards, intimidation of its employees and the assassination of a selected few when that intimidation failed. In March 1981, ETA sent death threats to 33 technicians working in the Lemoniz plant. The letter explained that the group would target all specialized personnel "because of [their] participation in the illegal Lemoniz project." The threats had little impact: the technicians continued working at the nuclear power plant, even in the wake of the assassinations of the chief engineer, Jose Maria Ryan, in January 1981, and of the project manager, Angel Pascual Mugica in May 1982.[26] The USA has not been immune to such threats either: in 1979, the FALN (*Fuerzas Armadas de Liberacion Nacioal*, or Armed Forces of the National Liberation), a Puerto Rican nationalist-separatist group, threatened to destroy the Indian Point nuclear plant in New York. In 1980, in solidarity with the seizure of the Dominican Republic's embassy in Bogata by M-19, the Marxist Colombian group, the FALN issued a further warning to the United States: "You must remember . . . that you have never experienced war in your vitals and that you have many nuclear reactors."[27]

As well as the greater opportunities for material diversion, the economic and political instability in the former Soviet Union has also caused an increased threat of attacks on the nuclear facilities themselves. Since 1992, there have been at least six attacks or credible threats directed against reactors in the post-Soviet states. In the fall of 1996, the Russian nuclear regulatory agency, Gosatomnadzor, received a warning that an armed group of Chechens was planning to target the Balakovo Nuclear Power Plant, a facility containing four VVER-1000 reactors. Both the MVD and the FSB were alerted, preparations were made to defend the plant, and a wider warning went out to facilities across Russia to be on their guard against an incursion. However, while a group of Chechens was moving along the Volga, they stopped well short of Balakovo and it was impossible to definitively determine whether they did plan an attack.[28] The threat was credible though because, since 1991, the Chechens had consistently made threats against Russian nuclear facilities and, in March 1996, their field commanders allegedly agreed to launch a series of such assaults.[29] The threat was indicative of a wider problem: security at Russian nuclear facilities. Both before and after this incident, Russian special forces, the FSB and MVD have been deployed, and held exercises, for protecting such establishments.[30] Motivations for threats to reactors also have included economic objectives. In March 1997, five men were apprehended at the plant generator of the Kursk Nuclear Power Station. They were hoping to seize the control room and disable the plant's reactor, allegedly as part of an extortion scheme. Their threat was not treated seriously by Russian authorities because they lacked the means to implement their plan.[31] Although details of the incident remain sketchy, its veracity is strongly supported by the fact that, only four months later, in July 1997, a new system of physical protection was unveiled at Kursk. Gennadiy Pshakin, head of the bureau of the international section of the state research center "Physical-Energy Institute" (Obninsk), stated that the new system will "substantially lower the risk of an unimpeded penetration" to the plant.[32] Ignalina Nuclear Power Plant in Lithuania has been especially prone to threats: there have been at least three since 1992. On 4 November 1994, Kestutis Mazuika, a Lithuanian national in Sweden threatened to destroy the facility at Ignalina unless a ransom of $8 million was paid to a secret organisation (NUC-41 "W") which he claimed to represent. His threat, which supposedly would be carried out by the NUC-41 "W"'s representatives at the power plant, was contained in a letter, handwritten in Russian, delivered to the Swedish Prime Minister's office. It demanded that $1 million be handed over to Mazuika on 7 November, with the balance to be deposited in a Swedish bank account. He was arrested on 7 November when he returned to the Prime Minister's office to collect the money. He later claimed that NUC-41 "W" forced him to commit the act.[33] The group was allegedly also responsible for the theft of fuel rods from the same facility in 1993.[34] Just a few days after the Mazuika incident, on 9 November, VATESI, the Lithuanian Nuclear Safety Inspectorate, was warned by the German Federal Ministry for Environment, Nature Conservation and Nuclear Safety of a further threat against the Ignalina installation. A local mafiya boss, Georgy Dekanidze, threatened to destroy the plant if his son, Boris, was sentenced to death in the contract murder he was then on trial for. On 10 November, the same German authorities advised that preparations for the sabotage had been made and would be committed by workers at Ignalina on 15 November if Boris Dekanidze received a death sentence. The Lithuanian prime minister then requested assistance from Sweden, which provided an expert search and bomb disposal team. They conducted a search between the 14 and 16 November, during which time Units One and Two of the nuclear plant were shut down and security around the reactor was strengthened. However, no indication of sabotage was uncovered. Boris Dekanidze was sentenced to death on 10 November and Georgy Dekanidze, unsurprisingly, denied all knowledge of the threat against Ignalina.[35] The threat caused the Ignalina to be shut down for three days and cost $10 million, while the reactors were thoroughly inspected for possible sabotage.[36] Since these threats, security at Ignalina has been improved: the perimeter of the plant is equipped with sensors and an observation system; entry into the facility requires a plastic card and access code which is unique for each of Ignalina's 5000 employees; and a computer monitors everybody's movements.[37] However, much of the danger continues to lie with the personnel of the nuclear industry, as well as with the technical aspects of protection.[38] If workers at nuclear facilities are demoralized and regularly denied their wages, they are likely to continue to pose a real threat to the security of these facilities.

In 2000, there were several low-level attacks on nuclear facilities. In January 2000, Steven James Romero, 27, telephoned the U.S. Nuclear Regulatory Commission three times and threatened to explode a nuclear facility. Romero called the headquarters in Bethesda, Maryland, twice as well as the regional headquarters in Lisle, Illinois.[39] Shortly after midnight on 5 November 2000, security officers conducting a random search at California's largest nuclear plant, at Diablo Canyon, discovered what initially appeared to be a bomb placed in a support building located on the premises. The incident subsequently emerged as a prank.[40] A bomb exploded on 6 March 2000 at the Scientific Research Institute of Nuclear

Physics in Rostov-na-Donu, Russia. The blast from the remote-controlled device, which injured two, was most likely tied to mafia in-fighting, officials stated.[41] On 29 March 2000, Japanese police reported that the Aum Shinrikyo cult had acquired information concerning nuclear facilities in Russia, Ukraine, Japan, and other countries. Aum stole the information by way of its computer software development companies.[42] On 6 April 2000, Sylvia Bergerova, 34, anonymously threatened to detonate a bomb at the nuclear power plant in Dukovany, south Moravia, Czech Republic. Trebic Police evacuated 1,200 people from the plant while they searched for three and a half hours for a device.[43]

The Insider Threat

One of the most common types of incident and, after the threat of truck or aircraft attacks, most potentially worrying is insider crime. Attacks by insiders are dangerous because they are, by their nature, hard to prevent and the perpetrators are more likely to know the facility's vulnerabilities.

In February 1992, Oleg Savchuk, a computer programmer, was arrested trying to introduce a computer virus into the Ignalina's system. This coincided with the breakdown of the cooling system of the station's first reactor, although no definitive link could be made. It is possible that Savchuk introduced the virus and then alerted authorities in order to receive an award for meritorius service.[44] Such a scenario would certainly be in accordance with the findings of several Rand reports, based on research in the United States, which concluded that a desire for recognition and approbation was a key factor, particularly in cases where the crime was committed by a lone insider. Conspiracies by several insiders, with no outside help, appear to be the least common variation of insider crime. Interestingly, in all of these conspiracies that were studied, the co-operation of employees appears to have voluntary, rather than compelled or otherwise coerced. As with the other types of insider crime, the overwhelming motivation for these acts was self-serving financial gain. An exception was the case of two employees of a commercial nuclear facility who vandalized fuel at the plant. They had both served on US Navy nuclear-powered vessels and this experience lead them to believe that the security at the powerplant was insufficient. Once they had vandalized the fuel, they then held a press conference to draw attention to the situation.[45] They appear to have been motivated by a mixture of altruism and idealism, so this case offers an interesting combination of both the insider and the nuclear protest action, for demonstration purposes.

The problem of insider crime, of workers within the nuclear industry attempting to exploit their position, has been extensively studied in the US, and numerically forms a major component of both nuclear material smuggling and reactor-related incidents. Obviously, insiders are capable of causing great damage and of embezzling vital material, either alone or acting in concert with other insiders or outsiders. One example of possible sabotage by an insider occurred at Turkey Point nuclear power station, in Florida, in 1983. There, someone shut the valve for the auxiliary feedwater system that supplied the two reactors at Turkey Point. If the main system was inoperable or only a small quantity of feedwater flow was required. This situation went unnoticed for five days, in spite of a requirement for checks twice per shift, partly because "out for maintenance" labels were placed on the valves. If the normal feedwater flow had been interrupted in those five days, severe damage, possibly even to the core, might have resulted. It is possible that this incident was simply the result of an error, rather than malicious intent, by a worker, but it still illustrates the possibilities for sabotage to have severe consequences and to go undetected for long periods of time.[46] The threat posed by insiders is almost impossible to defend against because it is so difficult to identify likely culprits before they act and because a measure of trust in employees is vital to the effective running of the facility. An additional problem is that the success of the insider often depends not on extensive planning, so much as on the exploitation of pre-existing flaws in security, which insiders are clearly in a unique position to recognise.[47] The NRC, in a 1980 report, found that security failures are often the result of people and not system failures; that non-adherence to security regimes was more often the problem than the intrinsic nature of the regime itself.[48] A 1990 Rand report found that, of the 62 insider crimes they analysed, 41% of crimes directed against guarded facilities were committed by those supposedly charged with protecting them, the guards,[49] a clear case of *Pone seram, cohibe; sed quis custodiet ipsos Custodes?*[50] Although much of the work, to date, is based on research from US nuclear facilities, it clearly has more widespread applicability.

The most serious type of insider threat is posed when the insider conspires with outsiders. This applies to embezzlement of nuclear material as well as to violent threats against nuclear facilities. In each case, the threat posed by the external group is considerably increased if it has reliable knowledge of the plant's security arrangements, procedures, operations, physical layout and the location of the material or vulnerable point in the facility. The most likely source for such information would be from someone who works at the site: an insider.[51] This concern would seem to particularly pertinent after 11 September as the attack clearly displayed a willingness to plan months, even years, ahead to train terrorists as pilots. It is precisely this type of patience and forethought that might encourage a terrorist group to infiltrate a member into the workforce of a nuclear facility, or to recruit a sympathetic pre-existing employee. Such a strategy would certainly increase the likelihood of terrorists succeeding in attacking a facility's vulnerabilities, either to sabotage or bombs.

However, in the RAND study, although the identity of these outsiders varied enormously, and included ideological extremists and major criminal organisations, in many cases the outsider was simply a friend or relation of the insider, someone with whom the insider already had a relationship. This is logical if the supposition is that most insiders do not come from a criminal background, but rather, they exploit the opportunity that is presented to them, so that it is unlikely that they would have pre-existing links with either criminal or ideologue groups. For this reason, and particularly in instances where the outsider did not initiate the conspiracy, the most common motivation in the Rand study was financial, rather than political gain.[52] Rand's study found only a small proportion of incidents in which outsiders approached an insider, with whom they had had no previous relationship, to assist them in their operation. However, this does not preclude such an event.

If the intent is simply to take the reactor off-line, there are far easier ways of doing so than a full-out attack on the reactor building itself. These methods include toppling a pylon on the reactor's primary distribution line, or sabotaging the transformers or switchgear at the reactor switchyard with a stand-off weapon. Other possibilities include damaging the feedwater and steam pipes or the reactor control mechanisms in the facility, using a shoulder-held rocket launcher, for example.[53] Such low-level attacks have formed the majority of terrorism against nuclear reactors to date and are still extremely expensive and disruptive to the power company.

Vulnerabilities Elsewhere Within the Nuclear Fuel Cycle

Nuclear reactors are obviously not the only parts of the nuclear complex that are vulnerable to attack. Enrichment, storage and spent fuel reprocessing facilities are also potential targets for an assault, as is the transport between them. The most dangerous target at a uranium enrichment plant would probably be the containers of liquid uranium hexafluoride at the feed end. An explosion releasing the liquid would cause it to solidify and about half would vaporize, reacting with the atmosphere to form a mixture of uranium oxide and fluorine compound (UO^2F^2) and hydrofluroric acid, the products of gaseous uranium hexafluoride.[54] The effect of such a release can be seen from the accident at a uranium processing plant in Oklahoma in 1986, in which one person died, 32 were injured, and several homes had to be evacuated when a tank of uranium hexafluoride ruptured, spilling its contents.[55] The opportunities to create an off-site radiation leak at a reprocessing facility may be limited. Although the radioactivity of the materials is considerable, and therefore potentially attractive for radiological terrorism, it also means that they are remotely handled and are inaccessible, even to operators, due to the necessity for extensive radiation shielding. Significant amounts of explosives might conceivably rupture the spent fuel storage pool, but the likelihood is that the radiation released by such a spill would be small since the gaseous fission products would mostly plate out on the interior of the building, or would be captured by the filtration system. However, if not only the pools or tanks were ruptured, but also the fabric of the building, then the explosion has the potential to throw large quantities of highly radioactive material into the atmosphere. If a plane crashed into a reprocessing facility, the resulting fire as the fuel burned would add to the radiological release. If the cooling system was also compromised in the explosion, then, potentially, the radioactive material could overheat and further material would be propelled into the atmosphere.[56]

The transport of spent fuel is the part of the nuclear cycle where material is seemingly at its most vulnerable. However, it would be far from straightforward for terrorists to exploit this: spent fuel is shipped in casks that protect the public from radiation, so the construction of the casks is extremely robust. Even enormous truck bombs, detonated within feet of the cask, may not be capable of penetrating it. However, Bunn and Steinhauser suggest that terrorists would have little difficulty acquiring and using anti-tank weapons capable of piercing the transport canisters.[57] Shaped charges probably could do so but by their nature, designed to penetrate deeply rather than to do massive damage, they are likely to rupture only the fuel pins directly in their path. Therefore, as with several other forms of radiological terrorism, the public reaction would probably be out of proportion to the true physical danger.[58] Nevertheless, such an attack would be a highly effective means of creating fear and disruption amongst a population. Key Russian Ministry of Defense (MOD) officials have indicated considerable concern about the possibility of nuclear weapons being stolen in transit or damaged in accidents on Russia's decaying railway system. Therefore, as part of the CTR program, supercontainers were shipped to the MOD to protect warheads in transit, as were five rail-mobile emergency support modules to help respond to attacks and accidents.[59]

Radiological Terrorism

If the terrorist group's intention is a radiological attack, then destroying a reactor is only one, albeit very public and dangerous, way to achieve this goal. Radiological materials in this category can be more easily stolen from nuclear, industrial and research facilities than can weapons-grade material.[60] The IAEA reports 380 incidents of radiological trafficking since 1993, only the minority of which involved "high end material."[61] Abel Gonzalez, the IAEA's director of radiation and waste safety reported in late October that "Security of radioactive materials has traditionally been relatively light . . . There are few security precautions on radiotherapy equipment and a large source could be removed quite easily, especially if those involved have no regard for their own health." Many such sources are presently without any regulatory control and are unaccounted for.[62] A radiological device would be extremely easy to construct (it need only be a aerosol can or a bomb with a radioactive coating or with a container of radioactive material next to it) and the materials for it are so widely available (cesium-137, for example, is commonly used in hospitals for X-rays). Even elements, such as cobalt-60 or cesium-137 which need a fierce fire to disperse them could be used effectively in radiological weapons if the material was surrounding a mixture of high-explosive and incendiary material. While a firebomb, of this variety, is technologically well within the reach of many terrorist organisations,[63] a group might also consider using military munitions for this purpose. Both thermite grenades and white phosphorus mortar or artillery shells could be used to ignite extremely hot fires that are resistant to water. White phosphorus would probably give greater dispersal, but does not burn as hot as thermite. However, variants of both are used by many military organisations and are therefore likely to be available on the black market.[64]

The technical feasibility of radiological terrorism, as a low-technology weapon, means that it is by far the most likely form of nuclear device, as well as the least catastrophic. However, it would still have considerable value as a terrorist weapon, since the mere fact of being nuclear would almost certainly ensure that it had a considerable impact on the publics imagination and fear, and thus on a governmental response. For the same reason, being nuclear, it conveys an added prestige and status on the perpetrators. Radiological terrorism would set a group apart and take its terrorism to a new level, so has considerable attractions. Furthermore, while the use of a radiological weapon would be more difficult than most "off the shelf" weaponry, and would be an example of technological innovation for terrorist groups, the arguments that make a nuclear-yield device an unlikely, if highly dangerous, threat apply to a much lesser degree for radiological weapons. While a nuclear-yield bomb would be an extremely expensive and difficult mass-casualty weapon, a radiological device would be an only moderately difficult (there might be material handling problems, for example).

It is almost impossible to generalise on the extent of the risk to the public from a radiological dispersal device: it depends so much on the material used, the means of dispersal, population density, weather conditions, and the period of public exposure. However, the International Physicians for the Prevention of Nuclear War (IPPNW), in their publication on crude nuclear weapons, argue that:

> . . . [T]he consequences of a radiological weapon using plutonium in amounts that are potentially available for a terrorist attack are very largely long-term in nature: primarily increased cancer incidence, particularly of lung, bone, and liver cancer . . . Thus in health effect terms, the impact of such a weapon would be hidden for several decades, and probably would not be dramatic. However, given the public aversion to cancer risk, and the fears engendered by plutonium as a potential carcinogen, there are likely to be immediate and dramatic responses by the emergency services.[65]

To a very large extent, though, the effects of a radiological weapon are dependent on the type of material used: while weapons-grade plutonium might cause limited damage, other elements, such as cesium, or even radioactive waste, are potentially lethal, very rapidly. In 1981, an environmental impact statement by the US Nuclear Regulatory Commission (NRC) estimated that a big truck bomb used against a reactor in a highly populated area could effectively turn the nuclear reactor into a large radiological weapon, causing up to 130,000 fatalities.[66] This is a highly pessimistic estimate. A more recent estimate of the implications of a catastrophic incident at the reprocessing facility at Sellafield, in northern England, was equally worrying. It found that up to half the 2400 kilograms of cesium-137 stored in the tanks at the site might be released into the atmosphere, causing up to 2 million cancer deaths in the following 50 years, assuming a similar pattern of exposure to that after the Chernobyl disaster.[67] Such claims are highly alarmist, not least because they present worst case scenarios as the likely outcome of any incident.

Where the cause is a radiological dispersal device rather than a disaster at a nuclear facility, the consequences appear substantially smaller. In 1987, in Goiana, Brazil, two adults broke open a cesium source, found abandoned in a clinic, and allowed children to play with the glowing material inside. Within days, four people died, and 249 others were contaminated. There was public hysteria, and thousands of cubic metres of soil had to be removed for decontamination.[68] Nevertheless, radiological devices are not ideal for creating mass casualties because the quantities of highly radioactive material required to cause powerful results over even a moderate area are likely to be so great that it would pose considerable problems for terrorists to acquire and then work with the material.[69] To achieve widespread casualties, terrorists would probably be obliged to find a way of manufacturing very small particles of radioactive material, exacerbating the handling and production risks and difficulties, or finding an effective means of dispersion, as discussed earlier. During the 1940s and 1950s, the US military experimented with radiological dispersal devices but ultimately decided that such weapons were not militarily useful. They found that disseminating gamma-emitting radiological agents in air posed considerable difficulties because of the heat generated by the material and the problems of dissipation.[70] Radiological weapons might, therefore, be used by groups as weapons of terror, rather than as an effective means of causing mass casualties for which other types of non-conventional weapon might be used instead.

Further questions about whether terrorists are likely to seek to use radiological weapons are raised by Brian Jenkins who noted over twenty years ago that:

> Scenarios involving the deliberate dispersal of toxic radiological material which could cause a number of immediate deaths, a greater number of serious and protracted illnesses, a statistical rise in the mortality rate, and ultimately an increase in the number of birth defects among the affected population do not appear to fit the pattern of any terrorist actions carried out thus far . . .

> Terrorist actions have tended to be aimed at producing immediate dramatic effects, a handful of violent deaths—not lingering illness, and certainly not a population of vengeance-seeking victims . . . If terrorists were to employ radioactive contaminants, they could not halt the continuing effects of their act, not even long after they may have achieved their ultimate political objectives. It has not been the style of terrorists to kill hundreds or thousands. To make hundreds or thousands of persons terminally ill would be even more out of character.[71]

Although recent reports of groups such as al-Qaida or Chechen separatists planning attacks with radiological weapons appears to undermine Jenkins argument, it is a worthwhile caveat that such attacks are not tactics that many terrorist groups have historically sought to use, and remain unlikely tactics for the majority of groups. Radiological weapons would have a vast impact and could, potentially, pose a considerable problem for an extended period. Therefore, an incident that is not intended to cause mass casualties, but is intended to achieve political or economic extortion, is the most plausible type of radiological terrorism. Once aware of the problem, it would probably be possible to clean up the radiological effects of a device, but restoring public confidence would be very difficult.[72] Clearly, the disruption would be immense and somewhat similar to the situation in Tokyo on April 15, 1995, when the Aum cult threatened fresh attacks on the subway, bringing the entire city to a grinding halt for the day, and mobilising an estimated one third of Japan's police force to defend the city. Commuters stayed at home, refusing to take the risk of being the victims of another sarin attack.[73]

The use of lower-grade nuclear material for terrorism or extortion is obviously already a reality. In April 1985, a letter addressed to mayor Ed Koch was sent to the New York City Water Authority, threatening to place plutonium trichloride in reservoirs serving New York. The perpetrator demanded that murder charges be dropped against Bernard Goetz, who shot four black youths allegedly attempting to mug him on the subway. When the U.S. Department of Energy tested the city's drinking water, they found elevated levels of plutonium, from the usual 0.1 to 0.6 femtocuries per litre to 21 femtocuries per litre. However, no proof of contamination, or a definitive link between the threat and the test results, was found. Moreover, the danger posed by this type of attack was small: the Federally-determined safe level for drinking water is 5000 femtocuries; and while plutonium trichloride is soluble, along with other types of plutonium, it is poorly absorbed through the stomach and intestinal walls compared to being inhaled.[74] Furthermore, most types of plutonium are largely insoluble, and so an ineffective means of contaminating water supplies.[75] The dubious effectiveness of such a tactic has not precluded other similar threats being made. In October 1974, the Italian Government announced that a plot, by right-wing terrorists, to contaminate a number of Italy's aqueducts with radioactive waste had been uncovered. The material was alleged to have been stolen from a nuclear centre in the north of the state. However, details of the attempt remained sketchy and no incident occurred.[76] Using radioactive material to contaminate water supplies has relatively little chance of causing fatalities: the quantities of material required to have a lethal effect, even in a small reservoir, are so vast that it seems a highly implausible tactic. However, as with other types of radiological terrorism, the effects on public confidence and behaviour are, potentially, enormous: in the New York case, purchases of bottled water doubled, despite the low risk to the public and the fact that the event was several months past before the public became aware of it.[77]

Additional cases of possible radiological terrorism include: the Russian mafiya alleged killing of a Moscow businessman in 1993, using gamma-ray emitting pellets, placed in his office[78] and the June 1996 attempt by three men in Long Island to kill local Republican Party officials, using radium placed in the victims' cars, food and, bizarrely, their toothpaste. The three perpetrators, John Ford, Joseph Mazzuchelli, and Edward Zabo, were members of the Long Island UFO Network and were enraged by a supposed conspiracy by Republican leader John Powell, Brookhaven town public safety director Anthony Gazzola and Legislator Fred Towle to hide evidence that a UFO had started a forest fire.

Ford had tried to run for office to reveal this conspiracy, but had been blocked by Powell. Zabo supplied the radium, which he claimed came from a friend, although Zabo worked as a Defense Department employee at Northrop Grumman and police found five storage canisters around his house. Ford was found unfit to stand trial; Zabo plead guilty to supplying the radium in exchange for a reduced sentence; and Mazzuchelli was convicted of second-degree conspiracy.[79] Incidents have also occurred outside the United States. On 17 April 1974, a man claiming to represent the "Justice Guerrillas" called police in Vienna, alleging that radioactive material had been placed on the train to Rome. Police found a large but non-lethal quantity of Iodine-131 under a seat in the first class compartment. The three packets of material had been stolen from Vienna's main railway station on April 12, from where they were due to be shipped to a hospital in Linz [Austria]. Police later arrested a man with a history of mental illness who claimed his actions were a protest against the treatment of mentally ill patients in Austria, rather than being politically motivated.[80] Radiological threats have also been issued in the USA: in 1975, a Puerto Rican group (probably the FALN) threatened to detonate 100 bombs against US targets, 25 of which would contain radiological material.[81]

The most important sub-state use of radiological material occurred on 23 November, 1995, when Chechen guerrilla leader, Shamyl Basayev, informed the Russian television network, NTV, that four cases of radioactive cesium had been hidden around Moscow. NTV discovered the 32 kg case, wrapped in a yellow plastic bag and giving off 310 times the normal amount of radioactivity in Ismailovo Park. Basayev had repeatedly threatened to attack Moscow with nuclear or chemical weapons, and had already proved his ability to create "terrorist spectaculars" by taking 1500 people hostage in Budennovsk in June. Russian officials largely dismissed the nuclear threat, claiming that the material was cesium 137, used in X-ray equipment or some industrial processes, capable of emitting only 100 times the background amount of radioactivity.[82] However, the truth about the material is less important than the credibility of the threat, as demonstrated by the precautions the Russian authorities took, sending emergency search teams out around the city with Geiger counters.[83] If the Chechens had sought to inflict harm on the city's residents, they could have left the container open, and allowed the contents to disseminate through the park. Dzhokar Dudayev, the Chechen leader, did claim that there were conventional explosives with the nuclear material, threatening radiological dispersal, but this was a hoax. Basayev was intent on displaying capability and on ensuring that this threats to launch further attacks against Moscow, unless Russia withdrew from Chechnya, were taken seriously.[84] His warning was plausible because the state of the Russian nuclear industry made it impossible to rule out the possibility that the Chechens had indeed acquired dangerously radioactive material.

In the wake of the 11 September attacks in the United States, it has also emerged that al Qaida may have sought the means to build a "dirty bomb".[85] Although there have been previous allegations relating to the organisation's attempts to acquire material to build a nuclear-yield bomb,[86] the claims over a radiological weapon represent a significant departure. British intelligence forces are currently investigating allegations, made by a Bulgarian businessman, Ivan Ivanov, that in April 2001 he was approached by a middleman for bin Laden, seeking to obtain radiological material. Ivanov allegedly had a series of meetings near Pakistani border with Afghanistan, including one with bin Laden. He then met with a "chemical engineer", near Rawalpindi, and was offered $200,000 to help the scientist acquire spent nuclear fuel rods from the Kozlodui nuclear electricity plant in Bulgaria. The plan would have involved buying the rods legally, through a newly established environmental front company that would deal with nuclear waste. Ivanov declined the opportunity and reported the contact once he returned to Europe.[87]

Earlier this year, customs officials seized 10 lead-lined containers on the border between Uzbekistan and Kazakhstan. The containers held a substantial quantity of radioactive material, ostensibly intended for a company in Quetta, Pakistan. The precise type of materials remains unclear, but it seems unlikely to have been a legitimate shipment and it does seem possible that bin Laden's al-Qaida was a potential end-user.[88] There must also be concerns that the main threat in this respect may not be leakage from the Former Soviet Union, but assistance to alQaida from Pakistani sources. In October, two key former members of Pakistan's nuclear program were detained as a result of their connections to the Taliban. Bashir uddin Mahmood was project director before Pakistan's 1998 tests and has since been running a relief organisation, sympathetic to the Afghan regime. Abdul Majid was a director of the Pakistan Atomic Energy Commission in 1999.[89]

Conclusion

The full implications of 11 September for nuclear security and the nuclear industry remain unclear. Although concerns at truck bomb attacks on reactors have been present for several decades, 11 September 2001 may be the closest example to date of an existential threat to a reactor. However, given that the uncertainty over where United Airlines flight 93 was being directed, it may equally be that nuclear reactors were simply one of several possible categories of target that were considered. It is possible to state though that 11 September indicates such attacks on reactors are more likely than had been thought previously. The attack represents a new level of high casualty, high profile, long-term action. Other groups may or may not follow al-Qaida's lead towards this new type of assault, but clearly an attack on a reactor, and potentially radiological terrorism, would fall within the patterns of action established by that network.

Mohamed ElBaradei, head of the IAEA, summed up the uncertain situation as follows: "The tragic terrorist attacks on the United States were a wake up call to us all. We cannot be complacent. We have to and will increase our efforts on all fronts—from combating illicit trafficking to ensuring the protection of nuclear materials—from nuclear installation design to withstand attacks to improving how we respond to nuclear emergencies."[90] Physical protection measures for nuclear materials and facilities varies widely from country to country, and even within states. It is vital that the security of both facilities and all nuclear materials (including those that might be used to make a radiological dispersal device) be ensured to the highest possible level. In the longer term, nuclear plants need to be built as target-hardened, stand-off facilities to combat the threat of truck bombs. New designs need to be considered as counters to the danger of aircraft being crashed into facilities. In the shorter term, more limited physical protection measures need to be pursued, but the problem of insider crime, with its potential for sabotage and theft, needs to be readdressed. In the new, uncertain, world of international terrorism, both facilities and material are simply too vulnerable to exploitation, with potentially devastating consequences. The IAEA needs to be at the forefront in calling for more effective physical protection for both facilities and materials. Dr. ElBaradi's statement to the United Nations General Assembly on 22 October is an important declaration of intent to prioritise these areas.[91] This has to be followed through, a process that is likely to require extended commitments of effort, money and thought to successfully implement. Nuclear security is too important to allow anything else.

References

1. Bruce Hoffman, "The Potential Terrorist Threat To Commercial Nuclear Facilities," *Rand Corporation Report P-7450*, Santa Monica, March 1988, p. 3.
2. *New York Times*, Information Bank Abstracts, 12 November 1972, p. 1. Lexis-Nexis Database, available from: http://web.lexis-nexis.com.
3. Sharon Waxman, "French Say Hijackers Target Was Paris," *Washington Post*, 28 December 1994, p. A1.
4. Nicholas Rufford, David Leppard, and Paul Eddy, "Crashed plane's target may have been reactor," *Sunday Times*, 21 October 2001, p. A9.
5. "Security concerns renew nuclear debate," *BBC News*, 1 November 2001, accessed at http://news.bbc.co.uk/hi/englisjh/world/americas/newsid_1631000/1631402.stm.
6. Mark Henderson, "Nuclear reactors vulnerable to attack," *The Times*, 27 September 2001, p. 4.
7. Ibid.
8. "US steps up nuclear security," *BBC News*, 31 October 2001, accessed at http://news.bbc.co.uk/hi/english/world/americas/newsid_1629000/1629367.stm.
9. Kitty Kay, "FBI fury as men with nuclear plan escape," *The Times*, 1 November 2001.
10. Nicholas Rufford, David Leppard, and Paul Eddy, "Crashed plane's target may have been reactor," *Sunday Times*, 21 October 2001, p. A9.
11. Melanie Brooks, "Terrorist eye nuclear plants, expert says: 'Ample evidence': Kuwaiti man had sensitive documents on N-plant, virus lab," *National Post*, 15 October 2001, www.nationalpost.com accessed 23/10/01.
12. Roland Watson, "FBI fears truck bombs are next terror weapon," *The Times*, 15 October 2001, p. 5.
13. Gerald L. Pollack, "Severe Accidents and Terrorist Threats at Nuclear Facilities" in Leventhal and Alexander, *Preventing Nuclear Terrorism*, pp. 66, 72.
14. Nuclear Control Institute/Committee to Bridge the Gap, "Experts Praise NRC Truck-Bomb Rule But Decry Delays and Shortcomings", Joint Press Release, 1 August 1994.
15. Nuclear Control Institute/Committee To Bridge The Gap, Letter To NRC Chair Jackson, 6 November 1995, accessed at: http://www.nci.org/nci/111695.html.
16. United States Nuclear Regulatory Commission, Letter to NCI, CGB from NRC Chair Jackson, 20 December 1995, accessed at: http://www.nci.org/nci/1122095a.html.
17. Cited in George Bunn and Fritz Steinhauser, "Guarding Nuclear Reactors and Material From Terrorists and Thieves," *Arms Control Today*, October 2001.
18. "Security concerns renew nuclear debate," *BBC News*, 1 November 2001, accessed at http://news.bbc.co.uk/hi/englisjh/world/americas/newsid_1631000/1631402.stm.
19. Matthew L. Wald, "Gate Crasher shakes Up Nuclear Debate", *New York Times*, 11 February 1993, p. A16.
20. *Los Angeles Times*, "FBI Seizes Nuclear Protester In Car Bombing At A-Weapons Lab", 8 April 1988, p. A32.
21. Frank J. Prial, "Antitank Rockets Are Fired At French Nuclear Reactor", *New York Times*, 20 January 1982, p. A3.
22. Brent L. Smith, *Terrorism In America: Pipe Bombs and Pipe Dreams*, (Albany, NY: SUNY Press, 1994), pp. 26–7 & 125–7.
23. Bruce Hoffman, "An Assessment of the Potential Terrorist Threat To Canadian Nuclear Power Plants," Ontario Court (General Division), 25 April 1993, p.5.
24. Richard Wigg, "Atom power station is sabotaged in France", *The Times*, 16 August 1975, p. 3.
25. *The New York Times*, Information Bank Abstracts, 4 May 1975, p. 7. Lexis-Nexis Database, available from: web.lexis-nexis.com.
26. Konrad Kellen, "Appendix: Nuclear-Related Terrorist Activities by Political Terrorists" in Leventhal and Alexander, *Preventing Nuclear Terrorism*, pp. 129–30. Robert Graham, "Basque

N-plant becomes political football," *Financial Times*, 4 February 1982. Robert Graham, "ETA's gunmen bring Basque N-project to a halt again," *Financial Times*, 14 May 1982, p. 3.

28. Hoffman, "The Potential", p.77.
29. Potter, "Less".
30. Sergei Shargorodsky, "Security Tightened at Nuclear Power Plant After Threat," *Associated Press*, 1 July 1995. "Chechen Rebels Decide To Target Nuclear Sites," *Ria Novosti*, 13 March 1996.
31. Alexander Khokhlov, "Chechnya, Winter, Disaster," *Komsomolskaya Pravda*, 26 October 1995, p. 1. "FSB Conducts Antiterrorism Exercise in Murmansk," *FBIS*, ID no. FTS19970827000308. "Discussion of FSB's Alfa, Vympel Antiterrorist Teams," *FBIS*, ID no. FTS19970923000805.
32. Potter, "Less".
33. "Kursk Nuclear Power Plant To Get New Protection System," *FBIS*, ID no. FTS19970714001024.
34. Potter, "Less". "Man threatening to blow up nuclear power station arrested in Sweden," *BBC Summary of World Broadcasts*, 12 November 1994.
35. Mattias Lufkens, "Paranoia Of Attack At Nuclear Plant In Lithuania," *Liberation*, 17 November 1994.
36. Potter, "Less". Seamus Martin, "Mafia threatens to bomb power station," *The Irish Times*, 14 November 1994, p. 15. *BBC Summary of World Broadcasts*, "Alleged terrorist denies plans to blow up Ignalina; bomb search fruitless," 16 November 1994. Ariane Sains, "Ignalina Sabotage Deadline Passes Without Blow-Up," *Nucleonics Week*, 17 November 1994, pp. 1–2.
37. *Associated Press*, "Lithuanian Nuclear Reactor Closed After Terrorist Threats," 15 November 1994. Benoit Thely, "Suspect held as threat forces closure of Lithuanian reactor," *Agence France Presse*, 15 November 1994. *Reuters*, "Lithuanian reactor shutdown costs $10 million," 16 November 1994. *Deutsche Presse-Agentur*, "Lithuanian reactor complex back on stream after bomb scare," 17 November 1994.
38. "Ignalina Power Plant Profiled," NTV, 3 April 1997, *FBIS* Document ID no: FTS19970414001108.
39. I am indebted to Scott Parrish for his comments and insights on the issue of security at nuclear facilities in the Former Soviet Union.
40. Gretchen Schuldt, "Man Admits He Made Phone Threats; Calls to Nuclear Regulatory Commission Traced to 3 Kenosha sites," *Milwaukee Journal Sentinel*, 21 January 2000, p. 3B. Center for Nonproliferation Studies (CNS), WMD Terrorism Database of Incidents Involving Sub-National Actors and Chemical, Biological, Radiological, or Nuclear Materials.
41. "Practical Joke Sparks Alert at Nuclear Plant," *Reuters* (7 November 2000); Internet, available from http://www.reuters.com/news_article, accessed on 11/7/00. Center for Nonproliferation Studies (CNS), WMD Terrorism Database of Incidents Involving Sub-National Actors and Chemical, Biological, Radiological, or Nuclear Materials.
42. Arkadiy Yuzhnyy, "Blast in Russian N-Center Seen Aimed at Businessman," *Segodnya* in Russian (10 March 2000); available from *FBIS*, document identification number CEP20000310000149. Center for Nonproliferation Studies (CNS), WMD Terrorism Database of Incidents Involving Sub-National Actors and Chemical, Biological, Radiological, or Nuclear Materials.
43. Vasily Golovin, "Aum Implicated in Nuclear Information Stealing," *ITAR-TASS News Agency* (29 March 2000). Mainichi Shimbun, "Aum Had Nuke-Plant Info," *Mainichi Daily News* (28 March 2000); Internet, available from http://www.mainichi.co, Center for Nonproliferation Studies (CNS), WMD Terrorism Database of Incidents Involving Sub-National Actors and Chemical, Biological, Radiological, or Nuclear Materials.
44. RTJ, "Police Detect Woman Who Caused Evacuation of Dukovany," *CTK National News Wire* (3 June 2000): General News. ICE, "Woman Causing Evacuation of Dukovany Invited for Excursion," *CTK National News Wire* (5 June 2000): General News. Center for Nonproliferation Studies (CNS), WMD Terrorism Database of Incidents Involving Sub-National Actors and Chemical, Biological, Radiological, or Nuclear Materials.
45. Potter, "Less". "Computer Sabotage Shuts Down Lithuanian Nuclear Plant," *MTI Hungarian news Agency*, 31 January 1992. "Technician accused of sabotage at Lithuanian nuclear plant," *BBC Summary of World Broadcasts*, 1 February 1992. Nikolai Lashkevich, "Malefactor at Ignalina Nuclear Plant," *Izvestia*, 3 February 1992, p. 8.

45. Hoffman, Meyer, Schwarz and Duncan, "Insider Crime", p. 47.
46. Daniel Hirsch, "The Truck Bomb and Insider Threats to Nuclear Facilities," in Paul Leventhal and Yonah Alexander (eds.), *Preventing Nuclear Terrorism*, (Lexington, Mass: Lexington Books, 1987), pp. 213–14.
47. Bruce Hoffman, Christina Meyer, Benjamin Schwarz, Jennifer Duncan, *"Insider Crime: The Threat To Nuclear Facilities and Programs,"* (Santa Monica, CA: RAND Corporation, R-3782-DOE, February 1990).
48. S.A. Mullen et al, "Potential Threat to Licensed Nuclear Activities from Insiders (Insider Study)", Division of Safeguards, *Office of Nuclear Material Safety and Safeguards, US Nuclear Regulatory Commission, NUREG-0703*, Washington DC, July 1980.
49. Hoffman, Meyer, Schwarz and Duncan, "Insider Crime", p. vi.
50. "Clap on a lock, keep watch and ward! But who the guards themselves shall guard?" Juvenal, *Satires*, 6, 347.
51. Hoffman, Meyer, Schwarz and Duncan, "Insider Crime", pp. 1–2.
52. Hoffman, Meyer, Schwarz and Duncan, "Insider Crime", pp. 38–41.
53. Robert K. Mullen, "Nuclear Violence" in Leventhal and Alexander, *Preventing Nuclear Terrorism*, pp. 237–40.
54. Mullen, "Nuclear Violence", p. 240.
55. William Robbins, "Untested Process Was In Use At Time Of Fatal Gas-Leak", *New York Times*, 6 January 1986, p. A1.
56. Rob Edwards, "The nightmare scenario," *New Scientist*, vol. 172 issue 2312, 13 October 2001, p. 10.
57. George Bunn and Fritz Steinhauser, "Guarding Nuclear Reactors and Material From Terrorists and Thieves," *Arms Control Today*, October 2001.
58. Mullen, "Nuclear Violence", pp. 241–2.
59. General Accounting Office, "Weapons of Mass Destruction".
60. Louis Freeh, Testimony to US Congress, 103rd Congress 2nd Session, "International Organized Crime and its Impact on the United States," *US Senate Governmental Affairs Committee, Permanent Subcommittee On Investigations*, Hearings Held 25 May 1994, p. 62.
61. Rob Edwards, "The nightmare scenario," *New Scientist*, vol. 172 issue 2312, 13 October 2001, p. 10.
62. Mark Henderson, "Terrorists 'could make atom bomb by raiding hospitals," *The Times*, 1 November 2001.
63. Barnaby, *Instruments of Terror*, pp. 172–4.
64. Correspondence with Major Ken Dombroski, US Army Artillery, (Ret.).
65. International Physicians for the Prevention of Nuclear War, "Crude," p. 38.
66. Cited in George Bunn and Fritz Steinhauser, "Guarding Nuclear Reactors and Material From Terrorists and Thieves," *Arms Control Today*, October 2001.
67. Rob Edwards, "The nightmare scenario," *New Scientist*, vol. 172 issue 2312, 13 October 2001, p. 10.
68. Sopko, "The Changing," pp. 7–8.
69. Falkenrath, Newman and Thayer, *America's Achilles Heel*, p. 15.
70. Jessica Stern, *The Ultimate Terrorists*, (Cambridge, MA: Harvard University Press, 1999), p.55.
71. Brian Jenkins, "Will Terrorists Go Nuclear?" (Santa Monica, CA: RAND, November 1975, P-5541), pp. 6–7.
72. Spector, Interview.
73. Kaplan and Marshall, *The Cult*, p. 271. Brackett, *Holy Terror*, p. 154.
74. Malcolm W. Browne, "Contaminant Called Extremely Rare", *New York Times*, 27 July 1985, Section 1, p. 27. "Traces of plutonium pour new puzzle into New York water woes", *The San Diego Union-Tribune*, 27 July 1985, p. A3.
75. Mark Hibbs, "Plutonium Thieves Pose No Threat to Drinking Water, LLNL Reports," *Nucleonics Week*, 36, no. 6 (9 February 1995), p. 13.
76. Rand-St Andrews Database.
77. Mullen, "Nuclear Violence", p. 243.
78. Phil Williams and Paul Woessner, "The Real Threat of Nuclear Smuggling," *Scientific American*, 274, no. 1 (January 1996), p. 30.

79. Michael Colton, "Out There They Thought UFOs Had landed. A Case of Hysteria, Politics, Poison and Toothpaste," *Washington Post*, 11 January 1998, p. F1. Chau Lam, "Guilty Plea in Anti-GOP Radium Plot," *Newsday*, 12 June 1997, p. A26. Olivia Winslow and Liam Pleven, "Radium Plot / 3 charged in plan to kill Suffolk GOP boss, others," *Newsday*, 14 June 1996, p. A5. John T. McQuiston, "Third Man Held In Plot To Use Radium To Kill N.Y. Officials," *New York Times*, 14 June 1996, p. B2.

80. Rand-St. Andrews Database.

81. Hoffman, "The Potential", p. 7.

82. *Agence France Presse*, 23 November 1995. Mark Hibbs, "Chechen Separatists Take Credit For Moscow Cesium-137 Threat," *Nuclear Fuel*, Volume 20 Number 25, 5 December 1995, p. 5.

83. Phil Reeves, "Moscow Tries To Play Down Radioactive Chechen Feat," *The Irish Times*, 25 November 1995, p. 11.

84. Stephane Orjollet, "Nuke package raises fear of Chechen attacks—but how real are they?" *Agence France Presse*, 24 November 1995.

85. Philip Webster and Roland Watson, "Bin Laden's Nuclear Threat," *The Times*, 26 October 2001, p. 1.

86. In September 1998, a deputy of bin Laden's, Mamdouh Mahmud Salim, was arrested in Germany, attempting to buy low grade reactor fuel. He was supposedly the victim of a criminal sting operation, believing he was purchasing material more readily usable to build a nuclear yield weapon. According to US court documents, Jamal al-Fadl, a former associate of bin Laden's, told the FBI that he had been offered uranium by a Sudanese intelligence officer for $1 million. He also stated that other al Qaida associates had sought enriched uranium throughout the mid-1990s, for the same purpose, to build a nuclear yield weapon. See Gavin Cameron, "Multi-track Microproliferation: Lessons from Aum Shinrikyo and Al Qaida," *Studies in Conflict & Terrorism*, 22/4 October-December 1999, pp. 287–9; Kimberly McCloud and Matthew Osborne, "WMD & Usama Bin Laden," Center for Nonproliferation Studies, http://cns.miis.edu/pubs/reports/binladen.htm accessed 23/10/01.

87. Adam Nathan and David Leppard, "Al-Qaeda's men held secret meetings to build 'dirty bomb'," *Sunday Times*, 14 October 2001, p. A5.

88. David Pugliese, "Police suspect bin Laden making 'dirty' nuclear bombs," *National Post*, 17 October 2001, www.nationalpost.com accessed 17/10/01.

89. Philip Webster and Roland Watson, "Bin Laden's Nuclear Threat," *The Times*, 26 October 2001, p. 1; "Nuclear Network: The need for action against bin Laden is sharper still," *The Times*, 26 October 2001, p. 21.

90. Cited in George Bunn and Fritz Steinhauser, "Guarding Nuclear Reactors and Material From Terrorists and Thieves," *Arms Control Today*, October 2001.

91. Dr. Mohamed ElBaradei, "Statement to the fifty-sixth regular session of the United Nations General Assembly," 22 October 2001, accessed on http://www.iaea.org/worldatom/Press/Statements/2001/ebsp2001n010.shtml.

Gavin Cameron is a fellow of the Centre for Military and Strategic Studies. He previously taught politics and contemporary history at the University of Salford, in the United Kingdom. He completed his doctorate at the University of St. Andrews, Scotland, and then held research posts at the Center for Nonproliferation Studies, part of the Monterey Institute of International Studies in California, and at the Belfer Center for Science and International Affairs, part of the Kennedy School of Government at Harvard University.

George Bunn and Chaim Braun

Terrorism Potential for Research Reactors Compared With Power Reactors: Nuclear Weapons, "Dirty Bombs," and Truck Bombs

Research Reactors

In statements about nuclear terrorism, there have been repeated expressions of concern about terrorists' attacks on nuclear power reactors but few about such attacks on research reactors. However, about half of the research reactors in the world contain highly enriched uranium that can be used for making nuclear weapons (International Atomic Energy Agency [IAEA], 2000). Highly enriched uranium (HEU) is enriched to 20% or more in uranium-235. Power reactors do not contain HEU, and their fuel cannot be made into nuclear weapons without enrichment of fresh fuel to HEU or separation of plutonium from spent fuel, major added technological undertakings.

Typical small university research reactors that burn HEU may contain less than one fifth of the nuclear material necessary to make a simple Hiroshima HEU gun-type nuclear weapon, the easiest for terrorists to make. They are likely to have additional irradiated or unirradiated HEU, or both, stored near the reactor. All but two U.S. university research reactors have been converted from HEU to low-enriched uranium (LEU), which is not weapon-usable without enrichment (Travelli, 2000). There are much larger U.S. government research reactors that still burn HEU, but they are thought to be well protected from theft and sabotage (National Council on Radiation Protection and Measurement [NCRP], 2002; National Research Council [NRC], 2002). Conversion of research reactors around the world from HEU to LEU has not been as successful as conversion of university reactors has been in the United States. There are almost 100 research reactors around the world using HEU of 90% or greater enrichment, and about 20 more that use 50% to 90% HEU (IAEA, 2000). Many countries besides the United States have government or industry research reactors containing much larger amounts of HEU than the 2 kg to 5 kg that university HEU research reactors typically burn (IAEA, 2000).

Research reactors in many countries around the world came from the United States pursuant to the "Atoms for Peace Program" proposed by President Eisenhower in 1953. He suggested that the Soviet Union and the United States transfer enriched uranium to a new international organization (what became the International Atomic Energy Agency or IAEA). These transfers would form an "atomic bank" from which other countries could withdraw uranium for their peaceful nuclear programs (Eisenhower, 1953). By then, in addition to the Soviet Union and the United States, Britain had tested a nuclear weapon, and Belgium, Canada, France, Sweden, Norway, Switzerland, and Italy had the beginnings of national nuclear programs (some had reactors for peaceful purposes and some had them for both peaceful and weapons purposes). The likelihood that Eisenhower's proposed program would produce proliferation of nuclear weapons, not just of peaceful uses of atomic energy, was apparently not considered seriously by Eisenhower and his top advisers before the speech was given. The possible connection between peaceful uses and weapons came as a surprise to Secretary of State Dulles after the speech was made. No physicists with knowledge about nuclear weapons had been consulted before it was given (G. Bunn, 1992; Smith, 1987). Eventually, however, after modifying the original U.S. proposal, the United States, then the Soviet Union, and then France and other countries supplied research reactors and weapon-usable HEU to burn in them to many countries around the world. In addition, the IAEA was formed to provide information, assistance, training, and safeguards for the peaceful development of atomic energy.

In 1978, the U.S. government started a program to convert the uranium it had supplied from HEU to LEU to prevent the HEU from being used to make nuclear weapons. At a conference on research reactors after September 11, Armando Travelli of Argonne National Laboratory, manager of the U.S. conversion program, had this to say (Travelli, 2002):

> In the past, our main concern [in the U.S. reactor conversion program] was that rogue nations or terrorist groups would develop nuclear weapons and that, by threatening to use those weapons, they would secure for themselves political and economic advantages that could drastically alter the world balance of power. . . . Today we know that if nuclear weapons were to fall in the hands of those who organized the September 11 attacks, there would be no threats or negotiations. . . . Innocent victims would die in a flash, without warning, killed by people driven by a twisted ideology and devoid of any respect for human life, including their own.

Research Reactors versus Power Reactors for Making Nuclear Weapons

There are many research reactors around the world. According to the IAEA (2000), there were 283 operating and 270 shutdown research reactors in 74 countries. The total of these two figures is higher than the total number of power reactors in operation and closed down around the world. Most reactors of both kinds use fresh fuel elements made of uranium. As we have seen, the LEU in power reactors is too low in its uranium-235 enrichment to be useful directly for making nuclear weapons. But, almost half of the operating research reactors in the world use HEU and most of those now shut down did so and may still contain HEU. There are hundreds of kg of HEU in operating and shutdown civilian research facilities in 58 countries, sometimes in quantities large enough in one facility to make a nuclear weapon (M. Bunn & G. Bunn, 2002). The total is enough to make many nuclear weapons.

The U.S. program begun in 1978 to convert reactors from HEU to LEU is called the Reduced Enrichment for Research and Test Reactors (RERTR) Program. Pursuant to it, 20 of the U.S.-supplied HEU research reactors outside the United States had been converted from HEU to LEU by March 2002. Except for one new HEU reactor in Germany, no new HEU research reactors have been built in the Western world since RERTR began. However, U.S.-supplied HEU reactors have not yet been converted in countries such as Argentina, Austria, Canada, France, Germany, Greece, Israel, Italy, Jamaica, Japan, Mexico, and Romania (Travelli, 2002).

In 1978, the Soviet Union launched its own program to reduce the enrichment of research reactor fuels it supplied to Eastern European countries and to Iraq, Libya, North Korea, and Vietnam. This program moved even more slowly than the U.S. program during the 1980s and 1990s. France also supplied large research reactors to other countries including Israel (uranium without enrichment) and Iraq (HEU fueled). According to the IAEA, government or industry research reactors with large HEU inventories were located in the year 2000 in Argentina, Australia, Austria, Belgium, Canada, Chile, China, Czech Republic, France, Germany, Greece, Hungary, Romania, Russia, South Africa, Switzerland, Taiwan, Ukraine, United Kingdom, United States, Uzbekistan, Vietnam, and Yugoslavia. Adding IAEA figures for operating research reactors to those that are shut down but may still house HEU fuel, there remain about as many HEU research reactors as LEU ones in the world (IAEA, 2000, 2002).

Delays in conversion of the HEU-fueled reactors to LEU fuel have resulted for technical and financial reasons. Designing LEU research reactor fuel that can accomplish the tasks that HEU fuel can accomplish has taken years of development that is still going on. Although the program started in 1978, funding was cut off for several years. There have been recent patent issues arising from the development effort that have held up some conversions (Civiak, 2002; Travelli, 2002). The similar Russian conversion program also was held up by funding problems and the need to develop an LEU fuel that would do essentially what the HEU fuels did for research purposes. Only recently, when funding became available from the United States, was it possible to conduct research on what LEU fuel could be substituted in Russian-built reactors. Thus, for many reasons, the conversion programs have not moved forward as fast as post–September 11 concerns suggest they should have.

As we have seen, to make a nuclear weapon from uranium, the weapon's uranium-235 content must be more than 20%. Moreover, a considerably higher percentage makes it easier to build a dependable weapon. This is particularly true for a terrorist group, which may not be well versed in the fine points of designing and manufacturing such weapons. Indeed, the higher the enrichment level of the HEU, the more manageable the weapon will be in size and the more likely to explode rather than fizzle. Assuming a simple Hiroshima gun-type nuclear weapon, something more than 50 kg (110 pounds) of HEU of 90% or greater enrichment in uranium-235 may be needed to make one nuclear weapon. More HEU would be needed if the uranium-235 enrichment level was lower than 90%. On the other hand, if 90% or higher enrichment in uranium-235 were used with a neutron reflector or in an implosion weapon using modern high-power explosives, the amount needed for a critical mass might be 15 kg to 25 kg.[1] According to DOE (1997),

> Several kilograms of plutonium, or several times that amount of HEU, are enough to make a bomb. With access to sufficient quantities of these materials, most nations and even some sub-national groups would be technically capable of producing a nuclear weapon.

Most research reactors do not contain 50 kg or even 15 kg of 90% or higher HEU, although some government and industry reactors do. However, combining the HEU within a medium-sized government or industry reactor with the inventories of fresh and irradiated fuel available at the site of the reactor might produce enough. Moreover, if more than one research reactor exists in a country, that country could use the combined fissile content of its reactors to produce one or more weapons in a nuclear breakout situation. Iraq was trying to produce a nuclear weapon out of fresh *and* irradiated HEU fuel rods from one French-supplied research reactor and another Russian-supplied research reactor at the end of the Gulf War (Travelli, 2002; von Hippel, 2001).

In 2000, there were almost 100 research reactors in the world with HEU enriched to 90% or more (IAEA, 2000). An earlier IAEA estimate was that HEU research reactors still outnumbered LEU reactors in Africa, the Middle East, Eastern Europe, Russia, and in the industrialized countries of the Western Pacific rim, but not in Western Europe (Ritchie, 1997).

Research reactor fuel becomes very radioactive if it is irradiated continuously for a long time in a high neutron-flux environment. However, research reactor experiments are often of short duration and the reactor may be shut down between experiments. Some research reactors also may operate at low power. Moreover, the radioactivity of irradiated fuel reduces over time if it is not burned again. Used fuel in a research reactor pool may well include assemblies that are very radioactive, assemblies that are not radioactive at all, and others in between. Some *irradiated* fuel from research reactors may thus be usable for making nuclear weapons if the enrichment is high enough and the radioactivity is not too high, as was the case for the Iraqi bomb-making attempt.

Power reactors typically operate more than 75% of the time. They are maintained in continuous operation as long as possible because they are needed to supply power and they are typically not shut down to reload fresh fuel until some of the fuel in the reactor has been burned for so long that its radioactivity has significantly increased. Thus, the spent fuel taken from power reactors is usually highly radioactive and dangerous to handle even for terrorists willing to take greater chances with their lives. Close exposure to the fuel for a short period could produce radiation sickness followed by painful death. On the other hand, as we have seen, research reactor fuel may be highly radioactive in some cases and much less radioactive in others. An educated terrorist with a dose rate meter could tell what used fuel could be handled with lower risk.

There was great concern about a research reactor holding at least 50 kg of HEU in Vinca, Serbia, during the fighting in the Balkans but the HEU was recently returned safely to Russia. Not counting countries having nuclear weapons, research reactors with more than 20 kg of 90% HEU content exist in Argentina, Belarus, Belgium, Germany, Italy, Japan, and Ukraine. The reactors in Belarus and Ukraine were built when those countries were part of the Soviet Union. The research reactor in Belarus has more than 370 kg of HEU, including enough enriched to 90% to make several bombs. One reactor in the Ukraine also contains large amounts of 90% HEU. Up to two kg of 90% HEU was reported to have disappeared from a research reactor in the Abkhazia region of the former Soviet republic of Georgia during civil resistance there. HEU of somewhat lower U-235 enrichment level, probably stolen from one of the research reactors in Obninsk, Russia, was seized by police in Western Europe when arresting the alleged thieves, and LEU fuel rods were stolen from a research reactor in the Congo (M. Bunn, Holdren, & Weir, 2002; Civiak, 2002; Steinhausler & Zaitseva, 2002).

In sum, HEU from research reactors, particularly the larger ones operated by government and industry, could well be the source of the explosive material for a terrorist nuclear weapon if the nuclear fuel could be successfully stolen from the reactor. But the LEU burned in power reactors and in an increasing number of research reactors cannot be directly used to make nuclear weapons.

Research Reactors versus Power Reactors for Making Radiological Weapons.

Radiological dispersal devices (RDDs), or "dirty bombs," are easier to make than nuclear weapons. One such potential device constructed by Chechens to scare the Russian authorities consisted of a container of radioactive material from medical or industrial sources attached to conventional explosives (Steinhausler & Zaitseva, 2002). The explosives were not exploded apparently because the Chechens wanted to gain Russian attention rather than cause major disruption by dispersing radioactive material. An RDD would probably not kill anyone not close enough to be killed by the high explosives. If effective as intended, however, it would disperse radioactive materials over a much wider area than the area in which people could be injured by the explosive force of the bomb. The size and shape of the area irradiated would depend on how large the explosion was, how well the radioactive particles were carried in the air, and what direction the wind was blowing. The dispersal could cause cancers eventually and, at the time, could cause panic in the irradiated area. It might require removal of the population from that area until the dispersed radioactive particles were cleaned away. The disruption to regular and business life and the economic loss could be great (NRC, 2002; Wald, 2002). In addition to being called dirty bombs, RDDs are sometimes referred to as weapons of "mass disruption" rather than "mass destruction."

Radioactive materials for making RDDs could probably be stolen from hospitals and industrial plants more easily than from research or power reactors. According to a committee of scientific experts, "Given the wide use of radiation sources in the United States and other countries, a determined terrorist would probably have little trouble obtaining material for use in an RDD" (NRC, 2002). However, typical hospital and industrial sources may contain only a few grams of easily available radioactive materials, and their dispersal by an explosion would be unlikely to cover a wide area. The area and concentration of dispersal of radioactivity might be too small and too low to cause major disruption. A knowledgeable radiological weapon maker who wanted major disruption would have to find a large quantity of radioactive materials.

He or she could perhaps find a large supply of Cobalt 90 or some similar radioactive material used in large quantities by industry or attempt to collect many grams of radioactivity from several industrial and hospital sources. Although small amounts of radioactive material from hospital and industry sources might be the easiest to acquire (large industrial sources are likely to be better protected), collecting many small sources from many places would likely be necessary. Doing so might well take longer and involve more risks of apprehension than stealing used fuel rods from a poorly protected, shutdown, university research reactor.

From a terrorist's point of view, the fact that the used fuel from such a reactor is likely not to be as highly radioactive as the spent fuel from a nuclear power plant may be an advantage. The NCRP (2002) had this to say about making radiological dispersion devices:

> The most likely scenarios involve the use of a solid radioactive material that would be of low enough activity that the construction and delivery of the RDD will not seriously inhibit the terrorist carrying out the attack. Large sources of penetrating radiation [such as irradiated power reactor fuel] are difficult to handle safely and without detection by authorities. Shielding materials that are adequate to protect both the individuals who construct the devices and those who are to deploy them complicate the design and fabrication of effective weapons. (p. 15)

Building an RDD from irradiated research reactor fuel may be within the reach of many terrorists, whereas making a nuclear weapon would take greater information and skill. The arrest of an alleged Al Qaeda terrorist who is reported to have studied how to make RDDs suggests the possible threat (Bridis, 2002).

Spent reactor fuel that has been recently removed from a power reactor will typically have been irradiated for a long time and will be too hot to handle even for suicidal terrorists. The same may be true of spent fuel from large government or industrial research reactors. If the gamma ray and neutron dosage is high enough, the radiation could affect the central nervous system fairly quickly and make the bomb maker unconscious. But this level of radioactivity typically results from the high burn-up that happens in power reactors and some large research reactors more often than in small university research reactors. Thus, for fashioning RDDs intended to frighten and disrupt, spent reactor fuel from small university reactors or from little-used government or industry research reactors could be more attractive to terrorists than spent fuel from power reactors.

With spent fuel from any reactor, terrorists would need to know the radioactive dose rate of the material to ensure against radiation sickness effects while working with it. Assuming the theft of research reactor fuel that had not been irradiated for too long a time or that had been out of the reactor long enough for its radioactivity to have cooled significantly—both of which are more likely with small university research reactors than with power reactors—making a radiological weapon out of used research reactor fuel seems more likely than making one from used power reactor fuel.

Research Reactors versus Power Reactors as Terrorist Attack Targets.

The typical power reactor is likely to have much more radioactive spent fuel in cooling ponds and to contain much more radioactivity within its core than the typical university research reactor or less-used large government or industry research reactor. A power reactor would likely be a more attractive target for a suicidal terrorist truck bomber or airplane pilot because the radioactive dispersal possibilities could be large—if the attack was successful in breaking through the reactor's containment building or into the spent fuel pool or in causing sufficient damage to other vital areas of the reactor. This dispersal seems far beyond what might be achieved in a successful terrorist attack involving a truck bomb or aircraft crash at a typical, less-well-protected research reactor. However, from the terrorists' point of view, a university reactor may appear much more vulnerable because its protection barriers against attack are likely to be much lower than those of power reactors or government or industry research reactors and it is more likely to be located within or near a populated area.

Protection Barriers for Nuclear Fuel in Research Reactors versus those for Power Reactor Fuel.

Both irradiated and fresh nuclear fuel are likely to be less well protected from terrorist attacks at university research reactors than at power reactors for many reasons.

First, typical research reactor fuel elements are much smaller than those for power reactors. The large size (perhaps 10 ft long) and weight (up to 1 ton) of power reactor fuel mean that a crane or other heavy machinery is needed to move an assembly. Taking it apart is not easy. On the other hand, research reactor fuel elements may be 4 ft long and weigh a few 10s of pounds. They can be disassembled more easily and can typically be moved by one person, properly shielded.

Second, university research reactors tend to be located in or near cities—in places where there are many people going back and forth. Government and industry research reactors are more likely to be somewhat removed from populations and surrounded by stronger fences or walls than university research reactors. Power reactors tend to be both farther from cities and more likely to be surrounded by fences, open areas, and walls, which can delay attackers and provide opportunity to observe them before the attack if guards are on duty, as is typical at power reactors.

Third, power reactors are ordinarily in operation all the time except for maintenance or when the fuel needs to be changed. Operating personnel are likely to be present during the day even when the reactor is shut down and guards are likely to be present both day and night. Many university research reactors are shut down and left unused for significant periods with only skeleton staff nearby. Power reactors are typically guarded by professional guards hired and trained for the purpose. That may also be true of government and industry research reactors, which are often in operation most of the time. University reactors, with intermittent operation, may rely on the university campus police who are usually present elsewhere and not trained adequately in antiterrorist procedures. When the research reactor is not in operation, they are not likely to check it often.

Fourth, as we have seen, the irradiated fuel removed from university research reactors is likely to be less radioactive than that from power reactors. Moreover, many research reactors are not used as much as their suppliers or owners originally expected or are operated at a lower power level than originally anticipated. Indeed, many university reactors are no longer operated. If the fuel has been removed, as is the practice in the United States, they are not likely to constitute a risk. But this is not a uniform practice. There is probably a great deal of irradiated research reactor fuel accumulated from many years of past operation that is stored in or near research reactors around the world, fuel that is easier to handle for terrorists than power reactor fuel would be.

Finally, research reactors, particularly those at universities, tend to have less effective security than power reactors and their fuel. Inadequate protection may result for several reasons.

1. There is no treaty requiring any level of protection for power or research reactors from terrorists. The relevant treaty, the Convention on Physical Protection of Nuclear Material, only provides protection standards to protect nuclear material from being stolen while it is in international transport. A consensus of most of the treaty's parties to amend it to cover material used or stored domestically, and prohibit sabotage as well as theft, was achieved in general terms in May 2001. However, except for some general principles, no specific standards for domestic protection were specified in this consensus agreement. Such standards exist in the treaty now for international transport and for storage while awaiting international transport. But the parties have been unable to agree to apply those or any other specific standards to regular domestic operations. Without such standards, the amendment has much less value (G. Bunn & Zaitseva, 2002; M. Bunn & Bunn, 2002; NRC, 2002).

2. In 1999, the IAEA issued revised recommendations for protecting nuclear material from sabotage. These are in IAEA Information Circular 225, Revision 4. This revision contains general provisions on sabotage, such as,

> The objective of the physical protection system should be to prevent or delay access to or control over the nuclear facility or nuclear material through the use of a set of protective measures including physical barriers or other technical means [e.g., security alarms,

closed-circuit TV cameras, electronic sensors, finger-print identification devices, etc.] or the use of guards and response forces so that the guards or response forces can respond in time to prevent the successful completion of sabotage.

This lists detailed recommendations on how to guard against sabotage of *power* reactors, but it contains no specific recommendations for sabotage to *research* reactors. Moreover, unless it is brought into force by the bilateral agreement of the reactor supplier and the recipient country, it remains only general recommendations. Unless national legislation or regulations or bilateral supply agreements require these recommendations, research reactor operators may ignore them.

3. IAEA Information Circular 225, Revision 4, also contains recommendations for protection against *theft* of nuclear material by terrorists. These apply wherever the nuclear materials are located within a country, including storage at or within research reactors. They say that the level of protection should be based on what *the country perceives the threat to be*. This is called the "design basis threat." Unlike the U.S. regulations issued for reactors by the U.S. Nuclear Regulatory Commission, these recommendations do not specify any minimum threat to guard against. Circular 225 divides nuclear material into categories and specifies the strongest protection recommendations for the most sensitive categories, one of which is HEU of 5 kg or more. Irradiated reactor fuel is not in this category but in the next most strongly protected category. The circular then sets forth some useful standards of protection against "unauthorized removal of nuclear material in use and storage." Again, however, these remain only recommendations except for countries subject to nuclear supply agreements where the supplier country has required adherence to them or where the country has otherwise adopted them through national regulations or legislation. In general, supply agreements suggest simply that the recipient country take these recommendations into account.

4. The Nuclear Suppliers' Guidelines (Nuclear Suppliers Group, 1996), negotiated among various nuclear suppliers to apply to what they supply to other countries, summarize what protection against unauthorized use should be provided by recipients. The guidelines say HEU and spent fuel rods should be used and stored within a *protected area*, "an area under constant surveillance by guards or electronic devices surrounded by a physical barrier with a limited number of points of entry under appropriate control, or any area with an equivalent level of physical protection." HEU of 5 kg or more should, in addition, be used and stored within a *highly protected area* inside the outer *protected area* with

access restricted to persons whose trustworthiness has been determined and which [area] is under surveillance by guards who are in communication with response forces. Specific measures taken in this context should have as their objective the detection and prevention of any assault, unauthorized access or unauthorized removal of material.

The guidelines suggest that these standards "should be" the subject of negotiation between the suppliers and recipients of nuclear reactors and nuclear fuel (Nuclear Suppliers' Group, 1996). Provisions relating to them appear in many supply agreements, but they are not public knowledge and are not required to be submitted to IAEA inspectors so that the inspectors can check whether the recommended protections have in fact been provided. Moreover, they are not applicable to small university-type research reactors unless the total HEU present in or near the reactor is 5 kg or more. Because of provisions in federal legislation and U.S. practice, U.S. agreements with foreign recipients usually call for the possibility of occasional U.S. inspections of the facility to observe, among other things, the protection the recipient provides (Nuclear Nonproliferation Act, 1978; Atomic Energy Act of 1954). The Nuclear Suppliers'Guidelines themselves do not call for inspections, and other suppliers may not ask for them. Moreover, this requirement did not prevent the theft of U.S.-supplied research reactor fuel from a reactor in the Congo.

5. National statutes and regulations on physical protection of reactors vary a great deal around the world. A survey by the Nuclear Energy Agency of the international Organization for Economic Cooperation and Development (OECD) showed major differences from country to country (OECD, 2000). The 29 countries in the survey, mostly well-developed countries with significant nuclear programs, seemed to have a wide variety of security requirements set forth in reactor licenses, regulations, statutes, and royal decrees. The summary did not compare the requirements to the regulatory recommendations of the IAEA, and it is not possible to do that effectively from the information provided. The variations in regulatory requirements raise questions about such compliance. In most cases, the OECD nuclear programs began long before the current IAEA physical protection recommendations and Nuclear Suppliers' Guidelines were issued, and some of the OECD respondents to the survey were themselves nuclear suppliers (OECD, 2000).

6. In a survey conducted by Stanford University, similar country variations appeared in actual physical protection practices for HEU research reactors (with 5 kg or more). Six of the responses to a questionnaire, mostly from less-developed countries than those covered by the OECD survey, relate to government research reactors. The countries were located in Latin America, Central and South Asia, and Eastern and Western Europe. Four of the five that answered questions on threat perception said their facilities faced major threats of armed violence from outsiders and that collusion by insiders (possibly involuntary collusion) with the outsiders was feared as well. However, despite considerable similarities in *threat perceptions*, there were great variations in the *level of protection* provided (barriers, sensors, etc.) for the protected area and the inner areas within the protected areas where the HEU was stored or used. For example, one respondent confirmed that the outer protected area could be accessed by climbing a wall or walking around the end of a fence or by crawling through a duct through a wall or something similar. Others described varying degrees of stronger protection. For the inner area where HEU should be kept, all said there were guards, at least during working hours. But two did not provide guns for the guards. Three said that during hours when the area was not in use for experiments or other purposes, there were "standard locks or better at critical access points" instead of guards. Another three, these with more nuclear experience and resources, said they used "ID actuated locks or better" when guards were not present. Contrast this with the Nuclear Suppliers Guidelines recommendation described above that recommend, for both spent fuel and HEU of more than 5 kg, "constant surveillance by guards or electronic/sensors" (G. Bunn, Steinhausler, & Zaitseva, 2002).

7. The variation in *actual* practices for protection despite IAEA recommendations or Nuclear Suppliers'Guidelines was confirmed by experts who were participants in the first 10 missions of the IAEA's "International Physical Protection Advisory Services" to review security at nuclear facilities—mostly in Eastern Europe where particular countries had requested assistance. The experts reported that their visits to nuclear sites showed that physical protection practices "*will vary from State to State. Differences in culture, perceived threat, financial and technical resources, and national laws* are some of the reasons for variations" (Soo Hoo et al., 2000).

8. Given these differences in the way states respond to similar threat perceptions; given the lower level of financial resources and importance usually provided to university and some little-used government research reactors as compared with power reactors; given the lack of specific provisions for protection from sabotage of research reactors in, for example, the Convention on Physical Protection of Nuclear Material and the IAEA recommendations; and given the intermittent operation of university and some government research reactors as compared with power reactors, it should not be surprising that the actual practices for protection of research reactors tend to be much weaker than those for power reactors.

Conclusion

Research reactors and their fuel are more likely than power reactors to be the targets of well-informed terrorists seeking to make dirty bombs or nuclear weapons. On the other hand, the fuel from many of them is likely to be much less radioactive than that from power reactors. This means that their fuel will usually be easier for the terrorists to handle, and it is less likely to be adequately protected from theft or from external attacks by truck bombs and aircraft.

Note

1. For the purposes of its safeguards system to account for all the uranium and plutonium in reactors of non-nuclear-weapon countries, the International Atomic Energy Agency (IAEA) has designated 25 kg of Highly enriched uranium (HEU) as a "significant quantity." According to the IAEA, this means that it is "the approximate quantity of nuclear material in respect to which, taking into account any conversion process involved, the possibility of manufacturing a nuclear explosive device cannot be excluded" (http://www.iaea.org/worldatom/inforesource/other/safeguars/pia3810.html). U.S. experts believe that something like 15 kg of HEU enriched to 90% or more in uranium-235 is sufficient to make a nuclear weapon. This helps to explain the Department of Energy (DOE) quotation in the text that follows this note.

References

Bridis, T. (2002, June 10). U.S. arrests alleged bomb terrorist. Associated Press.

Bunn, G. (1992). *Arms control by committee*. Stanford, CA: Stanford University Press.

Bunn, G., Steinhausler, F., & Zaitseva, L. (2002, June). *Could terrorists or thieves get weapons usable material from research reactors and facilities?* Proceedings of the 43rd annual meeting of Institute of Nuclear Materials Management, Northbrook, IL.

Bunn, G., & Zaitseva, L. (2002). Efforts to improve nuclear material and facility security. In *2002 SIPRI annual report* (App. 10D, pp. 11–14). Stockholm: Stockholm Institute of Peace Research.

Bunn, M., & Bunn, G. (2002, Spring). Strengthening nuclear security against post September 11 threats of theft and sabotage. *Journal of Nuclear Materials Management, 30*(3), 48.

Bunn, M., Holdren, J. P., & Weir, A. (2002). *Securing nuclear weapons and materials: Seven steps for immediate action*. Cambridge, MA: Kennedy School of Government, Harvard University Press.

Civiak, R. L. (2002). *Closing the gaps: Securing high enriched uranium in the Former Soviet Union and Eastern Europe*. Washington, DC: Federation of American Scientists.

Department of Energy, U.S. (DOE). (1997). *Final nonproliferation and arms control assessment of weapons-usable fissile material storage and excess plutonium disposition alternatives* (DOE/NN-0007, p. vii). Washington, DC: Author.

Department of Energy, U.S. (DOE). (2002). *FY 2003 budget request: Detailed budget justification. Defense nuclear nonproliferation*. Washington, DC: Author. Retrieved from http://www.cfo.doe.gov/budget/03budget/content/defnn/nuclenonpl.pdf

Eisenhower, D. E. (1953). *Atoms for peace proposal: Address of President Eisenhower to the U.N. General Assembly. U.S. Department of State, Documents on disarmament, 1945–1959*. Washington, DC: General Printing Office.

International Atomic Energy Agency (IAEA). (2000). *Nuclear research reactors of the world*. (Ref. Data Series 3, pp. 59–69).

International Atomic Energy Agency (IAEA). (2002). *Research reactor data base*. Retrieved from http://www.iaea.org

National Council on Radiation Protection and Measurement (NCRP). (2002). *Management of terrorist events involving radioactive material*.

National Research Council (NRC), Committee on science and technology in countering terrorism, division of engineering and physical sciences. (2002). *Making the nation safer: The role of science and technology in countering terrorism*.

Nuclear Nonproliferation Act of 1978, PL 95–242, 1978.

Nuclear Suppliers' Group. (1996). *Guidelines for nuclear transfers, IAEA Information Circular 254, Rev. 4*. [Pamphlet, Add. 1, par. 3 and Annex C]

Organization for Economic Cooperation and Development (OECD), Nuclear Energy Agency (2000). *Nuclear legislation: Analytical study. Regulatory and institutional framework for nuclear activities*.

Ritchie, I. (1997). Technical and administrative preparations required for shipment of research reactor spent fuel to its country of origin. IAEA-Argonne National Laboratory Training Course, Lecture L.1.2, text at Figs. 8, 9, 10.

Smith, G. C. (1987). *Adviser to Dulles*. In J. A. Thompson (Ed.), *Gerard Smith on arms control* (p. 117). College Park: University of Maryland Press.

Soo Hoo, M., Ek, D., Hageman, A., Jenkins, T., & Weiss, B. (2000). *International physical protection advisory service: Observations and recommendations for improvement*. Proceedings of the 42nd annual meeting of the Institute of Nuclear Materials Management, Northbrook, IL.

Steinhausler, F., & Zaitseva, L. (2002). *Database on nuclear smuggling, theft and orphan radiation sources*. Stanford, CA: Center for International Security and Cooperation, Stanford University.

Travelli, A. (2000). *Status and progress in the RERTR program in the year 2000*. Proceedings of the 2000 international meeting on reduced enrichment for research and test reactors, Las Vegas, NV.

Travelli, A. (2002). *Progress of the RERTR program in 2001*. Proceedings of the International Conference on Research Reactor Fuel Management, Ghent, Belgium.

von Hippel, F. (2001, November/December). Recommendations for preventing terrorism: FAS Public Interest Report. *Journal of the Federation of American Scientists, 54*(6).

Wald, M. L. (2002, June 11). Fear itself is the main threat of a dirty bomb, experts say. *New York Times*, pp. A–18.

George Bunn is a consulting professor at the Center for International Security and Cooperation at Stanford University. He was the first general counsel for the U.S. Arms Control and Disarmament Agency (ACDA; 1961–1969), helped negotiate the nuclear Non-Proliferation Treaty, and later became U.S. ambassador to the

Geneva Disarmament Conference. He has a degree in electrical engineering from the University of Wisconsin and a law degree from Columbia University.

Chaim Braun is a vice president of Altos Management Partners, Inc., and a Center for International Security Cooperation Science fellow and affiliate at Stanford University. He is a member of the Near-Term Deployment and the Economic Cross-Cut Working Groups of the Department of Energy (DOE) Generation IV Roadmap study.

Douglas M. Chapin et al.

Nuclear Power Plants and Their Fuel as Terrorist Targets

If you watch television or read repeated public statements of concern about nuclear power plants as terrorist targets, you would be justified in believing that spent nuclear fuel casks being shipped to Nevada for storage are each a nuclear catastrophe just waiting to be triggered. These casks have been called "mobile Chernobyls," and we are told they are capable of causing "tens of thousands of deaths" (*1*). What are the facts about the safety of nuclear shipments and power plants?

Since 11 September 2001, the U.S. nuclear industry and its regulators have been reevaluating plant and fuel shipment safety. These studies are being kept secret. But it is no secret that basic engineering facts and laws of nature limit the damage that can result. Extensive analysis, backed by full-scale field tests, show that there is virtually nothing one could do to these shipping casks that would cause a significant public hazard (*2, 3*). Before shipment, the fuel elements have been cooled for several years, so the decay heat and the short-lived radioactivity have died down. They cannot explode, and there is no liquid radioactivity to leak out. They are nearly indestructible, having been tested against collisions, explosives, fire, and water. Only the latest antitank artillery could breach them, and then, the result was to scatter a few chunks of spent fuel onto the ground. There seems to be no reason to expect harmful effects of the radiation any significant distance from the cask.

Similarly, we read that airplanes can fly through the reinforced, steel-lined 1.5-m-thick concrete walls surrounding a nuclear reactor and inevitably cause a meltdown resulting in "tens of thousands of deaths" and "make a huge area of the U.S. uninhabitable for centuries," to quote some recent stories (*4*). However, there seems to be no credible way to achieve that result (*5, 6*). No airplane, regardless of size, can fly through such a wall. This has been calculated in detail and tested in 1988 by flying an unmanned plane at 215 m/s (about 480 mph) into a test wall 3.6 m thick. The plane, including its fuel tanks, collapsed against the outside of the wall, penetrating a few centimeters. The engines were a better penetrator, but still dug in only 5 cm. Analyses show that larger planes fully offset their greater impact by absorbing more energy during their collapse. Higher speed increases the impact, but not enough to matter. And inside the containment wall are additional walls of concrete and steel protecting the reactor.

Is it possible to cause a nuclear reactor to melt down some other way? Yes, it happened at Three Mile Island (TMI) in 1979. Reactors are much improved since then, and the probability of such an accident is now much less. But suppose it happens, through terrorist action or other; what then? Well, the TMI meltdown caused no significant environmental degradation or increased injury to any person (*7–10*), not even to the plant operators who stayed on duty. It has been said that this lack of public impact was due primarily to the containment structure. But studies after the accident showed that nearly all of the harmful fission products dissolved in the water and condensed out on the inside containment surfaces. Even if containment had been severely breached, little radioactivity would have escaped. Few, if any, persons would have been harmed.

To test how far the 10 to 20 metric tons of molten reactor penetrated the 13-cm-thick bottom of the reactor vessel on which it rested, samples were machined out of the vessel and examined. The molten mass did not even fully penetrate the 0.5-cm cladding, confirming tests in Karlsruhe, Germany, and in Idaho, that the "China syndrome" is not a credible possibility (8–10).

The accident at Chernobyl in 1986 is simply not applicable to American reactors. The burning graphite dispersed most of the fission products directly into the atmosphere. Even in that situation, with no evacuation for several days, the United Nations' carefully documented investigation UNSCEAR-2000 (11) reported that there were 30 deaths to plant operators and firefighters, but no significant increase in mortality or cancer due to irradiation of the public have been observed (12,13). A possible link between exposure and thyroid cancer is still under study (14). The terrible and widespread consequences of that accident— increased suicide, alcoholism, depression, and unemployment (15), plus 100,000 unnecessary abortions (16)—were caused primarily by fear of radiation and by poor planning based on that fear. The evacuated lands are generally now no more radioactive than the natural background levels where many people have lived healthily for generations.

It's not surprising that some people overstate the concern about radiation, for whatever reason. But it is surprising that most nuclear advocates are reluctant to challenge such claims. They say they just want to be cautious. But striving for maximum caution leads to the assertion that we should act as if even the tiniest amount of radiation might be harmful, despite the large body of good scientific evidence that it is not (17–22). This policy has scared people away from mammograms and other life-saving treatments and has caused many Americans to die each year from pathogens that could have been killed by food irradiation (23). It has piled regulations on nuclear medicine facilities that caused many of them to shut down. And now, "permissible doses" have been pushed below those found in natural radiation backgrounds (24–26).

Such cautiousness has drawbacks when applied to design and operation of nuclear facilities. But it is particularly dangerous when applied to terrorism. To tell people that they and the Earth are in mortal danger from events that cannot cause significant public harm is to play into the hands of terrorists by making a minor event a cause for life-endangering panic. Now is the time to clear the air and speak a few simple scientific and engineering truths.

References and Notes

1. "[A] major fire is possible which could release 25 times more radioactive material than Chernobyl . . . such a fire could render 29,000 square miles uninhabitable…cause 28,000 cancer deaths and $59 billion in damage." B. C. Smith, *The Tech*, 1 May 2002. Available at: www-tech.mit.edu/V122/N22/col22brice.22c.html.
2. The shipping casks and the spent fuel are described in the 207-page Appendix J of the *Yucca Mountain Environmental Impact Statement* (DOE/EIS-0250, Government Printing Office, Washington, DC, 2002); available at: www.ymp.gov/documents/feis_a/vol_2/eis_j_bm.pdf
3. For an independent analysis, see J. L. Sprung et al., *Re-examination of Spent Fuel Shipment Risk Estimates* (NUREG/CR-6672, Sandia National Laboratory, Albuquerque, NM, 2000); available at http://ttd.sandia.gov/nrc/nuregcr6672/chap1.pdf
4. "You could have tens of thousands to hundreds of thousands of fatalities from cancer . . . the downwind path from these types of casualties could extend for hundreds of miles."

P. Leventhal, Director of Nuclear Control Institute, on the Cable News Network, 1 February 2002; "Nuclear specialist Mark Gaffney said that an attack on a plant could make a huge area of the US uninhabitable for centuries." D. Nelson, in OneWorld UK, 2 November 2001 (www.oneworld.net/uk). To which the Government reportedly responded, "Of course it would be a big mess. Would it lead to multiple tens of thousands of deaths? That's much less certain." B. Henderson, Nuclear Regulatory Commission (NRC) representative, in K. Davidson, *San Francisco Chronicle*, 5 October 2001, p. A6. NRC Commissioner Nils Diaz recognized the need to correct this situation in his plenary talk at the American Nuclear Society Conference, Hollywood, FL, 10 June 2002: "I do not believe nuclear power is being portrayed in a balanced manner. . . . This is probably the fault of all of us who know better . . . public health and safety consequences might very well be nuclear power and radiation technology's strongest and most favorable arguments when comparing risks and benefits." But on 5 August 2002, the Associated Press reported that NRC declared that "the best available way" to prevent a public health hazard is "controlling the airspace over atomic power plants."

5. "A hijacked commercial airliner loaded with explosive jet fuel like the one that hit the Pentagon on September 11 could not penetrate a U.S. nuclear power reactor and release deadly radiation," from a Reuters report, 17 June 2002, of a National Press Foundation Seminar. The report, commissioned by the Nuclear Energy Institute of independent contractors, is being reviewed by industry experts and will be completed this fall. The study reports detailed computer modeling, confirmed by large-scale tests.

6. Videotapes of tests of an unmanned airplane impacting a mockup of a section of containment wall can be seen at www.sandia.gov/media/NRgallery00-03.htm.

7. J. G. Kemeny, Chairman, *The Need for Change: The Legacy of TMI*, Report of the President's Commission on the accident at Three Mile Island, October 1979 (Government Printing Office, Washington, DC, 1979), 179 pp.

8. Organization for Economic Cooperation and Development (OECD), *Three Mile Island Reactor Pressure Vessel Investigation Project: Achievements and Significant Results*, Proceedings of an open forum sponsored by the OECD Nuclear Energy Agency and the U.S. Nuclear Regulatory Commission, Boston, MA, 20 to 23 October 1993.

9. See especially N. Cole, T. Friderichs, B. Lipford, pp. 81–91 of (*8*), "Specimens Removed from the Damaged TMI Reactor Vessel."

10. N. Cole, *"TMI-2, A learning experience: Assessing the damage"* (MPR-889, MPR Associates, Alexandria, VA, 1985).

11. *Sources and Effects of Ionizing Radiation: UNSCEAR 2000 Report to the General Assembly, with Scientific Annexes* (U.N. Scientific Committee on the Effects of Atomic Radiation, U.N. Publications, New York, 2000); available at www.unscear.org/reports.htm. See especially "The Chernobyl accident," vol. 1, p. 13 and the extensive scientific annexes, specifically vol. 2, Annex J, "Exposures and effects of the Chernobyl accident."

12. This report (*11*) was reviewed and the conclusions on Chernobyl reaffirmed in the 3rd International Conference, Health Effects of the Chernobyl Accident: Results of 15 Years of Follow-Up Studies, Kiev, Ukraine, 4 to 8 June 2001, sponsored by UNSCEAR; the World Health Organization; other U.N. agencies; and Ukraine, Belarus, and Russia; available at www.unscear.org/chernobyl.htm. Z. Jaworowski, member and former chairman of UNSCEAR, discusses the significance of these findings in *Phys. Today* 52, 24 (1999).

13. Z. Jaworowski, *Science* 293, 605 (2002).

14. See D. Williams, *Nature Rev. Cancer* 2, 543 (2002) and recent news coverage [R. Service, *Science* 292, 420 (20 April 2001)].

15. *The Human Consequences of the Chernobyl Nuclear Accident: A Strategy for Recovery, A Report Commissioned by UNDP and UNICEF, with the support of UN-OCHA and WHO* (25 January 2002). The report (356KB) is summarized in a U.N. news release at www.undp.org/dpa/frontpagearchive/2002/february/7feb02/ and is available for download at that URL.

16. G. Walinder, *"Has radiation protection become a health hazard?"* (Swedish Nuclear Training and Safety Center, Nykoping, 1995).

17. H. F. Henry, *JAMA* 176, 671 (1961).

18. A. M. Brues, *Science* 128, 693 (1958).

19. L. Gerber et al., *Q. Rev. Biol.* 74 (no. 3), 273 (1999).

20. R. S. Yalow, *The Scientist* 2 (13 June), 11 (1988).

21. L. E. Feinendegen, M. Pollycove, *J. Nucl. Med.* 42 (no. 7), 17N (2001).

22. M. Pollycove, L. E. Feinendegen, *J. Nucl. Med.* 42 (no. 9), 26N (2001).

23. The FDA site on Food Irradiation, www.fda.gov/fdac/features/1998/398_rad.html states, "A May 1997 presidential report, 'Food Safety from Farm to Table,' estimates that 'millions' of Americans are stricken by food-borne illness each year and some 9,000, mostly the very young and elderly, die as a result." There is general agreement that this number could be reduced markedly by food irradiation, but reliable estimates will not be available until irradiation is in widespread use.

24. The U.S. Environmental Protection Agency set an annual limit on radioactivity in primary drinking water, based on a permissible annual dose of 0.04 mSv/year [65 Fed. Reg. 76708 (7 December 2000), with technical justification in the Notice of Data Availability, 65 Fed. Reg. 21576 (21 April 2000) and its Technical Support Document]. Natural radiation background typically varies from less than 1 mSv/year to about 10 mSv/year. The U.S. average is about 3 mSv/year. (NCRP Report no. 94, available from the National Council on Radiation Protection and Measurements, 7910 Woodmont Avenue, Bethesda, MD 20814, USA.) In high-background regions, doses to populations range up to several hundred mSv/year, with no indications of adverse health effects. [UNSCEAR 2000, cited in (*11*), vol. 1, Annex B.]

25. *Low Level Radiation Health Effects: Compiling the Data*, J. Muckerheide, Ed. [Radiation, Science, and Health (RSH), Needham, MA, ed. 2, 1998]; with revisions and preliminary contents for the 3rd ed.; available at http://cnts.wpi.edu/rsh/docs, with access to UN reports on the Chernobyl accident health effects provided by the Center for Nuclear Technology and Society (CNTS) at Worcester Polytechnic Institute. James Muckerheide, Director of CNTS and Massachusetts State Nuclear Engineer, contributed to authoring this statement. RSH, along with the Nuclear Energy Institute, the National Mining Association, and several municipal water districts are currently suing the U.S. Environmental Protection Agency, charging that by basing its rules on the premise that low-dose radiation is harmful at any level, EPA is arbitrarily and capriciously failing to follow the best peer-reviewed science as required by law.

26. The most comprehensive compilation and evaluations of the biology and health effects of low-dose ionizing radiation from 1898 to 1988 are T. D. Luckey, *Hormesis with Ionizing Radiation* (CRC Press, Boca Raton, FL, 1980) and *Radiation Hormesis* (CRC Press, Boca Raton, FL, 1991).

27. The authors are all members of the National Academy of Engineering, but this statement does not constitute an official statement of the academy.

Douglas M. Chapin is a principal officer of MPR Associates Inc. (an engineering firm in Alexandria, Virginia) and chairman of the board on Energy and Environmental Systems, a unit in the National Academy of Engineering under the auspices of the National Research Council.

Chapter 2.4

Bioterrorism

David Franz

Bioterrorism Defense: Controlling the Unknown

The world has changed. The Soviet army charging through the Fulda Gap is no longer our greatest threat. Wide oceans and friendly neighbors to the north and south still protect us from many threats, but after the attacks of 2001, we are acutely aware of our vulnerability even within the continental United States. Those who would harm us are real and their weapons and methods have changed. We now face a far different threat than we did during the Cold War. At the same time, the developed nations of the world are experiencing a revolution in biotechnology—a good thing—and it is spreading to the rest of the world quickly. Unfortunately, like most technologies, biotechnology can be used for either good or harm.

The Anthrax Letters and the U.S. Government's Response

Thus far, terrorists worldwide have primarily used kinetic weapons, possibly because they understand them. At the same time, terrorists worldwide watched as a few grams of anthrax powder paralyzed the U.S. Senate and much of our postal system. That incident in 2001—which quietly killed five Americans, in the shadow of the violent World Trade Center attacks—totally changed our sense of vulnerability regarding biological attack. Our response was not surprising. We went from a total U.S. budget for biodefense of $137 million in 1997 to nearly $6 billion shortly after the anthrax letter attacks. While military biodefense budgets remained level, we increased the budget of the National Institutes of Health for basic research and medical countermeasures more than we had when the HIV/AIDS pandemic caught us by surprise in the 80s. We stood up university centers of excellence funded by NIH and the Department of Homeland Security. We started nearly from scratch to develop a national bioforensics program, and installed aerosol sensors in more than 30 of our largest cities. We trained emergency responders and physicians to recognize and assist patients with likely threat disease manifestations. Five years later, we are spending approximately $29 billion annually on biodefense, and there hasn't been another major incident. Have we been lucky, or are we truly safer?

Although the risk of a biological attack is still probably quite low, the potential impact is just too great to ignore. Technical barriers to the use of biology as a weapon are falling. We can do little to control the growing population worldwide, in academe and industry, that will understand the technology necessary to manipulate things biological; however, we must understand how to prepare, respond, recover and reduce the number of (or limit the technical capabilities of) those individuals or groups with the intent to harm our citizens or our economy with the traditional microbial weapons or products of the biotech revolution. We can't afford to impede the progress for good, but we must do everything we can to control and eliminate the intent to harm. By understanding the history of the abuse of biology and the legitimate world of biological research, development and production around us today, we will be better able to make sound decisions regarding the protection of our citizens from this low-likelihood, potentially high-impact threat, for which risk assessment is extremely difficult.

A Short History of Biodefense in the U.S.

Pre-1990—Biological Weapons: A Back-Burner Concern

After unilaterally halting our offensive biological weapons (BW) program in 1969 and signing and ratifying the Biological Weapons Convention (BWC) in 1972 and 1975 respectively, the U.S. relegated BW defense to low priority. Because we still possessed an offensive chemical weapons (CW) capability during much of the period, we continued to develop medical and non-medical countermeasures to CW agents. In 1969, when President Nixon stopped the offensive BW program, his statements had explicitly directed the continuation of defensive work against biological threats. Knowing little of the enormous Soviet BW program—which was actually scaled up throughout the 80s, after they ratified the BWC—we assumed our passive chemical protective gear, developed by the Department of Defense (DoD), would serve against the poorly understood biological threat. We had essentially stopped BW field sensor research in the 1960s. We also maintained a small (roughly $15–20 million per year) medical countermeasures research program at Fort Detrick, Maryland. Although a suspicious outbreak of inhalational anthrax occurred in the Soviet Union in 1979, and there was concern regarding the possible use of toxin weapons by the Soviets in Cambodia shortly thereafter, we did little to improve our defenses. This period could be characterized as one of naïveté and intelligence failure.

1990–1998—Just Protecting the Military on the Battlefield . . .

The first Gulf War triggered a new interest in passive biological defense within the DoD. Efforts were focused at Edgewood Arsenal, Dugway Proving Ground and Fort Detrick, the former two on environmental detection, physical protection and decontamination, and the latter on vaccines, drugs and diagnostics. During this period, biological and chemical defense doctrine was seen as one interrelated whole. Experts in chemical detection, where we already had significant capabilities to warn troops before concentrations reached toxic levels, retooled to detect biological agents in the air. "Detect to warn" sensors and protective clothing were touted as the likely solution to the biological problem as well. After 7–8 years of basic research and field testing, we realized that "bio" was not "chem" and "detect to treat" might be the best we could do with sensors, for the near term. The DoD medical technology base developed 10–15 new vaccine candidates but, for lack of funding, took them only through pre-clinical testing (most in non-human primates). The DoD also developed diagnostic and reference laboratory identification capabilities, to include chain of custody and forensics support, primarily in response to the numerous "anthrax hoaxes" which occured during the late 1990s. In 1997, only the DoD was seriously involved in biodefense. The Centers for Disease Control (CDC) was involved only peripherally, essentially unfunded for biodefense and focused on its public health mission.

The Department of Energy (DoE), its nuclear mission reduced, began collaborating with DoD laboratories on biodefense research, actively placing key personnel in DoD leadership positions and seeking to contribute at the national (DoE) laboratories as well. Some in the international community were suspicious of U.S. intentions due to the growth of our biodefense R&D effort, continued work with dangerous pathogens and toxins and our unwillingness to agree, in Geneva, to any type of enforcement regime or legally-binding protocol for the BWC. This "post-Iraq" period was characterized by increased awareness of the battlefield threat and the widely held belief that physical countermeasures were the key to protection of the force; however, concern about protecting civilians at home was developing.

1998–2001—Protecting Civilians and Seeking Public Health Buy-in

The Department of Justice (DoJ) and the Federal Emergency Management Agency (FEMA) were given responsibility for "crisis management" and "consequence management," respectively. In the fall of 1998, after the president read Richard Preston's "The Cobra Event," the CDC was given around $150 million to develop a biodefense capability. These resources funded laboratory upgrades, education and a fledgling national pharmaceutical stockpile. The increased role of public health in national defense probably resulted from the general change in our appreciation, not of the magnitude of the threat, but the character of the solution. Before this time, "bio" had been perceived as simply a new form of "chem;" therefore, a HAZMAT problem, not the public health threat it is. That perception changed gradually.

Several years after the sarin chemical attacks on the Tokyo subway (1995)[1] and ongoing "anthrax" hoaxes (having begun about 1997) in the U.S.—and the collapse of the former Soviet Union—we began to think more about biological terrorism in our cities than biological warfare on the battlefield. Within the DoD, along with environmental detection programs, the medical technology base budget was doubled (1998) to roughly $40–50 milllion annually. However, neither the complexities nor the cost of advanced development of medical countermeasures (vaccines) were well appreciated, so vaccine candidates remained in the technology base, years from licensure. The DoD's actual mission in a domestic bioterrorism event was not clearly defined, and our non-military agencies were not yet focused on biological terrorism defense. In the area of policy, the U.S. increased its efforts by encouraging criminalization and the establishment of an international norm condemning the use of biology for other than legitimate purposes. We had begun to appreciate biological *terrorism* as a threat against our civilian population, and our public health infrastructure as an important part of the solution.

2001–2004—Serious National Preparation . . .

The events of 2001 prompted many new biodefense initiatives within the U.S.—more outside the DoD than within. That fall, following the "anthrax letters" and five deaths by inhalational anthrax, the U.S. Government became serious about preparation for a bioterrorist attack against our population. The DoD's lead laboratory for medical biological defense, having prepared to support forensic identification in the late 1990s, processed more suspect samples than any other laboratory immediately post-October 2001. DoD experts supported the programs of the Department of Health and Human Services (DHHS) and the DoJ—and later, the Department of Homeland Security (DHS)—as they scrambled to catch up.

The 2003 President's budget specifically for biodefense soared to $5.8 billion. The National Institutes of Allergy and Infectious Disease (NIAID) harvested the best of the DoD tech-based vaccine candidates of the 1990s and moved the next generation anthrax and smallpox vaccines into advanced development and production. CDC budgets were increased for further development of state and local laboratory capabilities. The DHS was formed in March of 2003, consolidating anti-terrorism assets—including many for biodefense—within one department. DoE's laboratory programs, managed by DHS, increased their role in non-medical biological research and development, while the DHHS expanded its tech-based medical programs, to include construction of high-containment laboratories regionally within academic centers. The DoD's medical and non-medical tech-base budgets for biodefense remained relatively flat. The transition from thinking about and preparing to counter a biological *terrorism* threat, vs. a traditional biological *warfare* threat, had been difficult, but considerable progress was made.

2005–Present—Settling in for the Longer Term ...

After a rush to harvest real and perceived low-hanging fruit and rapidly building a new cadre of "experts," we are beginning, as a nation, to better understand the complexity of the biodefense challenge. As a result, we are refining our approach to protecting our population. Just the understanding that "bio" isn't "chem" was a huge step forward; it led to our awareness of the importance of public health, and changed preparedness and response approaches significantly. However, even understanding that, we have focused on very specific medical countermeasures and relatively simple, but expensive, aerosol sensors in cities to warn of attack. We believed that technical tools alone would protect us. Now, thought leaders within the U.S. are realizing that it's just not that simple. This problem—the possible abuse of biology—has some very unique characteristics: potentially extremely small footprints (the weapon and the lab or production facility within which it is produced); scores of suitable agents available in nature, thus impossible to control; low-tech (or no-tech) requirements for use of some, especially in the case of the contagious agents; and the inherent vulnerabilities of human, animal and plant populations in a free society. The best medical solutions against these potential threats—vaccines—must for the most part be given prophylactically, and there may be more behavioral barriers to their use than technical, because vaccines carry their own, if minimal, risk; regulatory barriers to developing medical countermeasures are significant and costly—and many of the products have relatively short shelf lives. Specific intelligence regarding the threat is extremely scarce, and the real risk of this low-likelihood but potentially very high-impact event is almost impossible to measure.

Now, we appear to be taking pause and giving another look at the way ahead. As the difficulty of the task sinks in, we are considering more "broad spectrum" solutions. Examples include research on non-specific immune modulators rather than very specific "one-bug" vaccines, and involving citizen-teams in response rather than depending on emergency professionals alone. Both are excellent proposals, but not quick or easy fixes. After an initial rush to technical solutions, there is now more talk of the non-technical: building international understanding and norms regarding the potential abuse of biotechnology, cooperation in deterrence and response, joint education and awareness programs and integration of species-neutral disease surveillance internationally. This evolution in thinking about biodefense is not occurring in the U.S. alone. A number of nations have recognized the unique challenges of the biological threat and the importance of an approach that significantly improves cooperation and coordination between public health and medical, law enforcement and first responder communities at the local, state, federal and international levels. We are learning that the problem of bioterrorism is too complex for simple technical solutions, that preparing specifically for each agent or even each incident is too expensive, that the potential for abuse of biology will likely become greater in the future, and that protecting our citizens without strong international cooperation in technical—and especially non-technical—areas may be impossible.

In 1998, Nobel Laureate Joshua Lederberg offered a prophetic observation that continues to ring true nearly 10 years later: "There is no technical solution to the problem of biological weapons. It needs an ethical, human and moral solution if it's going to happen at all. Don't ask me what the odds are for an ethical solution, but there is no other solution." Then, he added, "But would an ethical solution appeal to a sociopath?"[2]

Rethinking the Fundamentals

Biology is not Chemistry

Biological agents are living things (bacteria or viruses) or non-living substances (toxins) produced by microbes, animals or plants. Biological agents differ from chemicals (non-living manmade substances) in that they are not volatile, nor are they dermally active (they are not typically absorbed through intact skin). Also, unlike many chemical agents, which can cause illness within minutes after exposure, bacteria and viruses usually do not cause disease for days—although a few toxins can cause disease in hours or even minutes. For those interested in protecting our soldiers or citizens, the delayed onset of illness following biological exposure makes it more difficult to understand who was exposed, when and where, or who disseminated the agent which caused the illness.

These simple differences in physical characteristics of biological and chemical agents have enormous implications for both the weaponeer and those seeking to protect a population. The weaponeer need only release a volatile, highly toxic chemical into the vicinity of humans or crudely spray them with droplets of the material to cause illness or death. The same method of delivery for even the most infectious biological agents would typically not be effective. A pool of infectious virus or bacteria or even the most deadly biological toxin on the floor at your feet is not necessarily hazardous. These agents must typically be inhaled, injected or ingested to cause illness or death. Infecting large numbers of people is even more difficult because the agent must be inhaled, which means the weaponeer must find a way to aerosolize it. This is possible, but not easy. The weaponeer must either dry the microbes into very small particles for powder delivery, or spray them as a liquid using mechanical systems typically requiring high pressures that may kill the organism. Finally, the efficacy of an aerosol attack is also very dependent on a rather unique set of meteorological conditions.

The Threat Agent Spectrum

We have traditionally categorized "biological" agents as bacteria, viruses or toxins. But advances in biotechnology and new capabilities to synthesize designer agents may change the way we think about these categories in the future. Chemical and biological threats may eventually merge as we understand more about small, "manufacturable" molecules that can subtly alter human behavior.

The organism which causes anthrax—the most well known of biological threat agents—is a bacterium. What makes it special is its life cycle, which involves both the typical vegetative form (quite fragile) and the very stable spore form. The latter was found in the "anthrax letters" of October 2001.[3] Spores can survive significant environmental exposure and can be stored for years—even centuries—in a cool, dark, dry environment. The spore stage is rather rare among bacteria. Bacteria differ from viruses in that they can grow and multiply "by themselves" in the proper environment. Viruses don't have the genetic machinery to multiply, so they must live inside human, plant or animal cells, sharing the living cell's genetic systems to multiply. The newly made viral particles are excreted from a cell to infect other cells. These requirements for replication have implications for the weaponeer; while bacteria may be grown in something like a broth, viruses must be grown in cultures of living cell—or, as the Soviets did with the Marburg virus, in thousands of guinea pigs.

Besides ease of production for the weaponeer and environmental stability, other characteristics are important to the exposed population. Some microorganisms are highly "infectious," meaning it doesn't take many organisms to produce infection. Examples are the viruses Ebola, Marburg and probably variola, the virus that causes the disease smallpox. Some bacteria, such as the species that causes Q fever (*Coxella burnetti*) or the one that causes tularemia (*Pasturella tularensis*), may cause infection with as few as 1–10 organisms inhaled or injected. On the other hand, *Bacillus anthracis*—which causes the disease anthrax—is thought to require some thousands of spores inhaled, by the average person, to cause disease. "Transmissibility" or "contagiousness" relates to how easily disease is transmitted from one person to another. Fortunately, few of the traditional weapons agents are contagious; those that are include the virus which causes smallpox [eradicated from the globe as a natural disease in the early 1980s] and the bacterium which causes plague, *Yersinia pestis*. Smallpox is quite contagious; you probably don't want to be in the same room with a coughing patient. Plague might only be spread to those within 6–8 feet of a coughing victim.

Biological toxins are quite difficult to weaponize. The best known, historically, in weapons programs are the botulinum toxin family, which are the most toxic substances known to man; SEB (Staphalococcal enteroxin B), saxitoxin and ricin. Though it has been a popular candidate, the U.S., the U.S.S.R. and Iraq eventually dropped botulinum toxin as a weapon because it was significantly less toxic by the aerosol route than by injection. The U.S. did complete development of SEB and demonstrated it's effectiveness in a large field trial in the Pacific. Saxitoxin-filled small arms rounds were tested as assassination weapons by the U.S. and ricin—just not toxic enough to use as a mass-exposure aerosol agent—was also tested and discontinued by the U.S.—and by Iraq. We think of the toxins as "natural chemicals;" severity of illness and time to onset of illness are typically dose-dependent.

The Concept of Dual-Use

We often hear the term "dual-use" in the context of biological warfare and terrorism. The term was coined, in this context, in the mid-1990s to describe the fact that legitimate facilities, equipment and scientists could be used for illegitimate (biowarfare) purposes. The best example of a dual-use facility, intended to support a biological warfare program, may be Al Hakam, which was located about 80km outside of Baghdad in the early 1990s. It could have been a legitimate agricultural production facility, but it was used to make weapons agents. Likewise, the legitimate foot and mouth disease vaccine plant, built by the French near Al Manal, was used by Iraq to produce botulinum toxin for explosive bombs. One of the most complicating realities confounding our understanding of the biological threat is the fact that legitimate facilities can be used to make weapons. Thus, the "dual-use" problem makes enforcing the Biological Weapons Convention of 1972—which prohibits the development of biological weapons—virtually impossible.

There is another side to "dual-use" in the context of biological terrorism. Although we have some understanding of threat, vulnerability and impact of a biological attack, risk is impossible to quantify. Therefore, knowing how to allocate precious resources to prepare for an unknown biological terrorism attack is most difficult. By thinking of bioterrorism as *"emerging infectious disease + intent to harm,"* we can prepare, generally, for both. History suggests that diseases will continue to emerge and reemerge. If we prepare diagnostics, disease surveillance systems, drugs and vaccine platforms, public health and hospital capacity to deal with the very likely (but unknown) naturally emerging disease, we will be quite well-prepared to deal with the unknowns of bioterrorism. This is "dual-use" of countermeasures in bioterrorism defense.

Capability and Intent

Making a kilogram of high quality, dry anthrax spores at a concentration of 10^{12} spores per gram in an improvised facility, and surviving to talk about it, is not a trivial undertaking. The same is true of genetically engineering a virulent strain of influenza. Delivering a liquid slurry of any number of agents to thousands of unknowing civilians would not be easy either. It is considerably easier for a terrorist or sub-national group to use explosives (which they understand very well) or toxic industrial chemicals (which they probably understand reasonably well) than biological agents.

Why haven't we seen more bioterrorist attacks? To some degree, technical barriers and/or a lack of understanding of biological agents may have deterred potential terrorists from using them in the past, but that does not tell the whole story. The virus that causes foot and mouth disease in cloven-hoofed livestock is 1) readily available in nature on three continents, 2) not a human pathogen (and thus safe for humans to collect, handle and transport). and 3) would spread rapidly through our naïve livestock population with devastating economic impact. That no terrorist has used foot and mouth disease as an economic weapon suggests that technical barriers alone do not explain why we have not had a major biological attack in the United States. Indeed, as other chapters of this volume explore in greater detail, intent is a critical dimension to understanding of the WMD terrorism threat. Nevertheless, we are now in the age of biotechnology. Our capabilities to manipulate life forms expand daily, allowing more people in more places to more simply use the new tools more effectively for good or harm.

The population of individuals with this "capability" will continue to expand. We do not know the population of humans with the intent to harm us, but because we will not—

nor do we wish to—significantly limit the expanding circle of capability to use biology for good, we must seek ways to address the circle that represents intent to harm.

Surveillance and Situational Awareness

Whether a disease is naturally, accidentally or intentionally introduced into human, animal or plant populations, the most important thing we can do is discover it as early as possible. Furthermore, because more than 75% of emerging or traditionally weaponized agents are zoonotics [transmissible between humans and animals], we must look for disease wherever it is found, not just in humans. Because transportation of humans and animals—and microbes—is becoming ever more rapid, we must discover a disease in the country or region of origin before it spreads. Finally, during an outbreak or after a known exposure, we need to know who to treat, who to segregate or what areas to make off-limits.

Mechanical, air monitoring sensors for biological agents seem at first glance to be an excellent means of early warning. Chemical sensors can warn our military troops—often before concentrations reach toxic levels—to don protective mask or other gear. [Protecting just the airways and the eyes is often enough in the case of biological agents, unlike for chemical agents, where the skin may also need protection.] If we could warn people early enough, maybe a mask to guard the airways or even a folded cloth over the mouth and nose might be enough to protect the population and greatly reduce the biological threat. We have learned, however, that biological agents pose numerous challenges to the "sensor solution:" 1) a definitive sensor should be designed for a specific agent, limiting the number of sensors we can field; 2) the time required for the sensor to identify an agent is probably 5–10 minutes at the very best, and can be 30 minutes or more [individuals in the immediate area would be exposed in that time, limiting the value of warning for physical protection]; 3) unlike many chemical sensors, which use the chemical of concern to trigger a reaction in a stable transducer, most biological sensors need special reagents which must be constantly replenished; and 4) depending on the infectivity [number of organisms needed to cause disease], attaining adequate sensitivity with an air collector of practical size may be impossible. We have air sensors distributed throughout more than 30 U.S. cities, in an attempt to quickly detect an aerosolized biological agent. Early detection is critical; it would allow as much as a day or two head-start on therapy, and thus save lives. Sensors must be at the right place and time, and they are very expensive to install and monitor. If we do not have an attack in the next 10 years, will we be willing to bear the cost of such a system?

An alternative, dual-use solution is to monitor the human population for signs of disease. Because it takes hours or even days to make a definitive diagnosis on any single case, we could look for increased numbers of patients reporting to the hospital or doctors' offices with the same or similar syndrome [a loosely defined group of clinical signs of disease]. However, one problem with this approach is that it can be difficult to recognize the increased incidence of a syndrome if individuals with the same symptoms report to different doctors. An electronic system to collect information from all doctors and collate the information for public health decision makers could solve the problem. Such systems are available, but have not yet been widely accepted because of cost, efficiency and political factors. Finally, education and awareness are valuable and extremely cost-effective in preparing our physicians and emergency responders—and even our citizens—to recognize unusual disease presentations. In the end, education may be the most important of a combination of useful solutions.

Physical Countermeasures

Protective masks are valuable and practical protection from biological aerosols. Unlike chemical protective masks, which must contain activated charcoal beds to adsorb chemical vapors, the non-volatile biological particulates can be captured in simple filters [often called "HEPA" for High Efficiency Particulate Air filters]. Even improvised masks, fabricated from paper or cloth, can be effective in providing temporary protection from biological—but not chemical—aerosols. The problem with a plan that depends on protective masks for protection is knowing when to don them, which is why so much effort has been put into the development of sensors.

Decontamination after a biological incident or attack is, in some respects, less important than decontamination following a chemical attack. However, it may be far more complex. The cloud of biological agent produced by the most efficient disseminator or munition is not uniform in particle size. Some percentage of the material may be released in the respirable range (1 to 10 or 15 microns) and the rest as larger particles. Depending on meteorological conditions, the respirable cloud—called the "primary aerosol"—may travel many miles downwind, exposing everything inhaling air in its path. Although the primary aerosol is of great immediate concern, the larger particles which remain behind, mostly nearer the munition, are a decontamination problem.[4]

Most biological agents are eventually killed by the elements. UV radiation is destructive to biological agents, killing even resistent spores in hours. Therefore, the major focus regarding decontamination of a city would be inside buildings. Furthermore, knowing "where" and "how much" to decontaminate is a more difficult problem than "how" to decontaminate. We have analytical tools (such as polymerase chain reaction or "PCR") which are fast and highly sensitive for locating nucleic acids (DNA or RNA) from an agent, but these tests don't tell us if the agent is still alive. We just don't yet have the right "real time" tools yet. During the clean-up of the U.S. Senate and Post Office buildings in Washington, D.C. following the anthrax letters of October 2001, the gold standard evaluation tool was a simple culture on nutrient media known since the mid-19th century. Finally, although we normally think only about killing the organism in decontamination, we should remember that the real issue is the relationship between organism and humans, and that there may be times—especially in facilities needed to "restart" a city—when it is more efficient to protect the returning human (physically or medically), at least for a time, than attempting to assure that *all* of the organisms have been killed. Particle size is important; in theory, a "particle" of viable anthrax spores the size of a baseball would be no hazard, because it could not be inhaled, yet as individuals—or very small clumps—these same spores could be deadly.

Medical Countermeasures

Biological agent medical countermeasures differ from those needed for chemical agents, because while chemical agents can generally be lumped into classes requiring similar drug treatment—nerve, blister, blood, etc.—biological agents often demand very specific preparations. This is especially true for vaccines. Vaccines can be developed for bacteria, viruses or toxins, and must—in all but very rare cases—be given prophylactically. Antibiotics (for bacterial therapy) can cover multiple agents. Antivirals can be effective against classes of viruses; however, few licensed antivirals exist today.

During the Cold War, when protecting a military force rather than civilians was our primary concern, the DoD's biodefense laboratory at Fort Detrick worked at developing vaccines for the dozen highest threat agents, along with the diagnostic tools and antiviral therapies for these and others. The regulatory requirements for medical countermeasures (diagnostics, but especially vaccines and drugs) are much more severe than are requirements for advanced development of non-medical products and other military materiel. Vaccines provide the best way to protect an individual from biological agent attack; however, because of the complexity and cost of advanced development and production [up to $500 million and 10–15 years], only two are generally available for the military today: those which protect against anthrax and smallpox.

Throughout the 1990s, the DoD developed numerous vaccines for the key threat agents, but did not attempt to license them. After 9/11, the Department of Health and Human Services has taken the anthrax and smallpox vaccines—developed by the DoD—into advanced development and production for stockpiling. With the increased concerns about biological terrorism, rather than battlefield biological warfare, the national focus of medical countermeasures development has changed from vaccines (for the troops) to diagnostics and antimicrobial drugs, which may be used after an attack. The list of threat agents has increased dramatically, along with the concern for protecting civilians in addition to the military, further complicating development of countermeasures. Funding within the DoD has recently increased for non-specific, immunomodulating drugs [drugs which might not be totally protective, but would generally make the population more resistant to disease] and remained generally flat for vaccines and diagnostics post-9/11. Funding for basic research and the purchase of drugs and vaccines for stockpile has increased dramatically within the DHHS over the last 5 years.

Whether protecting the force or the civilian population, the goal is to discover the agent or the disease as early as possible after attack (using environmental sensors or disease surveillance systems), identify the affected population (through diagnostics) and treat (with antibiotics or antiviral drugs) those infected.

Intelligence and Attribution

The dual-use nature of facilities, equipment and people [for good or harm] has made discovery of Cold War programs such as that of the former Soviet Union extremely difficult. At that time, we were looking for buildings half the size of a football field and complexes the size of a college campus. In this age of terrorism, the size of the weapon and the footprint of the facility in which it might be produced has shrunk dramatically, making it an even more difficult intelligence target.

The facility needed to produce a few grams of dried spores, like those found in the anthrax letters, might be the size of an ordinary kitchen; a facility needed to produce a kilo or two is not much larger. A few kilos of dried anthrax could be easily transported or stored for years virtually anywhere. This amount of material, dispersed in a major city, might infect hundreds of thousands of people, causing illness and death tens of miles downwind.

The amount of chemical agent needed to have this impact would be orders of magnitude greater and much more easily discovered.

The way we think about intelligence is changing. While we focused on "collecting secrets" during the Cold War, we now realize that collecting secrets about dual-use facilities, equipment and people is just too hard. The biotech revolution is increasing the capability of almost anyone to produce biological weapons. The key is intent! One way to facilitate intelligence gathering is to encourage communication and collaboration among scientists worldwide. If we understand the biotechnological capabilities and legitimate activities of nations, sub-national entities and even small groups and individuals, we will have a matrix on which to hang what few "secrets" we might stumble across.

Attribution of a biological attack, as we have seen following the anthrax letters of 2001, is extremely difficult. Following that incident, we have worked hard to develop accredited microbial forensics laboratories with trained and certified personnel, as well as validated laboratory and field tools. We have described the biological, physical and chemical characteristics of the spores found in the letters and even reverse-engineered their production. The FBI has interviewed and conducted polygraphs on hundreds of individuals, yet no arrests have been made five years later.

Identification of the perpetrator(s) and attribution of the crime would likely have a significant deterrent effect. Unlike a crime with a firearm, where matching lands and grooves on the bullet often lead to the weapon, even the best molecular description does not identify the equipment or personnel that created the agent. Only by collecting identical samples in the field and in a lab can we track an agent's source. Developing biological forensics is critical, but traditional tools (fiber, hair, fingerprint analysis and testimony of observers) will likely be as critical to the eventual solution of a bio-crime or bioterrorist incident as they are to a traditional criminal investigation.

Non-Proliferation

The Soviet Union and the United States signed and ratified the Biological Weapons Convention (BWC) in 1972 and 1975, respectively. Iraq signed it in 1972 and ratified it in the early 1990s. Nevertheless, although the U.S. halted its offensive program in 1969, the convention did not stop Russia or Iraq.

The Clinton administration supported efforts to build a "verification protocol" for the BWC through much of the 1990s, but these efforts ceased when the George W. Bush administration pulled out of the talks. Many experts agree that verification of compliance with the BWC is not possible. Some have turned to creative alternatives. In the fall of 1992, Senators Nunn and Lugar sponsored a bill to support a program called "Cooperative Threat Reduction" (or CTR) in Russia and the Newly Independent States. The purpose was initially to keep former Russian bioweaponeers occupied at home so that they would not leave Russia and lend their support to rogue states interested in developing a biological weapons program. This program has had some unintended benefits. From the sometimes almost artificial attempts to involve former weapons scientists in legitimate collaborations with Americans in academe, industry or government have grown professional friendships and some lasting understanding. We have learned that working together on hard science and public health problems tears down walls, while attempts to "negotiate away" the threat across conference tables builds walls and may actually increase misunderstanding and mistrust.

In recent years, the focus of CTR programs has moved away from branding "former weaponeers" and keeping them at home, and toward building international teams of biological scientists to solve difficult problems related to emerging disease and public health. It is the same facilities, equipment and people needed to reduce the burden of infectious disease on their populations that could be involved in developing biological weapons. Thus, the CTR programs have served the dual purpose of solving some real-world health problems, improving human security, gainfully employing former weaponeers, and undermining the popular support for terrorism generally, while providing a deterrent to the misuse of biological technologies by building understanding and transparency between potential adversaries.

Public Resilience

Protecting our population from biological terrorism is not a trivial or short-term undertaking. There is a broad spectrum of rather specific options for preparation and response. There are also options related to preventing or deterring an attack. Finally, should all of these fail, a resilient public will handle an attack better than an unprepared one. Resilience should not be confused with invulnerability. Rather, it is the ability of a population or group to bounce back after receiving a shock to the system, thereby limiting the long-term impact of the shock. A resilient society is better able to "heal" itself quickly after an attack and to return to a sense of normalcy. Resilience is related to beliefs, attitudes, behaviors and possibly genetic factors affecting physiology and emotion.

Building resilience can involve many factors, but information and understanding of the threat and the appropriate response are at its core. Therefore, education is a central activity in building resilience. Humans must be able to make realistic plans and carry them out, be able to communicate within and outside the group, and have the capacity to manage strong feelings and concerns, accept change as a part of life, keep things in perspective and take care of one's self and one's family. At the time of an incident, policymakers, government spokespersons and the media can impact resilience—for good or ill—so they must be prepared to do and say the right things at the right time. Recent examples of leadership that apparently bolstered public resilience are President Bush, standing with a bull-horn on the rubble of the world trade center, and Mayor Giuliani, generally leading his city in recovering from the 9/11 attacks. Biological weapons may be attractive to terrorists because of the increased psychological impact of a non-traditional, "invisible" weapon. By building a resilient public, we may both prepare them to "heal" more quickly after an attack, and also "harden the target," making the would-be terrorist think twice before attacking.

The Future

How can we know we are doing the right thing to protect our citizens from biological threats without a real attack? We can't know for sure what our state of readiness is, but because bioterrorism would introduce disease into the human or animal populations, we can probably look at similar natural occurrences and assess ourselves and our discovery, response and recovery efforts. We can make the case for dual-use preparations, even with the relative rarity of a biological attack. Our current preparations vary significantly in their degree of "dual-useness." Our public health infrastructure is one of the best examples. How quickly do we discover an outbreak of an emergent disease? How rapidly do we identify the size and scope of a naturally occurring outbreak? How automated is our healthcare and medical records system, and how rapidly can we recognize trends in the health of the population? How do our hospitals deal with an unexpectedly large number of patients following a natural disaster or major industrial accident? Do we have enough vaccine for the annual flu season? How long does it take us to solve major crimes against individuals or organizations? What is our nation's rate of development and FDA approval of new diagnostics, drugs and vaccines for chronic and emerging disease? How well do our cities deal with widespread power outage or flooding? How credible are our leaders and government agencies during major social disruptions? What is our general state of public health and discipline?

It is safe to assume that the "capabilities" of biotechnology will continue to grow and spread across the globe for the next 20–30 years; manipulating biology will only get easier and faster. The complex human factors that define the size and scope of "intent to harm with biology," and its relationship to capabilities, are at once theoretically more controllable and less likely to be controlled than the technical aspects that contribute to the elusive risk analysis. As we attempt to make right decisions regarding the protection of our citizens from the panoply of interrelated biological threats we will face in the future, we must understand the technical and behavioral challenges, deal with them systematically with balance and, whenever possible, educate at home, communicate internationally and take the long view.

DAVID FRANZ is Vice President and Senior Biological Scientist at the Midwest Research Institute, Director of the National Agricultural Biosecurity Center at Kansas State University, and a Senior Fellow with the Combating Terrorism Center at West Point. He is a retired Colonel in the U.S. Army, having served 23 of his 27 years on active duty in the U.S. Army Medical Research and Material Command. He has served as both deputy commander and commander of the U.S. Army medical Research Institute of Infectious Diseases and as Deputy Commander of the Medical Research and Materiel Command. He also served as veterinarian for the 10th Special Forces Group (Airborne). In addition to his time on active-duty, Franz served as chief inspector for three U.N. Special Commission biological warfare inspection missions to Iraq and was a member of the first two U.S./U.K. teams that visited Russia to support the trilateral Joint Statement on Biological Weapons. He has served on numerous governmental advisory committees on bioterrorism.

Suggested Readings:

Alibek, Ken with Stephen Handelman. *Biohazard: The Chilling True Story of the Largest Covert Biological Weapons Program in the World.* New York: Dell Publishing, 1999

Mangold, Tom and Jeff Goldberg. *Plague Wars: The Terrifying Reality of Biological Warfare.* New York: St. Martin's Press, 1999.

Miller, Judith, Stephen Engelberg and William Broad. *Germs: Biological Weapons and America's Secret War.* New York: Simon & Schuster, 2001.

Nye, Joseph S. Jr. *Soft Power: The Means to Success in World Politics.* New York: Public Affairs, 2004.

Preston, Richard. *The Hot Zone.* New York: Random House, 1994.

Sidell, Frederick R., Ernest T. Takafuji, and David R. Franz. "Medical Aspects of Chemical and Biological Warfare." In *Textbook of Military Medicine: Medical Aspects of Chemical and Biological Warfare* ("Part I, Warfare, Weapons, and the Casualty") edited by Russ Zajtchuk and Ronald F. Bellamy. Washington, DC: Office of the Surgeon General, Walter Reed Army Medical Center, 1997.

Trevan, Tim. *Saddam's Secrets: The Hunt for Iraq's Hidden Weapons.* New York: Harper Collins Publishers, 1999.

Zelicoff, Alan P. and Michael Bellomo. *Microbe: Are We Ready for the Next Plague?* New York: AMACOM Books, 2005.

Danzig, Richard. *Catastrophic Bioterrorism—What Is To Be Done?* Center for Technology and National Security Policy, National Defense University, Washington, D.C., August 2003.

Journal

Biosecurity and Bioterrorism. Biodefense Strategy, Practice, and Science. Mary Ann Liebert, Inc. (www.liebertpub. com).

National Research Council of the National Academies Publications: The National Academies Press (www.nap.edu)

Reopening Public Facilities After A Biological Attack, 2005. Committee on Standards and Policies for Decontaminating Public Facilities Affected by Exposure to Harmful Biological Agents: How Clean is Safe?

Countering Agricultural Terrorism, 2003. Committee on Biological Threats to Agricultural Plans and Animals.

Biotechnology Research in an Age of Terrorism, 2004. Committee on Research Standards and Practices to Prevent the Destructive Application of Biotechnology.

Sensor Systems for Biological Agent Attacks, 2005. Protecting Buildings and Military Bases. Committee on Materials and Manufacturing Processes for Advanced Sensors.

Institute of Medicine and National Research Council of the National Academies:

Globalization, Biosecurity, and the Future of the Life Sciences, 2006. Committee on Advances in Technology and the Prevention of Their Application to Next Generation Biowarfare Threats.

Countering Bioterrorism: The Role of Science and Technology, 2002. Excerpted from Making the Nation Safer: The Role of Science and Technology. Panel on Biological Issues, Committee on Science and Technology for Countering Terrorism.

Notes

1. For more on this, please see the chapter on Aum Shinrikyo by William Rosenau in this volume.
2. Richard Preston, "Annals of Warfare" *The New Yorker* (9 March 1998).
3. For a detailed analysis of this event and the government's response, please see the chapter by Elin Gursky, Thomas V. Inglesby and Tara O'Toole in his volume.
4. Note that, although the primary aerosol cloud may only be on-site at any downwind location for a matter of minutes, equilibration in buildings will vary with the degree of building seal. The time-weighted average concentration inside and outside a building may be very similar.

Dave Franz is vice president and senior biological scientist at the Midwest Research Institute, director of the National Agricultural Biosecurity Center and Kansas State University, and a senior fellow with the Combating Terrorism Center at West Point. He is a retired colonel in the U.S. Army, having served 23 of his 27 years on active duty in the U.S. Army Medical Research and Material Command.

Christopher F. Chyba and Alex L. Greninger

Biotechnology and Bioterrorism: An Unprecedented World

In March 1963, President John F. Kennedy told the American people that he was haunted by the prospect of '15 or 20' nuclear powers by 1975.[1] Come that year, in a world with still only six nuclear states, the strategist Albert Wohlstetter warned that we could nevertheless soon face 'life in a nuclear armed crowd'.[2] Yet the web of measures that comprise the nuclear non-proliferation regime continues to hold that crowd at bay. The number of nuclear weapon states in 2004 stands at only eight or nine, and assertive steps may yet keep this figure from rising.

Barring theft, would-be nuclear proliferators must confront the challenging task of producing highly enriched uranium or weapons-grade plutonium. Even the most proliferation-friendly nuclear materials production technology — gas centrifuge enrichment — remains beyond the capacity of non-state groups. By aggressively confronting centrifuge proliferation and other threats to the non-proliferation regime, we can hope to continue to shape our nuclear future, moving it away from Kennedy's nightmare.

But biological proliferation is a different beast. Biotechnological capacity is increasing and spreading rapidly. This trend seems unstoppable, since the economic, medical and food-security benefits of genetic manipulation appear so great. As a consequence, thresholds for the artificial enhancement or creation of dangerous pathogens — disease causing organisms — will steadily drop. The revolution in biotechnology will therefore almost inevitably place greater destructive power in the hands of smaller groups of the technically competent: those with skills sufficient to make use of the advances of the international scientific community. This future is being driven not primarily by military programmes, but rather by open, legitimate private and academic research.

Lessons from the past half-century of relative success in blocking nuclear proliferation cannot be easily applied to the twenty-first century challenge of biological proliferation. Neither Cold War bilateral arms control nor multilateral non-proliferation provide good models for how we are to manage this new challenge. Much more than in the nuclear case, civilisation will have to cope with, rather than shape, its biological future. In the biological realm, we are entering an unprecedented world.

The new biosecurity landscape

Four trends came together in the 1990s to confront civilisation with a new and challenging biological security landscape. Each had earlier manifestations, yet each became salient during that decade.

Emerging Infectious Diseases.

Of course HIV/ADS and many other catastrophic pandemics preceded the 1990s. But the recognition that over the previous two decades a new disease had emerged into the human population roughly every year, coupled with dramatic outbreaks of diseases, such as ebola overseas and hantavirus within the United States, and the evolution of multi-drug resistant versions of well-known diseases, such as tuberculosis, led to the US National Academy of Sciences and, subsequently, the US government, focusing attention on this threat.[3] The centrality of improving domestic and international disease surveillance and response was embraced intellectually. But the Global Pathogens Surveillance Act, a US Senate initiative to improve capacity in the developing world to detect, monitor, and respond to sudden disease outbreaks, has yet to become law.[4] Somehow the imagination stops at international borders, even after the 2003 SARS epidemic. SARS provided an especially vivid example of an emerging disease that could spread globally on the short timescales of international flight schedules.

Mass-Casualty Terrorism.

There were historical precedents, but with the first attempt, in February 1993, to bring down a World Trade Center tower, the March 1995 sarin nerve-gas attack by Aum Shinrikyo in the Tokyo metro system and the April 1995 Oklahoma City bombing it became clear that a variety of groups aimed at mass murder. Attempts by Aum Shinrikyo to spray the anthrax bacterium throughout downtown Tokyo in 1993 demonstrated that at least some terrorist groups were willing to attempt mass casualty urban biological attacks, even if they were insufficiently competent to succeed. And then came 11 September 2001.

Gross Violations of the BWC.

Impressive violations of the 1972 Biological and Toxin Weapons Convention (BWC) came to light as a result of the end of the Cold War and the first Gulf War. States parties to the BWC pledge not to 'develop, produce, stockpile or otherwise acquire or retain' biological agents, toxins, or weapons. Yet Iraq, which had signed the BWC (but did not ratify it until 1991) had conducted a covert production programme with anthrax and other agents, and largely hidden it until invasive post-Gulf War UN inspections and high-level defectors revealed many of its details. More disturbing, the Soviet Union had built an illegal programme on a continental scale subsequent to signing the BWC in 1972, employing tens of thousands of people. Certain Russian facilities that had been part of this complex remain closed to outsiders. Equally disturbing were multiple reports that the Soviet programme had weaponised smallpox, a highly contagious agent. For this reason, smallpox had been considered of little interest to military programmes, because of the danger that it might 'boomerang' against one's own troops or populations', but clearly it was of potential interest to apocalyptic terrorist groups.[5] Concern over the ease with which the BWC had been violated for the two decades following its entry into force led to a six-year international negotiation of a compliance protocol to the BWC. In July 2001, the administration of George W. Bush withdrew from these negotiations and has declared the BWC to be 'inherently unverifiable'.[6] Suspicions persist that a number of BWC signatories are involved in illegal activities.[7]

Dramatic Advances in Biotechnology.[8]

Human beings have engaged in genetic engineering for millennia, breeding new strains of both plants and animals. However, the discovery of the structure of DNA in 1953 and, almost 20 years later, the invention of recombinant DNA technology permitted for the first time the direct manipulation of the genomes of organisms to achieve specific goals.[9] Biotechnological inventions, such as the polymerase chain reaction (PCR) in the 1980s, 'DNA shuffling' in the 1990s and other technologies that automate copying, mutating, sequencing and otherwise manipulating DNA, introduced enormous numerical power into molecular biology.[10] The resulting techniques of directed molecular evolution permit investigators to evolve capabilities without having to know beforehand what exact DNA modifications are necessary to achieve the desired result. Instead, it is now possible to engineer via trial and error, in which each step can involve populations of up to trillions of trial DNA molecules.[11] Simultaneously, automation of key techniques has substantially lowered the threshold for performing these experiments. In part as a consequence of these advances, between 1993 and 1999 the biotechnology industry in the United States doubled in size. An industry-sponsored group estimates that by the turn of the century, biotechnology contributed nearly half a million jobs and $47 billion in business revenue annually to the US economy.[12] At the same time, biotechnology has spread rapidly around the world. For example, China now has some 20,000 people working in 200 biotechnology laboratories.[13] In January 2004, a member of the Pakistani Atomic Energy Commission (PAEC) concluded a two-week training workshop on 'advanced techniques in biotechnology' in Faisalabad with the statement that the PAEC is committed to with the statement that the PAEC is committed to training scientists from Muslim countries in biotechnology.[14] And Singapore is investing billions of dollars in biotechnology, declaring it to be the 'fourth pillar' of its economy.[15]

The globalisation of biotechnology is being driven not only by national decisions, but also by biotechnology firms' growing use of international subcontracting and technological cooperation agreements to further their research — including their biodefence-related research, such as vaccine development for potential bio-terrorist agents.[16]

Necessary and Insufficient

By the turn of the twentieth century, the implications of these four trends had led to a re-conceptualisation of the biological terrorism threat, away from misplaced analogies to nuclear or chemical weapons and towards placing the threat in the context of the public health measures needed to combat disease. If non-proliferation efforts were inherently more difficult in the biological than in the nuclear case, and if deterrence by the threat of punishment was of questionable utility against certain terrorist groups, then it made sense to place greater reliance on defence, in the form of improvements in disease surveillance and response. Many (although not all) of the required measures would have the significant advantage of being intrinsically dual-use, bolstering defences against naturally occurring epidemics as well as intentional attacks.[17] Because most dangerous contagious pathogens (smallpox, plague, SARS) have incubation periods longer than international flight travel times, it is crucial that international disease surveillance and response be improved along with its domestic counterpart.[18]

An emphasis on disease surveillance and response does not mean that the realm of prevention should be neglected. Aum Shinrikyo's failed anthrax attacks in Tokyo in 1993 are a reminder that even a group with substantial financial resources and some scientific training did not find it easy to carry out an effective biological attack. Aum Shinrikyo obtained both the wrong strain (a generally non-lethal vaccine strain) of the anthrax bacterium, and it did not master aerosolisation technology.[19] It is clear that efforts to restrict the availability of the worst pathogens and key weaponisation technologies should not be abandoned. We must resist the 'silver bullet fallacy' — the notion that if a particular step does not magically solve a problem in its entirety, it is not worth pursuing. Rather, we must construct a web of measures to make biological terrorism more difficult. Therefore, even as we improve disease surveillance and response, we should work to stem proliferation where possible by, for example, maintaining and extending Australia Group suppliers' export standards that impede state and non-state weapons programmes. We should also improve the international security of the most dangerous pathogen stocks, to deprive would-be terrorists of the surest and easiest path to just the right disease organism.[20] But such steps will have only limited impact, and if not pursued wisely could unduly constrain legitimate biodefence research.[21]

In addition to broad improvements in prevention, surveillance and response, specific defensive measures against the most likely threat scenarios are also necessary. There is a large array of viruses and bacteria that can cause disease in humans, animals and crops. Even greater are the number of scenarios, from the subtle to the apocalyptic, that analysts can spin about possible terrorist attacks. An effective defence requires setting priorities; these should include identifying the most likely near-term threats and implementing research, detection and response agendas designed to take these off the table in the near future.[22]

The decision to stockpile enough smallpox vaccine for every American is an example of a step in this direction. To remove known strains of smallpox as a potential threat, however, this step must be supplemented either by research to develop a vaccine that is sufficiently safe so that widespread pre-attack vaccination is possible, or by the capability to vaccinate vast numbers of citizens rapidly after the earliest signs of an outbreak. (And here, too, a safer vaccine would be valuable.) Similarly, an effective and easily administered vaccine against anthrax, coupled with existing antibiotic stockpiles and a realistic and tested plan to distribute these rapidly and widely after an attack, would help to remove another of the most serious near-term threats. The biomedical research needed to achieve these and other high-priority objectives is being funded by a $1.5bn expansion in the National Institutes of Health annual biodefence research budget, and Bush's ten-year $5.6bn Bioshield initiative.[23]

But these near-term steps, while necessary, will not by themselves cope with the longer-term threats we face. For example, developing a strain of anthrax that is resistant to a particular antibiotic requires only standard microbiological techniques. And experiments published in the open scientific literature in 2001 suggest a way to modify the smallpox virus so that it could overwhelm the immune systems of even those who have been vaccinated against it. Steps taken today to prepare for the greatest biological threats risk committing the 'fallacy of the last move' — the failure to realise that a defensive measure taken to counter a particular offensive threat might in turn be circumvented by a competent adversary.[24] In fact, one lesson of experiments published in the open scientific literature over the past few years is that the capabilities for overcoming biodefence measures are becoming more widespread and available to groups of the technically competent. Each defensive move may be placed at risk by an offensive counter-move. The short- and medium-term steps we take now are still needed to protect us against the most immediate and severe threats, but they may be insufficient to meet the longer-term challenge.

Shots Across the Bow

Experiments performed and published over the last decade already demonstrate that biological power for constructing dangerous pathogens is becoming widespread. New examples now appear frequently in the open scientific literature. Describing a few of the experiments of concern illustrates what is to come.

In 2001 the *Journal of Virology* published a paper describing experiments conducted at the Australian National University with the mousepox virus, a smallpox-analogue virus that infects rodents.[25] Seeking to find a contagious contraceptive to suppress the wild mouse population, researchers spliced into the mousepox genome the gene for a mouse protein called interleukin-4 (IL-4), a signalling protein that is used by the mouse's immune system to regulate its response to infection. IL-4 suppresses the antiviral immune response, so the effect was to give the mousepox virus the ability to shut down the relevant part of the mouse's immune system. The modified virus proved far deadlier, killing mice that were naturally immune or that had been vaccinated against mousepox.

Since mousepox is the rodent analogue to smallpox, and since mouse IL-4 is analogous to the IL-4 used by the human immune system, there is reason to suspect that a similar experiment carried out with the human smallpox virus could lead to a virus that would circumvent the existing smallpox vaccine. The techniques used by the Australian researchers are not sophisticated; a recent report by the National Research Council of the US National Academies of Science, Engineering and Medicine describes them as 'standard and quite simple procedures'.[26] Of course, any terrorist group wishing to modify smallpox in this way would face the hurdle that, at least officially, the smallpox virus exists in only two well monitored and protected locations in the United States and Russia. Nevertheless, this experiment, and previously published related research, points the way to modifying a variety of viruses to subvert the human immune system. At the same time, these results also give researchers the knowledge needed to pursue countermeasures to such engineered — and some naturally occurring — pathogens.

Smallpox is the first, and so far only, virus to be eliminated from the natural world; the World Health Organization and other health agencies are working to ensure that polio soon follows it into oblivion. However, a recent experiment dramatised the fact that extinction is not necessarily forever in the case of the polio virus. A group of scientists working at the State University of New York (SUNY) published a paper in 2002 that showed they could synthesise an infectious polio virus from scratch using chemicals purchased on the open market.[27] Therefore, even if the polio virus is eliminated from the natural world, it could be reconstructed in the private laboratory. The SUNY team took three years to synthesise the virus; research by a group at the Institute for Biological Energy Alternatives in Rockville, Maryland in 2003, armed with the most sophisticated techniques available, reduced the time to manufacture a virus of comparable genomic size to two weeks.[28] The smallpox virus has a genome 25 times as large as that of the polio virus, and cannot reconstitute itself from its DNA alone, so it constitutes a fundamentally greater challenge. But many other viruses could now be synthesised in the laboratory.

One of the great killers of the twentieth century is the influenza virus, with a genome about twice the size of polio. The 1918–19 strain was especially virulent, killing at least 20–40m people worldwide. Research based in part on samples preserved from 1918 is now revealing the reasons why the strain was especially lethal.[29] This research may prove vital to protecting humanity against new strains of deadly influenza, but will also suggest modifications needed to convert the genome of contemporary influenza viruses to ones that could be especially deadly, were modern antiviral drugs to prove ineffective or be insufficiently available.

Nor are viruses the only disease agents that can be manipulated for greater lethality. Using classical microbiological techniques, the Soviet state bioweapons programme reportedly developed multiple-antibiotic-resistant strains of the bacteria responsible for anthrax and pneumonic plague.[30] Modern engineering techniques will confer more subtle capabilities. A US–Japanese academic team published in the *Proceedings of the National Academy of Sciences* in 2003 their creation of a 'hypervirulent mutant' of the bacterium responsible for tuberculosis; genetic manipulation yielded a deadlier strain that side-stepped the mouse's immune system.[31] The research is important for understanding why natural tuberculosis remains latent and asymptomatic in some of its infected victims; once again the capacity for harm is a by-product of the attempt to understand, and hence combat, a major human disease. Enhanced virulence had earlier been produced by other research groups, including the 2001 creation of a 'hypervirulent' version of the protozoan parasite responsible for the disease leishmaniasis.[32]

The recent outbreak of SARS was a reminder that the natural world continues to challenge the human population with novel and deadly diseases, independent of whatever human beings may engineer. Over 11m people die annually from infectious and parasitic diseases, suggesting that the benefits of fundamental research on disease organisms currently likely far outweigh the dangers.[33] The good news is that SARS was contained, even though no vaccine or cure for it exists. Traditional methods of contact-tracing and quarantine proved sufficient, albeit after more than 800 deaths and major economic consequences.[34] However, success in containing the SARS outbreak should not be misinterpreted to mean that concerns over designer contagious pathogens for which no cures or vaccines exist are overblown. Engineered pathogens could have worse characteristics than SARS, for example, much longer incubation periods or greater communicability. In fact, in a recent review paper in the journal *Science*, influenza researchers warned that 'because epidemiological modelling has suggested that it is much more infectious than SARS, influenza is unlikely to be controllable by SARS-like quarantine measures'.[35]

The dangers posed by advances in biotechnological research do not derive merely from experiments with pathogenic micro-organisms. The mousepox experimenters relied on research on the nature of the immune system to show them how to create a virus to subvert the mouse's immune response. Similarly, basic medical research into the human immune system or the human genome itself will inevitably point the way towards increasingly powerful and possibly quite subtle methods to cause human disease. Essentially all of this knowledge will be in the public domain.

The increasing ease with which micro-organisms may be given deadly modifications emphasises how even more misleading the moniker 'weapons of mass destruction' (WMD) will become in the future. The term already misleads by glossing over profound differences in the applicability of non-proliferation, deterrence, and defence to nuclear, chemical, or biological weapons, as well as in the consequences of their use.[36] But because it also fails to capture the disparate future trajectories of the technologies underlying these weapons, it will become ever more misleading over time.

It is important to distinguish between diseases that are contagious— capable of spreading from person to person, like smallpox, influenza or pneumonic plague—and those that are not (such as anthrax). To cause mass casualties, non-contagious biological agents will still require aerosolisation—the processing of the agent into an extremely fine powder or mist, and its effective dissemination. Aum Shinrikyo's failure with this technology is a reminder that, without specialised knowledge or a research and development programme, mastering these techniques is not easily done. However, contagious agents could be used by terrorists to cause widespread outbreaks on the basis of person-to-person transmission, possibly skipping the aerosolisation step. Given this fact, the kinds of experiments just surveyed suggest that, in future, in the realm of biology, we could face a 'banalisation' of WMD capacity. Many laboratories may have the capability to modify or synthesise deadly contagious pathogens, albeit with substantial risk to the researchers in the absence of proper containment facilities. This is altogether different from the hurdles facing those who would make nuclear weapons-usable material. It will be important, in a world where WMD capabilities may be the cause of war, to distinguish clearly between biological, chemical and nuclear weapons or 'WMD programme-related activities'.[37] Chemical and biological weapons, and 'programme-related activities' pertaining to these weapons, while of great concern, will often pose far lesser threats than nuclear weapons, so any call for war on the basis of 'WMD' should distinguish clearly between these possibilities, rather than conflating them.

Of course, it will remain of the highest importance to prevent proliferation of nuclear weapons capabilities. We do not want our nuclear future to begin to resemble our biological future.

Global Review

It is unclear how we should cope with the ongoing proliferation of biotechnology, and the prospects for non- or sub-state terrorism that will result. One suggested approach is oversight of potentially high-consequence biological research. A recent report by the National Research Council recommends several measures, including:[38]

Review of Plans for Experiments.

The Department of Health and Human Services should establish a review system for seven classes of experiments with microbiological agents that raise concern. Precedent exists in three-decades-old measures taken to review the safety of potentially hazardous recombinant DNA experiments. However, the recommended review would be binding only for those funded by federal research grants; private companies not supported by the National Institutes of Health would subscribe on a voluntary basis.

Publication Review.

Scientists and the editors of science journals would review their own publications for potential national security risks. In some cases, certain information might be withheld from publication.

Harmonised International Oversight

The United States would pursue harmonised national, regional and international measures to provide a counterpart to its own review system.

The most important aspect of these recommendations may be the recognition by the scientific community that biotechnology requires greater attention to the ways in which their research could be misused. Nevertheless, even the full implementation of the system recommended by the National Research Council would leave tremendous gaps: domestically, in those private laboratories that were not federally funded and chose to remain outside the system of review; internationally due to a 'crazy-quilt' pattern of oversight that would likely vary from country to country, and could be nonexistent in practice in countries of greatest concern. John Steinbruner and his colleagues at the University of Maryland's Center for International and Security Studies have instead elaborated a truly global system of internationally agreed rules for the oversight of high-consequence biological research.[39] But any such system would face at least three challenges:

Global Implementation

How would such a system be effectively and widely implemented? Admittedly, such a system may come to seem less utopian after a first major engineered pandemic killed vast numbers of people. After that kind of horror, implementing such a system could move from the realm of the incredible to the realm of the mandatory. But we are in a far better position now to engage in careful thinking about how such a system should balance conflicting interests than we would be in that post-attack world.

Capturing Bad Actors

In the absence of remarkably invasive oversight, the envisioned regime could fail to capture those bad actors of greatest concern. Legitimate research might be hamstrung while illicit research would proceed covertly without constraints. But to some extent this objection misapprehends the problem. Most non-state terrorist groups are unlikely to conduct sophisticated biotechnology research and development programmes. Rather, most will, at best, follow in the scientific literature those discoveries made by legitimate scientists, then attempt to implement those techniques. Therefore, by overseeing certain high-consequence work in the legitimate scientific community, we might hope to diminish the threat of misuse by bad actors.

Defining High-Consequence Research

A great deal of high-consequence work has nothing to do with pathogen manipulation, but rather lies in the realm of fundamental understanding of the human organism. In this sense, a vast amount of biomedical research is potentially of high consequence. Yet again we must resist the silver-bullet fallacy, if restrictions on the manipulation of pathogens would prove valuable. Even in this case, it may prove difficult to give a detailed account of those experiments that are of the greatest concern without in effect providing hints to less competent groups about the directions they should go in to achieve deadly results. A balance will need to be struck.

Despite these difficulties, we should not conclude that it is best simply to do nothing. Oversight regimes should continue to be explored, so that a detailed understanding of their promise and drawbacks is gained. Meanwhile, the production of biological agents for terrorism should be criminalised worldwide, and so-called 'societal verification'—the encouragement of scientists and other citizens to blow the whistle on illicit biological weapons activity—should be fostered. Finally, biotechnologically competent intelligence gathering and analysis must keep pace with the latest research.

An Eternal Arms Race?

In the absence of a comprehensive and effective system of global review of potential high-consequence research, we are instead trapped in a kind of offence–defence arms race. Even as legitimate biomedical researchers develop defences against biological pathogens, bad actors could in turn engineer countermeasures in a kind of directed version of the way natural pathogens evolve resistance to anti-microbial drugs. The mousepox case provides a harbinger of what is to come: just as the United States was stockpiling 300m doses of smallpox vaccine as a defence against a terrorist smallpox attack, experimental modification of the mousepox virus showed how the vaccine could possibly be circumvented. The United States is now funding research on antiviral drugs and other ways of combating smallpox that might be effective against the engineered organism. Yet there are indications that smallpox can be made resistant to one of the few known antiviral drugs. The future has the appearance of an eternal arms race of measures and countermeasures.

The 'arms race' metaphor should be used with caution; it too is in danger of calling up misleading analogies to the nuclear arms race of the Cold War. First, the biological arms race is an offence–defence race, rather than a competition between offensive means. Under the BWC, only defensive research is legitimate. But more fundamentally, the driver of de facto offensive capabilities in this arms race is not primarily a particular adversary, but rather the ongoing global advance of microbiological and biomedical research. Defensive measures are in a race with nefarious applications of basic research, much of which is itself undertaken for protection against natural disease. In a sense, we are in an arms race with ourselves.

It is hard to see how this arms race is stable—an offence granted comparable resources would seem to be necessarily favoured. As with ballistic missile defence, particular defensive measures may be defeated by offensive countermeasures. In the biological case, implementing defensive measures will require not only research but drug development and distribution plans. Offensive measures need not exercise this care, although fortunately they will likely face comparative resource constraints (especially if not associated with a state programme), and may find that some approaches (for example, to confer antibiotic resistance) have the simultaneous effect of inadvertently reducing a pathogen's virulence. The defence must always guard against committing the fallacy of the last move, whereas the offence may embrace the view of the Irish Republican Army after it failed to assassinate the British cabinet in the 1984 Brighton bombing: 'Today we were unlucky, but remember we have only to be lucky once—you will have to be lucky always'.[40] At the very least, the defence will have to be vigilant and collectively smarter than the offence.

The only way for the defence to win convincingly in the biological arms race would seem to be to succeed in discovering and implementing certain de facto last-move defences, at least on an organism-by-organism basis. Perhaps there are defences, or a web of defences, that will prove too difficult for any plausible non-state actor to engineer around. Whether such defences exist is unclear at this time, but their exploration should be a long-term research goal of US biodefence efforts. Progress might also have an important impact on international public health. One of the 'Grand Challenges' identified by the Bill and Melinda Gates Foundation in its $200m initiative to improve global health calls for the discovery of drugs that minimise the emergence of drug resistance — a kind of 'last move' defence against the evolutionary countermeasures of natural microbes.[41] Should a collection of such defensive moves prove possible, bioterrorism might ultimately succumb to a kind of globalised dissuasion by denial:[42] non-state groups would calculate that they could not hope to achieve dramatic results through biological programmes and would choose to direct their efforts elsewhere.

The objection might be raised that the vision of an eternal arms race smacks too much of technological determinism; after all, Kennedy and Wohlstetter foresaw a world replete with nuclear weapons, yet this world has so far been averted — and would not have been averted had we given in to claims of its inevitability. But biotechnology is fundamentally different from nuclear-weapons technology in its broad availability, and once again, the analogy to the nuclear case fails.

Given the proliferation of capabilities described here, greater weight must necessarily be placed on addressing the possible motivations of terrorist groups. After all, remarkably few non-state groups have ever attempted biological attacks. Understanding why this is so, to what extent it has been due to motivations as opposed to means, and working to preserve whatever inhibitions have been at play, should receive high priority.

Racing Against Ourselves

Short of de facto last-move defences, another way for the defence to try to maintain an advantage is for it to classify its most important countermoves. These might still be described publicly in broad terms so that some dissuasive benefit could be gained. Such an approach may seem natural, almost automatic, to the national security community—although it is not the approach that has been taken for smallpox biodefence research, which is overseen by the World Health Organization (WHO). But in fact, classified defence research carries dangers in the biological case that should not be overlooked.

First, from an ethical point of view, it would simply be unacceptable to keep secret certain potentially effective defensive measures. For example, in an era when certain strains of bacteria are already resistant to all known antibiotics, and with antibiotic resistance spreading rapidly, keeping a newly developed effective antibiotic in reserve for the event of a biological attack would lead immediately to avoidable deaths due to naturally occurring diseases. Only in a future where there were a huge variety of effective antibiotics available for infectious disease would such a biodefence strategy be acceptable. (And even then, one would worry whether such a stockpile could be kept secure against the small theft needed to permit biological countermeasures to be explored.) Our insufficient effort against naturally occurring disease and increasing antibiotic resistance currently limits our strategies for bioweapons defences.

Second, it will be vital from a strategic perspective to consider carefully what types of biodefence work should be classified, and whether some international transparency will be needed even in these cases. According to the *New York Times*, some classified research in the United States has involved genetically engineering pathogens in order to replicate steps believed to have been taken in the Soviet biowarfare programme.[43] Such work would be legally permitted under the BWC as legitimate biodefence research; however, if it were conducted in secret and news of it leaked, other nations might wonder whether the US had an offensive programme involving genetic modifications underway.

A more difficult question is whether it would be legal and wise to have classified biodefence research produce genetically modified pathogens that, to our knowledge, no adversary has yet created. On the one hand, we should know how to defend ourselves against such potential threats that we can already anticipate. On the other, such research risks making the US government a primary driver of the very biological arms race we hope to avoid, and risks convincing other nations of our offensive intent. Strategic decisions must be made about what biological weapons research the US or any other government will conduct in the name of biodefence, how much of this research will be classified and how that programme will be publicly described.

A congressional or presidential commission should be created to advise on these issues, while defusing international concern that the US is secretly pursuing an offensive weapons programme. A 'trigger list' of research that government agencies may only perform with White House approval and congressional oversight should ultimately be promulgated, to ensure that classified biological weapons research of potential high consequence anywhere within the US government is not conducted without its strategic and legal ramifications being weighed. A permanent body, with access to classified biodefence information government-wide, and responsibility to both the executive and legislative branches, should be created to ensure that this vigilance is in fact exercised. This body would go beyond intra-agency legal reviews such as those now conducted by the Department of Defense Compliance Review Group;[44] it would be both government-wide and have the mandate to make recommendations to the president regarding the strategic wisdom of lines of research. The body would combine the independence and access of the president's Foreign Intelligence Advisory Board with accountability to both the executive and legislative branches. The scientific community would have to play a central role for such steps to be realistic, current and viewed as legitimate.

The United States should carefully consider what classified biodefence research will be performed and do so in as transparent a way as possible consistent with national security, to reassure the world of its commitment to the BWC. In this way the US would seek to minimise incentives for other states to pursue or accelerate illegal offensive programmes. Rather, broad-based and publicly acknowledged biodefence research would aim to globalise dissuasion, convincing non-state terrorist groups that they cannot hope to counter the entire array of defences that the world's legitimate biodefence research community has arrayed against them. With research on de facto 'last-move' defences, the biodefence community should thereby endeavour to circumvent, or at least mitigate, an otherwise endless biological arms race.

Notes

1. President John F. Kennedy, News Conference Number 52, 21 March 1963, John F. Kennedy Library and Museum, Washington DC, http://www.jfklibrary.org/jfk_press_conference_630321.html. While this authorisation legislation has had some success in the United States Senate, it has faced more difficulty in the US House of Representatives.

2. Albert Wohlstetter, *Moving Toward Life in a Nuclear Armed Crowd?* ACDA/PAB-263, prepared by Pan Heuristics Division of Science Applications Inc., Los Angeles, December 1975, revised April 1976. A subsequent version may be found as Chapter 6, 'Life in a Nuclear Armed Crowd', in Albert Wohlstetter, Thomas A. Brown, Gregory S. Jones, Henry Rowen, Vince Taylor and Roberta Wohlstetter, *Swords from Plowshares* (Chicago: University of Chicago Press, 1979), pp. 126–150.

3. Much of this history is reviewed in Christopher F. Chyba, 'Biological Terrorism and Public Health', *Survival*, vol. 43, no. 1, spring 2001, pp. 93–106. For statistics on disease emergence over the past two decades, see Jonathan R. Davis and Joshua Lederberg (eds), *Emerging Infectious Diseases from the Global to the Local Perspective: A Summary of a Workshop of the Forum on Emerging Infections* (Washington DC: National Academy Press, 2001).

4. Global Pathogens Surveillance Act of 2003, S. 871, 108th Congress, 1st Session, http://www.theorator.com/bills108/s871.html.

5. This history and that of mass-casualty terrorism in the 1990s is reviewed in Christopher F. Chyba, 'Biological Terrorism and Public Health'.

6. US Assistant Secretary of State for Arms Control Stephen Rademaker, quoted in Brad Knickerbocker, 'In an age of biowarfare, US sees new role for nukes', *The Christian Science Monitor*, 26 November 2002, http://www.csmonitor.com/2002/1126/p02s02-usmi.htm. Also quoted in Wendy Lubetkin, 'US Welcomes Biological Weapons Convention Work Plan', http://www.globalsecurity.org/wmd/library/news/usa/2002/usa-021115-usia01.htm.

7. For one assessment of those states in various stages of biological weapons programmes, see Milton Leitenberg, 'An Assessment of the Biological Weapons Threat to the United States', *Journal of Homeland Security*, January 2001, http://www.homelandsecurity.org/journal/Articles/Leitenberg.htm. For the US State Department list of countries not in compliance with the BWC, see US Department of State, *Adherence to and Compliance with Arms Control and Nonproliferation Agreements and Commitments* (Washington DC: Bureau of Verification and Compliance, 2002), available at http://www.state.gov/documents/organization/22466.pdf.

8. Reviews of the bioweapons that genetic engineering might make possible include: Steven M. Block, 'Living nightmares: Biological threats enabled by molecular biology', in Sidney D. Drell, Abraham D. Sofaer and George D. Wilson, *The New Terror: Facing the Threat of Biological and Chemical Weapons* (Stanford: Hoover Institution Press, 1999), pp. 39–75; Claire M. Fraser and Malcolm R. Dando, 'Genomics and future biological weapons: The need for preventive action by the biomedical community', *Nature Genetics*, vol. 29, November 2001, pp. 253–256; and Mark Wheelis, 'Biotechnology and biochemical weapons', *The Nonproliferation Review*, Spring 2002, pp. 48–53.

9. 'Recombinant DNA' refers to DNA produced by recombining fragments of DNA from different organisms. For a review of the policy debates engendered by recombinant DNA research, see Christopher Chyba, 'The recombinant DNA debate and the precedent of Leo Szilard', in Sanford A. Lakoff (ed.), *Science and Ethical Responsibility* (New York: Addison-Wesley, 1980), pp. 251–264.

10 For illustrations of the capabilities provided by recent techniques, see, for example, Andreas Crameri, Sun-Ali Raillard, Ericka Bermudez and Willem P.C. Stemmer, 'DNA shuffling of a family of genes from diverse species accelerates directed evolution', *Nature*, vol. 391, 15 January 1998, pp. 288–291; Nay-Wei Soong, Laurel Nomura, Katja Pekrun, Margaret Reed, Liana Sheppard, Glenn Dawes and Willem P.C. Stemmer, 'Molecular breeding of viruses', *Nature Genetics*, vol. 25, August 2000, pp. 436–439; Ying-Xin Zhang, Kim Perry, Victor A. Vinci, Keith Powell, Willem P.C. Stemmer and Stephen B. del Cardayré, 'Genome shuffling leads to rapid phenotypic improvement in bacteria', *Nature*, vol. 415, 7 February 2002, pp. 644–646.

11. Gerald F. Joyce, 'Directed molecular evolution', *Scientific American*, December 1992, pp. 90–97; Ronald R. Breaker and Gerald F. Joyce, 'Inventing and improving ribozyme function: rational design versus iterative selection methods', *Trends in Biotechnology*, vol. 12, July 1994, pp. 268–275.

12. Ernst & Young Economics Consulting and Quantitative Analysis, prepared for the Biotechnology Industry Organization, *The Economic Contributions of the Biotechnology Industry to the US Economy*, May 2000, http://www.bio.org/news/ernstyoung.pdf.

13. David Barboza, 'Development of Biotech Crops is Booming in Asia', *New York Times*, 21 February 2003.

14. Staff report, 'PAEC to Train Foreign Muslim Scientists', *The Daily Times, Lahore*, 17 January 2004.

15. Wayne Arnold, 'Singapore goes for Biotech: A $280 Million Complex, Complete with Mice', *New York Times* 26 August 2003.

16. Kendall Hoyt and Stephen G. Brooks, 'A Double-Edged Sword: Globalization and Biosecurity', *International Security*, vol. 28, no. 3, Winter 2003–04, pp. 123–148.

17. See, for example, Christopher F. Chyba, *Biological Terrorism, Emerging Diseases, and National Security*, (New York: Rockefeller Brothers Fund Project on World Security, 1998), http://rbf.org/publications/sec.html and Christopher F. Chyba, 'Biological Terrorism and Public Health'.

18. Christopher F. Chyba, 'Toward Biological Security', *Foreign Affairs*, vol. 81, no. 3, May/June 2002, pp. 122–136.

19. The BW capabilities and mistakes of Aum Shinrikyo have been assessed by Milton Leitenberg, 'An Assessment of the Biological Weapons Threat to the United States', *Journal of Homeland Security*.

20. See, for example, Jonathan B. Tucker, 'Preventing the Misuse of Pathogens: The Need for Global Biosecurity Standards', *Arms Control Today*, June 2003, http://www.armscontrol.org/act/2003_06/tucker_june03.asp.

21. See, for example, Gerald Epstein, 'Controlling Biological Warfare Threats: Resolving Potential Tensions Among the Research Community, Industry and the National Security Community', *Critical Reviews in Microbiology*, vol. 27, no. 4 (2001), pp. 321–354.

22. A specific example of this approach is Richard Danzig, *Catastrophic Bioterrorism — What Is to Be Done?* Center for Technology and National Security Policy, August 2003.

23. For more information on these programmes, see *The NIAID Biodefense Research Agenda for CDC Category A Agents: Progress Report*, August 2003, accessible at http://www2.niaid.nih.gov/biodefense/research/strat_plan.aspx, and The White House, 'President Details Project Bioshield', http://www.whitehouse.gov/news/releases/2003/02/20030203.html.

24. The term 'fallacy of the last move' was, to our knowledge, first used in Herbert York, *Race to Oblivion* (New York: Simon & Schuster, 1970), p. 211.

25. Ronald J. Jackson et al., 'Expression of a mouse interleukin-4 by a recombinant ectromelia virus suppresses cytolytic lymphocyte responses and overcomes genetic resistance to mousepox', *Journal of Virology*, vol. 75, no. 3, February 2001, pp. 1,205–1,210. For a less technical historical account, see Jon Cohen, 'Designer Bugs', *The Atlantic Monthly*, July/August 2002, http://www.theatlantic.com/cgi-bin/send.cgi?page=http%3A//www.theatlantic.com/issues/2002/07/cohen-j.htm.

26. National Research Council, *Biotechnology Research in an Age of Terrorism*, (Washington DC: National Academies Press, 2004), p. 26.

27. Jeronimo Cello, Aniko V. Pau, and Eckard Wimmer, 'Chemical synthesis of poliovirus cDNA: Generation of Infectious Virus in the Absence of Natural Template', *Science* vol. 297, pp. 1,016–1,018, 9 August 2002,. See also Steven M. Block, 'A Not-So-Cheap Stunt', *Science Online*, vol. 297, 2 August 2002, pp. 769–770.

28. Hamilton O. Smith, Clyde A. Hutchison III, Cynthia Ftannkoch, and J. Craig Venter, 'Generating a synthetic genome by whole genome assembly: fX174 bacteriophage from synthetic oligonucleotides', *Proceedings of the National Academy of Sciences USA Early Edition*, http://www/pnas.org/cgi/doi/10.1073.pnas.2237126100.

29. James Stevens et al., 'Structure of the Uncleaved Human H1 Hemagglutinin from the Extinct 1918 Influenza Virus', *Science*, vol. 303, 19 March 2004, pp. 1,866–1,870. For a less technical perspective, see Edward C. Holmes, '1918 and All That', *Science*, vol. 303, 19 March 2004, pp. 1,787–1,788.

30. For some of these claims, see Ken Alibek, *Biohazard* (New York: Dell Publishing, 1999), p. 173; Sergei Popov, *NOVA Online Bioterror Sergei Popov*, http://www.pbs.org/wgbh/nova/bioterror/biow_popov.html.
31. Nobuyuki Shimono et al., 'Hypervirulent mutant of *Mycobacterium tuberculosis* resulting from disruption of the mce1 operon', *Proceedings of the National Academy of Sciences*, vol. 100, no. 26, 23 December 2003, pp. 15,918–15,923.
32. Mark L. Cunningham, Richard G. Titus, Salvatore J. Turco, and Stephen M. Beverley, 'Regulation of differentiation to the infective state of the protozoan parasite *Leishmania major* by tetrahydrobiopterin', *Science*, vol. 292, 13 April 2001, pp. 285–287.
33. World Health Organization, *The World Health Report 2003 — Shaping the Future*, Annex 2: Deaths by cause, sex and mortality stratum in WHO Regions, estimates for 2002, http://www.who.int/whr/2003/annex/en/.
34. World Health Organization, *The World Health Report 2003 — Shaping the Future*, Chapter 5: SARS: Lessons from a New Disease, http://www.who.int/whr/2003/chapter5/en/
35. Richard J. Webby and Robert G. Webster, 'Are We Ready for Pandemic Influenza', *Science* vol. 302, 28 November 2003, pp. 1,519–1,522.
36. Christopher F. Chyba, 'Toward Biological Security'.
37. In his January 2004 State of the Union speech, President George W. Bush stated that 'dozens of weapons of mass destruction-related program activities' had been identified by postwar inspections in Iraq. See, The White House, 'State of the Union Address', United States Capitol, Washington DC, 20 January 2004, http://www.whitehouse.gov/news/releases/2004/01/20040120-7.html.
38. National Research Council, *Biotechnology Research in an Age of Terrorism*, (Washington DC: National Academies Press, 2004).
39. John Steinbruner, Eisa D. Harris, Nancy Gallagher and Stacy Gunther, *Controlling Dangerous Pathogens: A Prototype Protective Oversight System*, September 2003, http://www.cissm.umd.edu/documents/pathogensmonograph.pdf.
40. Quoted in Art MacEoin, 'IRA Bombs British Cabinet in Brighton', *An Phoblacht/Republican News*, 11 October 2001, http://republican-news.org/archive/2001/October11/11hist.html.
41. Harold Varmus et al., 'Grand Challenges in Global Health', *Science* vol. 302, 17 October 2003, pp. 398–399.
42. 'Dissuasion by denial' has sometimes been called 'deterrence by denial'; we accept the distinction that 'deterrence' refers exclusively to prevention by the threat of punishment, so that 'dissuasion' is appropriate here. For a discussion of this terminology, see Scott D. Sagan and Kenneth N. Waltz, *The Spread of Nuclear Weapons: A Debate* (New York: W.W. Norton & Co., 1995), pp. 3–4.
43. Judith Miller, Stephen Engelberg and William J. Broad, 'US Germ Warfare Research Pushes Treaty Limits', *New York Times*, 4 September 2001; see also Judith Miller, Stephen Engelberg and William Broad, *Germs: Biological Weapons and America's Secret War* (New York: Simon & Schuster, 2001), pp. 287–314.
44. See Department of Defense, 'Department of Defense Directive Number 2060.1', 24 November 2003, http://www.dtic.mil/whs/directives/corres/pdf/d20601_010901/d20601p.pdf.

Christopher F. Chyba is co-director of the Center for International Security and Cooperation at Stanford University, the Stanford Institute for International Studies, and an associate professor at Stanford University. A graduate of Swarthmore College, Chyba studied as a Marshall Scholar at the University of Cambridge and received his Ph.D. in planetary science from Cornell University in 1991. He served on the White House staff from 1993 to 1995, entering as a White House fellow, working on the National Security Council staff and then in the National Security Division of the Office of Science and Technology Policy.

Alex L. Greninger completed his M.S. in biology and his Center for International Security and Cooperation honors thesis at Stanford University in 2003.

Chapter 2.5

Chemical Terrorism

Jonathan B. Tucker

Chemical Terrorism: Assessing Threats and Responses

Efforts to enhance the nation's ability to prevent and respond to acts of chemical terrorism are warranted by the fact that hazardous chemicals are ubiquitous in modern industrial society and hence are more accessible to terrorists than either biological or fissile materials. Four possible types of chemical terrorism have been identified:

1. Release of a military-grade chemical warfare agent against a civilian target with the intent to inflict indiscriminate casualties;

2. Sabotage of a chemical manufacturing plant or storage facility (including a rail tank car) in which toxic materials are held in gaseous or liquid form, or as solids, which have the capability of reacting with air or water to release toxic gases or vapors;

3. Contamination of public water or food supplies with toxic agents; and

4. Targeted use of a chemical agent to assassinate specific individuals.

Terrorists intent on acquiring chemical weapons have two options: buying or stealing them from existing national stockpiles, or manufacturing them independently. Because the synthesis of military-grade agents entails significant technical hurdles and risks, the acquisition of toxic industrial chemicals is more likely. Although such chemicals are hundreds of times less lethal than nerve agents, they could still inflict significant casualties if released in an enclosed space or outdoors under optimal atmospheric conditions. This paper assesses the threat of chemical terrorism and examines strategies of prevention and response.

Chemical Threat Agents

Chemical warfare (CW) agents are poisonous, man-made gases, liquids, or powders that, when absorbed through the lungs or skin, have incapacitating or lethal effects on humans and animals. Although many CW agents are liquids, the explosion of a munition can transform a liquid agent into an aerosol (a fine mist of tiny droplets) and then a vapor. Most warfare agents fall into five broad categories: blister, nerve, choking, blood, and incapacitating. Beyond their differing physiological effects, CW agents vary in their persistency and volatility, or tendency to evaporate. Nonpersistent agents dissipate within a few hours and pose mainly an inhalation threat, whereas persistent agents remain hazardous for as long as a month when deposited on terrain, vegetation, or objects, and pose primarily a skin contamination threat.

Blister agents, such as sulfur mustard and lewisite, are liquids that cause chemical burns. When absorbed by direct contact with the skin or eyes or by inhalation of aerosol or vapor, sulfur mustard induces painful skin blisters, blindness, and severe damage to lung tissue after an asymptomatic "latent period" of from one to eight hours. Mustard exposure also has harmful effects on the blood-forming tissues of the bone marrow, the lining of the gastrointestinal tract, and the central nervous system. Lewisite causes skin blistering similar to that of mustard, but its effects are immediate rather than delayed. Historical evidence from World War I and the Iran-Iraq War suggests that blister agents can inflict large numbers of casualties, although less than 5 percent are generally fatal. No effective treatment is available.

Nerve agents, such as sarin and VX, are the most lethal chemical poisons known: they disrupt the functioning of the human nervous system and can kill within minutes. Sarin is the most volatile of the nerve agents, evaporating at about the same rate as water. In an enclosed space with poor ventilation, the evaporation of a few liters of sarin can generate a lethal concentration in the air. Outdoors, however, much larger quantities are required to offset the dispersive effects of wind and air turbulence. VX is an oily liquid that persists in the environment for days or weeks, depending on ambient temperature, and acts primarily by penetrating the skin. The lethal dose is about 10 mg.

Because of the extreme hazards associated with handling and disseminating nerve agents, terrorists might seek to develop "binary" weapons, which are safer to produce, store, and transport. In a binary system, two relatively nontoxic ingredients are stored separately and mixed together before use to generate the lethal agent. Sarin, for example, can be produced in a binary system by reacting isopropanol (rubbing alcohol) with methylphosphonic difluoride (DF). Nevertheless, the synthesis of DF is complex and difficult. Terrorists would also have to mix the precursor chemicals manually before use—an extremely hazardous operation—or attempt to design a remote-controlled device that would carry out the mixing and dispersal steps, a task requiring considerable technical expertise.

Although nerve agents have by far the greatest lethality, terrorists might employ other classes of toxic chemicals effectively. For example, choking agents (e.g., chlorine, phosgene gas) and blood agents (hydrogen cyanide, cyanogen chloride) were used on a large scale during World War I. These chemicals dissipate rapidly outdoors, but they could potentially cause mass casualties if released by terrorists in an enclosed space, such as a subway station or an indoor sports arena.[1]

The Case of Aum Shinrikyo

Much of the current concern about chemical terrorism stems from the case of the Japanese cult Aum Shinrikyo, which conducted sarin attacks in Matsumoto in 1994 and Tokyo in 1995. Founded in 1987, the quasi-Buddhist sect attracted young intellectuals in their late twenties and thirties who were disillusioned with mainstream society. Aum had some 40,000 members by 1995, most of them in Japan and Russia. The cult ran a variety of legitimate businesses and also engaged in land fraud, drug dealing, and other criminal activities, enabling it to accumulate a net worth of about $1 billion.[2] Aum leader Shoko Asahara planned to use a large-scale chemical attack to trigger a major war between the United States and Japan that cult members would survive, enabling them to seize control of the Japanese government. In pursuit of this mad scheme, Aum aggressively recruited scientists and technicians from Japanese universities to work on the development and production of chemical weapons as part of a "chemical brigade" within the cult's "Ministry of Science and Technology."[3]

Aum chemists chose to manufacture sarin because of its relative ease of production compared with other nerve agents, its volatility, and the fact that the necessary ingredients could be obtained from commercial suppliers. The cult purchased a Swiss-made pilot plant with computerized process controls, normally used by industry to prototype chemicals. Installed at Aum's headquarters near Mount Fuji, this plant produced some 30 kg of sarin over a two-year period. Cult members successfully tested the nerve agent on sheep at a remote ranch that the cult had purchased in Western Australia.[4]

Asahara planned to acquire a stockpile of 70 tons of sarin and then employ a Russian military helicopter to spray the deadly agent over downtown Tokyo. On June 27, 1994, Aum staged a trial nerve gas attack in a residential area of Matsumoto, a city about 125 miles northwest of Tokyo. The primary targets were three judges who were about to reach a verdict against the cult in a fraud case brought by local landowners. Aum members drove to Matsumoto in a truck that was equipped with an electric hot plate, which they used to vaporize drops of sarin, and a fan and nozzle to vent the toxic fumes. Over a period of about 25 minutes, the team vaporized 3 liters of sarin, generating a toxic cloud that drifted downwind over a residential neighborhood. The Matsumoto attack killed seven and injured 144 others, including the three targeted judges. Initially, the police authorities did not suspect terrorism and blamed the incident on a local resident who was falsely accused of synthesizing pesticides in his backyard.

For the subsequent terrorist attack on the Tokyo subway on March 20, 1995, Aum chemists synthesized 24 liters of sarin on short notice. Asahara ordered the subway attack as a diversionary tactic in response to a tip from informants that the police were training for an imminent raid on Aum headquarters. Because the sarin was not distilled, it was only about 25 percent pure. The agent was also diluted with acetonitrile to reduce its volatility and thus give the perpetrators time to escape.[5] This solution was poured into 11 two-ply nylon-polyester bags, which were then heat-sealed.

During the morning rush hour on March 20, cult members boarded five different cars on three lines of the Tokyo subway system, carrying the sarin-filled plastic bags wrapped in newspapers. The trains were scheduled to arrive at the central Kasumigaseki Station within a few minutes of each other. At the appointed time, cult members placed the plastic bags on the floor, punctured them with sharpened umbrella tips, and quickly left the trains. The punctured bags released puddles of liquid sarin that slowly evaporated, generating toxic fumes. In addition to 12 fatalities, 17 victims were in critical condition requiring intensive care, 37 suffered from severe symptoms of nerve agent exposure such as miosis (pinpoint pupils), shortness of breath, muscular twitching, and gastrointestinal problems; and 984 had miosis only.[6] Had the sarin been purer and disseminated in aerosol form, the attack would have caused many more deaths.

A few weeks later, on May 5, 1995, Aum staged another chemical attack in a Tokyo subway station, this time using a crude binary weapon. The device consisted of two plastic pouches, one containing 2 kg of sodium cyanide crystals and the other filled with 1.5 liters of dilute sulfuric acid. A primitive fusing system ignited the sodium-cyanide pouch after a time delay. The two pouches were arranged so that as the flames from the first spread to the second, the cyanide crystals would react with the sulfuric acid to form deadly hydrogen cyanide gas. Cult members placed the jury-rigged chemical bomb in the men's room at Shinjuku subway station, Tokyo's busiest, but the device malfunctioned. Although four subway workers who doused the flames were overcome by toxic fumes and hospitalized briefly, the station was evacuated before anyone else was hurt.[7]

Aum also employed nerve agents as an assassination weapon. In late 1993, cult hit squads used sarin in two failed attempts on the life of the leader of a rival religious sect. Then, in December 1994 and January 1995, the cult reportedly carried out three assassination attempts with VX, one of which was successful. In each case, a small amount of liquid agent was sprayed with a hypodermic syringe in the victim's face. The targeted individuals included an anti-Aum attorney and an old man who had harbored an Aum defector.[8]

Assessing the Threat of Chemical Terrorism

Other than Aum Shinrikyo, relatively few terrorist groups have engaged in chemical terrorism. According to a database compiled by the Monterey Institute's Center for Nonproliferation Studies, only 125 incidents were reported worldwide between January 1960 and May 2001 involving the politically or ideologically motivated use of toxic chemicals. Responsibility for these incidents was distributed among the following types of groups: nationalist-separatist (18); religious (16); single issue, such as antiabortion or animal rights (14); lone actor (9); left wing (10); and right wing (4). In the remaining 54 cases, press accounts did not identify the perpetrators. Of the 125 reported incidents, most were small scale: only 6 caused 10 or more fatalities, and 12 caused more than 10 injuries.[9]

One possible explanation for this historical pattern is that few terrorist organizations are motivated to inflict indiscriminate casualties, particularly with weapons that are widely viewed as abhorrent. Staging a chemical attack would alienate a terrorist group's political constituency and bring down on the perpetrators the full repressive wrath of the government authorities.[10] Nevertheless, terrorist groups lacking outside supporters, such as apocalyptic cults or religious fanatics who believe they are acting on divine commands, may be more inclined to employ indiscriminate weapons such as toxic chemicals. It is still too early to tell whether Aum Shinrikyo was a bizarre aberration or the harbinger of a new trend in terrorism. But Osama bin Laden has declared that it is his "religious duty" to acquire chemical and other nonconventional weapons for use against U.S. targets.

In addition to the motivational side of the equation, technical impediments to the acquisition of military-grade CW agents, such as sarin and VX, seem likely to prevent the large majority of terrorist groups from producing and employing these weapons. Synthesis of nerve agents requires the use of high temperatures and corrosive and dangerous chemicals, and would not be feasible for terrorists untrained in synthetic organic chemistry. Blister agents such as sulfur mustard could be produced more easily if the necessary ingredients were available, but ordering large quantities of a key precursor chemical such as thiodiglycol from a commercial supplier would arouse suspicion and might lead the requested company to notify law enforcement authorities.

In at least one known case, however, an individual with expertise in chemistry managed to produce blister agents and other powerful poisons in a clandestine laboratory. Valery Borzov, a 40-year-old Russian chemist, was arrested in Moscow on August 6, 1998, for attempting to sell a sample of nitrogen mustard to an undercover police officer. After having been fired from the Moscow Scientific Research Institute of Reagents in 1997, Borzov set up a sophisticated chemical laboratory in his apartment and synthesized mustard agent and other unspecified poisons for sale to the Russian mafia and other criminal buyers, charging his customers $1,500 a vial. After his arrest, a police search of his apartment uncovered chemical equipment, 50 liters of "strong poisons," 400 ml of mustard agent, and a thick notebook containing recipes for the manufacture of toxic substances. Borzov was found mentally incompetent to stand trial, diagnosed with schizophrenia, and committed to a treatment facility.[11]

Even if chemical warfare agents can be produced successfully, they are difficult and hazardous to handle and deliver. "Weaponization" of a toxic chemical includes the addition of stabilizers to extend its shelf-life and the development of a system for delivering the agent to the target population by mechanical, pneumatic, or explosive means. The most effective but technically challenging delivery system is an aerosol generator, which disperses the agent as tiny droplets that float in the air and are inhaled by the victims. According to a report by the General Accounting Office, an analytical agency of the U.S. Congress, CW agents "must be released effectively as a vapor, or aerosol, for inhalation exposure, or they need to be in a spray of large droplets or liquid for skin penetration. To serve as terrorist weapons, chemical agents require high toxicity and volatility . . . and need to maintain their strength during storage and release."[12] For example, introducing sarin into the air-handling system of a large building to kill those inside would require a leak-proof container that was small enough to be easily carried by one person yet could deliver a high enough concentration of agent in aerosol or vapor form to inflict widespread casualties. A device possessing such characteristics would be technically complex, probably exceeding the design and manufacturing capabilities of most terrorist groups, even those that managed to attract university-trained scientists.[13] These hurdles might be overcome, however, by a wealthy terrorist organization that recruited military scientists and engineers who had been formerly employed in a state-level chemical weapons program.

As an alternative to synthesizing military-grade CW agents, terrorists might acquire toxic household or industrial chemicals such as sulfur dioxide, ammonia, phosgene, arsenic compounds, hydrogen cyanide, or methyl isocyanate. Cyanides, for example, are employed in a wide variety of industrial applications including electroplating, mineral extraction, dyeing, printing, photography, agriculture, and the production of paper, textiles, and plastics. The United States alone produces 300,000 metric tons of cyanides a year for peaceful purposes.[14] In addition, tens of thousands of toxic organic chemicals are produced by the commercial chemical industry. According to one estimate, the number of organophosphate compounds—a category that includes nerve agents, pesticides, and fire retardants—exceeds 50,000.[15] Thus, toxic industrial chemicals are widely accessible in a way that the materials needed to produce military-grade CW agents are not.

The Monterey Institute database suggests that, historically, terrorists have tended to employ "off-the-shelf" chemicals that are readily available. Of the 125 chemical attacks reported worldwide between January 1960 and May 2001, the toxic weapon was identified in 86 cases. Of this total, only nine incidents—most of them linked to Aum Shinrikyo—involved the use of a military CW agent. Instead, the great majority of attacks were carried out with household or industrial chemicals, such as cyanides (22), butyric acid (21), tear gas (19), insecticide or pesticide (6), sulfuric acid (3), rat poison (2), mercury and mercury compounds (2), arsenic compounds (1), and weed killer (1).[16]

The delivery system, when known, was often equally low-tech: direct contact with the target (34 cases), spray or aerosol (24), contamination of food or drink (15), consumer product tampering (10), explosive device (8), contamination of the water supply (6), jug or jar (5), letter or package (4), injection or projectile (2), and insertion into a building ventilation system (1).[17] Using a toxic chemical to poison a large urban reservoir would be difficult, because it would take impractically large quantities of agent to overcome the effects of dilution and filtration. Food and drink, however, are potentially more vulnerable. In 1999, for example, chickens in Belgium were unintentionally given animal feed that had been contaminated with a dioxin, a cancer-causing chemical. Because the contamination was not discovered for months, dioxin was probably present in chicken meat and eggs sold in Europe in early 1999.[18] This experience suggests that other toxic chemicals could be used to poison the food supply, by way of either animal feed, a food-processing facility, or direct product tampering.

A terrorist incident involving the deliberate poisoning of a beverage took place in Dushanbe, the capital of the former Soviet republic of Tajikistan, on December 31, 1994. Six Russian peacekeeping soldiers, three civilians, and the wife of a Russian embassy worker died after drinking champagne that had been laced with a cyanide. The locally produced champagne had been sold at a kiosk near the Russian military compound. It is not known how many bottles were poisoned.[19]

Sabotage of Chemical Industry Plants

Another possible form of chemical terrorism is sabotage of a commercial industry plant engaged in the production, processing, or storage of a highly toxic chemical, causing its release and the exposure of a nearby populated area. Such an attack might involve penetration of the plant site by outside terrorists or an inside job by disgruntled plant workers. The deliberate release of a hazardous chemical could be brought about by detonating a conventional explosive to rupture a storage tank or, alternatively, by manipulating the manufacturing process to cause a runaway reaction. In the latter case, if no group claimed responsibility, it might be difficult for investigators to distinguish a terrorist attack from an industrial accident. Terrorists might also use an improvised explosive device to puncture a railroad tank car carrying a hazardous chemical.

According to an estimate by the U.S. Environmental Protection Agency (EPA), approximately 15,000 facilities in the United States, many of them in urban areas, produce or store hazardous or extremely hazardous chemicals.[20] Phosgene, for example, was used as a chemical warfare agent in World War I, yet today more than 1 billion pounds of phosgene are produced and consumed in the United States each year for the production of plastics.[21] Another highly toxic industrial chemical, methyl isocyanate (MIC), is an intermediate in pesticide production and was responsible for the 1984 accident at a Union Carbide plant in Bhopal, India, that caused more than 2,500 deaths. The Bhopal disaster, allegedly the result of sabotage by a disgruntled employee, occurred just after midnight on December 3, 1984. Over a period of a few hours, an estimated 30 to 40 metric tons of MIC in vapor and liquid form escaped from a holding tank at the plant, forming a toxic cloud that blanketed an area of more than 10 square miles, including densely populated shantytowns. An estimated 500 people died before getting treatment, 2000 more died within the first week, and roughly 60,000 people were seriously injured.[22]

An example of a toxic release in the United States resulting from deliberate sabotage took place on February 28, 2000, at a chemical plant near the town of Pleasant Hill, Missouri. At about 4:00 a.m., an unknown individual opened a valve in a storage tank, causing 200 gallons of anhydrous ammonia to leak out. The chemical formed a cloud of poisonous vapor that spread through the down-town area, forcing the evacuation of more than 250 residents. Although the perpetrator and motive remain unknown, the facility manager speculated that the individual might have wanted ammonia to produce methamphetamines.[23] According to the EPA, a toxic release from any of more than 2000 facilities in the United States could affect at least 100,000 people.

Preventing Chemical Terrorism

Government authorities can take a number of measures to reduce the risk of chemical terrorism. First, state and local emergency management officials should conduct vulnerability assessments of the chemical manufacturing plants within their jurisdictions and encourage the owners to improve security at sites that produce or store toxic chemicals. At the same time, the locations of these plants and the associated vulnerability assessments should not be made public because of the risk that such information could fall into the wrong hands.

Second, the federal government should tighten restrictions on the sale by commercial suppliers to private individuals (either U.S. citizens or foreigners) of dual-use chemicals that can serve as precursors for chemical warfare agents. Although the United States controls the export of 54 precursor chemicals to countries of proliferation concern, domestic sales of these chemicals are not currently regulated.

Third, federal law enforcement agencies such as the Federal Bureau of Investigation (FBI) and the Bureau of Alcohol, Tobacco, and Firearms (ATF) should enhance their cooperation with state and local law enforcement agencies. To this end, the FBI and the ATF should reassess the balance between securing classified information about unconventional terrorism and sharing it with state and local agencies when it is relevant to preventing an incipient attack.

Responding to Chemical Terrorism

Unlike biological agents, which have an incubation period of days to weeks before clinical symptoms appear, chemical agents induce incapacitating or lethal symptoms within minutes after exposure—with the sole exception of sulfur mustard, whose clinical manifestations are delayed up to several hours. Whereas explosives generate instantaneous destructive forces that are difficult to defend against, the toxic effects of some classes of chemical agents can be reversed or mitigated through the prompt administration of antidotes and other drugs. Antidotes are available only for a few types of chemical agents, however, and the time window for effective treatment is limited. Although much of the historical experience with the emergency response to chemical terrorism derives from the 1995 Tokyo subway incident, one can also draw important lessons from industrial accidents involving toxic chemicals.

First Responders

During the Tokyo sarin incident, the city fire department received the first call about a medical emergency in the subway within minutes of the attack. Additional calls flowed in from 15 subway stations in rapid succession, yet it took more than an hour before emergency dispatchers realized that a single event was responsible rather than a series of unrelated incidents. As the crisis mounted, police, firefighters, 131 ambulances, and 1364 emergency medical technicians (EMTs) were dispatched to downtown subway stations on the three affected lines.[24] They arrived to find a chaotic scene. Critically injured casualties littered the sidewalks and subway entrances, vomiting or convulsing, and scores of less seriously affected commuters stumbled about, vision impaired and struggling to breathe. EMTs sought to triage the victims and offer some medical assistance, but they did not administer antidotes, intubate serious cases at the scene, or attempt to decontaminate the victims or even remove their sarin-saturated clothes.[25]

The Tokyo subway incident demonstrated that first responders to an incident of chemical terrorism who lack personal protective equipment (such as police, paramedics, and ordinary firefighters) are at considerable risk of becoming victims themselves.[26] Indeed, some observers have called police officers "blue canaries" because they would probably succumb to the toxic agent shortly after arriving on the scene. Because of this vulnerability, first responders lacking gas masks and protective clothing must resist the initial instinct to run to the rescue. Instead they must stand back, upwind and uphill of the spreading toxic cloud, and use loudspeakers and public address systems to direct the victims to safety. The first group to enter the danger zone should be members of the local hazardous material (Hazmat) team, who are equipped with personal protective equipment. Most fire departments in major U.S. cities have well-trained Hazmat teams with extensive experience in handling spills of toxic industrial chemicals, such as chlorine and organophosphate pesticides.

The first step in responding to an incident of chemical terrorism is for police and firefighters to establish a perimeter around the danger zone to prevent more people from becoming exposed. A complicating factor, however, is that the danger zone can move. Although volatile gases such as chlorine or phosgene dissipate rapidly, more persistent agents such as sarin can form clouds that last for hours, drifting with the breeze to form an elongated plume downwind from the point of release. In an urban environment, the air turbulence generated by tall buildings can redistribute the agent plume into zones of high and low concentration, creating "hot spots" in unexpected locations. Moreover, ventilation systems can spread a toxic gas throughout a building, and subway cars can force an agent cloud down tunnels, spreading it from one station to the next.

Rapid detection and identification of the toxic agent are crucial to ensure the prompt medical treatment of those who have been exposed and to reassure those who have not. Most fire departments, however, lack the specialized equipment needed to detect and analyze chemical warfare agents. Thus, a sample of the agent—itself highly toxic—would have to be collected and sent to a chemical laboratory for analysis. In a small, isolated U.S. city, several hours might elapse before the agent could be identified. To address this problem, scientists at the U.S. National Laboratories are developing handheld detectors that first responders could use to identify about a dozen different CW agents.[27] Until the toxic agent has been identified, medical practitioners should treat exposed persons according to the resulting clinical syndrome (cluster of symptoms), such as chemical burns, pulmonary edema, cardiorespiratory failure, neurological damage, or shock.[28]

At the same time that first responders are treating the casualties of a chemical attack, law enforcement officials will have to conduct a criminal investigation in order to identify and arrest the perpetrators. Careful coordination among the FBI, state and local police, and other agencies will be necessary to avoid destroying valuable forensic evidence while delivering urgently needed medical care. Another key task for state and local emergency responders is to inform the public and the news media immediately and continuously after a chemical incident has occurred, so as to prevent widespread confusion and panic. In particular, the authorities must be prepared to explain the cause of the disaster, what the victims should do, how long the crisis will last, where to obtain help, and how people can avoid exposure.

Decontamination

After the local Hazmat team is in place, the next challenge for emergency workers is to decontaminate the victims before they are evacuated for treatment. If people have come in contact with liquid agent or concentrated vapor, they will carry traces of the toxic substance on their clothes and bodies. Accordingly, decontamination is needed not only to prevent further absorption of the toxic agent through the skin or by inhalation of vapor, but also to prevent the victims from contaminating other people and the interior of cars and ambulances.

During the Tokyo subway incident, police were slow in establishing a perimeter around the affected zone and did not decontaminate victims on-site. As a result, many cases of secondary exposure resulted from the off-gassing of sarin from patients in cramped ambulances and poorly ventilated hospital rooms. Of a total of 1364 EMTs who transported victims to hospitals by ambulance, 135 (10 percent) developed symptoms of sarin exposure and had to receive treatment themselves. Moreover, although many patients were directed to a shower upon arrival at a hospital and their contaminated clothes were removed and sealed in plastic bags, 110 hospital staff members (23 percent) complained of symptoms of sarin poisoning in a follow-up questionnaire.[29]

In general, water is the best decontamination solution, with soap recommended for oily or otherwise adherent chemicals.[30] Decontaminating large crowds poses complex logistical challenges, however, and the various methods offer different strengths and weaknesses. The usual approach is to direct the victims to "decontamination corridors" where they strip off their outer clothing and shower. Even so, persuading a frightened and mixed-gender group of strangers—many of them scared, sick, blinded, or choking—to undress and leave their valuables behind could easily result in panic and chaos. Special decontamination trucks or trailers containing showers are commercially available, but this equipment is expensive and time-consuming to set up. Some cities plan to use ordinary fire hoses to spray victims, yet that approach would expose them to public view and, in winter, might cause hypothermia. Other approaches to decontamination problems include the use of protective tarpaulins, inflatable heated tents, and plans to commandeer the nearest large building equipped with showers, such as a high school or college.[31]

Medical Treatment

Medical treatment for victims for chemical terrorism varies depending on the type of toxic agent involved. In general, the prompt onset of symptoms after chemical exposure puts a premium on rapid response. If a nerve agent is used, the administration of antidotes within several minutes to an hour can save lives. Although those exposed to a massive dose would probably die before they could be treated, victims on the periphery of the attack who received sublethal doses would benefit from receiving antidotes. The U.S. Army's nerve agent antidote kit contains atropine and an oxime (2-PAM [praloxidime] chloride), plus diazepam to prevent seizures. Such drugs may be in short supply: most ambulances carry atropine for treating heart attacks, but only in doses less than a tenth of what a nerve gas victim requires. Thus, each major U.S. city should acquire and maintain a stockpile of nerve agent antidotes.

In the event of exposure to hydrogen cyanide, immediate treatment with antidotes that bind cyanide ions in the blood can accelerate detoxification. But no antidotes currently exist for exposure to choking or blister agents, which must be treated symptomatically. Inhalation of choking agents typically results in pulmonary edema, which can be managed by administering oxygen, cortisone, and a drug to widen the bronchial tubes. Mechanical ventilators may also be required to keep victims breathing while their damaged lungs recover, although such equipment is rare and expensive. Because the cost of stockpiling specialized antidotes and ventilators in quantities sufficient for a mass-casualty incident is too high for any city to bear, the U.S. Department of Health and Human Services has established a two-tiered stockpile system. At least in theory, enough materials for 5000 victims can be made ready within hours to be flown to the site of a terrorist attack, and more would be en route the following day.

In a serious incident of chemical terrorism, the only option may be triage: giving priority to patients who have the best chance of survival in view of the resources available to treat them. For this reason, ambulatory patients should be among the first to be decontaminated and evacuated.[32] If thousands of people are affected, rapid triage and holding sites may have to be established where patients are decontaminated and given initial treatment; seriously ill patients would then be evacuated to appropriate care facilities. Within the triage areas, medical staff would work in full protective clothing.

Hospital Care

The U.S. medical system is poorly equipped to treat the mass casualties that might arise from a chemical attack. In the age of "managed care," most urban hospitals are private-sector entities that are under strong pressure from insurance companies to contain costs and thus run at full or excess capacity even under normal conditions. As a result, they have little room to accept an influx of casualties from a terrorist attack. A survey of nearly 200 hospital emergency departments conducted by the U.S. Public Health Service found that less than 20 percent had plans or equipment for dealing with even 50 victims of a nerve agent attack, such as an isolated decontamination unit. Only 29 percent of the hospitals surveyed had adequate supplies of atropine to treat 50 patients, and just 6 percent had all of the "minimum recommended physical resources" to deal with a release of sarin by terrorists. Urban hospitals were three times more likely than rural hospitals to have a plan for responding to chemical terrorism.[33]

Given these statistics, it is likely that in the event of a major incident of chemical terrorism, the local supply of hospital beds would rapidly be exhausted. To avoid chaos and overcrowding, it is essential for cities to plan for satellite treatment areas in sports centers, schools, armories, and other public buildings equipped with central heating, hot and cold running water, and telephones. At these locations, medical personnel and equipment could be brought in and a large number of patients treated.[34] Another problem would be finding enough health care personnel to care for the injured. Some cities are creating databases of doctors or nurses who have retired, moved into administrative jobs, or changed careers but could be called up in an emergency. Such systems may not be rapid enough, however, to cope with a major incident of chemical terrorism.

To augment local medical response capabilities, the Metropolitan Medical Response System (MMRS) links federal emergency services with first responders, public health officials, and private hospitals into an integrated community disaster plan. As part of this program, the Department of Health and Human Services (HHS) has provided 97 U.S. cities with an average of $600,000 each in seed money, although the cities must expend their own resources to continue training and exercising people and to maintain equipment. Another federal program managed by HHS, the National Disaster Medical System (NDMS), would be activated after a major incident of chemical terrorism. More than 70 Disaster Medical Assistance Teams (DMATs), each consisting of up to 100 medical personnel, have volunteered to deploy to disasters ranging from earthquakes to terrorist attacks. These teams would probably take several hours to mobilize, however. NDMS can also transfer overflow patients, by medical airlift if necessary, to veterans' hospitals and 2000 participating private hospitals nationwide.

Psychosocial Impact

Another problem that will inevitably arise during an incident of chemical terrorism is that a large number of people will experience psychogenic symptoms or extreme anxiety and self-report to hospitals and doctors' offices for treatment. During the 1995 Tokyo subway incident, roughly 80 percent of the casualties who arrived at hospitals (about 4000 people) had no chemical injuries but still demanded medical attention. This influx of "worried well" swamped the available medical resources. Thus, after a major incident of chemical terrorism, physicians and other health care providers will have to distinguish real from psychogenic casualties so as to deliver priority treatment to those most urgently requiring it.

It is also clear that in the event of a large-scale chemical attack, survivors of and responders to the incident will experience extreme psychological trauma. For more than a week after the Tokyo subway incident, dozens of city residents continued to arrive at local hospitals complaining of various symptoms. Even months later, survivors sought treatment for posttraumatic stress disorder (PTSD), including panic attacks and fear of riding the subway.[35] Thus, psychiatrists, clinical psychologists, and social workers will have to treat the widespread incidence of PTSD and other psychological sequelae.

Organizational Issues

Because of the short time window available for medical response, the most cost-effective way to address the threat of chemical terrorism is to enhance local capabilities that can be brought to bear during the first critical minutes and hours after an attack. City and state governments have an institutional infrastructure for responding to chemical incidents, such as Hazmat teams and public health departments, that can be leveraged for enhanced domestic preparedness against terrorism. But although Hazmat specialists deal routinely with spills and accidental releases of toxic industrial chemicals, they require additional training to safely contain military-grade agents and to decontaminate and treat large crowds of victims.

The Defense Against Weapons of Mass Destruction Act of 1996, sponsored by Senators Sam Nunn, Richard Lugar, and Pete Domenici, tasked the Department of Defense (in conjunction with other federal agencies) with providing training, expert advice, and $300,000 worth of protective gear, detection, and decontamination equipment to emergency responders in the nation's 120 largest cities. This effort, known as the Domestic Preparedness Program, was designed to give each participating city a limited response capability and enable it to keep training after completion of the program. On October 1, 2000, lead responsibility was transferred from the Pentagon to the Department of Justice (DOJ), which has shifted the program's focus from the 120 cities to all 50 states. To be eligible for federal funds, each state must perform a comprehensive self-assessment to identify likely terrorist targets and threats, and must develop a three-year domestic preparedness plan. DOJ has also established a Center for Domestic Preparedness, based at the former U.S. Army chemical school in Anniston, Alabama, to give Hazmat specialists hands-on experience with military CW agents that might be used in a terrorist attack.

In recent years, however, spending priorities have drifted away from the original intent of the Nunn-Lugar-Domenici legislation. Of the $1.4 billion allocated to terrorism preparedness programs in fiscal year 2000, only about $315 million (22 percent) went to first responders in the form of training, equipment grants, and planning assistance.[36] With 46 different federal agencies seeking a piece of the counterterrorism pie, and eight congressional committees and seven subcommittees with jurisdiction over terrorism issues, the Domestic Preparedness Program has become a hodgepodge of overlapping and often duplicative programs. For example, a host of redundant federal response teams have been established, including the Marine Corps' Chemical/Biological Incident Response Force, the FBI's Hazardous Materials Response Unit, the Army's Chemical-Biological Rapid Response Team, the EPA's Emergency Response Team, HHS's National Medical Response Team, and the National Guard's Weapons of Mass Destruction Civil Support Teams, among others.

Given the fact that most of these teams would take several hours to deploy to the scene of an incident of chemical terrorism in a small to medium-sized city, it makes little sense to invest a large proportion of domestic preparedness resources in such efforts.[37] Instead, the federal government should return to its original strategy of leveraging existing state and local assets by training and equipping first responders, while giving those agencies that have technical expertise in dealing with toxic chemicals, such as the U.S. Army and the EPA, a support role in the event of a massive attack.

Conclusions

The historical record indicates that most incidents of chemical terrorism have involved the use of household or industrial chemicals. Although such compounds are far less toxic than military-grade agents, the Bhopal disaster demonstrates the deadly potential that could result from the sabotage of a commercial chemical plant or a series of railroad tank cars. It therefore makes sense to devote more resources to addressing forms of chemical terrorism that would be less catastrophic but are more likely, such as industrial sabotage, rather than focusing exclusively on worst-case scenarios involving the large-scale release of a military nerve agent. Improving the security of chemical plants and the transportation infrastructure will require cooperative efforts by government and the private sector.

With respect to consequence management of a chemical terrorist attack, greater emphasis and funding should go to training and exercising local and state first responders, particularly Hazmat teams, and improving their capabilities for crowd decontamination, medical triage, and treatment of large numbers of casualties. At the same time, federal assets such as information hotlines, drug stockpiles, and rapid response teams should be better coordinated, rationalized, and streamlined, with the primary aim of providing support to state and local authorities.

Notes

1. Sidell, Fred. 1996. Testimony in Proceedings of the Seminar on Responding to the Consequences of Chemical and Biological Terrorism, July 11–14, 1995, sponsored by the U.S. Public Health Service, Office of Emergency Preparedness. Washington, D.C.: U.S. Government Printing Office, pp. 1–66.
2. Kaplan, David E. Aum Shinrikyo. 2000. *Toxic Terror: Assessing Terrorist Use of Chemical and Biological Weapons*, Jonathan B. Tucker, ed. Cambridge, Mass.: MIT Press, pp. 208–210.
3. Murakami, Haruki. 2001. *Underground: The Tokyo Gas Attack and the Japanese Psyche*. New York: Vintage International, p. 118.
4. Kaplan, op. cit., p. 214.
5. Murakami, op. cit., p. 217.
6. Sidell testimony, p. 2–32.
7. U.S. Senate, October 21, 1995. Committee on Governmental Affairs, Permanent Subcommittee on Investigations. Staff Statement: Hearings on Global Proliferation of Weapons of Mass Destruction: A Case Study on Aum Shinrikyo.
8. Kaplan, op. cit., p. 222.
9. Monterey Institute of International Studies, Center for Nonproliferation Studies, WMD Terrorism Database, data as of May 7, 2001.
10. Tucker, Jonathan B. 2000. Chemical and biological terrorism: how real a threat? Current History 99(636):147–153.
11. Viktorov, Andrey, Stepan Krivosheyev, 1998. Moscow gangsters were preparing for chemical war: mad genius devoted lifetime to chemical warfare development. Moskva Segodnya (in Russian), September 11, 1998, p. 7; translated in FBIS document FTS19981001001057, October 1, 1998. See also Associated Press. September 11, 1998. Russian man arrested for manufacturing, selling chemical weapons.
12. U.S. General Accounting Office. 1999. Combating terrorism: observations on the threat of chemical and biological terrorism. Statement of Henry L. Hinton, Jr., Assistant Comptroller General, National Security and International Affairs Division Report No. GAO/T-NSIAD-00-50, October 20, 1999, p. 4.
13. Zilinskas, Raymond A. 1996. Aum Shinrikyo's chemical/biological terrorism as a paradigm? *Politics and the Life Sciences 15*(2):238.
14. Schmid, Alex P. 2001. Chemical terrorism: precedents and prospects. *OPCW Synthesis* (Summer/June): 12.
15. Mullen, Robert K. 1978. Mass destruction and terrorism. *Journal of International Affairs 32*(1):69.
16. Monterey Institute of International Studies, Center for Nonproliferation Studies, WMD Terrorism Database, data as of May 7, 2001.
17. Ibid.
18. U.S. Centers for Disease Control and Prevention, Strategic Planning Workgroup. 2000. Chemical and biological terrorism: strategic plan for preparedness and response. *Morbidity and Mortality Weekly Report* 49(April 21):1–14.
19. *Los Angeles Times*. January 3, 1995. Poisoned champagne kills 10 in Tajikistan, p. A18.
20. Begley, Sharon. 2001. Chemical plants: go well beyond "well prepared." *Newsweek*, p. 33.
21. National Research Council. 1999. *Chemical and Biological Terrorism: Research and Development to Improve Civilian Medical Response*. Washington, D.C.: National Academy Press, p. 127.
22. Jackson, Richard, M.D., M.P.H., Director, National Center for Environmental Health. Statement before the U.S. Senate Committee on Appropriations, Subcommittee on Labor, Health and Human Services, June 2, 1998.
23. Reuters. February 28, 2000. Dozens flee deliberate poison cloud.

24. Smithson, Amy E., and Leslie-Anne Levy. 2000. *Ataxia: The Chemical and Biological Terrorism Threat and the U.S. Response*. Washington: Henry L. Stimson Center, Report No. 35, pp. 91–102.

25. For vivid eyewitness descriptions of the Tokyo subway attack, see Murakami, op. cit.

26. U.S. Department of Health and Human Services. 1996. Planning Considerations for Health and Medical Services Response to Nuclear/Biological/Chemical Terrorism. Washington, D.C.: U.S. Department of Health and Human Services, p. 2.

27. U.S. Department of Energy, National Nuclear Security Administration, Office of Nonproliferation Research and Engineering. 2001. Chemical & Biological National Security Program, FY00 Annual Report DOE/NN-0015. Washington, D.C.: pp. 67–76.

28. U.S. Centers for Disease Control and Prevention, Strategic Planning Workgroup, op. cit.

29. National Research Council, op. cit., p. 102.

30. Ibid., p. 100.

31. Freedberg, Sidney J., Jr. 2001. Feds prepare state, local governments for terrorist attacks. *National Journal*, March 15, 2001. On-line at www.govexcc.com/dailyfcd/0301/031501nj/htm.

32. National Research Council, op. cit., p. 108.

33. *American Journal of Public Health 91* (May 2001):710–717. Cited in Reuters. May 1, 2001. Study: U.S. hospitals not prepared for bioterrorism.

34. Lorin, H.G., P.E.J. Kulling. 1986. The Bhopal tragedy—what has Swedish disaster medicine planning learned from it? Journal of Emergency Medicine 4:311–316.

35. Smithson and Levy, op. cit., p. 101.

36. Ibid., p. 289.

37. Green, Joshua. 2001. Weapons of mass confusion: how pork trumps preparedness in the fight against terrorism. *Washington Monthly* (May 2001):15–21.

Jonathan B. Tucker is a senior fellow at the Washington, D.C. office of the Center for Non-Proliferation Studies (CNS), where he specializes in chemical and biological weapons issues. Dr. Tucker holds a B.S. in biology from Yale University and a Ph.D. in political science from the Massachusetts Institute of Technology with a concentration in defense and arms control studies.

Chapter 2.6

Food Security and Agricultural Terrorism

Mark Wheelis, Rocco Casagrande, and Laurence V. Madden

Biological Attack on Agriculture: Low-Tech, High-Impact Bioterrorism

Most of the concern over the last decade about US vulnerability to bioterrorism has focused on terrorist use of pathogens to attack the civilian population. This concern increased in the wake of the September 11 terrorist attacks on the World Trade Towers and the Pentagon and the anthrax letter attacks on US Senate offices and the media. However, a number of analysts have pointed out that terrorist attacks on livestock or crops, although unlikely to cause terror, are also a concern because they could be executed much more easily and could have serious economic consequences (Frazier and Richardson 1999, Horn and Breeze 1999, Casagrande 2000, Wheelis 2000). It is worth considering the consequences for the US economy had there been a widespread and sudden outbreak of foot-and-mouth disease (FMD) shortly after September 11. The stock market probably would have plunged even further, and its recovery could have been significantly delayed. More substantial consequences are easy to imagine. This article will give an overview of US vulnerability to agricultural bioterrorism and biocrimes; the accompanying articles and a previous article in this journal (Madden and van den Bosch 2002) examine individual facets in more detail. See Whitby and Rogers (1997), Schaad et al. (1999), Wheelis (1999a), Wilson et al. (2000), and Whitby (2002) for a historical overview of attacks on agriculture with biological weapons, a subject that is beyond the scope of this article.

Diseases have a Significant Negative Impact on Agricultural Productivity

The burden on agriculture of endemic and naturally imported epidemic disease is high, confirming the capacity of animal and plant diseases to cause economic harm. The United States is free of many globally significant livestock diseases because of effective surveillance of herds and imports and aggressive eradication campaigns. Even so, approximately $17.5 billion dollars are lost each year because of diseased livestock and poultry. In general, losses from animal disease account for 17% of the production costs of animal products in the developed world and nearly twice that amount in the developing world (ARS 2002).

The total cost of crop diseases to the US economy has been estimated to be in excess of $30 billion per year (Pimentel et al. 2000). The costs include reduction in the quantity (e.g., reduced bushels per acre) and quality (e.g., blemished fruit, toxins in grain) of yield; short-term costs of control (e.g., cost of purchasing and applying pesticides) and long-term costs (e.g., development of resistant varieties of crops through breeding and development of new pesticides); extra costs of harvesting and grading diseased agricultural products (e.g., separating diseased from disease-free fruit); costs of replanting blighted fields; costs of growing less desirable crops that are not susceptible to the dominant plant pathogens in an area; higher food prices; unavailable foods; trade disruptions; and public and animal health costs caused by the production of toxins by some plant pathogens (Zadoks and Schein 1979, James et al. 1991, Madden and Nutter 1995).

In contrast to the sweeping campaigns undertaken to eliminate the most virulent diseases of livestock, efforts generally have not been made to eradicate diseases of crops (Strange 1993). One goal of plant disease control has been to maintain most indigenous diseases at a low or very low incidence level through a range of management techniques (Fry 1982). The exception is when a disease has a very narrow geographic distribution (as would a newly introduced exotic disease), spores are not dispersed great distances, and disease incidence is low. In such a situation, eradication may be feasible.

Despite the high toll endemic disease and periodic incursions of epidemic disease exact on agriculture, many pathogens have not appeared in the United States at all, while others have made only very rare appearances, and still others were eradicated decades ago (especially with animals); many of these are considered to be serious threats to agriculture (Brown and Slenning 1996, Madden 2001). Thus, the exotic, highly contagious pathogens causing these diseases could be chosen as bioweapons for the large economic consequences that could result from their introduction. Pathogens that cause diseases such as FMD, rinderpest, African swine fever (ASF), soybean rust, Philippine downy mildew of maize, potato wart, and citrus greening could, if introduced into the continental United States, have serious consequences for the US economy.

Agricultural Bioterrorist Attack can have Severe Economic Consequences

Even a massive outbreak of plant or animal disease in the United States would not cause famine; the agricultural sector is too diverse, too productive, and too closely regulated for that to be a realistic possibility. However, a successful attack could have severe economic consequences. The most substantial impact would be the loss of international markets for animal or plant materials. Member nations of the World Trade Organization are entitled to ban imports of plant or animal materials that may introduce exotic diseases into their territories (Wheelis 1999b, FAS 2001). Thus, importing countries that are themselves free of a particular highly contagious animal or plant disease will routinely impose sanitary or phytosanitary restrictions on trade with countries in which that disease breaks out. This can result in billions of dollars of lost trade.

For instance, as soon as the first case of FMD was reported in the United Kingdom last year, the European Union (and other countries) immediately blocked imports of British beef, sheep, and swine and products derived from them. The total sum of lost revenues from contracted international markets has not yet been determined, but it will certainly be billions of dollars. For the United States, with $41 billion of beef, $19 billion of diary, and $14 billion in pork sales annually (USDA 1997), the trade consequences of an outbreak of FMD could be much larger. A recent study of the impact that an outbreak of FMD would have on California agriculture concluded that losses, using conservative estimates, would be $6 billion to $13 billion even if the outbreak were contained within California and eradicated within 5 to 12 weeks (Ekboir 1999).

Karnal bunt of wheat, caused by the fungus *Tilletia indica,* provides another example of severe economic consequences caused by agricultural disease. About 80 countries ban wheat imports from regions with karnal bunt infections, even though the disease does not have a large direct effect on crop yield (Bandyopadhyay and Frederiksen 1999). When the disease was discovered in Arizona and surrounding areas in 1996 (probably from an accidental introduction from Mexico), there was an immediate threat to the overall $6 billion per year US wheat crop, since about 50% of produced wheat is exported. Because of this threat, the Animal and Plant Health Inspection Service (APHIS) of the US Department of Agriculture (USDA) immediately mobilized efforts to contain the outbreak within the original small area and to eradicate the disease. From 1996 to 1998, APHIS spent over $60 million on the effort, and growers in this small affected area lost well over $100 million from lost sales and increases in production costs (Bandyopadhyay and Frederiksen 1999; John Neesen [APHIS], personal communication, 2 April 2002). In this case, the localized nature of the outbreak allowed the United States to convince its trading partners that none of the contaminated wheat was entering the market, and wheat exports continued from the rest of the country. Unfortunately, karnal bunt was recently discovered again, this time in Texas (AgNet 2001), and a new round of containment and eradication efforts has been initiated.

In some cases, domestic demand can also be significantly affected. Even minor outbreaks of disease that can potentially infect people can have severe economic consequences. Since September 11, a mere three cases of mad cow disease have been found in Japan; yet as a consequence, Japanese beef sales dropped approximately 50% during this period (Watts 2001).

In addition to the costs that result from reduced international and domestic demand, the costs of containment can be quite substantial, as the examples discussed above make clear. Thus, even for commodities that are not exported in large amounts, an outbreak of disease that provokes vigorous eradication efforts may have a substantial economic effect. Taiwan, for instance, spent about $4 billion in an unsuccessful effort to eradicate FMD after it was introduced to the country in 1997 (Wilson et al. 2000).

Containment, Eradication, or Control?

As demonstrated in the examples above, introductions of exotic pathogens that cause highly contagious animal or plant diseases may elicit rapid and aggressive attempts to contain and eradicate them, and these measures commonly cause more economic damage in the short term than the disease itself. Despite the costs, such intervention is often justified, since if exotic highly infectious diseases become endemic, the long-term costs would be much greater than the costs of containment.

Containment and eradication of exotic animal diseases is commonly done by culling all potentially exposed animals to break the chain of transmission (Ferguson et al. 2001a, 2001b). Thus, small numbers of infected animals can lead to the slaughter of large numbers of healthy ones. Many of the animal diseases that are potential bioterrorist threats are caused by viruses, for which there is no practical therapy once the animal is infected. Therefore, transmission cannot be interrupted by treatment, but only by culling diseased and exposed animals or by vaccination (when that is an option—see below). In contrast, about 75% of plant diseases are caused by fungi, and these can be controlled, with varying degrees of effectiveness, by the application of fungicides (Strange 1993, Agrios 1997). For many high-value-per-acre crops (e.g., fruit and vegetables, ornamentals), fungicides are used in routine control of endemic diseases. Some fungicides actually move systemically within plants and can arrest the infection process during the early phases of infection. More commonly, however, fungicides are applied to the surface of plants and are used prophylactically to provide short-term protection from fungal infection (Fry 1982). When an introduced disease is discovered, infected and possibly exposed plants are culled ("rogued"), and fungicides can be used to treat plants in surrounding areas (even for low-value-per-acre plants) to prevent infection. This method is expensive, it fails to prevent all infections, and it can have negative environmental consequences.

Transmission of bacterial and viral crop diseases is difficult to control with chemical pesticides, unless such diseases are transmitted by insect vectors, in which case insecticides may be useful (Madden et al. 2000). Because of these difficulties, containment and eradication of bacterial pathogens depend heavily on quarantining infected areas and removing all infected and exposed plants.

The only chance of successfully containing and eradicating a crop pathogen is to start the process relatively soon after introduction, when the focus of infection is small, there are few infected individuals, and the dispersal distance of spores is short. For some diseases, such as rust of several crops (e.g., stem rust of wheat, caused by *Puccinia graminis* f. sp. *tritici),* spores can be dispersed very long distances (thousands of kilometers), so the spread of disease can be substantial before the pathogen is discovered (Campbell and Madden 1990). For these reasons, eradication is generally not attempted.

Agricultural Bioterrorist Attack Requires Relatively Little Expertise or Technology

One of the reasons that a bioterrorist attack on human populations is difficult is that the development of an effective bioweapon is a technically daunting task (Falkenrath et al. 1998). Many of the antipersonnel agents that have been used as weapons ("weaponized") are poorly transmitted among humans (e.g., anthrax), so a large amount has to be disseminated at once to cause large numbers of casualties. The only effective way to infect large numbers of people simultaneously is to generate a respirable aerosol. However, aerosol preparation to a particle size that is effective in causing inhalational disease is quite difficult, and once so prepared, it is highly hazardous to the perpetrators themselves (unless they are vaccinated and taking prophylactic antibiotics).

Other anti-human agents are contagious (e.g.,*Yersinia pestis,* the causative agent of plague), but they too have to be disseminated in large quantities for widespread infections, because agent transmission can be interrupted by antibiotic treatment. Since organisms such as *Y. pestis* do not form the highly resistant spore form that *Bacillus* does, it is technically quite challenging (and dangerous) to prepare a large stockpile of the agent. Still other agents are viral rather than bacterial, and their preparation and weaponization is even more challenging because of the more demanding technologies needed for laboratory culture.

In some special situations, highly contagious viruses could be effectively introduced by voluntarily infected terrorists who would travel to the target area during the incubation period of the disease. This reportedly was done a number of times in the 1950s and 1960s in an effort to infect Native Americans in the Matto Grosso of Brazil, by land speculators who would be able to purchase tribal lands once the natives no longer inhabited them (Davis 1977). However, in the developed world, for any disease other than smallpox, it is unlikely that such a low-tech method would be effective. Thus, the technical expertise required to mount a mass-casualty biological attack on the human population is formidable and probably beyond the capabilities of most terrorist groups (and indeed of many nations). However, the recent anthrax infections have clearly shown that only a few cases are sufficient to produce a large psychological impact on the population.

Unfortunately, the same difficulties do not exist for many of the diseases that would make effective agricultural bioterrorist weapons. These diseases of animals and crops are highly contagious and spread effectively from a point source, as the recent FMD outbreak in the United Kingdom dramatically confirms. Moreover, humans can safely handle the causative organisms, with no risk of becoming infected. None of the plant pathogens of concern, nor most of the animal pathogens, cause disease in humans. Thus, there is no need for vaccination, prophylactic antibiotic use, or special precautions to prevent infection of the perpetrators.

Although a small outbreak may not produce a large psychological impact (relative to a single person dying of anthrax or smallpox), several of these pathogens owe much of their economic impact to trade sanctions that are imposed in response to a few cases; thus, even small outbreaks can have very large economic effects. A few cases of FMD scattered around the country could interrupt much of US animal product exports for several months, even if the outbreaks were promptly contained (importing countries would want to wait several weeks or months to verify that the outbreak was truly contained before resuming imports). Obviously it is technically easier to cause a few scattered cases of disease than to prepare a kilogram-sized stockpile of weaponized agent for aerosol distribution.

Material to initiate an outbreak of plant or animal disease therefore does not have to be prepared in large quantity—a few milligrams could be sufficient to initiate multiple outbreaks in widely separated locations—if the goal is to disrupt international trade, or if the terrorists are sufficiently patient to allow a crop disease to develop over several months by transmission from individual to individual. And the agent does not necessarily have to be grown in the laboratory or otherwise manipulated—a small amount of natural material taken from a diseased animal or plant can serve without any additional manipulation. For instance, a few hundred microliters of scrapings from the blistered mucosa of an FMD-infected animal, or blood from an animal hemorrhaging from ASF, or a handful of wheat tillers heavily infected by the stem rust pathogen can provide more than enough agent to initiate an epidemic. Such materials are readily available in many places in the world where the diseases of concern are endemic, and they can be obtained and transported without any particular expertise other than what is necessary to recognize the disease symptoms with confidence. Since only small amounts are needed, they can be easily smuggled into the country with essentially no chance of detection.

Dissemination of many introduced pathogens likewise requires relatively little expertise. Animal virus preparations could be diluted and disseminated with a simple atomizer in close proximity to target animals, or the preparation smeared directly on the nostrils or mouths of a small number of animals. This could be done from rural roads with essentially no chance of detection. Dissemination of animal diseases could also be done surreptitiously at an animal auction or near barns where animals are densely penned (as in chicken houses or piggeries). For plant diseases, simply exposing a mass of sporulating fungi to the air immediately upwind of a target field could be effective, if environmental conditions were favorable for infection. The biggest challenge of introducing a plant pathogen is probably timing the release with the appropriate weather conditions (Campbell and Madden 1990). If pathogens are released immediately before the start of a dry period, few, if any, infections are likely to result. However, if released at the start of a rainy period, these pathogens could cause a major epidemic.

The technical ease of introducing many agricultural pathogens makes it more likely that terrorists or criminals would release pathogens in several locations in an attempt to initiate multiple, simultaneous outbreaks. This would ensure that trade sanctions would be imposed, because it would undermine any argument that the outbreaks are localized and do not jeopardize importing countries. It would also be more likely to overwhelm the response capacity and lead to the uncontrollable spread of disease. This is the principal way in which a bioterrorist attack would differ from a natural disease introduction, and it raises the question whether a system designed to respond to natural introductions can deal effectively with sudden, multifocal outbreaks.

Under some circumstances, a pathogen could be effectively introduced without the perpetrators entering the country. This is, of course, true of crops planted on both sides of an international border, such as sorghum along the Mexican border or wheat and barley along the Canadian and Mexican borders. These crops have experienced disease outbreaks that spread from acreage outside the United States—sorghum ergot, karnal bunt of wheat, and barley stripe rust, for example (Chen et al. 1995, Bandyopadhyay and Frederiksen 1999). Thus, such pathogens could be deliberately introduced in an adjacent country, a potential advantage to a terrorist if disease surveillance and control programs were less effective there. Multiplication of the pathogen in the foreign acreage could lead to large numbers of spores blowing across the border and initiating an outbreak that could very quickly become very large. International movements of animals also provide opportunities for the introduction of an animal pathogen without the perpetrator having to enter the country. For instance, the very serious 1997–1998 outbreak of classical swine fever in the Netherlands was due to inadequate disinfection of a swine shipment from Germany (GreiserWilke et al. 2000). However, this is an unlikely route for bioterrorist attack, because its effectiveness requires a failure of quarantine or disinfection procedures.

International trade in nonliving agricultural materials can also introduce disease. An example is the 2000 outbreak of FMD in Japan, which occurred simultaneously in two widely separated locations. Investigation suggested that at least one of these locations was infected by straw imported from China (where the FMD virus is endemic) and used as bedding for cattle (Matsubara 2000). Although this particular event appears to have been natural, it shows that deliberate contamination of materials such as bedding or fodder could initiate simultaneous outbreaks at widely scattered locations, making containment extremely difficult. The invasive Asian long-horned beetle, a pest of trees, probably arrived in the United States from China via a similar route, from eggs laid in wooden packing material. If this pest becomes established in the United States, the damage to fruit, lumber, and tourism industries is expected to exceed $40 billion (APHIS 2002). For crops, seeds present similar vulnerability. Many plant pathogens either infect or reside on seeds (Agrios 1997), and a considerable (and increasing) amount of seed for US crops is produced outside the United States (Condon 1997).

Finally, there is a substantial moral difference between killing people and killing plants and animals, and a corresponding difference in the intensity of expected law enforcement response and legal consequence. Thus moral norms and legal consequences can be expected to constitute less of a disincentive to the agricultural bioterrorist than to the bioterrorist who targets people.

Agricultural Bioterrorists Could have a Variety of Motives

We normally think of a terrorist attack as being ideologically motivated, and this is certainly one motive for attacking the agricultural sector. The immense potential for economic damage could make this kind of attack attractive to enemies of the United States, particularly because it is relatively easy and safe for the perpetrators. Given the escalating scale of terrorist attacks on the United States, this is cause for serious concern.

In addition to the political and religious ideological motivations for terrorism, agriculture provides some new ones (Casagrande 2000). There is considerable opposition to the increasing use of genetically modified (GM) crop plants and domestic animals, which have been largely developed in the United States and are most widely used here. For instance, GM soybeans accounted for 63% of the crop grown in the United States in 2001 (Bohan 2001).Worldwide, over 130 million acres are planted with GM crops, because they possess increased resistance to herbicides or insects. The United States alone cultivates almost 70% of the total acreage of GM crops (James 2001). Opposition to the use of GM crops and animals has sometimes taken the form of vandalism and destruction (Greenstone 2001), and it is quite possible that some activists will at some point turn to diseases as weapons to attack GM organisms. Radical animal rights groups may wish to attack animal agriculture to prevent corporations from profiting from animal suffering. Ingrid Newkirk, president of People for the Ethical Treatment of Animals, stated recently that she openly hoped "that it [FMD] comes here [the United States]. It will bring economic harm only for those who profit from giving people heart attacks and giving animals a concentration camp-like existence. It would be good for animals, good for human health, and good for the environment" (Elsner 2001).

Attacks on the agricultural sector could also be motivated by greed, properly termed "biocriminality"rather than bioterrorism. The major shifts in agricultural markets and commodity prices that could result from a successful attack could provide such economic motivation. Profit could be made by the manipulation of futures markets, selling short the stock of major agrochemical companies, or intentionally sabotaging overseas competitors to capture lost import markets. For instance, outbreaks of FMD have changed global dominance in the export of pork. In the 1980s, Denmark supplied most of the pork imported by Japan. After a 1982 FMD outbreak halted pork exports from Denmark, Taiwan filled Japan's need for pork and continued to be its primary supplier even after Denmark was declared free of FMD. After the 1997 FMD outbreak in Taiwan, the United States captured the Japanese pork market and continues to supply Japan with most of its imported pork (FAS 1997). Corporations, individuals, organized crime groups, and even national governments might be attracted to the very large financial gain that is at least theoretically achievable from the judicious use of plant or animal diseases to manipulate markets or commodity prices.

Another possible motive is revenge. The United States and the United Nations Drug Control Program have supported research and development of the use of plant pathogens for killing or reducing yields of opium poppy, coca, and cannabis (Kleiner 1999, Jelsma 2001). The programs involved selection of virulent strains of fungi, consideration of large-scale production of fungal spores, and testing of the most efficient ways of delivering the spores. The work is exactly analogous to the anticrop biological weapons programs of the former Soviet Union and the United States during the cold war (Whitby and Rogers 1997). Because of various political and social pressures, these programs are on hold or moving very slowly. However, if the deliberate release of plant pathogens to destroy drug crops did ever go ahead, there could be a powerful incentive for those in the illicit drug business to retaliate by releasing plant pathogens into US crops (Stone 2000).

Prevention and Response

In response to a 1998 Presidential Decision Directive (White House 1998), and especially to the attacks on September 11 and the subsequent anthrax infections, considerable effort is now being expended to reduce the vulnerability of the United States to bioterrorist attack. A small part of this effort is aimed at protecting crops and livestock. Among other things, a National Research Council committee is evaluating the vulnerability of US agriculture to biological attack and determining strategies for dealing with that vulnerability. USDA and other federal departments and agencies are in the process of making many changes, and it is premature to comment on their effectiveness. However, it is worth making a few general points and sketching the scientific agenda as we see it.

Aggressive counterterrorism measures and greater international intelligence sharing can be expected to reduce the likelihood of a bioterrorist attack on agriculture. Severe criminal penalties may also act as a deterrent. The 1989 Biological Weapons Antiterrorism Act prohibits the development, production, and stockpiling of biological agents for use as a weapon, and it explicitly applies to anti-plant and anti-animal agents. Violation incurs penalties up to life imprisonment. Nevertheless, no measures, singly or in combination, can eliminate the threat. And a bioterrorist attack on the agricultural sector, because of its relative ease, safety, and minimal technical requirements, is probably less likely to be deterred than an attack on human targets. Since agricultural bioterrorist attacks cannot be prevented altogether, an effective response plan to minimize the effects is essential. Knowledge that the United States can respond quickly and effectively to terrorist attacks, and can minimize their impact, would itself serve as an additional deterrent.

An effective response to an agricultural bioterrorist attack is in principle no different from effective response to a natural introduction of exotic diseases. The differences are largely quantitative: A bioterrorist attack is more likely to be multi-focal, and it is more likely to begin explosively (because larger numbers of pathogens could be initially involved). These considerations suggest that at a minimum, existing response strategies should be evaluated and improved to deal with the more demanding outbreak situations that would most likely result from a bioterrorist attack.

However, there is good reason to question whether our existing response capabilities are adequate even to deal effectively with fully natural disease introductions. The experience of the United Kingdom in 2000 and Taiwan in 1997 with FMD, or the Netherlands with classical swine fever in 1997–1998, shows that even developed countries with advanced agricultural health services can be overwhelmed by some outbreaks. This suggests that more radical changes in the way we approach outbreak control may be necessary.

Effective preparation for a bioterrorist attack has several components. Probably most important is early detection. However, US farmers, veterinarians, plant pathologists, and agricultural extension agents are generally not well prepared to rapidly identify exotic animal and plant diseases. Thus a significant educational task confronts us. It is hard to overestimate the importance of that task; even a couple of days' delay in identifying an exotic animal disease can mean the difference between an easily controllable outbreak and one that escalates out of control because of rapid transmission. The UK FMD outbreak is thought to have been as serious as it was largely because of the failure to identify infected sheep for more than a week, during which time the sheep were transported and the disease spread throughout the country (DEFRA 2001, Ferguson et al. 2001a, 2001b).

For crop diseases, there is an additional problem: Crops are grown over millions of acres, and there is no way of carefully observing a very large proportion of individual plants. The first plants with symptoms typically are observed only after substantial spread has already occurred; 0.1% or more of the plants in an area may need to be infected before symptoms are first noticed (Campbell and Madden 1990). This may be too late for successful eradication, especially for highly contagious diseases such as rusts, which have spores that travel long distances. Long-term efforts are needed to develop strategies and technologies to reduce the time to discovery.

Confirmation of a diagnosis of most of the diseases of concern is done with accurate, sensitive molecular techniques, but samples may have to be shipped across the country, consequently delaying confirmation of a diagnosis for days. Expanded local capacity, at least at the state or regional level, to diagnose relevant exotic diseases is therefore important. Complicating the problem, diagnostic laboratories for plant pests (diseases and insects) are typically run by land grant universities and state departments of agriculture. These are often underfunded and understaffed, and they may not have the facilities or supplies to run molecular or biochemical assays or to provide rapid turnaround times. These labs need to be better supported to deal quickly with exotic pathogens.

Beyond the need to expand local capacity is the necessity that diagnostic technology be able to detect diseased animals or plants before they are symptomatic or contagious. This will be especially important after a disease outbreak is established and intensive containment and eradication efforts are being pursued. This would allow earlier culling of infected herds or fields, thereby greatly limiting pathogen transmission. It would also allow the culling of exposed herds or fields to be delayed until there was evidence of infection, since there would then still be time for culling before further disease transmission occurred. These measures could dramatically reduce unnecessary culling and thus reduce containment costs. Such technology has been developed for FMD, for example, but it is not yet widely available.

Diagnosis of presymptomatic plants is practical only for systemic diseases, those in which the pathogen is transported throughout the plant by the vascular tissue. Many threatening plant pathogens, however, are not systemic, and infection is localized; in these cases, tests on samples of plant material will not reliably detect infection. This limitation to presymptomatic diagnostic testing has hindered eradication efforts for citrus canker (Gottwald et al. 2001, Schubert et al. 2001), a bacterial disease discovered in Florida in 1995 that has global quarantine significance.

Rapid and accurate diagnosis is the cornerstone of effective control, but comprehensive planning for response is also required. Many of the decisions about control strategies can be (and should be) made in advance, so that action can be taken immediately upon notification of an outbreak. Response plans obviously will be specific for each disease of concern. For animals, these will be almost exclusively diseases on List A of the Office International des Epizooties's (OIE 2000). However, for crops, there is no worldwide consensus on the most threatening pathogens that could be used as biological weapons (MacKenzie 1999, Schaad et al. 1999, Madden 2001). Developing a consensus for a list of the major bioterrorist threats is thus the first priority in protecting crops. Such a list is necessary to guide the development of surveillance plans, diagnostic tests, and response plans for best containing and eradicating an introduced pathogen.

Probably the most important technical development for animal disease control would be to develop effective vaccines for all diseases of concern. FMD vaccines, for instance, are each protective against only one of the various strains of FMD virus, and they give only limited protection, requiring revaccination every six months or so (Ferguson 2001a, 2001b). A polyva-lent, long-lasting vaccine could provide valuable control options. Vaccines also need to be designed such that a vaccinated animal can be reliably distinguished from a previously infected animal, because seriological evidence is used to document disease-free status for the purpose of international trade. These vaccines could be donated to international efforts for disease control, thereby keeping stockpiles renewed, production capacity busy, and the risk of importation of disease low.

Control strategies for crop diseases depend on the epidemiology of the particular disease (Vanderplank 1963, Fry 1982, Madden and van den Bosch 2002) and on the cropping system. For field crops such as wheat, for example, breeding for resistance is a fundamental approach for control of many diseases. However, breeding is done only for endemic diseases, because it is too expensive to develop resistant varieties for pathogens that are not present. Clearly, efforts must be made to at least identify sources of resistance for threatening pathogens so that the time it takes to develop new varieties is reduced. Genomics should speed this process considerably through the eventual development of plant cultivars that have general resistance to multiple plant pathogens.

Genomic technologies should also facilitate the development of a new generation of pesticides that combine high specificity, high effectiveness, and low environmental and health risks (for a discussion of genomics and drug discovery, see Wheelis 2002). Because plant disease control will very likely continue to rely heavily on pesticide use, substantial research and development efforts are warranted, including genome sequencing of important current and potential pests and their hosts.

The United States currently responds to large outbreaks of agricultural disease by deploying teams of specialists to assist in the diagnosis, containment, and eradication of the disease (APHIS 1998, USDA 2002). There are too few of these teams in the United States to effectively control a large or multifocal outbreak of highly contagious disease (as would probably be the case with an intentional disease introduction). Having more of these teams would increase our capability to respond quickly and effectively to large disease outbreaks, whether the outbreak is intentionally or unintentionally caused.

Because the United States normally has few outbreaks of disease that require such a response, these teams could be deployed internationally to combat disease outbreaks. This international deployment would have several benefits. The members of these teams would gain valuable experience in the diagnosis and containment of diseases that do not often occur in the United States, experience that they could not otherwise acquire. These internationally deployed professional teams could limit the extent of serious animal diseases in other countries, thereby diminishing the chances of an accidental introduction of that disease into the United States and minimizing the opportunities for a terrorist to obtain the pathogen from the environment. Plant diseases, for reasons discussed above, are less likely to be eradicated or contained globally, and thus the benefits of international deployment of specialists may be less obvious for them. Even so, the experience the teams gain would be valuable in itself, and the humanitarian benefit to developing countries would bring valuable goodwill.

Conclusion

Despite our best efforts, this country will continue to be vulnerable to deliberate introductions of exotic plant and animal diseases by terrorist groups with an ideological agenda or by governments, corporations, or individuals with a profit motive. The vulnerability to agricultural bioterrorist attack is a consequence of the intrinsically low security of agricultural targets, the technical ease of introducing consequential diseases, and the large economic repercussions of even small outbreaks. It is exacerbated by structural features of US agriculture that are unlikely to change without forceful government intervention: low genetic diversity of plants and animals, extensive monoculture, and highly concentrated animal husbandry.

While the vulnerability cannot be eliminated, effective response can minimize the damage from both intentionally and naturally introduced disease. We have suggested an aggressive scientific agenda: continuing education programs for farmers, veterinarians, and extension specialists; development of new diagnostics, vaccines, and pesticides; development of new sensing technologies for early identification of plant disease outbreaks; development of plant varieties resistant to diseases not yet endemic; and an increase in the number of outbreak control specialists assigned to international disease control efforts. This is an expensive agenda, but cost-effective in context—a single serious outbreak prevented or quickly controlled could pay for the program several times over. Given the ever-increasing international traffic in agricultural commodities combined with decreasing transit times, we can expect continued natural introductions of exotic plant and animal diseases. These will easily justify the cost of the programs that we recommend. Clearly, aggressive action is warranted to address the deficiencies of our current response system, for both naturally and deliberately introduced plant and animal diseases, given the billions of dollars at stake.

References Cited

AgNet. 2001. Karnal bunt in the news again. Canadian Phytopathological Society. (20 May 2002; *www.cps-scp. ca/karnalbunt.htm*)

Agrios GN. 1997. *Plant Pathology*. 4th ed. New York: Academic Press.

[APHIS] Animal and Plant Health Inspection Service, US Department of Agriculture. 1998. APHIS' role in animal health and trade. *USDA APHIS Factsheet*, August. (20 May 2002; *www.aphis.usda.gov/oa/pubs/ fsprotect.html*)

———. 2002. Asian longhorned beetle *(Anoplophora glabripennis)*. *USDA APHIS Factsheet*, January. (20 May 2002; *www.aphis.usda.gov/oa/ pubs/fsalb.html*)

[ARS] Agricultural Research Service, US Department of Agriculture. 2002. ARS National Programs, Animal Health. (20 May 2002; *http://nps.ars. usda.gov/programs/programs.htm?npnumber=103*)

Bandyopadhyay R, Frederiksen RA. 1999. Contemporary global movement of emerging plant diseases. Pages 28–36 in Frazier TW, Richardson DC, eds. Food and Agricultural Security: Guarding against Natural Threats and Terrorist Attacks Affecting Health, National Food Supplies, and Agricultural Economics. New York: New York Academy of Sciences.

Bohan P. 2001. GMO crops here to stay or gone with the wind? Reuters Online, 5 November. Document HA2001115130000011. (6 June 2002; *http://special.northernlight.com/gmfoods/gone_with_the_wind.htm*)

Brown CC, Slenning BD. 1996. Impact and risk of foreign animal diseases. *JAVMA* 208: 1038–1040.

Campbell CL, Madden LV. 1990. Introduction to Plant Disease Epidemiology. New York: John Wiley and Sons.

Casagrande R. 2000. Biological terrorism targeted at agriculture: The threat to US national security. *Nonproliferation Review* 7: 98–99.

Chen X, Line RF, Leung H. 1995. Virulence and polymorphic DNA relationships of *Puccinia striiformis* f. sp. *hordei* to other rusts. *Phytopathology* 85: 1335–1342.

Condon M. 1997. Implications of plant pathogens to international trading of seeds. Pages 17–30 in McGee DC, ed. Plant Pathogens and the Worldwide Movement of Seeds. St. Paul (MN): APS Press.

Davis SH. 1977. Victims of the Miracle: Development and the Indians of Brazil. New York: Cambridge University Press.

[DEFRA] Department for Environment, Food, and Rural Affairs. 2001. How the 2001 outbreak of foot and mouth began. *DEFRA Factsheet*, 1 May. (28 May 2002; *www.defra.gov.uk/animalh/diseases/fmd/about/current/source.asp*)

Ekboir JM. 1999. Potential Impact of Foot-and-Mouth-Disease in California: The Role and Contribution of Animal Health Surveillance and Monitoring Services. Davis: University of California, Agricultural Issues Center.

Elsner A. 2001. PETA cheers disease spread. Boston Globe, 3 April, p. A5.

Falkenrath R, Newman R, Thayer B. 1998. America's Achilles' Heel. Cambridge (MA): MIT Press.

[FAS] Foreign Agricultural Service, US Department of Agriculture. 1997. Foot-and-mouth disease spreads chaos in pork markets. FASonline, October. (20 May 2002; *www.fas.usda.gov/dlp2/circular/1997/97-10LP/taiwanfmd.htm*)

———. 2001. The World Trade Organization and U.S. agriculture. FASon-line, Fact Sheet, March. (20 May 2002; *www.fas.usda.gov/info/ factsheets/wto.html*)

Ferguson NM, Donnelly CA, Anderson RM. 2001a. Transmission intensity and impact of control policies on the foot-and-mouth epidemic in Great Britain. *Nature* 413: 542–548.

———. 2001b. The foot-and-mouth epidemic in Great Britain: Pattern of spread and impact of interventions. Science 292: 1155–1160.

Frazier TW, Richardson DC, eds. 1999. Food and Agricultural Security: Guarding against Natural Threats and Terrorist Attacks Affecting Health, National Food Supplies, and Agricultural Economics. New York: New York Academy of Sciences.

Fry WE. 1982. Principles of Plant Disease Management. New York: Academic Press.

Gottwald TR, Hughes G, Graham JH, Sun X, Riley T. 2001. The citrus canker epidemic in Florida: The scientific basis of regulatory eradication policy for an invasive species. *Phytopathology* 91: 30–34.

Greiser-Wilke I, Fritzemeier J, Koenen F, Vanderhallen H, Rutili D, De Mia G, Romero L, Rosell R, Sanchez-Vizcaino J, San Gabriel A. 2000. Molecular epidemiology of a large classical swine fever epidemic in the European Union in 1997–1998. *Veterinary Microbiology* 77: 17–27.

Horn FP, Breeze RG. 1999. Agriculture and food security. Pages 9–17 in Frazier TW, Richardson DC, eds. Food and Agricultural Security: Guarding against Natural Threats and Terrorist Attacks Affecting Health, National Food Supplies, and Agricultural Economics. New York: New York Academy of Sciences

Greenstone MH. 2001. GMOs: Tree hackers, bathwater, and the free lunch. *BioScience* 51: 899.

James C. 2001. Global review of commercialized transgenic crops: 2001. *ISAAA Briefs* 24: Preview. (17 May 2001; *www.isaaa.org/publications/briefs/ Brief_24.htm*)

James WC, Teng PS, Nutter FW. 1991. Estimated losses of crops from plant pathogens. Pages 15–51 in Pimentel D, ed. CRC Handbook of Pest Management in Agriculture. Boca Raton (FL): CRC Press.

Jelsma M. 2001. Vicious Circle: *The Chemical and Biological 'War on Drugs.'* Amsterdam: Transnational Institute. (17 May 2001; *www.tni.org/drugs/*)

Kleiner K. 1999. Operation eradicate. *New Scientist* 163 (2203): 20.

MacKenzie D. 1999. Run, radish, run. *New Scientist* 164 (2217): 36–39.

Madden LV. 2001. What are the nonindigenous plant pathogens that threaten U.S. crops and forests? APS*net* feature. (17 May 2002; *www.apsnet.org/ online/feature/exotic/*)

Madden LV, Nutter FW. 1995. Modeling crop losses at the field scale. *Canadian Journal of Plant Pathology* 17: 124–137.

Madden LV, van den Bosch F. 2002. A population-dynamic approach to assess the threat of plant pathogens as biological weapons against annual crops. *BioScience* 52: 65–74.

Madden LV, Jeger MJ, van den Bosch F. 2000. A theoretical assessment of the effects of vector-virus transmission mechanism on plant virus disease epidemics. *Phytopathology* 90: 576–594.

Matsubara K. 2000. Final Eradication of Foot and Mouth Disease in Japan. Tokyo: Ministry of Agriculture.

[OIE] Office International des Epizooties. 2000. OIE classification of diseases. (20 May 2002; *www.oie.int/eng/ maladies/en_classification.htm*)

Pimentel D, Lach L, Zuniga R, Morrison D. 2000. Environmental and economic costs of nonindigenous species in the United States. *BioScience* 50: 53–65.

Schaad NW, Shaw JJ, Vidaver A, Leach J, Erlick BJ. 1999. Crop Biosecurity. APS*net* feature. (20 May 2002; *www.apsnet.org/online/feature/ Biosecurity/Top.html*)

Schubert TS, Rizvi SA, Sun X, Gottwald TR, Graham JH, Dixon WN. 2001. Meeting the challenge of eradicating citrus canker in Florida—again. *Plant Disease* 85: 340–356.

Stone R. 2000. Experts call fungus threat poppycock. *Science* 290: 246.

Strange RN. 1993. Plant Disease Control. London: Chapman and Hall.

[USDA] US Department of Agriculture. 1997. Profile of the nation's agriculture. (14 June 2002; *www.nass.usda. gov/census/census97/volume1/ us-51/us1figs.pdf*)

———. 2002. Emergency Programs Manual. Washington (DC): USDA, APHIS, Plant Protection and Quarantine. (20 May 2002; *www.aphis. usda.gov/ppq/emergencyprograms/manual.pdf*)

Vanderplank JE. 1963. Plant Diseases: Epidemics and Control. New York: Academic Press.

Watts J. 2001. Japan's government tries to allay BSE fears. *Lancet* 358: 2057.

Wheelis M. 1999a. Biological sabotage in World War I. Pages 35–62 in Geissler E, Moon JEvC, eds. Biological and Toxin Weapons: Research, Development and Use from the Middle Ages to 1945. Oxford (UK): Oxford University Press.

———. 1999b. Outbreaks of Disease: Current Official Reporting. Bradford (UK): University of Bradford, Department of Peace Studies. Briefing Paper No. 21. (20 May 2002; *www.brad.ac.uk/acad/sbtwc/briefing/ bp21.htm*)

———. 2000. Agricultural Biowarfare and Bioterrorism. Edmonds (WA): Edmonds Institute. (20 May 2002; *www.fas.org/bwc/agr/main.htm*)

———. 2002. Biotechnology and biochemical weapons. *Nonproliferation Review* 9: 48–53.

Whitby SM. 2002. Biological Warfare against Crops. Hampshire (UK): Palgrave.

Whitby S, Rogers P. 1997. Anti-crop biological warfare—implications of the Iraqi and US programs. Defense Analysis 13: 303–318.

White House. 1998. Combating terrorism: Presidential Decision Directive 62. Critical Infrastructure Assurance Office, *Fact Sheet* 62. (20 May 2002; *www.info-sec.com/ciao/62factsheet.html*)

Wilson TM, Logan-Henfrey L, Weller R, Kellman B. 2000. A review of agroterrorism, biological crimes, and biological warfare targeting animal agriculture. Pages 23–57 in Brown C, Bolin CA. Emerging Diseases of Animals. Washington (DC): ASM Press.

Zadoks JC, Schein RD. 1979. Epidemiology and Plant Disease Management. New York: Oxford University Press.

Mark Wheelis works in the Section of Microbiology at the University of California, Davis. His research interests are in the history of biological warfare and the scientific aspects of biological and chemical arms control. He has a Ph.D. in bacteriology from the University of California, Berkeley.

Rocco Casagrande is the director of the Homeland Security program for ABT in Cambridge Massachusetts. His research interests are in the development and testing of devices to detect and analyze biological weapons and in biological defense policy. Dr. Casagrande holds a B.A. in chemistry and a B.A. in biology from Cornell University where he graduated magna cum laude and a Ph.D. in experimental biology from MIT.

Laurence V. Madden is a professor with the department of plant pathology, Ohio State University in Wooster, Ohio. He received his M.A. and Ph.D. degrees in plant pathology from Pennsylvania State University.

Gavin Cameron, Jason Pate, and Kathleen Vogel

Planting Fear: How Real Is the Threat of Agricultural Terrorism?

Between February 20 and July 14 of this year, 1,844 cases of foot-and-mouth disease were reported by the British Department of Environment, Food and Rural Affairs, with a smaller number of possible cases reported in France, the Netherlands, and Ireland. As Britain struggled to contain this extremely infectious disease, spread by both direct and indirect contact, an estimated three and a half million cattle, swine, sheep, and goats were slaughtered, and many British farmers faced economic ruin.

This foot-and-mouth outbreak coincides with increasing concern over the potential for agricultural bioterrorism—the malicious use of plant or animal pathogens to cause devastating disease in the agricultural sector. The perception of increased risk stems from recent natural outbreaks (like that of foot-and-mouth and the spread of the West Nile virus in the eastern United States), from an increased focus on "asymmetric" weapons, and in the United States in particular, from heightened worries about domestic terrorism.

Agricultural attack could seem appealing to a broad range of rogue actors, including politically motivated single-issue groups and criminal organizations seeking financial gain. Impacts could be short-or long-term, with a wide range of costs.

One-sixth of the U.S. gross domestic product and one-eighth of all jobs are connected to agriculture, either directly or indirectly. The destruction of crops and/or livestock has a direct financial impact on the grower or breeder, but it also hurts shippers, stockyards, slaughterhouses, distributors, and so on. Attacks may also impact consumers, threatening not only their pocketbooks, but their confidence in the safety of the food supply as well.

Apart from immediate revenue losses, producers may lose future market share if distributors, wholesalers, and retailers choose alternative suppliers. Worse yet, the price of replacing entire crops or herds of livestock—or, depending on the pathogen used in an attack, the need to decontaminate an entire area—could put individual farmers' recovery beyond reach. In addition, seemingly unrelated industries could be affected. For instance, although estimates vary, this year's foot-and-mouth outbreak is expected to cost the British tourism industry at least $5 billion.

Agricultural bioterrorism has received increased attention and discussion within academic, media, and government circles, with most recent studies arguing that agricultural bioterrorism represents a new and dire threat to U.S. national security. [1] But are these studies accurate? Many of their conclusions are pure conjecture, based on worst-case scenarios. Both the threat and consequences of bioterrorism aimed at agriculture remain poorly understood.

However, the threat may not be as dire as alarmists claim, and increased vigilance and institutional reforms could lessen the consequences of either an intentional attack or a naturally occurring disease outbreak.

In the Hands of Terrorists

There is little empirical data regarding attacks, particularly those by sub-state actors, so analysts and policy-makers have been left to discuss the threat based on assumptions about vulnerability. But what, in fact, can we learn based on the motivations of past terrorists?

The "Database of Incidents Involving Sub-National Actors and Chemical, Biological, Radiological, or Nuclear Materials," maintained by the Center for Nonproliferation Studies at the Monterey Institute of International Studies, lists all terrorist incidents in the last century. It includes 21 incidents that might be classified as examples of sub-state attacks against agriculture. The earliest of these was perpetrated in 1952 by the Mau Mau, a violent nationalist-separatist movement in Kenya, which used a toxin from the African milk bush to kill cattle during their rebellion against British rule.

Most of the 21 incidents were unsophisticated and ineffective, lacking significant impact. Only five occurred in the United States, and almost all attacks were very small scale, involving mostly chemical rather than biological materials. Five attacks were criminal rather than political in nature, and several of the others were purely personal (motivated mainly by revenge). The majority of these incidents might more appropriately be described as product tampering rather than agricultural terrorism.

In 1974 the "Revolutionary Command," a radical Palestinian group, claimed to have contaminated grapefruit exported from Israel to Italy; in 1978 another Palestinian outfit, the "Arab Revolutionary Council," targeted Israeli citrus fruit, using liquid mercury as an agent; and in 1988, Israeli grapefruit exports were again threatened with contamination. In 1999 and 2000, Israeli eggs sold domestically were contaminated with salmonella. In this incident, two people died and many others were sickened. Although people had been injured in the earlier attacks on Israeli goods, economic disruption seemed to be the primary goal.

Of the 21 incidents, three hoaxes, three actual incidents, and one ambiguous event involved biological agents. The hoaxes involved foot-and-mouth disease, necrotizing fasciitis, and an unnamed biological agent. A 1984 threat to use the foot-and-mouth disease virus in Australia, although a hoax, elicited considerable alarm. But there was no evidence that the perpetrator possessed or had access to the virus.

In 1989, there were allegations that a group called the Breeders had released Mediterranean fruit flies to protest the use of pesticides on crops in California. The "Medfly" infestation was particularly damaging to citrus fruit. No one was apprehended in the case, but the number of flies was particularly high in California that year, leading authorities to suspect that some had been deliberately released. But it is impossible to say that the Medfly was used as a terrorist instrument.

It is difficult to extrapolate from such a small number of incidents, but the evidence seems to suggest that sub-state groups and individuals motivated by revenge or financial considerations have been the most likely to use or threaten to use biological agents against agricultural products. The record also shows that these attacks have been low-level efforts with limited impact.

State Bioweapons Programs

In contrast to what is known about sub-state actors, a good deal of information is available regarding state-run biological weapons programs.

During World War I, German agents infected horses that were being shipped to Europe from the United States, Argentina, and Morocco with glanders and anthrax bacteria. This was accomplished by feeding the horses contaminated sugar cubes or wiping their noses with disease agent. The purpose was sabotage, intended to undermine the Allied war effort rather than to achieve the widespread contamination of livestock. There is no detailed record of animal deaths, suggesting that the attacks were not very effective.

Germany conducted research into plant and animal pathogens during World War II, but it appears not to have used them. Germany also investigated the use of potato beetles and worked on foot-and-mouth virus (including its weaponization) as well as on a range of anti-crop pathogens.

Before World War II, France also experimented with Colorado beetles and researched the rinderpest virus for attack on cattle, but there is no evidence that either agent was ever used. During the war, the United States, Britain, and Canada coordinated their efforts to produce anthrax bacteria for use against German cattle. The British researched foot-and-mouth disease virus, fowl plague bacteria, and pathogens lethal to sugar beets. The United States developed a viral agent to be used against the Japanese rice crop, conducted research into diseases such as the avian Newcastle, rinderpest, and fowl plague, and pathogens directed against rice, potatoes, and wheat. None of these agents were used during the war.

The Japanese biological weapons program during World War II, although most noted for its attacks against the Chinese people, was also directed against agriculture. Japan's anti-agriculture work was based in Manchuria, and to a lesser extent in Southeast Asia. The details of the program remain vague, although it also included research into diseases such as anthrax, glanders, "nose ulcers," sheep pox, ox plague, and numerous anti-crop agents, directed particularly against certain grains and vegetables. The Japanese used these anti-crop and anti-livestock pathogens in sabotage efforts in Manchuria.

After World War II, the U.S. agricultural program focused on large-scale production and weaponization of anti-crop agents. By the time the United States unilaterally renounced all forms of biological warfare in 1969, it had conducted research and development on wheat stem rust, rice blast, rye stem rust, foot-and-mouth, rinderpest, and brucellosis (a porcine form was intended to incapacitate humans). As late as the 1950s, the American program's dissemination methods for some anti-agriculture agents involved bomblets filled with an agent-and-feather mix. Later, the American program developed spray systems.

The most widespread effort to develop anti-agriculture pathogens may have been that of the Soviet Union, with agents directed primarily at livestock—foot-and-mouth, rinderpest, and African swine fever.[2] Anthrax and psittacosis bacteria were directed at both livestock and human targets, and pathogens such as wheat rust, rice blast, and rye blast were developed as anti-crop agents. There are allegations from a key Soviet defector that Soviet forces unsuccessfully used glanders in the campaign in Afghanistan in the 1980s, but these allegation cannot be substantiated. The Soviets apparently did not mass produce or stockpile anti-agriculture agents; instead, they maintained the ability to expand production rapidly if desired.

Other states may have considered biological agents as weapons against agriculture. South Africa has been accused of using anthrax bacteria as an anti-animal agent in Zimbabwe in the mid-to late 1970s during the Rhodesian civil war, but the outbreak could also have been a natural occurrence. The Iraqi bioweapons program of the early 1990s included agents like cover smut (an anti-wheat fungal agent) and camel pox. Neither appears to have been mass produced or weaponized. Iraq, however, did weaponize anthrax bacteria, botulinum toxin, and aflatoxins, although details remain sketchy.

Most national efforts outside the United States and the Soviet Union were not technically sophisticated. The German sabotage program of World War I relied on infecting individual horses. The Japanese studied climatic and geographical factors that might affect their use of biological pathogens, but they appear to have made minimal efforts to find effective dissemination techniques.

The Technical Details

A look at various countries' programs suggests that the development and weaponization of effective anti-agriculture agents is not straightforward—it requires dedicated infrastructure, personnel, and resources.

A successful agricultural attack would require: acquiring and propagating the proper pathogen; processing it for delivery; constructing an appropriate delivery device; and developing a range of techniques to deal with varying meteorological conditions.

No detailed discussion of these factors has been published in the open-source literature, but a determined terrorist could find a great deal of factual information on animal or plant pathogens. Using it to produce a successful disease outbreak, however, would not be straightforward. It would require some degree of scientific sophistication.

Although the United States and other nations place export and/or trade restrictions on dangerous foreign animal and plant pathogens, it is still possible to obtain them from various international laboratories or repositories.[3] Alternatively, pathogens can be isolated from infected animals or diseased crops. Small quantities of pathogens could easily be carried across a customs checkpoint or an unregulated border area, or sent through international mail. Only a few of these pathogens are zoonotic (communicable from animals to humans), so there would be little risk of infection to the carrier. In a globalized society, increased travel by humans and increased transport of agricultural and other goods have already unintentionally spread some pathogens.

Obtaining a strain of a virus or a fungus does not necessarily mean, however, that it can be used directly as a biological weapon. For example, different strains of the rinderpest virus are immunologically similar, but they vary widely in pathogenicity, lethality, ease of transmission, and host affinity.[4] Such variations, which occur in all animal and plant pathogens, complicate the selection of a weapons-usable strain. In most cases, a terrorist would need the right strain to cause a significant disease outbreak.

Some foreign animal pathogens, like the foot-and-mouth disease virus, are highly infectious and would not need to be cultured—a vial of material might be enough to cause an epidemic. But that is not always the case. Depending on the pathogen, different infective doses would be needed. And infectivity varies even between different isolates of the same viral strain and for different routes of infection (ingestion versus inhalation). If widespread destruction is the goal, moderate or high levels of scientific expertise may be needed to grow, handle, and store larger quantities. Certain parameters involving nutrients and growth conditions would need to be determined experimentally for individual pathogens.

Some animal pathogens are highly infectious and environmentally hardy, so processing—microencapsulation, milling, and drying—might not be necessary. But most plant pathogens and several animal pathogens are sensitive to environmental conditions;

protective coatings would need to be applied to increase their survival upon dissemination. Developing such coatings would involve sophisticated scientific skills that are not likely to be available to terrorists. For example, specific microencapsulation techniques used with bio-control agents (fungicides, bacteria) against the Late Blight pathogen have been found to protect potatoes only in local, targeted plots, not over widespread areas.[5]

With highly infectious pathogens, there may be no need to develop elaborate delivery devices. Historically, commercially available spray devices have been used in various state-level anti-crop and anti-livestock bioweapon programs. However, it is easier to deliver a pathogen to cause an epidemic in animals; plant disease epidemics are highly dependent on environmental conditions.

Environmental and Meteorological Conditions

Both animal and plant pathogens are susceptible to environmental conditions. Infection of crops with plant pathogens would be less dependent on the skill of the terrorist than on specific environmental conditions like temperature and moisture. If the proper weather conditions are not present, typically no plant-disease epidemic will occur no matter how much agent is disseminated. And weather is impossible to control. For example, a 1999 drought in the eastern United States prevented scores of expert university plant pathologists from creating epidemics of the Late Blight disease in research plots—even when growing potatoes that were susceptible and using strains of pathogen that were particularly virulent.[6]

Environmental testing would require a dedicated effort involving sophisticated technical expertise and the kind of financial resources that are likely to be available only to state-supported bioweapons programs. The environmental determinants in plant disease outbreaks could be a virtual chokepoint for terrorists trying to utilize potent anti-crop weapons. Although foreign animal pathogens are less sensitive to environmental conditions, many are also vulnerable to temperature changes, sunlight, and disinfectants.

It would be extremely difficult to cause the widespread destruction of a crop because most plants are not grown in isolation.[7] They have already encountered a variety of plant pathogens, and these earlier contacts have increased their resistance. There are only a few cases, such as that of the Late Blight disease that caused potato crop failures in nineteenth century Ireland, where a crop has remained isolated and has therefore been highly vulnerable. There are a few foreign strains of plant pathogens, however, against which current crops have no resistance; some of these pathogens are highly resistant to fungicides. On the other hand, the issue of isolation is more serious in the case of livestock. The United States has quarantined livestock against several foreign animal diseases, making American livestock extremely vulnerable.

All in all, serious technical issues would confront terrorists attempting to launch an "agricultural armageddon." But blanket statements on technical feasibility are not sufficient to assess the threat—they must be qualified by examining each of the factors involved in turning a living organism into a biological weapon. In contrast to sensationalist reports on the threat of agricultural bioterrorism, terrorists would face many difficult technical hurdles before obtaining the capability of unleashing this sort of bioweapon.

Prevention

The capability to attack has existed for years, so why have so few attacks occurred? The historical record shows that only a handful of terrorists have used economic targeting and attacks against property.

On the other hand, future terrorist groups may be attracted to agricultural bioterrorism because it may be easier for them to justify the killing of plants rather than people. And it is possible that publicizing the idea of agricultural bioterrorism through sensationalist reporting could promote attacks. Media, academic, and government groups should exercise prudence when discussing this subject in public forums.

As with any act of terrorism, there are political, social, and psychological effects that go beyond those who are immediately affected. For instance, would the use of an anti-agricultural agent increase public fear of direct attacks on humans? And how might political life be affected? Britain postponed national elections and restructured a government agency following the foot-and-mouth disease outbreak. The Ministry of Agriculture, Food, and Fisheries was abolished, replaced by the Department of Environment, Food and Rural Affairs, and the secretary of agriculture was sacked from the Cabinet. In spite of these upheavals, the Labour Party won re-election in June.

Another complication is the difficulty of differentiating between a naturally occurring outbreak and a deliberately induced one. For example, Cuba has repeatedly alleged that the U.S. military has targeted Cuban crops such as sugar cane, tobacco, and coffee with plant pathogens, but it has offered no credible proof that these diseases were anything other than naturally occurring outbreaks.

It is extremely unlikely that any agricultural bioterrorist could fatally wound the entire U.S. agricultural sector or national economy, both of which are strong and diversified. Local, regional, and national effects, however, could be significant. Even to the extent that the United States is vulnerable, it is unlikely that terrorists could strike successfully. An advanced, state-level bioweapons program, however, might be able to overcome or circumvent some technical hurdles. Given the bioweapons programs of Iraq and the Soviet Union, it is possible that state programs might explore agricultural options in the future.

While our examination of open-source historical and technical information demonstrates that the threat of agricultural bioterrorism has been exaggerated, Britain's recent foot-and-mouth outbreak has revealed the devastating effects of agricultural disease outbreaks. In an increasingly globalized society, the potential for more outbreaks can only grow. Given their potential impact, more efforts should be directed at disease prevention and response. Several specific steps should be taken:

Communication among scientists concerned with animal, human, and plant diseases should be increased. Currently, there are limited interactions, linkages, and institutional mechanisms for communication between the public health and veterinary sectors. This problem became apparent during the 1999 West Nile virus outbreak, when the existing surveillance and response structures between public health, veterinary, and other scientific communities failed to appreciate the connection between outbreaks in birds at the Bronx zoo and human cases. [8] In addition, some plant diseases have been found to cause disease in immune-compromised humans. Increased contact and communication could assist in earlier identification of disease outbreaks.

Interaction among veterinarians is frequently limited to concerns with livestock and domestic animals, overlooking the fact that finding diseases in wildlife can serve as an early warning system. Many emerging diseases originate in the wild, and it is important to support increased surveillance and study of disease outbreaks among wildlife populations.

National and international disease surveillance networks need to extend down to the individual farm and facility. Many times, farmers and local veterinarians are the first to deal with and diagnose animal diseases. Since most local veterinarians and farmers will never see a case of foot-and-mouth disease, increased education, from the grassroots to the university level, would increase the prospect of accurate disease diagnosis and rapid response.

Many local and state public health and veterinary laboratory systems are not equipped or structured to allow rapid diagnosis of animal samples. Neither the Centers for Disease Control and Prevention nor the U.S. Army Medical Research Institute of Infectious Diseases is prepared or willing to test animal samples regularly—nor should they necessarily be, considering that they are primarily research facilities. But absent adequate lab capabilities elsewhere, there is currently no alternative. In the face of a massive outbreak of foot-and-mouth or another disease, existing laboratories may be overwhelmed. Additional mechanisms are needed for diagnostics in emergency situations.

Funding for work related to foreign animal and plant diseases should be increased. There is a great deal of funding available for human pathogen research, even for diseases considered extremely unlikely to surface, such as smallpox. At the same time, funding on foreign animal and plant disease has been relegated to the background. Such research, however, offers enormous benefits for U.S. public health.

The Soviet bioweapons program employed hundreds to thousands of scientific specialists devoted to animal diseases like foot-and-mouth and West Nile, as well as expert plant pathologists. Due to restrictions, few U.S. or European facilities and scientists are permitted to work on these pathogens, yet Russia and several other former Soviet republics have unique facilities and scientific expertise. The U.S. Defense and State Departments have been working to redirect former Soviet bioweapons efforts toward the development of medical treatments and other responses to protect against foreign animal and plant diseases. U.S. support and funding for these programs' scientists (administered under the Nunn–Lugar program) should be increased.

Current agricultural practices—the use of monocultures, and intensive livestock production in which animals are closely confined—should be reevaluated. These practices increase U.S. vulnerability to disease outbreaks. Although the costs of making significant changes may be too high, it should be possible to evaluate whether some aspects could be changed in a cost-effective manner.

Additional response structures are needed to address the problems involved in differentiating between natural and intentionally induced disease outbreaks. This might include the formation of objective, independent response teams modeled after the National Transportation Safety Board teams, which investigate catastrophic transportation accidents. These teams could ensure that the investigative process is not cut short or neglected in the face of economic and political pressures to control the outbreak.

Additional research on offensive state bioweapons programs and a strengthened verification protocol for the Biological and Toxin Weapons Convention would also be helpful. Understanding the past and present can help us to better assess future bioweapon threats. Scholarly research on why countries have pursued anti-agricultural bioweapons programs, policies, and strategies, coupled with support for a verification protocol, will make it more costly and time consuming for states to conduct prohibited activities and thus strengthen the international norm against bioweapon development and use.

References

1. Jim Drinkard, "Foot-and-mouth 'Probable' in U.S.," *USA Today*, April 16, 2001; *Food and Agricultural Security*, Thomas W. Frazier and Drew C. Richardson, eds., *Annals of the New York Academy of Sciences*, vol. 894 (1999); Panel to Assess the Capabilities for Domestic Response to Terrorist Acts Involving Weapons of Mass Destruction, Washington, D.C., September 22, 1999 (www.rand.org/nsrd/terrpanel/minutes/minutes.9.22.html); Paul Rogers, Simon M. Whitby, and Malcolm Dando, "Biological Warfare Against Crops," *Scientific American*, June 1999, pp. 70–75; U.S. Senate, Committee on Armed Services, Subcommittee on Emerging Threats, Hearing on the Agricultural Biological Weapons Threat to the United States, October 27, 1999.
2. Ken Alibek with Stephen Handelman, *Biohazard: The Chilling True Story of the Largest Covert Biological Weapons Program in the World—Told From the Inside By the Man Who Ran It* (New York: Random House, 1999), pp. 37–38, 301; Kenneth Alibek, "The Soviet Union's Anti-Agricultural Biological Weapons," in *Food and Agricultural Security*, Thomas W. Frazier and Drew C. Richardson, eds., *Annals of the New York Academy of Sciences,* vol. 894 (1999), pp. 18–19; Jonathan Ban, "Agricultural Biological Warfare: An Overview," *The Arena* (Chemical and Biological Arms Control Institute), no. 9, June 2000.
3. Foreign animal and plant pathogens are defined here as those that are not endemic to the United States and cause transmissible diseases that have the potential for very serious and rapid spread, that are of serious public health and socio-economic consequence, and that are of major importance in the international trade of animals, plants, and their products.
4. U.S. Department of Agriculture, Animal and Plant Health Inspection Service, Foreign Animal Disease Training Module, "Keeping America Free from Foreign Animal Diseases, Rinderpest, Volume 6" (www.aphis.usda.gov/vs/ep/fad_training/Petitvol6vol6index.htm).
5. Interview with William Fry, plant pathologist, Department of Plant Science, Cornell University, January 2001.
6. William Fry, "Technical Feasibility of Anti-Crop Terrorism," in Conference Proceedings, "Agro-terrorism: What is the Threat?" November 12–13, 2000, at Cornell University (forthcoming).
7. Interview with William Fry, January 2001.
8. Jason Pate, "Better Plan Needed for Curbing Epidemics," November 29, 2000, (cns.miis.edu/pubs/reports/patend.htm).

Gavin Cameron is a fellow of the Centre for Military and Strategic Studies. He previously taught politics and contemporary history at the University of Salford, in the United Kingdom. He completed his doctorate at the University of St. Andrews, Scotland, and then held research posts at the Center for Nonproliferation Studies, part of the Monterey Institute of International Studies in California, and at the Belfer Center for Science and International Affairs, part of the Kennedy School of Government at Harvard University.

Kathleen Vogel is a post-doctoral fellow at the Center for Nonproliferation Studies at the Monterey Institute of International Studies. She received a Ph.D. in chemistry from Princeton University.

Jason Pate is an independent global security researcher. At the time this chapter was written, Pate was a senior research associate and WMD terrorism database manager at the Center for Nonproliferation Studies (CNS) at the Monterey Institute of International Studies.

Chapter 2.7

Cyberterrorism

James A. Lewis

Cybersecurity and Critical Infrastructure Protection

Cybersecurity entails safeguarding computer networks and the information they contain from penetration and from malicious damage or disruption. Since the use of computer networks has become a major element in governmental and business activities, tampering with these networks can have serious consequences for agencies, firms, and individuals. The question is to what degree these individual-level consequences translate into risk for critical infrastructure.

Analyses of asymmetric, unconventional attacks at first assumed that potential opponents would be drawn to the use of cyber weapons. These opponents could include traditional nation-state opponents and "non-state actors." Cyber weapons were considered attractive because they could offer low-cost means of exploiting the vulnerabilities that are found in most computer networks. Some analysts go further and argue that a cyber weapon could create destruction equal to a kinetic or blast weapon, or could amplify the effects of an attack with these kinds of weapons.

The term "Digital Pearl Harbor" appeared in the mid-1990s, coinciding with the commercialization of the Internet. Digital Pearl Harbor scenarios predicted a world where hackers would plunge cities into blackness, open floodgates, poison water supplies, and cause airplanes to crash into each other. But no cyber attack—and there have been tens of thousands of cyber attacks in the last ten years—has produced these results. The dire predictions of the 1990s arose from a lack of insight into the operations of complex systems, from a gross overestimation of both the interconnectedness of critical infrastructures, and the power and utility of software as a weapon to be used against them.

Determining the actual degree of risk posed by computer network vulnerabilities requires an estimate of the probability that a computer malfunction will damage a critical infrastructure in ways that will affect the national interest. For this to occur, a number of simultaneous or sequential events must take place to let a digital attack in cyberspace have a physical effect. This is not a simple transformation. Computer networks are indeed vulnerable, but this does not mean that the critical infrastructures these networks support are equally vulnerable. Terrorists are attracted to different kinds of weapons, particularly explosives, which are more reliable and which better meet their political and psychological need for violence. Infrastructures are robust and resilient, capable of absorbing damage without interrupting operations, and accustomed to doing so after natural disasters, floods, or other extreme weather conditions. In short, the cyber threat to critical infrastructure has been overstated, particularly in the context of terrorism.[1]

This initial overstatement does not mean, however, that cybersecurity can be entirely ignored in planning for critical infrastructure protection. First, as the use of computer networks grows, vulnerabilities may increase. Second, a more sophisticated opponent will not seek to cause physical damage or terror, but instead will target the information stored within the computer networks. Nation-states are likely to be attracted to this approach: penetrate networks, collect information, and observe activities without arousing suspicion and, should a conflict begin, use that access to disrupt the databases and networks that support key activities. This is a different kind of threat from what much of the planning and organization for critical infrastructure protection at first had in mind, and addressing it may require a reorientation of our thinking and our actions on cybersecurity. This chapter discusses reasons and goals for reorientation.

Political Context for Cybersecurity and Critical Infrastructure Protection

Cybersecurity was, at the end of the 1990s, the dominant theme in policy documents and public discussions of critical infrastructure protection. There is now a general recognition that cybersecurity was overemphasized.[2]

The overemphasis was the result of several factors. Critical infrastructure came of age in the era when the Internet seemed to have upended all rules. The mentality of the dotcom era underlay many of the assumptions on the scope and linkages of critical infrastructure and cybersecurity. The newness of critical infrastructure protection as an area for security analysis—the United States had not contemplated attacks on infrastructure (other than by strategic nuclear weapons) for decades—introduced a degree of imprecision into early analyses. The heightened concern over Y2K, when information technology (IT) experts warned that ancient programming errors associated with the millennial change would make computers around the world go haywire at the stroke of midnight on New Year's Day, plunging the globe into chaos, helped focus attention on cyber networks as a new and dangerous vulnerability.

Analyses of critical infrastructure protection were also shaped (and continue to be shaped) by a change in American political culture. Evidence for this change is (as yet) diffuse and anecdotal, but American government has become progressively more risk-averse since the 1970s. The reasons for this include a loss of confidence among governing elites, decreased public trust of government (with concomitant increases in cumbersome accountability and oversight requirements that act to chill initiative), and a more partisan and punitive political environment. The consequences of a more risk-averse political culture are far-reaching and have yet to fully play out for the United States, but an increased aversion to risk affects the discussion of strategies for critical infrastructure protection (even if the actual implementation of those strategies is at times lax enough to appear to welcome risk with open arms).

This set of political changes is important for understanding critical infrastructure protection and cybersecurity's place in it. Planning for critical infrastructure protection involves an assessment of risk (the probability that a damaging attack can be made). A risk-averse individual will estimate the probability of a damaging attack as higher than a more neutral approach might suggest. This overestimation of risk has been a standard element of discussions of cybersecurity.

Assessing Risk

Determining the importance of cybersecurity for critical infrastructure protection must begin with an estimate of risk. This has proven to be difficult to do, for some of the reasons suggested above. A neutral approach to estimating risk would look at the record of previous attacks to gain an understanding of their causes and consequences. It would estimate the likelihood of a potential attacker selecting a target and which kind of weapon an attacker would be likely to use against it (and this involves an understanding of the attackers' motives, preferences, strategic rationale, goals, capabilities, and experience). It would match attacker goals and capabilities against potential infrastructure vulnerabilities, in effect duplicating the analysis and planning process of potential attackers, as they identify targets and estimate the likelihood of success in achieving their goals with an attack using a particular weapon and tactics.

The importance of cybersecurity revolves around how risk is defined, and how much risk a government or society is willing to accept. Homeland Security Policy Directive 7 (HSPD-7), which lays out federal priorities for critical infrastructure protection, begins by noting that it is impossible for the United States to eliminate all risk and calls on the Secretary of Homeland Security to give priority to efforts that would reduce risk in "critical infrastructure and key resources that could be exploited to cause catastrophic health effects or mass casualties comparable to those from the use of a weapon of mass destruction."[3] For the purposes of this article, the definition of risk used to assess the need for cybersecurity is the probability of an outcome that (a) causes death and injuries, (b) affects the economic performance of the United States, and (c) damages U.S. military capabilities.

Using these criteria, there have been no successful cyber attacks against critical infrastructure (much less attacks that produced terror among the population). Even if we use a minimal definition of risk, that an attack results in a disruption in the provision of critical services that harms the national economy and rises above the level of annoyance, there still have been no successful cyber attacks on critical infrastructure.[4]

An even more rigorous approach would limit risk to outcomes that affect the macroeconomic performance of the United States and reduce U.S. military capabilities. Every society has the ability to absorb a certain amount of death and destruction without serious consequence. The year 2005 saw Hurricane Katrina lay waste to much of the Gulf coast and cost perhaps 2,000 lives (initial and hysterical claims by local officials that Katrina would close New Orleans for years and cost 10,000 deaths were very wrong). Despite the damage and suffering, there was only a temporary dip in national income (economists suggest that U.S. economic growth would have reached 4 percent instead of 3.8 percent if not for Katrina), and there was no degradation of military capabilities.

One way to estimate the effect of a cyber attack is to ask whether a foreign power, using cyber weapons, could stop U.S. military forces from deploying. How, for example, could China use cyber weapons to prevent a carrier battle group in San Diego or Hawaii from heading for the Taiwan Straits? Interfering with the telecommunications systems might slow the recall of crew members on leave (if China was able to successfully disrupt the multiple cellular networks in addition to the fixed telecom network and e-mail). Interfering with the traffic signals could make it more difficult for the crews to assemble, as could interfering with the electrical grid, which could also complicate and slow preparing the ships for departure. Hackers could take over broadcast radio and TV stations to play Chinese propaganda or to change broadcast parameters in the hopes of creating radio interference.

But this is a poor start to securing naval victory. If China or another opponent were able to turn off telecommunications, electricity, and the traffic light system, it would have little effect on the ability of the carriers to deploy. Further, this sort of attack creates the risk for nation-states (as opposed to nonstate actors) of exacerbating tensions or widening conflict in exchange for very little benefit.

The counterargument to these neutral approaches is that they ignore the political effects of a successful attack. The most important of these political effects are the damage to a government's credibility and influence and the risk of an overreaction by security forces that does more damage than the attack itself.[5] Some scenarios even contemplate nonstate actors launching a cyber attack with the knowledge that while its actual effect would be feeble, the overreaction by security forces would be damaging (the history of the Transportation Security Agency and the air passenger business, where large costs to consumers and taxpayers are traded for a modest reduction in risk, demonstrates this effect). While the "self-inflicting strategy" may not appeal to violence-prone attackers like al Qaeda or other jihadi groups, it is one scenario where the subtle use of cyber attack by a national state could trigger long-term economic damage.

But the political consequences of an attack, cyber or otherwise, can be hard to predict. We know that in many instances, the effect of an attack is to actually harden resistance and increase support for an incumbent government. Even unpopular governments will benefit.[6] Political leaders who put forth the right message of steadfast resolve in the face of attacks will actually improve their standings. While the political investigations that followed September 11 called into question the competence of both the Bush and the Clinton Administrations, the immediate political effect was to generate a wave of support for the incumbent president. This support can be lost if the response to an attack is seen as ineffective, but if a government puts forward the right messages, avoids self-inflicted damage, and is seen as making progress in reducing risks of further attacks, any political harm may very well be limited.

Computer Networks and Critical Infrastructures

The United States has identified a long list of industries as critical. They include, according to the National Infrastructure Protection Plan, food and water systems, agriculture, health systems and emergency services, information technology and telecommunications, banking and finance, energy (electrical, nuclear, gas and oil, dams), transportation (air, road, ports, waterways), the chemical and defense industries, postal and shipping entities, and national monuments and icons.[7] The nature and operations of most of these infrastructures suggests that cybersecurity is not a serious problem for them.

An infrastructure is judged to be critical because it meets some standard of importance for the national interest—in that the goods or services it provides are essential to national security, economic vitality, and way of life. To meet this standard, there is an implicit assumption that the disruption of the infrastructures would reduce the flow of essential goods or services and create hardship or impede important government or economic operations. In the interest of deciding where cybersecurity makes a useful contribution to critical infrastructure protection, we can refine this standard by introducing two additional concepts—time and location.

Time and location help explain why cybersecurity is not of primary concern for many critical infrastructures. If there are immediate problems when a system goes off-line, not problems that emerge after weeks or months, that system is critical. Problems that take longer to appear allow organizations to identify solutions and organize and marshal resources to respond, and thus do not present a crisis. The ability of industrial societies to respond to problems, to innovate, and to develop alternative solutions or technologies suggests that in those infrastructures where disruption does not produce immediate danger and is not prolonged for an unreasonable period of time, there would be little effect on national security or the economy.

There is also a geographic element to criticality. National infrastructures are composed of many local pieces, not all of which are equally critical. Specific elements of the larger infrastructure provide critical support to key economic and governmental functions, not entire networks or industries. It is harsh to say, but Hurricane Katrina in 2005 demonstrated that large cities or sections of the country can be taken off-line and, if the political consequences are managed, have little effect on national power—either economic or military. Certain high-value targets—the national capital region, military facilities, a few major cities, or nuclear power plants—require greater attention, while other areas, where disruption or destruction would not impair key national capabilities, can be assigned a lower priority.

The concerns of cybersecurity can transcend this geographic focus in some instances. There are a few, very few networks that are national in scope and interconnect thousands of entities in ways that make them mutually dependent. These networks—finance, telecommunications, electrical power—are among the most critical for national security and economic health, and their interconnectedness, national scope, and criticality may make them more attractive targets for cyber attack.[8] Fedwire, the financial settlement system operated by the Federal Reserve, is one example of this kind of system. Fedwire provides a critical service to banks. Interfering with Fedwire would cripple (temporarily) the U.S. banking system. The Federal Reserve has expended considerable effort to harden FedWire, and the Fed's desire to prevent online bank robbery provides an incentive to continue these efforts.

The U.S. electrical system is composed of several thousand public and private utilities organized into ten large regional grids. There is a substantial degree of interconnection within these grids, and computer networks play an important role in managing grid operation and the production of electrical power. The grids themselves suffer from the consequences of underinvestment and deregulation. Newer industrial control systems used by the electric power industry are based on commercial computer operating systems and Internet protocols because these are cheaper and easier to use. But they replace older control systems that used specialized proprietary software and dedicated networks that were difficult for hackers to access and exploit. The move to commercial software and IP increases vulnerability.

Vulnerability is not the same as risk, however, and a number of factors limit the increase in risk created by this transition to "off-the-shelf" control systems. There have been thousands of hacking incidents aimed at power companies, but as of yet, none have produced a blackout.[9] In the larger national context, blackouts are common in the United States and often do not even attract national attention. In 2002, an ice storm blacked out the twentieth largest city in the United States with a population of 600,000 for several days. The event had no effect on economic or military power and barely merited attention in the national press. Power companies cooperate to respond quickly to these events. Many critical facilities have installed backup power generation equipment. A localized blackout outside of a few major cities can be of minor importance to the nation—witness the recent Los Angeles blackout. The real risk may lie in interconnection, and the ability of an attacker to access one vulnerable producer and cascade this attack into a blackout of one of the big regional grids, but an attack that succeeds in blacking out a low-value target would only be an annoyance.

Telecommunications services are another national-level network. The telecom backbone that supports the Internet and voice communications comprises a number of large networks. An attack that disrupted the services provided by several of these large networks could disrupt communications traffic. However, the presence of multiple over-lapping connections means that there is no single point of failure. The use of satellites in communications services also introduces a degree of redundancy. Since the 1970s, telecommunications networks have been hardened to allow for some continuity of service even after a strategic nuclear exchange.

Additionally, telephone companies developed and use packet switching technology (which breaks messages into many small "packets" of data that can be sent separately) to allow voice communications to persist without a continuous end-to-end connection. The Internet relies on packet switching and benefits from the robustness provided by this technology. The Internet itself was designed to automatically route around damage to complete transmissions. Communications may be slowed or disrupted, but there is no single point for hackers to attack that would allow the national telecommunication system to be disabled.

Before deregulation and the breakup of the national monopoly, the U.S. telecom network was built (with federal guidance) to provide survivability and redundancy in the event of attack, accident, or system failure. After deregulation, when telecom companies were less able to make investments solely to meet the requirements of national security, a highly competitive environment and rapid technological development became the source of a high level of redundancy. In contrast to an attack that destroyed facilities, a cyber attack (a) would require sustained, successful reattack to overcome network operators' repair efforts, and (b) would have to disable multiple communications systems (wireless, fixed line, Internet) to effectively degrade communications.

The complexity of successfully carrying out a cyber attack against national infra-structures like telecommunications or the electrical grid, combined with a lower probabil-ity of success than a physical attack, may make it unattractive to terrorists. Terrorists want screaming people to run in terror past mangled bodies in the street—an attack that produces only a busy signal is likely to be dissatisfying. In theory, the idea of a cyber attack against telecommunications systems in coordination with a physical attack is attractive, as it could compound damage and terror, but coordinating two simultaneous attacks adds a degree of complexity that may overwhelm a terrorist cell's planning capabilities while increasing the chances of detection.

The same constraints do not apply to a nation-state attacker. Such an attacker would have the resources for coordinated attacks. Surreptitious economic warfare during peace-time may be attractive to a nation-state, but the benefits of an attack that produced a long term drag on the target's economy would have to be weighed against the risk and damage of discovery. In the event of a conflict, however, a nation-state opponent is likely to be tempted to use cyber weapons to attempt to disrupt these large U.S. national networks.

The Internet as a Critical Infrastructure

Some point to the Internet as a single large infrastructure that could be attacked with cyber weapons.[10] The first point to bear in mind, however, is that it is a shared global network. An attack against it will affect both target and attacker. An attacker may calculate that the United States might suffer more as a result, or it could plan to use some alternative or backup system to replace the Internet while the target struggled to respond, giving it a temporary advantage. Neither calculation seems particularly compelling.

The Internet is very robust. It is a network designed to continue to function after a strategic nuclear exchange between the United States and the Soviet Union. Its design and architecture emphasize survivability. The Internet (building on earlier technological improvements created by the telecommunications industry) could deal with disruption by automatically rerouting to ensure that a message would arrive despite the complete destruction of key nodes from the network. The Internet addressing system, which is critical to the operations of the system, is multilayered, decentralized, and can continue to operate (albeit with slow degradation of service) even if updating the routing tables that provide the addressing function is interrupted for several days. Some of the core protocols upon which the Internet depends appear vulnerable to attack. BGP (Border Gateway Protocol) is responsible for routing traffic, and a number of tests suggest that BGP is vulnerable to attack but an attacker faces the immense redundancy contained in a network comprising tens of thousands of subsidiary networks.

There has been at least one effort to attack the Internet. An October 2002 attack by unknown parties used a Distributed Denial of Service attack against the 13 "root servers" that govern Internet addresses. The attacks forced 8 of the 13 servers off-line. The attack on the Domain Name System (DNS) system did not noticeably degrade Internet performance and went unnoticed by most of the public, but had it been continued for a longer period of time (and if the perpetrators remained undetected) there could have been a significant slowdown in traffic. A successful attack on the Internet's DNS system, if successful, would slowly degrade that system's ability to route traffic, but this would take several days to have any effect. In response to the attack, the DNS system has been strengthened since the 2002 attack by dispersing some root servers to different locations and by using new software and routing techniques. The new redundancy makes shutting down the DNS system a difficult task for an attacker.

The difficulty of estimating the actual cost of damages from a cyber attack adds complexity to planning for critical infrastructure protection. Estimates of damage from cyber attacks at times reflect the heritage of the dot.com boom in cybersecurity—they generally overestimate or exaggerate damage. Damage estimates are derived by taking a sample of the costs of damage to a few users and then extrapolating them to the affected user population. In some cases, the sample of costs is itself an estimate. These estimates of the economic damages of cyber attack show considerable variation in the value they ascribe to cyber incidents. There is also considerable variation in the methodologies used to calculate cost estimates, and they are often not made public. Few if any of these efforts use the sampling techniques derived from statistical analysis that could ensure greater reliability. Statements that cybersecurity is crucial because of the risk of economic losses that could total in the millions, hundred of millions, or billions of dollars should not be accepted at face value.

It is important to disaggregate the effects of an attack. The Slammer worm is often cited as a damaging cyber attack, but its effects were, from a national perspective, inconsequential. One frequently cited example about the damage of Slammer tells how it affected automatic teller machines (ATM) across the northwest, putting 13,000 of them out of service. What is important to note, however, is that Slammer affected only one bank and its ATM network. Other banks were unaffected, and the other major bank in the region did not see its ATM network go off-line at all. In this instance, customers of the first bank were inconvenienced. The first bank lost revenue and suffered reputational damage. But the bank's competitors were, in one sense, rewarded for practicing better cybersecurity, as some transactions that would have been made on the first bank's ATM network were instead conducted on their machines.

Another example involves a railroad forced by the "sobig" virus to suspend operations on 23,000 miles of track—but no other railroad was forced to suspend operations.[11] If a cyber attack damages one company in a critical sector but leaves its competitors operational, it limits the overall risk to critical national functions. It is difficult to think of a case where a cyber attack affecting one firm and not others would pose a risk to security.

We do not want to extrapolate the misfortunes of a single company to an entire sector in estimating the risk to critical infrastructure from a cyber attack. Similarly, we also want to disaggregate the estimates of opportunity cost to determine whether it is a single company that suffers or the entire economy. In this case, opportunity cost refers to the income (or production) lost when a resource cannot be used, a sale made, or a service provided because of cyber attack. Most of the estimates of the cost of the damage from cyber attacks include opportunity cost, and this often makes up a large portion of the estimated damages from an attack.

Opportunity cost can be misleading for security analysis. If one online merchant is forced off-line by a cyber attack, but its competitors remain in operation, customers may choose to go to the site that works to make their purchase. The vendor forced off-line has lost income, but national income remains unaffected. Other customers may choose to wait and make their purchase later. Again, national accounts are ultimately unaffected. In other cases, a manufacturer may see its Web site or corporate e-mail network go off-line but be able to maintain production—in one case involving an auto manufacturer whose corporate e-mail systems was affected by a virus, the rate of production for cars and trucks was unaffected.[12]

This is not to disparage the effects of cybercrime, which can be costly for an individual or company. However, most cybercrime involves losses in the thousands of dollars (there are anecdotal reports that a few major banks have experienced much larger losses, but they have not made these losses public for fear of reputation damage). Cybercrime is prevalent and increasing, but this does not mean that the risk to critical infrastructure is similarly increasing. Cybercriminals want money. Their favored tactics include theft of valuable data or extortion (e.g., the threat to launch denial of service attacks or disrupt networks unless paid). Their first question is how to turn a threat to a national infrastructure into financial gain without risk of arrest. Threatening an attack against multiple firms may either be operationally too difficult or attract too much attention from law enforcement agencies.

In view of their motives and incentives, attacks against infrastructure by cybercriminals seems unlikely, but nation-states may adopt the hacking tools and "bot nets" developed by cybercriminals for use in cyber war efforts. The sophisticated "shareware" available for cybercrime from hacker or "warez" sites can give even inexperienced attackers access to advanced automated tools and techniques. These range from online hacking manuals and do-it-yourself virus kits to sophisticated attack tools that require some computer expertise to use.

The most interesting of these tools allow a hacker to surreptitiously place malevolent programs on a computer without the user's knowledge. The program can then execute damaging instructions, transmit data or an external address, or provide increased (and invisible) access and control to the hacker. This "malware" can infect computers through the opening of malicious e-mail attachments, downloading seemingly harmless programs, or simply through visiting a malicious Web site. Cybercriminals assemble networks of these infected computers for use in denial of service attacks, for spamming, or for advertising and tracking. Using these tools, an attacker could attempt to disrupt networks or damage or erase data.

But not all networks are equally vulnerable to the tools of cybercrime. The botnets mainly infect consumer systems using always-on connections. Damaging these consumer computers would be annoying, but not threatening to national security or long-term economic health. Second, cybercrime tools are not aimed at physical infrastructure. Infecting a computer does not automatically become a risk to an associated infrastructure. This means that while cybercrime can increase, and it is a growing problem for law enforcement, that does not mean that the risk for critical infrastructure is also increasing.

One benefit that has come from the attention paid to cybercrime is that the measures that improve cybersecurity to protect against criminals will also reduce any risk to critical infrastructure. The use of regular software patching, defensive software (such as intrusion detection systems and antivirus and antispyware software), better authentication of users, and encryption of sensitive data will make an attacker's job more difficult. Improved law enforcement capabilities to arrest and prosecute cyber criminals will also reduce the attractiveness of cyber attacks against critical infrastructure. Companies are more likely to spend money to protect themselves from criminal attacks, since this offers a direct and immediate benefit to their bottom line. Defense is a "public good,"[13] and the private sector routinely undersupplies public goods. This is a particularly important point given the U.S. dependence on the private sector for critical-infrastructure protection. A reading of economic incentives suggests that companies will spend to improve cybersecurity to prevent cybercrime more than they would for a nebulous threat to homeland security.

The importance of cybersecurity in protecting critical infrastructures other than finance, electrical power, or telecommunications rests on the assumption that critical infrastructures are dependent on computer networks for their operations. The chief flaw in this reasoning is that while computer networks are vulnerable to attack, the critical infrastructures they support are not equally vulnerable. Early proponents of cyber attack assumed that many public services, economic activities, and security functions were much more dependent on computer networks than they are in their actual operation. While the dependence on computer networks continues to grow, many critical functions remain insulated from cyber attack or capable of continuing to operate even when computer networks are degraded. It may be more accurate to say that critical infrastructures are dependent on their human operators, whose actions are supported, reinforced, or carried out using computers and networks. This human element reduces the risk of cyberattack to critical infrastructures.

An example of the difference between computer vulnerability and system vulnerability again comes from the 2003 release of the Slammer worm. The worm affected database software. Some police departments in Washington State saw the computers used in their 911 emergency response systems slow to the point of uselessness as the worm spread and implemented its instructions. These departments compensated by using paper notes to record calls, allowing 911 services to continue uninterrupted.[14] The computers were vulnerable and affected, but the critical service was not.

The debate today in how to approach this task is whether cybersecurity should be an element of a larger critical infrastructure strategy or whether it deserves its own independent approach. While the first phase of planning for critical infrastructure protection made cybersecurity of primary importance, the second phase of thinking about critical infrastructure protection assumed that cybersecurity made sense only when it was embedded in a larger strategy focused on physical protection. Had the 911 centers in Washington State been the subject of physical attack or damage, they might very well have had to shut down and 911 services would have been disrupted (as was the case in New Orleans during the post-Katrina flooding). Incidents like this seem to show that risk comes primarily from physical attack.

While this new approach to critical infrastructure protection has dominated federal planning for the past few years, it is not universally accepted. There are reasons for this lack of universal acceptance, some good, some less sensible. The IT industry did not like being downgraded from the central place it occupied in the 1990s in critical infrastructure protection. A more cogent argument for a separate approach to cybersecurity involves recognition of the inability of differing security communities to implement a strategy that unifies cyber and physical security. A chief security officer in a corporation often thinks in terms of "guns, gates, and guards." The chief information security officer thinks in terms of fire-walls and software. In most companies, neither is well placed to execute a unified strategy.

A third approach to critical infrastructure protection might be to recognize that the importance of cybersecurity varies from infrastructure to infrastructure and with the nature of the attacker. We should not be surprised that the distribution of vulnerability is not uniform among or across infrastructures. Cybersecurity is more important for a few networked, interconnected national infrastructures and less important for many disaggregated infrastructures. Cybersecurity is less important in planning to defend against terrorist attacks, since these are less likely to use cyber weapons, but more important in planning for conflict with a national state opponent. Critical infrastructure protection could distinguish among the many places where cybersecurity is a tertiary source of risk and the few places where it is of central importance. These key facilities could be "hardened" with a combination of redundancy, contingency plans for responding to computer disruption, maintaining non-networked controls for key functions, and ensuring additional monitoring of computer and network activities.

Conclusion

HSPD-7 asserts that "Terrorists seek to destroy, incapacitate, or exploit critical infrastructure and key resources across the United States." This assertion is not entirely accurate. While terrorists do exploit western infrastructure for transport and communications to obtain a global presence and capability, it is not clear that they seek to destroy or incapacitate critical infrastructures. Their strategies do not emphasize economic warfare, but favor a blend of military and psychological actions that they believe will produce political change. Cyberspace is a valuable tool for coordination and propaganda for terrorists, but it is not a weapon.[15]

Nation-states who are potential opponents may see more opportunity in cyberspace. Intelligence gathering will prompt them to penetrate U.S. computer networks. In the event of a conflict, nation-states will likely try to use the skills and access gained in intelligence operations to disrupt crucial information systems. This disruption will also affect critical infrastructures and, potentially, degrade the services they provide. It remains unclear, however, if even a skilled opponent can translate the degradation of key infrastructure services into military advantage for a conflict whose combat phase is likely to be of short duration and depend more on existing inventories.

The best path to better cybersecurity may lay outside of critical infrastructure protection. It is hard to motivate people to defend when risks are obscure or appear exaggerated. However, the risks of espionage (including economic espionage) and cybercrime are very real for individuals, firms, and agencies. A security agenda that focused on measures to respond to cybercrime and espionage would produce tangible benefits, win greater support, and reduce many vulnerabilities in computer networks used by critical infrastructure. If an emphasis on cybercrime and counterespionage is the key to better cybersecurity, this suggests that the core of the problem lies with law enforcement.

Critical infrastructure protection began by making cybersecurity the cornerstone of defense. This chapter suggests that, in fact, if we calculate the risk from cyber attack for most infrastructures, it is a tertiary concern. The history of critical infrastructure protection has been to develop expansive plans to cover a broad list of targets and then, in the effort to protect many things with few resources, achieve little in terms of risk mitigation. Putting cybersecurity in the context of more precise assessments of the actual threat could help overcome some of this difficulty by allowing a federal strategy to focus on the few networks of real concern.

Notes

1. "Assessing the Risks of Cyber Terror, Cyber War and Other Threats" provides the fuller discussion of the likelihood of cyber terrorism, http://www.csis.org/media/csis/pubs/021101_risks_of_cyberterror.pdf.
2. The Joint Security Commission was the first in a series of commissions to identify cybersecurity as a primary challenge, saying "The Commission considers the security of information systems and networks to be the major security challenge of this decade and possibly the next century . . ." Joint Security Commission, "Redefining Security: A Report to the Secretary of Defense and the Director of Central Intelligence," February 28, 1994, Chap. 1, "Approaching the Next Century."
3. "Homeland Security Presidential Directive/HSPD-7: Critical Infrastructure Identification, Prioritization, and Protection," December 17, 2003, http://www.whitehouse.gov/news/releases/2003/12/20031217-5.html.
4. A fuller discussion of this claim, and use of the concept of "opportunity cost" in assessing economic harm, follows below.
5. This conclusion reflects the results of government-sponsored cyber war games.
6. The first study to confirm this counterintuitive effect was the U.S. Strategic Bombing Survey, but later studies have found a similar reaction among target populations. U.S. Strategic Bombing Survey, Summary Report (European War), 1945. See also Stephen T. Hosmer, "Psychological Effects of U.S. Air Operations in Four Wars," (Rand, 1996).
7. The earlier PDD-63 (May 1998) identified the task as protecting "the nation's critical infrastructures from intentional acts that would significantly diminish the abilities of: the Federal Government to perform essential national security missions; and to ensure the general public health and safety; state and local governments to maintain order and to deliver minimum

essential public services; and the private sector to ensure the orderly functioning of the economy and the delivery of essential telecommunications, energy, financial and transportation services." The PATRIOT Act and HSPD-7 also provide similar but not identical lists of infrastructures deemed critical.

8. Oil and gas pipelines could be considered a national network, but there are alternative transport modes that could mitigate an attack. Air traffic control may appear national, but is conducted in discrete segments on a local and regional basis.

9. "Energy and power companies experienced an average of 1,280 significant attacks each in the last six months, according to security firm Riptech Inc. . . . The number of cyber attacks on energy companies increased 77 percent this year (2002)." CBS News, "Hackers Hit Power Companies," July 8, 2002, http://www.cbsnews.com/stories/2002/07/08/tech/main514426.shtml.

10. For more on this, please see Chapter 19 in this volume by Aaron Mannes.

11. National Infrastructure Advisory Council, "Prioritizing Cyber Vulnerabilities," October 2004, 5, http://www.dhs.gov/interweb/assetlibrary/NIAC_CyberVulnerabilitiesPaper_Feb05.pdf.

12. The Ford Motor Company received 140,000 contaminated e-mail messages in three hours. It was forced to shut down its e-mail network. E-mail service within the company was disrupted for almost a week. Ford reported, "the rogue program appears to have caused only limited permanent damage. None of its 114 factories stopped production. Computerized engineering blueprints and other technical data were unaffected. Ford was still able to post information for dealers and auto parts suppliers on Web sites that it uses for that purpose." Keith Bradsher, "With Its E-Mail Infected, Ford Scrambled and Caught Up," *The New York Times,* May 8, 2000.

13. A "public good" provides benefits to an entire society with very little incentive for any one person to pay for it.

14. R.M. Wells, "Dispatchers Go Low-Tech as Bug Bites Computers," *Seattle Times,* January 27, 2003, http://archives.seattletimes.nwsource.com/cgi-bin/texis.cgi/web/vortex/display?slug=webworm27m&date=20030127.

15. See, for example, Office of the Director of National Intelligence, "Letter from al-Zawahiri to al-Zarqawi," October 11, 2005, http://www.dni.gov/letter_in_english.pdf.

James A. Lewis is director of the technology and public policy program for the Center for Strategic and International Studies in Washington. He received his Ph.D. from the University of Chicago.

Chapter 2.8

Case Studies

Bruce Hoffman

CBRN Terrorism Post-9/11

The terrorist attacks on 11 September 2001 dramatically re-cast global perceptions of threat and vulnerability. Long-standing assumptions that terrorists were more interested in publicity than in killing were dramatically swept aside that morning in a crescendo of death and destruction. The deaths of some 3,000 persons at the World Trade Center, the Pentagon and aboard the hijacked aircraft were without parallel in the annals of terrorism.[1] Indeed, throughout the entire 20th century only 14 terrorist incidents had killed more than 100 persons[2] and, until 9/11, no terrorist operation had ever killed more than 500 persons.[3] To put the day's death toll in perspective: more than twice as many Americans perished on 9/11 than had been killed by terrorists since 1968[4]—the year acknowledged as marking the advent of modern, international terrorism.

So massive and consequential a terrorist onslaught naturally gave rise to fears that a profound threshold in terrorist constraint and lethality had been crossed. The attacks renewed fears and concerns were in turn generated that terrorists would now embrace an array of deadly non-conventional weapons in order to inflict even greater levels of lethality than occurred on 9/11. Attention focused especially on terrorist use of weapons of mass destruction (WMD), reflected in a new doctrine derived from Vice President Dick Cheney's reported statement that "If there's a one percent chance that Pakistani scientists are helping al Qaeda build or develop a nuclear weapon, we have to treat it as a certainly in terms of our response."[5] What the "one percent doctrine" meant in practical terms, one observer has argued, is that, "Even if there's just a one percent chance of the unimaginable coming due, act as if it's a certainty."[6] Countering the threat of non-conventional weapons proliferation thus became one of the central pillars of America's post-9/11 national security strategy—whether by rogue states arrayed in an "axis of evil" or by terrorists who might acquire such weapons from these same states or develop them on their own.

This chapter assesses the post-9/11 WMD terrorist threat. However, it eschews the terminology of WMD and instead uses the more helpful nomenclature of CBRN[7]—chemical, biological, radiological[8] or nuclear weapons. The chapter argues that we face a two-fold challenge from both al Qaeda, given its longstanding and documented ambitions to develop capabilities spanning all four weapons categories—chemical, biological, radiological, and nuclear—as well as from associated and affiliated jihadis, who are attracted to these weapons not necessarily because of their putative killing potential, but because of the profoundly corrosive and unsettling psychological effects that even a limited, discrete attack using a chemical, biological, or radiological weapon could have on a targeted society and nation. We begin by examining the conventional wisdom on terrorist use of CBRN weapons before 9/11, and then turn to a brief analysis of al Qaeda's long-standing ambitions and recent, important activities in this arena by its affiliates and associates.

The Pre-9/11 Conventional Wisdom on CBRN Terrorism

Until 9/11, most thinking on terrorism in general and CBRN terrorism in particular was arguably seen through an anachronistic Cold War–era prism. This meant that many of our most basic assumptions about terrorists and terrorism—and, more critically, many governmental policies—had largely ossified during the 30 years since terrorism first emerged as a global security problem. These assumptions had originated and taken hold at a time of very different circumstances and dynamics, when radical left-wing terrorist groups and militant ethno-nationalist organizations were widely regarded as posing the most serious threats to Western security.[9] The only significant modification to this thinking or "fine-tuning" of government policies did not really occur until President Bill Clinton's second administration during the final years of the 20th century.[10] At the time, fears of the former Soviet Union's nuclear stockpile falling into terrorist hands—coupled with the 1995 nerve gas attack on the Tokyo by a Japanese religious cult, the Aum Shinrikyo—galvanized fears that terrorists would employ non-conventional weapons, which set in motion increased federal spending and new programs designed to counter this menace. However, these developments notwithstanding, on the eve of 9/11 the threat of potential terrorist use of CBRN weapons remained poorly understood and the efforts to counter it necessarily inchoate. In particular, the implications of terrorism motivated by a religious imperative, in contrast to the secular terrorism that hitherto had dominated this phenomenon throughout the entire Cold War era, was also as unappreciated as it was misunderstood.

Since the French Revolution at the end of the 19th century, terrorism had been practiced mostly by groups and persons motivated mostly by ideological or ethno-nationalist and separatist motivations.[11] Radical leftist (i.e., Marxist-Leninist/Maoist/Stalinist movements) organizations such as the Japanese Red Army, the Red Army Faction in Germany, and the Red Brigades in Italy, as well as ethno-nationalist terrorist movements like the Palestine Liberation Organization (PLO), Palestinian splinter groups like the Abu Nidal Organization, the Irish Republican Army (IRA), and the Basque separatist group ETA generally engaged in highly selective and mostly discriminate acts of violence. They chose to attack various symbolic targets representing the source of their animus (i.e., embassies, banks, national airline carriers, etc.) with conventional bombs, or kidnapped and assassinated specific persons whom they blamed for economic exploitation or political repression in order to attract attention to themselves and their causes. In this respect, their violence was deliberately kept within the bounds of what the terrorists believed the prevailing political order and their core constituency of sympathizers and supporters deemed "acceptable." Terrorists, therefore, were seen as being careful not to undertake actions that might foreclose negotiations with their opponents, alienate them from the global political order that they sought to become a part of, or brook censure, condemnation or worse from their actual or perceived constituency. They appeared to recognize that acts of mass destruction or bloodshed might result not only in international and domestic revulsion and castigation but, equally as important, that it might trigger severe governmental reprisals or countermeasures as well. In this now arguably anachronistic context, terrorists were seen as wanting to have a "seat at the table" and not, as former director of Central Intelligence James Woolsey was famously quoted in the report issued by the National Commission on Terrorism in 2000, now "want[ing] to destroy the table and everyone sitting at it."[12] In sum, mass, indiscriminate murder—such as that involving

CBRN terrorism—consequently would alienate the very audience that the traditional type of terrorists sought to mobilize or influence. Further, it also risked creating a crisis that governments could seize upon to justify the severest repressive measures imaginable in order to eliminate completely any organization that dared to employ such heinous weapons.

For this reason, the violence used by left-wing terrorists, for instance, was always narrowly proscribed. Their self-styled crusade for social justice therefore was often typically directed against governmental or commercial institutions or persons whom they believed represented capitalist exploitation and repression. Specific individuals—including wealthy industrialists such as Hans Martin Schleyer, who was kidnapped and murdered by the German Red Army Faction (RAF) in 1977, or distinguished parliamentarians like Aldo Moro, whom the Italian Red Brigades similarly abducted and executed the following year, alongside lower-ranking government officials, factory managers or ordinary civil servants—were most often targeted. When the left did resort to bombing, the violence was conceived in equally "symbolic" terms. In this sense, although the damage and destruction that often resulted were certainly not symbolic, the act itself was meant to dramatize or call attention to the terrorists' grievances or political cause by striking at targets emblematic or symbolic of the terrorists' grievance and fundamental raison d'etre.

This approach was not entirely dissimilar from that taken by the more prominent ethno-nationalist and separatist groups of that era: the PLO, IRA, and ETA. Although acts of terrorism committed by this category of terrorists were frequently more destructive and caused more casualties than those of their left-wing counterparts, the same self-imposed constraints and balancing act of finding a level of violence acceptable to their actual or perceived constituents while still conforming (however elastically) to the international political community's acceptable boundaries of tolerance was clearly evident. In a broader sense, ethno-nationalist and separatist terrorism was often specifically designed to appeal to international as well as internal opinion in support of the terrorists' irredentist or nationalist aims. Hence, to continue to receive the support of their constituency, generate sympathy among the international community and forestall massive governmental countermeasures, these terrorists also strove to regulate and calibrate their violence. The vast majority of their targets, accordingly, were often individuals—usually confined to low-ranking government officials, ordinary soldiers or policemen, other so-called "agents of the state," and members of rival communities or ethnic groups.

Finally, however radical or revolutionary these groups were politically, the vast majority were also equally conservative in their operations. These types of terrorists were said to be demonstrably more "imitative than innovative," having a very limited tactical repertoire that was mostly directed against a similarly narrow target set.[13] They were judged as hesitant to take advantage of new situations, let alone to create new opportunities. Accordingly, what little innovation that was observed was more in the terrorists' choice of targets[14] or in the methods used to conceal and detonate explosive devices than in any particularly innovative tactics, much less in their use of non-conventional weapons— particularly chemical, biological, radiological or nuclear.

Although various terrorist groups—including Germany's RAF,[15] Italy's Red Brigades, and some Palestinian organizations—reportedly had toyed with the idea of using such indiscriminately lethal weapons, none had ever crossed the critical threshold of actually implementing their heinous daydreams or executing their half-baked plots. For example, it was occasionally reported that these groups had at one time or another "recruited microbiologists, purchased bacteriological experimentation equipment and dabbled in sending toxins such as anthrax to potential victims."[16] What is known conclusively is that in 1979 Palestinian terrorists were suspected of having poisoned some Jaffa oranges exported to Europe in hopes of sabotaging Israel's economy; then in 1984, followers of the Bhagwan Shree Rajneesh contaminated the salad bars of ten restaurants with salmonella bacteria; and six years later, the Liberation Tigers of Tamil Eelam (LTTE) used chlorine gas in an attack on a Sri Lankan military camp at East Kiran.[17] But these three isolated incidents represented virtually the total extent of either *actual* use or serious *attempts* at the use by terrorists of such non-conventional weapons and tactics.

Instead, most terrorists seemed almost content with the limited killing potential of their handguns and machine-guns and the slightly higher rates that their bombs achieved. Like most people, terrorists themselves appeared to fear powerful contaminants and toxins they knew little about and were uncertain how to fabricate and safely handle, much less effectively deploy and disperse. Indeed, of some 12,000 incidents recorded in the RAND Terrorism Incident Database between 1968 and 1998, perhaps only 60 or so evidenced any indication[18] of terrorists *seriously* plotting such attacks, attempting to use chemical or biological agents or intending to steal, or otherwise fabricate their own nuclear devices.

Perhaps the main reason that terrorist use of CBRN was discounted before 9/11 was because terrorists, it was repeatedly argued, were fundamentally rational.[19] There were few realistic demands that terrorists could make by threatening the use of such indiscriminate weapons. There were also few objectives that terrorists sought which could not be obtained by less extreme measures than the detonation of a nuclear device or dispersal of radioactive materials[20] or by attacks employing either biological or chemical warfare agents. In perhaps the most important book written on the subject in the 1970s, Walter Laqueur unambiguously concluded that, "It can be taken for granted that most of the terrorist groups existing at present will not use this option, either as a matter of political principle or because it would defeat their purpose."[21]

The terrorists' perceived obsession with controlling events was also regarded as an important constraint.[22] "Terrorists, like war planners," one unidentified expert opined at a mid-1980s symposium on the subject of nuclear terrorism, "believe they can control what they start . . . and CB [chemical and biological agents] seems too uncontrollable." Hence, this line of argument went, terrorists would abjure from using weapons that could not be discriminately directed against their enemies only, and that therefore could also harm their ethnic brethren, co-religionists, or that often declared but indistinctly amorphous constituency, the so-called "people." Of equal significance was that while terrorists had mastered all the components of operations using conventional weapons, they were thought to be wary of venturing into such terra incognita as WMD. Hence, like most ordinary people, terrorists also harbored profound fears about dangerous substances which they knew little about and, if handled improperly, would affect them as adversely as it would their intended target(s).

Even when experts in the 1970s thought about possible terrorist use of WMD, the prevailing consensus was that terrorists would axiomatically prefer nuclear or radiological weapons over chemical or biological ones.[23] As Brian Jenkins—perhaps that era's leading terrorism analyst—explained in a paper presented at the same conference noted above:

> Terrorists imitate governments, and nuclear weapons are in the arsenals of the world's major powers. That makes them "legitimate." Chemical and biological weapons also may be found in the arsenals of many nations, but their use has been widely condemned by public opinion and proscribed by treaty, although in recent years the constraints against use seem to be eroding.[24]

But most importantly, there was a general acceptance of the observation made famous by Jenkins that "Terrorists want a lot of people watching and a lot of people listening and not a lot of people dead."[25] This maxim was applied directly to potential terrorist use of WMD and in turn was often used to explain the paucity of actual known plots, much less verifiable incidents. Writing in 1975 with reference to potential terrorist use of radiological or nuclear weapons, Jenkins argued that

> Scenarios involving the deliberate dispersal of toxic radioactive material . . . do not appear to fit the pattern of any terrorist actions carried out thus far. . . . Terrorist actions have tended to be aimed at producing immediate dramatic effects, a handful of violent deaths—not lingering illness, and certainly not a population of ill, vengeance-seeking victims. . . . If terrorists were to employ radioactive contaminants, they could not halt the continuing effects of their act, not even long after they may have achieved their ultimate political objectives. It has not been the style of terrorists to kill hundreds or thousands. To make hundreds or thousands of persons terminally ill would be even more out of character.[26]

This was also the conclusion reached by a contemporary of Jenkins, the noted authority on sub-national conflict, J. Bowyer Bell. He too dismissed the possibility that terrorists might target a commercial nuclear power plant in hopes of engineering a meltdown or large-scale atmospheric release of radioactive materials on similar grounds of political expediency and logical instrumentality. "[T]here is no evidence," Bell wrote in 1978,

> that terrorists have any interest in killing large numbers of people with a meltdown. The new transnational television terrorists want media exposure, not exposure of the masses to radioactive fallout. And finally, the technological capacities of organizations with sufficient military skills to launch an attack . . . are not great. The mix of motive, military and technological skills, resources, and perceived vulnerability simply does not exist.[27]

Despite the events of the mid-1980s—when a series of high profile and particularly lethal suicide car and truck bombings were directed against American diplomatic and military targets in the Middle East (in one instance resulting in the deaths of 241 Marines)—many analysts saw no need to revise these arguments. In 1985, Jenkins, for example, again reiterated that, "simply killing a lot of people has seldom been one terrorist objective . . . Terrorists operate on the principle of the minimum force necessary. They find it unnecessary to kill many, as long as killing a few suffices for their purposes."[28] In the revised version of his earlier work, Laqueur similarly emphasized that

> Groups such as the German, Italian, French, Turkish or Latin American terrorists are unlikely to use nuclear, chemical or bacteriological weapons, assuming that they have any political sense at all—an assumption that cannot always be taken for granted. They claim to act on behalf of the people, they aspire to popular support, and clearly the use of arms of mass destruction would not add to their popularity.[29]

In sum, the conventional wisdom on terrorism prior to 9/11 held that terrorists were not interested in killing, but in publicity. Violence was employed less as a means of causing mass death and destruction than as a way to attract supporters, focus attention on the terrorists and their causes or attain a tangible political aim or concession—for example, the release of imprisoned brethren, some measure of political autonomy, independence for an historical homeland or a change of government. Terrorists therefore believed that only if their violence were calculated or regulated would they be able to obtain the popular support or international recognition they craved or attain the political ends they desired. Indeed, as one IRA fighter from this previous era of terrorism once explained, "You don't just bloody well kill people for the sake of killing them."[30]

Both the 9/11 attacks themselves, along with the evidence that has come to light since about al Qaeda's grandiose ambitions spanning the entire CBRN spectrum, have now effectively refuted these longstanding assumptions. Indeed, as Laqueur warned in a seminal reassessment of terrorism trends and thinking published in 1996, "Proliferation of weapons of mass destruction does not mean that most terrorists are likely to use them in the foreseeable future, but some almost certainly will, in spite of all the reasons militating against it."[31] It is al Qaeda's efforts in chemical, biological, radiological, and nuclear weapons development that is the focus of the next section.

Al Qaeda's CBRN Weapons Ambitions and Intentions

Usama Bin Laden's interest in acquiring a nuclear weapon reportedly began as long ago as 1992, and an attempt by an al Qaeda agent to purchase uranium from South Africa was reportedly made either late the following year or early in 1994 without success.[32] Four years later, al Qaeda operatives were still engaged in this quest when Mamdouh Mahmud Salim, a senior official in the organization, was arrested in Germany while attempting to buy enriched uranium. Bin Laden, however, appears to have been undeterred by these initial failures. Indeed in May 1998, he issued a proclamation in the name of the "International Islamic Front for Fighting the Jews and Crusaders," titled "The Nuclear Bomb of Islam." In it, the al Qaeda leader unambiguously declared that "it is the duty of Muslims to prepare as much force as possible to terrorize the enemies of God."[33] When asked several months later by a Pakistani journalist whether al Qaeda was "in a position to develop chemical weapons and try to purchase nuclear material for weapons" Bin Laden replied: "In answer, I would say that acquiring weapons for the defense of Muslims is a religious duty."[34]

Evidence of bin Laden's continued interest in nuclear weaponry again surfaced just six weeks after the 9/11 attacks with the arrests of two Pakistani nuclear scientists—Sultan Bashiruddin Mahmood and Abdul Majeed. In August 2001, the scientists had held three days of meetings with bin Laden, Zawahiri and other top al Qaeda officials at its secret headquarters located near Kabul, Afghanistan. Although their discussions ranged widely to include chemical and biological weapons, Mahmood told his interrogators that bin Laden was specifically interested in nuclear weapons. Al Qaeda supposedly had acquired some nuclear material from an affiliated jihadi movement in Central Asia, the Islamic Movement of Uzbekistan (IMU), and Mahmood's opinion was solicited on its suitability for use in an explosive device. According to Graham Allison,

> Mahmood explained to his hosts that the material in question could be used in a dirty bomb but could not produce a nuclear explosion. Al-Zawahiri and the others then sought Mahmood's help in recruiting other Pakistani nuclear experts who could provide uranium of the required purity, as well as assistance in constructing a nuclear weapon. Though Mahmood characterized the discussions as "academic," Pakistani officials indicated that Mahmood and Majeed "spoke extensively about weapons of mass destruction" and provided detailed responses to bin Laden's questions about the manufacture of nuclear, biological, and chemical weapons.[35]

Al Qaeda's desire to develop at least some kind of nuclear weapons capability were again revealed in January 2002 when CNN reporters discovered in Kabul a 25-page document containing designs for such a device.[36] Further, more recent evidence suggests that bin Laden has not completely abandoned his quest to acquire a nuclear weapon, with many statements posted to various Internet forums over the last several years encouraging followers to aid in this quest. He also points to a religious sanction for this—as Michael Scheuer, the former head of the CIA's bin Laden unit and author of the seminal work on bin Laden, *Through Our Enemies' Eyes*, noted in a 2004 interview broadcast on the CBS investigative news show "60 Minutes," the al Qaeda leader received permission in May 2003 from an influential Saudi cleric, Sheikh Nasir bin Mahid al-Fahd, to use precisely such a weapon against the U.S.[37]

In addition to its nuclear ambitions, al Qaeda has also actively sought to develop a variety of chemical and biological weaponry.[38] It was of course bin Laden's alleged development of chemical warfare agents for use against U.S. forces in Saudi Arabia that was cited by the Clinton Administration in August 1998 to justify the controversial American cruise missile attack on the al-Shifa pharmaceutical plant in Khartoum, Sudan.[39] The movement's efforts in the biological warfare realm appear to have begun in earnest with a memo written by al-Zawahiri on 15 April 1999 to Muhammad Atef, then-deputy commander of al Qaeda's military committee. Citing articles published in *Science*, the *Journal of Immunology*, and the *New England Journal of Medicine*, as well as information gleaned from books such as *Tomorrow's Weapons* (1964), *Peace or Pestilence* (1949), and *Chemical Warfare* (1924), Zawahiri outlined his thoughts on the particular attraction of biological weapons ad seriatim:

a) The enemy started thinking about these weapons before WWI. Despite their extreme danger, we only became aware of them when the enemy drew our attention to them by repeatedly expressing concerns that they can be produced simply with easily available materials. . . .

b) The destructive power of these weapons is no less than that of nuclear weapons.

c) A germ attack is often detected days after it occurs, which raises the number of victims.

d) Defense against such weapons is very difficult, particularly if large quantities are used . . .

I would like to emphasize what we previously discussed—that looking for a specialist is the fastest, safest, and cheapest way [to embark on a biological- and chemical-weapons program].[40]

One of the specialists thus recruited was a U.S.-trained Malaysian microbiologist named Yazid Sufaat. A former captain in the Malaysian army, Sufaat graduated from California State University in 1987 with a degree in biological sciences. He later joined al-Jemaah al-Islamiya (the "Islamic Group"), an al Qaeda affiliate operating in Southeast Asia, and worked closely with its military operations chief, Riduan Isamuddin—better known as Hambali—and with Hambali's al Qaeda handler, Khalid Sheikh Mohammed (KSM). In January 2000, Sufaat also played host to two of the 9/11 hijackers, Khalid Almihdar and Nawaf Alhazmi, who stayed in his Kuala Lumpur condominium. Later that year, Zacarias Moussaoui, the alleged "20th hijacker" who was sentenced in 2006 to life imprisonment by a federal district court in Alexandria, Virginia, stayed with Sufaat, too. Under KSM's direction,

Hambali and Sufaat set up shop at an al Qaeda camp in Kandahar, Afghanistan, where their efforts focused on the weaponization of anthrax.[41] Although the two made some progress, bio-warfare experts believe that on the eve of 9/11 al Qaeda was still at least two to three years away from producing a sufficient quantity of anthrax to use as a weapon.[42] Sufaat's arrest in late 2001, however, may not have entirely de-railed al Qaeda's bio-terror efforts. When KSM himself was apprehended two years later, he was found hiding in the Rawalpindi home of a Pakistani bacteriologist—who has since disappeared.[43]

Prior to 9/11, a separate team of al Qaeda operatives reportedly had been engaged in a parallel R&D effort to produce ricin and chemical warfare agents at the movement's Derunta camp, near the eastern Afghan city of Jalalabad. The Derunta facility reportedly included laboratories and a school that trained a handpicked group of terrorists in the use of chemical and biological weapons. Its director was an Egyptian, Midhat Mursi (also known as Abu Kebab), and the school's teachers included Sufaat and a Pakistani microbiologist. When U.S. military forces overran the camp, they found equipment required to produce the toxin ricin as well as castor oil (ricin is derived from castor beans). Both Mursi and a colleague named Menad Benchellali managed to avoid capture. Although Mursi remains at large, Benchellali, a French national of Algerian heritage, was arrested in 2002. After fleeing Afghanistan, he had initially settled in the Pankisi Gorge, an area in Georgia that borders Chechnya, but became homesick. Once back in France, Benchellali became involved in a terrorist cell that had planned to bomb the Russian Embassy in Paris. Acting on information provided by French authorities following Bechellai's arrest, police in Britain and Spain detained 29 suspects from North African countries suspected of ties to al Qaeda and an affiliated Kurdish-Iraqi terrorist group, Ansar al-Islam.[44] Evidence seized by British police in the search of one suspect's apartment in North London included both recipes and ingredients for several toxins—including ricin, cyanide, and botulinum.[45] British authorities believe that the ricin production instructions had been downloaded from an American white supremacist website and then photocopied on a machine at a well-known radical London mosque.[46] A police raid the previous year on a house in Norfolk used by another cell of Northern Africans also found recipes for ricin and other poisons along with information about explosives and instructions for making bombs.[47]

A common thread in all these cases—whether involving actual al Qaeda operatives or others with potential links to the movement—is a strong interest in, and clear willingness to use, these non-conventional weapons that was not, however, always matched by the capabilities required either to fabricate or effectively disseminate them. As CBRN terrorism expert John Parachini argued,

> Demonstrating interest in something is far different both from, first, experimenting with it and, second, mastering the procedures to execute an attack. Gaining access to materials is certainly a major barrier, but it is not the only one. Delivering toxic materials to targets in sufficient quantities to kill in the same fashion as explosives is not easy.[48]

Indeed, as mesmerizingly attractive as these non-conventional weapons are to some terrorists, they have historically proven frustratingly disappointing to whoever has tried to use them. Despite the extensive use of poison gas during World War I, for instance, this weapon accounted for only five percent of all casualties in that epic conflict. Even in more recent times, such as during the 1980s when Iraq used chemical weapons in its war against Iran, less than one percent (5,000) of the 600,000 Iranians who perished were killed by gas. The wartime use of biological weapons has a similarly checkered record. On at least eleven occasions before and during World War II, the Imperial Japanese Army employed germ agents as diverse as cholera, dysentery, bubonic plague, anthrax and paratyphoid, disseminated in both water and air. Not only did these fail to kill as many Chinese soldiers as the Japanese had hoped, but on at least one occasion—the 1942 assault on Chekiang—10,000 Japanese soldiers themselves were affected, of whom some 1,700 died. "The Japanese program's principal defect, a problem to all efforts so far," David Rapoport concluded, was "an ineffective delivery system."[49] The difficulties of using germs as weapons are further substantiated by the work of Seth Carus, a researcher at the National Defense University in Washington, D.C. Over the past decade, Carus has compiled perhaps the most authoritative accounting of the use of biological agents by a wide range of adversaries, including terrorists, government operatives, ordinary criminals, and the mentally unstable. His exhaustive database, which begins in 1900, reveals that during the 20th century a grand total of ten people were killed and fewer than 900 made ill as a result of some 180 acts of either bioterrorism or bio-crime. The majority of these incidents, moreover, involved the selective poisoning of specific people rather than the wholesale, indiscriminate attacks most often imagined.[50]

The Newly Emerging Terrorist CBRN Paradigm: Shaking Society's Foundations

Significantly, the post-9/11 generation of al Qaeda terrorists does not appear to have been deterred either by the formidable challenges of fabricating and then effectively weaponizing and disseminating biological agents. Indeed, two separate plots that were uncovered and derailed in the United Kingdom respectively in 2003 and 2004 underscore how biological and radiological weapons continue to attract terrorist interest despite these hurdles and how such weapons are admired perhaps even more for their psychological impact than lethal potential.

The first incident, which was cited in the brief discussion above concerning al Qaeda's biological weapons efforts, involves the so-called "ricin plot" orchestrated by a 31-year-old al Qaeda operative named Kamel Bourgass. From what we know of Bourgass, he was born in May 1973 in the Algerian province of Souk Haras: interestingly, when interrogated by authorities, he was unable to provide a specific day for his birth. Conscripted into the national police, where he served for a year, Bourgass subsequently fled Algeria for Britain. He arrived illegally in Dover on the back of a truck in January 2000 and immediately made his way to London's then-notorious Finsbury Park Mosque—a well-known center of Islamist extremism, where Richard Reid (the "shoe bomber" who tried to blow up an American Airlines plane bound from Paris to Miami in December 2001 with explosives concealed in his sneaker) and Zacarias Moussaoui (the alleged "20th 9/11 hijacker") had also worshipped. Bourgass applied for asylum using the name of Nadir Habra, but his claim was rejected and then denied on appeal in November 2001. Bourgass then disappeared. According to his testimony in court, he claimed to have spent the following three years working in a London pizzeria and selling clothes. What is known is that throughout that time he drew state welfare benefits and supplemented his income with petty thievery. Indeed, in the summer of 2002 Bourgass was arrested for shoplifting in Romford, Essex. Presenting false documentation to the police and court, he avoided identification and thus deportation by giving his name as Kamel Bourgass and not Nadir Habra—the name he used on his asylum application.[51]

Coincidentally, about the same time that Bourgass was being charged with shoplifting, British anti-terrorist police in July 2002 began an investigation into North African criminal networks working in Britain suspected of credit card fraud. Their attention had been drawn to these gangs by reports that the proceeds were being used to fund terrorism. Meanwhile, a parallel investigation was unfolding that same month that led to the aforementioned police raid on a house in Thetford, Norfolk, where the recipes for ricin and other poisons were discovered. A third—simultaneous, but unrelated—police operation, also cited above, had resulted in the arrest of an Algerian named Mohamed Meguerba. But, after making bail, Meguerba decamped to Algeria, where he was arrested by police there two months later. Under interrogation, Meguerba told the Algerian authorities that he and a group of fellow expatriates in London had been planning to carry out attacks using ricin in Britain and that sufficient quantities of the biological weapon had been produced to fill two small jars of skin cream. The plot's leader, Meguerba claimed, was Bourgass.[52]

Based on information that Meguerba provided to his Algerian interrogators, in January2003 British police raided the apartment in north London where Bourgass allegedly had made ricin. Initial reports that small amounts of the biological agent were discovered by police in the apartment were later proven false following detailed scientific analysis. However, even if no actual ricin was found, the means and utensils required to produce it were certainly present. In addition to four sets of recipes or instructions in Arabic for making ricin[53] as well as other toxins, along with a mortar and pestle which appeared to contain chemical residue, 20 castor beans (the raw ingredient needed to produce ricin), cherry and apple seeds (which are used in the production of cyanide), and a CD-ROM containing instructions for the fabrication of homemade explosives were seized by police. A nationwide manhunt was subsequently launched for Bourgass. Coincidentally, nine days later police staged what they believed to be a routine raid on an apartment in Manchester where illegal immigrants were thought to be living. Unaware that Bourgass himself was among the persons apprehended at the apartment, the arresting police officers neglected to take any of the special precautions that are standard operating procedure for handling terrorist suspects, failing even to handcuff Bourgass or any of the others. Desperate to escape before he could be identified, Bourgass suddenly grabbed a kitchen knife from a table around which he and the officers were gathered, and in the ensuing struggle he stabbed one policeman to death and wounded three others. In June 2004, Bourgass was convicted of murder and the following April was convicted of "conspiracy to commit a public nuisance by the use of poisons, and/or explosives." However, he was acquitted of charges of conspiracy to commit murder using ricin—as were his four indicted co-conspirators from the London apartment.[54]

According to police documents and testimony at his second trial, Bourgass's plan was to target businessmen and holidaymakers using the Heathrow Express, the train that travels throughout the day between Heathrow Airport and London's Paddington Station. Maps of its route were found in the home of one of Bourgass's co-conspirators. Their plan was to surreptitiously paint or swab door handles on the train with the ricin in hopes of poisoning the victims when they touched the substance with the fingers and palms of their hand.[55] Their objective, according to prosecutors, was not necessarily to kill as much as to "cause mayhem and widespread panic."[56] Indeed, according to the FBI, ricin is ranked as the third most toxic known substance, behind only plutonium and botulism, and a minute amount of it can kill in minutes if inhaled, ingested or absorbed through the skin. However, the agent's molecules are in fact too large to be easily absorbed through the skin from ordinary tactile contact, and thus as lethal as ricin is, it is a more difficult weapon with which to kill or injure than is commonly assumed. "Although the ricin might not have killed anyone," a British Home Office official explained, "it would still have been regarded as a major terror coup" to carry out an attack with such a weapon.[57] This was also the conclusion reached by Peter Clarke, Deputy Assistant Commissioner at Scotland Yard and the head of the police anti-terrorist branch. "It is clear had Bourgass been allowed to continue his plot undetected," he noted, "some people would have been made very ill and quite possibly have died. [Furthermore] It would have been hard to underestimate the fear and disruption this plot could have caused across the country."[58]

Significantly, the plot had al Qaeda's fingerprints all over it. British authorities are convinced that Bourgass left the UK at some point during the three years specifically to travel to Afghanistan to train in an al Qaeda facility and thereby acquire the expertise necessary to concoct and disseminate ricin and other poisons. Indeed, according to intelligence sources, witnesses claimed that Bourgass had been singled out by al Qaeda commanders for specialized, advanced training in the making and use of poisons.[59] Further, Meguerba himself also confessed to having been trained in al Qaeda camps in Afghanistan and to have "had numerous personal meetings with al Qaeda chief Osama bin Laden" as well.[60] Hence, rather than the homegrown, organic radicalization problem that is often assumed to be behind many of the most recent European terrorist attacks and plots, the evidence linking Bourgass and Meguerba to al Qaeda arguably suggests a more conscious and deliberate strategy of subversion and the insertion of terrorist sleepers into Western society and Muslim Diaspora communities. Equally disturbing is the realization that less than a decade ago, the same group of terrorists would more likely have been sitting in a basement attempting to fabricate crude pipe bombs and other conventional, explosive devices and not concoct and disseminate highly toxic biological weapons like ricin.

In sum, today's jihadi terrorists not only seem to be thinking increasingly in terms of non-conventional weapons, but they also appear to fully appreciate the potentially corrosive and unsettling psychological impact that such attacks can have on society—even if such weapons fail to kill or physically harm large numbers of persons. Prominent in their calculations is the likely assumption that attacks with these weapons can substantially enhance the fear and intimidation that terrorism (by definition) seeks to produce in a targeted society. Doubtless present in their calculations as well are the potential effects that such non-conventional weapons could have in undermining public confidence and trust in the ability of the government and authorities to prevent and protect society against such attacks. "This was a hugely serious plot," Peter Clarke noted, "because what it had the potential to do was to cause real panic, fear, disruption and possibly even death to the public."[61]

The conviction in November 2006 of Dhiren Barot (also known as Issa al-Hindi or Issa al-Britani), an al Qaeda operative who planned to use a radioactive "dirty bomb" in a series of attacks on both public gathering places and key economic targets in both Britain and U.S.—another UK terrorist plot involving a clear al Qaeda pedigree—underscores contemporary terrorists' affinity to such a strategy. According to prosecutors in Barot's case, his motive was indeed less wanton, homicidal killing than the creation of "injury, fear, terror and chaos."[62] Moreover, Barot and his cell's attraction to a non-conventional weapon paradoxically may have been a reflection of, or to compensate for, their inability to stage a more sophisticated or lethal conventional attack. Accordingly, the non-conventional weapons threat today may counter-intuitively be not as much ruthless terrorist use of some mass destruction weapon against an entire city and its population as the discrete, calculated terrorist use of some chemical, biological or radiological device to achieve far-reaching psychological effects or provoke a specific reaction from the targeted country.

Conclusion

The CBRN threat we face today from al Qaeda is thus two-pronged: attacks using non-conventional weapons that are meant to kill and injure en masse alongside less lethal attacks, conceived less for their killing potential than for their de-stabilizing psychological repercussions. In this respect, it should be stressed that a limited terrorist attack involving not a WMD per se, but a deliberately small scale non-conventional chemical, biological or radiological weapon, could have disproportionately enormous consequences, generating unprecedented fear and alarm and thus serving the terrorists' purpose(s) just as well as a larger weapon or more ambitious attack with massive casualties could. Accordingly, the issue here may not be as much ruthless terrorist use of some WMD as calculated terrorist use of some unconventional weapon to achieve far-reaching psychological effects in a particular target audience. We may therefore be missing the point and sidestepping the real threat posed by terrorists in this regard. It will likely not be the destruction of an entire city—as portrayed by fictional thriller-writers and government officials alike—but the far more deliberate and delicately planned use of a chemical, biological or radiological agent for more discreet purposes.

Notes

1. The exact number of deaths caused by the 9/11 attacks is believed to be 2,976. Of these, the New York City Medical Examiner's Office concluded that 2,752 were killed by American Airlines Flight 11 and United Airlines Flight 75 that struck the World Trade Center towers. Forty people were killed when United Airlines Flight 93 crashed into a rural field in Somerset County, Pennsylvania, and 184 persons were killed when American Airlines Flight 77 struck the Pentagon. The numbers of persons seriously injured was surprisingly low and defied initially dire expectations. According to a RAND Corporation estimate, no more than about 250 persons required hospitalization for one day or more as a result of the attacks. See Lloyd Dixon and Rachel Kaganoff Stern, *Compensation Losses From The 9/11 Attacks* (Santa Monica, CA: RAND Corporation, MG-264-ICJ, 2004), pp. 15–16. The RAND report cites New York City Medical Examiner's Office, Office of Chief Medical Examiner, 'World Trade Center Operational Statistics', April 2004 as the source from which this data was obtained. See also, National Commission on Terrorist Attacks Upon the United States, *The 9/11 Commission Report: Final Report of the National Commission on Terrorist Attacks Upon the United States, Authorized Edition* (New York & London: W.W. Norton, 2004), p. 552, footnote 188.
2. Brian M. Jenkins, 'The Organization Men: Anatomy of a Terrorist Attack,' in James F. Hoge, Jr. and Gideon Rose, *How Did This Happen? Terrorism and the New War* (NY: Public Affairs, 2001), p.5.
3. Some 440 persons perished in a 1978 fire deliberately set by terrorists at a movie theater in Abadan, Iran.
4. Bruce Hoffman, *Lessons of 9/11: Statement Submitted for the Committee Record to the United States Joint September 11, 2001 Inquiry Staff of the House and Senate Select Committees on Intelligence, 8 October 2002* (Santa Monica, CA: RAND Corporation, 2002), p. 2.
5. Quoted in Ron Suskind, *The One Percent Doctrine: Deep Inside America's Pursuit of Its Enemies Since 9/11* (New York: Simon & Schuster, 2006), p. 62.
6. Ibid.
7. For reasons of clarity and precision, the term CBRN is preferred to the more commonly used, yet potentially misleading term, "weapons of mass destruction" or WMD. With the exception

of nuclear weapons, none of these unconventional weapons by itself is, in fact, capable of wreaking mass destruction, at least not in structural terms. Indeed the terminology "weapons of mass casualties" may be a more accurate depiction of the potentially lethal power that could be unleashed by chemical, biological, or non-explosive radiological weapons. The distinction is more than rhetorical and is critical to understanding the vastly different levels of technological skills and capabilities, weapons expertise, production requirements, and dissemination or delivery methods needed to undertake an effective attack using either chemical or biological weapons in particular. See Advisory Panel to Assess Domestic Response Capabilities for Terrorism Involving Weapons of Mass Destruction, *First Annual Report to The President and The Congress* (Washington, D.C.: RAND Corporation, 15 December 1999), pp. ii–iii.

8. Radiological terrorism involves *contamination* with readily avail able radioactive materials, for instance those used in medicine and commerce, as compared with nuclear terrorism, which implies an explosion caused by the chain reaction created by fissionable materials.

9. Some observers argued that these groups were in fact part of a world-wide communist plot against the West orchestrated by Moscow and implemented by its client states. See especially Claire Sterling, *The Terror Network: The Secret War of International Terrorism* (New York: Holt, Rinehart and Winston, 1981).

10. See, for instance, "Remarks By The President to 17th Annual Legislative Conference Of The International Association of Fire Fighters," Hyatt Regency Hotel, Washington, D.C., 15 March 1999, p. 3 at http://www.usia.gov/topical/ pol/terror/99031502.html, where President Clinton explained: "Since 1996, the number of weapons of mass destruction threats called in to fire fighters, police and the FBI has increased fivefold. The threat comes not just from conventional weapons, like the bomb used in Oklahoma City, but also from chemical weapons, like the nerve gas agent that killed 12, but injured thousands in Tokyo, in the subway, just four years ago; and even from biological weapons that could spread deadly disease before anyone even realized that attack has occurred. I have been stressing the importance of this issue, now, for some time. As I have said repeatedly, and I want to say again to you, I am not trying to put any American into a panic over this, but I am determined to see that we have a serious, deliberate, disciplined, long-term response to a legitimate potential threat to the lives and safety of the American people."

11. See Bruce Hoffman, *Inside Terrorism* (New York: Columbia University Press, 2nd edition, 2006), pp. 81–86.

12. Quoted in the Report of the National Commission on Terrorism p. 2. XXX

13. Brian Michael Jenkins, *International Terrorism: The Other World War* (Santa Monica, CA: The RAND Corporation, R-3302-AF, November 1985), p. 12.

14. For example, the 1985 hijacking of the Italian cruise ship, the *Achille Lauro,* by Palestinian terrorists as opposed to the more typical terrorist hijacking of passenger aircraft.

15. For example, it was reported in 1979 that German Red Army Faction terrorists were being trained at Palestinian camps in Lebanon in the use of bacteriological weapons. Additional information of the group's reputed interests in this respect came to light as a result of a police raid of an RAF safe-house in Paris that uncovered a miniature laboratory containing a culture of Clostridium botulinum, used to create a botulinum toxin, alongside earlier threats by the group to poison water supplies in 20 Germany towns if three radical lawyers were not permitted to defend an imprisoned RAF member. Subsequent investigation, however, revealed that these efforts likely never occurred. For the most authoritative account and analysis, see Terence Taylor and Tim Trevan, "The Red Army Faction (1980)," in Jonathan B. Tucker (ed.), Toxic Terror: Assessing Terrorist Use of Chemical and Biological Weapons (Cambridge, MA: MIT Press, 2000), pp. 107–113.

16. See "Violence: a buyer's market," *Jane's Defence Weekly*, 12 May 1990, pp. 909–911. A similar report is detailed in W. Seth Carus, *Bioterrorism and Biocrimes: The Illicit Use of Biological Agents in the 20th Century* (Washington, D.C.: Center for Counterproliferation Research, National Defense University, August 1998, pp. 175–176.

17. The attack—like Aum's five years later—was relatively crude: thus again suggesting the impediments to mounting more sophisticated operations employing CBRN weapons. In this instance, several large drums of the chemical were transported from a nearby paper mill and positioned around the camp's perimeter. When the wind currents were judged right, the attackers

released the gas, which wafted into the camp. The use of this weapon was verified personally by the author who visited the destroyed encampment in December 1997 and saw the drums of chlorine gas used in the attack, that had been left on the outskirts of the camp. It was further confirmed in the course of in-depth interviews with more than a dozen serving or retired senior Sri Lankan military commanders (including an officer who was present at the East Kiran camp when the attack occurred), intelligence officials, police officers and captured LTTE cadre conducted in Colombo, Jaffna, and Batticoloa, Sri Lanka by the author in December 1997 and January 2000.

18. Admittedly, these were only those incidents or plots that we both *definitely* knew about and that were also been reported in open, published sources.

19. See, for example, the studies conducted by The RAND Corporation during the 1970s for Sandia National Laboratories and in particular, Gail Bass, Brian Jenkins, et. al, *Motivations and Possible Actions of Potential Criminal Adversaries of U.S. Nuclear Programs* (Santa Monica, CA: The RAND Corporation, R-2554-SL, February 1980).

20. See, for example, the discussion in Peter deLeon,Bruce Hoffman, et al., *The Threat of Nuclear Terrorism: A Reexamination* (Santa Monica, CA: The RAND Corporation, N-2706, January 1988), pp. 4–6.

21. Walter Laqueur, *Terrorism* (London; Weidenfeld and Nicolson, 1977), p. 231.

22. Jeffrey D. Simon, *Terrorists and the Potential Use of Biological Weapons: A Discussion of Possibilities* (Santa Monica, CA: RAND, R-3771-AFMIC, December 1989), p. 12.

23. Robert L. Beckman, "Rapporteur's Summary," in Alexander and Leventhal, *Nuclear Terrorism: Defining the Threat*, p. 13.

24. Brian M. Jenkins, "Is Nuclear Terrorism Plausible?" in Ibid., p. 31.

25. Brian Michael Jenkins, "International Terrorism: A New Mode of Conflict" in David Carlton and Carlo Schaerf (eds.), *International Terrorism and World Security* (London: Croom Helm, 1975), p. 15.

26. Brian Jenkins, *Will Terrorists Go Nuclear?* California Seminar on Arms Control and Foreign Policy, paper no. 64 (Los Angeles: Crescent Publications, 1975)—also published under the same title as P-5541 (November 1975) in the RAND Corporation Paper series, pp. 6–7.

27. J. Bowyer Bell, *A Time of Terror: How Democratic Societies Respond to Revolutionary Violence* (New York: Basic Books, 1978), p. 121.

28. Brian Michael Jenkins, *The Likelihood of Nuclear Terrorism* (Santa Monica, CA: The RAND Corporation, P-7119, July 1985), p. 6.

29. Walter Laqueur, *The Age of Terrorism* (Boston & Toronto: Little, Brown, 1987), p. 319.

30. Quoted in Gerald McKnight, *The Mind of the Terrorist* (London: Michael Joseph, 1974), p. 179.

31. Walter Laqueur, 'Postmodern Terrorism,' *Foreign Affairs*, vol. 75, no. 5 (September-October 1996), p. 34.

32. See Graham Allison, *Nuclear Terrorism: The Ultimate Preventable Catastrophe* (New York: Times Books, 2004), p. 3; Peter Bergen, "The Bin Laden Trial: What Did We Learn?," *Studies in Conflict & Terrorism*, vol. 24, no. 6 (November-December 2001), p. 431; Benjamin Weiser, "U.S. Says Bin Laden Aide Tried to Get Nuclear Material," *New York Times*, 26 September 1998; and, Michael Grunwald, "U.S. Says Bin Laden Sought Nuclear Arms," *Washington Post*, 26 September 1998.

33. Quoted in Ben Venzke and Aimee Ibrahim, *The al-Qaeda Threat: An Analytical Guide to al-Qaeda's Tactics and Targets* (Alexandria, VA: Tempest Publishing, 2003), p. 52.

34. "Osama bin Laden—Interview—23 December 1998, Rahimullah Yusufzai Interview" in Ibid., p. 53.

35. Allison, *Nuclear Terrorism*, pp. 20–23.

36. CNN.Com, "Live From Afghanistan—Was Al Qaeda Working on a Super Bomb?" 24 January 2004 accessed at http://www.isis-online.org/publications/terrorism/transcript.html.

37. See Dafna Linzer, "Nuclear Capabilities May Elude Terrorists, Experts Say," *Washington Post*, 29 December 2004; and, "Bin Laden seeking nukes," *Toronto Star*, 24 November 2004.

38. John Parachini, 'Putting WMD Terrorism into Perspective,' *The Washington Quarterly*, vol. 26, no. 4 (Autumn 2003), p. 44

39. See both the contemporary accounts of the explanation for the strike by Barbara Crossette, et al., "U.S. Says Iraq Aided Production of Chemical Weapons in Sudan," *New York Times*, 25

August 1998; Michael Evans, "Iraqis linked to Sudan Plant," *The Times* (London), 25 August 1998; James Risen, "New Evidence Ties Sudanese To Bin Laden, U.S. Asserts," *New York Times*, 4 October 1998; Gregory L. Vistica and Daniel Klaidman, "Tracking Terror," *Newsweek*, 19 October 1998 and the "insider" account published by two members of President Clinton's National Security Council staff, Daniel Benjamin and Steven Simon, *The Age of Sacred Terror* (New York: Random House, 2002), pp. 259–262 & 353–365.

40. Quoted in Alan Cullison, "Inside Al-Qaeda's Hard Drive," *The Atlantic Monthly*, vol. 294, no. 2 (September 2004), p. 62.

41. Alan Sipress, "Key Player in Nuclear Trade Ring Found Hospitable Base in Malaysia," *Washington Post*, 24 February 2004; and, Judith Miller, "U.S. Has New Concerns About Anthrax Readiness," *New York Times*, 28 December 2003.

42. Eric Lipton, "Qaeda Letters Are Said to Show Pre-9/11 Anthrax Plans," *New York Times*, 21 May 2005.

43. Barton Gellman, "Al Qaeda Near Biological, Chemical Arms Production," *Washington Post*, 23 March 2003.

44. Ibid.; and, Joby Warrick, "An Al Qaeda 'Chemist' and the Quest for Ricin,: *Washington Post*, 5 May 2004.

45. Alan Cowell, 'One Conviction in Plot to Spread Deadly Toxins, but 8 Go Free,' *New York Times*, 13 April 2005.

46. Information provided by British authorities.

47. Duncan Campbell and Rosie Cowan, "Ricin Plot: Terror trail that led from Algeria to London," *The Guardian* (London), 14 April 2005.

48. John Parachini, "Putting WMD Terrorism into Perspective," *Washington Quarterly*, vol. 26, no. 4 (Autumn 2003), p. 39.

49. David Rapoport, "Terrorism and Weapons of the Apocalypse," *National Security Studies Quarterly*, vol. v, issue 3 (Summer 1999), pp. 52–54.

50. W. Seth Carus, *Working Paper: Bioterrorism and Biocrimes: The Illicit Use of Biological Agents Since 1900* (Washington, D.C.: Center for Counterproliferation Research, National Defense University, February 2001 Revision), pp. v, 10, 11, & 21.

51. See "The Many names of danger man Bourgass," *Manchester Evening News*, 15 April 2005; "Pack of lies told by a ruthless killer," *Manchester Evening News*, 15 April 2005; "Ricin plot: The Bourgass case—How the parties compare," *The Guardian* (London), 15 April 2005; Neville Dean and Nick Allen, "Mosque's Terrorist Roll Call," *Press Association Newswire*, 7 February 2006; and, John Steele and Sue Clough, "How Jihad network's tentacles reached the back streets of Gloucester," *Daily Telegraph* (London), 14 April 2005.

52. "CHRONOLOGY—Britain's thwarted chemical attack plot," Reuters (London), 14 April 2005. See also, Rosie Cowan and Duncan Campbell, "Detective murdered by an obsessive loner," *The Guardian*, 14 April 2005; Karen McVeigh, "Killer and the chemical weapons factory in a kitchen." *The Scotsman* (Edinburgh), 14 April 2005; Kate Southern, "Terror plot man had Wood Green Base," *Newsquest Media Group Newspapers*, 15 April 2005; "Terror police find deadly poison," *BBC News World Edition*, 7 January 2003 accessed at http://www.bc.co.uk/2/hi/uk_news/2636099.stm; and, James Tourgout, "Killer was on the ruin in Weymouth," *Newsquest Media Group Newspapers*, 15 April 2005.

53. During the trial, evidence was presented that scientists working at the British Ministry of Defence's chemical warfare laboratories at Porton Down in Wiltshire were able to produce enough ricin and cyanide using Bourgass's recipes to kill hundreds of people if properly employed. McVeigh, "Killer and the chemical weapons factory in a kitchen." 14 April 2005.

54. Ibid. See also, Ben English, "Plot to poison London," *Herald Sun* (Victoria, Australia), 15 April 2005; and, "Man admits UK-US terror bomb plot," 12 October 2006 http://newsvote.bbc.co.uk/mpapps/pagetools/print/news.bbc.co.uk/2/hi/uk_news/6044.

55. Michael Isikoff ahnd Mark Hosenball, "Terror Watch: What Ricin? Colin Powell and British Authorities pointed to a poison lot as justification for the war on Iraq. But a jury says the case didn't add up," *Newsweek Web Exclusive*, 13 April 2005.

56. Southern, "Terror plot man had Wood Green Base," 15 April 2006.

57. Quoted in Roddy Ashworth, "Ricin gang targeted Heathrow Express," *The Express on Sunday*, 17 April 2005.
58. Southern, "Terror plot man had Wood Green Base," 15 April 2005.
59. Jenny Booth, "Profile: true identity of ricin plotter remains a mystery," *Times Online*, 13 April 2005 accessed at http://www.timesonline.co.uk/printFriendly/0,,1-2-1567904-2,00.html. See also, Rosie Cowan and Duncan Campbell, "Detective murdered by an obsessive loner," *The Guardian*, 14 April 2005; McVeigh, "Killer and the chemical weapons factory in a kitchen." 14 April 2005; and, Tourgout, "Killer was on the ruin in Weymouth," 15 April 2005.
60. McVeigh, "Killer and the chemical weapons factory in a kitchen." 14 April 2005.
61. Quoted in Ibid.
62. BBC News, "Man admits UK-US terror bomb plot," 12 October 2006 accessed at http:newsvote.bbc.co.uk/mpapps/pagetools/print/news.bbc.co.uk/2/hi/uk_news/6044. See also Alan Cowell, "British Muslim Sentenced in Terror Attacks," *New York Times*, 8 November 2006.

Bruce Hoffman is a professor at the Edmund A. Walsh School of Foreign Service at Georgetown University and one of the world's preeminent terrorism experts. He is the recipient of the U.S. Intelligence Community Seal Medallion, the highest level of commendation given to a non-government employee and a senior fellow at the Combating Terrorism Center at West Point.

Adam Dolnik and Rohan Gunaratna

Jemaah Islamiyah and the Threat of Chemical and Biological Terrorism

Over the course of the past decade, the possibility of the use of chemical and biological weapons (CBW) by non-state actors has been a topic of extensive academic and public debate. Originally, this debate concentrated primarily on capabilities, where the ease of acquisition of CBW materials after the breakup of the Soviet Union, as well as more widespread availability of information needed for the production and weaponization of CBW agents, were the sources of major concern. Relatively recently, the debate was brought to a more realistic level through the acknowledgment of technical hurdles associated with the successful delivery of CBW agents, as well as the possible motivational constraints involved in the decision of terrorist groups to use such weapons. Another shift in the debate was represented by the claim that the rise of religious terrorism had eroded these constraints. According to this argument, religious terrorists whose operations have been observed to be responsible for the vast majority of all casualties in terrorist attacks worldwide are believed to be unconstrained by political considerations, as their only constituency is God. Further, the ability of religious terrorists to dehumanize indiscriminately their enemies is strengthened by the perceived divine sanction of their actions.[1]

A prominent example of religious terrorism is seen in Jemaah Islamiyah (JI or "Islamic community"), a group in Indonesia which generally supports the global Islamic caliphate vision and anti-Western ideology of al Qaeda. In light of the October 2003 discovery of a JI chemical and biological manual in the apartment of top operative Taufiq Rifqi in Cotabato City in southern Mindanao,[2] the CBW threat has become an issue of an increased importance in the Southeast Asia region. This chapter will analyze the level of this threat by assessing both the motivational and capability aspects of CBW terrorism, followed by the application of this framework to the Jemaah Islamiyah case. Particular attention will be devoted to the assessment of the JI CBW manual, as it provides a unique insight into the current capability level of the organization. In this section, the chemical and biological agents considered by JI will be surveyed, followed by an assessment of the group's knowledge level with respect to those agents. An overall evaluation of the JI CBW threat will be presented in the conclusion.

Motivation

Terrorism: Old vs. "New"

At the most basic level, terrorists that will succeed in killing thousands of people with chemical or biological weapons must possess the ability to acquire and weaponize successfully lethal agents, as well as the motivation to inflict indiscriminate mass casualties.[3] But despite the fact that terrorism does typically involve killing and destruction, most terrorists practice a level of restraint on their activities. Traditionally, terrorists have not necessarily been interested in killing a lot of people, but rather in spreading fear among the general population by killing only the necessary few. Possibly for this particular reason, terrorists have traditionally not been very interested in CBW because such weapons were deemed too large-scale to serve any purpose useful to the terrorists.[4] Mass casualties are likely to be counterproductive for terrorists who typically strive to attract popular support in order to force a political change, such as creation of a homeland or implementation of social justice norms within the targeted state. Mass killing would likely hinder such support, rather than attract it. Moreover, a large-scale attack might also strengthen the affected government's resolve to track down and punish the terrorists, and may thus jeopardize the group's very existence.

While this traditional interpretation of terrorism has been the consensus for decades, many authors have observed that over the past 20 years, the phenomenon has experienced disturbing new trends. These indicate the rise of violent activities motivated by a religious imperative, as opposed to the still lethal but arguably more comprehensible motives of ethnic nationalism and revolutionary ideologies.[5] Some authors have claimed that religious terrorists are not constrained by the traditional political concerns, such as popular image or the reaction of the constituency or the targeted state. Rather, since they base their justifications for using violence on the sanction of a supernatural authority whose will is absolute, the "new" terrorists are less rational, and therefore more prone to indiscriminate mass-casualty violence.[6] While this logical and widely accepted interpretation of the new trends in terrorism makes intuitive sense, a grave danger lies in its mechanical application to threat assessment without further inquiry into the nature of a given organization's belief system.[7]

It is true that terrorist attacks have over the last two decades become more lethal. It is also true that following the end of the Cold War, religion replaced secular ideologies as the dominant philosophical basis for justifying terrorist violence. However, we should recognize that underlying motives in the belief systems of the majority of today's terrorists have *not* changed. Even the religious fanatic sees his violent activity as an essentially altruistic act of self-defense. It is still the perception of victimization and injustice that drives the so-called "religious terrorist," rather than a perceived universal command from God. The use of holy rhetoric by most groups commonly labeled "religious" serves much more as a uniting and morale-boosting tool than as a universal justification for acts of unrestrained violence.[8] As a result, the commonly defined characteristics of the "new terrorists" as religious fanatics who do not seek to benefit a constituency and whose violent actions are not a means to an end but rather a self-serving end in itself, do not apply to the absolute majority of today's terrorists. Implicitly, many of the organizations that are included in the statistics that show the rise of indiscriminate, divinely sanctioned violence do not belong into this narrowly defined category, rendering the alarmist interpretation of such statistics much less useful than generally believed.[9]

So how do we assess JI's motivational potential to use CBW weapons? The record is clearly mixed. Let us first look at the motivational characteristics suggesting that the JI CBW threat may not be imminent. The most important in this respect is the political nature of the group's objectives. JI clearly does not fall into the category of organizations that lack a constituency and are thus immune to possible public opinion backlash associated with killing a large number of people with weapons that are universally regarded as inhumane. JI does have a community of sympathizers and shows a great concern for the enlargement of this constituency base by paying special attention to religious training, in order to create a favorable environment for taking over power with the eventual goal of establishing an Islamic state in Southeast Asia.

The emphasis placed on building political influence can be documented by the institution of Majelis Mujahidin Indonesia (MMI), a political umbrella organization headed by Abu Bakar Ba'asyir, the JI's spiritual leader. MMI essentially seeks to unite members of various radical groups in Indonesia with the intent of lobbying for the implementation of the *sharia* through the legitimate political process. This effort documents the willingness of the JI leadership under Ba'asyir to embrace a political solution in order to achieve the group's goals, an aspect that strongly distinguishes JI from the apocalyptically-minded groups that have throughout history shown the greatest propensity toward the use of chemical and biological weapons. From this perspective, it could be argued that the political nature of JI's objectives has a restraining influence on the strategy and tactics the group uses in its armed campaign. This is especially true in the case of the political sensitivity of killing innocent Muslims. Even the first Bali bombing, which was clearly designed to kill as many people as possible, was intended to avoid casualties among locals by the specific timing of the attack, and the selection of targets that were essentially "off limits" to locals.[10]

Even Imam Samudra, one of the key perpetrators of the attack, later expressed his regret about the fact that some locals were killed, and stated that he "seeks forgiveness from God for the 'human error.'"[11] Similarly, the reaction to a wave of popular resentment against the perpetrators of the 2004 Australian Embassy bombing in Jakarta, in which all of the 11 fatalities were Indonesian Muslims, demonstrated JI's sensitivity on this issue. Far from ideologically and strategically immune to this backlash, in its next attack the group decided to move its next operation to Bali, where in the organizers' own words it had a grater chance of success in being more discriminate in killing only "white people."[12] These examples indicate that an indiscriminate mass casualty attack might be viewed as politically too risky even among the more violent elements within the group.

On the other hand, there are many alarming indicators as well. From this point of view, the religious nature of the organization seems to provide the group with an enhanced level of enemy dehumanization, which ultimately leads to an escalating spiral of violence and the associated inclination toward producing an increasingly large number of casualties. This trend seems to be confirmed by the operational progression JI has undergone over the past several years. Inspired by the Darul Islam (DI) movement—which was established in 1967 by a group of activists seeking to engage in *dakwah* (or proselytizing) in order to turn Indonesians into better Muslims—and founded with the intent of creating a regional Islamic government in Southeast Asia, Jemaah Islamiyah originally focused its wrath against local sectarian targets such as Christian churches. But the JI leadership's willingness to become a public political organization had contributed to an ideological split within the group, which effectively triggered the escalation of JI tactics on behalf of the more radical faction under the operational command of Hambali.[13]

In December 2000, JI operatives conducted 38 bomb attacks throughout Indonesia targeting Christian churches, on one hand maintaining the group's targeting logic but on the other introducing elements of synchronization and grandiosity at a scale previously unknown.[14] The Christmas 2000 church bombings clearly aimed for a much higher level of fatalities then JI had ever produced in the past, and despite the fact that the coordinated attack resulted in the death of "only" 19 people and injuries to 120 others, the *modus operandi* that was used in the attacks represented a significant shift. Further, when one of cells during the operation encountered a problem with their target—the church they selected was not having a Christmas Eve service—it had been advised by Jabir[15] to select any location such as a discotheque or other establishment, as long as it was either *kafir* (infidel) or Chinese.[16] This suggestion was a good indication of where the JI elements under Hambali were heading. Only six days later, JI launched its first successful attack against transportation infrastructure in the Philippines, killing 14 people on a light railway train and wounding some 70 others by a series of explosions in Metro Manila.[17] This attack again was a sign of an increasingly daring attempt at mass casualties.

For Operation JIBRIL, in which multiple suicide bombers were supposed to detonate truck bombs in Singapore, only Western or *kafir* targets such as embassies and government buildings would be selected. After the failure of Operation JIBRIL due to the swift arrests of the Singapore cell's members in December 2001, yet another important shift in JI's targeting preferences took place. Under pressure to deliver a strike that would finally succeed, at the next meeting held in January 2002 in Thailand, Hambali called for a revision of targeting procedures to focus on "soft targets" associated with the West, such as nightclubs, bars and hotels.[18] On October 12, 2002, a man detonated a suicide belt in Patty's Bar in Bali. As people fled out onto the street in panic, another suicide bomber detonated a van loaded with explosives in the middle of the quickly forming crowd. According to one of the terrorists, the bomb weighed 1,000 kilograms as a symbolic payback for the one-ton bombs America has repeatedly dropped on Muslims in the Middle East.[19]

The shift from hard government targets to soft tourist targets represents a significant escalatory progression—due partly to the difficulty of successfully attacking heavily protected government targets, the terrorists now started considering innocent civilians to be a guilty party in the conflict, regressing their attribution of guilt to the lowest possible common denominator: anyone but themselves and their co-religionists. Indeed, Hambali reportedly distributed bin Ladin's fatwa advocating precisely this targeting logic among the operatives of the Bali attack. In the bin Ladin text, anyone who supports the infidel governments by paying taxes is declared guilty of the resulting oppression of Muslims, and therefore a legitimate target. Besides embracing this legitimization of indiscriminate violence, JI has also shown the desire to kill in bulk—the Bali bombings killed 202 people, which at the time marked the ninth highest total in a single attack conducted throughout the history of terrorism. Only nine months after the Bali attack, suicide terror would reach the Indonesian capital, when on 5 August 2003, a car bomb exploded outside the J.W. Marriott Hotel in Jakarta, killing 12 people and wounding 150 others.[20] The link between the two attacks was immediately obvious. As in the Bali bombing, the perpetrators in Jakarta used the same kind of explosives, as well as mobile phones for the purposes of remote detonation.

The Jakarta Marriot hotel bombing killed "only" 12, which was considerably fewer than in the Bali attack, but this was largely due to the malfunction of the bomb, as opposed to a lack of intent.[21] Another thirteen months later, on 9 September 2004, a nearly identical suicide truck bombing took place at the Australian Embassy in Jakarta, killing11 people and injuring more than 180 others.[22] The attack was a clear demonstration of the fact that despite the apprehension of Hambali in August 2003, the pro-al-Qa'ida wing in the JI was still a potent force. Just in case there was any doubt, on October 1, 2005, three suicide bombers detonated their belts at the seaside area of Jimbaran Bay and the bar and shopping hub of Kuta, killing 26 people and wounding 102 more.[23] By this time it was clearly established that the principle organizers behind the attacks in Indonesia were two Malaysians, Dr. Azahari bin Husin and Noordin Mohammed Top, both members of Hambali's pro-al-Qa'ida faction within the JI.[24] According to Nasir Abbas, who was a key JI operative until his arrest in 2003, members of this faction "see themselves as fighting a new world battle. . . . They say, we can attack civilians anywhere, just as Americans attack Muslim civilians all over the world."[25]

The above chronology carries several important lessons and implications. The first implication stems from the JI ideology, which at least in the interpretation of the more radical wing provides a justification that favors operations that can maximize damage and casualties. In this light, the popular (though often mistaken) perception of CBW as "weapons of mass destruction" provides a logical choice for the group. Furthermore, even the more mainstream faction of JI may be motivated to go down this path, although not necessarily due to the promise of mass fatalities, but more for the purposes of deterrence. Consider Abu Bakar Ba'asyir's reply to the question of whether the use of nuclear weapons was justified: "Yes, if necessary. But the Islamic Ummah should seek to minimize [the intensity of the fighting]. Allah has said in verse 8 chapter 60 that we should equip ourselves with weapon power—that is an order—but preferably to scare and not to kill our enemy. The main goal is to scare them."[26] From this perspective, CBW would provide an ideal weapon of choice, as most attacks with CBW agents would likely result in limited casualties, but also in the spread of a highly disproportionate level of fear and panic.

Motivation Assessment

JI as an organization is a fairly diverse entity, in which the motivations of various factions need to be analyzed differently. With regard to the motivation to use chemical or biological weapons, we need to look at two elements. The first is an inclination to mass casualty violence, a threshold which at least one faction within the organization has been able to overcome. The second component is the motivation to use chemical or biological agents over conventional weapons as a means to kill a large number of people. If the desire is indeed to kill as many people as possible, why not just attack more often, at more locations, and on a greater scale with weapons that are available and have proven to be effective? Why invest a massive amount of precious resources into a new technology that only few if any know how to use and that could potentially end up killing the perpetrators themselves—all without any guarantee of success? Why risk a negative public reaction and a possibly devastating retaliation likely to be associated with the use of non-conventional weapons?

As we can see from the complexity of these questions, there is clearly an additional element besides the desire to kill on a large scale that plays a decisive role in the equation. Empirically speaking, organizations that have in the past gone beyond merely expressing interest in chemical and biological agents have been groups for whom these weapons had a strong expressive or emotional value, such as the desire to kill without shedding blood or the interpretation of poisons and plagues as God's tools. An example of this is the frequent reference to biblical plagues commonly used by various radical Christian groups, or the strange fascination of Aum Shinrikyo's leader Shoko Asahara who wrote poems about sarin. Alternatively, environmentalist cults—such as the Church of Euthanasia, the Voluntary Human Extinction Movement, and the Gaia Liberation Front—have interpreted diseases as "natural" tools used by Mother Nature to eliminate the human race that has through technological advances and an inconsiderate use of natural resources caused a natural imbalance, which according to the group could only be restored by an elimination of the world's most destructive species.[27]

What is important to emphasize is that despite the fact that JI belongs to the many organizations that have inquired into the possibility of using CBW because of their theoretical potential to kill on a large scale and in a way that would succeed in spreading a high level of fear, it seems to lack the all-important emotional/expressive attraction to CBW per se. As a result, even if JI decides to progress to an even higher level of casualties in the future, such operations are much more likely to utilize multiple large explosive devices rather then exotic poisons.

Capability

Achieving a chemical and biological weapons capability consists of two main steps: the acquisition of a chemical or biological agent in a sufficient quantity, and the acquisition of an efficient delivery system that will allow an effective dispersal of this agent. Acquiring classical warfare agents is certainly not an easy task, although state sponsors of terrorist organizations that possess such agents could serve as a potential source. At the same time, history shows that despite compatible goals and a common enemy, state sponsors have quite rationally been reluctant to provide terrorist groups with more than relatively basic conventional armaments.[28] Not only could terrorist use of relatively sophisticated technologies provide evidence of state involvement in the attack, but terrorist groups could also be very difficult to control and may potentially turn the given technology against the sponsoring state itself.[29] Another possible source for acquisition of biological warfare agents is their purchase or theft from laboratories associated with state-level biological weapons programs. But even more importantly, many biological agents have legitimate uses and are therefore widely available through commercial repositories that isolate, preserve and distribute cultures. Even though the security of many repositories has recently been tightened, there are still many unsecured culture collections around the world from which pathogens can be purchased with few questions asked.[30] Another factor that makes the acquisition of biological agents possible is the relative ease with which even small amounts of biological materials can be converted into large quantities. Moreover, the boom of information technologies and the Internet makes the necessary know-how for successful procurement of cultures more widely available. The acquisition of low-level chemical agents such as cyanide, chlorine or various pesticides is also relatively easy, considering the dual-use nature of these substances. A much more challenging task is the acquisition of ready-made nerve agents or key precursor chemicals needed for the production of such compounds. Other significant challenges include the safety issues involved in handling chemical agents and the difficulties of stabilizing such agents for storage purposes.[31]

The term "weaponization" refers to the process of producing an effective delivery system for the acquired agent. Generally, two basic scenarios for a chemical or biological terrorist attack exist. One is a relatively crude, small-scale delivery along the lines of the 2001 anthrax letters in the U.S., which can succeed in causing massive panic and disruption, but lacks the potential of inflicting significant damage in terms of loss of human life. The other scenario is a mass-casualty attack, which is much less likely but which could potentially be catastrophic. It is the latter type of attack that is the primary focus of this chapter.

The difficulty of weaponizing chemical and biological substances varies greatly based on the agent of choice. Inflicting mass casualties with chemical and non-contagious biological agents such as anthrax or tularemia requires a high-tech delivery, as every victim has to come into direct contact with the agent in order to be affected. Contagious agents on the other hand, allow for a much less efficient delivery, as it is only necessary to infect a small group of people, who can then spread the disease by secondary transmission. At the same time, the likelihood of the spread of a contagious disease beyond the desired target population is likely to be viewed by most terrorist groups as a liability, rather than an asset, due to the lack of control over the final outcome.[32]

The JI CBW Manual

The JI manual is a 26-page document consisting of hand-written notes, apparently compiled from a number of different sources. One of the main sources appears to be the *Mujahidin Poison's Handbook,* a sourcebook compiled by anonymous *jihad* sympathizers from open source literature and widely distributed over the Internet. It appears to be the case that the author(s) of the Bahasa-written JI manual had directly copied parts of the more extensive English-written *Mujahidin* handbook. The two publications not only share the same format for listing agents, they also cite common experimental data. On the other hand, some of the information about production procedures is in many cases significantly different, suggesting either the lack of attention on the part of the note taker or alternatively, the consultation of additional source(s) that were deemed as more reliable. The manual itself covers a number of toxins as well as chemical agents, pesticides and even narcotics. All of the agents are discussed in a uniform structural manner, describing the materials and the procedures needed for the production of the given agent, expected effects, dosage, experimental results, and in some cases, delivery methods. The following section will explore the agents covered in the manual in more detail.

With regards to the scope of the chemical agents listed, it is noteworthy that with the exception of phosgene—one of the agents that were developed and used for assassination purposes by the Aum Shinrikyo—none of the listed substances can be accurately described as warfare agents. The chemical substances covered in the manual include hydrogen cyanide, hydrogen sulfide, phosgene, chlorine, and arsenic, which are each described in some detail. The manual also discusses various less threatening or completely unusable agents such as potassium ferrocyanide, potassium permanganate, chloroform, and aniline, as well as a number of narcotics including cocaine, heroin and morphine. These agents are discussed in less detail, omitting the information on composition, manufacture and weaponization.

Hydrogen cyanide, the blood agent that was used in the Nazi gas chambers under the name Zyclone-B, is the one substance that is covered in most detail. The manual expresses optimism that a victim exposed to this agent would die in less than 30 seconds, also showing a considerable level of excitement over the fact that hydrogen cyanide is extremely easy to produce—it consists of only a simple mixture of ingredients that are easily accessibly on the open market (potassium or sodium cyanide and sulfuric acid). The manual also spends a considerable amount of space describing two "firing devices" for this agent, one of which utilizes a close up release consisting of a mechanical break of a glass plate separating the binary components, triggering their mixture and immediate release. The other firing device relies on the use of a table tennis ball as a delay mechanism. In this scenario the ball injected with sulfuric acid is placed into an open container filled with potassium or sodium cyanide, relying on the acid to eat through the plastic in order to combine with the other ingredient. Having described the production and delivery, the manual moves on to prescribing ideal targets, focusing mainly on buildings that are air-conditioned in order to "achieve a more rapid spread of the gas." Overall, the production as well as delivery mechanisms for hydrogen cyanide are described accurately, but the author(s)' descriptions contain some logical flaws—e.g., when they indicate that a human being would be killed by the same dose and in the same amount of time as a rabbit.

Two other agents are discussed in the same category—hydrogen sulfide and phosgene, the most widely used choking agent of World War I. The whole group of agents is then analyzed collectively, suggesting that hydrogen cyanide should be the agent of choice because of its ease of production, also referring to the favorable characteristics of the above described delivery system, which is praised for the possibility of delayed action. What the authors apparently do not realize is that the same delivery system could be used for both of the other two agents as well. Also, the manual at this point makes several important mistakes, such as the statement that: "in post-operation, the firing device is difficult to detect, and they will keep asking who the real culprits are."

Another mistake is the reference to a precedent in the use of hydrogen cyanide, when the manual states that "[the agent] was used in a Japanese railway several years ago killing a number of people." This statement is highly inaccurate—it refers to the 5 May 1995 incident in the bathroom of the Shinjuku subway station, where two plastic bags containing 1.5 liters of diluted sulfuric acid and 2 liters of powdered sodium cyanide, respectively, were found on fire. The objective of the attack (which was later ascribed to Aum Shinrikyo) was the production of hydrogen cyanide with the hope that the air-conditioning system would suck in the gas, dispersing it over the platform. The delivery system in this incident was particularly interesting: mixing of the two chemicals was to be achieved by the means of fire, triggered by an incendiary system consisting of two condoms placed inside each other and filled with sodium chlorate and sulfuric acid, respectively. The sulfuric acid eats through the rubber and combines with the sodium chlorate to produce fire.[33] The attack however failed to impact anyone, nor did the three duplicate attempts that took place later during the same year. Overall, the chemical weapons section of the manual discusses fairly accurately the production of several highly potent agents that could theoretically cause the death of a large number of people. At the same time, only agents which can be produced about as easily as making Kool-Aid are considered in further detail—the manual completely omits the category of nerve agents, which are the most potent but also most difficult to produce. The chemical weapons section also pays little attention to the concept of effective weaponization. While crude methods for releasing hydrogen cyanide into the open are discussed in some detail, other agents are either to be directly injected into the victims' body or smeared onto the skin, which makes them about as lethal as a knife or an axe, in the sense that the attacker must approach each victim individually and up-close in order to kill. As a result, some of the methods described in the CW section could potentially be used to kill kidnapped victims, but their use to produce hundreds of fatalities is extremely unlikely. It is clear from the language used in the manual that the authors do not understand this fact.

In the category of biological agents, the JI manual focuses only on toxins (poisons produced by living organisms) such as botulinum toxin, nicotine, toxins from poisonous mushrooms and potato buds. In comparison to the time and space devoted to chemical agents, this section is considerably less extensive and consists mainly of the description of production procedures and results of tests on various animals. In terms of agent selection, only substances that can be easily produced from conventional materials such as cigarettes, potatoes, castor beans, mushrooms, or meat are considered. The described production methods are fairly accurate, but it is crucially important to note that the lethal doses stated throughout the document refer to agents with a high level of purity—a level that is unachievable through the prescribed production methods. For instance, the ricin recipe describes how castor beans with a removed seed coat (the nontrivial procedure for removing the coat is omitted) should be grounded in a blender or coffee grinder with acetone and then filtered through a coffee filter to remove the oil. After repeating this step several times, the remaining extract is air-dried to a fine powder. This preparation is purported to be a highly toxic material capable of killing within a few minutes, namely through skin contact when mixed with a suitable lotion or carrier solvent such as dimethylsulfoxide (DMSO). According to experts, however, if such an approach were followed it would produce a crude mixture the trans-dermal toxicity of which would be negligible, as large proteins of this nature do not readily cross the skin even in a carrier solvent. As a result, following the ricin recipe from the JI manual would not yield any usable results.[34]

Another problem with this manual is the complete lack of mass-casualty capable delivery systems for a biological terror attack. In contrast to chemical agents, where some (albeit extremely crude) methods are suggested, the toxins described in the manual would be of little use, even if produced successfully.

The JI manual is noteworthy in that there is no discussion at all of contagious pathogens that could theoretically be delivered by a human carrier via secondary transmission. The non-inclusion of contagious agents is by no means a surprise—the lack of control over the outcome of the attack makes them highly unattractive for terrorist purposes, unless of course the perpetrators desire to kill everyone including themselves, their constituency and even their own family members.

Capability Assessment

The JI manual provides useful insights into the CBW capability of the group. On the one hand, the document surveys several agents of disturbing potency and expresses considerable optimism and fascination with regard to how miniscule amounts of the respective agent are theoretically needed to kill a large number of people. When discussing botulinum toxin, for instance, the manual states that "30 ml of the agent can kill 60 million people, God willing!!!" Further the manual provides chilling details on the killing of mammals such as rabbits or dogs during experiments with the described agents.

On the other hand, the author(s) of the manual are in many respects only re-inventing the wheel by presenting advice that falls into a "no-brainer" category. For instance, the manual instructs the group's members on obvious safety considerations (e.g., "stand against the wind when dispersing a lethal agent" or "don't smell the highly toxic substance [you just produced]") and provides ridiculous "insights" on dosage, such as stating that when using pesticides, "the dosage for people will need to be different than the prescribed amount for insects." Also the author(s) demonstrate a lack of understanding of the differences between individual agents and their effects, combining blood and choking agents into the same category for comparison. In addition, the cited experiments—despite being described in a familiar way—were in all probability not conducted directly by the author(s), as they are word-by-word descriptions plagiarized from standard open-source literature. Moreover, the author(s) commit a number of elementary mistakes, such as in the conversion of the dosage needed to kill a rabbit versus a human, or the suggestion that "every poison can be placed upon the skin with lethal results." And finally, the manual reflects a complete lack of knowledge with regards to efficient delivery of the produced agents. While in some cases very simple but mass-casualty incapable methods are suggested, in most cases ambiguous statements such as "there is a specific way of making the potential victim take this poison" or "one has to think of an effective way to apply it on the target" are used. To conclude, the "manual" more closely resembles an initial survey of openly available literature, as opposed to an operational cookbook.

Another element that is critical to assessing the CBW capability characteristics of a group is its innovativeness, defined as the ability to improve operationally. Quite simply, since achieving CBW capability constitutes a point of considerable innovation for any existing terrorist organization, understanding the capacity of a group to suddenly alter its established *modus operandi* in a creative way is an absolutely essential component of predictive threat assessment. From this perspective, the JI's tactical repertoire has been a relatively modest one, at least when comparing to other major contemporary terrorist organizations. Virtually all of the group's operations have involved the use of explosive devices, detonated either remotely or by suicide bombers.

Even in the area of explosive devices JI has been rather conservative, settling for the design that has worked in the past accompanied by minor incremental improvements over time.[35] These improvements were essentially the result of a "learning from failure" approach. For instance, during the 2000 Christmas church bombings the explosive devices were made out of carbon, potassium, sulfur and TNT,[36] wrapped in gift paper and rigged to mobile phones for remote detonation. In this case however, a number of the bombs malfunctioned, either failing to detonate completely or detonating at the wrong time. This has resulted in the death of several JI operatives including Hambali's close friend Jabir, who forgot to change his SIM card and died in an explosion triggered by an unexpected phone call.[37] JI bomb makers reviewed their mistakes and during the next major attack in Bali, not only were the destructive effects of the large bomb enhanced by packing the delivery vehicle with a dozen plastic filing cabinets filled with a mix of explosive materials; the device was also rigged with four separate detonation mechanisms (remote, timing, manual and anti-handling mechanism) to ensure that it would detonate as planned.[38] Although the 1,000 kg bomb was only 30 percent efficient—that is, according to Australian authorities, only about 30 percent of the chemical mixture exploded, while the rest simply burned—it produced a large enough explosion and subsequent fire to kill 202 people. According to interrogation reports, the Bali terrorists originally planned for even greater carnage, by incorporating a third suicide bomber who was supposed to ride a motorcycle through the doors of the packed Sari Club and detonate himself. The plan was abandoned only after it was discovered the man chosen for the suicide task could not properly operate a motorcycle.[39]

The explosive device used in the bombing of the J.W. Marriot in Jakarta was identical to the one used in Bali, and although it was considerably smaller consisting of six plastic boxes weighing 19 kilograms each,[40] it was still clear the attack was aimed to create as many casualties as possible. In order to increase lethality, the terrorists attached dozens of bars of laundry soap to containers of inflammable liquid which were placed next to the bomb. The mixture of sodium and fatty acids in the soap helped create fireballs which engulfed some of the victims.[41] According to investigators, the bomb was personally detonated via a mobile phone by Dr. Azahari bin Husin, JI's top bomb maker who escaped from the scene on the back of a motorcycle. The explosion produced a two-meter wide crater, penetrating through 32-centimeter thick concrete into the basement, and the suicide bomber's head was catapulted all the way to the hotel's 5th floor. As earlier in Bali, in this attack the perpetrators tried to prevent easy attribution by attempting to scrape off the identification numbers on the vehicles used so they would not be easily traceable to the original owner.[42] However, in both of these cases as well as in the case of the Australian Embassy bombing, the Indonesian authorities were still able to recover and reconstruct the registration number from the debris, leading to the arrest of many of the JI members involved in the bombings.[43] This fact, along with the failure to achieve significant damage to the Australian Embassy due to anti-vehicle barriers installed in front of the building, apparently led to a change in JI's bombing approach. Instead of using trucks packed with explosives which had trouble approaching their targets, the group adopted the use of suicide backpacks, which would not only be more difficult to trace, but could also be more successful in reaching the desired target.

Such devices were not only used in the second Bali bombing, but were also recovered from the hideouts of Dr. Azahari during his elimination in Malang in November 2005, and even more importantly, in the safe house of Noordin Mohammed Top during the unsuccessful apprehension attempt in Wonosobo in May 2006.[44] The Wonosobo discovery is particularly significant, as it demonstrates JI's ability to construct these explosive devices even after the demise of Azahari, the group's chief bomb maker. Nevertheless, there has been only a limited amount of operational innovativeness involved in the JI campaign so far. The points of shift that did occur assumed the form of incremental improvements in the construction and delivery of explosive devices, as opposed to radical innovation involving the adoption of weaponry or tactics that the group had not used before. This is another reason why JI's operational capacity to attack with chemical or biological agents on a large scale is currently rather low.

Could this reality suddenly change? History tells us that terrorist organizations rarely alter their established *modus operandi,* and when they do, these changes are driven by very specific reasons.[45] The first such reason comes in the event of an introduction of government countermeasures, such as target hardening efforts that serve as a direct obstruction to the tactics used by terrorists in the past. While most groups can be expected to respond by selecting substitute targets, an innovative organization will refuse go down this path of least resistance in order to increase its probability of success. Instead, such a group will work to overcome these countermeasures by means that have not been accounted for by the enemy, often placing an emphasis on projecting an image of invincibility as well as mocking the state for failing to stop the attack despite all of its resources. This is not a profile that would fit the JI in the current state. The group has responded to government countermeasures in the past precisely in a regressive fashion, by refocusing their target preferences to less challenging targets such as tourist spots, while making only minor incremental improvements along the way in their tactics and weapons.

Another scenario in which a group can be expected to alter its operational methods in a novel direction comes in the presence of an inherent ideological pre-determination toward using certain technologies or the need to innovate in order to obtain the capability to match the level of violence associated with the respective ideological and strategic preferences.[46] This is not the case of JI at this moment; Azahari—whose personal technological zeal was one of the major drivers of the incremental improvements in explosive devices—is no longer available, and the group is dependent on the codification of his knowledge via various manuals and past training. For this reason, it is highly unlikely that JI's *modus operandi* will change because of ideological or strategic reasons, especially given the limited resources and capability of the group.

The third relevant scenario of a trigger to terrorist adaptation of new operational methods is an incidental or unintended acquisition of a particular human or material resource. This is a real threat. If, for instance, a highly skilled microbiologist decided to ally himself with the JI, this would be a considerable boost to the group's biological weapons program. At the same time, even such a development would still leave the group miles away from launching a feasible *mass casualty* biological weapons plot. This was clearly demonstrated by the interaction of JI and al-Qa'ida with regards to the latter's biological weapons program. As far back as 1999, al-Qa'ida initiated the so-called "Project Yogurt," a secret plan to develop chemical and biological weapons.[47] In the initial stages, the plan was to conduct a survey of literature while the organization looked to recruit a scientist to run the program. In 2001, al-Qa'ida's third in command, Mohammed Atef, approached Hambali with a request to find a scientist that would take over the program. Hambali introduced Yazid Sufaat, a U.S. trained bio-chemist and former Malaysia military officer, who subsequently spent several months attempting to cultivate anthrax in a laboratory near the Kandahar airport.[48]

Plans were also established to set up another laboratory in Malaysia and a third lab in Bandung, Indonesia, through Sufaat's company called Green Laboratories Medicine.[49] In addition, on August 1, 2006, the Philippine military raided an Abu Sayyaf Group hideout in Jolo, Sulu Province, and recovered a detailed 2004 proposal from JI to build a chemical lab in the Philippines. The project was shelved due to the difficulty of procuring the necessary precursor chemicals and the comparatively high costs.[50] But while this intent may sound scary on paper, it is interesting to compare the logistics and expertise of al-Qa'ida's biological weapons program with that of the Aum Shinrikyo, the apocalyptic cult that in 1995 became famous for its sarin nerve agent attacks in the Tokyo subway. Prior to deciding on the production of chemical agents, Aum Shinrikyo had conducted no less then 10 attacks with biological agents, particularly *bacillus anthracis* and botulinum toxin. Aum's biological weapons program was founded in 1990 under the direction of Dr. Seichi Endo, a molecular biologist with a degree in genetic engineering, genetics, and medicine from the prestigious Kyoto University.[51] Even though the group had at its disposal an unrivaled amount of resources equaling nearly $1 billion, a team of no less then 20 graduate level scientists, and state of the art laboratories and equipment, it failed to kill a *single* person with a *biological* weapon. Compare that with al-Qa'ida's project Yogurt, which had the startup budget of only $2–$4,000, was based on an initial survey of literature from the 1920s to 1960s,[52] and its chief "scientist" only had a bachelors degree in biological sciences and a minor in chemistry from Cal State University in Sacramento.[53] What does this comparison tell us about the capacity of JI or al-Qa'ida to kill thousands of people with biological agents?

Conclusion

The likelihood of a JI terrorist attack using chemical or biological weapons needs to be assessed both at the level of motivation and capability. At the motivational level there are at least some segments within the JI that have embraced bin Ladin's ideas, both in the sense of deliberately targeting westerners and the propensity toward launching high-profile, synchronized attacks using suicide bombers, with the objective of inflicting a large number of casualties. This faction of JI can be expected to search for increasingly destructive means in order to keep escalating their struggle. At the same time, given the considerable sacrifices JI has invested (both in terms or resources and personnel) into achieving a sufficient expertise with manufacturing and handling explosives, JI can be expected to make use of suicide truck bombs and not CBW in its future operations. This is especially true in the absence of an expressive fascination with nonconventional weapons that could override the costs associated with these technologies in an otherwise rational cost-benefit calculation. This, ironically, can be seen as a circumstance that is rather unfortunate.

Judging by the manual, the group is nowhere near a noteworthy CBW capability. At best, the group may be able to mount a small scale hydrogen cyanide attack that may succeed in killing a handful of individuals, but even this is doubtful. The manual suggests that JI clearly lacks the knowledge to produce CBW agents in the necessary level of purity, and lacks the knowledge to achieve a reliable weaponization of these materials. Further, JI operatives have demonstrated an extremely low level of improvisational skills, at least with respect to producing explosive materials for their past operations. For instance, both of the potassium chlorate mixtures used in the Bali and Jakarta bombings were relatively inefficient, due to mistakes in the recipe that was blindly followed to the last detail. If the same lack of improvisation and tacit knowledge transpires during the production of CBW agents following the manual discussed above, the process will almost certainly fail to produce usable results.

In conclusion, JI's motivation and capability to use CBW do not overlap, making the prospect of JI successfully using such agents on a large scale a very low probability. And while a small scale attack using very simple chemical mixtures cannot be ruled out completely, it is critical to emphasize that such an attack would represent a regression, as opposed to a progression in terms of the lethality of JI's operations.

Notes

1. Hoffman, Bruce, *Inside Terrorism* (New York: Orion Publishing Co. 1998) p. 205.
2. Sunstar: Bio-weapons traces found in JI hideout Tuesday, October 21, 2003. Internet. Available at: http://www.sunstar.com.ph/static/net/2003/10/21/bio.weapons.traces.found.in.ji.hideout. html (accessed on 12.May 2006).
3. Dolnik Adam, "The Age of Superterrorism" in Gunaratna, Rohan, *Combating Terrorism*, (Singapore: Marshall Cavendish Academic, 2005).
4. Tucker, Jonathan B., *Toxic Terror: Assessing Terrorist Use of Chemical and Biological Weapons*, (Cambridge, Mass: MIT Press, 2000).
5. Jurgensmeyer, Mark, "The Logic of Religious Violence" in David C. Rapoport: *Inside Terrorist Organizations* (London: Frank Cass, 2001) p. 185–190.
6. Hoffman, Bruce, *Inside Terrorism* (New York: Orion Publishing Co. 1998) p. 201.
7. Dolnik, Adam, "All God's Poisons? Re-evaluating the Threat of Religious Terrorism with Regards to CBRN Weapons," in Howard & Sawyer, *Terrorism and Conterterrorism, 2nd Edition,* (McGraw-Hill, 2003).

8. Ibid.

9. For more on this argument see: Dolnik, Adam, All God's Poisons? Re-evaluating the Threat of Religious Terrorism with Regards to CBRN Weapons in Howard, Russ and Sawyer, Reid: *Terrorism and Counterterrorism, 2nd Edition* (McGraw-Hill, 2003).

10. Paddy's Bar did not allow locals to enter at all, the Sari night club had free entry for foreigners, while local would have to pay a ridiculous cover charge to enter.

11. Imam Samudra, *Aku Melawan Teroris*, Jazeera, Solo, 2004.

12. Azhari, Husin, "The Bali Project," 34-page document found on Azhari's computer.

13. Whether this split actually exists is still a topic of some academic debate.

14. Ressa, Maria A., *The Seeds of Terror*, (New York: Free Press, 2003) p. 103.

15. Jabir, whose real name is Enjang Bastaman, was the close friend of Hambali. Both were fellow Afghan veterans who had also been associates in Malaysia.

16. Hidayat Gunadi and Ida Farida, "Bandung Xmas Eve 2000 Bombers Also Used Mobile Phones," *FBIS SEP20021113000117 Jakarta Gatra*, 6 January 2001.

17. Christina Mendez and Bong Fabe, "Police Say a Detained MILF Terrorist Admitted Leading Bombing in Manila in 2000," *FBIS SEP20030530000022 The Philippine Star*, 30 May 2003.

18. Ibid. p. 182.

19. Miller, Wayne, Bali attack delayed a day, mastermind reveals, The Age, July 5 2003.

20. BBC: Bomb wrecks top Jakarta Hotel (August 5, 2003) Internet, available at http://news.bbc.co.uk/2/hi/asia-pacific/3124919.stm.

21. One reviewer of an earlier version of this article suggested the JW Marriott bomb did not malfunction; the steep incline of the driveway absorbed most of the blast, lowering the death toll.

22. BBC: Massive blast at Jakarta Embassy, (September, 2004). Internet, available at http://news.bbc.co.uk/2/hi/asia-pacific/3639922.stm.

23. BBC: Bali bomb attacks claim 26 lives (October 2, 2005) Internet, available at http://news.bbc.co.uk/1/hi/world/asia-pacific/4300274.stm.

24. Interview with Sidney Jones: "The hardliners are called Thoifah Muqatilah". Tempo Magazine October 18–24, 2005.

25. McDowell, Robin, Indonesians ask why fellow Muslims are turning to suicide bombings. Associated Press, December 4, 2005.

26. Atran, Scott, The Emir: An Interview with Abu Bakar Ba'asyir, Alleged Leader of the Southeast Asian Jemaah Islamiyah Organization. Spotlight on Terror, Volume 3, Issue 9 (September 15, 2005) Internet, available at http://jamestown.org/terrorism/news/article.php?articleid=2369782.

27. Dolnik, Adam, *Understanding Terrorist Innovation: Technology, Tactics and Global Trends* (Routledge, forthcoming in 2007).

28. For example the Soviet Union, despite providing regular shipments of AK-47s, RPGs, and latest top-of- the-line night vision equipment to Ahmed Jibril's PFLP-GC, allegedly refused to provide the group with potentially highly destructive items such as the SA-9 Gaskin surface-to-air missiles. (Samuel M. Katz, *Israel versus Jibril*, New York: Paragon House 1993, p. 80–81).

29. An example of this phenomenon is the Abu Nidal Organization, which turned against its former sponsor Libya, following Khaddafi's decision to seize his support for the group's terrorist activities.

30. For instance, in 2001 Sunday Times reporters pretending to be Moroccan businessmen were able to order botulinum toxin from a Czech veterinary hospital culture collection with no questions asked.

31. For more detailed discussion see Croddy, Eric, *Chemical and Biological Warfare: A Comprehensive Survey for the Concerned Citizen* (Springer, 2001).

32. Dolnik, Adam, Die and Let Die: Exploring Links between Suicide Terrorism and Terrorist Use of Chemical, Biological, Radiological, and Nuclear Weapons. *Studies in Conflict and Terrorism* Vol. 26, No.1 (January–February 2003), pp. 17–35.

33. Center for Nonproliferation Studies: *Chronology of Aum Shinrikyo's CBW Activities*, (March 2001), Internet, available at http://cns.miis.edu/pubs/reports/aum_chrn.htm (Accessed on 12/12/02).

34. Following the reviewers' recommendation, the exact technical details were removed from the final version of this paper.

35. Baker, John C., "Jemaah Islamiya" in Jackson, Brian, et al.: *Aptitude for Destruction Volume 2: Case Studies of Organizational Learning in Five Terrorist Groups.* (Santa Monica: RAND 2005) p. 74.

36. Ressa (2002) p. 102.

37. Turnbull, Wayne, *A Tangled Web of Southeast Asian Islamic Terrorism: The Jemaah Islamiyah Terrorist Network.* Monterey Institute of International Studies, Monterey, California, July 31, 2003

38 Ressa (2002) p. 186–187.

39. Wockner, Cindy, Third suicide bomber planned, *The Advertiser*, 23. July 2003.

40. Harsanto, Damar, Reenactment traces bomb assembly, *The Jakarta Post,* December 10, 2003.

41. Harsanto, Damar and Unidjaja, Fabiola Desy, *The Jakarta Post*, 12 August 2003.

42. CBS news: Jakarta Bomber: Qaeda Group Link. August 8, 2003.

43. Baker in Jackson (2005) p. 84.

44. Stratfor: "Indonesia: Missing a Chance at a 'Top' Militant." Stratfor Daily Terrorism Brief 05.01.2006.

45. Dolnik, Adam, *Understanding Terrorist Innovation: Technology, Tactics and Global Trends* (Routledge, forthcoming in 2007).

46. Ibid.

47. Cullison, Alan, Inside al Qaeda's Hard Drive. *Atlantic Monthly.* September 2004.

48. 9–11 Commission Report, p. 151.

49. Australian Broadcasting Corporation: Al Qaeda analyst on cricket terrorist plot claims. (10/10/2006) Full transcript of the interview with Zachary Abuza is available at: http://www.abc.net.au/lateline/content/2006/s1759229.htm (accessed on 12/10/06).

50. Final Report, Document Exploitation of Operation Ultimatum, Task Force Comet (104th Bde of the Philippine Army, 3MBDE of the Philippine Marine Corps, MIG9, ISAFP) Global Pathfinder Database, International Centre for Political Violence and Terrorism Research, Nanyang Technological University, Singapore, October 2006.

51. Miller, Judith, *Germs: Biological Weapons and America's Secret War,* (New York: Touchstone, 2002) p. 160.

52. Cullison, Alan, Inside al Qaeda's Hard Drive. *Atlantic Monthly.* September 2004.

53. Cal State in Sacramento.

Adam Dolnik is the director of Research Development at the Center for Transnational Crime Prevention (CTCP) at the University of Wollongong, Australia. He received a B.A. in political science from the Masaryk University in Brno, Czech Republic, M.A. in international policy studies from the Monterey Institute of International Studies in California, and Ph.D. in strategic studies from the Institute of Defense and Strategic Studies in Singapore.

Rohan Gunaratna is the head of the International Centre for Terrorism and Political Violence Research (ICTPVR) at the Nanyang Technological University, Singapore and senior fellow, The Fletcher School for Law and Diplomacy's Jebsen Centre for Counter Terrorism Studies at the Fletcher School at Tufts University. An internationally recognized terrorism expert, he received his Ph.D. from Saint Andrews University in Scotland.

Lewis A. Dunn

Can al Qaeda Be Deterred from Using Nuclear Weapons?

The terrorist use of a nuclear weapon would be the ultimate al Qaeda outrage.[1] Over the past decade, however, the prevailing assessment about the likelihood of terrorist acquisition and use of chemical, biological, radiological or (specifically) nuclear weapons (CBRN) has been reversed.[2] In the 1990s, most policymakers and analysts were highly skeptical of warnings about a terrorist use of these weapons. Today, it is very widely assumed that acquisition of CBRN by al Qaeda would be rapidly followed by the use of those weapons—that is, employment via the release of a biological or chemical agent, the dispersal of radiological materials, or the detonation of a nuclear explosive. This chapter examines that proposition, and in so doing, seeks to illuminate the conditions and calculations that could shape al Qaeda's posture regarding the employment of CBRN, and highlights the possible contribution of deterrence to the overall U.S. war on terrorism.

Al Qaeda Use of Weapons of Mass Destruction—Is There Even a Question?

It is currently assumed by American officials and others within the defense and foreign policy communities that acquisition of chemical, biological, radiological, or nuclear weapons by al Qaeda would be tantamount to the employment of those weapons. This judgment largely reflects a perception that the overriding goal of Osama bin Laden and the organization's other senior leaders and followers is "to kill us before we kill them." Nuclear weapons and more lethal, contagious biological weapons agents promise more loss of American life than even the death and destruction wrought by the suicide bombers on September 11, 2001. In addition, the proven readiness of al Qaeda members to die for their cause reinforces a judgment that there is little if anything that can be done to deter al Qaeda's leaders and followers from that course. As President George W. Bush noted in his February 11, 2004 address at the National Defense University:

> In the past, enemies of America required massed armies, and great navies, powerful air forces to put our nation, our people, our friends and allies at risk. In the Cold War, Americans lived under the threat of weapons of mass destruction, but believed that deterrents made those weapons a last resort. What has changed in the 21st century is that, in the hands of terrorists, weapons of mass destruction would be a first resort — the preferred means to further their ideology of suicide and random murder.[3]

This belief that acquisition equals employment and the wider consensus it reflects may very well be correct. At a minimum, prudent policymaking demands that officials assume so—and that the U.S. government take all steps to prevent al Qaeda's access to CBRN weapons. But for several reasons beyond taking a "contrarian approach," it may be valuable to pause and assess this prevailing judgment.

First, today's consensus stands in contrast to earlier skepticism about terrorist use of these weapons. That skepticism reflected an assessment that CBRN use would clash with the political and temporal objectives of the terrorist groups in question—from the Irish Republican Army to the Tamil Tigers of Sri Lanka. Second, it is important to reexamine this issue because there are important policy implications *if* under certain conditions acquisition might not necessarily mean employment. Actions to enhance deterrence would take on greater importance, including efforts to shape perceptions within the al Qaeda leadership of the possibility that nuclear or biological weapons use could backfire, alienating the very audience the organization seeks to rally to its side—the wider Islamic community. Third, over the past several decades, many U.S. national security policy blunders have been rooted in prevalent "mindsets" about specific realities. For that reason as well, it is useful to step back and assess contemporary assumptions. Finally, exploring this judgment helps to generate propositions about how Osama bin Laden and his closest associates—or what may be termed the "al Qaeda center—might view the purposes to be served by different types of weapon use, how al Qaeda might undertake these different uses, and the relative usability (under various conditions) of the different types of unconventional weapons.

Four different but complementary approaches are used in this chapter. First, the publicly-available ground truth is examined—that is, the evidence of attempted, aborted, and alleged al Qaeda terrorist attacks as well as in their planning and preparations. Second, this chapter focuses on the personnel make-up of al Qaeda—that is, the different individuals that comprise this organization and *their* readiness to jump to new levels of violence. Third, it assesses the extent to which CBRN use would be consistent with al Qaeda's "operational code"—its established way of conducting the "business" of terrorism. Finally, the chapter examines the consistency of CBRN employment with Osama bin Laden's overall vision of an Islamic revival and restoration from the Gulf to Southeast Asia—and in particular, whether a nuclear detonation would help or hurt realization of that vision.

What's the Ground Truth—Much Smoke, Some Fire?

Publicly-available information shows continuing interest and efforts by Osama bin Laden and al Qaeda to develop or acquire CBRN weaponry. As summarized by Table 1, this information ranges from hard evidence to reports and allegations. There have also been publicly-reported aborted plots or operations entailing the possible use of chemical, biological, or radiological weapons.

Reports and Allegations

Since the late 1990s, there have been continuing reports and allegations of al Qaeda's efforts to purchase nuclear weapons, nuclear weapons materials, biological and chemical weapons, and nuclear waste or other material for use in radiological dispersal devices (RDD). Sometimes, it is alleged that al Qaeda has already successfully purchased or produced CBRN weaponry. In some instances, these reports apparently have been based on leaked assessments of one or another intelligence agency.

Hard Evidence

Materials seized and activities uncovered after the U.S.-led military action against al Qaeda and the Taliban government of Afghanistan provide hard and credible evidence of al Qaeda's interest in acquiring CBRN. Perhaps the most graphic evidence was a videotape obtained by CNN news after the war which showed testing of a poison gas on three dogs.[4] Analysts speculated that the gas was cyanide. Still other evidence demonstrated actual production of biological agents (including ricin and botulinum toxin). Research and experiments (as well as written analyses) for nuclear weapons were also uncovered. Contacts with Pakistani nuclear weapon scientists provided further evidence of this exploration of nuclear weaponry.[5] Officials derived more confirming evidence from the interrogation of al Qaeda detainees (in and outside of Afghanistan) as well as from trial testimony of arrested al Qaeda personnel. However, the evidenced has indicated significant gaps in al Qaeda's CBRN know-how and capabilities.

Table 1

Al Qaeda and CBRN Weaponry—A Partial "Snapshot"

Type/Status	Nuclear	Biological	Chemical	Radiological
Reports & allegations	• Attempted or successful purchase—suitcase bomb (1998, 2001, 2002, 2004) • Attempted purchase—nuclear materials (1998, 2000, 2001) • Claim to Pakistan journalist of nuclear possession by al-Zawahiri (2004)	• Successful purchase—anthrax, plague, other (1997, 1999, 2000, 2001, 2002, 2003) • Training & experiments in Afghanistan, Iraq by Ansar al-Islam (2001, 2002) • Lab in Iraq to produce ricin (2004)	• Attempted or successful purchase—chemical agents (1997, 1998, 1999, 2002, 2003) • Production in Sudan or Afghanistan (1997, 1998, 1999, 2002) • Training in Afghanistan (2001) • Lab in Iraq to produce cyanide (2004)	• Production of Radiological Dispersal Device (2002, 2003, 2004) • Attempted purchase of nuclear waste, radiological materials—Russia, elsewhere (2001, 2002, 2004) • Warnings (2004)
Hard evidence	• Contacts with Pakistani nuclear scientists (2001) • Afghanistan—seized documents (2001, 2002) • Arrests, interrogations, & detainee testimony (1998, 2001, 2002, 2003, 2004)	• Afghanistan—seized training manuals, files, planning documents, labs—ricin, botulinum toxin, overall bio program (2001, 2002) • Arrests, interrogations, & detainee testimony (2002, 2003, 2004)	• Afghanistan—seized training manuals, files, planning documents, experiments on dogs, labs—cyanide, other (2001, 2002) • Arrests, interrogations, & detainee testimony (2002)	• Afghanistan—seized documents (2002) • Arrests, interrogations, & detainee testimony (2002)

(continued)

Type/Status	Nuclear	Biological	Chemical	Radiological
Aborted Plots & Operations		• Ricin, London (2003)	• Cyanide, London Subway (2002) • Rome, U.S. Embassy (2002) • NYC Subway (2002) • Amman, Jordan—unspecified (2004) • London (2004)	• Arrest of Jose Padilla (2002)

This table draws on a wide range of press reporting, as well as on "Chart: Al-Qa'ida's WMD Activities," Center for Nonproliferation Studies, Monterey Institute of International Studies, Updated: May 13, 2005. Dates in parenthesis refer to year of report, usually close in time to when the event occurred.

Aborted Plots or Operations

Several aborted attempts by al Qaeda-linked individuals to use biological or chemical weapons in terrorist attacks are summarized on Table 1. A plot in 2003 to use ricin was disrupted by the British authorities,[6] as was an earlier plot to release cyanide in the London subway. It also has been reported and confirmed by former U.S. officials that a 2003 plan to use hydrogen cyanide gas in New York City subway trains was called off by the al Qaeda leadership (specifically, Ayman al-Zawahari) for unknown reasons.[7] Jordanian authorities also claimed in April 2004 to have disrupted an al Qaeda plot to release a chemical agent in Amman. (However, an al Qaeda released tape recording denied that any such chemical attack had been planned.[8]) And U.S. authorities have stated that Jose Padilla's arrest in 2002 prevented a terrorist attack that would have involved a radiological weapon.

One Initial Bottom Line

Overall, the "ground truth" leaves little doubt of the continuing efforts of Osama bin Laden and al Qaeda's senior leadership to produce or purchase CBRN weaponry or materials, and this bears directly on the question of whether acquisition equals employment. Specifically:

Lethal Chemical, Non-Contagious Biological—Yes but. . .

For employment of either high-lethality but non-contagious biological agents (e.g., ricin) and chemical agents (e.g., cyanide), the aborted plots for the most part support a judgment that acquisition does equal employment. Only effective police work in London, Paris, Rome, and Amman prevented the use of chemical and biological agents. But the apparent decision to abort the cyanide attack on the New York subway suggests that the calculus of al Qaeda's leadership may be somewhat more complicated. (We can only speculate on what led to that decision, but it could have included concern that such use would backfire for some reason.) Moreover, the record also still leaves open, whether the acquisition of *contagious* biological agents (e.g., smallpox) would mean their employment.

Radiological Weapons—Perhaps, but Why Not Yet . . . ?

Both Jose Padilla's arrest in 2002 (who was charged with planning an RDD attack), as well as more recent authoritative warnings of planned radiological attacks,[9] appear to confirm the judgment that acquisition would equal employment. If so, it is somewhat surprising that no RDD terrorist attack has yet occurred, especially becuase radiological source materials are so widely available in medicine and industry. Relatively straightforward means exist to disperse the material using readily available explosives. Though inefficient, even crude dispersal of radioactive materials would trigger considerable public panic and psychological disruption, along with (albeit limited) long-term environmental damage.

However, detonation of a simple RDD would lack one important characteristic from al Qaeda's perspective—that is, the type of "visually pleasing destruction" that has so often characterized its attacks, not the least the September 11th attacks on the World Trade Center and Pentagon. Such dramatic destruction is especially important to al Qaeda if its main audience is not the American public but instead the publics in many Islamic nations around the globe.[10] So viewed, the jury may still be out on whether possession would equal employment of a radiological weapon.[11]

Nuclear Weapons—Means Still Lacking, or Anything Else at Work . . . ?

Given the evidence of interest, it would not be unreasonable to assume that only the lack of means explains why al Qaeda has not used an improvised nuclear weapon. But the absence of aborted plots or operations to use a nuclear weapon—despite the many allegations of al Qaeda's attempts to purchase nuclear weapons or materials—stands in partial contrast to this conclusion. The lack of publicly-known detainee statements or testimony of involvement in preparations for a nuclear attack also may be important. Thus, this mix of reports and allegations suffices to create a presumption that nuclear acquisition would equal employment—but questions persist.

Who Is "al Qaeda"—Do Personnel Types Matter for CBRN Employment?

Turning to the second approach, which focuses on al Qaeda's personnel, there is no single "al Qaeda"—indeed, this organization is far from monolithic. There are also many different individuals tightly or loosely linked to al Qaeda for a variety of reasons. At least for some individuals associated with al Qaeda, their readiness to employ CBRN could be conditional on the perceived personal risks of doing so, and therefore, some deterrence leverage points may exist.

Organizational Fluidity and Personnel Diversity

Al Qaeda's core comprises the remnants and associates of the previously described al Qaeda center, still typified by Osama bin Laden and his deputy Ayman al-Zawahiri, both now presumed to be hiding somewhere on the Pakistan-Afghanistan border. At the same time, other terrorist organizations around the globe are loosely affiliated with the al Qaeda center. They share a basic commitment to an anti-Western jihad and may cooperate tactically with the al Qaeda center (receiving technical, financial, or recruiting support), but are not subject to direct command. Still other isolated terrorist cells and mini-movements take their inspiration from bin Laden's vision of jihad.

Across this network of terrorist entities, the individuals also range widely. Beyond bin Laden and al-Zawahiri, active al Qaeda members appear to fall into the following personnel types: center-level operational coordinators; center-level specialists (e.g., for explosives or communications); field-level operation coordinators; field-level specialists (e.g., surveillance, logistics, explosives); "soldiers and muscle;" and suicide operatives. These types have their counterparts in other terrorist groups that have direct or indirect linkages to the al Qaeda center.

Underlying al Qaeda's active membership, a wider supporting personnel infrastructure exists of fellow travelers, sympathizers, and individuals prepared to look the other way, providing financial, operational, technical, recruiting, and political support. In some instances, these individuals may be either "sleepers" (waiting to be called to action) or "insiders" (able to provide physical or other access to key organizations or targets). Especially with regard to nuclear terrorism, outside technical experts for hire could prove important as well.

Implications for CBRN Employment

Fear of a U.S. or Western response is most unlikely to be a compelling reason for bin Laden, al-Zawahiri, or any of the core operatives in the al Qaeda center to hesitate before using CBRN weapons.[12] This applies, as well, to the field operatives and the suicide operatives, carrying out directions from the center. Not only have the suicide operatives shown little (if any) fear of personnel retribution, but, for the most part, so have the other operatives. Their commitment to the jihadist cause has made the sacrifice of their lives simply a way station to a new life after death. Some field operatives or coordinators apparently have sought to save their own lives rather than dying in a specific suicide attack. However, given the efforts now underway to kill or capture al Qaeda members, it is hard to believe that much more could be done to enhance deterrence specifically of such members' participation in CBRN attacks.

By contrast, fear of retribution could be more compelling for many of those individuals that make up al Qaeda's supporting infrastructure. In other words, perceived risks of helping al Qaeda carry out a CBRN attack could matter significantly for financial supporters, for fellow-travelers providing access to safe houses and surveillance information (and otherwise facilitating a possible nuclear terrorist attack), for senior officials in specific states, and for insiders located in target countries or elsewhere. Fear of discovery and retribution could also be a significant constraint on potential technical experts for hire.

Al Qaeda's Operational Code—Implications for CBRN Employment?

The record of al Qaeda or al Qaeda-linked terrorist attacks since the early 1990s reveals a fairly clear set of preferences, characteristics, or standard operating procedures—or what may be labeled an operational code.[13] It comprises three broad sets of activities associated with executing a terrorist attack—targeting, operational preparations, and attack profile. To answer the primary question addressed in this chapter, a full discussion of this operational code is not needed. However, several important dimensions stand out, particularly the consistencies and inconsistencies in al Qaeda's operational code as it pertains to the use of CBRN weaponry.

CBRN Use and al Qaeda's Operational Code—"Targeting"

Some of the more important features of al Qaeda's operational code related to targeting are summarized in Table 2. Consider some of the consistencies and inconsistencies first for use of nuclear weapons, then for use of biological, chemical, or radiological weapons.

With regard to consistencies—from the failed 1995 "Bojinka" plot to bring down, nearly simultaneously, 12 American aircraft on flights from Asia, through its successful September 11, 2001 attacks to the planned attack on up to a dozen airliners flying from the United Kingdom to the United States—pursuit of spectacular effects has been a consistent characteristic of al Qaeda and the global jihadist movement it inspires.[14] Further, many of its attacks have reflected a desire for graphic destruction that would pulsate across the global mass media. Detonation of a nuclear weapon would meet both conditions. Nuclear use would also almost certainly wreak unprecedented economic damage, another targeting criteria of al Qaeda's operations, especially in recent years. In addition, detonation of a

Table 2

Al Qaeda's Operational Code—Targeting

Category	Some Distinguishing Features
Decision-making	• Multiple levels, from bin Laden-initiated and -directed to lower-level initiated attacks inspired by bin Laden's vision
Criteria for Target Choice	• Top preference for: ⇒ High symbolic impact targets ⇒ Spectacular effects & visually pleasing destruction • Economic damage a more secondary consideration—but may be growing in importance, e.g., with attempts on oil targets • Focused primarily on external audience—not in the targeted country • Finishing the job and persistence, e.g., attempted bombings of airliners in flight
Target Types: People & Organizations	• Sporadic attacks on officials & leaders • Inflicting mass casualties more an exception (World Trade Center) than the rule (embassy and hotel bombings) • Continuing attacks on military units
Target Types: Sites & Structures	• Repeated attacks on public & private buildings • Increasing attacks on religious sites • Increasing attacks on oil-related sites, e.g., refineries
Target Types: Systems & Institutions	• Repeated attacks against air and land transport
Target Protection	• Often but not exclusively "soft", with little inherent protection

stolen nuclear device would provide a highly effective means to attack public and official sites as well as leaders, while overcoming increased security at such sites.

Despite this fit between nuclear use and al Qaeda's targeting, there could be some tension between al Qaeda's targeting code and the levels of death expected from the successful use of a nuclear weapon. The use of an improvised nuclear device could result in many tens of thousands of casualties, while the use of a stolen nuclear weapon could result in hundreds of thousands if not millions dead. The attacks of 9/11 killed several thousand persons while the aborted Bojinka and London airline plots could have led to comparable loss of life. This potential discrepancy between the very high number of casualties that could result from a nuclear detonation (even compared to the claims of Ramzi Yusuf that he wanted to kill 50,000 people in the first attack on the World Trade Center) and al Qaeda's past attacks may only reflect technical limitations. That is, limited casualties may only demonstrate the difficulty but not impossibility of inflicting mass casualties using only traditional kinetic means.

In turn, it is suggestive that in the specific instances in which al Qaeda operatives so far have sought to use biological agents, the agent chosen—ricin—does not lend itself to inflicting mass casualties. By contrast, though alleged since the late 1990s to already possess the highly lethal biological agent anthrax, al Qaeda has yet to claim an attack involving the release of this agent.[15] Al Qaeda may simply be awaiting the right moment to use anthrax, or it may believe it still lacks the technical capability to disseminate anthrax effectively; or perhaps, killing several hundreds of thousands of persons may not be seen at this point in time to serve its overall objectives. Further, Al Qaeda operatives also have denied the charges by Jordanian officials that it was planning to mount a chemical attack in Amman that could have killed upwards of 30,000 Jordanian civilians. Whatever the truth, the fact is that al Qaeda perceived a need to make such a denial.[16] Further, as noted above, Ayman al-Zawahiri is reported to have aborted attacking New York City subways with cyanide, for reasons that remain unexplained. Thus, without making too much of this possibility, is it conceivable that there could be some concerns about the level of civilian deaths expected to be involved with nuclear violence?

On the one hand, bin Laden's own statements have justified and accepted the loss of life among innocent civilian bystanders that resulted from past al Qaeda attacks. Moreover, a May 2003 fatwa by a cleric associated with al Qaeda, Nasir bin Hamd al-Fahd—"A Treatise on the Legal Status of Using Weapons of Mass Destruction against Infidels"—argued for the permissibility of using such weapons. More specifically, according to this treatise, use of WMD would be a legitimate means of retaliation for "Muslims [already] killed directly or indirectly by their weapons," a number of deaths that bin Hamd al-Fahd puts at "nearly ten million."[17] In addition, this fatwa argues that according to Islamic law, an argument of necessity also legitimizes use of WMD if ". . . the evil of the infidels can be repelled only by attacking them at night with weapons of mass destruction. . . ."[18] Further, this treatise concludes by arguing against what it terms three "specious arguments" against the use of WMD—specifically, that WMD is proscribed by "the ban on killing women and children," by "the ban on sowing corruption in the land," and by the fact "that these weapons will kill some Muslims." For each, necessity is again seen to be an overriding justification for WMD use.

On the other hand, the very fact that it was thought necessary to issue that fatwa appears to indicate some sensitivity to the types of "specious arguments" it addresses against the use of weapons intended to inflict mass casualties on civilians. (The criticism by Ayman al-Zawahiri of Abu Musab Zarqawai's indiscriminate violence in Iraq as well as the calling off of the cyanide attack on the NYC subway also suggests concern over how actions will be perceived by the broader Muslim community.) Moreover, the argument of the fatwa is that when necessary or required, WMD use is legitimate and permissible. However, the possibility raised here of lingering concerns among al Qaeda's leadership about CBRN use need not reflect any moral uneasiness or questions about the "legitimacy" of using these weapons in the global *jihad*. Rather, that possibility rests on "self-interested calculations" over whether the use of CBRN would be seen as necessary and desirable to achieve the organization's goals. This possibility calls for further exploration in light of the criteria for targeting implicit in al Qaeda's past attacks.

Bin Laden's principal audience is not only the government and population of the targeted country but the broader Islamic community. For some, the use of a nuclear weapon would almost certainly be welcomed as part of the ongoing defensive jihad against the West. Muslims around the world could also be awed by bin Laden's capability to inflict such destruction. But the use of nuclear weapons could provoke revulsion among the very communities that bin Laden is seeking to rally to his restored Muslim Caliphate.[19] Thus, al Qaeda's concerns over the impact of attacks on the broader Islamic audience could raise questions about the desirability of mass killing on the nuclear violence level. Put most starkly, the use of a nuclear weapon could be regarded as fully permissible in principle, but in practice a nuclear attack could be seen as not contributing to the achievement of al Qaeda's goals.

In contrast to a nuclear attack, biological, chemical, or radiological weapons do not promise the spectacular and graphic destruction so characteristic of the targeting dimension of al Qaeda's operational code. A biological weapons attack would look similar—except in scale—to a major flu outbreak. While requiring the detonation of conventional explosives, an RDD would offer little additional visual destructiveness than a more straightforward car bomb. Further, when striking the typical al Qaeda target types (officials and leaders, public and private buildings, military personnel and units, or air and land transport) highlighted in Table 2, biological, chemical and radiological weaponry may be a less effective means as well as more technically demanding. In each of these ways, therefore, the use of these weapons would be inconsistent with past targeting practices.

However, al Qaeda's targeting pattern of "finishing the job" has important implications for the possibility of a future attack using these weapons. That pattern was highlighted most dramatically in the organization's successful September 11th attack, which followed its unsuccessful 1993 attack against the World Trade Center. At least from this perspective, either al Qaeda's leadership or an affiliated cell could well try again to use ricin to attack either individuals or mass transit systems.

CBRN Use and al Qaeda's Operational Code—"Operational Preparations"

Several dimensions of al Qaeda's past pattern of operational preparations, summarized by Table 3, also have implications, perhaps less for the question of whether acquisition would equal use than for the possible modalities of CBRN weapons possession. This includes: the personnel-operational mix, the duration of preparations, and the patterns for acquisition of means.

Table 3

Al Qaeda's Operational Code—Operational Preparations

Category	Some Distinguishing Features
Recruitment Patterns	• Reliance on experience in Afghan training camps had dominated; recently, recruitment of disaffected individuals in Western Europe
Personnel Characteristics	• Reliance on Arab nationals increasingly supplemented by reliance on= non-Arab nationals, Western converts to Islam, and disaffected second-generation Muslim immigrants in Western countries
	• Reliance on men for operations
	• Limited use of women, mostly for cover & logistics
Operational Mix	• Field leadership distinct from suicide operatives
	• Some operational specialization, e.g., attacks on ships
	• Some technical specialization, e.g., logistics, weaponeers
	• Some senior and field leaders with technical backgrounds, e.g., engineering
	• Some evidence of "sleepers"
	• Some evidence of "insiders"
Financing	• Multiple sources & financial flows, including use of legitimate businesses and charities
Training, Rehearsal, & Surveillance	• Still drawing on operatives with Afghan camp backgrounds
	• Reliance on one-on-one training, including from al Qaeda center but also from non-affiliated experts
	• Surveillance often long in advance of attack
	• Impact of Iraq insurgency as training ground uncertain, e.g., for attacks on oil infrastructure, for use of explosives
Duration of Preparations	• 1–2 years was not atypical for al Qaeda center, may remain so
	• 3–5 years preparations not precluded
Acquisition of Means	• Theft much less prevalent than production (e.g., bombs) or purchase (materials and components, less so weapons)

Overall, al Qaeda's *personnel-operational mix,* leans very heavily toward the traditional terrorist activities of using conventional means to blow things up and kill people. Enraged Muslim young men, quite a few of whom have experience either in defeating the Soviet Union in Afghanistan or in the ensuing period of Taliban-al Qaeda cohabitation, have carried out several attacks. Some technical specialization is also evident in past attacks, most often in explosives and logistics. In addition, some senior and field leaders have technical backgrounds—for example, in civil and other engineering specialties, medicine, agricultural operations, and so on. As noted above, in the Afghan training camps, research and experimentation in nuclear, biological, and chemical weapons production were underway.[20] Western citizens—sometimes converts to Islam, sometimes children of immigrants from Islamic countries—have become more apparent in operations since the transformation of counter-terrorist actions after 9/11. Officials have also encountered some sleeper cells, as well as possible "fellow-traveling" insiders.[21]

Given the strong bias in this personnel-operational mix toward kinetic action, *outside technical assistance* could be an important input to al Qaeda's successful transition to more sophisticated CBRN terrorism. For example, at one end of the spectrum, outside technical assistance could be essential to overcoming internal control mechanisms on a stolen Russian nuclear weapon or to aerosolize anthrax effectively. At the other end of the spectrum, production of ricin and its dissemination via relatively unsophisticated methods already appears to have been within reach.

Al Qaeda's operational preparations have frequently taken many years. This *long duration of preparations* would be consistent with patient, multi-year efforts to carry out an eventual nuclear terrorist attack. But how the al Qaeda center would orchestrate a nuclear attack is uncertain. Would al Qaeda's leadership only seek to purchase or steal a nuclear weapon once it had done all of the planning and put in place all of the subsidiary operational elements for that weapon's use? In that case, possession would truly equal employment. Alternatively, would the organization always be on the lookout for successful acquisition, regardless of any specific plans or assets in place for its use?[22]

Finally, the pattern of past preparations again highlights the long-term horizon of al Qaeda's jihad against the West. But given that lengthy timeline, pressures to detonate a nuclear weapon as soon as possible could be considerably less. Instead, Osama bin Laden would almost certainly think in terms of how best to leverage possession of a nuclear weapon to serve the longer-term goal of an Islamic revival and restoration. Pursuit of that goal might be served by inflicting nuclear death and destruction on the United States. But there could be other ways, as discussed below, in which possession of a nuclear weapon—but not its employment—might be better suited to serve the longer-term goal.

Concerning the *acquisition of CBRN means,* U.S. and other officials and analysts have focused most of their attention on steps to make it harder for al Qaeda or any terrorist organization to steal or purchase CBRN weapons, agents, or directly usable materials. Nonetheless, the outlying possibility should not be excluded that the al Qaeda center could set up its own nuclear production complex. This would require a safe location; overcoming obstacles to purchase or theft; access to turn-key components and expertise, typified by the types of activities conducted by the A.Q. Khan nuclear supply network;[23] a long-time horizon; and, if the experience of other nuclear weapon programs is any indication, one or two individuals with some technical expertise and administrative competence to drive the program along. Increasingly, it is no longer unthinkable to assume that this set of conditions could exist. Assuming the production (instead of the purchase or theft) of a nuclear weapon, al Qaeda could approach successful acquisition not as a terrorist organization might (that is, by using that weapon immediately) but as a state would (that is, by thinking in terms of the political gains to be achieved vis-à-vis nuclear possession).

CBRN Use and al Qaeda's Operational Code—"Attack Profile"

The attack profile of past strikes, as summarized by Table 4, comprises the baseline for future al Qaeda operations. Three dimensions offer particularly useful insight: the scope and complexity of past attacks, repeated recourse to bombs of different sorts, and a persistence of efforts.

Table 4

Al Qaeda's Operational Code—Attack Profile

Category	Some Distinguishing Features
Scope & Complexity of Attack	• Many times a single target
	• But simultaneous attacks on several targets in one country or in one city increasingly prevalent
	• Simultaneous attacks on several targets within a region still an exception
	• No simultaneous attacks yet on several targets around the globe
Personnel Levels	• Range from single individuals to small teams (~5–7) to paramilitary units (201)
Conventional Kinetic Means of Attack	• Explosives dominate—car bombs, boat bombs, concealed bombs repeatedly used
	• Suicide delivery but not only method
	• Long interest prior to 9–11 in use of aircraft as bombs
	• Continuing interest in surface-to-air missiles (SAMs)
Non-Kinetic Means of Attack	• Evidence of interest in cyber-attack but no actions
Unconventional Means of Attack	• Clear evidence of readiness to use high-lethality, low dissemination bio (ricin)
	• Evidence of experimentation with chemical agents in Afghanistan
	• Credible reports of aborted chemical attacks
	• Reports of aborted RDD attack plans
	• Long-term interest in nuclear weapons

In scope and complexity, al Qaeda's early attack profile included mainly isolated attacks on single targets. However, in recent years this attack profile increasingly appears to involve *simultaneous attacks on multiple targets*. From the 1998 attacks on two U.S. embassies in East Africa to the April, 2004 Madrid train bombings and the 2005 London transit bombings, multiple attacks in at least one country have increasingly become the norm.[24] Simultaneous attacks increase the level of destruction and terror—and they demonstrate operational sophistication to members, potential recruits, other outsiders, and opponents. After the defeat of the Taliban in Afghanistan, multiple attacks also demonstrated that al Qaeda and its affiliates are still in operation.

A single use of CBRN weapons—including an attack carried out by affiliated organizations or individuals—would be consistent with al Qaeda's past experience with isolated attacks. It also would fit al Qaeda's operational code to execute attacks with dramatic impact. Al Qaeda might even prepare a single attack with the intent of delaying it rather than simply making use of whatever capability it had acquired as soon as it had done so. Multiple CBRN attacks in the United States—using RDDs, for example—would in principle not be difficult and would add to the psychological impact. Multiple uses of chemical or biological weapons would have a particularly powerful force multiplier effect. Thus, the fact that no single attack has yet occurred may simply indicate that preparations for a more spectacular multi-attack effort are underway.

Assuming the acquisition of a nuclear weapon, the al Qaeda center (as a most likely acquiring group) could again face a choice between using its first nuclear weapon right away or waiting. Many of the same considerations that appear to have led to a growing emphasis on multiple attacks—such as an increased effect, demonstration of technical sophistication, or potential impact on the target and observing audiences—would suggest waiting. Furthermore, multiple detonations would signal even more powerfully, "we're back." On the other hand, procurement constraints (only one weapon available or likely to be available) and operational risks (increased risk of detection and disruption) could force a mentality of "get it and use it."

Turning to means, what stands out most is al Qaeda's *preference for bombs of all kinds* in executing its attacks—car bombs, boat bombs, concealed bombs, aircraft as bombs, and human bombs. From this perspective, the use of chemical, biological, and radiological weapons would be inconsistent with this aspect of its operational code. By contrast, the use of a nuclear weapon would be very consistent with this proven al Qaeda preference for bombs.

A final aspect of al Qaeda's attack profile—and indeed, its overall operational code—is *persistence in doing what it knows and does well*. Its recurrent reliance on bombs exemplifies that feature. Similarly, its choice of targets also reflects a tried and true—even if very diverse—set of targets over the years. Persistence has not meant stagnation. Al Qaeda's second attack on the World Trade Center showed an ability to learn from its initial failure and to find and adopt a new, more effective operational approach—one which entailed the use of aircraft as bombs.

By contrast, the use of CBRN weapons would entail trying something new—switching to a new, unproven, and untested means of attack. This does not mean that al Qaeda center or its affiliates would not take that step, but it might do so at first in a more limited and constrained manner—as reflected in the aborted plots to use ricin. This preference for the tried and true also could demand close scrutiny of the potential risks and benefits of shifting to CBRN attacks (and the comparative advantage in terms of achieving the organization's goals).[25] Finally, this preference could direct al Qaeda's leadership to think carefully about the best way to leverage nuclear weapon acquisition to serve their overall goals in the long-term struggle.

Al Qaeda's Operational Code and Use of CBRN—Is there a Bottom Line?

There are consistencies and inconsistencies, as summarized by Table 5, between the different elements of al Qaeda's operational code and the use of nuclear, biological, chemical, or radiological weapons. At the very least, this conclusion justifies continued exploration of the proposition that acquisition of nuclear weapons need not equal their use. Equally as important are some important uncertainties, such as the reaction of the wider Islamic audience to the death and destruction that would be caused by a nuclear weapon. Would a nuclear attack serve Osama bin Laden's over-arching goal of rallying the faithful to a new Muslim Caliphate? This last question may be the most critical issue of all.

Table 5

Al Qaeda's Operational Code and Does NBC or R Acquisition Equal Use?

	Consistent with Acquisition = Use	Inconsistent with Acquisition = Use	Uncertainties & Other Implications:
Targeting	• Nuclear use as spectacular attack, with graphic destruction	• Past attacks (excepting WTC as well as aborted plans to blow up airliners) not caused at mass casualties— even then not comparable to nuclear use	• Reaction of external audience in Islamic world to large-scale nuclear or biological weapons destruction—if seen as excessive undercuts goal of rallying the Muslim world
	• Nuclear weapon, high-coverage, high-lethality bio offers orders of magnitude more fatalities than even WTC		
		• Constrained use in aborted ricin plots	
	• Finishing the job suggests continued efforts at Ricin use, chemical use	• Bio, chem, RDD do not offer spectacular, graphic destruction	
Operational Preparations	• Long duration of preparations + allegations-reports suggests use could be only matter of time	• Traditional personnel-operational mix more in line with "kinetic attacks"	• Technical expertise to disable nuclear weapon control means
		• Taking long view of struggle, no rush to use nuclear weapon (even assuming acquisition)	• Importance of insider assistance for nuclear, aerosolized bio
			• At what point in attack cycle, seek to procure nuclear weapon—early, late

	Consistent with Acquisition = Use	Inconsistent with Acquisition = Use	Uncertainties & Other Implications:
		• "State-like" behavior implied by nuclear production opens up alternatives to rapid use once acquired	• Though nuclear theft or purchase most likely pathway, production is a wild card
Attack Profile	• Preference for bombs— nuclear weapon simply bigger bomb	• Logic behind multiple attacks suggests no rush to use nuclear weapons	• Could simultaneous NBC or R attacks occur
	• As al Qaeda affiliates take on prominence, lower-level initiative more likely in using chemical or bio agents	• Persistence in doing what knows & does well—or for lower levels, following past successes	• Campaigns of use of biological, chemical, or radiological weapons

Bin Laden, a Restored Islamic Caliphate, and a Nuclear Blackmail-Deterrence Strategy

The likelihood that Osama bin Laden is himself a factor in the debate over nuclear weapon use provides a final perspective. Bin Laden's statements about nuclear weapons (and defensive jihad), a look at his goals, and "state-like" action by al Qaeda provide useful points of initial inquiry. From all three points of view, bin Laden and his immediate lieutenants might—under some conditions—regard nuclear weapons as "too valuable to detonate."[26] Instead, possession of those weapons could offer a new means of blackmail and deterrence—or use as political instruments of power.

"A Religious Duty"

Bin Laden's pronouncements on the *acquisition* of NBC weapons are very straightforward. Responding to a question, he stated in a 1998 interview that:

> [to] seek to possess the weapons that would counter those of the infidels is a religious duty. ... It would be a sin for Muslims not to try to possess the weapons that would prevent the infidels from inflicting harm on Muslims. But how we would use these weapons if we possess them is up to us.[27]

Bin Laden leaves open the question of how such weapons would be used to prevent "harm on Muslims." Elsewhere, bin Laden has talked of "punishing [enemies such as world Christianity, Zionist Jewry, and the United States, Britain, and Israel] using the same means as it is pursuing us with."[28] Moreover, as discussed earlier, the May 2003 "Treatise on the Legal Status of Using Weapons of Mass Destruction Against Infidels" argued that use of these weapons was permissible in retaliation or if necessary to defeat the Infidels. These statements suggest a readiness to use CBRN weaponry as soon as bin Laden had acquired it.

From another perspective, the emphasis on using these weapons to prevent harm as well as to inflict punishment-in-kind raises the possibility that nuclear weapons could be used instead as a deterrent. In that regard, prior to Operation *Enduring Freedom* in Afghanistan, bin Laden stated in an interview with a Pakistani journalist: "I wish to declare that if America used chemical or nuclear weapons against us, then we may retort with chemical and nuclear weapons. We have the weapons as a deterrent."[29] In retrospect, this claim was bravado or disinformation. But it also reflects a possible attempt to leverage uncertainty about al Qaeda's CBRN capabilities for deterrence. In turn, such "deterrent use" would be fully consistent with the May, 2003 "Treatise."

Nuclear Use—and the New Caliphate

One of Osama bin Laden's goals is to wage a "defensive jihad" to expel the United States and the modern "crusaders" from the Arabian Peninsula and the Holy Places in Jerusalem. Another of bin Laden's goals is to force Israel to withdrawal from Palestinian territory, if not the complete destruction of Israel itself. Bin Laden is also seeking to rally the Islamic faithful and to galvanize an Islamic revival that will restore the faith, right living, and ultimately, power of Islam at its zenith. So viewed, bin Laden's ultimate goal is to recreate the Islamic Caliphate combining religious, social, economic, and political power in a great sweep across the Islamic crescent from Saudi Arabia to Southeast Asia.[30] For bin Laden, the use of a nuclear weapon against the United States could be seen both to support and to undermine the pursuit of these goals. Nuclear possession but non-use also could open up new options.

On the one hand, *immediate detonation* of a nuclear weapon in a major American city could be seen as a means to inflict an even more damaging blow to the U.S. polity, economy, and society. In that regard, it would differ significantly from the use of chemical, radiological, and probably non-contagious biological weapons, whose direct (if not psychological) effects could be more readily contained. A successful nuclear attack also could divert U.S. energies to recovery, thereby disrupting counter-terrorist actions. This might especially be the case in the event of an attack against Washington, D.C. A nuclear attack could be seen as the pinnacle of "visually pleasing destruction" and thus, as an even more potent means than the 9/11 attacks to rally the Islamic "street" and to demonstrate Islamic power. Further, as mentioned previously, the May 2003 "Treatise" argues that nuclear use is permissible if regarded as a necessary means to pursue *jihad*.

On the other hand, *other longer-term considerations could well outweigh these immediate perceived payoffs of nuclear weapon detonation.* Almost certainly, global anti-terrorist cooperation would be reinvigorated and intensified. Short-term disruption and diversion of U.S. efforts quite probably would give way to intense mobilization of U.S. energies, resources, and public support for a truly no-holds barred approach. Very large-scale loss of life among innocent civilians, including women and children, also could trigger a backlash among those Muslim faithful whose adherence is needed for Islamic revival and restoration. This latter possibility may be of most concern despite the fact that bin Laden has repeatedly justified killing innocent non-Muslim civilians as well as killing innocent Muslim bystanders (either on the grounds of their collaboration with the United States or of the larger Islamic cause). Indeed, the very need to make public statements justifying such losses of life—and the May 2003 "Treatise" to address the permissibility of use of WMD under Islamic law—suggests concern that excessive taking of innocent lives could repulse thse Islamic faithful.[31]

Perhaps even most important, *possession but non-employment of nuclear weapons* would increase significantly bin Laden's options to pursue a restored Caliphate. Assuming that the realization of this goal will ultimately require al Qaeda to seize power in at least one Islamic state, nuclear possession could be seen as a means of deterring military action by the United States and other countries—after such a seizure of power. Possession but non-employment of nuclear weapons could rally the Islamic faithful without running the risk of backlash. Bin Laden could also leverage possession to blackmail other countries in order to undermine their global anti-terrorist actions.

Successful reliance on nuclear weapons as a means of deterrence, rallying support, and blackmail would require bin Laden to demonstrate convincingly actual possession of nuclear weaponry, as well as a capability and will to employ them. One way to do so would be to carry out an initial nuclear attack. To repeat, there are significant risks of doing so if bin Laden's goal is not simply to kill Americans. Other means exist to demonstrate possession—from inviting scientists and media to confirm possession, to releasing technical, security, and other unique data in the case of a stolen warhead.

Bin Laden, al Qaeda, and "State-like" Behavior

Possession, non-employment, and use as a means of deterrence and blackmail would be consistent with a continuing strain of state-like behavior on the part of bin Laden and the al Qaeda center. Indeed, with its various committees and sub-entities as well as its secure base and network of associated organizations, al Qaeda—prior to the American invasion of Afghanistan—had already adopted some state-like characteristics. Each of bin Laden's major pronouncements in 2004 confirms the al Qaeda center's view of itself as a state-in-progress.

Specifically, shortly after the March 11, 2004 bombings of commuter trains in Madrid, the Arabic news network *al-Arabiya* obtained and broadcasted a new bin Laden tape which rejected the label of "terrorism" and returned to the argument that al Qaeda's actions are a "reaction to your own acts. . . ." In turn, bin Laden went on to state:

> I also offer a reconciliation initiative to them [the European peoples], whose essence is our commitment to stopping operations against every country that commits itself to not attacking Muslims or interfering in their affairs—including the U.S. conspiracy on the greater Muslim world.[32]

Bin Laden's November 1, 2004 tape again struck this note. Most of that speech consisted of a long explanation and justification of the September 11, 2001 attacks as being rooted in the Israeli occupation of Lebanon:

> And as I looked at those demolished towers in Lebanon, it entered my mind that we should punish the oppressor in kind and that we should destroy towers in America in order that they taste some of what we tasted and that they be deterred from killing our women and children.

Bin Laden concludes by asserting "[y]our security is in your own hands. And every state that doesn't play with our security has automatically guaranteed its own security."[33] This theme has persisted in periodic al Qaeda statements.

Any one these statements and tapes could be written off as the egocentric ramblings of a religious fanatic. But they also reflect a well-honed capability to appeal to a wider Islamic audience, providing both a statement of purpose and a call to further action. In turn, those statements are part of bin Laden's own continuing psychological campaign to divide the anti-terrorist coalition and undermine public support not only for the U.S.-led war in Iraq, but the wider global actions to defeat al Qaeda linked terrorism. In both the April and November, 2004 statements, bin Laden sets out a clear deterrent message: "[y]our security is in your own hands." It would be only a short step from that implicit threat of unspecified future destruction to a more explicit use of nuclear weapons as instruments of blackmail and deterrence. By taking that step (and assuming possession but not immediate employment of a nuclear weapon), bin Laden could hope to regain sanctuary status or protect that status by deterring direct attack, to undermine public and official resolve, to rally supporters and encourage his vision of Islamic revival, and ultimately to make more possible the emergence of a restored Muslim Caliphate.

Bin Laden, al Qaeda, and CBRN Weapons—Some Implications for U.S. Posture and Policy

Prudence demands that U.S. policy and posture assume that once in possession, Osama bin Laden and al Qaeda would be fully prepared to use nuclear, biological, chemical, or radiological weapons. Credible reports of al Qaeda's efforts to acquire such weapons, statements by bin Laden and other senior leaders, and past failed attempts to use chemical and non-contagious biological weapons all support that assumption. The United States and other countries need to act accordingly—from intensified actions to destroy al Qaeda, through enhanced international cooperation to block terrorist access to CBRN weaponry, to strengthened capabilities to contain the consequences of a terrorist CBRN attack.

However, the preceding analysis also suggests three other complementary lines of U.S. response, especially to al Qaeda's successful acquisition of nuclear weapons. First, we must pursue concerted actions to work potential deterrence leverage points in order to make acquisition of any form of CBRN weaponry more difficult. Second, actions to enhance "self-deterrence," at least on the part of bin Laden, are needed. And third, we must be prepared to counter attempted nuclear blackmail as well as deterrence by bin Laden.

Deterrence Leverage Points

Three potential deterrence leverage points stand out from the preceding discussion: technical assistance from black marketeers as well as from individuals with insider access; funding and logistics support from al Qaeda fellow-travelers; and official or governmental direct or indirect support for al Qaeda's acquisition of CBRN weaponry.

To begin with, the United States can continue pressing other countries to put in place necessary national controls, penalties, and enforcement mechanisms to heighten the risk of detection and punishment of individuals providing technical assistance, financial support, or logistics to al Qaeda or other terrorist groups. United Nations Security Council Resolution (UNSC) 1540 provides a foundation to do so, by declaring that "All states . . . shall adopt and enforce effective laws which prohibit any non-State actor to manufacture, acquire, possess, develop, transport, transfer or use nuclear, chemical or biological weapons and their means of delivery."[34]

Further, public statements by the United States and other countries should emphasize the potential risks to individuals of providing such assistance as well as the commitment to hold individuals accountable for doing so. Public diplomacy and information operations could be complemented by covert and clandestine operations against individual conduits, operations that if successful could then be leaked after the fact to have a continuing deterrent impact.

The successful U.S. operation against the Taliban regime and al Qaeda in Operation Enduring Freedom sent a strong signal to other governments about the risks of supporting or harboring al Qaeda. By contrast, the continuing insurgency after the overthrow of Saddam Hussein—and an expectation that the United States would not soon take comparable military action again—may well have weakened that signal. Regardless, part of U.S. strategy should continue to focus on deterring governments from supporting the acquisition of CBRN weapons by al Qaeda—or, for that matter, any terrorist group. Here, too, UNSC 1540 offers support by its statement that *"All States shall refrain from providing any form of support to non-State actors that attempt to develop, acquire, manufacture, possess, transport, transfer or use nuclear, chemical or biological weapons or their means of delivery."*[35]

The United States and its friends and allies, as well as follow-on Security Council resolutions, should seek to strengthen the international consensus that support for CBRN terrorism is unacceptable to the civilized world. For its part, the United States should explicitly make clear its readiness—with broad international support if possible, but without that support if needed—*to hold accountable any leaders linked to al Qaeda's or any other terrorist group's use of CBRN weapons.* The overall impact of convincing other countries of the risks of assistance would depend ultimately on the role of state support for terrorist acquisition and use of CBRN weapons. Suffice it to suggest that in some instances outside support could well be the critical distinguishing feature between a failed or ineffective terrorist attack with CBRN and a successful one.

Heightening bin Laden's "Self-Deterrence"

The United States should also take steps aimed at influencing the assessment of bin Laden and the al Qaeda center of whether nuclear employment would help or hurt their longer-term goals of a global Islamic revival and restoration of the Islamic Caliphate. In particular, declarations from a broad spectrum of Islamic clerics, leaders, and organizations condemning indiscriminate violence and the taking of innocent civilian lives would be one element. In addition, moderate clerics should be encouraged to refute the May, 2003 bin Hamd al-Fahd "Treatise." A potential terrorist act involving use of chemical or biological weapons must be condemned by all religions.

Such declarations condemning mass violence and refuting the argument that the use of WMD is a permissible means of *jihad* would reinforce any concerns among the al Qaeda center that employment of a nuclear weapon would serve not to rally Islamic publics but to repulse them. The impact on bin Laden and his closest lieutenants of these declarations is uncertain. Bin Laden has repeatedly argued that the taking of innocent Western civilian lives is a legitimate response to the taking of innocent Muslim civilian lives. He has also publicly justified the loss of life of innocent Muslims during al Qaeda's attacks. Nonetheless, that bin Laden personally thought it necessary to provide these justifications—and that he may have been the animating force behind the 2003 fatwa—indicates a concern that some members of the global Islamic community could be turned off by al Qaeda's excessive killing. In any case, there would be few if any drawbacks to eliciting such condemnations of mass violence.

Countering a Bin Laden Nuclear Blackmail-Deterrence Strategy

Assuming bin Laden and the al Qaeda center might seek to use possession of one or more nuclear weapons as a means of blackmail and deterrence, it is none too soon to begin thinking through how bin Laden might implement such a strategy operationally—and ways to counter it. Issues would range from how bin Laden would prove possession of nuclear weapons to what types of threats might be made and in what manner. Existing U.S. capabilities to evaluate the credibility of nuclear weapon designs and threats need to be assessed against this particular bin Laden threat. Officials also need to identify and assess options for U.S. counter-deterrence strategies. Some key issues include what information to make public and when, how to surge detection and defenses, what private posture to adopt, and how to respond in the absence (unlike state deterrence) of a known "return address." A G-8 or wider consensus not to concede to nuclear blackmail would undercut a nuclear blackmail strategy and should be pursued as well. But in that case, bin Laden's incentive to employ a nuclear weapon rather than use it as blackmail or deterrence could paradoxically be heightened.

A Concluding Thought

No one will be surprised if Osama bin Laden and his al Qaeda associates gain possession of a nuclear weapon and employ it to wreak grave damage on the United States. By contrast, many officials and observers would likely be very surprised if bin Laden and al Qaeda were to exploit possession of nuclear weapons as a means of deterrence or blackmail—whether to regain a secure sanctuary or head off military action to reverse seizure of power in an Islamic state, to undermine the counter-terrorist coalition, or by acting in a state-like manner to further the goal of an Islamic revival and restoration across many regions. However, Osama bin Laden and his closest lieutenants have repeatedly demonstrated a capability to act in unexpected and surprising ways, the attacks of September 11, 2001 being but one of many examples. For that reason alone, it would be ill-advised to reject out of hand the possibility that for Osama bin Laden nuclear weapons could be too valuable to detonate.

Notes

1. This chapter originally appeared in 2005 in the monograph series of the Center for the Study of WMD of the U.S. National Defense University. The author thanks the NDU Center for its support of this analysis and for its permission to reprint it here. Some updates have been made but the chapter's argument remains essentially unchanged.
2. This chapter does not use the phrase "weapons of mass destruction, or WMD." That term melds together very different types of weapons capable of inflicting mass casualties and destruction. But those weapons differ in many respects—ease of acquisition, level of destructiveness, potential utility for purposes other than inflicting death and destruction, and overall "gestalt." Instead, the chapter will refer to nuclear, biological, chemical, or radiological agents, materials, or weapons, or NBC/R. It also will disaggregate its discussion of these different weapons, even while focusing most attention on the most destructive weapons—nuclear weapons. Its use of NBC/R rather than the currently in vogue CBRN is intended to highlight the chapter's primary focus on nuclear weapons as well as the fact that these weapons are the most destructive.

3. Remarks by the President on Weapons of Mass Destruction, Fort Lesley J. McNair—National Defense University, Washington, D.C., February 11, 2004.

4. "Tapes shed new light on bin Laden's network", from Nic Robertson, CNN.com, August 19, 2002; "Disturbing scenes of death show capability with chemical gas," from Nic Roberstson, CNN.com, August 19, 2002.

5. For more on this, please see the chapter by David Albright and Cory Hinderstein on the AQ Khan network in this volume.

6. See the chapter by Bruce Hoffman on the London ricin plot in this volume.

7. "Report: Al Qaeda planned N.Y. subway attack", CNN.com, June 18, 2006.

8. "Al Qaeda denies Jordan WMD plot," BBC News World Edition, 30 April 2004.

9. "Concerns Grow over Possible 'Dirty Bomb' Attack," Global Security Newswire, May 10, 2004.

10. My colleague Jeff Cooper first highlighted for me both the importance of what he labeled "visually pleasing destruction" and the fact that for al Qaeda there is an important difference between its target and its audience.

11. There may have been successfully aborted plots to detonate a RDD not made public. Even so, given the interest and relative ease, it still is somewhat surprising that no successful attack has yet taken place.

12. This still leaves open the question, discussed below, of whether there are any other considerations that could lead bin Laden to decide not to detonate a nuclear weapon—even once in possession of one.

13. This assessment is summarized in Lewis A. Dunn, "Terrorist Adaptation—a Framework and Some al Qaeda Possibilities," Briefing, March, 2004.

14. For a detailed analysis of this plot, please see Rohan Gunaratna, "Al Qaeda's Lose and Learn Doctrine: The Trajectory from Oplan Bojinka to 9/11," in *Teaching Terror: Strategic and Tactical Learning in the Terrorist World,* edited by James JF Forest (Lanham, MD: Rowman & Littlefield, 2006), p, 171–187. The Bojinka Plot was uncovered by accident when there was an accident in the process of making the explosives. It had included a test explosion on a flight within Asia. Ramzi Yousef (the planner for the 1993 attack on the World Trade Center) and Khalid Sheik Mohammad (the mastermind of the 9/11 attacks on the Trade Center and the Pentagon) were the key al Qaeda operatives.

15. Airborne dissemination of very small amount of anthrax (on the order of one kilogram) in a densely populated area could result in upwards of 500,000–1 million civilian fatalities. In that way, anthrax resembles nuclear weaponry.

16. See "Zarqawi Among 13 Indicted by Jordan in Plot," *Washington Post,* October 18, 2004.

17. Article by Nasir bin Hamd al-Fahd: "A Treatise on the Legal Status of Using Weapons of Mass Destruction against Infidels," Internet text in Arabic 01 May 03, p. 9.

18 Ibid., p. 12.

19. For instance, after the 9–11 attacks, there was considerable sympathy for the United States even among the wider Islamic populations around the globe.

20. The WMD-related discoveries made in Afghanistan as well as many other related activities are summarized in Center for Nonproliferation Studies, "Chart: Al-Qa'ida's WMD Activities," Updated: May 13, 2005.

21. The sleeper cell detected in Lackawanna, N.Y. may be typical. It comprised Muslim men who had gone to Afghanistan to meet with bin Laden and then returned to the United States. They provided no special technical expertise and brought only a diffuse interest in supporting bin Laden's cause.

22. Gary Stradling of Los Alamos National Laboratory has argued for the former pathway in conversations with me.

23. For more on this, please see the chapter by David Albright and Cory Hinderstein on the AQ Khan network in this volume.

24. Some other examples include: the 2002 attacks on a hotel and an aircraft taking-off in Mombassa, Kenya; the 2003 attacks on several housing complexes in Riyadh; simultaneous 2003 attacks on Riyadh and Casablanca as well as multiple attacks in Casablanca; the 2004 multiple attacks

on the United Kingdom Consulate, the UGS bank, and other buildings in Istanbul, Turkey; and the 2003 attacks on Jewish synagogues in Istanbul, Turkey.

25. This preference for doing what it does well also could partly explain (along with effective counter-terrorist operations) why there has yet to be an RDD attack—despite the relatively widespread availability of necessary means.

26. However, to repeat an earlier point, any such calculation need not—indeed, probably would not apply—to al Qaeda's membership overall. For suicide bombers, mid-level planner and operatives, and others concerned only with striking out against the United States and Western influences, nuclear use could well be seen as an even more effective means of doing so.

27. Statement quoted in Anonymous, Through Our Enemies' Eyes: Osama bin Laden, Radical Islam, and the Future of America (Washington, D.C.: Brassey's, Inc., 2002), p. 66.

28. Ibid., p. 67.

29 Hamid Mir, "Osama Claims He Has Nukes: If U.S. Uses N-arms It Will Get Same Response," *Dawn* (Islamabad) Internet Edition, November 10, 2001, accessed at http://www.dawn.com/2001/11/10/top1.htm.

30. Brad Roberts of the Institute for Defense Analyses first stressed to me this aspect of bin Laden's goals.

31. This possible adverse impact on bin Laden's own goals could well provide a compelling reason not to use contagious biological weapons, e.g., smallpox. Once released, smallpox almost certainly would sweep around the globe and quite possibly kill many tens of millions of Muslims along with others.

32. Text of tape broadcast on al-Arabiya, BBC News, April 15, 2004.

33. Full transcript of bin Laden's speech, 01 November 2004, Aljazeera.Net.

34. United Nations Security Council, S/Res/1540 (2004)—adopted on 28 April 2004.

35. United Nations Security Council, S/Res/1540 (2004)—adopted on 28 April 2004.

Lewis A. Dunn is a senior vice president at Science Applications International Corporation. A former senior U.S. government official, he has provided analytic support on deterrence and other counter-proliferation issues to the U.S. Department of Defense, the Military Commands, the National Nuclear Security Administration, and the Intelligence Community. He received his Ph.D. from the University of Chicago.

David Albright and Corey Hinderstein

Unraveling the A.Q. Khan and Future Proliferation Networks

The most disturbing aspect of the international nuclear smuggling network headed by Abdul Qadeer Khan, widely viewed as the father of Pakistan's nuclear weapons, is how poorly the nuclear nonproliferation regime fared in exposing and stopping the network's operation. Khan, with the help of associates on four continents, managed to buy and sell key nuclear weapons capabilities for more than two decades while eluding the world's best intelligence agencies and nonproliferation institutions and organizations. Despite a wide range of hints and leads, the United States and its allies failed to thwart this network throughout the 1980s and 1990s as it sold the equipment and expertise needed to produce nuclear weapons to major U.S. enemies including Iran, Libya, and North Korea.

By 2000, U.S. intelligence had at least partially penetrated the network's operations, leading to many revelations and ultimately, in October 2003, the dramatic seizure of uranium-enrichment gas-centrifuge components bound for Libya's secret nuclear weapons program aboard the German-owned ship BBC China. Libya's subsequent renunciation of nuclear weapons led to further discoveries about the network's operations and the arrest of many of its key players, including Khan himself.

The Khan network has caused enormous damage to efforts aimed at stopping the spread of nuclear weapons, to U.S. national security, and to international peace and stability. Without assistance from the network, it is unlikely that Iran would have been able to develop the ability to enrich uranium using gas centrifuges—now that country's most advanced and threatening nuclear program. Suspicions also remain that members of the network may have helped Al Qaeda obtain nuclear secrets prior to the fall of the Taliban regime in Afghanistan. The damage caused by this network led former CIA director George Tenet to reportedly describe Khan as being "at least as dangerous as Osama bin Laden."[1] The Khan network succeeded for many years by exploiting weaknesses in export control systems and recruiting suppliers, including some in states that were members of the Nuclear Suppliers Group (NSG). The network's key customers were states contemptuous of NSG controls and committed to violating the Nuclear Non-Proliferation Treaty (NPT) in their quest for secret nuclear capabilities. In essence, the network adapted to and benefited from the discriminatory and voluntary export control regime that was embodied in the NSG and complementary national export control systems. There is little confidence that other networks do not or will not exist or that elements of the Khan network will not reconstitute themselves in the future.

Yet, the international response thus far has not been sufficiently effective. Although revelations about the Khan network have reenergized support for a range of reforms, more extensive improvements to the international non-proliferation regime are still needed to block the emergence of new networks and to detect them promptly if they do arise. The United States, with the help of its allies, needs to pursue a broad range of foreign policy, intelligence, nonproliferation, export control, and law enforcement initiatives, as well as policies designed to close down nuclear smugglers' access to civilian industries in newly emerging industrial states.

The Khan Network

The Khan network is, first and foremost, an elaborate and highly successful illicit procurement network that Khan created in the 1970s to supply Pakistan's gas-centrifuge program, which has been used to produce weapons-grade uranium for Pakistan's nuclear weapons program. Khan and his associates slowly expanded their import operation, however, into a transnational illegal network that also exported gas centrifuges and production capabilities, as well as designs for nuclear weapons, to other, mostly Muslim countries to turn a profit and provide additional business for their international collaborators. In addition to money, Khan was also motivated by pan-Islamism and hostility to Western controls on nuclear technology.[2]

Khan's Customers

Khan's contempt for Western controls on nuclear technology was demonstrated early, in articles in technical journals in the late 1980s. They were among the first hints that Khan was willing to disseminate sensitive nuclear information and may also have served to advertise what Khan was willing to offer to would-be customers. Indeed, Khan appears to have attracted his first major customer when Iran received centrifuge assistance in 1987, during a period in which relations between Iran and Pakistan were briefly warming.[3] Even though Western intelligence agencies first suspected that Pakistan was providing aid to Iran's centrifuge program by the early 1990s, little was done to stop it.[4] During the 1990s, the Khan network expanded and became more capable, evolving into an organization that could provide "one-stop shopping" both for the technology needed to produce weapons-grade uranium and nuclear weapons designs.

In late 1990, shortly after Saddam Hussein seized Kuwait and the UN Security Council imposed an embargo on Iraq, Khan offered to help Baghdad produce gas centrifuges and design nuclear weapons. Iraqi nuclear officials, ironically suspecting that the offer was a sting operation because Pakistan was a U.S. ally, proceeded cautiously and requested a sample of what Khan could provide. In the mid-1990s, when Khan's offer was discovered by International Atomic Energy Agency (IAEA) weapons inspectors, the Iraqis told UN inspectors that they did not receive anything.[5]

Little information is available about Khan's assistance to North Korea in the 1990s and early 2000s. Pyongyang has denied that it has a gas-centrifuge program, and Pakistan seems reluctant to divulge details about its nuclear dealings with North Korea. Nonetheless, evidence strongly suggests that North Korea has at least received centrifuge designs, a few sample centrifuges, and lists of potential suppliers from the network.[6]

The network has also offered aid to Egypt and Syria. Egypt is believed to have turned down the assistance.[7] Pakistani investigators reportedly found that Khan's middlemen offered help to Syria but never provided assistance in the end.[8] This assertion is still subject to scrutiny. Other countries, notably Saudi Arabia, may also have received offers of assistance.[9] Khan traveled extensively, and his visits to 18 countries between 1997 and 2003 have furthered speculation about potential clients.[10] His visit to Afghanistan during this period has added to suspicions that Khan or his associates may have offered nuclear aid to Al Qaeda or other terrorist organizations that were based in Afghanistan at the time.

The network's most ambitious customer, however, was Libya, which ordered a gas-centrifuge plant sufficient to produce enough highly enriched uranium to turn out roughly 10 nuclear weapons annually. The network intended to provide Libya with a turnkey gas-centrifuge facility, something typically reserved for states or large corporations in industrialized nations with full government support and knowledge.[11] The network also offered ongoing technical assistance to help overcome any obstacles in assembling and operating the plant. If Libya had continued to pursue its nuclear ambitions and the network had not been exposed, it could have succeeded in assembling the centrifuge plant in about four or five years and produced significant amounts of highly enriched uranium.

In addition to the means to produce fissile material, the Khan network also gave Libya the information necessary to build a nuclear weapon, including detailed nuclear weapons component designs, component fabrication information, and nuclear weapons assembly instructions.[12] The documents appear to have been information that Pakistan had received in China in the early 1980s. They include detailed, dated, handwritten notes in English taken during lectures given by Chinese weapons experts who were named by the notetakers. These notetakers appear to have been working for Khan, based on their cryptic notations deriding a rival Pakistani nuclear weapons program led by Munir Khan, the chairman of the Pakistan Atomic Energy Organization.[13] The design appears to be for a Chinese warhead that was tested on a missile, has a mass of about 500 kilograms, and measures less than a meter in diameter. Although this design would have been too large for Libyan Scud missiles, it could have been airdropped or intended for a more advanced missile system that Libya may have been seeking. Indeed, the design would fit on existing Iranian and North Korean missiles.

Iran and North Korea have both denied receiving any weapon designs. The Pakistani government has told the IAEA that Khan claimed that the network had not provided any such designs to Iran. Nonetheless, as a result of the assistance provided to Libya and Iraq, suspicions remain that the network routinely offered these designs to its customers.

Inner Workings

By 2003, when the Khan network was exposed to the public, it had become a truly transnational organization. The key providers of the necessary technology and several of the network's leaders, including Khan, were located in Pakistan, but other leaders were spread throughout the world, including in Switzerland, the United Kingdom, the United Arab Emirates (UAE), Turkey, South Africa, and Malaysia. The network also depended on unwitting manufacturing companies and suppliers in many countries. It sold what the Pakistanis have called the P1 and P2 centrifuges—the first two centrifuges that Pakistan deployed in large numbers. The P1 centrifuge uses an aluminum rotor, and the P2 centrifuge uses a maraging steel rotor, which is stronger, spins faster, and therefore enriches more uranium per machine than the P1 centrifuge's aluminum rotor. Initial exports of the P1 centrifuges to Iran in the mid-1990s included 500 machines retired from Pakistan's nuclear program or made under contract by the network. This quantity of P1 centrifuges would only be able to produce about one quarter of a bomb's worth of weapons-grade uranium in a year.

In the Libyan case, the network focused on producing P2 components outside of Pakistan. The Libyans have stated to the IAEA that they placed an order for 10,000 P2 machines.[14] Because each centrifuge has roughly one hundred different components, this order translates into a total of about one million components—a staggering number of parts given the sophistication of gas-centrifuge components. Thus, it is clear that Khan's network was assembling an impressive cast of technical experts, companies, suppliers, and workshops.

The workshops contracted to manufacture components for the network typically imported the necessary items, such as metals, equipment, or subcomponents. After the facilities produced the item, they would send it to Dubai under a false end-user certificate, where it would be repackaged and sent to Libya. According to Mohamed ElBaradei, director general of the IAEA, "Nuclear components designed in one country could be manufactured in another, shipped through a third (which may have appeared to be a legitimate user), assembled in a fourth, and designated for eventual turnkey use in a fifth."[15]

Initial information found in Libya identified roughly a half-dozen key workshops spread across at least Africa, Asia, and the Middle East that were making the centrifuge components. The network selected a workshop based on the type of centrifuge component needed and the materials and equipment involved in making those particular components. The most publicly known facility—Scomi Precision Engineering (SCOPE) in Malaysia—made stationary aluminum components and was the source of 15 percent of the total number of components destined for Libya, including the centrifuge components seized on the *BBC China.*

Workshops in Turkey importing subcomponents from Europe and elsewhere assembled other key parts of the centrifuges, including centrifuge motors, power supplies, and ring magnets. Tradefin Engineering, a company in South Africa, produced the elaborate equipment needed to insert and withdraw the uranium hexafluoride gas that is enriched in centrifuges. Tradefin also attempted unsuccessfully to make the sensitive maraging steel rotors for the P2 centrifuges.[16]

At some point after the initial order, Libya may have changed its initial plan to buy all the centrifuge components overseas and instead planned to build the components itself. Libya could have accomplished this objective because it also ordered from the network a sophisticated manufacturing center, code-named Workshop 1001, to produce centrifuge components. The original plan called for this center to make additional centrifuges either to replace broken ones or add to the total number after the network delivered the first 10,000 machines, but if the network encountered problems in making a component for the original 10,000 machines, Libya's manufacturing center may have had to accomplish that task as well. Most of the equipment for the center came from Europe, particularly from or through Spain and Italy, and was sent to Libya via Dubai. The network had also supplied detailed manufacturing information for many of the parts.

Pakistan Gets Cornered

After the seizure of the *BBC China* and Libya's subsequent cooperation after its decision to renounce its efforts to produce nuclear weapons, the Khan network was exposed, and Pakistan came under intense pressure to deal with Khan and his associates. Pressure had already been building on Pakistan to rein in Khan. In September 2003, the IAEA Board of Governors passed a resolution requesting all countries (diplomatic code for Pakistan) to help the IAEA resolve questions about procurements for Iran's secret centrifuge program tied to Pakistan that had risen independently of the *BBC China* and Libyan cases.

The Pakistani government nonetheless initially resisted arresting Khan, whom most Pakistanis considered a national hero. U.S. secretary of state Colin Powell recalled in December 2004 that he had called President Gen. Pervez Musharraf in early 2004, telling him, "We know so much about this that we're going to go public with it, and within a few weeks, okay? And you needed to deal with this before you have to deal with it publicly." According to Powell, "[T]he next thing we knew, A. Q. Khan had been put in custody."[17] After his arrest in February 2004, Khan confessed to selling sensitive technology and equipment to Libya, Iran, and North Korea. He received a conditional pardon and today remains under house arrest with very little access to outsiders. Khan also maintained that he alone was responsible and had acted independently of current and previous Pakistani governments—a statement that many experts view with skepticism as apparently intended to prevent Islamabad's further embarrassment.[18]

Although many Pakistanis have been detained since the scandal broke, none have been prosecuted. The Pakistani government has provided the IAEA and foreign governments with information about Khan's activities but has not allowed anyone outside the Pakistani government to interview Khan or the others that were detained. Although the IAEA has been allowed to submit written questions that Khan will answer, this type of exchange is not a substitute for direct access to Khan and his associates.

The Investigation Widens

Absent major breakthroughs in Pakistan, attention has been focused on investigations conducted by national authorities and the IAEA in an effort to fully understand the network, its key suppliers, and its operations, as well as the history and procurement activities of the network's customers.

Prosecutions, which may provide the only way to fill in the remaining knowledge gaps, are in fact taking place in many countries, particularly in France, Germany, Japan, Malaysia, the Netherlands, South Africa, Spain, Switzerland, Turkey, and the United Kingdom. Many of these prosecutions have been slow to start, however, and some face tough challenges in proving the charges against the accused individuals and companies. In some cases, prosecutors or government investigators have been unaware of information that has been uncovered about their citizens through investigations in other countries. Because the network operated transnationally, information sharing among the key states remains critical.

Nonetheless, investigations in Malaysia, South Africa, Germany, Switzerland, and the UAE have already revealed a great deal about the Khan network. For instance, a Malaysian police investigation of SCOPE, the source of the centrifuge components seized on the *BBC China*, showed how the network exploited Malaysia's weak national export control system as well as SCOPE's owners, who seemed unaware of the network's activities.[19] The Malaysian government detained B. S. A. Tahir, a Sri Lankan living in Dubai, for his role in coordinating the manufacturing operation, but no charges have been made public. Tahir has been identified as the chief organizer and "money man" for the Khan network's sales to Iran, Libya, and perhaps other countries. As of early 2005, however, the Malaysian government had not allowed the IAEA access to him.

In September 2004, South Africa arrested Johan Meyer of Tradefin on suspicion of manufacturing centrifuge parts and equipment for Libya. Meyer admitted to prosecutors that he knew that the items were for a uranium-enrichment plant.[20] Based on his testimony, other individuals were arrested, including Gerhard Wisser, a German citizen and owner of Krisch Engineering in South Africa, who had a long history of involvement with other members of the network. Wisser had been arrested a month earlier in Germany for his alleged role in producing centrifuge parts in South Africa for delivery to Libya but had been released on bail.

In early October 2004, German prosecutors also nabbed Urs Tinner, a 39-year-old Swiss citizen who was mentioned in the Malaysian police report as being allegedly responsible for overseeing the production of centrifuge parts at SCOPE for shipment to Libya. Urs Tinner is the son of Friedrich Tinner, who had previously been suspected of supplying Pakistan and Iraq with centrifuge-related items and is reportedly suspected by authorities of having played a key role in the Khan network's activities over the years. Friedrich Tinner remains free, although investigations into his activities continue.

In November 2004, the Swiss government arrested Gotthard Lerch, a German citizen. In the 1970s and early 1980s, Lerch was employed by Leybold Heraeus, a German company that developed and produced vacuum products and technology. Before undergoing significant internal reform in the early 1990s, Leybold Heraeus and its sister companies had been major suppliers to many secret nuclear weapons programs, including those in Iraq, Iran, South Africa, and Pakistan. Mentioned in the same Malaysian police report that cited Tinner, Lerch was allegedly involved in trying to obtain centrifuge parts for Libya from South Africa. There are indications that Germany asked Switzerland to arrest Lerch so that he would not be free when Wisser was released on bail by South African authorities who had sought to hold Wisser but lost on appeal. Investigators in the United Kingdom and the UAE, the principal transshipment point for much of the equipment bound for Libya, are investigating Peter and Paul Griffin, a British father and son team also named in the Malaysian police report, both of whom have allegedly had a long history of involvement with Khan.

At this point, many questions about the extent of the network still remain unanswered. Investigators worldwide believe that other key participants may not yet have been identified. Questions also remain about the full extent of these individuals' activities in manufacturing and supplying centrifuges and associated equipment. Whether or not all the key workshops and companies have been identified also remains unknown. Moreover, it is possible that components for uranium-enrichment plants have been produced but were not delivered to Libya. Perhaps they have been sent to other unknown customers.

The key to the success of Khan's network was its virtual library of centrifuge designs and detailed manufacturing manuals. An important task for investigators is to retrieve as much of this information as possible. That effort requires, in turn, tracking down and prosecuting the members of the network with this kind of sensitive centrifuge information. Given the ease of copying and hiding documents and digital files, this centrifuge information may form the core of a future network aimed at secretly producing or selling gas centrifuges.

Rolling Up the Khan Network

The Khan network could not have evolved into such a dangerous supplier without the utter corruption and dishonesty of successive Pakistani governments which, for almost two decades, were quick to deny any involvement by its scientists in illicit procurement. They blocked internal investigations and hindered outside investigations of known cases. Pakistani leaders routinely denied that Khan was involved in any transfers of gas centrifuges, despite frequent reports to the contrary, including many that mentioned him by name.

Despite the pressure Washington applied to stop Khan, the United States must also share part of the blame for the network's successful operation over so many years. The United States and its allies failed to act on many hints about the network's activities, such as evidence of Pakistan's help to Iran and Khan's offer to Iraq. Too often in the 1980s and 1990s, the United States put other priorities ahead of exposing Khan and putting him out of business. Even today, the United States has not demonstrated that it places an equal priority on unraveling the activities of the Pakistani members of the Khan network as it does on maintaining Islamabad's support for hunting down Al Qaeda terrorists in Pakistan. Unraveling the activities of the network and ensuring that it is shut down require the Pakistani government to provide more assistance to investigators, including giving the IAEA direct access to question Khan and his associates verbally. Greater cooperation from Pakistan would allow the IAEA, the United States, and other affected governments to conduct more thorough investigations, to pursue criminal prosecutions of individuals involved in the network, and to recover physical remnants of the illicit procurement network that have not yet been found and that could provide the seeds for future, secret nuclear weapons programs.

Although Pakistan has taken steps to create a national export control system and to place additional controls over its nuclear scientists, Islamabad has not faced up to the difficult task of actually implementing an effective control system. One necessary step is to prosecute Pakistani members of the network to send a clear signal that Pakistan will punish illegal exporters severely and thereby reduce the likelihood that someone will step into Khan's shoes.

The successes of the Khan network should shatter any complacency about how effective national and international export controls have been in stopping illegal nuclear or nuclear-related materials. Some countries, such as South Africa and Turkey, were NSG members. Investigations have shown that these countries did not adequately implement their national export control and nuclear nonproliferation laws, despite their commitments as NSG members. Indeed, because of their countries' NSG membership, companies assisting the network could receive items from other NSG members essentially without checks on their potential end use. The failure of these NSG countries to stop the illicit manufacture of centrifuge components is one of the most embarrassing aspects of this scandal.

The network was also masterful in identifying countries that had sufficient industrial capability and were eager to make direct-use nuclear items, yet had little knowledge of nuclear technology or inadequate national export laws, making them oblivious or indifferent to the actual nature of items. Revelations about the network have in fact highlighted the risk posed by states such as Malaysia that are outside the NSG. Because these states are not members, their governments and companies were poorly prepared to resist the Khan network's lucrative offers. Although many of the network's suppliers were not aware of the actual purpose of the materials they provided or the parts they were contracted to make, they were often located in countries whose authorities were unlikely to scrutinize exports carefully or to encourage curiosity about the actual end use of an item. In many cases, the companies themselves had little motivation arising from either conscience or threat of punishment to confirm the cover stories they were given by members of the network.

Members of the network even knew how to exploit loopholes in much more stringent European export control systems to obtain necessary subcomponents, materials, machine tools, and other manufacturing equipment. For instance, the network depended on complicated transportation arrangements, mainly to confuse suppliers about the true end use of the item and to evade prying intelligence agencies or deceive them about the final destination for its products. The international free zone in Dubai, through which shipments are still subject to few meaningful controls, was particularly critical to the network. Indeed, most items found in Libya were transported through Dubai, in some cases more than once.

Efforts to Prevent Future Networks

Public revelations about the Khan network intensified support in 2003 and 2004 to improve the regimes already in place to address nuclear proliferation. In particular, the network's exposure reenergized efforts to strengthen inspections and national and international export controls. These efforts had gained international support in 2002 as a result of an IAEA investigation proving that Pakistan had provided substantial assistance to Iran's nuclear program. Nonetheless, significant progress had to await revelations about the extent of Khan's activities.

In direct response to the activities of the Khan network, President George W. Bush called for a wide set of reforms in a February 2004 speech at the National Defense University in Washington, D.C., proposing a broad strategy to strengthen and improve both domestic and international nonproliferation efforts as well as new measures designed to enable the United States and the international community to increase the likelihood of detecting illicit trade in nuclear-related materials.[21] Among these steps were expanding the Proliferation Security Initiative (PSI); strengthening the legal framework governing proliferation, in particular through a UN Security Council resolution requiring states to criminalize proliferation, enact strict export controls, and secure sensitive materials; expanding efforts to secure nuclear material in the former Soviet Union and other states; denying enrichment and reprocessing technology to any states that do not already possess them; requiring countries to implement the IAEA's advanced safeguards Additional Protocol as a necessary condition for supplying equipment and materials for civilian nuclear programs; and reforming the IAEA to improve its capability to enforce states' obligations. The international community also responded with the adoption of various measures by separate bodies including the passage of UN Security Council Resolution 1540, reforms considered by the NSG, expansion of the PSI, the G-8 Global Partnership's Action Plan on Nonproliferation, and proposed steps to strengthen IAEA investigations.

Un Security Council Resolution 1540

In April 2004, the UN Security Council passed Resolution 1540, which requires all states to criminalize proliferation to nonstate actors and to establish, review, and maintain appropriate and effective export control systems. This resolution, which the United States had first proposed in September 2003, fills an important gap in existing nonproliferation regimes by including an export control law requirement for all 191 UN member states and targeting nonstate actors. Because its requirements apply to all states, this resolution offers a remedy for some of the problems resulting from the NSG's voluntary, limited membership.

The UN resolution has several problems, however, in terms of its implementation. Some states, particularly in the developing world, may resist its main provisions, believing that the obligations should have been established through treaty negotiations. It will also likely be applied unevenly among even the most well-intentioned states because many, without extensive assistance, will experience difficulties in enacting, implementing, and enforcing effective export control legislation.

Nuclear Suppliers Group

The NSG has considered steps designed to address weaknesses in its system that contributed to the Khan network's success, including implementing a so-called catch-all provision to give member states additional discretion to deny suspicious but not clearly controlled exports, making the IAEA Additional Protocol a condition for supplying nuclear technology for civilian use, expanding NSG membership, and increasing communication and information sharing among NSG countries as well as with the IAEA. The status of these initiatives, however, varies.

At the May 2004 NSG plenary meeting in Goteborg, Sweden, the NSG decided to establish the first measure—that, as part of their national export control laws, all member states should adopt a catch-all mechanism. This would directly target a tactic used by the Khan network to obtain dual-use items for its customers from several NSG countries. This useful tool, which is already in place in many countries including the United States, gives NSG members the legal authority to refuse to allow an item to be exported, even if it is not included on a control list, if that item might be intended for use in a nuclear weapons program. It also commits states to consider additional factors such as specifications of the requested item that may fall just below those requiring controls and known information about the imports and proliferation credentials of the recipient country. In addition, NSG members debated adopting the second measure, requiring states to implement the IAEA Additional Protocol as a condition for supplying nuclear items for civilian use. Agreement on this issue is likely to be reached at the NSG plenary meeting in 2005.

The NSG has also considered the third measure—expanding its membership—but remains hesitant to do so. The Khan network has shown that some states, such as Malaysia, that are not generally considered actual or potential suppliers of nuclear items have advanced industrial infrastructures that can be exploited to produce direct-use nuclear items such as centrifuge components. Expanding membership in the NSG would enable additional countries to improve their export control systems and receive help from more experienced members. The NSG has already expanded significantly over the last decade, however, and as the cases of South Africa and Turkey highlight, many current NSG members cannot implement the controls they accepted when they joined the organization. Thus, leading members of the NSG, including the United States, are reluctant to expand the group until controls among all existing members are improved. At a minimum, the United States should dramatically step up its efforts to bring NSG members up to acceptable standards so that the group can increase membership in an effective manner.

The NSG is committed to implementing the final measure, improving information sharing among its members, strengthening its relationship with the IAEA, and increasing the amount of information NSG members share with the agency. At the 2004 plenary meeting, NSG members made a commitment to improve information exchange, to reinforce contacts with states outside the NSG, and to strengthen the relationship between the NSG and the IAEA. Currently, members share information with each other on export denials but not approvals of key items. The IAEA does not routinely receive notice of denials. The NSG needs to start sharing key approvals among its members, and the IAEA should be notified of denials as well as approvals. This step would help members of the NSG and the IAEA develop a better picture of a potential proliferant state's overall nuclear capability, hopefully leading to earlier warnings of a state's undeclared nuclear activities.

Proliferation Security Initiative

Another policy area undergoing change as a result of the revelations about the Khan network is the PSI, which the U.S. Department of State defines as "a global effort that aims to stop shipments of weapons of mass destruction (WMD), their delivery systems, and related materials worldwide."[22] This initiative is pursued primarily through international coordination of efforts to interdict shipments of WMD-related items.

The successful seizure of the *BBC China* demonstrated the importance of the PSI as an enforcement tool that complements existing national and international export controls. The event also highlighted some of the PSI's weaknesses and controversies. Because it is a set of activities and not an organization, the PSI may be vulnerable to changes in administration. For example, the program is not directly funded but is supported through existing diplomatic resources.[23] In addition, the PSI can suffer from lack of intelligence. Even though the PSI was responsible for the successful seizure of Malaysian-made centrifuge parts on the *BBC China*, the ship also contained many centrifuge parts made in Turkey that were not intercepted by the United States and its allies. Although no damage was done in this case—the parts eventually reached Libya, which turned them over to the IAEA and the United States—it revealed how critically the PSI depends on intelligence that, even in optimum cases, can be incomplete.

In fact, the premature release of information about the *BBC China* seizure may have damaged investigations into key members and suppliers of the Khan network. It is now suspected that members of the network realized that their activities had been discovered, leading some of them to destroy critical evidence. In apparent recognition of this risk, a State Department official noted that keeping PSI successes secret is important to preserve the integrity of investigations.[24]

As part of the PSI, Bush, in his February 2004 speech, called for using Interpol and other mechanisms to strengthen coordination among countries in their efforts to bring those who traffic in deadly weapons to justice—to shut down their labs, to seize their materials, and to freeze their assets. Toward this goal, the United States has undertaken a range of discussions with its allies aimed at building on existing international law enforcement cooperative efforts that have been successful in other areas. As of early 2004, however, few concrete results had been achieved.

G-8 Global Partnership

Drawing from Bush's February 2004 speech, the G-8 Global Partnership reached agreement on an Action Plan on Nonproliferation at the Sea Island summit in July 2004.[25] The G-8 partners agreed that exporting "sensitive items with proliferation potential" should be allowed only in a manner consistent with nonproliferation norms and limited to states committed to these norms. In the action plan, the G-8 members made a commitment to pursue these goals by amending the NSG guidelines as appropriate and by working to gain wide support for these measures. While pursuing these efforts, the G-8 partners agreed not to initiate any new contracts to provide reprocessing or uranium-enrichment equipment and technologies to additional states for one year. This was a weaker commitment than the one that Bush had called for and that the U.S. delegation reportedly lobbied the G-8 to adopt. A complete, long-term ban on providing reprocessing and enrichment technology to new states will be difficult to achieve within either the framework of the G-8 or the NSG, although the United States is expected to continue to work toward achieving this important goal.

International Atomic Energy Agency

The Khan network confirmed the weaknesses of traditional IAEA inspections in detecting undeclared nuclear facilities and materials and the need for all states to implement the Additional Protocol in order to increase reporting of information by states and expand the rights of inspectors to verify that information. This case has also shown the need for the IAEA to receive more information from states about their exports and imports of key sensitive dual-use items. In the cases of Iran and Libya, the IAEA has retroactively received a wide variety of information about their imports of sensitive dual-use equipment, materials, and technology. The agency is now in a much stronger position to perform its responsibilities in those states, to make a determination about Iran's and Libya's compliance with the NPT, and to take the steps necessary to develop confidence that there are no undeclared nuclear activities or materials in these two countries.

Because Iran and Libya lied to the IAEA about their nuclear activities, they were under intense international pressure to be more transparent with the IAEA. Under normal circumstances, however, the IAEA receives limited information about countries' exports and imports. The IAEA's Additional Protocol does require states to report on exports of direct-use nuclear items. In practice, however, nuclear smuggling networks can be expected to export those items illegally—hiding their true purpose—as the Khan network frequently did. Thus, states would receive false information and could not report such items to the IAEA as being of direct use.

Reports of exports of nuclear dual-use items would be more useful. These items would be more likely to be exported with a license, albeit with a false end-use declaration, and thus reportable to the IAEA and subject to scrutiny aimed at revealing undeclared activities in a country of concern. Requiring states to report on a wider variety of exports and imports would be a logical extension of the current safeguards that place great emphasis on developing a broader picture of a state's nuclear and nuclear-capable infrastructure. These new reporting requirements should be seen as a necessary component of implementing credible safeguards.

Such a reform could be implemented on a case-by-case basis, as has been done with regard to Libya and Iran. Additionally, it could be achieved by amending the Additional Protocol to require states to report more exports and imports to the IAEA. In either case, the IAEA must allocate more resources to retrieving and analyzing import and export information.

A New System to Improve Export Controls

Beyond these existing reforms, ElBaradei has called for a formal international arrangement to control exports and imports. In January 2004, ElBaradei said that "export controls must be dramatically improved and, in contrast to the past, must be carried out within an international framework."[26] A month later, he urged the establishment of universal, "binding, treaty-based controls."[27] ElBaradei did not provide any details about a potential treaty, and he also apparently recognized the difficulty of achieving such a treaty in practice. Nonetheless, his proposal warrants further study because it could solve many of the problems in the current system of export controls, making it significantly more difficult for nuclear smuggling to occur.

A universal treaty-based system controlling nuclear export activities would be binding on states and would include a means to verify compliance. Under such a treaty, countries would implement a set of nuclear and nuclear-related export control laws and criminalization procedures, similar in nature to those required by Resolution 1540. The agreement, however, would also require an organization to verify compliance, ensure the adequacy of a state's laws, and investigate illicit procurement activities. Signatories to the agreement would inform this organization of sensitive nuclear or nuclear-related exports, and it would have the mandate and legal right to verify that the transactions are indeed legal. The organization would also verify the accuracy and completeness of a country's declaration about its nuclear or nuclear-related exports or imports. In addition, a treaty-based system of export controls and verification would impose new requirements on all states, even those that have not implemented the Additional Protocol.

The IAEA is a logical choice to undertake this role because, as part of its safeguard responsibilities under the NPT, it is already pursuing investigations of illicit procurement activities by Iran and Libya. These investigations include taking inventories of all centrifuge equipment and components in Iran and Libya and verifying their accuracy and completeness, determining the network's suppliers and manufacturing activities, cooperating with a range of governments on the network's activities, receiving information about suppliers from member states, and meeting with Pakistani investigators. These investigations involve receiving more information from states than the IAEA's Additional Protocol requires.

By more formally linking its safeguards system with export control verification and monitoring, the IAEA would be in far better position to assure the absence of undeclared nuclear activities and to detect cheating in a timely manner. A treaty-based export control system would allow the IAEA to perform a task that governments have been unable to do and thereby significantly increase the security of the United States and the international community.

As it is, the A. Q. Khan network exploited loopholes in the existing nationally based system and created a network of suppliers, manufacturers, and shippers that provided secret nuclear technology to Iran, Libya, North Korea, and perhaps others. Iran and Libya would have been severely hindered in their efforts to achieve nuclear weapons capability absent assistance from the Khan network. These transfers went largely undetected, and any hints of these dangerous activities were not pursued aggressively until relatively recently. With the international community increasingly aware of the damage done by the Khan network, it needs to take further steps to uncover all aspects of the network and prevent future nuclear smuggling.

Notes

1. Douglas Jehl, "CIA Says Pakistanis Gave Iran Nuclear Aid," *New York Times*, November 24, 2004.
2. See William J. Broad, David Sanger, and Raymond Bonner, "How Pakistani's Network Offered the Whole Kit," *New York Times*, February 13, 2004.
3. International Atomic Energy Agency (IAEA) Board of Governors, "Implementation of the NPT Safeguards Agreement in the Islamic Republic of Iran: Report by the Director General," GOV/2004/83, November 15, 2004, http://www.iaea.org/Publications/Documents/Board/2004/gov2004-83_derestrict.pdf (accessed January 30, 2005).
4. David Albright, "An Iranian Bomb," *Bulletin of the Atomic Scientist* 51, no. 4 (July/ August 1995): 20–26.
5. For more information, see David Albright and Corey Hinderstein, "Documents Indicate A.Q. Khan Offered Nuclear Weapon Designs to Iraq in 1990: Did He Approach Other Countries?" February 4, 2004, http://www.isis-online.org/publications/southasia/khan_memo.html (accessed January 30, 2005).
6. Anonymous government official, interview with author.
7. Anonymous source, interview with author.
8. Kamran Khan, "Pakistanis Exploited Nuclear Network," *Washington Post*, January 28, 2004.
9. "Khan Gave Nuke Tech to Three More Nations," *Press Trust of India*, January 2, 2005.
10. William J. Broad and David E. Sanger, "As Nuclear Secrets Emerge, More Are Suspected," *New York Times*, December 26, 2004.
11. International Atomic Energy Agency (IAEA) Board of Governors, "Implementation of the NPT Safeguards Agreement of the Socialist People's Libyan Arab Jamahiriya," GOV/2004/59, August 30, 2004, http://www.iaea.org/Publications/Documents/Board/2004/gov2004-59.pdf (accessed February 1, 2005).
12. Ibid.
13. Anonymous government officials, interviews with author.
14. IAEA Board of Governors, GOV/2004/59.
15. Mohamed ElBaradei, "Nuclear Non-Proliferation: Global Security in a Rapidly Changing World" (speech, Carnegie International Non-proliferation Conference, Washington, D.C., June 21, 2004), http://www.ceip.org/files/projects/npp/resources/2004conference/speeches/ElBaradei.doc (accessed January 30, 2004).
16 Johan Andries Muller Meyer, sworn statement, Pretoria, September 8, 2004 (given to police in Vanderbijlpark, South Africa, in the presence of Benjamin Nel, captain, South African Police Department) (unofficial translation) (hereinafter Meyer statement).
17. *Christian Science Monitor* Newsmaker press briefing, Washington, D.C., December 21, 2004.
18. *Dawn*, February 5, 2004 (transcription of Khan's statement of February 4, 2004).
19. "Press Release by Inspector General of Police [Malaysia] in Relation to Investigation on the Alleged Production of Components for Libya's Uranium-Enrichment Programme," February 20, 2004, http://www.rmp.gov.my/rmp03/040220scomi_eng.htm (accessed January 30, 2005).
20. Meyer statement.
21. Office of the Press Secretary, The White House, "President Announces New Measures to Counter the Threat of WMD," Washington, D.C., February 11, 2004, http://www.whitehouse.gov/news/releases/2004/02/20040211-4.html (accessed January 30, 2005).
22. Bureau of Nonproliferation, U.S. Department of State, "The Proliferation Security Initiative," July 28, 2004, http://www.state.gov/t/np/rls/other/34726.htm (accessed January 30, 2005). See Andrew C. Winner, "The Proliferation Security Initiative: The New Face of Interdiction," *The Washington Quarterly* 28, no. 2 (Spring 2005): 129–143.
23. Mark Fitzpatrick, testimony before the U.S. Senate, Governmental Affairs Subcommittee on Financial Management, the Budget, and International Security, *Hearing on International Smuggling Networks: Weapons of Mass Destruction Counterproliferation Initiatives*, Washington, D.C., June 23, 2004.
24. Ibid.

25. "G8 Action Plan on Nonproliferation," Sea Island, Georgia, June 9, 2004, http://www.g8usa. gov/d_060904d.htm (accessed January 30, 2005).
26. Erich Follath, Juergen Kremb, and Georg Mascolo, "Nuclear War Is Getting Closer," *Der Spiegel*, January 26, 2004, available in "IAEA Director General: Danger of Nuclear War 'Has Never Been Greater Than Today,'" FBIS Document EUP20040124000085.
27. Mohamed ElBaradei, "Saving Ourselves From Self-Destruction," *New York Times*, February 12, 2004.

David Albright is president of the Institute for Science and International Security (ISIS) in Washington, D.C. Mr. Albright holds an M.S. in physics from Indiana University and an M.S. in mathematics from Wright State University.

Corey Hinderstein is deputy director of the Institute for Science and International Security (ISIS) in Washington, D.C. Ms. Hinderstein is a Phi Beta Kappa graduate of Clark University and is a member of the Northeast Regional Board of Directors of the Institute for Nuclear Materials Management.

Unit III

Responding to the Threat

It is one of today's great paradoxes that the most powerful nation in the world, having invested more in its military and defense than any nation in history, faces the challenges described in the preceding sections of this volume. Clearly, preventing, preparing for and responding to a WMD terror attack has not always been a priority of U.S. public policy, but this has changed since September 2001. The chapters of this section examine issues of strategic deterrence, domestic and global cooperation, and interagency coordination, emphasizing the need for an effectively networked community of agencies and individuals committed to nonproliferation and countering the global threat of WMD and terrorism.

First, Daniel Whiteneck—a researcher at the Center for Naval Analysis—highlights the complexities of deterrence in his critical assessment of the Bush administration's Nuclear Posture Review. Because terrorist groups like al Qaeda are not interested in protecting territory, traditional means of deterrence—for example, the threat of retaliation—is limited, and thus it is tempting to assert that the only feasible ways to counter a WMD attack is prevention, by denying terrorist groups access to WMD through nonproliferation efforts, safeguards, and interdictions. Certainly, denying access to technology, safeguarding WMD facilities, and conducting inspections at borders and ports should be considered important tools to lower the likelihood of successful WMD acquisition and attack by terrorists. However, he argues, such tools will always be somewhat unreliable as long as a dedicated group of trained individuals can construct at least crude CBRN weapons. Further, the United States cannot guarantee the ability of all countries (such those of the former Soviet Union) to protect CBRN materials and weapons located within their borders, despite Washington's continued urgings and financial support. Similarly, border defenses and inspections can be porous and sometimes impractical. As a result, Whiteneck concludes, current tools are necessary but insufficient measures to contain the WMD terrorist threat, and thus achieving some level of deterrence against such attacks is desirable as a complementary layer of security.

Next, Vera L. Zakem and Danielle R. Miller—national security policy analysts in the Washington, DC area—examine the motivations of violent non-state actors (VNSAs) to acquire and use weapons of mass destruction. Their analysis also highlights the characteristics of terrorist groups and VNSAs that might enable them to acquire and use nuclear weapons and technology. The chapter then assesses whether or not VNSAs can be deterred, and whether or not sovereign states and criminal groups within transitional/failed states can help VNSAs acquire nuclear technology. Overall, their analysis contributes to the debate over whether *acquisition* actually leads to a group's decision to *use* weapons of mass destruction.

Next, Natasha Bajema of the Fletcher School at Tufts University examines the role of non-proliferation regimes in countering the threat of WMD terrorism. She argues that without significant re-engagement by member states and U.S. leadership, nonproliferation regimes are now facing the danger of collapse, and asks whether this would have damaging effects on strategies to counter WMD terrorism. Further, she asks, how should the nonproliferation regimes be strengthened to reduce the risk of WMD terrorism? Nonproliferation regimes help to coordinate national policies on law enforcement, extradition, export controls, and security and safety of WMD-related materials and facilities; thus, it is clear that an absence of these regimes would present a far more complicated world in which to prevent acts of WMD terrorism. Without nonproliferation regimes, all states would be free to develop WMD according to their capabilities. Thus, she concludes, nonproliferation regimes are relevant for countering the threat of WMD terrorism for three reasons: first, the counterproliferation toolbox contains a wide range of tools, all of which are necessary for a comprehensive strategy against WMD terrorism; second, the nonproliferation treaties provide a legal framework that is essential for countering the threat of WMD terrorism; and third, the norms established by the nonproliferation regimes underpin all other international efforts designed to counter threats posed by WMD.

In the next chapter, Emma Belcher—also of the Fletcher School at Tufts University—describes the practical measures of law enforcement in countering terrorism. She examines three initiatives that attempt to provide practical means to deal with the WMD terrorism threat: the Proliferation Security Initiative (PSI), the Container Security Initiative (CSI), and the Customs-Trade Partnership Against Terrorism (C-TPAT). The PSI uses international and legal principles in a creative manner and the CSI and C-TPAT use a risk-based approach in partnership with states and businesses to minimize the risk of WMD terrorism to the U.S. while enabling the timely flow of legitimate trade. However, she argues, all three initiatives could be strengthened. In particular, the PSI is faced with limits under international law and political realities, while the CSI and C-TPAT could use better tools to assist law enforcement officials. Overall, she concludes, these initiatives make it more difficult for terrorists to achieve their aims, but because terrorists are constantly seeking new means for achieving their goals, the PSI, CSI and C-TPAT will need to constantly evolve.

Three case studies complete this section and provide readers with "how to respond" guidance and policy advice. The first of these—authored by Elin Gursky of the ANSER Institute for Homeland Security, and Thomas Inglesby and Tara O'Toole of the Center for Biosecurity of the University of Pittsburgh Medical Center—explores issues of disease surveillance, diagnostics and detection, drawing from observations of the medical and public health response to the 2001 anthrax attacks. Despite the commitment and hard work of the individuals in these professional communities, they argue, the anthrax attacks revealed an unacceptable level of fragility in systems now properly recognized as vital to national defense. Too many citizens, elected leaders, and national security officials still have a limited understanding of the degree to which 22 cases of anthrax rocked the public health agencies and hospitals involved in the response to this small bioterrorist attack. Further, most of the vulnerabilities in the medical and public health systems revealed by the response remain unaddressed. In striving to help improve these response systems, the authors identify the strategic and organizational successes and shortcomings of the nation's response to the anthrax attacks so that medical and public health communities as well as elected officials can learn from this crisis.

Next, Crystal Franco of the Center for Biosecurity of the University of Pittsburgh Medical Center leads a group of senior scientists in examining the medical community's response in the aftermath of the 2005 Hurricane Katrina in New Orleans. What their analysis reveals is nothing short of systemic collapse: federal, state, and local disaster plans did not include provisions for keeping hospitals functioning during a large-scale emergency; the National Disaster Medical System was ill-prepared for providing medical care to patients who needed it; there was no coordinated system for recruiting, deploying, and managing volunteers; and many Gulf Coast residents were separated from their medical records. They conclude the chapter with a series of recommendations, including mandating that all hospitals identify the critical systems that are essential for facility operations and make plans to preserve those systems throughout a disaster or public health emergency. They also call for a national system of electronic health records, greater regional coordination among hospitals with the federal government and with the private sector, and for the U.S. Department of Health and Human Services to take the lead role on coordinating and deploying all medical volunteers in a federally declared emergency. Overall, they recommend placing a higher priority on hospital preparedness in all community and government disaster planning.

The final case study of this section examines the consequence management response to the 1995 sarin gas attacks on the Tokyo subway system. Here, Robyn Pangi of the Executive Session on Domestic Preparedness reveals a series of missed opportunities for Japanese authorities to preempt the attack or mitigate its effects. Many of the lessons learned in Japan also offer insights for the United States. For example, relationships between various agencies need to be established and nurtured, and telecommunications infrastructure must be strengthened at the local and international levels. In addition, medical surge capacity should be enhanced, laws are needed to enable appropriate surveillance and prosecution methods, and psychological care capabilities need improvement. Pangi concludes that United States has already confronted several of these challenges, some with greater vigor and success than others, and calls for greater efforts in all areas.

This collection of chapters highlights several of the most important components of the debate over how to effectively respond to the threat of WMD terrorism. Each chapter is a potentially useful learning tool for policymakers and emergency response professionals seeking to form a coherent domestic preparedness strategy, and will hopefully promote creativity and new ideas to improve our nation's security.

Chapter 3.1

Deterrence and Preemption

Daniel Whiteneck

Deterring Terrorists: Thoughts on a Framework

Seeking to deter terrorists, especially committed, utopian groups such as Al Qaeda willing to use weapons of mass destruction (WMD), poses significant challenges.[1] Against what would one threaten to retaliate? What do these groups value? Unlike traditional states preoccupied with protecting territory and regime survival, terrorist groups use different scales to weigh costs and benefits, often calculating risks and evaluating rewards in ideological and religious terms.[2] Evidence suggests, for example, that Al Qaeda might not only use WMD simply to demonstrate the magnitude of its capability but that it might actually welcome the escalation of a strong U.S. response, especially if it included catalytic effects on governments and societies in the Muslim world.[3] An adversary that prefers escalation regardless of the consequences cannot be deterred.

Given the inadequacy of traditional state-based deterrence, it is tempting to assert that the only feasible ways to counter a WMD attack is prevention, by denying terrorist groups access to WMD through nonproliferation efforts, safeguards, and interdictions.[4] Certainly, denying access to technology, safeguarding WMD facilities, and conducting inspections at borders and ports should be considered important tools to lower the likelihood of successful WMD acquisition and attack by terrorists. Yet, such tools will always be somewhat unreliable as long as a dedicated group of trained individuals can construct at least crude WMD; the United States cannot guarantee the security culture to protect WMD located in all countries, such as Russia, despite Washington's continued urgings and financial support; and border defenses and inspections can be porous and sometimes impractical. As a result, these tools are necessary but insufficient measures to contain the WMD terrorist threat. Achieving some level of deterrence against such attacks is desirable as a complementary layer of security.

Similarly, although this analysis will focus on how to maximize the effectiveness of deterrence, this tool should be considered part of a broader strategy against terrorism whose pieces improve each other's effectiveness. International norms against terrorism, for example, are not only important, but they can be established and even observed more widely with the enforcement provided by coercion.[5] Rather than abandoning deterrence, it can be redefined as providing influence against moral, spiritual, educational, recruiting, and financial support of WMD terrorism by one of two sets of actors, either by states or nongovernmental, transnational, societal elements also referred to as the "Al Qaeda system,"[6] consisting of religious figures and institutions, political leaders and movements, financiers, less ambitious or less global terrorist groups and guerrillas, and other entities that provide either direct or indirect assistance to Al Qaeda's operations.

Deterring State Sponsorship

Although no convincing evidence yet exists that Al Qaeda currently possesses WMD or that any state knowingly assisted Al Qaeda in acquiring such weapons, reasons for such cooperation at the very least can be posited. Rogue regimes and terrorist groups have a history of military cooperation, including Al Qaeda's assassination of Northern Alliance leader and Taliban rival Ahmad Shah Masud two days before the September 11 attacks.[7] States may directly seek out a terrorist group to become a de facto extension of a state's military, acting as irregular or special forces for its WMD operations. Another more indirect linkage could be from a state that provides general assistance to a group, perhaps through basing support, general financial or material support, or training, but does not specifically conspire in WMD deployments or attacks.

The United States and its allies should communicate a clear message that states that provide either direct or indirect sponsorship of terrorism will be punished based on reasonable evidence of state linkage. In the aftermath of an attack, the response to a state that supported or even tolerated WMD acquisition on its soil would be powerful and sustained and would violate that state's sovereignty as necessary.[8]

One way that states might traditionally be warned is through the U.S. government's official list of state sponsors of terrorism. Such a tool could be perceived to convey Washington's clear and present threat to the states on the list. The list, however, is a separate declaratory statement aimed at states sponsoring a variety of terrorist-related activities and is used as a political tool to impel international scrutiny or sanction of the state in question. The state's activities may or may not include actions that contribute to the distribution of WMD materials or related knowledge or to the financing of terrorist groups that want to attack the United States. Being on the list does not necessarily make a state a U.S. target, nor would a state absent from the list be in any way exempt from a U.S. military response if it supported a terrorist attack on the United States, especially an attack involving WMD. With this potential for misperceptions, it is debatable whether the list helps or hinders the coherence of Washington's messages and threats to would-be state sponsors of terrorism and also whether it aids deterrence.

To make the deterrent threat clearer and to maximize its credibility, an adversary must be able to predict soundly what the scope of a state's response to an attack could be, not just what it would be.[9] The most fearsome, rather than the most likely, military response may hold sufficient credibility to deter an opponent. The requirement is not necessarily for the adversary to be completely certain that the threat will be carried out, but rather that escalation would be a reasonable, plausible military option in response to the defined provocation. During the Cold War, for example, the United States threatened to use tactical nuclear weapons against a conventional Soviet invasion of Western Europe. Many believe that Washington would not have ultimately followed through on the threat. In fact, in the 1960s, Secretary of State Henry Kissinger told NATO representatives "not to count on" a U.S. nuclear response to a conventional Soviet attack.[10] Nevertheless, deterrence in Europe did not fail because the adversary perceived the stakes to be high enough and the dangers of escalation to be catastrophic.

The Bush Doctrine

Today, the United States has set forth a definitive, overwhelming, and credible policy to deter state sponsorship of WMD terrorism through three declarations. The president's September 20, 2001, speech before a joint session of Congress, just days after the September 11 attacks, announced the so-called Bush Doctrine, which noted that "[the United States] will pursue nations that provide aid or safe haven to terrorism" and that "any nation that continues to harbor or support terrorism will be regarded by the United States as a hostile regime."[11] The September 2002 *National Security Strategy of the United States of America* authorizes the use of force to preempt WMD acquisition.[12] Finally, the December 2002 *National Strategy to Combat Weapons of Mass Destruction* threatens that "[t]he United States will continue to make clear that it reserves the right to respond with overwhelming force—including through resort to all our options—to the use of WMD against the United States, our forces abroad, and friends and allies."[13]

Although many despair of the growing global perception of a newly and inappropriately aggressive United States, such concern enhances the credibility of the Bush Doctrine's threat. A nation that has launched two major military interventions in the last three years—tied in large measure to supporting terrorism or WMD proliferation—and that has publicly articulated a willingness to preempt WMD acquisition or operations by states increases the credibility that it could be more than willing to respond in the same or greater magnitude after it has been attacked.

Of course, this is not to say that the United States can or should actually hold every state accountable for the acts of terrorists who have used the state's territory or have otherwise exploited the state's resources. Terrorists may choose to encamp within a state whose government is too weak to maintain its sovereignty or that lacks the resources to defend all of its borders. It is possible for a state to have a compartmented government, in which one agency may support terrorist activities independent of oversight by the head of state. Furthermore, WMD or WMD materials may simply be stolen from a state's weapons cache.

Although the United States can demand that no state knowingly provide a terrorist group with the material or technology required to develop WMD and insist that states be vigilant in controlling the use of their territory, particularly if Washington is willing to provide military or law enforcement assistance when necessary, it cannot expect poor states to install domestic intelligence-gathering capabilities similar to those of the United States or other Western nations. Less-developed African countries have little capability to control their borders. Similarly, in Asia and possibly even South America, some states do not have sufficient resources to detect discrete terrorist cell activities in large cities, let alone in the more remote areas of their territories. Nevertheless, given the seriousness of WMD consequences, the commitments the United States and its allies are willing to devote to help other states' counterterrorism efforts, and the footprint that terrorist WMD activities would likely leave in a state, it is reasonable to threaten states willing to support terrorism and actually to hold certain states accountable under specific circumstances.

Enhancing the Bush Doctrine

Terrorist use of WMD justifies and most likely requires the threat of a major military response. Through the Bush Doctrine, the scope of the U.S. threat certainly includes forcibly expelling regimes that are responsible for or support such attacks, by using conventional forces to invade and temporarily occupy an offending state. Limiting options to a unilateral, conventional response, however, would place great strains on U.S. forces, even more so if dispersed networks and responsible regimes exist in more than one country, potentially straining the credibility of a deterrent threat. The initial length and difficulties of U.S. operations in Iraq may reduce U.S. credibility to effect regime change in countries with large populations, strong nationalist backgrounds, and a large, anti-American extremist core. On the other hand, the demonstration of U.S. and allied commitment and the progress in Afghanistan as well as Iraq reinforce the credibility of U.S. threats to effect regime change in any state supporting terrorist use of WMD against the United States.

Alliances can play a role in stretching and magnifying a conventional military capacity to respond forcefully against a state that had sponsored a WMD terrorist attack. The good news is that, although the United States and its European allies have had serious disagreements about the war in Iraq, allied cohesion in the global war on terrorism has been generally strong, from NATO forces in Afghanistan to the allied presence in the Horn of Africa and the Strait of Gibraltar. International coordination of intelligence has led to arrests around the world by national police forces from North America, Europe, and Asia. In response to a state-sponsored WMD terrorist attack on the United States, NATO would almost certainly mobilize to assist the U.S. counterattack as best it could. NATO forces are not necessarily huge force multipliers for such a war, however, and they are heavily committed to other theaters, similar to U.S. forces. Even with NATO assistance and deep call-ups from the U.S. Reserve Corps and the National Guard, it is still not clear that the actual number of combined forces would be sufficient to remove regimes such as those in Iran, North Korea, or even Syria.

One possible way to increase the power of alliances could be to expand them. The inclusion of more states in U.S.-led alliances that share threat assessments, information and intelligence, and military operational risks provide increased power for counterterrorism operations outside of the traditional alliance strongholds in Europe and Northeast Asia. In principle, an expanded alliance could help make conventional deterrence more credible by exhibiting both greater political cohesion and increased military options. Several key questions, including the specific capabilities of each potential coalition member, would have to be considered before expanding an alliance such as NATO. Would other states that might also be vulnerable to a WMD terrorist attack, such as Russia, India, or Pakistan, be persuaded to join such a coalition? Conversely, would the United States and NATO agree to join forces with Russia? What if the state sponsor of the attack is a friend or an ally of another state in the coalition? Will new members of the coalition accept the U.S. standard of evidence that a particular state was behind the attack, or will the coalition become more conservative with expansion?

A Nuclear Deterrent?

Another option to fill military gaps in current U.S. and NATO conventional capabilities would be to consider threatening to use nuclear weapons against states that sponsor or conduct WMD attacks. The operational need for nuclear use increases as a target's "hardness"—its ability to limit and defend against the effects of blasts—or the difficulty of destroying what may be buried deep underground increases. Subsequently, the need promptly to destroy these targets grows, and the availability or feasibility of conventional alternatives decreases. Conventional alternatives can require a debilitating and costly process of establishing dominance on the ground or in the air and perhaps both. Yet, do nuclear threats serve as credible deterrents to rogue regimes?

Regardless of U.S. capabilities, any state might question Washington's willingness to use a nuclear weapon, even in retaliation to an attack on the U.S. homeland. Some states might decide that U.S. political considerations would completely rule out the use of nuclear weapons, despite Washington's public declarations to the contrary. The primary political and ethical consideration for the United States and its allies is the fear of causing massive civilian casualties. Even more tailored nuclear capabilities, such as smaller yields combined with more accurate bombs and warheads, cannot eliminate the incidence of casualties unless the targets are extremely remote. Moreover, the fallout pattern from even small-yield weapons is substantial at ground level.[14] These risks could cause rational adversaries to doubt Washington's intent to use nuclear weapons.

Deterrence involves communicating what might happen, rather than what will happen. The loss of civilian life in the United States from a WMD attack, combined with the seriousness of the breach of international rules and evidence of state involvement, would provide a strong justification for any U.S. government to threaten to respond with a nuclear attack. Any state would have a high degree of uncertainty as to its ability to escape responsibility and avoid the consequences of a U.S. response.

Demonstrating the link between a state and a terrorist group convincingly enough to justify any military action, let alone a nuclear reprisal, is no trivial undertaking. Given the variety of technical and human resources that the United States and its close allies have at their disposal, it is difficult to believe that a rogue state could convince itself that its direct or indirect support of a WMD attack on the United States would have no possibility of being detected.[15] In addition, the state would likely be unable to convince itself that the United States would not act on strong suspicion alone. Nevertheless, the credibility of a nuclear response remains an issue. In reality, a state—terrorist group linkage that contains significant uncertainty would constrain U.S. use of nuclear weapons much more than it would constrain the use of conventional forces. A mistaken linkage that led to a tailored, conventional response would be less damaging to U.S. prestige than one that led to a much more blunt and incendiary nuclear response.

The Bush Doctrine, through its many public and diplomatic statements, ongoing transformation of U.S. strategic forces, and demonstrated willingness to use military force against perceived threats to U.S. vital interests, has reinforced its deterrent posture against states. Without explicitly threatening nuclear retaliation, states that consider sponsoring terrorist actions must take into account that they jeopardize the survival of their regime and the future of their country and that the United States may accomplish these goals with conventional forces alone or with a combination of conventional and nuclear forces.

Deterring the Larger Society from WMD Sponsorship

If acts of WMD terrorism required state support, the problem of deterring WMD terrorism would be much simpler: deter the state and you deter the terrorist. Yet, several options for terrorist groups can make stateless nuclear terrorism a real possibility. Terrorist networks can exploit insufficient security over nuclear weapons and weapons-grade materials, identify and recruit persons experienced in international smuggling, and access people capable of putting together very simple WMD devices with components available in thousands of discrete locations throughout the world. The same options are available for terrorists to gain access to biological agents, except that smuggling or manufacturing biological weapons would be even easier than nuclear ones. For example, inhalational anthrax can be manufactured by a handful of trained personnel who simply have several dual-use industrial items delivered to a small building.[16] Stateless WMD terrorist attacks could be as likely as or perhaps even more likely than WMD attacks that have state support.

These stateless terrorist networks are embedded in a larger society that may include some elements that may only be vaguely aware of a terrorist group's specific plans to use WMD. The core of Al Qaeda, for example, may be less than 1,000 people. It typically utilizes other terrorist groups for attack logistics and other purposes but likely does not share the entire plot with these more locally oriented groups. Even these other Islamists and terrorist groups, along with broader societal supporters, that broadly share Al Qaeda's goals are likely to be more moderate and risk averse than Al Qaeda itself, less interested in using WMD against the United States, and much less willing to risk a U.S. response to a WMD terrorist attack, whether they are targeted directly or just caught in major collateral repercussions.[17]

How to define and understand deterrence of these larger societal sponsors (networks of financiers, supporters, scientists, smugglers) of WMD terrorism is much murkier than deterring sovereign states. Deterring elements in the larger society would require developing new policies and techniques to determine the target audience, the appropriate message, and how to convey it. One extreme possibility is to directly threaten the interests of society broadly, such as the state's infrastructure (its power, transportation, water, and information support systems).[18] Such blunt threats, although not very credible, could lead to more active efforts by the societal elements themselves to curtail support for terrorist groups or at least to dissuade them directly from WMD attacks. Other options that might be considered could be to threaten to destroy schools and religious centers that promote terrorist objectives, assassinate religious leaders or teachers who sympathize with terrorists, or even harm terrorists' family members to try to maximize potential deterrence. Realistically, however, even if such extreme options may enhance deterrence, they violate core American values that have been observed even in times of war, regional conflicts, or threats to the U.S. homeland, as well as accepted conceptions of "just war" theories[19] that have evolved over the course of the past centuries in the conduct of war between and among nations, with recognized and condemned notable exceptions.[20]

One potential uncertainty worth considering is whether those values would continue to hold during the potentially panicked or rabid response to a nuclear or biological attack that inflicted severe casualties on the U.S. homeland.[21] Precisely because it is impossible to predict how the U.S. government and public would react after such a tragic time, it is important to assess analytically the consequence of such a U.S. response now. Quite simply, attacking civilian targets such as religious educational centers or terrorists' families could lead to events and consequences so catalytic that both short-term and long-term effects could well swamp any benefits that might be derived from such a strike. Options to deter the larger society from supporting terrorist WMD attacks have to be more subtle than these blunt measures. The United States might be left seeking the smaller objective to deter the flow of resources such as money and recruits to Al Qaeda or other terrorist organizations seeking to use WMD.

The Exceptional Case of Weapons of Mass Destruction

For deterrence to work against this larger society, it may be necessary to adopt the concept of a limited war. This concept asserts that stopping terrorism involving WMD is more important than stopping smaller, less devastating acts of terrorism. A state might function reasonably well when it is under assault from traditional forms of terrorism with minimal changes in civil rights, the use of domestic law enforcement, the functioning of courts, and the carrying out of daily government activities, as was the case in Western Europe in the 1970s. It is clearly very difficult to argue the same when it is under an attack from nuclear weapons, for example. Even the threat of catastrophic terrorist attacks involving any WMD or mass-casualty assault can dramatically alter the normal functioning of a state. The United States has changed policies on everything from the routine importation of cargo containers to border controls to judicial procedures and financial record transparency.

In a limited war, coercive diplomacy works best when demands are limited to stopping the most egregious acts, those that are crucial for one side to prevent but are not crucial for the other side to commit. This "limits" war or conflict by drawing lines that both sides believe would lead to unacceptable conflict if crossed. Studies have demonstrated that extending threats to inhibit all undesirable actions drives credibility downward.[22] Using WMD is not easy to justify in the eyes of the larger society. Those that lend financial, educational, or other support to terrorist organizations seek to engage the state in hopes of producing political results, such as changes in domestic power structures or alterations in foreign policies, while avoiding an overwhelming response from the state that could destroy the terrorists and perhaps also their cause.[23] WMD use thwarts their objective by losing any international support or goodwill, hardening military resistance to terrorism, raising the stakes to the survival level, putting the entire larger group in an outlaw status, and making a political solution more unlikely.

Although communicating the message that some types of terrorism are worse than others risks legitimizing the more moderate but still lethal kind of terrorism to some degree, some states might choose to address non-WMD terrorism through law enforcement operations, interdiction, and public diplomacy, among other techniques, justifying such approaches with the rationalization that terrorism can be reduced to an "acceptable" level but cannot be totally defeated. This is not the case for WMD terrorism, thus raising the importance of a clearly conveyed deterrent message. That message seeks to threaten the larger society directly so that it will seek more limited means to achieve more moderate goals than those terrorists that seek to use WMD.

Clearly Communicating Deterrent Threats

Implementing a deterrent strategy, either against states or against elements of the larger society, depends on clearly and successfully communicating coercive threats. Broad, strongly worded political statements about preventing terrorism easily gain consensus internationally, but it is more difficult to achieve international agreement on specific policies and threats. Effective deterrence may not require international agreement. An attack on the

United States or its forces would provide sufficient justification for a unilateral response and the likely pretext for at least diplomatic support from most of its allies.

Coercive messages can be communicated in many ways but must be clearly and coherently tailored to the target audience. To deter a state, acceptable options might include initiating or shifting deployments of weapons or troops; publicly providing details of specific military planning related to survivable and credible response capabilities that could be easily understood by a potential adversary; declaring U.S. policy statements publicly or by using private channels of diplomacy, including back channels; and strengthening and forming alliances to demonstrate resolve and broad military capability. All of these steps signal the U.S. commitment to prevent an adversary from escalating a crisis, enhance U.S. credibility with allies and other nations, and broadcast capabilities to make the consequences of any escalation unacceptable to the adversary. When devising deterrent strategies for specific states, it is crucial to remember that what deters one foreign government might not deter another.

Two postulated approaches could deter the larger society. The first would attempt to influence more moderate elements within terrorist networks themselves. Less-ambitious groups may encourage elements of Al Qaeda to refrain from spectacular attacks on the United States that would require using WMD. These more risk-averse groups might seek the more traditional view of terrorism as a valuable tool, but one that is better focused on regional political goals and also moderate in its use of violence. Whether such groups could influence their Al Qaeda colleagues to exercise restraint remains to be seen, but they might at least end their alliance with Al Qaeda to avoid an attack by an aggrieved United States. In the future, such a separation could cause Al Qaeda to lose much of its logistics aid. The United States could consider using restraint against "moderate elements" in exchange for intelligence on any planned WMD or mass-casualty attacks by Al Qaeda against the United States or its allies.

The difficulty is identifying "moderate elements" and then deciding what combination of threats and incentives are available to separate them from the rest of the terrorist network. Would the United States target individuals on a case-by-case basis and leave others in a terrorist network alive to assume a more responsible position in the future? Such a policy seems highly unlikely, given the current nature and structure of the relevant terrorist groups, the lack of actionable intelligence, and the need to demonstrate U.S. credibility and resolve for a long-term global war on terrorism.

The second potential strategy is a variation of public diplomacy that seeks to influence the Arab and Muslim world more generally. It is doubtful that the general population of the Middle East or other Muslim countries is aware of the marked effects that a WMD attack could have on the U.S. economy and psyche, as well as on the support for an assertive foreign policy against distant threats to U.S. citizens. Making the general population aware that they might pay a large proportion of the "costs" of a terrorist attack against the United States may support the larger deterrent aims. A population educated about the capabilities of U.S. strategic forces might restrain those elements of society that support extremist actions. The members of that society would recognize that, although those horrors might be visited in some measure on a portion of the U.S. population, they would be at even greater risk of a much more devastating response with long-lasting consequences for their society. Although general suspicions of U.S. intentions might still complicate their perceptions and reactions, this would have to be weighed against the costs of continued support for the terrorists who would start this catastrophic chain of events in motion.

In sum, deterrence is a tool that the United States should not ignore. In the wake of the September 11 attacks, the prevailing thought has been that terrorists cannot be deterred because of their own nihilistic beliefs, the absence of a capability to target the individuals responsible, and the lack of a credible response to a WMD attack without causing unacceptable levels of collateral damage. To remedy this situation, the United States has used public diplomacy to threaten all those who might be connected to such attacks with a devastating U.S. response, and it has explored new capabilities for its nuclear forces that would restore the credibility of its deterrent force.

Yet, this is not enough. The United States can hold state sponsors of terrorism responsible as a first step, but it must then go further. Instead of abandoning deterrence or limiting it to state sponsors of terrorism such as Syria or Iran, who cannot be treated equally but have their own motivations and interests to be held at risk, the key is to extend deterrence using conventional and nuclear forces to the societal elements that support terrorism. A new deterrent aimed at those elements must identify the interests and vulnerabilities of the sponsors of terrorism, and it needs the credibility of diplomacy and capabilities to coerce those sponsors into ceasing their support. The new era of WMD terrorism can then be met with all of the critical tools at the U.S. government's command: deterrence, defense, and denial.

Notes

1. For a more detailed examination of deterring terrorists, including while the groups are evolving, see Brad Roberts, *Terrorist Campaigns and Prolonged Wars of Mutual Coercion* (Washington, D.C.: Institute for Defense Analysis, June 2002).
2. *The 9/11 Commission Report: Final Report of the National Commission on Terrorist Attacks Upon the United States* (Washington, D.C.: Government Printing Office, 2004).
3. Daniel Byman, "Al Qaeda as an Adversary," *World Politics* 56, no. 1 (October 2003): 139–164.
4. For a discussion of the difficulties of traditional deterrence in the modern age, see Keith Payne, *Deterrence in the Second Nuclear Age* (Lexington, Ky.: University of Kentucky Press, 1996), pp. 17–35.
5. For a discussion on the importance of establishing norms against terrorism both at societal and government levels and the role of deterrence or "fear" in reinforcing such norms, see Steve Simon and Jeff Martini, "Terrorism: Denying Al Qaeda Its Popular Support," *The Washington Quarterly* 28, no. 1 (Winter 2004–05): 131–145.
6. Paul K. Davis and Brian Michael Jenkins, *Deterrence and Influence in Counterterrorism* (Santa Monica, Calif.: RAND, 2002), pp. 1–19.
7. See Ahmed Rashid, "Afghanistan: Inside the Taliban," *Far Eastern Economic Review,* October 18, 2001.
8. Davis and Jenkins, *Deterrence and Influence in Counterterrorism.*
9. See Thomas C. Schelling, *Arms and Influence* (New Haven, Conn.: Yale University Press, 1966), pp. 2–3.
10. George Rathjens and Marvin Miller, "Nuclear Proliferation After the Cold War," *MIT Technology Review,* August-September 1991, pp. 25–32.
11. Office of the Press Secretary, The White House, "Address to a Joint Session of Congress and the American People," September 20, 2001, http://www.whitehouse.gov/news/releases/2001/09/20010920-8.html.
12. *The National Security Strategy of the United States of America,* September 2002, www.whitehouse.gov/nsc/nss.pdf.

13. See *National Strategy to Combat Weapons of Mass Destruction,* December 2002, p. 3.
14. See Michael A. Levi, *Fire in the Hole: Nuclear and Non-Nuclear Options for Counter-Proliferation* (New York: Carnegie Endowment for International Peace, November 2002), p. 31. See also Samuel Glasstone and Philip J. Dolan, *The Effects of Nuclear Weapons* (Washington, D.C.: U.S. Department of Defense, 1977).
15. For a concise discussion of the technical aspects of nuclear attribution after an attack, as well as the technical issues of counterproliferation, see John R.Harvey, *Deterrence and Beyond: Strategic Responses* (presentation, Los Alamos Conference on Nuclear and Conventional Forces: Issues for National Security, Science and Technology, Los Alamos, New Mexico, April 28-May 1, 2003).
16. See Office of Technology Assessment, U.S. Congress, *Technologies Underlying Weapons of Mass Destruction,* OTA-BP-ISC-115 (Washington D.C.: U.S. Government Printing Office, December 1993).
17. Byman, "Al Qaeda as an Adversary." See Simon and Martini, "Terrorism"; Institute for Defense Analysis, "Deterring Terrorism: Exploring Theory and Methods," *IDA Paper P-3717,* Washington, D.C., August 2002.
18. For example, estimates of civilian deaths in Iraq for the first 18 months of the war range from 10,000 to 100,000, with a more methodical study tending toward the higher number. See "More Iraq Civilian Deaths Seen in Study: *Lancet* Report Based on Family Interviews," *Boston Globe,* October 29, 2004.
19. For the best treatment of this subject, see Michael Walzer, *Just and Unjust Wars: A Moral Argument With Historical Illustrations* (New York: Basic Books, 1977).
20. Davis and Jenkins, *Deterrence and Influence in Counterterrorism.*
21. For the scope of casualties and economic effects of a nuclear attack on a U.S. city, see Jonathan Medalia, "Nuclear Terrorism: A Brief Review of Threats and Responses," *CRS Report for Congress,* RL32595, September 22, 2004. See also Ira Helfand, Lachland Forrow, and Jaya Tiwari, "Nuclear Terrorism," *British Medical Journal,* no. 24 (February 9, 2002): 356.
22. Alexander George, David Hall, and William Simon, *The Limits of Coercive Diplomacy: Laos, Cuba, Vietnam* (Boston: Little Brown, 1971).
23. Roberts, *Terrorist Campaigns and Prolonged Wars of Mutual Coercion.*

Daniel Whiteneck is a research analyst at the Center for Naval Analysis.

Vera L. Zakem and Danielle R. Miller

Stop or Else: Basic Concepts to Deter Violent Non-State Actors

As the United States considers the global security environment, the nexus of rogue/failed states, international terrorists, and proliferation of weapons of mass destruction is the challenge that demands the primary attention of the U.S. foreign and national security policy communities. According to Ambassador Robert A. Joseph, Undersecretary of State for Arms Control and International Security, "the spread of WMD by rogue states and terrorists is widely recognized as the greatest security threat that we face as a nation." Joseph's remarks echo the oft-repeated judgment of President Bush that the United States cannot afford to allow the world's most dangerous weapons to fall into the hands of the world's most violent and irresponsible groups. Since the terrorist attacks of September 11th, 2001, much has been written about violent non-state actors (VNSAs) and the characteristics, motivation, and behavior of VNSAs. Additionally, many scholars have focused on the proliferation of weapons of mass destruction (WMD). This chapter attempts to merge the two fields of studies to determine the impact of nuclear weapons in the hands of VNSAs.

This chapter summarizes our review of various studies and articles published over the last five years on VNSA motivations to acquire and use weapons of mass destruction and what this analysis means for the development of United States' policies to effectively prevent, dissuade, and deter VNSA's from acquiring and utilizing a nuclear weapon. Nuclear weapons are a class apart from other weapons of mass destruction, yet among the published studies we reviewed they appear to have received less attention than other kinds of WMD.

This chapter will examine several important issues that have been discovered in the studies and articles that have been reviewed: the characteristics of terrorist groups and VNSAs that might enable them to acquire and use nuclear weapons and technology; whether or not VNSAs can be deterred; whether or not sovereign states and criminal groups within transitional/failed states can help VNSAs acquire nuclear technology; and whether acquisition actually leads to a decision to use such weapons. Finally, we propose a set of recommendations for United States decision makers to consider in an effort to deter VNSAs as an entity, and deter them from acquiring and using nuclear weapons.

Why Do VNSAs Want Nuclear Weapons?

There are many reasons why VNSAs might want to acquire WMD, particularly nuclear weapons. The motives may be ideological, religious, political, or operational in nature. The literature in the field has collapsed all these issues under the rubric of examining the strategic cultures and operational codes of VNSAs. For a VNSA that wants to inflict large numbers of casualties, a nuclear weapon might appear to be the most appropriate weapon to employ since even a rudimentary, entry-level weapon can cause enormous casualties. Furthermore, the shock of such an attack would inevitably "command worldwide media attention."[1]

While there appears to be some debate within Islam about the religious underpinnings concerning nuclear weapons possession and use, it seems certain that within the more radical fringes of Islam, such as al-Qaida, there is little doubt that the acquisition of nuclear weapons is viewed as a religious obligation and would be a symbol of immense power. As Osama bin Laden declared during a 1998 interview:

> [To] seek to possess the weapons that would counter those of the infidels is a religious duty. . . . It would be a sin for Muslims not to try to possess the weapons that would prevent the infidels from inflicting harm on Muslims. But how we would use these weapons if we possess them is up to us.[2]

Moreover, al-Qaida may want to acquire nuclear weapons for political or retaliatory purposes similar to those attributed to states. The group's leaders have made several statements over the years that their duty is to kill as many people as possible in retaliation for U.S. policy in the Middle East and the U.S.-led wars in Afghanistan and Iraq. Sulaiman Abu Ghaith, press spokesman for Osama bin Ladin, stated that al-Qaida seeks "to kill four million Americans, including one million children," in response to Muslim casualties inflicted by the United States and its allies.[3] According to the recently arrested al-Qaida operative Mustafa Setmariam Nasar, defeating the U.S. and its allies using conventional weapons and insurgency tactics are no longer sufficient, as this type of strategy would take "many years and enormous sacrifices." According to Nasar, nuclear weapons alone will not solve the problem either. "An attack on the United States with WMD has become necessary . . . by means of decisive strategic operations with weapons of mass destruction including nuclear, chemical or biological weapons."[4] Although there is little evidence in the literature to support the idea, analysts in the field openly speculate that Osama bin Laden and others in the al-Qaida hierarchy seek nuclear weapons to make themselves more secure against the relentless attacks against their command section that have occurred in response to 9/11. Thus, the expectation among many analysts appears to be that al-Qaida's leadership has—or is capable of gaining—a means of deterrence as it is understood among the nuclear powers.

Characteristics of a VNSA and Acquisition of Nuclear Weapons

In the last five years, Western analysts have failed to reach consensus regarding whether VNSAs are deterrable or not. To better address this question, we examined the characteristics of VNSA organizations that potentially would reveal their capabilities and indicate their likelihood of using a nuclear weapon, if successfully acquired. Table 1 presents six qualitative factors to help us assess the threat of VNSAs acquiring and using nuclear weapons.

According to Thomas Badey, one of the pioneers in analyzing the issue of nuclear terrorism, the likelihood of VNSAs acquiring and using a nuclear weapon is not as high as most people would expect. For instance, to obtain nuclear technology and materials on the black market is cost prohibitive. "In 1995, according to press accounts, an Italian

Figure 1   Threat Assessment Scale for Nuclear Terrorism[30]

Factors that may indicate the potential for the use of nuclear devices by non-state actors such as international terrorists. While some factors may weigh more heavily than others, like most risk assessments this scale is based on the premise that the more factors are identified, the more likely the use of nuclear devices by a non-state actor may be.

1. Access to fissile material
    a. Access to nuclear device
    b. Access to weapons grade uranium or plutonium
    c. Access to financial resources
    d. Access to transport/shipping capability

2. Access to nuclear-related technologies
    a. Weapons components
    b. Delivery systems or components thereof
    c. Detonators or detonation systems
    d. Processing and handling technologies
    e. Measuring and detection equipment

3. Access to skilled personnel willing to work for non-state actors
    a. Nuclear technology skills
    b. Weapons design skills
    c. Operation/planning skills

4. Organization factors
    a. Covert organization
    b. Significant infrastructure and established logistics capability
    c. Operational experience

5. Geographic factors
    a. Extraterritorial enemy
    b. Proximity relative to source of materials and to target
    c. Geographic identity of perpetrator

intelligence official attempted to sell 7.5 kg of osmium (at $63,000 per gram) for $472 million."[5] At these prices, a terrorist organization would require significant financial resources to be able to purchase nuclear technology and materials, resources that would likely attract attention and result in state-led seizure actions. Moreover, even if a VNSA organization were somehow able to discretely obtain enough money to purchase nuclear technology, the VNSA still would require technical expertise in order to produce a nuclear weapon. Thus, the terrorist organization must attract experts with technological, operational, planning, and weapon design expertise, and couple this with materials and technologies that are relatively rare, a prospect which is difficult for states to ascertain. In certain parts of the world, it is conceivable that a nuclear scientist with financial hardships and/or ideological convictions in line with those of certain VNSAs might be vulnerable to recruitment by VNSAs. It is equally likely that if a nuclear scientist has worked for a government institution and does not have strong ideological convictions, his/her vulnerability to recruitment by a VNSA could be considerably less.[6]

A VNSA's access to WMD materials will most likely determine the nature and scope of a WMD attack. For instance, Aum Shinrikyo was an organization with a millennial worldview. The group's charismatic leader Shoko Asahara preached that the United States would attack Japan with nuclear weapons, sparking the beginning of Armageddon. In order to trigger the end of days, Ashara and his follower began an intensive campaign to either acquire the technological know-how to build a nuclear weapon or the connections to purchase an existing weapon. Despite the membership of more than 300 scientists and the recruitment of two Russian nuclear scientists, they were unable to acquire nuclear capabilities. As a result the group launched the 1995 Sarin attack on the Tokyo subway.[7]

To orchestrate a nuclear attack on a major Western city, a VNSA must consider the following questions:

- Will it be detonated properly and produce the desired effect?
- Will it hit the appropriate symbolic targets?
- Will it be capable of targeting a large portion of the population?
- What type of retaliation can be expected from such an attack?

The uncertainties surrounding these questions would lead many VNSA leaders to be cautious about the merits of acquiring weapons of mass destruction, particularly nuclear weapons. Indeed, analysis of VNSA organizational objectives suggest that only those groups with global terrorist aspirations are likely to turn to weapons of mass destruction. The lost of territorial ties to a specific population appears to free the planners from any concern regarding "what will happen to any population that supports them."[8]

Al-Qaida as an Organization

Describing al-Qaida as a transnational organization is a fairly straightforward proposition. Most estimates suggest that the organization has operations in 60 countries. Accurately capturing the group's organizational structure is far more difficult. Al-Qaida is not a transparent or easily defined entity; it does not mirror the top-down organizational construct that dominates governments and militaries. Nor is the group a cult of personality. Members are not mere drones programmed to do the bidding of a charismatic leader. Rather, al-Qaida represents a network of individuals coalescing around a common cause.[9] Marc Sageman argues that al-Qaida has been subsumed into a larger Salafi jihad movement. According to Sageman:

> Al-Qaida is really a social movement. People think of it as a hierarchical organization, like a military organization, but [it] was never that. [It] was always a network, like a peace movement; coalescing together for a peace demonstration . . . That is the model . . . [it] has very fuzzy boundaries. Some people are part of it, some people are not. To think of [it] as having a fixed membership is an illusion.[10]

This amorphous structure is the key to al-Qaida's continued vitality in the face of the 2001 United States-led invasion of Afghanistan. As Audrey Kurth Cronin observes:

> Benefiting from Osama bin Laden's considerable experience in business, the organization is said to be structured like a modern corporation, reflective of management concepts of the early 1990s, including bottom-up and top-down networks, a common "mission statement," and entrepreneurial thinking even at the lowest levels.[11]

James Phillips posits that al-Qaida can be divided into three tiers. The first tier he refers to as al-Qaida Central (AQC) and is composed a core group of the highly-trained professionals dedicated to achieving the organization's objectives. The second tier's membership includes associate groups. These groups are dispersed across the globe and are loosely tied to al-Qaida Central. The final tier is inspired by al-Qaida but organized locally without any connection to al-Qaida Central.[12]

What affect does al-Qaida Central's position in the global Salafi jihad movement have on its calculus to employ a nuclear weapon? Al-Qaida currently acts as the voice of the movement and as the inspiration for others driven to act against the perceived tyranny and derogation of the West and the apostate governments in the Middle East. This role is fungible. For instance, it could be argued that Hizballah's position vis-à-vis al-Qaida has increased since the August 2006 conflict with Israel; due to Hizballah's sustained engagement with and ability to withstand Israel's (and indirectly the West's) assault.

To maintain its premier position, al-Qaida Central must be perceived as a credible and effective counterforce. Having orchestrated the September 11, 2001 attacks—the most spectacular terrorist events in the past 50 years—future attacks must at a minimum meet this threshold. Any assault on a lesser scale would look weak and ineffectual to al-Qaida's audience. Accordingly, an attack with a nuclear device would create devastating psychological and physical damage.

State Sponsorship of VNSAs

When examining whether a sovereign state might assist a VNSA in acquiring nuclear technology and/or nuclear weapons, it is important to understand the reasons behind the state's support for a VNSA. Perhaps no other region has a more classic case of state sponsorship of violent non-state actors than the Middle East region. In this region, Syria and the Islamic Republic of Iran have been actively sponsoring several VNSAs such as Hizballah, as well as VNSAs operating out of Palestinian Territories, namely the Islamic Resistance Movement (Hamas), Palestinian Islamic Jihad (PIJ), Palestinian Front Liberation Party (PFLP) and others. Syria has been involved in state sponsorship of VNSAs' terrorist activities for quite some time. Over the last several decades, Syria has shown its active support for groups such as Hizballah and Hamas. Syria is known to support Hizballah militarily and financially. With regards to Hamas, Syria also supports the organization via political means by housing Khaled Mashal, Hamas' political leader. As senior U.S. government officials have pointed out, Syria continues to harbor and support these terrorist groups. This is the primary reason for the complex relationship between the U.S. and Syria.[13] Since Syria does not have key economic and natural resources that Iran has, Syria uses the "terrorism card" with the international community and in negotiations with Israel. According to Ambassador Dennis Ross, the Syrians also use Hizballah as a negotiating card for the "right circumstances"[14] on issues such as the Golan Heights, Syria's presence in the international community, and better economic incentives.

Iran has been involved in sponsoring several VNSAs for a very long time, primarily Hizballah, Palestinian Islamic Jihad, and Hamas. Most notably, Hasan Nasrallah—the leader of Hizballah—has used Iran as a model when creating a vision for his organization. He was inspired by Iran after it was able to bring to power a Shia dominant theocratic regime after the Iranian Revolution of 1979. Iran is a key financial and military supplier of Hizballah's weapons and its social infrastructure in Lebanon. For instance, it is believed that Iran has been supplying Hizballah the Shahab 3 missiles that it has repeatedly used in its attacks against Northern Israel. According to most estimates, Iran has been providing Hizballah roughly $100 million a year to help support its social services and infrastructure programs, though some diplomats and policymakers believe that the figure is closer to $200 million a year. The reason Iran has a keen interest in funding Hizballah is because Iran sees Hizballah as a tool in "undermining prospects for Israeli-Palestinian peace, and Hizballah's growing role as Iran's proxy to achieve this goal."[15] Since the start of the Intifada, Iran has also been supporting the Palestinian VNSAs. In 2002, the Israeli Navy intercepted a ship carrying 50 tons of Iranian weapons to the Palestinian territories. This incident demonstrated to the international community Iran's assistance in supporting Palestinian terrorism and violent extremism. However, Iran has a somewhat different relationship with the Palestinian VNSAs than its relationship with Hizballah. Iran only rewards Palestinian groups like Hamas and Palestinian Islamic Jihad with additional funds when they carry out successful terrorist attacks against Israel. As Matthew Levitt, the current Deputy Assistant Secretary for Intelligence and Analysis at the Department of Treasury points out, "Iranian funding to terrorist groups like Hamas and Islamic Jihad (most often funneled via Hizballah) increases when they carry out successful attacks and decreases when they fail, are thwarted or are postponed due to ceasefires or other political considerations."[16]

In addition, Iran has shown many times during the course of the Intifada its support for the Palestinian uprising through many events like Al-Quds Day (Jerusalem Day). Most recently, the international community has been under the impression that one of the reasons Iran gave Hizballah the green light to kidnap Israeli soldiers was due to the desire to draw more international attention to the Palestinian cause.

The Role of Sovereign States in Assisting VNSAs in Acquiring Nuclear Weapons

A debate exists among analysts over whether VNSAs have the ability to gain access to nuclear technology and weapons from a sovereign state. As Thomas Badey argues, despite the evidence that a number of nuclear weapon facilities in the former Soviet Union are not well protected, the risk of a terrorist organization gaining access to one of these facilities— in order to acquire nuclear material for a weapon—remains relatively low. He writes:

> Governments that have nuclear capability tend to be, for obvious reasons, extremely protective of these weapons systems. Even in situations where complete weapons systems may be left vulnerable, as in a much-cited incident in which Russian Ministry of Defense inspectors found an SS-25 nuclear missile battery abandoned by its operators in search of food, the risk of the theft or wrongful acquisition of such systems by non-state actors is relatively low.[17]

Furthermore, contrary to expectations among many policymakers, Badey argues that the chances of a terrorist organization acquiring nuclear weapons and/or technology from rogue states such as North Korea and Iran are also low. His conclusion is based on the fact that rogue states have invested significant financial and human capital in their nuclear weapon programs. For these countries, nuclear weapons represent prestige and power, and serve as a deterrent in their respective regions. After investing so much in their nuclear weapon programs, Badey argues, it is unlikely these countries would want to sell their hard-earned nuclear technology and/or weapons to terrorist organizations. Moreover, if a rogue state were to sell a nuclear weapon to a terrorist organization, and that group orchestrated an attack against Western interests, the West would likely conclude the rogue state was also culpable in the attack. For example, were Tehran to give a nuclear weapon to the Hizballah terrorist organization for use in attacking Israel, it would be reasonable for Israel and the United States to conclude that Iran had aided and abetted the attack and shared equally in any guilt for the attack. Iran would be foolish to expect that it could avoid retaliation for its support to nuclear terrorism. The same logic would apply to North Korea.

Conversely, John Parachini suggests that VNSAs can expect the support of rogue states, or radicalized failed states, if they have nuclear aspirations. He believes that VNSAs often receive support for terrorist operations from such states, which allow VNSAs to operate from within their territories. "Weak, failing, or supportive states not only enable terrorist groups to thrive but also enable their ability to acquire unconventional capabilities with sufficient scale for truly catastrophic attacks."[18] In some cases, weak states cannot effectively safeguard their nuclear facilities and control terrorist activities in their territories due to lack of civic and political order, and economic constraints. The A.Q. Kahn network of nuclear smuggling based in Pakistan is the classic example of how nuclear technologies can be shared among like-minded states.[19] To see similar sharing with like-minded VNSAs would be a difference in degree, not kind.

Rogue and transitional states and organized criminal networks can aide a terrorist organization in acquiring nuclear weapons by smuggling nuclear materials and/or weapons for the group. Robert Orttung and Louise Shelley of American University conducted a case study on organized crime in the Chelyabinsk Oblast region of Russia. Within Chelyabinsk, there are closed cities[20] that house nuclear facilities, and these cities have serious internal problems that make them vulnerable to organized crime, including illegal entry of outsiders; corruption; poverty and "command" economies; major drug trafficking and usage; and presence of terrorist propaganda and recruitment.[21]

Because of these factors in the Chelyabinsk Oblast and elsewhere in the region, criminal groups operate largely unhindered by local law enforcement and are well-positioned to facilitate VNSA efforts to steal materials and/or weapons from nuclear facilities. In many of these regions smuggling is a time-honored profession, and these criminal groups are organized to assist VNSAs in smuggling nuclear materials out of the area. The criminal elements involved could range from common thieves and drug traffickers to corrupt officials and nuclear facility guards. Poverty among those guarding nuclear facilities entices these individuals to consider bribes from what can be well-funded VNSAs. These criminals can either band together using existing networks or develop new ones to help VNSAs smuggle their precious cargo.

Figure 2 displays a network diagram of the Chelyabinsk Oblast region and shows how a terrorist organization might create a network made of local institutions, corrupt officials, drug traffickers, and criminals to acquire and transport nuclear weapons from a closed city. In this diagram, the circle represents a closed city. The boxes inside the circle are potential sources of nuclear material. The three boxes on the line of the circle represent possible actors who could transport material out of the closed city. The next four boxes represent criminal groups that could provide transportation services for the material to the terrorist organization.

As this diagram shows, it is conceivable that a terrorist group with links back to the closed city sources through prisons, extremist recruiters, and organized crime could use

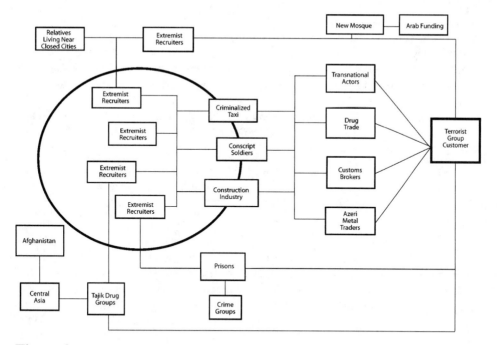

Figure 2   Chelyabinsk Corruption

relatively modest funds to bribe and purchase access and influence. The fact that the city is "closed" by the Russian government actually appears to have little impact on the situation; indeed, it could actually facilitate terrorist efforts, since the local population becomes more vulnerable to financial incentives to look the other way. Because of this kind of environment, Parachini believes the probability of a VNSA acquiring nuclear technology and/or weapons remains relatively high.

Although something must clearly be done to minimize the chances of this occurring, completely eradicating terrorist organizations operating inside sovereign states is unrealistic. As a consequence, analysts have wondered whether a terrorist organization aspiring to conduct nuclear operations could be controlled via a deterrence strategy.

Can VNSAs Be Deterred from Using Nuclear Weapons?

Mohammed El-Baradei, the head of the International Atomic Energy Agency (IAEA), recently commented to international efforts to deter VNSAs from obtaining and using nuclear weapons, saying that "we are actually having a race against time which I don't think we can afford."[22] Given this race and the strong intent and impressive resources of several VNSAs, a key question to answer is whether the United States and its allies can do anything to deter VNSAs from acquiring and using nuclear weapons? One camp of policymakers and analysts believes terrorist organizations cannot be deterred, because they will stop at nothing to try to kill their enemies. Moreover, any attempt to negotiate or provide concessions will not moderate the behavior of VNSAs. As Emily Hunt argues, "Concessions simultaneously weaken a state's position vis-à-vis the terrorists and undermine the international human rights framework by acknowledging attacks on civilians as a legitimate and effective tool of diplomacy."[23] Subsequently, the only way to stop them is to kill them first. Vice President Richard Cheney is a prominent member of this camp. Mr. Cheney once stated that traditional Cold War deterrence strategy simply will not work against VNSAs. According to him, a VNSA is not a sovereign state to which one can offer political and economic incentives in hopes of deterring it from acquiring and using nuclear weapons. Many others also support this point of view, including Monty Sagi:

> With respect to the al-Qaida organization, or to a terrorist who is committed to jihad, who is out to kill infidels and who is prepared to sacrifice his life in the process, the whole notion of deterrence is meaningless. There isn't anything they value highly enough that you can put at risk that would lead them to decide they wanted to change their policy.[24]

However, there are others who believe that deterrence may still work. For several years, a small group of analysts has questioned the assumption that VNSAs are undeterrable. The basis of their analysis is modern neuroscience, which traces the perception of fear to changes in brain chemistry produced by the involuntary nervous system. They believe that human beings are unable to control feelings of fear, and if they can be made to feel fear, they can be deterred. This school of thought believes that even highly-motivated terrorists bent on suicidal attack may be deterred when confronted with the prospect of death, capture, or failure. Moreover, these analysts suspect that terrorist decision-makers may be deterred by a conclusion that their WMD attacks will be thwarted, will be unsuccessful, or will result in unintended consequences counterproductive to their cause.

Surprisingly, traditional deterrence theory has not elaborated the protocols for dealing with VNSAs. There seems to be no reason to assume *a priori* that deterrence cannot work. It is an assumption that must be examined.

The basic root of deterrence is fear of loss. The loss of something of value such as life, property, or power often drives one to be dissuaded or deterred from action. This is likely an involuntary action and thus exploitable. The conventional wisdom is that for deterrence to work, one must discover the enemy's center of gravity and value system, and hold that at risk. The vexing problem with VNSAs is determining what to hold at risk. This difficulty is compounded by the cultural gulf that separates the Western Judeo-Christian value system that permeates much of modern societies, and the complex multi-faceted value systems within Islam. Suicide bombers represent a unique deterrence challenge. Since the terrorists in this case are willing to end their lives, threatening their lives or livelihoods with destruction is not a viable option. The long-term effect of killing or capturing terrorist seems to increase the ranks of terrorists rather than deterring future generations.

Since VNSAs by definition do not hold land and are not part of the nation-state system, it is impossible to threaten their destruction as a state entity, or even their leadership within the state, in order to deter them. The shadowy, disconnected nature of VNSAs is what makes efforts to deter or dissuade them so difficult. They do not present lucrative targets for diplomacy or warfare. Their ability to strike fear in the minds of their contemporaries through intimidation and random acts of violence further frustrate U.S. efforts to use societal pressure to deter and dissuade VNSAs.

These features lead to an important set of questions. Do VNSAs really have nothing of value that we can hold at risk? Or have we just not discovered what they value, or have not taken the time and effort to discover important centers of gravity to hold at risk? To the extent one believes terrorists cannot be deterred, there is only one alternative: their destruction or capture. However, if their destruction or capture refuels the ranks of passionately committed terrorists seeking new ways to survive and attack on America and its friends, eventually one realizes that a strategy of terrorist eradication will be too costly and, in the end, unsuccessful. At some point, an alternative to terrorist eradication will need to be discovered that may require the restoration of deterrence.

If the establishment of a deterrence relationship with VSNAs is deemed necessary, and possible, it should be pursued on terms that are as favorable as possible to the United States and its allies. Finding an approach that can deter VNSAs from action is a worthy endeavor, as is an effort to define the most favorable outcome in this kind of relationship.

Deterring VNSAs

The first step in devising a VNSA deterrence strategy is to recognize that VNSAs are not homogeneous entities. Hizballah, al-Qaida, and the Tamil Tigers are each a distinct organization with different organizational constructs and objectives. Their common denominator is the utilization of violence to achieve a political objective. Why do these organizations choose violence? Simply stated, because terrorism works.[25] The effectiveness of political violence is rarely discussed but needs to be understood to effectively deter a VNSA.

VNSAs do not pursue violence for the sake of violence but as part of a larger political objective. Exploiting the organization's political goals may be an opportunity for deterrence. The leadership of a VNSA may be less willing to operationalize an attack if it will fundamentally hurt their purported goals. Rober F. Trager and Dessie P. Zagorchev argue that targeting political goals will be the most effective course for modern deterrence strategies. "From a policy perspective, the ability to hold political ends at risk is a crucial point, because doing so stands by the far the best chance of fracturing the global terrorist network, one of the most important objectives of counterterrorism policy."[26] Within the framework of counterterrorism, Trager and Zagorchev recast the definition of deterrence.

> A deterrence strategy . . . consists of the following two elements: (1) a threat or action designed to increase an adversary's perceived costs of engaging in particular behavior, and (2) an implicit or explicit offer of a state of affairs if the adversary refrains from that behavior.[27]

Determining the criteria that a terrorist utilizes to make a cost-benefit analysis remains elusive. As in all decision models, information symmetries complicate and reduce the reliability of any behavior modification calculus. However, to summarily dismiss deterrence as an acceptable counterterrorism approach due to its level of complexity and difficulty may needlessly remove a potentially effective tool from a necessarily multi-layered policy.

An effective deterrence strategy may require the international community to engage in dialogue with VNSAs. Due to the diverse nature of VNSAs, the utility of dialogue will depend on the unique traits of each organization. For example, Hamas and Hizballah may present potential opportunities to establish a dialogue due to their role in local politics, dependence on and bond with a local population, and state sponsorship, while al-Qaida—as the front of a disparate social movement—may represent less of an opportunity. In the case of Hizballah, opening negotiations with Iran and Syria could have possible implications for undercutting a source of military and financial support. Furthermore, deterring an organization may differ from deterring individual actors.

Once again, differing violent political movements can directly influence how a terrorist operative is recruited and trained. According to Scott Atran:

> There also appear[s] to be a clear profound difference between secular nationalist groups such as the Tamil Tigers, who fight to expel occupiers from their homeland, and global jihadis, who fight perceived global domination. For example, Tamil suicide operatives are actively selected by recruiters and cannot withdraw from the planned operations without fear of retaliation against their families, whereas the martyrs for the al-Qaida network are mostly self-recruiting and deeply committed to global ideology through strong network ties of friendship and kinship so that events anywhere in jihad's planetary theater may directly impact actions anywhere else.[28]

In the case of the Tamil Tigers, suicide bombers are being deterred from aborting the mission via threats to their families, while the al-Qaida operatives are self-selected and acting due to their deep commitment to their faith, friends, and families. In both cases, the operative fears inaction. Furthermore, individual terrorists have rationalized that violence is necessary to meet their ultimate objectives. Once an individual commits to a terrorist lifestyle, the ability to question the use of violence becomes increasingly difficult.[29] Deterring individual actors will be a long-term process that will depend on public diplomacy and shifting world views. This effort will not be dependent on the United States alone but will require international commitment.

Recommendations

There are specific steps that the United States can take to develop an effective deterrence policy, such as identifying and exploiting a VNSA's center of gravity, reducing their ideological resonance, influencing the behavior of rogue states, and control access to materials necessary for developing weapons of mass destruction.

Identify and Exploit the Center of Gravity

The first step that the United States may want to take is identifying VNSAs' political centers of gravity and identifying ways to exploit these in order to deter terrorist organizations from planning and implementing an attack. For example, al-Qaida Central's political agenda is well documented. The organization's purported objectives are to remove the West's presence and influence in the Middle East, overthrow apostate regimes in the region, and establish a new Caliphate reminiscence of the Golden Age of Islam. One way to undermine the appeal of these objectives is to ensure that the United States' role in the region is not seen as exploitive. The Palestinian Parliament elections in January 2006 provided an opportunity to begin undermining some of al-Qaida's appeal by recognizing the election results. But instead, the United States response to the election only reinforces beliefs that the U.S. is only interested in ensuring Israel's survival rather than a fair solution to the Middle East conflict. Hizballah's political center of gravity is to establish a Shia dominant Lebanon and eliminate Israel. One way that the U.S. could exploit these goals is by undermining financial and military support Hizballah receives from Syria and Iran. The U.S. can do so via two channels: effective counterterrorism measures that aim to undermine the funds that Hizballah receives from these countries, and attempts to deter Syria's and Iran's support to the organization.

Reduce the Ideological Resonance

The United States needs to begin implementing a well-strategized public policy and public diplomacy campaign within the Middle East. This may include activities meant to address perceived grievances. The objective of this program should be to reduce the appeal of terrorist organizations to individual actors. This is especially important for individuals and groups who are self-motivated to act, meaning that they are influenced by—but have no direct contact—with an established VNSA. To marginalize the appeal of al-Qaida, Hizballah or other terrorist groups the campaign must address perceived grievances. To do so, the U.S. and a particular country in the Middle East should design activities that focus on trying to understand each other's culture, society, and politics. This will enable the U.S. to formulate effective policies in the region. Simply attempting to democratize a region that has shown a propensity to be somewhat hostile to the Western democratization process will not address these grievances, and as a result, ultimately worsen America's standing in the region. Above all, the U.S. should quickly and effectively initiate economic and reconstruction programs aimed at improving the quality of life in the Middle East before rogue states engage these countries first and win the hearts and minds of the region. The U.S. and the international community took some time to approve funds for relief and reconstruction in Lebanon. While the money was being approved, Iran responded quickly by immediately promising substantial funds to rebuild Lebanon, and now Hizballah and Iran enjoy significant popular support throughout the country.

Explore New Ways to Influence Rogue State Behavior

Since the events of September 11th, there has not been a time that negotiations with rogue states—and via them, violent non-state actors—have appeared so important. Given the rise of anti-Americanism in the world and the validation that military operations no longer bring stability and security to the region, negotiations and diplomatic approaches are needed. Specifically, it may be time to open negotiations with rogue states that sponsor VNSAs, especially those that operate like a "state within a state" and have political and territorial ambitions.

In the Middle East, the United States and the international community could open negotiations with Iran and Syria, two countries that are primary sponsors of VNSAs' terrorist activities. The U.S. and its allies would need to use two distinct negotiation strategies with these two countries. For example, the United States and its international allies could provide Iran with major economic and political incentives, and assist them with domestic reforms if it halts production of nuclear technology and support for terrorist organizations like Hizballah, Hamas, and the Palestinian Islamic Jihad. If Iran walks away from the negotiation table and continues on its current path, then their loss would be tremendous. Iran may find itself under attack via economic sanctions and military actions. At that point, Iran would have to ask itself whether it values stability in the Middle East and Persian civilization or nuclear weapons and terrorism. With Syria, the U.S. could pursue a different type of negotiation strategy, since it has different political objectives than Iran. Since Syria's primary interest is to be a major and respected player on the international stage, the U.S. could provide Syria with a combination of economic and political incentives if it renounces assistance to VNSAs. If Syria is willing to act favorably in this regard, the U.S. could offer to mediate possible negotiations between Israel and Syria on the Golan Heights issue. Through the negotiating process, the United States may realize that it will not only help the image of its foreign policy, it will also help its security. By finding new ways to impact rogue state behavior, the U.S. will be able to demonstrate the rogues' weakness to the world. As a result, it will be able to take appropriate security measures.

Control Access to Materials

Preventing VNSA's from acquiring nuclear weapons will require the United States to lead the effort in the international community to reducing access to nuclear materials. This includes strengthening non-proliferation regimes and programs that will reduce the availability of highly enriched uranium (HEU) and other fissile materials. As Aum Shinrikyo and al-Qaida have demonstrated, the United States and other nations may not be able to control the desire of an organization to utilize a nuclear weapon, but they can limit the option by controlling access to the necessary materials. Programs such as the Cooperative Threat Reduction (CTR) program already exist; however these programs need to be more effective. For instance, through their connections with members of VNSAs, Russian criminal networks threaten the security of nuclear facilities. Not only does the problem of physical security at these facilities need to be addressed, but so do other problems such as poverty and unemployment that drives citizens of Russian "closed cities" to join these criminal networks.

Formulate a New Deterrence Strategy

The United States Department of Defense ought to look at a new policy framework that examines the issue of deterrence in a new light. The Cold War era approach to deterrence may have been easier to understand and deal with because it involved two nation-states that tried to contain each other. The new post-9/11 security environment gives the opportunity for the U.S. to rethink its traditional way of looking at deterrence, taking into account the fact that we are now dealing with both states and VNSAs—as well as criminal networks—that need to be deterred from acquiring nuclear weapons and achieving their objectives. Therefore, the U.S. Department of Defense should create a deterrence strategy that looks at all dimensions of deterrence in the age of a Global War on Terrorism: state to state; state to non-state; non-state to non-state; and non-state to criminal network. Once the United States has developed a deterrence strategy that examines all of these actors, we and our allies will be able to better prevent terrorism, violent extremism, and the acquisition and use of nuclear weapons.

Bibliography

Allison, Graham, "How to Stop Nuclear Terror," *Foreign Affairs*, January/February 2004, 1.

Atran, Scott. "The Moral Logic and Growth of Suicide Terrorism." *The Washington Quarterly* 29, no. 2 (Spring, 2006), p. 137.

Badey, Thomas, "Nuclear Terrorism: Actor-Based Threat Assessment," *Intelligence and National Security*, vol. 16, no. 2 (Summer 2001), 43.

Black Cofer, "Syria and Terrorism," remarks to the Senate Foreign Relations Committee, October 30, 2003, Washington, DC, accessed on September 13, 2006 http://www.state.gov/s/ct/rls/rm/2003/25778.htm

Cronin, Audrey Kurth. "Al Qaeda after the Iraq Conflict" *CRS Report for Congress*. May 23, 2003 p. 3–4.

Cruickshank, Paul and Hage Ali, Mohanad, "Jihadist of Mass Destruction," *Washington Post*, June 11, 2006, p. B02.

Daly, Sara; Parachini, John; Rosenau, William. "Aum Shinrikyo, Al Qaeda, and the Kinshasa Reactor: Implications of Three Case Studies for Combating Nuclear Terrorism." Rand: Project Air Forces. Accessed August 16, 2006 http://www.rand.org/pubs/documented_briefings/2005/RAND_DB458.pdf.

Ganor, Boaz, *Non-Conventional Terrorism: Chemical, Nuclear, Biological* (Hertzilya, Israel: The Institute for Counter Terrorism, Interdisciplinary Center, April 25, 1998), p. 1.

Hunt, Emily, "Concessions will not Defeat Terrorism." The Washington Institute for near East Policy. Accessed August 8, 2006 http://www.washingtoninstitute.org.

Kydd, Andrew H and Walter, Barbara F, "The Strategies of Terrorism." *International Security*, Vol. 31, No. 1 (Summer 2006), p. 49–80.

Levitt, Matthew "Iranian State Sponsorship of Terror: Threatening U.S. Security, Global Stability, and Regional Peace," Testimony before the House Committee on International Relations, Subcommittee on the Middle East and Central Asia, and the Subcommittee on International Terrorism and Nonproliferation, February 16, 2005, Washington, DC, accessed on September 13, 2006, http://www.washingtoninstitute.org/templateC07.php?CID=228

Marion, Russ and Uhl-Bien, Mary. "Complexity Theory and Al-Qaeda: Examining Complex Leadership. *Emergence* 5(1) 2003, p. 54–76.

Parachini, John, "Putting WMD Terrorism into Perspective," *The Washington Quarterly*, Autumn 2003, p. 47.

Phillips, James, "The Evolving Al-Qaeda Threat." *Heritage Lectures, No. 928. Delivered February 16, 2006.* The Heritage Foundation. Accessed August 22, 2006 http://www.heritage.org/research/nationalsecurity/hl928.cfm

Orttung, Robert and Shelley, Louise, "Linkages Between Terrorist and Organized Crime Groups in Nuclear Smuggling: A Case Study of Chelyabinsk Oblast," PONARS Policy Memo No. 392, Center for Strategic and International Studies, December 2005, 160.

Ross, Dennis, "A Cease-Fire Reality: Dealing with Syria," *The Washington Post*, Opinions, August 17, 2006, www.washingtonpost.com)

Sageman, Marc. *Understanding Terror Networks*. University of Pennsylvania: Philadelphia, PA. 2004.

Sagi, Monty, "Ticking Bomb: Has the countdown to nuclear terrorism already begun?" (The Institute for Counter-Terrorism at the Interdisciplinary Center for Herzliya, Israel, September 11, 2004), p. 2

Taylor, Maxwell and Quayle, Ethel. *Terrorist Lives*. Brassey's: Washington. 1994.

Telvick, Marlena. "Al-Qaeda Today: The new face of the global jihad." Frontline. Accessed August 22, 2006. http://www.pbs.org

Notes

1. Ganor, Boaz, *Non-Conventional Terrorism: Chemical, Nuclear, Biological* (Hertzilya, Israel: The Institute for Counter Terrorism, Interdisciplinary Center, April 25,1998), p. 1.
2. Dunn, Lewis, "Must Acquisition Equal Employment: Can al-Qaida be Deterred from Using Nuclear Weapons?" paper for Science Applications International Corporation, McLean, Virginia, May 2005. Quoted in Anonymous, *Through Our Enemies' Eyes: Osama bin Laden, Radical Islam, and the Future of America* (Washington, DC: Brassey's, Inc, 2002). P. 18.
3. Allison, Graham, "How to Stop Nuclear Terror," *Foreign Affairs,* January/February 2004, p. 1.
4. Cruickshank, Paul and Hage Ali, Mohanad, "Jihadist of Mass Destruction," *Washington Post,* June 11, 2006, p. B02.
5. Ibid., p. 45.
6. Ibid., p. 48.

7. Daly, Sara; Parachini, John; Rosenau, William. "Aum Shinrikyo, Al Qaeda, and the Kinshasa Reactor: Imlications of Three Case Studies for Combating Nuclear Terrorism." Rand: Project Air Forces. Accessed August 16, 2006 http://www.rand.org/pubs/documented_briefings/2005/RAND_DB458.pdf.

8. Atran, Scott. "The Moral Logic and Growth of Suicide Terrorism." *The Washington Quarterly* 29, no. 2 (Spring 2006), p. 137.

9. See Marion, Russ and Uhl-Bien, Mary. "Complexity Theory and Al-Qaeda: Examining Complex Leadership. *Emergence* 5, no. 1 (2003), p. 54–76 and Sageman, Marc. *Understanding Terror Networks*

10. Telvick, Marlena. "Al-Qaeda Today: The new face of the global jihad." Frontline. Accessed August 22, 2006. http://www.pbs.org

11. Cronin, Audrey Kurth. "Al Qaeda after the Iraq Conflict" *CRS Report for Congress.* May 23, 2003, p. 3–4.

12. Phillips, James, "The Evolving Al-Qaeda Threat." Heritage Lectures, No. 928. Delivered February 16, 2006. The Heritage Foundation. Accessed August 22, 2006 http://www.heritage.org/research/nationalsecurity/hl928.cfm p. 1

13. Black, Cofer, "Syria and Terrorism," remarks to the Senate Foreign Relations Committee, October 30, 2003, Washington, DC, accessed on September 13, 2006 http://www.state.gov/s/ct/rls/rm/2003/25778.htm

14. Ross, Dennis, "A Cease-Fire Reality: Dealing with Syria," *The Washington Post,* Opinions, August 17, 2006, accessed via www.washingtonpost.com

15. Levitt, Matthew "Iranian State Sponsorship of Terror: Threatening U.S. Security, Global Stability, and Regional Peace," Testimony before the House Committee on International Relations, Subcommittee on the Middle East and Central Asia, and the Subcommittee on International Terrorism and Nonproliferation, February 16, 2005. Washington, DC, accessed on September 13, 2006, http://www.washingtoninstitute.org/templateC07.php?CID=228

16. Ibid

17. Badey, p. 44

18. Parachini, John, "Putting WMD Terrorism into Perspective," *The Washington Quarterly,* Autumn 2003, p. 47.

19. For more on this, please see the chapter on the A.Q. Khan network by David Albright and Cory Hinderstein.

20. Closed cities are cities in Russia that have high security as a result of nuclear facilities.

21. Orttung, Robert and Shelley, Louise, "Linkages Between Terrorist and Organized Crime Groups in Nuclear Smuggling: A Case Study of Chelyabinsk Oblast," PONARS Policy Memo No. 392, Center for Strategic and International Studies, December 2005, p. 160.

22. Sagi, Monty, "Ticking Bomb: Has the countdown to nuclear terrorism already begun?" (The Institute for Counter-Terrorism at the Interdisciplinary Center for Herzliya, Israel, September 11, 2004) 2

23. Hunt, Emily., "Concessions will not Defeat Terrorism." The Washington Institute for Near East Policy. Accessed August 8, 2006 http://www.washingtoninstitute.org.

24. Sagi, Monty, "Ticking Bomb: Has the countdown to nuclear terrorism already begun?" (The Institute for Counter-Terrorism at the Interdisciplinary Center for Herzliya, Israel, September 11, 2004), p. 2

25. For a discussion of the success of terrorist campaigns and specific terrorist strategies, please see Kydd, Andrew H and Walter, Barbara F. "The Strategies of Terrorism." *International Security,* Vol. 31, No. 1 (Summer 2006), p. 49–80.

26. Trager, Robert F and Zagorcheva, Dessie P. "Deterring Terrorism: It can be done." *International Security* Vol 30, Issue 3 Winter 2005/2006. Accessed August 22, 2006 http://www.columbia.edu/ rt184/Terrorism_article.doc.

27. Ibid.

28. Atran, Scott. "The Moral Logic and Growth of Suicide Terrorism." *The Washington Quarterly,* Spring 2006. p. 131.

29. Please see Taylor, Maxwell and Quayle, Ethel. *Terrorist Lives.* Brassey's: Washington. 1994 for a more in-depth discussion on the rationalization of violence.

30. Badey, Thomas, "Nuclear Terrorism: Actor-Based Threat Assessment," *Intelligence and National Security,* vol. 16, no. 2 (Summer 2001), p. 43.

Vera L. Zakem is a national security policy analyst in the Washington, D.C. area. Her research focuses on non-proliferation, terrorism, and arms control. She holds a B.A. in politics with emphasis in international relations from the University of San Francisco. She will be receiving an M.A. in government with emphasis in international security policy from the Johns Hopkins University.

Danielle R. Miller is a national security policy analyst in the Washington, D.C. area. Her research focuses on the developments in arms control, non-proliferation, and counter-proliferation. She holds a B.A. in international studies from Wright State University and an M.A. in international affairs from Florida State University.

Chapter 3.2

Nonproliferation Regimes

Natasha E. Bajema

Assessing the Role of the Nonproliferation Regimes: Are They Relevant Tools for Countering WMD Terrorism?

The 9/11 terrorist attacks dramatically transformed threat assessments with regard to weapons of mass destruction (WMD) and terrorism, shifted priorities on the international agenda and imposed new expectations on the nonproliferation regimes, i.e. multilateral treaties and export control regimes. Since 9/11, many common calculations regarding the threat of WMD terrorism have been overturned. In the past, scholars assumed that most terrorists would be restrained in terms of the scale of attack and their choice of weapons for reasons including technical obstacles, the fear of retaliation, or moral constraints.[1] Although terrorists have been known to copy effective modes of attack rather than to innovate, the 9/11 attacks demonstrated the willingness of terrorists to cause mass casualties and have crossed a threshold that may make acts of WMD terrorism more likely in the future. Arguably then, the central goal of the nonproliferation regimes, i.e. preventing the further spread of WMD, has become more relevant than ever. In fact, the 9/11 attacks might have even been expected to provide significant impetus for repairing long-standing weaknesses in the nonproliferation regimes. Yet so far, the political momentum to address the threat of WMD terrorism has not led to treaty negotiations to strengthen these regimes. Instead, the prevailing threat perception with regards to WMD, the major threat being acquisition of WMD by rogue states and non-state actors, appears to have negative implications for the future viability of the nonproliferation regimes. Without significant re-engagement by member states and U.S. leadership, the nonproliferation regimes are now facing the danger of collapse. Would the collapse of the nonproliferation regimes have damaging effects on strategies to counter WMD terrorism? How should the nonproliferation regimes be strengthened to reduce the risk of WMD terrorism? This chapter will address these questions by providing an overview of the nonproliferation regimes and evaluating the shortcomings of the regimes for addressing WMD terrorism.

Post Cold War Era: A Rapidly Changing Security Environment

The end of the Cold War generated a flurry of multilateral activity and much optimism about prospect of a new world order. With the threat of a global nuclear war between superpowers removed, the proliferation of WMD emerged as a major priority on the international agenda with the nonproliferation regimes at the forefront of efforts to deal with the threat.[2] The early to mid-1990s produced many nonproliferation successes. Several states including South Africa, Brazil and Argentina renounced nuclear weapons and joined the Nuclear Nonproliferation Treaty (NPT). New treaties were negotiated, adopted and ratified. After many years of negotiation, states were finally able to adopt the Chemical Weapons Convention in 1993, thus creating the chemical weapons regime. The long sought-after Comprehensive Nuclear Test Ban Treaty was successfully adopted in 1996. Guidelines for export control regimes were tightened. The Nuclear Suppliers Group adopted full-scope safeguards as a condition of supply, while the Australia Group added dual-use items related to biological weapons to its control lists. States renewed their support for the nuclear nonproliferation regime. The NPT, set to expire after 25 years, was indefinitely extended in 1995. Closing a key gap in the regime, the IAEA strengthened its safeguards system with the approval of the Additional Protocol by its Board of Governors in 1997.

By the late 1990s, the tide was beginning to turn for the nonproliferation regimes. Uncertainty about the effectiveness of the nonproliferation regimes for preventing proliferation against a rapidly evolving security environment began to increase due to gaps in the regimes, grievous treaty violations of Iraq and North Korea, widespread diffusion of technology and information, nuclear testing by India and Pakistan in 1998, a growing threat of ballistic missiles, and an emerging concern about non-state actors gaining access and using WMD. Towards the end of the 1990s, progress toward strengthening the nonproliferation regimes to address these new threats was being impeded in part by a lack of U.S. leadership, but also by legitimate questions pertaining to their role in countering WMD terrorism.

Skepticism about the viability of the nonproliferation regimes continued under the Bush administration in early 2001 and focused primarily on their effectiveness for monitoring and regulating state behavior. The nonproliferation regimes are seen by the Bush administration as limited tools for addressing urgent proliferation threats or regulating the behavior of rogue states. Under the nonproliferation treaties, enforcement action against a proliferating state party typically requires a finding of non-compliance and a referral to the UN Security Council, a process which is both lengthy and fraught with political obstacles.[3] Demonstrating its lack of confidence in these tools, the Bush administration refused to resubmit the Comprehensive Nuclear Test Ban Treaty to US Congress for ratification and withdrew from negotiations to strengthen the Biological Weapons Convention by rejecting the draft verification protocol in July 2001. The rejection of the draft protocol was not based on the growing threat of biological terrorism, but rather on concerns that the protocol was on one hand too weak to provide credible verification of state compliance and would at the same time seriously jeopardize U.S. national security and confidentiality of commercial information.[4]

After 9/11, the Bush administration shifted its priorities with regards to threats posed by WMD, which had mixed implications for the international nonproliferation agenda. Following the terrorist attacks, the Bush administration significantly increased its efforts in addressing the threat of WMD, but was more concerned with urgent and specific threats than with the long-term goal of preventing widespread proliferation of WMD among all states. The U.S. National Security Strategy in 2002 defined the threat as the nexus between rogue states, terrorists and WMD.[5] Accordingly, U.S. strategy to combat WMD includes three pillars: (1) proactive counterproliferation efforts including the tool of preemption;

(2) strengthened nonproliferation efforts to prevent rogue states and terrorists from acquiring the materials, technologies, and expertise necessary for WMD; and (3) consequence management.[6] Based on this threat assessment, the Bush administration has refrained from directly strengthening the nonproliferation treaties and chosen instead to supplement the regimes by creating new measures such as the G8 Global Partnership, the Proliferation Security Initiative and UN Security Council resolution 1540.[7] Despite increased engagement on the part of the U.S. with respect to the threat of WMD, the process to strengthen the nonproliferation treaties, in particular the NPT and the BWC, has reached a stalemate.[8] The continuing relevance of the nonproliferation regimes appears to hinge for a large part on their effectiveness for addressing the threat of WMD terrorism.

An Overview of the Nonproliferation Regimes

During the Cold War, the nonproliferation regimes mainly consisted of multilateral treaties and export control regimes. Since the end of the Cold War, however, the nonproliferation regimes have each evolved to encompass an intricate web of multilateral, plurilateral, and bilateral agreements and activities. Furthermore, the regimes have become increasingly interconnected by instruments and activities that address more than one class of weapons or all WMD as well as their delivery systems.[9] The multilateral treaties and export control regimes are often now referred to as the *traditional components* of the nonproliferation regimes and are the main focus of this chapter.

Each of the nonproliferation regimes is based on a multilateral treaty. Multilateral treaties are agreements among states that are designed to regulate the *behavior of states* by proscribing and prescribing certain actions. A multilateral treaty takes years to negotiate, is inherently difficult to amend, and thus offers a low level of formal adaptability to new threats. A treaty typically requires some type of domestic implementation by states, establishes at minimum a secretariat to administer the treaty or at most a formal organization to monitor compliance, and provides for review conferences at which the treaty may be informally strengthened or formally amended.[10] The nonproliferation treaties are based on the assumption that proliferation begets proliferation.[11] In other words, when states can be assured that other states renounce WMD, they will also forgo the development of such weapons.

The nonproliferation treaties are supplemented by export control regimes. An export control regime involves a political agreement (i.e. voluntary) that seeks to coordinate the national transfer policies of participants and ideally results in a harmonized system of export controls. Export controls are national measures designed to regulate the international transfer of certain weapons systems and their components.[12] Since participation in export control regimes is not legally binding, there is no verification mechanism. Each member state agrees to implement guidelines in its national legislation, and thus retains full control over its national export controls. As a result, the performance of export control regimes depends on the effectiveness of each member's national export control system. The members of export control regimes argue that harmonizing export controls is vital to the implementation of the nonproliferation treaties, in particular for preventing trade in dual-use materials, technology and equipment from being diverted to weapons purposes. However, developing states who are not members of these regimes view these instruments as supply cartels impeding their access to peaceful uses of dual-use technology.

Nuclear Nonproliferation Regime

Serving as the cornerstone of the nuclear nonproliferation regime, the NPT was adopted in 1968 and currently has 188 states parties.[13] The NPT creates two categories of states: nuclear-weapon states and non-nuclear-weapon states. Nuclear-weapon states are prohibited from transferring nuclear weapons or related technology to non-nuclear weapon states. Nuclear-weapon states are also obligated to pursue negotiations on nuclear disarmament and to transfer technology to non-nuclear-weapon states for peaceful uses of nuclear energy. Non-nuclear-weapon states are prohibited from developing nuclear weapons, but are allowed to develop the full-range of nuclear technology for peaceful purposes. These states are required to conclude safeguards agreements with the IAEA to provide assurance that they are complying with their treaty obligations.

IAEA safeguards are designed not to *prevent* a state from diverting nuclear technology and materials to nuclear weapons programs or from engaging in clandestine nuclear activities, but rather are intended to *detect* such diversion and clandestine activities. The IAEA declares states in compliance with safeguards by verifying that the data in state declarations matches the data obtained through inspections, open source analysis, satellite imagery and third-party information. Any inconsistencies are clarified between inspectors and states through additional inspections and information from states. The IAEA Director General reports unresolved consistencies to the IAEA Board of Governors, which has the authority to declare a state in non-compliance with safeguards. Cases of non-compliance are referred to the UN Security Council for possible enforcement measures.

The tools available to the IAEA for assessing the compliance with safeguards obligations vary depending on the standard of safeguards accepted by states. Since 1997, there are three different standards for safeguards measures under the NPT: comprehensive safeguards, Additional Protocol and Small Quantities Protocol. The type of safeguards agreement required for fulfilling NPT safeguards obligations was adopted in 1971 and is now known as a comprehensive safeguards agreement or full-scope safeguards. Under a comprehensive safeguards agreement, the IAEA is "obliged to ensure that safeguards are applied to all nuclear material in all peaceful nuclear activities."[14] Under these agreements, IAEA inspections are limited to locations containing nuclear material that has been declared by states. The IAEA does not have the authority to inspect locations beyond those that contain declared nuclear material. This restriction has significantly hindered the IAEA's ability to verify the absence of undeclared nuclear material and activities.

After discoveries of Iraq's and North Korea's safeguards violations, the IAEA initiated a process to strengthen the efficiency and effectiveness of the safeguards system and adopted the Additional Protocol in 1997. The Additional Protocol provides the IAEA with more comprehensive information on the nuclear activities of a state and extends the authority of the IAEA to inspect beyond locations containing declared nuclear material to ensure the absence of undeclared activities.[15] Although the Additional Protocol provides a higher standard of safeguards compliance, concluding an Additional Protocol remains voluntary for states party to the NPT.

The lowest standard for safeguards compliance with the NPT has recently come under increased scrutiny.[16] States with small quantities of nuclear material may sign a Small Quantities Protocol (SQP) to their safeguards agreement, which holds most safeguard measures in abeyance for that state.[17] Since small quantities of fissile material are not large enough to be diverted to building a nuclear weapon, inspections were viewed as unnecessary. In practice, these agreements reduce the authority of the IAEA to evaluate the nuclear program (or lack thereof) in such states or even verify that the state continues to qualify for the SQP exemption. Although the IAEA Board of Governors determined in 2005 that IAEA has "the right to conduct inspections in SQP States," the scope of these inspections remains limited.[18]

Shortly after the entry into force of the NPT in 1970, nuclear supplier states party to the NPT became concerned that variations in export controls could lead to unintentional proliferation of nuclear weapons. These states formed the Zangger Committee in 1971 to harmonize export controls to ensure that commercial competition in nuclear technology did not lead to the spread of nuclear weapons. In 1974, the Committee developed a so-called "trigger list", which represents a list of nuclear-related items that trigger the requirement for IAEA safeguards and guidelines to regulate the export of those items to states not party to the NPT. Given the nearly universal membership of the NPT, the Zangger Committee still exists but has been in practice replaced by the Nuclear Suppliers Group (NSG).

Founded in 1975, the NSG incorporates and expands upon the trigger lists established by the Zangger Committee. The trigger list for the Zangger Committee is limited to items that are especially designed for use in nuclear activities. The NSG extends its trigger list to include dual-use items that can be used in other industries besides the nuclear industry. In addition, whereas the trigger list for the Zangger Committee only applies to states which are not party to the NPT, the NSG guidelines are applied to all importing states.

In recent years, the NSG has increasingly tightened its guidelines on the transfer of items related to the peaceful uses of nuclear energy. In 1992, the NSG decided to use full-scope IAEA safeguards as a condition of supply for nuclear materials and technology. In May 2004, the NSG established a "catch-all" mechanism to provide a national legal basis to control the export of nuclear-related items that are not on the control lists, when such items are or may be intended for use in connection with a nuclear weapons program. Catch-all controls are intended to prevent end-users of concern, whether states or non-state actors, from obtaining dual use materials, equipment and technology.[19]

Biological Weapons Regime

The biological weapons regime is based on two multilateral treaties. The Geneva Protocol, signed in 1925, prohibits the use of chemical and biological weapons in war. The Biological Weapons Convention (BWC), signed in 1972, establishes international norms against the possession or development of biological weapons and represents the first multilateral treaty banning an entire category of weapons.[20] Despite this achievement, the BWC lacks the robustness of the other nonproliferation treaties and is considered little more than a gentlemen's agreement.

Under the BWC, all states are prohibited from developing, producing, stockpiling, acquiring or retaining biological agents, toxins, weapons or means of delivery. States are further obligated not to transfer these items to any recipient, group of states or international organization. States are required to implement the provisions of the convention by adopting national legislation and taking measures to prohibit and prevent the development, production, stockpiling, acquisition, or retention of biological weapons within its territory or under its jurisdiction anywhere.

Despite imposing ambitious obligations on states parties, the BWC did not establish an organization or even a secretariat responsible for administration, implementation or monitoring of the convention. Furthermore, the BWC also does not contain any provisions for verifying compliance or enforcement in the case of non-compliance. In contrast to the NPT the CWC and, the BWC lacks provisions for verifying compliance with the treaty. At the time of negotiation, states did not perceive a need for a verification regime. It was believed that states would abide by their obligations without a verification regime due to the lack of military utility for biological weapons and political costs involved with non-compliance.[21]

During 1990s, negotiations had been underway to strengthen the verification components of the BWC. After the U.S. rejected the verification protocol in July 2001, these negotiations were suspended and replaced by a pragmatic interim process to strengthen implementation of the BWC.[22] Since 2002, the interim process has refocused the efforts of states on the types of national legislation and measures that are necessary for implementing the convention at the domestic level. Although the interim process has involved productive consultations among states and led to a greater understanding of implementation issues for the BWC, it is unlikely that states will return to negotiations on a verification protocol at the BWC Review Conference in November 2006.

The BWC is supplemented by an export control regime, the Australia Group. The Australia Group (AG) was first created in 1985 to ensure, through the harmonization of export controls and licensing procedures, that trade in certain chemicals and dual-use equipment by industries, would not lead to a proliferation of chemical weapons. In 1990, the AG adopted its first guidelines on biological weapons, which now include extensive control lists for pathogens, toxins and equipment. The AG maintains a set of guidelines or "control lists" for controlling transfers that could contribute to the development of biological and chemical weapons programs by states and non-state actors. Each member state agrees to deny requests for export licenses for items on the lists if there is a concern that the materials or equipment may be diverted to the development of a biological or chemical weapons program. Among the most recent guidelines, members of the Australia Group abide by "catch-all controls," which are intended prevent end-users of concern from obtaining a dual-use materials, equipment and technology related to chemical or biological weapons.

Chemical Weapons Regime

Since toxins are considered to be both biological and chemical weapons, there has always been overlap between the biological and chemical weapons regimes. Both regimes include the Geneva Protocol and Australia Group described above. In fact, states originally intended to deal with biological and chemical weapons in a single convention. However, the proven utility of chemical weapons on the battlefield made it more difficult for states to reach consensus on banning them. Furthermore, the existence of effective chemical weapons arsenals made the treaty negotiations more labor-intensive due to the need for a dismantlement process and adequate provisions for verification.[23] Difficulties in reaching agreement on verification delayed the negotiation of the Chemical Weapons Convention (CWC) until the 1980s.

The chemical weapons regime was formally established by the CWC in 1997.[24] The CWC boasts a comprehensive and sound treaty structure, near universality, and few challenges to the norm against possession, acquisition and development of chemical weapons.[25] The CWC prohibits all states from developing, acquiring, stockpiling, retaining or transferring chemical weapons to anyone. The CWC establishes clear criteria for the national implementation of its provisions. In particular, the CWC calls for the criminalization (penal legislation) of offensive activities involving chemical weapons and requires legislation that establishes jurisdiction for committed crimes.

The CWC established the Organization for the Prohibition of Chemical Weapons (OPCW) to implement the treaty and monitor and verify compliance with the treaty. The CWC verification system differs from the NPT/IAEA system in several respects. Since the CWC requires all states parties to declare all chemical weapons stockpiles and chemical weapons production facilities, the inspections regime must verify the destruction of chemical weapons programs, non-diversion from the chemical industry and the absence of clandestine activities. This means that the OPCW must evaluate two types of state declarations during its inspections: declarations on status of the destruction of chemical weapons programs and declarations on commercial and industrial activity related to dual-use chemicals.

The CWC also contains extensive procedures for investigating suspected cases of non-compliance. States are encouraged to resolve disputes and questions through bilateral consultations. If these do not suffice, a state party may request clarification from the OPCW Executive Council for any situation that is unclear or may be related to non-compliance. If the requested clarification is deemed inadequate, the state may also request a challenge inspection of the facilities in question. In addition, the CWC authorizes the OPCW to investigate alleged use of chemical weapons upon request by a state party.

The OPCW Conference of the States Parties and Executive Council both have the authority to address cases of non-compliance that are identified through the inspections process. Punitive measures for non-compliance can include restriction or suspension of a state party's rights and privileges under the convention (e.g. trade in dual-use chemicals). If a state is found to be in non-compliance the Executive Council may refer the case to the Conference of the States Parties or directly to the UN Security Council in extraordinary cases for enforcement measures.

The Australia Group establishes harmonized export controls on dual-use chemicals, equipment and technology. The CWC is the only nonproliferation treaty to contain provisions on the transfers of dual-use materials. The provisions of the CWC are complemented by the guidelines of the Australia Group. The CWC establishes criteria and regulations for three categories or "Schedules" of chemicals, Schedule 1 containing chemicals that pose the highest risk. For all three Schedules, states parties are required to report transfers (imports and exports) of the listed chemicals. States parties are prohibited from transferring Schedule 1 and 2 chemicals to states not party to the convention. Despite these provisions, the regulations in the CWC do not constitute an export control regime. The transfer regulations do not apply to equipment and technology that could be used to develop chemical weapons. Moreover, once a state is party to the CWC, it can import any of the chemicals restricted by the convention, including Schedule 1 chemicals.

Assessing the Shortcomings of the Nonproliferation Regimes for addressing WMD Terrorism

Since the end of the Cold War, the nonproliferation regimes have been confronted with significant challenges not only to their effectiveness for regulating state behavior, but also to their capacity for addressing the complete menu of threats posed by weapons of mass destruction (e.g. rogue states and non-state actors). The nonproliferation regimes for nuclear, biological and chemical weapons differ greatly in their history, structure, procedures and technical aspects. Since the overall effectiveness of each regime for countering WMD terrorism depends on these factors, each regime should ideally be assessed separately. Due to limited space, however, this chapter will instead highlight the main shortcomings of the nonproliferation regimes for addressing the threat of non-state actors gaining access to and using weapons or materials of mass destruction.

The most obvious shortcoming of nonproliferation regimes is that the treaties are designed to regulate, monitor and verify the actions of states, i.e. to prevent state proliferation, and not to curb activities of non-state actors. Negotiated respectively in the late 1960s and early 1970s, the NPT and the Biological Weapons Convention (BWC) contain no reference to potential threats posed by non-state actors.[26] Consequently, the provisions of the treaty have little bearing on the threat of non-state actors. Although the treaties serve to establish global norms against the acquisition, development and use of WMD, terrorists do not consider themselves bound by international treaties nor by the norms established by them. The enforcement measures or reputational costs imposed on states by the treaties in the case of violation also are not applicable to terrorists. Thus, the main question to consider, is whether or not there is any spillover from efforts to prevent WMD proliferation among states to addressing the non-state actor problem.

It can be argued that the fewer the states involved in developing WMD, the less likely that such weapons will be stolen by non-state actors, sold to the black market by disgruntled guards, or intentionally diverted by states to terrorist groups. Graham Allison argues that preventing new states from joining the nuclear club remains a critical component of a strategy to counter nuclear terrorism.[27] Other scholars are less convinced that restraining state proliferation will necessarily prevent nuclear terrorism due to the multifaceted nature of the threat.[28] Such skepticism, though unintentionally, implies that there are one-size-fits-all approaches for countering WMD terrorism. While restraining state proliferation of WMD is definitely not sufficient for countering the multidimensional threat of WMD terrorism, this chapter argues that limiting the spread of WMD among states makes a critical contribution in this direction. Based on this assumption, the nature of the role that nonproliferation regimes in countering WMD terrorism depends on their effectiveness for regulating state behavior. The analysis in this section will assess the weaknesses of the nonproliferation regimes for containing the spread of WMD and thus indirectly for containing the threats of WMD terrorism.

Lack of Universality

The nonproliferation regimes face serious challenges in regulating state behavior on a global scale. Although the nonproliferation treaties are nearly universal, there are important holdouts to each treaty. For example, the Chemical Weapons Convention (CWC) has 178 states parties. States that have not signed or ratified the CWC include North Korea and Syria. North Korea has been known to widely trade its ballistic missile technology and under the pressure of additional economic sanctions, may also trade its nuclear technology to the highest bidder.[29] Syria has a history of providing weapons to non-state actors including Hizbollah. As long as key states fail to sign and adhere to the nonproliferation treaties, these states will provide possible access points to more advanced level technology to non-state actors.

Compounding the issue of universality, the widespread diffusion of technology has compromised efforts to control of exports of WMD-related technology. Export control regimes such as the Nuclear Suppliers Group are by design exclusive rather than universal in their membership structure. Membership in the NSG is limited to major suppliers of nuclear technology who meet certain criteria including adherence to the NPT. The exclusion of states with advanced nuclear technology such as India, Israel, Pakistan, Iran and North Korea has given rise to the threat of second-tier proliferation, which Chaim Braun and Christopher Chyba define as proliferation "in which states in the developing world with varying technical capabilities trade among themselves to bolster one another's nuclear and strategic weapons efforts."[30] Pakistan, an important hold-out to the NPT was discovered in 2004 to be a critical node in an illicit trading network for advanced nuclear technology among states such as Iran, Libya, and North Korea. In other words, states that are most likely to proliferate WMD and sell technology related to WMD to non-state actors are becoming able to operate completely outside of the nonproliferation regimes in so-called proliferation rings.[31]

Weaknesses in Treaty Structures

While not directly applicable to the threat of non-state actors, any weaknesses in the structures of nonproliferation treaties will have negative implications for the goal of containing the threat of WMD proliferation. The more widespread that WMD are proliferated among states, the more likely it is that non-state actors will be able gain access to WMD or related materials.

Though not all nonproliferation treaties are created with equal structures, each nonproliferation treaty faces significant challenges with regard to enforcement in the case of non-compliance. Ideally, nonproliferation treaties are designed to regulate state behavior through a verification process that entails the submission of state declarations, inspections by an independent agency, impartial conclusions on the compliance of states, and enforcement in cases of intentional non-compliance.[32] Both the NPT and the CWC create relatively robust verification mechanisms. Moreover, NPT/IAEA and the CWC/OPCW procedures include the possibility of referral to the UN Security Council for enforcement. However, the inconsistent record of the UN Security Council in enforcing nonproliferation norms and the difficulty in reaching agreement among the major states on punitive measures indicate that the question about what happens after detection of violations remains fundamentally unanswered.[33]

Lacking a mechanism for verification, the BWC has by far the weakest treaty structure. The process to strengthen the verification component of the BWC began with the establishment of confidence-building measures at the Review Conferences in 1986 and 1991.[34] The confidence-building measures are politically binding and aim to increase transparency and confidence that all states are complying with their obligations under the BWC through the exchange of information. Lacking legal status, however, the confidence building measures have failed to significantly enhance transparency or confidence with regards to the BWC. As few as 11 states parties have made annual declarations on a consistent basis since 1987.[35] In the early 1990s, revelations that the former Soviet Union, a depositary of the BWC, had developed a highly advanced bioweapons program, served as significant impetus for establishing an effective and legally binding verification mechanism for the BWC. In 1994, an Ad Hoc Group was created to develop a draft proposal for a verification protocol.[36] After almost seven years of negotiation, Tibor Tóth, chairman of the Ad Hoc Group, proposed a "composite text" for the protocol based on compromise language in March 2001. Three months later, the U.S. rejected the protocol. The absence of a verification mechanism for the BWC remains a critical gap in the biological weapons regime.

Challenges of Regulating the Behavior of Rogue States

Even with extensive monitoring and inspections, the nonproliferation regimes have not proven themselves effective tools for dealing with rogue states. Despite ratifying the NPT and concluding safeguards agreements, Iraq, North Korea, Libya and Iran have engaged in clandestine nuclear activities with the intent of developing nuclear weapons. The safeguards system under the NPT failed to detect non-compliance in the cases of Iraq, Iran and Libya. Iraq was found in compliance by the IAEA, but discovered to have developed a secret nuclear weapons program during the UNSCOM/IAEA inspections following the Gulf War. After a dissident group revealed the locations of two undeclared nuclear sites in 2002, Iran was found to be in non-compliance with its safeguards obligations by the IAEA Board of Governors three years later in 2005.

The case of North Korea demonstrates the necessity of the cooperation by the inspected states for the *effective implementation* of IAEA safeguards. Having ratified the NPT in 1985, North Korea waited until 1992 to submit its initial declaration and begin to fulfill its safeguards obligations. When the IAEA discovered inconsistencies in the declaration during ad hoc inspections and attempted to conduct a special inspection, North Korea refused to admit inspectors and announced its withdrawal from the NPT. After agreeing to suspend its withdrawal from the NPT, North Korea remained party to the NPT under the 1994 Agreed Framework, an agreement between the U.S. and North Korea, which provided generous incentives to North Korea to freeze its nuclear program including the construction of two nuclear power plants, provision of heavy fuel oil and negative security assurances. In 2002, the U.S. received information about a clandestine uranium enrichment program in North Korea in violation of the Agreed Framework, the NPT and IAEA safeguards. After confrontation by the U.S. regarding its violations, North Korea withdrew from the NPT in 2003 and went on to test its first nuclear device in October 2006. Although the IAEA strengthened its safeguards system in 1997 with the adoption of the Additional Protocol, the effectiveness of the new safeguards system for detecting non-compliance has yet to be tested, and adherence to the Additional Protocol remains voluntary for NPT states parties. Without the cooperation of inspected states, however, any level of IAEA safeguards remains ineffective for verifying compliance.

Materials of Mass Destruction: The Dual-Use Problem

The dual-use problem reveals a critical shortcoming of nonproliferation regimes for addressing the threat WMD proliferation: the inability of these regimes to control access to materials of mass destruction. Because the treaties are focused on state proliferation of WMD, they are weapons-based rather than materials-based. Though prohibiting states from developing *weapons*, nonproliferation treaties not only permit defense activities, but also promote peaceful activities involving dual-use materials, equipment and technology. The dual-use problem is especially acute for the biological and chemical weapons regimes.

The distinction between materials, technology and equipment for offensive or peaceful purposes is often non-existent or merely political, i.e. dependent on the offensive or peaceful intentions of the states themselves. For example, there is often little technical distinction between an offensive biological or chemical warfare program and defensive programs. The production of small quantities of biological and chemical warfare agents is required for testing the effectiveness of defensive gear or a vaccine. Moreover, many of the materials, equipment and technology used for developing WMD have diverse dual-use applications. For example, the equipment required for the production, stabilization and dissemination of biological agents can be acquired on the commercial market since it is used for legitimate applications by the pharmaceutical, food, cosmetics and pesticide industries. Jonathan Tucker argues that "most incidents of chemical terrorism have involved the use of household or industrial chemicals" such as cyanides, ammonia, insecticide or pesticide, arsenic, sulfuric acid, rat poison and weed killer.[37] In other words, terrorists have tended to employ "off-the-shelf" chemicals rather than develop or steal military-grade chemical warfare agents.[38]

The dual-use problem undermines the effectiveness of inspections for detecting diversion of materials by states or theft by non-state actors, especially in the case of chemical and biological weapons.[39] In contrast to the relative unavailability of fissile materials, dual-use materials for developing low-tech biological and chemical weapons are easy to acquire. Globalization and the information age have led not only to a widespread diffusion of dual-use technology and technical information related to WMD, but also an abundance of relevant facilities for inspections. While the IAEA is expected to verify compliance with safeguards at 923 nuclear facilities, the Organization for the Prohibition of Chemical Weapons (OPCW) is charged with verifying compliance with the CWC, a feat which requires providing assurance that no diversion is taking place at as many as 5,835 chemical facilities.[40] This number of facilities far surpasses the inspection capability of the OPCW. In 2005, the OPCW were able to conduct 381 inspections at 239 sites in 55 countries.[41] Biological materials can be acquired from an even more vast array of dual-use facilities including university labs, hospitals, pharmaceutical companies, biotech firms, etc. Christopher Chyba and Alex Greninger argue that the nonproliferation model is simply not adequate for addressing the challenge of managing the consequences of rapidly advancing area of biotechnology.[42] The sheer number of facilities alone would jeopardize the effectiveness of any verification regime devised for the BWC.

Threat of Latent Proliferation

Until recently, the dual-use problem has not been as acute for the nuclear nonproliferation regime. Christopher Chyba argues that the nonproliferation regime for nuclear weapons is comparatively robust when considering the entire spectrum of WMD.[43] The acquisition of fissile material represents the main obstacle for states or non-state actors who seek to develop nuclear weapons. Fissile material is not readily available, and weapons-useable fissile material has few legitimate peaceful applications.

The nuclear technology for developing weapons-grade material, on the other hand, is also used to develop fuel for nuclear power plants. In the past, access to advanced nuclear technology was limited. Although acquiring weapons-grade fissile material remains challenging even for states such as Iran, the technology for producing enriched uranium and for reprocessing plutonium is becoming more readily available. When the NPT was adopted in 1968, there were only a few countries capable of enriching uranium. Since then, as many as 18 states have the requisite technology for enriching uranium and 13 states the technology for reprocessing plutonium.[44] States with a commercial capacity to enrich uranium or reprocess plutonium can come within months of a nuclear weapon capability while remaining in compliance with the NPT. This possibility has given rise to the threat of latent proliferation, "in which a state adheres to, or at least for some time maintains a façade of adhering to, its formal obligations under the NPT while nevertheless developing the capabilities needed for a nuclear weapons program."[45] The threat of latent proliferation seriously undermines the NPT not only for curbing the proliferation of nuclear weapons, but also for reducing the risk of non-state actors gaining access to fissile material.

Countering WMD Terrorism: A Role for the Nonproliferation Regimes?

Based on the analysis thus far, the prospects for nonproliferation regimes to play a role in countering WMD terrorism let alone regulate state behavior appear rather bleak. If this indeed were the desired conclusion of this chapter, then it follows that a collapse of the nonproliferation regimes would not have a very profound impact on efforts to counter WMD terrorism. Thus, recommendations for addressing WMD terrorism would *at most* pay lip service to the nonproliferation regimes. However, before reaching a hasty conclusion, it is useful to consider the alternative, i.e. the nature of the threat of WMD terrorism in the absence of the nonproliferation regimes. Without the nonproliferation regimes, all states would be free to develop WMD according to their capabilities. There would be no international agency for conducting inspections to determine the peaceful or offensive nature of WMD-related programs. Without reliable information about the intentions of states, states who would otherwise forgo the development of WMD, might choose instead to do so. States would have no fora in which to coordinate their national policies on law enforcement, extradition, export controls, and security and safety of WMD-related materials and facilities. It is clear that the alternative presents a far more complicated world, in which to prevent acts of WMD terrorism. The nonproliferation regimes, insofar as they remain critical tools for regulating state behavior, are relevant for countering the threat of WMD terrorism for three reasons.

First, the counterproliferation toolbox contains a wide range of tools, all of which are necessary for a comprehensive strategy against WMD terrorism.[46] There is no one-size-fits-all approach to countering WMD terrorism. Given the many different threats posed WMD, a comprehensive requires a multilayered (e.g. demand, supply, etc.) and a multidimensional (e.g. nuclear, biological, chemical, etc.) approach. The nonproliferation treaties provide the first line of defense, establishing global norms against the possession, acquisition and development of WMD.[47] The norms established by the nonproliferation treaties help to contain the demand for WMD. Meanwhile, export control regimes as a second layer restrict the supply of WMD-related materials, equipment and technology.[48] Without these instruments, the proliferation of WMD would become even more unmanageable and thus compromise efforts to prevent WMD terrorism.

Second, the nonproliferation treaties provide a legal framework that is essential for countering the threat of WMD terrorism.[49] The more comprehensively these treaties are implemented at the domestic level, the more that these instruments have to offer for countering WMD terrorism. The creation of the export control regimes only scratch the surface in this regard. Both the CWC and BWC explicitly require national implementation of their provisions. Full implementation of the CWC and BWC might include a wide range of legislation that criminalizes activities involving the offensive use of chemical or biological materials, imposes minimum security standards on facilities containing sensitive materials, or requires licenses for access to dangerous materials. IAEA safeguards agreements require states to develop a system for the accounting and control of nuclear materials. The implementation of these requirements could be extended to include measures to ensure the safety and security of nuclear materials. The adoption of UN Security Council resolution 1540 in 2004 reinforces the importance of this feature of nonproliferation treaties. Resolution 1540 requires all UN member states to adopt legislation and measures to criminalize activities related to WMD terrorism and to implement measures to prevent WMD terrorism including export controls, minimum levels of physical protection on WMD-related materials, border controls, and transport regulations.[50]

Third, the norms established by the nonproliferation regimes underpin all other international efforts designed to counter threats posed by WMD. The existence of these norms remains critical for the effective functioning of activities such as the Cooperative Threat Reduction (CTR) program, G8 Global Partnership and newer instruments such as the Proliferation Security Initiative (PSI). Established by the U.S. Congress in 1991, the Nunn-Lugar Program, now known as CTR, initially aimed to assist with the safe and secure transportation, storage, and dismantlement of nuclear, chemical and other weapons in the former Soviet Union. CTR activities have evolved into a comprehensive threat reduction and nonproliferation effort that includes a wide range of activities from enhancing safety, security and control of WMD-related materials to the demilitarization, destruction and dismantlement of WMD themselves. The G8 Global Partnership aims to expand upon threat reduction activities undertaken by the U.S. and the European Union in Russia. The Global Partnership was established at the Kananaskis G8 Summit in 2002 to "prevent terrorists, or those that harbor them, from acquiring or developing nuclear, chemical, radiological and biological weapons; missiles; and related materials, equipment and technology." At the summit, G8 leaders pledged $20 billion over ten years to finance non-proliferation projects in Russia. Established by the U.S. in 2003, PSI involves a set of operational activities to interdict illicit shipments of WMD and related materials via sea, land and air. Serving as a complement to export control regimes, PSI plays an important role in addressing the problem of second-tier proliferation discussed earlier in this chapter and thus countering the threat of WMD terrorism.[51]

Given the important role that nonproliferation regimes play in regulating state behavior, the collapse of the nonproliferation regimes would have a profound effect on efforts to counter WMD terrorism. However, expending effort on lengthy negotiations to close legal gaps in existing nonproliferation treaties is not the only way to keep the nonproliferation regimes from collapsing, nor is it the best way to maximize their effectiveness for addressing WMD terrorism. Legal frameworks without national implementation are not effective tools for countering WMD terrorism. By adopting legislation and measures to prohibit activities involving dangerous materials, establishing minimum standards for the safety and security of WMD-related materials, equipment and technology, states can strengthen their capacity to counter WMD terrorism. Ensuring that states have effectively implemented the nonproliferation treaties in their domestic systems and have the capacity to enforce domestic legislation should be a priority. Despite a stalemate in the treaty-strengthening process, the norms against WMD are strong and continuously reinforced by the development of new measures and initiatives to address the threat posed by WMD. New initiatives such as the Global Threat Reduction Initiative and the Global Initiative to Combat Nuclear Terrorism are likely to be better placed to address the critical gaps in the nonproliferation regimes by focusing on the security of WMD-related materials.[52]

Suggested Readings

Braun, Chaim and Christopher F. Chyba. "Proliferation Rings: New Challenges to the Nuclear Nonproliferation Regime." *International Security* 29, no. 2 (Fall 2002): pp. 5–49.

Chyba, Christopher F. "Toward Biological Security." *Foreign Affairs* (May/June 2002).

Falkenrath, Richard A. Robert D. Newman, and Bradley A. Thayer, *America's Achilles' Heel: Nuclear, Biological and Chemical Terrorism and Covert Attack.* Cambridge, MA: MIT Press, 1998

Graham, Thomas Jr. *Commonsense on Weapons of Mass Destruction.* Seattle: Washington University Press, 2004.

Parachini, John. "Putting WMD Terrorism into Perspective." *The Washington Quarterly* 26, no. 4 (Autumn 2003): pp. 37–50.

Roberts, Brad. *Weapons Proliferation and World Order: After the Cold War.* The Hague, The Netherlands: Kluwer Law International, 1996.

Stern, Jessica. *The Ultimate Terrorists.* Cambridge, MA: Harvard University Press, 1999.

Notes

1. See for example, Richard A. Falkenrath, Robert D. Newman, and Bradley A. Thayer, "America's Achilles' Heel: Nuclear, Biological, and Chemical Terrorism and Covert Attack," in Robert J. Art and Kenneth N. Waltz, eds., *The Use of Force: Military Power and International Politics*, Sixth Edition, Lanham, MD: Rowman & Littlefield Publishers, Inc., 2004; See also Jessica Stern, *The Ultimate Terrorist*, Cambridge, MA: Harvard University Press, 1999.

2. In 1992, the UN Security Council declared that the proliferation of weapons of mass destruction (WMD) constitutes a threat to international peace and security. See UN document S/23500 (January 31, 1992).

3. Natasha Bajema, *Evolving Threats, Evolving Policy: U.S. Attitudes & Multilateral Institutions for Nuclear, Biological and Chemical Weapons*, Occasional Paper, Studies in Security Institutions, Vol. 2, New York: Center on International Cooperation, 2005, p. 4.

4. See Ambassador Donald Mahley, U.S. Special Negotiator for Chemical and Biological Arms Control Issues, *Statement by the United States to the Ad Hoc Group of the Biological Weapons Convention States Parties*, Geneva, Switzerland, 25 July 2001.

5. *National Security Strategy of the United States of America*, September 2002.

6. *National Strategy to Combat Weapons of Mass Destruction*, December 2002.

7. Bajema, p. 10.

8. Ibid.

9. Other export control regimes not covered in this chapter include the Missile Technology Control Regim and the Wassenaar Arrangement.

10. Bajema, p. 10.

11. Scott D. Sagan, "Why Do States Build Nuclear Weapons: Three Models in Search of a Bomb," *International Security* 21, no. 3 (Winter 1996/1997): pp. 54–86.; See also Ashton Carter, "How to Counter WMD," *Foreign Affairs*, September/October 2004.

12. Definitions from Steve Tulliu and Thomas Schmalberger, *Coming to Terms with Security: A Lexicon for Arms Control, Disarmament and Confidence-Building*, Geneva: UNIDIR, 2001, p. 128.

13. The NPT had 189 state parties until North Korea withdrew from treaty in 2003.
14. See IAEA, *The Safeguards System of the International Atomic Energy Agency*. Available from the IAEA website at http://www.iaea.org/OurWork/SV/Safeguards/safeg_system.pdf.
15. As of October 2006, 78 states have ratified Additional Protocols. See IAEA website for updates.
16. See International Atomic Energy Agency, "Board Moves to Strengthen Nuclear Safeguards System," Staff Report, 23 September 2005. Available at http://www.iaea.org/NewsCenter/News/2005/strengthening_sg.html.
17. Pierre Goldschmidt, "Strengthening the Nuclear Non-Proliferation Regime: The Need For Broad Information and Access Rights," Paper presented at the Carnegie International Nonproliferation Conference, 22 June 2004, Washington D.C.
18. International Atomic Energy Agency, "Board Moves to Strengthen Nuclear Safeguards System," Staff Report, 23 September 2005. Available at http://www.iaea.org/NewsCenter/News/2005/strengthening_sg.html.
19. See Bajema, p. 12.
20. The BWC was opened for signature in 1972 and entered into force in 1975. The BWC currently has 155 states parties.
21. Trevor Findlay, *Biological Weapons: Minding the Verification Gap*, VERTIC Brief No. 4, London: The Verification Research, Training and Information Centre (VERTIC), February 2004. Available at http://www.vertic.org/assets/BP4_Findlay.pdf.
22. John Borrie, "The Limits of Modest Progress: The Rise, Fall and Return of Efforts to Strengthen the Biological Weapons Convention," *Arms Control Today*, October 2006.
23. See Findlay.
24. The Chemical Weapons Convention was adopted in the Conference on Disarmament in 1992, open for signature in 1993 and entered into force in 1997.
25. The CWC has 178 states parties. See the OPCW website for updates. http://www.opcw.org/
26. The CWC does not make a specific reference to terrorism. However, article X of the CWC offers states parties assistance and protection against the use or threat of use of chemical weapons.
27. See Graham Allison, "How to Stop Nuclear Terror," *Foreign Affairs*, January/February 2004.
28. William C. Potter, Charles D. Ferguson, and Leonard S. Spector, "The Four Faces of Nuclear Terror and the Ned for a Prioritized Response," *Foreign Affairs*, May/June 2004.
29. See Graham Allison.
30. Chaim Braun and Christopher F. Chyba, "Proliferation Rings: New Challenges to the Nuclear Nonproliferation Regime," *International Security* 29, no. 2 (Fall 2004): pp. 5–6.
31. Braun and Chyba, p. 6.
32. See Natasha Bajema and Mary Beth Nikitin, "Assessing Nuclear Maturity: Determining which States should have Access to what Nuclear Technology," *The Fletcher Forum of World Affairs* 28, no. 2 (Summer 2004): p. 167.
33. Fred Ikle, "After Detection—What?" *Foreign Affairs* 39, no. 2 (January 1961).
34. Jonathan Tucker, "The BWC New Process: A Preliminary Assessment," *The Nonproliferation Review* 11, no. 1 (Spring 2004): pp. 26–39.
35. Marie I. Chevrier, "Doubts About Confidence: The Potential and Limits of Confidence-Building Measures for the Biological Weapons Convention," *Biological Weapons Proliferation: Reasons for Concern, Courses of Action*, Report no. 18, Washington D.C.: The Henry L. Stimson Center, 1998. Available at http://www.stimson.org/cbw/pdf/report24-entire.pdf.
36. Biological Weapons Convention, Special Conference 1994, *Final Declaration*, BWC/SPCONF/1.
37. Jonathan Tucker, "Chemical Terrorism: Assessing Threats and Responses," *High-Impact Terrorism: Proceedings of a Russian-American Workshop*, pp. 122–123, 131.
38. Tucker, p. 122.
39. Christopher Chyba, "Toward Biological Security," *Foreign Affairs*, May/June 2002.
40. See IAEA website at http://www.iaea.org/Publications/Reports/Anrep2004/table_a19.pdf.
41. Organization for the Prohibition of Chemical Weapons, Draft Annual Report, Available at http://www.opcw.org/docs/csp/csp11/en/ec4603c11crp01.pdf.

42. Christopher F. Chyba and Alex L. Greninger, "Biotechnology and Bioterrorism: An Unprecedented World," *Survival* 46, no. 2 (Summer 2004): p. 144.
43. Christopher Chyba, "Toward Biological Security," *Foreign Affairs*, May/June 2002.
44. IAEA, *Country Nuclear Cycle Profiles*, Technical Reports Series No. 404, Vienna, Austria: IAEA, 2001, pp. 5–6.
45. See Braun and Chyba.
46. Ashton Carter, "How To Counter WMD," *Foreign Affairs*, September/October 2004.
47. See Jason D. Ellis, "The Best Defense: Counterproliferation and U.S. National Security," *The Washington Quarterly* 26, no. 2 (Spring 2003): p. 128.
48. See Bajema; See also Braun and Chyba; See United Nations High Level Panel on Threats, Challenges and Change, A More Secure World: Our Shared Responsibility, 2 December 2005, Available at http://www.un.org/secureworld/.
49. Ashton B. Carter, John Deutch, and Philip Zelikow, "Catastrophic Terrorism: Tackling the New Danger," *Foreign Affairs*, November/December 1998.
50. United Nations Security Council, Resolution 1540 adopted on 18 April 2004, UN Document S/RES/1540 (2004).
51. Chyba.
52. For more information, see the White House website, *Fact Sheet: The Global Initiative to Combat Nuclear Terrorism*, July 15, 2006, Available at http://www.whitehouse.gov/news/releases/2006/07/20060715-3.html.

Natasha E. Bajema is a Ph.D. Candidate at the Fletcher School at Tufts University. Before coming to Fletcher, she was a research associate at the Center on International Cooperation at New York University. She holds an M.A. in international policy and a Certificate in Nonproliferation Studies from the Monterey Institute of International Studies.

Chapter 3.3

Interdiction and Law Enforcement

Emma Belcher

Interdiction and Law Enforcement to Counter WMD-Terrorism: Practical Measures that Should be Strengthened

W hile states have made good progress in adapting their security strategies to account for non-state actors, practical measures at the operational level could be strengthened, particularly regarding the threat of weapons of mass destruction (WMD) terrorism. Terrorists have exploited global trade dynamics and new technologies to gain knowledge that was previously in the domain of states. Their illicit networks have converged with transnational crime as terrorists receive assistance from those who benefit financially from the supply chain of WMD-related materials and delivery means. Terrorists use banking systems, financial markets, front companies, partnerships with legitimate businesses (some unwitting) to create complex webs that disguise the end user of WMD-related materials. Many of the items used to make WMD and their delivery systems are of dual-use—they have legitimate use in other industries—and are difficult to identify and then prove that they are intended for WMD use. The sheer number of transactions that take place on a daily basis makes it difficult for those who find themselves on the front line. Increasingly, those on the front line are law enforcement officials, for whom this threat presents a new role and accompanying challenges. Elements of the private sector are becoming increasingly involved in partnerships with government to achieve security and efficiency.

The tools developed to deal with WMD proliferation between states, such as the non-proliferation treaties, do not lend themselves to adaptation to the non-state actor problem (not to mention the difficulty they are experiencing with state proliferation among states parties). Moreover, traditional forms of deterrence do not have the same effect against apocalyptic terrorists. Should terrorists manage to assemble or gain access to WMD, states could not rely on the threat of annihilation to deter their use as they can with other states. Acquisition of just one weapon would likely mean detonation with disastrous effects. This raises the question of how to stop the flow of WMD and related materials to terrorists.

This chapter examines three initiatives that attempt to provide practical means to deal with the WMD terrorism threat—the Proliferation Security Initiative (PSI), the Container Security Initiative (CSI), and the Customs-Trade Partnership Against Terrorism (C-TPAT), through U.S. Border Control and Customs activity. The PSI operates in the murky arena of international law and international relations, whereas the CSI and the C-TPAT are based on contracts with the U.S. government that assists those willing and able. While all three initiatives address the WMD-terrorism threat, the bulk of this discussion will involve PSI, given that it is more open to interpretation.

Proliferation Security Initiative

Despite its short life, the PSI has already been credited with disrupting the A.Q. Khan illicit nuclear trade network, and some argue that its discovery of WMD-related shipments to Libya was a factor in Qaddafi's decision to renounce Libya's WMD program.[1]

The PSI is a loose network of states that aims to employ international and domestic legal principles to stem WMD proliferation to terrorists as well as states. It emerged in 2003 as an agreement between 11 core states—the United States, Australia, France, Germany, Italy, Japan, the Netherlands, Poland, Portugal, Spain, and the United Kingdom. Its membership has grown quickly, its structure has evolved, and it now boasts participants from over 70 states.[2] PSI participants pledge their commitment to enhance the nonproliferation regime by endorsing a set of principles.[3]

Its emergence reflected the reality of the gaps in the WMD nonproliferation regime.[4] None of the nonproliferation treaties—including the Nuclear Non-Proliferation Treaty, the Chemical Weapons Convention, and the Biological Weapons Convention—provides enforcement mechanisms for violation of the norm against WMD proliferation, and none of them was conceived at a time when non-state actors were part of the security equation.

PSI participants aim to fill these gaps by better coordinating their actions against WMD proliferation, and rely heavily on intelligence and information-sharing to inform their decisions. When the PSI began in 2003, participants envisaged working together to interdict vessels suspected of transporting WMD-related material and their means of delivery at sea, on land, or in the air, using the best legal authorities available to them. To date, PSI activities have been focused on interdiction at sea. They have recently widened the nature of their activities to address all aspects of WMD proliferation trade by "denying terrorists, rogue states, and their supplier networks access to WMD-related materials and delivery systems."[5] This broader view includes disruption of the supply chain, proliferation networks and financial networks.[6]

The PSI's aims of interdiction are aspirational, but how much authority does the PSI have to undertake such actions? In reality, on the interdiction at sea front, there are limited circumstances under which states can board ships legally, let alone seize any WMD-related material they might come across in a search. Another complicating factor is that the dual-use nature of much WMD-related equipment makes it difficult to recognize or prove that it is intended for terrorist use. If it could be proven that the equipment were intended for terrorist use, under whose laws would criminals be prosecuted?

These issues warrant investigation. Under maritime law, ships must be registered to a state and must display the flag of that state, known as the flag state. The flag state determines the conditions for granting its nationality and has jurisdiction over that ship. Once flagged, the ship is afforded certain protections from interdiction by other states. The norms of the freedom of the seas and the right of innocent passage, as codified under the United Nations Convention on the Law of the Sea (UNCLOS),[7] prohibit interdiction of vessels except for under a number of circumstances. Suspicion of WMD proliferation is not one of them.[8] The norm of freedom of the seas prevents ships from being interdicted on the high seas except in cases such as piracy, slavery, drug trafficking, broadcasting, or in the case of a flagless vessel.[9] The norm of innocent passage allows for a ship's uninterrupted passage through the territorial waters of a state when it is "not prejudicial to the peace, good order, or security of the coastal state."[10] The situations in which a ship's passage could be deemed prejudicial include a recognition that it threatens the sovereignty of the territorial state, illegal fishing activities, willful pollution, collecting information prejudicial to the security of the coastal state, or violation of principles of international law embodied in the United Nations charter.[11] Activities classed as prejudicial do not include transport of WMD.

As part of their efforts to stem WMD proliferation, PSI participants have pledged to consider boarding, searching and seizing the cargo of any ship flying its flag within its territorial waters or on the high seas that is suspected of transporting WMD or related materials. To circumvent the prohibition against interdiction by a state other than the flag state, PSI participants also pledge to consider giving consent to another participant to board, search and seize the cargo of a ship flying its flag.[12] In this way, they are signaling their intent to prevent WMD proliferation, while staying within the bounds of international law. In effect, this creates a network of association that can be called on when a case arises.

Bilateral ship boarding agreements between participants strengthen this network. Critically, the United States maintains ship-boarding agreements with several states—Panama, the Marshall Islands, Liberia, Cyprus, Croatia, and Belize. Some of these states have a history of being used for illicit activity, given that their maritime regulations and enforcement are less stringent than most other countries. These reciprocal agreements provide circumstances under which one state might board and search another's ships. They are based on request and consent, and must be executed within specific timeframes. As such, these agreements can serve to expedite consultation in times where swift action is needed.[13]

The nonproliferation regime was boosted recently through the amendment of the Suppression of Unlawful Acts Against the Safety of Maritime Navigation (SUA). At the conference in October 2005, the states parties agreed to amend the convention via protocols, outlawing *inter alia* the use of a ship as a weapon or to enable a terrorist attack, including the transport of terrorists or cargo to support WMD programs. The amendment also provide for ship boarding in the case of an offense being committed. This amendment adds weight to the argument of a norm against WMD transportation, although ship boarding still requires consent of the flag state.[14]

In the absence of state consent, PSI participants have explored is what is commonly referred to in law enforcement as tail lighting. PSI participants look for other grounds to interdict the ship they suspect is transporting WMD. This was the case with the *So San*, where Spain interdicted the ship under the rubric of falsified documents and because it had failed to submit to inspection. Ultimately, the *So San* and its cargo were released because the shipment of 50 SCUD missiles that was hidden under thousands of packets of cement powder was not prohibited under international law.

The *So San* incident prompted new thinking about the circumstances under which cargo could be seized and proliferators prosecuted. Upon creation of the PSI, participants examined their domestic legislation and export control regimes to see what means they had to seize cargo or prosecute proliferators and how they could strengthen their legislation to bring about the strictest proliferation penalties possible.[15]

It is conceivable that the timing, location, and assets involved in PSI activities could be determined to provide the greatest probability for an interdiction that resulted in prosecution. For example, once a suspect ship's route of travel were identified, PSI participants might be able to chose whether to commence the interdiction when it was traveling through country x, country y, or country z based on which had the strongest domestic nonproliferation laws. Further, there could be situations in which several states might be able claim jurisdiction and apply their own domestic law—depending on the flag state, the interdicting force and the nationalities of the proliferators, for example. PSI participants could determine where and by whom interdiction is undertaken to result in the strongest possible prosecution. While these techniques are less than perfect, and interdictions are no easy task to perform, in the absence of a norm of interdiction by any state on proliferation grounds, they reflect creative application of the best available means to address WMD proliferation. In order to maximize the potential of this approach, PSI participants need to deliver on their promise to strengthen their domestic law to allow for the maximum possible penalties for WMD proliferation.

To consolidate the PSI framework, members undertake interdiction exercises to build and strengthen relationships between countries that might need to cooperate efficiently during a real interdiction, as well as assist countries to sort out their domestic arrangements in the case of a real incident. Given the nature of the activity and the limited timeframes within which to act, efficiency is an essential component.

While creative law enforcement can delay—and frustrate attempts at—proliferation, PSI members acknowledge that gaps remain in the coverage of all of the stages of WMD proliferation. The fact that the PSI does not have global coverage lessens the impact of the agreements. China and South Korea are notably absent. However, despite these gaps, the extent of the coverage—over 70 states—means that there is likely to be some point of a cargo's shipment at which it passes through the jurisdiction of a PSI participant and is then captured in the PSI network. Also absent from the PSI participant list are Indonesia and Malaysia. The U.S. initially proposed the Regional Maritime Security Initiative to perform similar activities in the region, focusing on the Malacca Straits, which was rejected by Indonesia and Malaysia.[16] However, they have pledged to work with Singapore to address transnational maritime threats in the Asia Pacific. This captures a particularly vulnerable point in the global trading system—the Malacca Straits, a narrow waterway through which an enormous volume of trade passes, and where ships are particularly vulnerable to piracy and attractive to terrorists. Indonesia's and Malaysia's non-participation in the PSI reflects regional sensitivities surrounding sovereignty and international involvement in maritime affairs in the Asia Pacific region. However, their partnership strengthens coverage and signals their intent to tackle transnational crime and terrorism.[17] Unlike the PSI, the partnership between Singapore, Indonesia, and Malaysia incorporates a wider approach to maritime security in the region, involving local law enforcement as well as the region's military forces where necessary.

Interdictions have played a role enforcing the sanctions placed on North Korea by the United Nations following its atomic weapon test on October 9, 2006. Resolution 1718 authorized inspection of cargo entering and leaving North Korea. The PSI itself was not called upon to undertake interdictions, but no doubt some participants have taken part. It is noteworthy that, after initial reluctance, China agreed to take part in such interdictions. At the time of writing, North Korea had agreed to return to the Six Party Talks, likely in part due to the pressure applied by further sanctions. While pleased with this decision, the Bush administration says it will continue making sure the Security Council resolution is being upheld,[18] and it is likely that interdictions will continue to take place for the immediate future. Whatever the eventual outcome of this round of talks, the role of interdictions in supporting diplomatic processes is evident. It will be interesting to see whether this case has implications for the PSI.

The loose networked nature of the PSI gives it a certain amount of flexibility that might prove productive. While it is not an organization with binding requirements on its members, and it is largely a political statement and thus subject to politics of the day, it might enable states that were able to assist but did not want the surrounding publicity—for whatever domestic or international reason—the opportunity to do so effectively, even on a case-by-case basis. The lack of a bureaucracy frees the PSI from deadlock and potential stagnation, and focuses attention on its practical activities. Some PSI participants have also created partnerships with the maritime industry, an essential development if the goal of preventing proliferation has any hope of being achieved. At the third government-industry workshop, government and maritime industry representatives from 20 states met to discuss how to enhance operational capabilities and cooperation on issues of port governance, the disposition of cargo, and the roles of freight forwarders and shipping line owners and operators.[19] For the remaining gaps, interdiction principle three encourages participants to "work to strengthen when necessary relevant international law and frameworks in appropriate ways to support these commitments."[20] The United States has made clear its intention to work toward this goal: "While all actions will be taken consistent with existing national and international legal authorities, we are also seeking ways to expand those authorities."[21] One of those is to make WMD-related proliferation an exception against the freedom of the seas norm by establishing state practice for interdiction on the high seas to disrupt WMD proliferation and develop *opinio juris*. While no PSI-related instance has been reported that presents a challenge of interdiction on the high seas to date, when he was Undersecretary of State for Arms Control and International Security, John Bolton expressed his hope that state practice and customary international law might result.[22]

The PSI's success is difficult to gauge, given its reliance on intelligence and, accordingly, the secret nature of its activities. Some wonder whether it is merely a public relations exercise and others wonder whether it is anything new; claiming that it does not grant states additional powers in their arsenals against WMD proliferation. But its participants' cooperation and creative law enforcement might, given time and in conjunction with other international developments, do just that.

Container Security Initiative and Customs-Trade Partnership Against Terrorism

Unlike the PSI, the Container Security Initiative (CSI) and the Customs-Trade Partnership Against Terrorism (C-TPAT) deal with the specific threat of WMD terrorism to U.S. ports and have principles in common. Thus, they will be discussed together. Given the size of U.S. borders and the significant amounts of goods that are imported on a daily basis, patrolling these borders and screening cargo presents an enormous challenge. The CSI and C-TPAT aim to screen this cargo while enabling legitimate trade to flow unencumbered.

Announced in January 2002, the CSI is an association of agreements between states to work together to reduce the opportunity for WMD and related materials to be trafficked into the United States. It is an attempt to enhance security—minimizing the chance that material will end up in the busy ports of the United States where it could either be detonated or smuggled into U.S. cities—while maintaining an efficient trade system. CSI ports are operational in North America, Europe, Asia, Africa, the Middle East, and Latin and Central America.[23]

U.S. law enforcement officials are posted to ports with CSI agreements and prescreen containers that are destined for U.S. ports. They identify high-risk containers for prescreening and evaluation before they are shipped to the U.S. This is done as early as possible in the supply chain, mainly at the departure port. They use intelligence to identify targets and technology to screen targets without causing delays. The use of "smart" containers assists Customs and Border Protection (CBP) officers at United States ports of arrival to identify containers that have been tampered with during transit.[24] According to U.S. Customs and Border Protection, prescreening can be conducted while containers are sitting on docks waiting to be shipped, thus not slowing down a container's passage.[25] The CSI offers reciprocity by allowing officers of CSI participant countries to inspect outgoing containers from the U.S. to their own countries. Like the PSI, coverage is not complete. But, also like the PSI, it covers the areas of most risk, the busiest and most at-risk ports. Moreover, CBP aims to have 50 CSI ports operational by the end of fiscal year 2006, resulting in approximately 90 percent of all transatlantic and transpacific cargo that is imported into the United States subjected to prescreening.[26]

While the CSI provides a framework to minimize the risk that WMD will be shipped to the U.S., it is possible that weapons, or components of these weapons, will slip through these controls as attempts are made to smuggle them into cities of the United States. This is where border control plays an enormous role in the line of defense. U.S. Customs and Border Protection has developed a government-industry partnership whereby companies voluntarily implement security measures to their cargo, enabling officials to smooth the passage of known and trusted entities and focus on higher-risk entities. The C-TPAT is described by the U.S. as "partnerships to secure the supply chain."[27] Through these partnerships, importers, sea carriers, and highway carriers implement security measures at their facilities that enable their cargos to be processed more rapidly.[28] This ultimately benefits businesses as they experience reduced wait times at borders and priority inspection.

The aims of these initiatives are sensible and, arguably, a creative approach to risk-based management. It likely represents an effective and reasonable effort to prevent against diversion of materials to WMD terrorism, taking into account security imperatives and the practicalities of everyday use of dual-use items. They minimize the potential for a WMD attack on the U.S. via transport of WMD—which could cripple global trade, not to mention the worldwide transport industry—while minimizing the delay to legitimate business. This type of activity is another example of the joint efforts of governments and the private sector in working together to combat terrorism. Such a practice serves the trade industry as well as the government and, ultimately, the population.

Nevertheless, the CSI and C-TPAT are not without their problems. For example, smaller ports and businesses that might not be able to afford such measures and could be at a disadvantage within their industry. Some are critical of the impression that the CSI simply serves to extend U.S. borders and push the threat onto others.[29] Further, concerns that not all of the security measures that businesses implement to obtain participation in the C-TPAT program are verified by CBP are valid.[30] However, this likely represents another risk-based approach to achieve efficiency in face of an overwhelming task. Getting the right balance between the number of facilities physically inspected, thus providing a credible threat of inspection, and efficiency will be crucial.

Activities such as the CSI and C-TPAT highlight a potential weakness in border security activities worldwide, related to the fact that the contemporary terrorist threat requires the involvement of new players. Law enforcement officials are now at the front line of WMD proliferation and must be educated about what they are looking for when conducting their searches. Previously, such personnel were searching for guns, boxes that ticked, or drugs—obvious dangerous materials.[31] The types of materials that are used in WMD production are difficult to identify, particularly when broken down into components. Moreover, their dual-use nature makes it hard to determine whether they are being shipped for WMD production. While U.S. programs educate those now involved in border protection activities in some states of high risk, there are thousands of law enforcement officials working at states' borders that deal with thousands of packages on a daily basis. Thus, it is essential that effective education takes place worldwide.

Furthermore, while officers can be educated about what they are looking for and how many of one particular item might be required for peaceful purposes and how many might indicate illicit activity, officers conducting a search of suspect cargo are not necessarily getting the big picture. Some traffickers involved in the proliferation network attempt to disguise their activity by importing parts they require in small batches and from different places. By making their cargo appear legitimate, they are able to increase their chances of avoiding suspicion.[32] While a box of parts might appear innocent, if many boxes are ordered by one entity from around the globe, this could suggest something more sinister. What a law enforcement officer in one country might not know is that identical boxes are being sent to the same recipient from another country.

What is needed is a real-time global database into which officials can enter details surrounding suspect or dual-use items, including point of origin and point of destination. Flags could be raised when aggregate cargo indicates suspicious activity, providing officials at the front line an accurate picture of the cargo they are inspecting.[33] In this way, states increase their chances of uncovering illicit activity and could possibly break up a proliferation ring. Such tools have been used for customs and border protection and should be developed for use against WMD proliferation. With a global WMD database, perhaps run through Interpol, more intelligence could be created, upon which these systems rely. While it would be a difficult task, resources would be well directed toward such an effort.

Conclusion

As the nature of governments' understanding of the terrorist threat has evolved, governments have adapted their approaches to address the threat. An increasing number of practical new tools are being employed, ushering in new players in the fight against terrorism, including law enforcement and the private sector. The PSI, CSI, and C-TPAT are some of these tools that aim to prevent the proliferation of WMD to terrorists and states alike. The PSI uses international and legal principles in a creative manner, and the CSI and C-TPAT use a risk-based approach in partnership with states and businesses to minimize the risk of WMD terrorism to the U.S. while enabling the timely flow of legitimate trade. All three initiatives, however, could be strengthened.

The PSI is faced with limits under international law and political realities. The CSI and C-TPAT could use better tools to assist law enforcement officials. The best approach for the PSI is to develop the tools they have identified to their full potential. Participants should strengthen their domestic laws to ensure they maintain harsh penalties for WMD proliferation in order to make it less attractive to those who currently profit such activity. However, doing so will likely push those intent on continuing these activities to conduct them under the jurisdictions of those states that are not PSI participants and are unlikely to provide boarding consent on an ad hoc basis. Thus, the PSI need to pursue WMD proliferators where possible and, in doing so, strengthen the norm against proliferation to make WMD proliferation an interdictable offense on the high seas without the consent of the flag state. Meanwhile, the best approach for the CSI and C-TPAT is to ensure that those on the front line have the best training possible to identify WMD-related cargo and to make a strong case for the development of a global database to give those on the front line an accurate picture of proliferation activities. For all three of these initiatives, reliable intelligence will be key.

Undoubtedly, terrorists will adapt their practices to circumvent these procedures, but this is a start in making it more difficult for terrorists to achieve their aims. As governments work domestically and multilaterally to reduce the opportunities for successful terrorist attacks, terrorists will likely look to other, previously discarded or postponed, means for achieving their goals. Like the PSI, the CSI and C-TPAT will need to constantly evolve.

Notes

1. Conversation with U.S. government official, April 2004 about the interdiction by the U.S., UK, Germany and Italy—acting under PSI auspices—of an illicit cargo of centrifuge parts for uranium enrichment en route to Libya. The U.S. official suggested that, when confronted, the evidence might have added to Qaddafi's reasons for his pledge to halt Libya's WMD program.
2. As of 5 September 2006, participants include: Afghanistan, Albania, Angola, Argentina, Armenia, Australia, Austria, Azerbaijan, Bahrain, Belarus, Belgium, Belize, Bosnia, Brunei Darussalam, Bulgaria, Cambodia, Canada, Croatia, Cyprus, Czech Republic, Denmark, El Salvador, Estonia, Finland, France, Georgia, Germany, Greece, Holy See, Honduras, Hungary, Iceland, Iraq, Ireland, Israel, Italy, Japan, Jordan, Kazakhstan, Kuwait, Latvia, Liberia, Libya, Lithuania, Luxembourg, Macedonia, Malta, Marshall Islands, Moldova, Mongolia, The Netherlands, New Zealand, Norway, Oman, Panama, Philippines, Poland, Portugal, Romania, Russia, Serbia, Singapore, Slovakia, Slovenia, Spain, Sweden, Switzerland, Tajikistan, Tunisia, Turkey, Turkmenistan, Ukraine, United Arab Emirates, United Kingdom, United States, Uzbekistan, Yemen. Source: "Proliferation Security Initiative Participants," Bureau of International Security and Nonproliferation (ISN), Washington, DC, September 6, 2006, available at http://www.state.gov/t/isn/71884.htm, accessed 30 September 2006.
3. Proliferation Security Initiative: Statement of Interdiction Principles, available at http://www. state.gov/t/isn/rls/fs/23764.htm, accessed 1 October 2006.
4. U.S. President George W. Bush announced the formation of the PSI in May 2003, in response to the December 2002 U.S. *National Strategy to Combat the Proliferation of Weapons of Mass Destruction*. For more on this, please see the chapter by Natasha Bajema in this volume.
5. "President's Statement on Proliferation Security Initiative," *Released by the White House Office of the Press Secretary June 23, 2006*, available at http://www.state.gov/t/isn/68267.htm, accessed 30 September 2006.
6. ibid
7. While not all PSI participants are signatories of the PSI, they all recognize freedom of the seas and the norm of innocent passage under customary international law.
8. In fact, Article 23 of the Convention explicitly grants ships carrying nuclear weapons the right of innocent passage.
9. United Nations Convention on the Law of the Sea (UNCLOS) Part VII High Seas

10. UNCLOS Part II Territorial Sea and Contiguous Zone

11. UNCLOS Article 19(2)

12. Principle four, clause c, "Proliferation Security Initiative: Statement of Interdiction Principles," available at http://www.state.gov/t/isn/rls/fs/23764.htm, accessed 1 October 2006.

13. Interestingly, some of these agreements were based on ship boarding agreements the U.S. maintained with such states during its war on drugs, as the so-called flag of convenience states an attractive jurisdiction for drug smugglers under which to register their vessels. John Bolton, former Undersecretary of State for Arms Control and International Security, explained that the relationship of trust that had been built between the U.S. and other countries through their cooperation in the war on drugs enabled them to develop similar agreements for WMD proliferation. To address WMD proliferation, the U.S. then built on these ship boarding agreements, based on the premise that these same jurisdictions would be attractive to those attempting clandestine terrorist activity also.

14. Protocols to the United Nations Convention on the Suppression of Unlawful Acts Against the Safety of Maritime Navigation. The SUA Protocol will come into force 90 days after signature by the 12th state.

15. "Proliferation Security Initiative: Chairman's Statement" from PSI meeting in Brisbane, Australia from 9-10 July 2003, available at http://www.dfat.gov.au/globalissues/psi/chair_statement_0603.html, accessed 14 November 2006.

16. "Future Unknown: the Terrorist Threat to Australian Maritime Security," Australian Strategic Policy Institute, available at http://www.aspi.org.au/21139maritimesecurity/chapter03.html, accessed 1 October 2006.

17. In July 2004, Indonesia, Malaysia, and Singapore commenced patrolling the Malacca Straits to combat piracy and terrorism.

18. "North Korea Talks to Money," available at http://www.cnn.com/2006/WORLD/asiapcf/10/31/north.korea/index.html, accessed October 31, 2006.

19. "London PSI Meeting Advances Public-Private Partnership to Combat WMD Proliferation," from US Department of State website, available at http://www.state.gov/r/pa/prs/ps/2006/73177.htm, accessed 14 November 2006. Representatives were from Argentina, Australia, Canada, Denmark, France, Germany, Greece, Italy, Japan, the Netherlands, New Zealand, Norway, Poland, Portugal, Russia, Singapore, Spain, Turkey, the United Kingdom and the United States.

20. "Proliferation Security Initiative: Statement of Interdiction Principles," Principle 3.

21. Remarks by National Security Advisor Dr. Condoleezza Rice to the National Legal Center for the Public Interest, New York NY <http://www.whitehouse.gov/news/releases/2003/10/20031031-5.html> (accessed April 2004).

22. ibid

23. According to U.S. Customs and Border Control, operational ports are: In the Americas and Caribbean: Montreal, Vancouver & Halifax, Canada; Santos, Brazil; Buenos Aires, Argentina; Puerto Cortes, Honduras; Caucedo, Dominican Republic; Kingston, Jamaica; Freeport, The Bahamas. In Europe: Rotterdam, The Netherlands; Bremerhaven & Hamburg, Germany; Antwerp and Zeebrugge, Belgium; Le Havre and Marseille, France; Gothenburg, Sweden; La Spezia, Genoa, Naples, Gioia Tauro, and Livorno, Italy; Felixstowe, Liverpool, Thamesport, Tilbury, and Southampton, United Kingdom; Piraeus, Greece; Algeciras, Barcelona, and Valencia, Spain Lisbon, Portugal. In Asia and the East: Singapore; Yokohama, Tokyo, Nagoya and Kobe, Japan; Hong Kong; Pusan, South Korea; Port Klang and Tanjung Pelepas, Malaysia; Laem Chabang, Thailand; Dubai, United Arab Emirates (UAE); Shenzhen and Shanghai; Kaohsiung and Chi-Lung; Colombo, Sri Lanka Port Salalah, Oman. In Africa:Durban, South Africa. Available at http://www.cbp.gov/xp/cgov/border_security/international_activities/csi/ports_in_csi.xml; accessed 1 October 2006.

24. "Fact Sheet," Press Office, U.S. Department of Homeland Security, March 29, 2006.

25. ibid

26. "CSI in Brief," available at http://www.cbp.gov/xp/cgov/border_security/international_activities/csi/csi_in_brief.xml, accessed 1 October 2006.

27. "Customs-Trade Partnership Against Terrorism (C-TPAT): Partnership to Secure the Supply Chain," http://www.cbp.gov/xp/cgov/import/commercial_enforcement/ctpat/ (accessed 25 August 2006).

28. ibid

29. "Future Unknown: the Terrorist Threat to Australian Maritime Security," Australian Strategic Policy Institute, available at http://www.aspi.org.au/21139maritimesecurity/chapter03.html, accessed 1 October 2006.

30. "Container Security Initiative (CSI)", available at http://www.globalsecurity.org/security/systems/carg_inspect.htm, accessed 1 October 2006.

31. Conversation on 29 September 2006 with Australian Government law enforcement official.

32. Conversation on 29 September 2006 with Australian Government law enforcement official.

33. Suggested by Australian Government law enforcement official.

Emma L. Belcher is a Ph.D. candidate at the Fletcher School. She recently served as a policy adviser in the National Security Division of Australia's Department of the Prime Minister and Cabinet.

Chapter 3.4

Case Studies

Elin Gursky, Thomas V. Inglesby, and Tara O'Toole

Anthrax 2001: Observations on the Medical and Public Health Response

Introduction

This Article Describes Aspects of the medical and public health response to the 2001 anthrax attacks based on interviews with individuals who were directly involved in the response. It has been more than 18 months since *B. anthracis* spores were discovered in letters sent through the U.S. postal system. The specific purpose and perpetrator(s) of these attacks remain unknown. A total of 22 people developed anthrax as a result of the mailings, 11 suffered from the inhalational form of the disease, and 5 of these people died. Thousands of workers—including health care, public health, environmental, and law enforcement professionals—participated in the response to the attacks. Thousands more were directly affected, including individuals working in facilities contaminated by the attacks and their families. The immediate and continuing medical and public health response to the anthrax attacks of 2001 represents a singular episode in the history of public health.

After-action assessments of the response to the anthrax attacks could offer invaluable opportunities to better understand and remedy the systemic vulnerabilities revealed by America's only experience with an anthrax attack. Yet there still has been no comprehensive published analysis of the response to these events. In December 2001, the Center for Strategic International Studies convened a meeting, which included high-level government officials directly involved in managing the crisis, to discuss the response and review lessons learned. The report describing this meeting has been withheld from public distribution by the Department of Defense, which supported the meeting, on the grounds that the document contains sensitive information.[1]

The "response" to the anthrax attacks was extremely complex, and any analysis that purports to assess the response must account for this complexity. The unprecedented nature of the attacks and the context in which the response occurred are also crucial to understanding what happened and why. The long-standing neglect of federal, state, and local public health agencies, and the highly stressed condition of U.S. medical facilities, which routinely work at the limits of their capacity, are acknowledged by virtually all informed observers. That the medical and public health institutions involved in the response functioned as well as they did is a tribute to the extraordinary efforts of the individuals involved.

Despite the commitment and hard work of the individuals in these professional communities, what was revealed by the anthrax attacks was an unacceptable level of fragility in systems now properly recognized as vital to national defense. Too many citizens, elected leaders, and national security officials still have limited understanding of the degree to which 22 cases of anthrax rocked the public health agencies and hospitals involved in the response to this small bioterrorist attack. Most of the vulnerabilities in the medical and public health systems revealed by the response remain unaddressed. It is not the purpose of this article to praise or criticize individuals who responded to the 2001 anthrax attack. The emphasis here is on how to improve response *systems*. The article seeks to identify the strategic and organizational successes and shortcomings of the health response to the anthrax attacks so that medical and public health communities as well as elected officials can learn from this crisis.

The recent international spread of Severe Acute Respiratory Syndrome (SARS) is illustrating once more the importance of effective public health response systems. Initial impressions of the Centers for Disease Control and Prevention's response to SARS indicate that the agency has improved several aspects of epidemic response that were problematic in the aftermath of the 2001 anthrax attacks. Fortunately, because the numbers of SARS cases remain low, the state public health agencies' capacities to deal with a major epidemic have not been severely tested by SARS. It is hoped that other countries' experiences with SARS will offer useful lessons for outbreak response and bioterrorism preparedness.

This article provides a small window into the medical and public health response that followed the anthrax attacks of 2001. The authors recognize that since that time a number of actions have been taken by federal, state, and local public health agencies to improve bioterrorism preparedness. It is the authors' hope that the perspectives presented in this article will stimulate more comprehensive examinations of public health biopreparedness and help guide future bioterrorism planning efforts.

Methodology

The authors interviewed clinicians, public health professionals, government officials, journalists, union representatives, and others who were directly involved in the five geographic areas where anthrax attacks took place: Boca Raton, Florida; New York City; Washington, DC; Hamilton, New Jersey; and Oxford, Connecticut. A total of 37 individuals were interviewed from the period late 2001 through spring 2002. Study participants represented the following sectors: clinicians working in hospital settings or in private practice, including physicians who cared for victims of the attacks (n = 6); public health professionals working in local public health agencies (n = 9); public health professionals working in state health departments (n = 5); officials from public health laboratories (n = 2); public health professionals working at the Centers for Disease Control and Prevention (n = 3); other officials of the federal government (n = 2); media professionals in the private and public sector (n = 4); postal service managers and representatives of the postal workers' union (n = 3); and directors of not-for-profit health organizations (n = 3).

Participation was voluntary and nonremunerated. Interviews were confidential. All study participants were assured that their responses would not be attributed to them in ways that could identify interviewees. A small number of the interviews were conducted in person, but most interviews were conducted in prearranged telephone calls. Prepared interview questions were intended to bring to light specific challenges and successful strategies that interviewees had observed or identified during the response to the anthrax attacks. Participants were encouraged to offer additional comments and to suggest the names of other individuals whose involvement and insights might benefit the goals of this study.

Comments from interviewees were analyzed by the authors. Themes and findings that were common in the responses of multiple interviewees are reported below under

"Important Issues and Challenges." Quotes from the interviews are included when they illustrate these issues.

There are limitations to the methods employed here. The authors are mindful of the responsibility to distinguish between anecdote and analysis, and we have included only those issues or themes that were raised or commented on by several interviewees. This article does not focus on the actions taken by individual hospitals, though many hospitals had key roles in the response and published accounts of such institutional experiences would be of great value. Nor does this article offer an analysis of the decisions, processes, and

---

Chronology of Key Events following the Attacks

The following brief timeline of events following the anthrax attacks is synthesized from reports from public health agencies, news summaries and from statements of those interviewed in this study. It is not intended as an exhaustive account of events, but only as a synopsis of key developments that would enable readers of this article to place events and observations in some context.

October 2, 2001—An infectious disease physician recognized a possible case of inhalational anthrax in a man hospitalized in Palm Beach County, Florida. This physician contacted the local health officer in Palm Beach County, who immediately began a public health investigation. By October 2, there were already 7 persons with cutaneous anthrax in the northeastern U.S., but none had yet been diagnosed.

October 4—The microbiologic diagnosis of *B. anthracis* was confirmed by the Florida Department of Health (FDH) and the Centers for Disease Control and Prevention (CDC), and the diagnosis was made public.[2,3] Epidemiologic and environmental investigations were launched to determine the source of the patient's anthrax exposure. Evidence of contamination with *B. anthracis* was found at American Media Inc. (AMI) in Boca Raton, Florida, where this first victim worked as a photo editor.[4]

October 5—The first victim of the anthrax attacks died. A second AMI employee, who had been hospitalized for pneumonia on September 30, was diagnosed with inhalational anthrax. He was an employee in the AMI mailroom.

October 6—The Palm Beach County Health Department began to obtain nasal swabs from those who had been in the AMI building in an attempt to define exposure groups.[5] Because nasal swab testing was known to be an insensitive diagnostic test, the health department also recommended prophylactic antibiotics for all those people who had been in the AMI building for at least one hour since August 1 regardless of the results of their nasal swab tests.[6] Environmental samples taken from the mailroom showed evidence of *B. anthracis.*

October 7—A nasal swab was positive on another employee. A swab from the first victim's computer screen was positive. The AMI building was closed.

October 9—The New York City Department of Health notified CDC of a woman with a skin lesion consistent with cutaneous anthrax. The woman, an assistant to NBC anchor Tom Brokaw, had handled a powder-containing letter postmarked September 18 at her workplace.[7]

October 13—Another cutaneous case of anthrax was recognized in a 7-month-old infant who had visited his mother's workplace, the ABC office building on West 66th Street in Manhattan, on September 28.[8]

October 13—Symptoms of cutaneous and inhalational anthrax in New Jersey postal workers began to be observed and reported by physicians to the New York City Health Department. Diagnoses of anthrax are confirmed by the CDC on October 18 and 19.[9–11]

October 15—A staff member in the office of Senator Daschle in the Hart Senate Office Building opened a letter (postmarked October 9) which contained a powder and a note identifying the powder as anthrax. The powder tested positive for *B. anthracis* on October 16. Nasal swab testing of anthrax spores was performed on 340 Senate staff members and visitors to the building who potentially were exposed and to approximately 5,000 other people who self-referred for testing. This testing indicated exposure in 28 persons. Antimicrobial prophylaxis was administered on a broader scale and environmental testing was initiated.[12]

October 19—CDC linked the four confirmed cases of anthrax to "intentional delivery of *B. anthracis* spores through mailed letters or packages."[13]

October 19–22—Four postal workers at the Brentwood Mail Processing and Distribution Center in the District of Columbia were hospitalized with inhalational anthrax. The Brent-wood facility was closed on October 21. On October 22 two of these four postal workers died.[14]

October 24—CDC sent an advisory to state health officials via the Health Alert Network recommending antibiotic prophylaxis to prevent anthrax for all people who had been in the non-public mail operations area at the U.S. Postal Service's Brentwood Road Postal Distribution Center or who had worked in the non-public mail operations areas at postal facilities that had received mail directly from the Brentwood facility since October 11.[15]

October 27—A CDC alert recommended antibiotic prophylaxis for workers in the mail facilities that supplied the CIA, the House office buildings, the Supreme Court, Walter Reed Army Institute of Research, the White House, and the Southwest Postal Station after preliminary environmental sampling revealed *B. anthracis* contamination in these mailrooms.[16]

October 31—A 61-year-old female hospital stockroom worker in New York City died from inhalational anthrax after she had become ill with malaise and myalgias on October 25. The source of her exposure remains unknown despite extensive epidemiologic investigation.[17,18]

November 16—A 94-year-old woman residing in Oxford, Connecticut, was hospitalized with fever, cough, and weakness. She died on November 19. Her diagnosis was confirmed as *B. anthracis* on November 20 by the Connecticut Department of Public Health Laboratory. Subsequent environmental and epidemiological testing indicated exposure from cross-contaminated letters.[19]

actions occurring within the Centers for Disease Control and Prevention (CDC), the Department of Health and Human Services (DHHS), the Federal Bureau of Investigation (FBI), or other federal agencies engaged in the response to the anthrax attacks. Such analyses could provide very useful information and should remain a priority.

Much time and effort is being invested in the development of bioterrorism exercises and drills at multiple levels of government and in the private sector. A comprehensive analysis of what actually happened after the anthrax attacks informed by more voices and the willing cooperation of involved institutions would be useful.

A brief timeline of events following the anthrax attacks, synthesized from reports from public health agencies, news summaries, and statements of those interviewed in this study, is provided. . . . It is not intended as an exhaustive account of events, but only as a synopsis of key developments to enable readers of this article to place events and observations in some context.

Background: Context of the U.S. Public Health System

In the United States, public health functions are conducted by agencies at federal, state, and local (municipal, county, etc.) levels of government. These agencies vary in scope and capacity and are only loosely connected. The legal responsibility for many public health functions is vested in state governments. The level of state operational authority over local health departments varies across the country, but most state health departments provide disease control assistance when more than one local jurisdiction is involved or when local resources are insufficient.

There are approximately 3,000 local (i.e., municipal, county, city) health departments that routinely conduct restaurant inspections, environmental testing, and disease outbreak investigation and control.[20] Many of these agencies also deliver a broad spectrum of clinical services such as the provision of immunization, treatment of tuberculosis and sexually transmitted diseases, hypertension screening, and prenatal care. The median number of full-time staff in local health departments is 13 persons. Two-thirds of these local public health agencies are responsible for populations of fewer than 50,000 persons.[21]

The federal agency that deals with public health is the Centers for Disease Control and Prevention within the Department of Health and Human Services. Initially organized in 1946 to lead malaria control efforts, CDC now employees 8,500 people.[22] CDC serves as a source of scientific guidance and funding for many state and local public health programs. Traditionally, states formally request and receive assistance from CDC when a disease outbreak exceeds local skills and resources, or when an unusual health threat is involved which requires specialized expertise. CDC has limited formal authority within states or local jurisdictions unless public health problems arise that cross state borders.[23]

Important Issues and Challenges Identified by Interviewees

Public Health Decision-Making Processes

The 2001 anthrax attacks challenged traditional decision-making processes of federal, state, and local public health authorities. Historically, most outbreaks of naturally occurring disease are first recognized in a limited geographic region; laboratory and clinical methods for accurately diagnosing and treating cases of an unfamiliar illness (e.g., HIV/AIDS, Hanta virus, Legionnaire's Disease) often evolve over a period of months or even years. Data pertaining to the outbreak and the causes of the illness are collected and analyzed by scientists at CDC and other public health agencies and medical institutions, and these analyses are discussed in the academic public health and medical communities at conferences and in medical journals. With time, a consensus view usually emerges about the causes of the disease, who is at risk, and how the illness can best be diagnosed, treated, and prevented. These scientifically based guidelines often are published by CDC and/or professional medical societies and serve as the basis for state and local public health practice.

In October 2001, at the time of the initial discovery of a person with anthrax infection in Florida, public health officials worked closely with clinicians in Palm Beach County to rapidly confirm the medical diagnosis of anthrax and to initiate the epidemiologic investigation that followed. For many of the decisions and actions that would follow, traditional public health decision-making processes were not adequate to cope with the extent, pace, and complexities of events surrounding the attacks.

This was the first time that CDC had been called on to respond to outbreaks of illness occurring nearly simultaneously in five geographic epicenters. Because sending *B. anthracis* spores through the mail was clearly an act of terrorism, the FBI was involved, substantially increasing the number of people and organizations that needed to receive and interpret information pertinent to the disease investigation and remain "in the loop." In addition, because anthrax is virtually unknown in current medical practice, few local or federal public health officials had ever seen or been involved in evaluating a single case of *B. anthracis* infection, let alone a bioterrorist attack resulting in a series of cases.

Many public health policies—for example, whether to offer needle exchange programs to stem the spread of HIV/AIDs, or the nature and extent of prenatal care programs—routinely differ quite extensively from state to state and reflect variations in resources, expertise, and judgments about local priorities and needs. In the context of the anthrax attacks, however, policies and recommendations that differed between states, and between states and CDC, caused confusion. In some cases, inconsistencies in the response were interpreted as evidence of incompetence or inequitable treatment, rather than as nuanced reactions to local situations or principled disagreement about what was the best course of action.

Throughout the crisis, huge volumes of information related to the anthrax attacks arrived at federal and state public health agencies via email, phone, fax, and news media reports. The information came from disparate sources that included local and state health departments, postal distribution sites, unions, physicians, hospitals, clinics, and laboratories. At the same time these agencies were gathering and trying to make sense of available data, they faced enormous demands to rapidly produce clear and accurate information and guidance for both public and professional use. Those interviewed for this study acknowledged these daunting challenges. One public health official echoed the sentiments of many: "CDC was in a classic double bind. They have to be exactly right. And they have to be exactly right very quickly."

In some instances, state and local public health officials were reluctant to initiate public health actions, such as recommending prophylactic antibiotics, without benefit of specific CDC guidance. Other health departments made decisions prior to receiving CDC guidance, in some instances deciding to act in ways that conflicted with CDC recommendations. Such variations in states' decisions were especially notable in the context of determining who was at risk for exposure to *B. anthracis* spores and who should receive prophylactic antibiotics.

Confusion and contention surrounded both CDC's authority to mandate specific public health actions and state public health officials' responsibility to act on their own best judgments. Noted one state public health official, "We relied on CDC as a consultant. They gave us guidance and knowledge, but we used our own instincts. [We concluded that], if the environment had one spore, you are exposed." A local public health official expressed the view that although CDC's scientific expertise was valuable, CDC was "a research-based organization, far removed from how public health is delivered," and hence was not well placed to make operational decisions on the local level.

Some interviewees described disagreements that occurred between state public health officials and CDC. For example, New Jersey public health officials learned that three New Jersey postal workers had sought medical care for cutaneous anthrax between October 13 and 19. By October 19, state public health officials recognized that these cases likely were the result of exposures to at least two unopened anthrax-contaminated letters postmarked at the Trenton post office. State public health officials wanted to provide prophylaxis to postal workers in the facilities where these three cases of cutaneous anthrax had been diagnosed, but officials from CDC did not concur. One health official recalled, "CDC still believed [at that time] that only the material in opened letters could aerosolize, and therefore closed letters posed no risk. They still thought of anthrax spores like fomites—a disease contracted through touching something contaminated. We were left with the option of recommending antibiotic prophylaxis for postal workers on our own, or waiting until CDC came to this conclusion later. We went against CDC's advice." New Jersey officials released a health alert on October 19 recommending that all postal workers at the two implicated post offices begin a course of antibiotics. Because CDC did not agree with state health officials' decision, resources from the National Pharmaceutical Stockpile were not immediately released. State public health officials therefore instructed postal workers to obtain antibiotics from their private physicians.

On some occasions during the response to the anthrax attacks of 2001, confusion about who was at risk of developing anthrax and ambiguities about the extent of public health officials' authority resulted in public health actions being influenced by political pressures. Several of those interviewed reported that in some locations elected officials had directed which groups of people should receive preventive antibiotics. In at least one case, differences among state health departments' recommendations about who should receive antibiotic prophylaxis caused great concern among elected federal representatives. One public health official noted, "The media would compare our decisions to those made [elsewhere]. It was extremely uncomfortable. Elected officials came down on us regarding fairness. One elected official said, 'The only fair thing was to give every postal worker [in the state] Cipro' even though state public health officials believed that the information available warranted a more limited distribution of antibiotics."

Coordination and Sharing of Information within and across Health Organizations

In a number of areas targeted by the anthrax attacks, several different adjacent or overlapping public health agencies were simultaneously responding. City, county, and state health officials within states and across state borders, in many instances, had difficulty acquiring and sharing information and harmonizing their recommendations.

Medical and public health professionals from the greater Washington, DC, area reported many obstacles to reaching consensus decisions and to working collaboratively across the region. The Washington, DC, metropolitan area encompasses a complicated network of government jurisdictions. Many people who work in DC live in Maryland or Virginia.[24,25] Three different health departments (Maryland, Virginia, and DC) were involved in the 2001 anthrax investigation and response. Although each was responsible for actions in their respective jurisdictions, the people at risk and the issues at stake often crossed geopolitical boundaries. In some instances, local public health officials working in these different jurisdictions were receiving contradictory recommendations from different sources.

The District's recommendations regarding who needed prophylactic antibiotics and for how long were at odds with CDC's guidance, while Maryland and Virginia were following CDC guidance. One local public health official stated, "Since the majority of people who work in DC's federal buildings live outside of DC, there was a question of whose preventive treatment guidelines to follow: DC's, where people were exposed, or Virginia and Mary-land's, where people lived. Things didn't get resolved until the three health secretaries sat down to review the situation." Steps to resolve cross-jurisdictional problems in the nation's capital region were subsequently taken in May and September 2002 when representatives of the governments of Maryland, Virginia, and the District of Columbia signed agreements to coordinate disease surveillance, alerts, evacuation, and other emergency preparedness efforts.[26]

It also proved difficult to communicate environmental testing data across jurisdictions, so that public health officials could make informed decisions about who might have been exposed to anthrax and thus needed antibiotic prophylaxis. "We could not get enough information [about environmental exposure risk] to make clinical decisions on how to treat patients," noted a local public health official in Maryland. People would just show up at prophy [prophylaxis] clinics and expect to be treated stating, 'My boss told me to come here.' " Another public health official noted that in many cases the agency was unable to verify that an individual was in an identified risk group, so antibiotic prophylaxis often was initiated on the basis of the patient's judgment and wishes: "If they thought they were exposed, that person was treated."

There were also examples of great collaboration between different components of the public health and medical system. For example, in Palm Beach County, health department officials worked very closely with physicians, sending emails and faxes to all physicians in the county and inviting all infectious disease physicians to visit the health department.

In and around Washington, DC, members of the medical community initiated a process of coordinating clinical management of patients with suspected anthrax across the DC metropolitan jurisdictions. Morning conference calls were held by the DC Hospital Association, greatly facilitating information sharing among DC-area physicians. These conference calls proved to be a valuable tool during the crisis, allowing doctors who were treating anthrax victims to describe the clinical course of patients under care and to discuss medical management options. Information shared on these calls included epidemiologic data, such as what buildings and which floors showed evidence of contamination with anthrax spores. Participants exchanged information regarding diagnosis and treatment, such as the usefulness of chest CTs in detecting early signs of inhalational anthrax, the value of nasal swabs in making a diagnosis, the effectiveness of certain antibiotic regimens, and the numbers of days for which treatment should be prescribed. The calls also helped dispel rumors and contributed to the development of relationships within and outside of hospital systems. Even so, it was difficult to create a unified treatment plan. One physician noted, "There needed to be a consistent, citywide and regional [clinical] response to minimize the anxiety for caregivers and patients and lessen the chaos. We had hoped a consistent protocol would have emerged from the public health community and the CDC. [Instead different] protocols came out of Kaiser, GW [George Washington University Hospital], and the Washington Hospital Center."

Risk Communication in the Context of Scientific Uncertainty

CDC is a world-renowned source of scientific expertise on a broad range of diseases and public health issues. As of October 2001, however, CDC did not have extensive experience in dealing with *B. anthracis* disease; CDC's staff included few anthrax experts. The anthrax attacks immediately confronted CDC and state and local public health agencies with an array of scientific uncertainties. As one CDC official reported, "We lacked scientific data to address issues. We could not inform public health decision-making regarding issues such as exposure, isolated cases, letters in transit, [and] cross-contamination. Identifying the population at risk was the greatest problem."

CDC's usual approach to investigating disease outbreaks—a careful, step-by-step gathering of evidence followed by deliberate scientific analysis—was not feasible in the context of a high-profile attack occurring in multiple epicenters that potentially placed thousands at risk and was causing massive disruption of government, business, and citizens' routines. The analytical challenges were compounded by the complexities of the investigation. For example, the FBI was in charge of studying the anthrax powder found in the identified envelopes—material that immediately became evidence in a criminal investigation. It is unclear how soon CDC became aware that the anthrax powder found in the letter to Senator Daschle had different physical properties from the anthrax powder in letters sent to ABC, which had been examined earlier. The Daschle material was more refined, "fluffier," and more likely to remain airborne, thus posing a greater threat of inhalation.

Over the course of the response to the anthrax attacks, some public health officials began to question the technical guidance they were receiving from CDC. One local public health practitioner noted, "Things kept changing. CDC kept changing things. Simple swabs [for environmental surface testing] versus dust wipes. Dry swabs versus wet swabs. Yes to nasal swabs. No to nasal swabs." Another local government official stated, "We would ask CDC a question [about antibiotic treatment] and they would tell us 'It's not warranted.' We would ask why and they would answer, 'Not sure.' There was a lack of trust of CDC's knowledge. CDC was making recommendations that they could not initially justify. Later their guidance was disproved. They could not clearly answer questions about the latency of infection or why Cipro versus Doxy."

In the days immediately following the discovery of the first case of inhalational anthrax in Florida, CDC scientists had judged that only opened envelopes posed a risk of spore exposure. The investigation to date had revealed that no postal workers were ill in the Florida facility "up-stream" of the contaminated letter that was believed to have been the source of the first victim's exposure. Concerned about the potential side-effects of preventive antibiotics, and lacking information about what risks anthrax spores in sealed letters might pose to people working in the U.S. postal system, CDC initially recommended that only those in close proximity to *opened* anthrax-laden letters receive antibiotic prophylaxis. As the risks posed by sealed *B. anthracis*–laden envelopes and cross-contamination of envelopes became evident, prophylaxis recommendations were expanded to include mail handlers and others working in contaminated sites. A CDC official noted, "The greatest challenge was developing and communicating a set of recommendations for the public. It was difficult because we had to get all the [state and local] jurisdictions to agree and because there were different recommendations [for different risk groups]."

One hospital-based infectious disease expert said, "The public had better sense than CDC. They saw their co-workers getting sick and came for treatment. We had this really sick guy. We could not prophy him because he was not on the list. CDC would only let us prophy people who worked in the Brentwood postal office [as postal workers], not people who cleaned the air handlers there or filled the Coca-Cola machines." Other study participants faulted CDC for failing to solicit technical information from the postal workers themselves. As one postal employee noted, "Right after the Daschle letter, postal employees were voicing their concerns, but there was no guidance from the CDC. The first thing CDC said was, 'There is no danger unless the mail is opened." But as this postal employee noted, it was widely recognized by postal workers that "stuff leaks out of envelopes all the time. One machine handles 17,000 envelopes per hour. There is lots of capacity for aerosolization."

Postal workers also questioned the reliability of some of the CDC guidance. A representative of the postal workers noted, "The information [from CDC] changed every day. Nobody knew what was going on. I started a web page, but I would put something out and it would change. They said you need 10,000 spores to be ill, but we asked, 'Can't some people get sick with less?' They said, 'No. You have a better chance of getting hit by a bicycle.' We had a party [to celebrate] the end of 60 days [of Cipro] and then they came back [a few weeks later] and said there were spores still living in us. They held a lot of meetings. I sat in on each one. Every doctor and every story was different. They said the stuff [vaccine] was safe but we would have to sign all these papers and maybe we could lose our rights under workers comp. Then they said the military people used to get six shots, but we were going to get less. Even that doctor said she had the six. If six was good for her, why not for us?"

The confusion caused by these scientific uncertainties was compounded by the poor communication among public health officials and the media and the public. As the investigation first evolved and CDC learned more about the nature of the anthrax powder, the risk posed by unopened envelopes working their way through post office sorting machines, and other technical issues that bore on who was at risk and the nature of the public health response, the public heard little from top federal health officials. The lack of a consistent, credible message emanating from CDC in the early days after the anthrax attacks has yet to be fully explained.

CDC thus faced daunting challenges. The world expected CDC to provide detailed, authoritative information about a disease with which it was not familiar, in the context of a deliberate attack during a criminal investigation, the scope of which was larger than anything CDC had ever handled. Key aspects of the investigation were not under CDC's control, and it is unclear to what extent CDC officials were free to speak to the public or the media.

Information Dissemination to Professional Communities

Physicians interviewed for this study initially believed that they would be given rapid and specific instructions from public health officials regarding how to recognize and treat victims of the anthrax attacks. It quickly became clear that public health guidance was not being issued fast enough to guide many necessary clinical decisions. When no guidance was forthcoming, clinicians relied on their own medical judgment to make diagnoses and initiate treatment and, in some instances, published guidelines based on their experience. As one physician noted, "There were expectations of external support. We were told on October 20th that guidelines from CDC were forthcoming. They were [eventually] posted in the *Morbidity and Mortality Weekly Report* on the 26th. [Meanwhile] we wrote our own prophy guidelines and created a milieu for clinical decision-making. We created what we needed to create."

Many of those interviewed from the medical and public health communities spoke of the difficulty getting information about the number and location of confirmed or possible anthrax cases, the risk factors associated with anthrax exposure, or the latest CDC recommendations on diagnosis and treatment. Physicians reported being unable to get through to local or federal public health officials by phone. According to one local public health official, "Our phone lines were clogged by people who were confused about their risk of exposure and the worried well." When authoritative guidance from health officials was provided, it was often, as one clinician noted, "too little, too late." Many study participants reported that the media was the most consistent and rapid source of current information for physicians and public health practitioners.

A number of CDC's intended mechanisms for communicating with health care and public health professionals proved to be problematic vehicles for delivering information during the anthrax response. *Morbidity and Mortality Weekly Report (MMWR)* is a weekly bulletin that conveys important disease outbreak–related information to clinicians and public health officials. It is available by subscription through the mail and on CDC's website, and excerpts are printed in the weekly *Journal of the American Medical Association*.[27] But the *MMWR* weekly schedule was not designed to deliver updates of information that changed several times a day, and only a minority of physicians are regular readers. Those interviewed did not report that *MMWR* was a source of rapid clinical information during this crisis.

Epi-X, an encrypted electronic web-based communication, was launched in December 2000 to relay sensitive and urgent disease outbreak information to state and local public health departments. Most clinicians do not have access to Epi-X.[28] The utility of Epi-X for public health officials following the anthrax attacks was unclear; those interviewed in this study did not cite it as a source of information during the response.

In 1999, CDC initiated the Health Alert Network (HAN).[29] The HAN is envisioned as an electronic system linking CDC with state and local health departments, allowing electronic distribution of CDC health alerts and disease prevention guidelines. The HAN also would make it possible for state and local health officials to electronically report laboratory findings and disease surveillance data and to participate in distance learning modules. During the anthrax attacks of 2001, in most areas of the country the HAN was accessible only to public health agencies; the medical and hospital communities were not part of the HAN and could not receive its reports. Some local health departments passed

HAN alerts on by fax or shared HAN information through phone calls, but this was not a widespread practice.

Public health officials interviewed for this study indicated that even within the public health community, the HAN's usefulness during the anthrax attacks was limited. Constraints included limited access to the necessary technology, confusion about how information conveyed by the HAN should be used, and delays in moving the HAN information down the chain from CDC through state health agencies to local public health officials.

At the time of the 2001 anthrax attacks, only 60% of local health departments had the type of Internet access necessary to receive HAN alerts. In the first several weeks after the initial anthrax attacks, HAN alerts often were stopped or delayed at the state level before being distributed to local public health departments. Public health authorities at the federal and state levels were at times uncertain about how much information to send over the HAN. As one public health expert noted, "The HAN could have been the most reliable source of information for state and local public health officials during the anthrax outbreaks, but there were technical and philosophical problems. There were concerns about sharing HAN information. Should it be shared with local health officials? All physicians? What if the press got hold of HAN information?" When it became clear that information was not reaching many local health departments, CDC began distributing anthrax alerts and updates directly to all state and local health departments that had Internet access and were a part of the HAN.

CDC maintains a public website where much useful information that was pertinent to the anthrax attacks was posted. It crashed and went off-line twice during the anthrax response, in part because of heavy use and partly because it lacked redundancy.

Strategies for Responding to the Media

Many public health agencies were not prepared to meet media demands. A number of public health officials interviewed for this study found the media demands during the anthrax crisis extremely time-consuming and difficult to satisfy. Many public health officials did not consider media requests for information to be a priority. Most public health departments lacked prepared materials or detailed public communication plans. In many cases, educational fact sheets stating basic facts about anthrax were crafted in the midst of the crisis.

Public health practitioners spoke of the "tension" among elected officials and health officials trying to reach consensus about how much information should be released to the press. There were disputes about who should be responsible for releasing information: the local health department, the state health department, CDC, elected officials, or other government agencies. A number of public health professionals noted that they lacked the skills to prepare press statements or speak to the media. Some health officials were afraid to say anything in the midst of an unfolding investigation during which the facts changed so quickly. Several within the public health community stated that there were restraints placed on them regarding what information could be released. One local public health official stated, "My mayor told me what I could say and what I could not say to the media."

Some public health officials criticized their own colleagues for spending too much time with the press, saying that time spent with the media meant attention was being diverted from the anthrax investigation. Other public health officials disagreed with these sentiments and asserted the critical importance of speaking to the press. One of these officials said, "The community, country, and world needed a point of central knowledge. If you don't do interviews, the reporters will get information elsewhere and the source may not be as good."

Some health departments were clear leaders in their ability to develop information and summaries for public and professional community dissemination more quickly, and they were able to share this information broadly with other health departments. For example, New York City Department of Health officials placed a high priority on communication with the press. They issued timely alerts and updates to clinicians and public health officials in New York City, and these were regularly passed on to others across the country. The department also held regular briefings for the press. They judged that these press briefings were an important way to transmit current information and avoid misinformation. These officials knew they had the authority to speak to the press, because the authority had come from the top. Said one NYC public health official, "The mayor had a strong belief that you have to get information out and not keep things from the public."

The difficulties that public health agencies had communicating with the public were particularly serious in the Washington, DC, area, where communication failures led some to speculate that there were racial disparities in the treatment recommendations. When a letter containing anthrax spores was delivered to the office of Senator Daschle, the Capitol physician arranged for Capitol workers to receive nasal swab testing and instituted a course of ciprofloxacin antibiotic prophylaxis. One week later, when it became evident that Brentwood postal workers had been exposed to anthrax, CDC decided not to recommend nasal swabs because they had determined that this test was an unproven and possibly misleading measure of anthrax exposure. CDC had also begun to recommend doxycycline as an alternative antibiotic prophylaxis choice to ciprofloxacin ("Cipro"), because they judged it to be equally efficacious and more readily available. These recommendations led some to believe there was a double standard emerging. As one infectious disease physician in the DC area noted, "There was no printed guidance and a lot of what we did was fly by the seat of our pants. We attempted to be consistent, but CDC's recommendations and the Capitol physician's recommendations were different."

Ultimately, CDC did not succeed in convincing many of the Brentwood employees that the changing guidelines reflected public health officials' best judgments regarding prophylaxis and treatment. The variations in practice were perceived by many as evidence of a lack of equity. As one government official noted, "The Capitol physician's course was different from CDC. So people in DC felt they were getting less good care. It became an issue of poor black folks versus rich white folks."

Media lacked access to reliable information. The media reported great difficulty getting reliable information from public health authorities. Members of the media interviewed for this study reported that public health officials frequently ignored or did not return phone calls from the press. One newspaper journalist stated, "Finding out what was being done was incredibly difficult. Finding out what was happening at the national level was next to impossible. We couldn't get through, or no calls were returned. This went on for weeks. CDC was a disaster until one month later when they started daily telephone press briefings. [In addition], the top state officials were not accessible and they could not figure out how to do the press."

Journalists faced the challenge of reporting on a subject with which most public health experts had a limited scientific understanding and no firsthand experience. Reporters spoke of the frustration in dealing with changing recommendations and with the uncertainties of who would deliver the next installment of authoritative information and when. "Once we reached people, the quality [of information] varied, and every day we got different and conflicting information. The health department press offices didn't know the disease. I can't think of any other public health event like this."

Faced with either poor access to public health officials or inadequate information, reporters scanned websites, downloaded articles, and attempted to identify experts. Without information from public health authorities, one journalist noted that they had to assemble pieces of the anthrax puzzle from a variety of what they hoped would be credible sources. One reporter noted, "It was extremely difficult to get information out [of public health]. If I did not have a several-year relationship with officials, it would have been impossible. I have been in the business 25 years, but this was the fastest unfolding story. There was information, rumors, powders, and people on edge. It would have been useful to have a single person, point of contact, or continually updated website. Everyone was having meetings and things were hush-hush. They didn't know what was safe to say. The press relied on back channel contacts. We wanted to make sure we did not embellish. This took effort. The job of good reporting is a function of the reliability of data. There were many agencies involved that had conflicting information. You don't want reporters making scientific judgments."

Insufficient Personnel, Resources, and Operational Systems

The anthrax attacks of 2001 placed heavy and novel demands on a public health system that long has been recognized to lack resources commensurate with its responsibilities. Although some public health officials reported that experience with previous communicable disease outbreaks had helped to prepare them to respond to the anthrax attacks, most believed that the demands placed on public health authorities by the anthrax crisis made this different from past public health events. One state public health official noted, "Public health planning for West Nile Virus, Y2K and even 9/11 facilitated the development of systems and strategies, but we were un-prepared for the surge in demand [caused by the anthrax attacks]." A number of concerns were common across affected communities.

Communications technology was inadequate. Equipment widely requested on an emergency basis by public health officials during the attacks included computers, software applications, conference call capability, wireless email, broadcast fax, and cell phones. One Virginia public health official noted that cell phones were ordered when the anthrax attacks were discovered in the DC region, but the phones were delivered to fire departments and not public health agencies. Another study participant noted that cell phones finally arrived at the local public health department, but came with a service agreement that did not cover the health department's location.

Systems for emergency procurement of critical resources were lacking. Few public health departments had emergency procurement systems. Interviewees repeatedly noted the lengthy and cumbersome administrative processes they had to navigate to procure tools and equipment to manage the anthrax response. One public health laboratory director noted that he had adequate funds in his budget to purchase the additional safety cabinets needed to analyze suspect anthrax samples, but he was told that it would take the state's office of general services two months to process the request. A public health physician reported using a personal credit card to purchase plastic bags to package preventive medication doses for patients.

Public health laboratories were stretched. State public health laboratories across the country were highly stressed by the quantity of potentially contaminated items brought in for testing. CDC laboratorians worked around the clock, sometimes sleeping in the lab, to analyze clinical samples. One state public health laboratory director noted, "We handled over 2,000 [suspect] anthrax samples in two months." This lab previously had performed one anthrax test per year. "We worked 7 AM to midnight, seven days a week. Sometimes we worked until 2 or 4 in the morning. We eventually trained ten people, but then we did not have enough safety cabinets to work in."

Many public health officials noted there was a lack of space to store samples and inadequate procedures to receive them. A state laboratory director noted, "We had no teams to assess the risks of samples, so nothing got rejected. We got drum-sized things, large bags of mail, stuff that we could not get into safety cabinets. [Additionally] stuff just got walked in through the department lobby by Hazmat workers in their protective and contaminated garments. It was a risk for the laboratories."

Personnel limitations affected local public health surge capacity. Public health officials needed to perform a wide array of functions, including investigating all suspected cases; answering inquiries from other public health officials, clinicians, the public, and the media; coordinating clinical information from hospitals; conducting and tracking down environmental test results; and administering antibiotic prophylaxis clinics. States typically did not have the capacity to emergently credential health professionals from adjoining states. A public health physician noted, "Lots of people wanted to help. . . . We needed lots of people but we couldn't teach them while we were so involved." Most senior local and state public health officials noted that there were no systems in place to compensate their staff for the tremendous number of overtime hours worked.

There were not enough personnel to continue routine public health functions, so non-anthrax-related public health investigations and other laboratory studies were put aside. A senior local public health official noted, "If we had another simultaneous health problem we would have been in trouble." Five months after handling the anthrax investigation, a public health official at another site noted, "If there were a recurrence today we would be less able to respond. People are tired. They have been working seven days a week since October. We're in big trouble. We pulled out all the stops. If this were just the tiniest bit bigger, we would have been in trouble."

Organizational and personnel fatigue was further exacerbated in locales where public health personnel had participated in the response to the events of 9/11. And other public health emergencies required attention even as the anthrax response continued. For example, Florida health officials, in addition to investigating scores of "suspect powder" incidents, were also responding to the contamination of 500 pounds of grouper with ciguatera toxin, hurricane Michelle, and many other outbreak investigations.

Over the course of the anthrax response, CDC dispatched more than 350 employees to the five anthrax epicenters, but even this substantial deployment could not address all of the personnel shortages experienced by state and local health departments. Of the CDC staff deployed to states, 136 were Epidemiologic Intelligence Service (EIS) officers, representing 93% of the nation's active EIS.[30] Many public health officials interviewed were appreciative of CDC direction and support, acknowledging a lack of local expertise and inadequate numbers of human resources needed to respond to the attacks, but some noted that CDC personnel did not always match local needs. Some state and local health officials noted difficulty integrating CDC staff into local response efforts. One state health official noted, "I don't expect CDC to do community-based work. I just expect technical guidance."

Conclusions

These interviews with several dozen individuals directly involved in responding to or reporting on the 2001 anthrax attacks document the intense and sustained pace and pressures associated with the crisis response. These accounts reveal several themes that might usefully be considered by those responsible for bioterrorism preparedness and planning.

Expectations about Federal, State, and Local Public Health Responsibilities Require Clarification

Public health officials from state and local health departments appear to have differing, and sometimes contradictory, views about the type and extent of assistance that can or should be expected from CDC in the wake of a bioterrorist attack. Some were disappointed that CDC was unable to deliver more robust operational support on the ground. Others believed that CDC's resources and capabilities were more appropriate to the role of scientific advisor. Still others believed that CDC did not possess the medical expertise to guide clinical efforts or to adequately interface with the health care delivery community. It would be useful to have a national discussion regarding the expected role of CDC during large-scale public health crises.

If CDC is to serve as the authoritative source of scientific analysis, the agency's ability to quickly gather and make sense of information from many sources, including the medical community, will need to be greatly improved. It needs to be recognized that CDC's resources are insufficient to serve during a crisis simultaneously as the nation's scientific advisor in public health matters, as a provider of extensive operational assistance to state and local health departments, and as an authoritative source of clinical practice recommendations.

Dr. Julie Gerberding, who was appointed CDC Director in the summer of 2002, has noted that the agency has revised its emergency response strategy in an effort to improve CDC's ability to respond to future attacks in a more coordinated manner. Nonetheless, absent extensive investments in CDC staff and infrastructure, it is unrealistic to expect CDC to play a prominent operational role during a response to a bioterrorist attack, given limitations on the agency's resources and the potentially huge scope of bioterrorist attacks.

The type and extent of assistance that local health care institutions and public health agencies can expect from CDC and other federal agencies, as well as realistic timetables for delivering such aid need to be clarified. The Federal Response Plan and most other bioterrorism response templates acknowledge that responsibility for responding to terrorist acts resides with local authorities. It appears, however, that many in the responder community—particularly health care professionals—expected the federal government to provide immediate, scientifically accurate guidance in a bioterrorism emergency. Prudence requires that bioterrorism preparedness plans *assume* that state and local public health authorities will have to make judgments based on uncertain knowledge and without the guidance of federal authorities, at least initially. Provisions for gathering critical information, including input from relevant local experts, and for reaching coherent decisions and making the basis of these decisions known should be part of all local and state plans.

Medical Preparedness Requires better Communications among Physicians and between Medical and Public Health Communities

The 2001 anthrax response highlighted the challenges associated with managing the medical and public health aspects of bioterrorist attacks. Should future attacks occur, clinicians likely would be called on to exercise professional judgment in the face of unfamiliar illness and uncertain risk factors. The time pressures associated with caring for acutely ill patients will likely make it impossible for CDC or local health authorities to supply physicians with rapid, authoritative, and scientifically validated assessments of the nature of the attack and with the most current medical diagnostic and management recommendations, at least in the initial stages of response.

Public and Media must Recognize that Response to Bioterror Attacks will Evolve

Epidemics move at a pace that is unlike that of other crises and catastrophes. The full extent of future bioterrorist attacks will not be immediately apparent at the start of such crises; identifying the at-risk population and formulating effective recommendations for unfamiliar diseases occurring in never-before-seen contexts will take time, and initial impressions may be revised or rejected.

It is apparent that responders, the media, and the public were frustrated and confused by the evolving understanding of the risks posed by anthrax-laden letters and by shifting recommendations about who might be at risk for becoming sick and how such people should be treated. Some of this confusion is the result of inadequate public education regarding the nature of bioterrorism and of epidemics generally.

It is likely that recognition of the nature of and appropriate response to future bioterrorist attacks also will unfold over time. This is a difficult lesson in an age of 24/7 media coverage and expectations of instant answers. The media and the public must understand that the need for rapid decisions may be at odds with the desire for complete answers. As has been seen with the international outbreak of Severe Acute Respiratory Syndrome (SARS), it may be difficult to quickly answer even seemingly straightforward questions such as whether the number of victims is increasing or leveling off.

It is critical that leaders familiarize the public and the media with the likelihood that reliable answers to questions arising in future attacks will take time to assemble and validate. Government spokespeople must take great care to highlight uncertainties and to be explicit about what is known and what is not known or fully understood. If public health and medical recommendations that evolve or are revised are interpreted as revealing incompetence or as evidence that information is being withheld or that different populations are getting preferential treatment, the public may be unwilling to follow authorities' recommendations in times of crisis.

Health Officials Must Prepare to Handle the Media Storm

Most study participants acknowledged that the public health community, with some notable exceptions, did a poor job of meeting the media's demand for information, although study participants believed many of the reasons for this inadequate performance were beyond their personal control. The intention to provide accurate and comprehensive information (and in so doing, necessitating the time required to be accurate and comprehensive) was at odds with the media's—and the public's—desire to be informed about the attacks as soon as information became available.

Most public health agencies lacked sufficient numbers of technically credible, media-savvy professionals who could work constructively with the media. There was no evident media strategy within the federal government for several weeks into the crisis. The irregular and at times confused interactions between the federal government and the press during the crisis resulted in a loss of government credibility and an increasingly aggressive media feeding frenzy.

Past public health emergencies, notably those involving environmental crises, have yielded many well-tested lessons about how health risk information can reliably be communicated. The essence of these lessons is that authorities should tell the truth as they know it, when they know it; they should be forthright about what is not known; and they should explain what is being done to improve understanding of the situation and manage the problem. If the government does not find a way to embody these fundamental lessons, the public's willingness to accept the government's recommendations in future crises will be compromised.

Dr. Gerberding has noted that she intends to change CDC's traditional "evidence-based" style of communicating to an "adaptive style" more suited for fast-moving emergencies. "We'll tell you what we know today, and acknowledge that it may change by tomorrow," Dr. Gerberding is quoted as saying in a recent publication.[31]

Public Health Resources are Barely Adequate for a Small-Scale Bioterror Attack

The failure to create a detailed, after-action assessment of the public health and medical response to the 2001 anthrax attacks is a lost opportunity to illuminate, concretely and specifically, the fragile state of bioterrorism preparedness. The capacities of CDC and involved health departments and hospitals were highly stressed by the bioterror attacks of 2001, which resulted in 22 cases and involved one of the few bioagents for which there exist effective drugs and vaccine. The adequacy of the response was due in large part to the laudable efforts of individual clinicians and public health professionals who worked relentlessly for months to manage the response. This level of effort would not be sustainable over the long term (e.g., for the span of the 1918 flu epidemic). An attack involving more victims, or multiple attacks in different locations, likely would have overwhelmed the frail network of response capabilities.

The Bush Administration has significantly increased the federal resources available to state health departments for bioterrorism preparedness. By late fall 2002, HHS had dispersed the bulk of almost $1 billion in new funding to state governments, intending that state and local health departments spend this money to meet 17 "benchmark" criteria judged essential to epidemic response.[32–34] Many states and cities have hired bioterrorism coordinators and have undertaken drills and exercises to improve responsiveness. Hospital response has received less attention and much less money, but HHS officials have asserted that this is a high priority for future spending. Federal funding for research and development of drugs, vaccines, and biomedical research important to biodefense also has been appropriated.[35] Sufficient quantities of smallpox vaccine to immunize all Americans are being manufactured, and mass pre-event and event-related smallpox vaccination strategies are being developed.

These are welcome and appropriate steps. It must be remembered, however, that these federal funding streams are flowing into states whose own revenues are severely limited.[36] The smallpox immunization plan announced by the Administration in December 2002 has added great stress to public health agencies around the country. Many have reported that they will not be able to move forward in that effort without interruption of routine immunization or other public health prevention programs. More than 40 states are in recession, and most of these have placed a freeze on hiring. As history, and the current state of public health, has shown, public health preparedness is not necessarily a priority of governors and mayors. The Executive Director of the American Public Health Association, who was the Maryland Health Commissioner in 2001, has noted that overall funding for public health in the 50 states has declined, in spite of federal support for bioterrorism preparedness.[37]

It will take considerable vision and leadership—and sustained funding—to build the medical and public health systems needed to appreciably improve the nation's capacity to mitigate the consequences of bioterrorist attacks. The anthrax attacks of 2001 demonstrated the feasibility of the use of biological weapons upon civilian populations. The SARS outbreak has again demonstrated the great responsibilities and challenges that the medical and public health systems bear in confronting disease epidemics, even when the overall number of cases remains relatively modest. Assessments of the response to the 2001 anthrax attacks and to other disease outbreaks such as SARS are critical to making wise decisions and strategic investments at the local, state, and federal levels concerning bioterrorism preparedness and response. Establishing the policy priorities, resources, and institutional capabilities to practice public health at a level of sophistication consistent with 21st century science and technology and commensurate with the threat posed by catastrophic bioterrorism is the task before us.

Notes

1. Personal communication, David Heymann, Center for Strategic International Studies, Feb. 7, 2003.
2. Centers for Disease Control and Prevention. Notice to Readers: Ongoing Investigation of Anthrax—Florida, October 2001, *Morbidity and Mortality Weekly Report* 10/12/01, 50(40):877.

3. Centers for Disease Control and Prevention. Update: Investigation of Anthrax Associated with Intentional Exposure and Interim Public Health Guidelines, October 2001, *Morbidity and Mortality Weekly Report* 10/19/01, 50(41):889–893.

4. Ibid.

5. Ibid

6. Ibid.

7. Ibid

8. Ibid.

9. Centers for Disease Control and Prevention. Update: Investigation of Bioterrorism-Related Anthrax and Interim Guidelines for Clinical Evaluation of Persons with Possible Anthrax, *Morbidity and Mortality Weekly Report* 11/02/01, 50(43):941–948.

10. Jernigan DB, Raghunathan PL, Bell BP, et al. Investigation of Bioterrorism-Related Anthrax, United States 2001: Epidemiologic Findings, *Emerging Infectious Diseases* October 2002, 8:1019–1028.

11. New Jersey Department of Health and Senior Services. Anthrax Investigation Update in New Jersey. *News Release* November 5, 2001.

12. Op cit., note 9.

13. Op cit., note 2.

14. Centers for Disease Control and Prevention. Update: Investigation of Bioterrorism-Related Anthrax and Interim Guidelines for Exposure Management and Antimicrobial Therapy, October 2001, *Morbidity and Mortality Weekly Report* 2001;50(42):909–919.

15. Centers for Disease Control and Prevention. CDC Statement Regarding the Washington DC Processing and Distribution Center, and Postal and Mailroom Facilities Who Directly Receive and Distribute Mail from this Center, *Health Advisory* October 24, 2001.

16. Centers for Disease Control and Prevention. CDC Statement regarding postal and other mailroom facilities in the Metropolitan DC area, *Health Alert* October 27, 2001.

17. Op cit., note 8.

18. Mina B, Dym JP, Kuepper F et al. Fatal Inhalational Anthrax With Unknown Source of Exposure in a 61-Year Old Woman in New York City, *Journal American Medical Association* February 2002;287:858–862.

19. Centers for Disease Control and Prevention. Update: Investigation of Bioterrorism-Related Inhalational Anthrax—Connecticut, 2001, *Morbidity and Mortality Weekly Report* 11/30/01: 50(47):1049–1054.

20. National Association of City and County Health Officials. Local Public Health Agency Infrastructure: A Chartbook, October 2001. *www.naccho.org/general428.cfm*

21. Ibid.

22. www.cdc.gov/aboutcdc.htm

23. 42 CFR §70, 70.2.

24. U.S. Department of Transportation, Federal Highway Administration. Journey-To-Work Trends in the United States and its Major Metropolitan Areas, 1960–1990. Washington, DC.

25. Metropolitan Washington Council of Governments. COG Report: 2010 worker flows. Washington, DC: George Mason University of Public Policy, "Characteristics of the Northern Virginia Workforce and Labor Market," December 2001. Available at http://www.nvrp.org/whatnew/gmu-surveypdfs.html

26. Hsu S. Emergency Plan for Region Unveiled; COG Proposal Includes D.C. Evacuation System. *Washington Post* September 12, 2002.

27. www.cdc.gov/mmwr/about.html

28. www.cdc.gov/programs/research5.htm

29. www.phppo.cdc.gov/han

30. Centers for Disease Control and Prevention. Update: Largest-Ever Deployment of CDC Epidemic Intelligence Service Officers, *Press Release* January 25, 2002.

31. Boschert S. Most Clinical Labs Have Bioterror Detection Plan, but Gaps Remain, *Internal Medicine News* January 15, 2003;36(2):38.

32. United States Department of Health and Human Services. Bioterrorism Preparedness Grants, *Press Release* June 6, 2002. www.hhs.gov/news/press/2002pres/20020606b.html

33. United States Department of Health and Human Services. 17 Critical Benchmarks for Bioterrorism Preparedness Planning, *Press Release* June 6, 2002 http://www.hhs.gov/new/press/2002pres/20020606a.html

34. *Washington Fax.* Gerberding plans strategically for CDC's future while preparing for emergencies now, February 24, 2003.

35. Ibid.

36. Elliott VS. Public health funding: Feds Giveth but the States Taketh Away *amednews.com* October 28, 2002. www.ama-assn.org/sci-pubs/amnews/pick_02/hll21028.htm

37. Mulcahy N. Bioterror Prep Funds Don't Cover States' Cuts, *Internal Medicine News* January 15, 2003;36(2):38.

Elin Gursky is a senior fellow for Biodefense and Public Health at the ANSER Institute for Homeland Security, Arlington, Virginia. Dr. Gursky received a doctor of science degree (1985) from the Johns Hopkins University Bloomberg School of Public Health.

Thomas V. Inglesby is chief operating officer and deputy director, Center for Biosecurity of the University of Pittsburgh Medical Center (UPMC) and associate professor of medicine and public health, University of Pittsburgh Schools of Medicine and Public Health. He received his undergraduate degree from Georgetown University in 1988 and his M.D. from the Columbia University College of Physicians and Surgeons in 1992. He completed his internal medicine residency and infectious diseases fellowship training at the Johns Hopkins School of Medicine, and served as assistant chief of service in the Johns Hopkins department of medicine in 1996–97.

Tara O'Toole is the CEO and director, Center for Biosecurity of the University of Pittsburgh Medical Center (UPMC) and professor of medicine, University of Pittsburgh. She received her bachelors degree from Vassar College, her M.D. from the George Washington University, and a master of public health degree from Johns Hopkins University. She completed a residency in internal medicine at Yale, and a fellowship in occupational and environmental medicine at Johns Hopkins University.

Crystal Franco et al.

Systemic Collapse: Medical Care in the Aftermath of Hurricane Katrina

This article describes and analyzes key aspects of the medical response to Hurricane Katrina in New Orleans. It is based on interviews with individuals involved in the response and on analysis of published reports and news articles. Findings include: (1) federal, state, and local disaster plans did not include provisions for keeping hospitals functioning during a large-scale emergency; (2) the National Disaster Medical System (NDMS) was ill-prepared for providing medical care to patients who needed it; (3) there was no coordinated system for recruiting, deploying, and managing volunteers; and (4) many Gulf Coast residents were separated from their medical records. The article makes recommendations for improvement.

This article describes and analyzes key aspects of the medical response to Hurricane Katrina in New Orleans, based on interviews with individuals directly involved in the response and on an analysis of published reports and news articles. This article does not attempt to describe the dedicated and heroic individual efforts of the thousands of medical professionals from the New Orleans region and around the country who responded to Katrina. There is no doubt that their compassion and dedication saved countless lives. Rather, we focus on a number of the key institutional and systemic responses that were intended to provide medical care in large catastrophes and make suggestions for improving them in future disasters.

Methodology

Over the months following Hurricane Katrina, the authors gathered information for this article via telephone and email conversations with 22 physicians, nurses, hospital administrators, public health officials, government officials, and academic medical center staff, all of whom were involved in the medical response to the disaster. Many of the people interviewed were at the time actively involved on the ground in the medical response. Conversations took place between September 1, 2005 and January 2006; they were voluntary, unstructured, and nonremunerated. Respondents were assured that their comments would not be attributed to them in ways that could reveal their identities. Individuals contacted were chosen based on their expertise, their willingness to participate, and their knowledge of the medical systems and institutions involved in the response. In addition, we reviewed hundreds of newspaper articles, journal and magazine articles, government websites, government press releases and reports, healthcare organization websites, and scientific articles identified via PubMed to find information related to these issues.

Throughout the article, where quotes from individuals are specifically attributed, it is because the quote was acquired from a public news source or government document. Where comments or opinions are not attributed, they are from one or more of the individuals who were interviewed for this article under an assurance of anonymity.

We recognize that it may be difficult to generalize from some of the interviewee observations, but we concluded that many of the individual accounts of the events after Katrina are compelling and clear illustrations of where medical response systems succeeded and where they didn't.

We have made a serious effort to distinguish the facts in the historical record from individual views or accounts. Due to space limitations, not all of the complex and important issues related to the medical response could be discussed in a single article. We do not claim that this is an exhaustive account of the medical response in New Orleans. For example, the article does not attempt to examine how the American Red Cross or CDC's Strategic National Stockpile functioned in the crisis.

A number of government reports on Hurricane Katrina have provided important findings and recommendations on issues related to the response, particularly the White House report,[1] a report from the U.S. Senate Committee on Homeland Security and Governmental Affairs,[2] a report released by the U.S. House Select Bipartisan Committee to Investigate the Preparation for and Response to Hurricane Katrina,[3] and a report titled *Public Health and Medical Response* from the Congressional Research Service (CRS).[4] This article is meant to add to this existing body of information on these issues.

Under Key Findings, we discuss the most important common findings from the individual accounts and the literature review. In Conclusions and Recommendations, we reflect on how these findings should influence future planning of the medical system response to disasters.

Key Findings

KEY FINDING #1: Federal, state, and local disaster plans did not include strategies or provisions to keep hospitals functioning during a large-scale emergency such as Hurricane Katrina.

In the wake of Hurricane Katrina, 9 of New Orleans's 11 hospitals were incapacitated. Hospitals were isolated from local first responder assistance due to flooding, and the arrival of federal assets was delayed for days after the storm, leaving hospitals to fend for themselves.[5] Charity Hospital, Louisiana's largest healthcare facility, was left without power for 5 days, in 100 degree heat, and with little food and water.[6] Without electricity, it was impossible to deliver the usual standard of care for the sickest patients in hospital ICUs. There was no power for mechanical ventilators, bedside monitors, or dialysis machines; many functions had to be performed by hand or not at all.

Nearly every hospital in New Orleans faced security problems, as individuals attempted to raid what was left of hospital supplies and pharmaceuticals.[6] Security threats on the streets of the city forced doctors to move patients to upper floors of hospitals, and reports of snipers on nearby buildings (whether or not they would later prove to be true) hindered rooftop evacuation efforts. "At every [hospital], there are reports that as the helicopters come in people are shooting at them," confirmed Coast Guard Lt. Cmdr. Cheri Ben-Iesan, spokesman at the city emergency operations center.[7] Fear of this seemingly unstable situation outside the hospital no doubt slowed the evacuation process.

Prior to Katrina, New Orleans hospitals represented a critical and reliable community resource for the city's residents, but after the hurricane struck, most hospitals were no longer open as a place of refuge and care. "The hospital is the backbone of the community because the lights are always on," said Knox Andres, an emergency nurse and regional coordinator for a federal emergency preparedness grant covering Louisiana. "When hospitals can't take care of people and the rescuers need rescu[ing] there's no social fabric left."[7]

- Emergency plans did not ensure that critical hospital systems, such as electricity and backup power sources, would continue to be available. Without power, hospitals were unable to function and were forced to evacuate.

In years prior to Hurricane Katrina, hospitals in the Gulf Coast region experienced a number of storms that tested their disaster preparedness. For example, in 2001 Tropical Storm Allison stalled over Texas, unexpectedly dropping torrential rains that flooded Houston's bayous. Floodwaters filled Houston's Hermann Memorial Hospital with 5 feet of standing water, swamping the lower levels of the facility, which housed the hospital's emergency generators. The hospital lost electricity, its backup power source, running water, sewer services, and communications capabilities, and it had to evacuate 540 patients. In response to this experience and in preparation for future storms (including Hurricane Rita in 2005), Houston's Memorial Hospital moved its generators off of the first floor of the building and installed floodgates around the outside of the hospital.[8]

Yet most hospitals in New Orleans, including Charity Hospital, had emergency generators on the first floor of their buildings when the levees failed during Hurricane Katrina, 4 years after Houston Memorial Hospital's experience. According to one physician in a New Orleans hospital interviewed for this article, moving the generators to another floor of the hospital was something that could not have been done in the midst of the crisis, since it would have involved not only moving the generator unit but also moving and rewiring the electrical connections. For the hospitals in New Orleans, the lack of electricity to run essential equipment needed for patient care was the limiting factor that ultimately forced them to evacuate and close.

- New Orleans hospitals had little functioning backup communications equipment, and it was unclear which emergency response agency(s) they should call or rely on for help.

As has been the case in other major disasters, in Hurricane Katrina, the telephone communication infrastructure was one of the first casualties of the storm. By the time the hurricane had passed, many cell phone towers had been destroyed or disabled and most land telephone lines were dead. Some hospitals were without a backup communications system such as satellite phones or two-way radios. And according to one Louisiana physician, those hospitals that had backup equipment found it to be largely unreliable.

A few physicians whom we interviewed commented that ham radios were the one piece of communications equipment that could be consistently relied on, but there were very few of these radios and even fewer personnel who knew how to operate them. The result was that, in their time of greatest need, New Orleans hospitals had very little ability to contact the outside world. They were unable to request evacuation, to request additional staff and supplies, or to update other hospitals and local incident command on their status. Having gone 5 days without rescue, and after exhausting every other avenue of appeal, Dr. Norman McSwain, chief of trauma surgery at Charity Hospital, finally was able to contact the Associated Press with this message: "We have been trying to call the mayor's office, we have been trying to call the governor's office ... we have tried to use any inside pressure we can. . . . We need coordinated help from the government."[7]

Others interviewed relayed that when hospital staff could make use of functional communications equipment, or when they used messengers to relay information, they often did not know whom they should contact to communicate their needs. Was it the New Orleans or Louisiana State Emergency Operations Centers (EOC), the health department, a hospital association, or the federal government? Charity Hospital did not know whom to call or how to get in touch with the right people when they needed urgent assistance and evacuation of their patients.

Meanwhile, evacuation efforts by local, state, and federal responders were underway, but, without established lines of communication with hospitals, it was often unclear to responders which facilities were in need of assistance and which had already been evacuated. At one hospital, as staff and patients waited for evacuation, listening to news updates on a portable radio, they heard an announcement from the governor's office saying that their hospital had already been evacuated.[6]

- There was no regional hospital authority or entity able to provide coordination or serious assistance to New Orleans hospitals in the aftermath of Hurricane Katrina.

In many respects, the scale of destruction caused by Hurricane Katrina was beyond the ability of any individual hospital to prepare for or cope with. Hospitals that had good disaster plans were still surprised by the unanticipated and severe consequences of the storm. In the aftermath of the hurricane, there was no functioning regional emergency coordinating authority for hospitals. According to the Southeast Louisiana Catastrophic Hurricane Functional Plan and the State of Louisiana Emergency Operations Plan, the Louisiana State University Health Sciences Center (LSUHSC) was to have the lead role in coordinating hospital planning with private hospitals and other facilities under Emergency Support Function 8 (the entity charged with ESF-8 is responsible for public health and medical services in an emergency).[9]

While LSU successfully ran major medical response activities in Baton Rouge in the wake of the hurricane, it was unable to simultaneously coordinate emergency planning and response activities with its own health-care facilities and other private hospitals in the New Orleans area, since many of these facilities were isolated for days after the storm and unable to make contact with authorities to request evacuation. One physician from a Louisiana academic health center interviewed for this article commented that there was no one overarching authority or leader to provide assets or to ask who needed what during the response to Hurricane Katrina, and hospitals did not know whom to ask for help.

KEY FINDING #2: The National Disaster Medical System was a valuable source of dedicated medical professionals. But as a whole, it did not function as a system and was ill-prepared to provide medical care to the thousands of patients who needed it.

The National Disaster Medical System (NDMS) is cited by the U.S. Department of Homeland Security (DHS) as the U.S. federal government's primary civilian medical response asset (see sidebar). The mission of NDMS is to provide "state of the art medical care under any conditions at a disaster site, in transit from [an] impacted area, and into participating definitive care facilities."[10] With most New Orleans hospitals closed or inoperative, NDMS became the source of medical care for tens of thousands of displaced patients.

Medical Response Programs in Brief

The following are descriptions of and key facts about some of the existing systems that are intended to prepare for and respond to large-scale national medical emergencies. These descriptions are taken directly from the program websites.

National Disaster Medical System (NDMS)
From NDMS website: NDMS is a section within the U.S. Department of Homeland Security, Federal Emergency Management Agency, Response Division, Operations Branch. It is responsible for supporting federal agencies in the management and coordination of the federal medical response to major emergencies and federally declared disasters. NDMS teams (including Disaster Medical Assistance Teams [DMATs]) are designed to provide care under any conditions at a disaster site, in transit from the affected area, and into participating definitive care facilities.[29]
FY2006 Budget Estimate: $134 million[30]
Facts: Hospitals in large metropolitan areas (usually over 100 beds in size) partner with NDMS and commit a certain number of their acute care beds for NDMS patient care in an emergency.[31]

Medical Reserve Corps (MRC)
From MRC website: MRC is a specialized component of Citizen Corps, housed within the Office of the Surgeon General, Department of Health and Human Services (HHS). MRC units are community-based and function as a way to locally organize and utilize volunteers. MRC volunteers supplement existing emergency and public health resources. MRC units also can be called on to volunteer for national deployment in a federal emergency.[32]
FY2006 Budget Estimate: $10 million[33]
Facts: As of February 2006, MRC had 370 units based in 49 states, and more than 70,000 volunteers from around the country.[34]

Emergency System for Registration of Volunteer Health Professionals (ESAR-VHP)
From HRSA website: The ESAR-VHP system is a state-based electronic database of healthcare personnel who volunteer to provide aid in an emergency. An ESAR-VHP System must (1) register health volunteers, (2) apply emergency credentialing standards to registered volunteers, and (3) allow for the verification of the identity, credentials, and qualifications of registered volunteers in an emergency. The ESAR-VHP program is managed through the Health Resources and Services Administration (HRSA).[35]

Facts: 60 U.S. states and territories and the District of Columbia have all received funding (about $200,000 each) and guidance to begin development of an ESAR-VHP system.[34]

During Hurricane Katrina, 7 states that had not already developed systems each set up a temporary ESAR-VHP in order to facilitate volunteer credentialing and management.[36]

Emergency Management Assistance Compact (EMAC)

From EMAC website: EMAC is a congressionally ratified organization that provides form and structure to interstate mutual aid. Through EMAC, a disaster-affected state can request and receive assistance from other member states quickly and efficiently, resolving two key issues upfront: liability and reimbursement.[37]

Facts: 49 states, the District of Columbia, Puerto Rico, and the U.S. Virgin Islands have enacted EMAC legislation. Since 1999, EMAC has been activated 53 times for events such as hurricanes and terrorist attacks.[38]

Metropolitan Medical Response System (MMRS)

From the MMRS website: The MMRS began in 1996 and has been part of the U.S. Department of Homeland Security since March 1, 2003. The primary focus of the MMRS program is to develop or enhance existing emergency preparedness systems to effectively respond to a public health crisis, especially a weapons of mass destruction (WMD) event.[39]

FY2006 Budget Estimate: $30 million[30]

Facts: There are 125 MMRS jurisdictions.

MMRS jurisdictions are encouraged to establish and fund MRC units. Up to $25,000 of FY2006 funds for each jurisdiction may be used to support MRC units.[40]

NDMS Disaster Medical Assistance Teams (DMATs) came from around the nation to assist in the medical response to Hurricane Katrina. Nineteen DMATs and other NDMS teams were pre-positioned in the Gulf Coast area prior to Katrina; as the storm passed, those teams and others from around the country were able to move into affected regions.[11] The teams were trained to offer hospital-level specialty medical care, but patient numbers often so greatly outweighed the numbers of medical practitioners that DMATs had time only to triage patients and provide basic first aid. The New Orleans Airport became a mass triage site where 10 DMAT teams worked around the clock for nearly a week after the hurricane struck. At its busiest, the shelter was staffed by about 30 individual DMAT medical providers and 100 ancillary personnel. At its peak, it processed around 15,000 patients in a single day.

One DMAT physician recalled that all that could be done was to "provide the barest amount of comfort care." He said, "We practiced medical triage at its most basic, black-tagging the sickest people and [moving] them [away] from the masses so that they could die in a separate area."[12] The teams ran out of the most fundamental supplies and medications, including ventilators, and one Oregon-based DMAT's after-action report stated that "FEMA/NDMS operations at the airport were extremely disorganized and poorly managed."[13]

- Poor NDMS/FEMA logistics management of critical medical supplies and medical teams decreased DMATs' capabilities to respond.

Numerous DMAT members that we interviewed complained of insufficient federal planning for team transportation, poor coordination and communication regarding where teams were needed, and long delays in deployment of medical supplies and pharmaceuticals. Roy Alson, MD, Commander of DMAT North Carolina-1, testified to Congress that many problems DMATs had in the field during Hurricane Katrina stemmed from the basic lack of a DHS medical logistics support system to coordinate the transport and placement of NDMS assets. Dr. Alson pointed out that in the three DMAT deployments prior to Katrina, the Federal Emergency Management Agency (FEMA) had failed to deliver medical supplies to the teams in a timely manner.[12]

Emergency Medical Technician Bill Engler, whose Seattle-based DMAT flew into the Gulf Coast region prior to Hurricane Katrina, said in an interview with *USA Today* that pre-positioning his team made little difference, since the team's cache of medical supplies was not sent in with them. Supplies had to be shipped in from Washington State, and the team was forced to share medicines and equipment with other DMATs, depleting those supplies very quickly.[14]

Jake Jacoby, who leads a San Diego–based team that responded to Hurricane Katrina, also commented to *USA Today* on NDMS logistics management. "[NDMS] is a program that on paper looks very good, but [DMATs] are getting abused by being sent into disaster-relief scenes without proper supplies," he said.[14]

Additionally, some DMATs that wanted to be included in the Hurricane Katrina medical response were never deployed by NDMS because of lapses in coordination and internal NDMS communication. One mobile DMAT hospital that had been developed through the Office of Homeland Security after September 11, 2001, with 113 beds, digital radiology, satellite internet, ultrasound, and a full pharmacy with 100 surgeons and paramedics, was stranded for days outside of New Orleans with no authorization to deploy anywhere in the city. A trauma surgeon from Vanderbilt University reported to the Associated Press, "There are entire [DMAT] hospitals that need to take in patients, but they can't get through the bureaucracy. . . . [Y]ou've got millions of dollars in assets and it's not deployed."[14]

Despite these many difficulties and barriers, Hurricane Katrina did demonstrate the ability and commitment of the DMAT members to care for patients under harsh conditions. DMAT medical providers were highly flexible and able to improvise in many instances when standard medical equipment and facilities were unavailable.

> KEY FINDING #3: There was no one coordinated system to recruit, deploy, and manage volunteers during the medical response to Hurricane Katrina.

Many medical professionals attempted to volunteer in the wake of Hurricane Katrina. Offers of help came from academic health centers, the Medical Reserve Corps, medical associations, hospitals, ad hoc teams, and from individuals with no group affiliation. There was no single federal office or national database with the ability to register, track, and manage the thousands of medical volunteers who descended on the Gulf Coast, and many volunteers had trouble engaging constructively in the medical response.

- Academic medical centers had disaster response plans and resources that might have changed the medical outcomes of many patients, but most of these centers were unable to effectively bring those resources to bear.

In the medical response to Hurricane Katrina, academic medical centers and large healthcare systems were unable to contribute their considerable resources, because there were no clear mechanisms for integrating these systems into the federal, state, and local medical response structure. By September 8, 2005, approximately 100 medical schools had been designated as response units to assist the U.S. National Institutes of Health (NIH) in providing care to patients displaced by Hurricane Katrina.[15] One individual from an academic medical center we interviewed said his institution was prepared to send thousands of medical volunteers to the Gulf Coast, and they had offered to provide a wide array of equipment and supplies including helicopters and medical crews; pharmaceuticals, ventilators, and other medical equipment and supplies; trucks with mechanics, staff, food, and water; communications equipment; and more. This academic medical center as well as others tried to offer their resources by directly contacting FEMA officials. However, they were redirected to the American Hospital Association. Ultimately, most of this medical center's contributions were never employed by the federal government.

The LSU medical response to Hurricane Katrina in Baton Rouge is one example of the great potential benefit of bringing to bear the expertise and resources of academic medical centers in emergency planning and response. LSU established a field hospital at the Pete Maravich Assembly Center (PMAC) in Baton Rouge within hours after Hurricane Katrina. The PMAC became the site of the largest acute care field hospital in U.S. history, with an 800-bed facility and about 1,700 volunteer medical personnel. Over the course of its operations, about 6,000 patients were cared for in the PMAC, and more than 2,000 faculty, students, and staff on the LSU campus volunteered to assist evacuees, by providing volunteer hours, housing, and meals for evacuees and medical personnel.[16]

LSU attributes its successful Baton Rouge field operation to advance planning. LSU had sponsored and participated in numerous hurricane drills; had stockpiled supplies and medicines necessary for field hospital setup; and had recruited and trained both medical and nonmedical volunteers to staff the field operations. LSU was a key partner in developing Hurricane Pam, an exercise held in 2004 by Innovative Emergency Management in coordination with FEMA, which simulated a direct hit on New Orleans by a Category 3 hurricane. LSU was one of the few participants in the Hurricane Pam exercise to implement lessons derived from the drill. LSU determined that in the event of a catastrophic hurricane, large temporary hospitals would be needed to replace permanent medical facilities, which would be incapacitated either by damage from the storm, by flooding, or by the overwhelming influx of thousands of patients. Having made this judgment, LSU began to plan and drill to set up field hospitals. In fact, only 2 weeks prior to Hurricane Katrina, LSU had held its latest in a series of practice drills. Organizers felt that this advance planning and drilling had been key to LSU's successful Katrina response in Baton Rouge.[17]

- Medical Reserve Corps (MRC) units provided medical support to their own local communities in the aftermath of Hurricane Katrina, enabling other volunteer health professionals to respond to the crisis. MRC members also volunteered in the Gulf Coast area, yet a coordinated national MRC deployment could not be organized.

The MRC (see sidebar) played a unique role in the medical response to Hurricane Katrina. It not only rallied volunteers to travel to New Orleans and other affected areas, but MRC units also activated within their local communities and established medical needs shelters for Gulf Coast evacuees, provided medical support in evacuee shelters and clinics, and filled in at local hospitals for other volunteers who had been deployed to the Gulf Coast. Following Hurricane Katrina, an estimated 6,000 MRC volunteers around the country were activated at home to support local medical response efforts.[18]

Approximately 1,500 MRC team members were deployed to hurricane-affected areas of the Gulf Coast. This deployment was coordinated through state agencies, the American Red Cross, and HHS.[19] The national MRC response following Hurricane Katrina was less effective and less organized than the community MRC response, primarily because the MRC National Program Office did not have the capacity to act as an effective coordinating body for MRC units. MRC members assigned to Red Cross shelters were prohibited from providing any advanced medical care to sheltered individuals, because Red Cross liability allows only basic-level medical care within its shelters.[19] MRC units raised concerns that their teams were not utilized to their highest potential.

HHS launched its own website for medical and support volunteers both to rally volunteer support and to verify professional credentialing. However, many MRC volunteers were already registered and credentialed through the Health Resources and Services Administration's (HRSA) Emergency System for Advanced Registration of Volunteer Health Professionals (ESAR-VHP) program (see sidebar). Because HHS was operating more than one credentialing system, it was unclear to some MRC volunteers which system they were supposed to use.

- Professional medical associations were a potentially valuable resource, but they were not well utilized by the federal government.

In the immediate aftermath of Katrina, calls for volunteers to respond to the medical crisis in the Gulf Coast went out separately from organizations such as the American Hospital Association (AHA), the American Medical Association (AMA), the American Association of Medical Colleges (AAMC), the Federation of American Hospitals, the State, Regional and Metropolitan Hospital Associations, the National Association of Public Hospitals and Health Systems, and many more. But with so many associations calling for help, and with most health practitioners having multiple allegiances to and memberships with various organizations, it was difficult for members of the healthcare community to know how to plug in to the response efforts.

Some health professionals ultimately abandoned efforts to volunteer in any structured way and formed their own ad hoc medical teams, or they simply showed up in the Gulf Coast, hoping to offer their medical expertise in any way they could. Unfortunately, this kind of well-meaning but extemporized reaction often hampered other more organized efforts. One interviewed DMAT member commented that the physicians who just showed up in New Orleans seeking to help actually hindered relief efforts, because they didn't have the training to work in a disaster area.

On August 31, Secretary of HHS Michael Leavitt announced plans to create up to 40 federal emergency medical shelters with a total of 10,000 beds requiring 5,000 medical professionals to staff them. HHS could only staff the first 10 emergency medical shelters with Veterans Affairs and Defense Department medical personnel, DMAT teams, and MRC volunteers. HHS predicted that it would have to rely on private sector volunteers to staff an additional 10 medical shelters and to relieve the first contingent of medical responders.[19]

Also on August 31, Secretary Leavitt made an urgent call to the American Hospital Association to appeal for private sector hospital volunteers. The AHA collaborated with other hospital associations to create a website to collect information from hospitals interested in sending teams to staff the emergency shelters.[20] Ultimately, 480 hospitals responded to this call, and Secretary Leavitt was able to form 200 teams. Yet volunteers were delayed while HHS checked credentials and altered team deployment locations. Based on documents reviewed for this article (including HHS press releases), as well as on firsthand reports from volunteer health professionals interviewed for this analysis, it remains unclear whether HHS ever deployed the volunteer teams that were formed in response to the Secretary's August 31 request.

> KEY FINDING #4: Hurricane Katrina separated many Gulf Coast residents from their medical records, leaving volunteer health professionals without medical histories to help guide patient care.

Hurricane Katrina displaced about 1 million people from the Gulf Coast area, and most of them were separated from their medical records.[21] Both immediately after the storm and in the weeks to follow, medical providers had no way to know about or track patients' pre-existing medical conditions, medications, or allergies, and many times patients themselves were unable to provide accurate medical histories for a variety of reasons. Patients were evacuated from hospitals, shuttled between multiple temporary medical shelters, and often were relocated to out-of-state healthcare facilities, all without any form of durable medical records.

A New Orleans Health Department physician interviewed for this article stated that one of the biggest public health problems that medical providers faced in the wake of the storm was the lack of access to patient health information. In order to give patients the best chance of survival, doctors resorted to primitive methods of passing on medical information. At Charity Hospital, for example, the medical staff taped notes containing brief medical records summaries to each ICU patient's forearm before helicopters evacuated them to other locations.[6]

In sharp contrast, the Veterans Administration (VA), which has an extensive national electronic health records system, was able to provide care for its patients in the Gulf Coast with fewer logistical complications because all of its patients' medical records were electronic. Several hundred veterans were evacuated from VA medical centers in Biloxi, Mississippi, and New Orleans.[4] While this system was most likely not accessible from the heart of New Orleans, where basic infrastructure was down, VA patients could be tracked as they moved around the country, and their care (including histories of chronic conditions) could be maintained despite their changing locations.

Ten days after the landfall of Hurricane Katrina, HHS instituted a program to make pharmacy data from Gulf Coast residents affected by the storm available online on a secure database accessible by doctors.[22] This database includes patient medication histories from about 150 zip codes from the Gulf Coast region and has been a collaborative effort of HHS and participating pharmacies such as CVS, Rite Aid, Albertsons, Walgreens, and Wal-Mart. By having a history of patients' prescription medications easily accessible, doctors have been better able to provide treatment to patients who were separated from their medical records, possibly separated from their families or caretakers, and did not know the medications that they had been prescribed.[23]

Conclusions and Recommendations

1. Hospitals should identify the critical systems that are essential for facility operations and should make plans to preserve those systems throughout a disaster or public health emergency.

A hospital is far more than just the doctors and nurses who staff it. As was seen in Hurricane Katrina, the functioning of a hospital requires a wide array of nonmedical staff, the continued operation of the physical facility, the pharmaceutical supply chain, physical security, functioning medical equipment, electricity, and more. Hospitals are important and highly valued places of refuge for the citizens they serve, yet in New Orleans hospitals could not fulfill their community responsibility because they themselves were overwhelmed and were seeking rescue. Hospitals need to ensure that their disaster response plans provide for the continuity of systems that are crucial to facility operation and hospital function, such as sufficient medical and nonmedical staff, electricity and backup power, critical supply chains, security, communications, and the like.

2. Hospitals should form and participate in Regional Hospital Coordinating Groups.

A recent study found that only three-quarters of the nation's nonfederal short-stay hospitals are currently integrated into communitywide disaster plans, and fewer than half of all hospitals (41.6%) have memoranda of understanding with other hospitals in their community to accept inpatients during a declared disaster.[24] The structure of the U.S. healthcare system puts hospitals in a competitive stance that can make it difficult to create collaborative relationships. However, no single institution had enough resources to prepare for a disaster of the magnitude of Hurricane Katrina without the help of the community.

"The burden of preparation cannot fall [totally] on the hospital itself," said Joseph Cappiello, Vice President of the Joint Council on Accreditation of Health Care Organizations (JCAHO). "This is a community problem."[25] If hospitals are to prepare for the next disaster, and for the difficult but looming challenges of a possible influenza pandemic, or a bioterrorist attack, they will need to form community plans and partnerships that allow hospitals to plan collectively, to share resources and staff as necessary, and to communicate effectively in a crisis.

3. NDMS should be consolidated with other emergency medical response programs at HHS, and its stated missions, concept of operations, and staffing should be reexamined.

Under the National Response Plan (NRP), HHS has the lead role in federal medical and public health response and has the primary responsibility for implementing Emergency Support Function (ESF) #8—Public Health and Medical Services. Yet, in 2003, Congress moved NDMS to the newly created Department of Homeland Security, where it was placed within FEMA, an agency without a medical or public health mission. HHS still has the primary responsibility for implementing ESF-8, and it can call on NDMS teams to assist in a public health or medical emergency. But the oversight and organizational authority of NDMS is under the purview of DHS.

In light of HHS's role as the primary coordinator of the federal medical response, NDMS should be returned to HHS so that it can be directly overseen by the department with the greatest amount of medical resources and expertise. The U.S. House Select Bipartisan Committee to Investigate the Preparation and Response to Hurricane Katrina found that DHS and HHS did not share a common understanding of which agency is responsible for NDMS under ESF-8,[3] and the White House recommended moving NDMS to HHS as well.[1] Not only NDMS but all emergency medical response assets in HHS should be organized and consolidated within HHS to maximize their utility: It does not make sense to have volunteer programs in HRSA, the national pharmaceutical stockpile in CDC, and the Medical Reserve Corps in the Surgeon General's office.

Once back in HHS, NDMS's mission, organization, and staffing should be carefully reconsidered. Even if the primary mission of NDMS continues to be delimited to providing proper training to DMAT and other teams and to ensuring the efficient deployment, organization, and staffing of these teams, the NDMS national office staff is too small and lacking in expertise to execute this.

Since its move to DHS, NDMS staff has been reduced from 144 to 57, and, according to an internal DHS report, as of January 2005, that staff did not include a physician, medical planner, or logistician.[26] Jeffrey A. Lowell, MD, former DHS Senior Advisor to the Secretary for Medical Affairs, testified before Congress that, within the DHS Emergency Preparedness and Response Directorate, there are "few qualified medical personnel available to develop the requisite medical doctrine, policies and procedures."[27]

In the medical response to Hurricane Katrina, DMATs lacked sufficient direction, coordination, and logistical support from federal staff, and some DMAT members interviewed for this analysis felt that the absence of clear NDMS medical leadership and coordination led to a highly improvisational on-the-ground response that put teams at risk. Logistics systems that deliver and track necessary supplies and organize and ensure the communication of teams would need to be created in NDMS for future similar missions to be fulfilled.

If the future mission of NDMS were to be expanded to include the provision of widespread, perhaps sustained community medical care in the event of large natural or manmade disasters like hurricanes, pandemics, or bioterrorist attacks, NDMS will need to set expectations and train its teams accordingly and ensure the medical logistics associated with such a system are built. The NDMS website states: "DMATs . . . may serve to augment overloaded local health care staffs."[28] Perhaps this is true in the short term, but neither the NDMS, nor any other currently existing federal medical response program, is intended to provide long-term support for hospitals in stricken communities or widespread support for a hospital system under great duress in a crisis. DMATs typically prepare to deploy to disaster sites with enough supplies and equipment to sustain themselves for 72 hours.[29]

Many DMAT physicians are specialists who are not used to providing generalized patient care, and DMAT teams are ill-equipped to care for patients with chronic medical conditions. Before focusing on the creation of large numbers of difficult-to-staff and logistically complicated field hospitals, the federal government would be well-advised to make sure there is a robust program, be it in HHS or elsewhere, to do all that is possible to ensure the continuing operation of existing hospitals in communities in crisis by organizing its medical volunteers, its medical assets, and its logistics systems accordingly.

4. HHS should take the lead role on all medical volunteer coordination in a federally declared emergency, and it should have one office in charge of deploying medical volunteers.

Following the events of September 11, 2001, Congress began a program to establish a national database of licenses and credentials of volunteer health professionals, so that they can be verified during an emergency. This Emergency System for Advanced Registration of Volunteer Health Professionals (ESAR-VHP) is administered by HRSA and is operational in at least 13 states and is being developed in others. Sixty states and territories have received $200,000 each to develop ESAR-VHP systems based on national guidelines.

ESAR-VHP should be provided with sufficient funds to grow and support the state ESAR-VHP systems that are being developed, and ESAR-VHP should be completed quickly in all 60 states and territories. All health professionals who wish to volunteer within their communities or around the country should be required to register their licensing and credentials through their state ESAR-VHP system, and they should be encouraged to do so prior to an emergency. States should be required to make their systems interoperable, so that when there is a large-scale public health emergency requiring a nationwide response, the national ESAR-VHP office will have the ability to help manage a national volunteer health professional deployment effort.

HHS should create an Office of Citizen Engagement within the Office of Public Health Emergency Preparedness (OPHEP), which would be charged with helping communities to engage medical volunteers in planning and preparation prior to an emergency, mobilizing volunteer health professionals in a federally declared emergency, and managing a national volunteer deployment to affected locations around the country. This office would need to coordinate closely with other offices within HHS, possibly with Strategic National Stockpile (SNS) assets, and with other agencies such as DHS, as well as with the Red Cross and other nongovernmental disaster organizations. It would make great sense for the same office(s) in HHS to organize (and, where appropriate, consolidate) the various volunteer efforts that now exist in the NDMS, the Medical Reserve Corps (MRC), and ESAR-VHP.

5. The Medical Reserve Corps program should be restructured so that MRC units are required to report to the National Program Office.

If the MRC is to continue as a program distinct from other medical volunteer efforts, more clarity is needed in its concept of operations. During the MRC's response to Hurricane Katrina, there were organizational barriers that made the MRC's national response efforts less effective than they could have been. Since MRC units are community-based entities and are not designed for a national response, the MRC National Program Office is unable to mandate units to report on activities such as volunteer numbers, activation/deployment status in an emergency, and unit location.

If MRC units are going to be called on in the future to respond outside of their communities, they should be provided with the training, guidance, logistical capabilities, and liability protection to do so. The National Program Office should be able to organize unit deployment in a national emergency.

MRC units are currently ineligible for FEMA reimbursement and have to seek out funding to run their units from community sponsors or apply to receive funding via other federal grant mechanisms (sometimes through HRSA Bioterrorism grants). If FEMA reimbursement was made available to MRC units, then the MRC National Program Office could tie unit reporting requirements to reimbursement monies.

The MRC National Program Office should offer liability protection and workers' compensation to their MRC unit volunteers. Currently, MRC volunteers are not offered any form of liability protection by the federal government, and in order for MRC volunteers to obtain information on liability protection, they are instructed by the MRC National Program Office to contact a lawyer or their local office of volunteerism.

6. Leaders in both government and the private sector must continue to work toward developing a national system of electronic health records.

Much of the U.S. healthcare system today still uses paper medical records that must be physically transferred as patients change doctors and locations. It would have been immensely helpful to medical providers at various treating locations if evacuees and hospital patients who had been relocated had had an electronic medical record of their care. In fact, electronic medical records and the ability to efficiently move clinical information electronically between providers would be key in responding to many kinds of catastrophes.

The effort to make electronic medical records standard in the country is moving far too slowly. Congress should pass legislation that accelerates such efforts. Meanwhile, the HHS Office of the National Coordinator for Health Information Technology (ONCHIT) should continue to engage the private sector and to fund pilot projects to produce interoperable electronic medical records that can be implemented in hospitals throughout the country.

7. Place higher priority on hospital preparedness in all community and government disaster planning.

In most kinds of large disasters, there will be many sick people needing medical care, much of it necessarily serious enough that it ought to be delivered in one of the nation's 5,000 hospitals. This was certainly true after Hurricane Katrina, and it would be true in a pandemic, a smallpox outbreak, and the like. But despite this clear and central role in response, hospitals have been given relatively few resources and little technical guidance to prepare for the wide variety of natural or deliberate crises that they could face.

Those charged with disaster preparations at the federal or state government or local community level should pay increased attention to the critical role of hospitals. The Administration should make clear its commitment to these issues by convening hospital leaders to review these challenges. Congress should make clear its commitment to these issues by passing the Public Health Preparedness Re-Authorization bill that funds such efforts in keeping with the serious and complex nature of the challenges.

References

1. The White House. *The Federal Response to Hurricane Katrina: Lessons Learned.* Washington, DC: The White House; February 2006. Available at: http://www.white-house.gov/reports/katrina-lessons-learned.pdf Accessed on May 3, 2006.
2. U.S. Senate. *A Nation Still Unprepared: Report of the Committee on Homeland Security and Governmental Affairs.* Washington, DC: U.S. Senate; May 2006. Available at: http://hsgac.senate.gov/_files/Katrina/FullReport.pdf Accessed on May 3, 2006.
3. Select Bipartisan Committee to Investigate the Preparation for and Response to Hurricane Katrina. *A Failure of Initiative: The Final Report of the Select Bipartisan Committee to Investigate the Preparation for and Response to Hurricane Katrina.* Washington, DC: Select Bipartisan Committee; February 15, 2006. Available at: http://a257.g.akamaitech.net/7/257/2422/15feb20061230/www.gpoaccess.gov/katrinareport/medicalcare.pdf Accessed on May 3, 2006.
4. Lister SA. *2005 Gulf Coast Hurricanes: The Public Health and Medical Response.* Washington, DC: Congressional Research Service Report for Congress; October 5, 2005.
5. Kaiser J. After Katrina: struggling New Orleans universities cut hundreds of faculty. *Science* 2005;310:1753.
6. DeBoisblanc B. Black Hawk, please come down: reflections on a hospital's struggle to survive in the wake of Hurricane Katrina. *Am J Respir Crit Care Med* 2005;172: 1239–1240.

7. Two New Orleans hospitals plead for help. *Associated Press* September 1, 2005. Available at: http://www.msnbc.msn.com/id/9159903/ Accessed March 27, 2006.
8. Berger E. Charity Hospital and disaster preparedness. *Ann Emerg Med* 2006;1:47.
9. Innovative Emergency Management. *Southeast Louisiana Catastrophic Hurricane Functional Plan. Draft.* Baton Rouge, La: Innovative Emergency Management; August 6, 2004.
10. U.S. Department of Homeland Security. *The National Disaster Medical System.* Washington, DC: U.S. Department of Homeland Security; 2006. Available at: http://www.oep-ndms.dhhs.gov/ Accessed on March 13, 2006.
11. Alson R. *Mitigating Catastrophic Events through Effective Medical Response.* Testimony Before the House Committee on Homeland Security Subcommittee on Prevention of Nuclear and Biological Attack, October 20, 2005.
12. Vankawala HH. Doctor's message from Katrina's front lines. *NPR* September 8, 2005. Available at: http://www.npr.org/templates/story/story.php?storyID=4836926 Accessed March 27, 2006.
13. Hall M. Significant gaps reported in disaster responses. *USA Today* January 17, 2006. Available at: http://www. usatoday.com/printedition/news/20060118/a_emergency18.art.htm Accessed March 27, 2006.
14. Katrina medical help held up by red tape. *CNN–AP* September 4, 2005. Available at: http://www.freerepublic.com/focus/f-news/1477432/posts Accessed on March 27, 2006.
15. Association of American Medical Colleges. *Medical Schools with Designated Response Unit.* Washington, DC: Association of American Medical Colleges; September 8, 2005. Available at: http://www.aamc.org/katrina/school-sresponse.htm Accessed on March 27, 2006.
16. Louisiana State University. *LSU is site of largest acute-care field hospital in U.S. history* [press release]. Baton Rouge: Louisiana State University; September 8, 2005. Available at: http://www.lsu.edu/university_relations/mediacenter/nr/20050906_645p.htm Accessed March 27, 2006.
17. Dentzer S. Hurricane hospital challenges: a report from Baton Rouge, Louisiana, about how makeshift hospitals are coping with a surge of patients. *PBS* September 8, 2005. Available at: http://www.pbs.org/newshour//bb/weather/july-dec05/hospitals_9-8.html Accessed March 27, 2006.
18. Medical Reserve Corps. *The Medical Reserve Corps Response to Hurricanes Katrina & Rita. Interim Report.* Rockville, Md: Office of the Surgeon General; October 11, 2005. Available at: http://www.medicalreservecorps.gov/page.cfm?pageID=1047 Accessed March 27, 2006.
19. Cannon CM. Special report: learning from mistakes. *National Journal* September 10, 2005. Available at: http://nationaljournal.com/members/news/2005/09/0909nj1.htm Accessed March 27, 2006.
20. HHS to seek hospitals' help in staffing emergency medical centers. *AHA News Now* August 31, 2005. Available at: http://www.ahanews.com/ahanews/hospitalconnect/search /article.jsp?dcrpath=AHANEWS/AHANewsNow Article/data/ann_050831_HHS&domain=AHANEWS Accessed March 27, 2006.
21. Leavitt promotes health care IT uses in national emergencies. *American Health Line* September 9, 2005.
22. KatrinaHealth.org. Available at: http://www.katrinahealth.org/ Accessed on April 28, 2006.
23. Krim J. Health records of evacuees go online. *Washington Post* September 14, 2005. Available at: http://www.wash-ingtonpost.com/wp-dyn/content/article/2005/09/13/ AR2005091302128.html Accessed March 27, 2006.
24. U.S. Centers for Disease Control and Prevention. *Bioterrorism and Mass Casualty Preparedness In Hospitals: United States, 2003.* CDC Advance Data: 364. Atlanta: U.S. Centers for Disease Control and Prevention; September 27, 2005. Available at: http://www.cdc.gov/nchs/data/ ad/ad364.pdf Accessed March 27, 2006.
25. Community bears burden for preparedness. *USA Today* January 23, 2006. Available at: http://26.www.usatoday.com/news/nation/2006-01-23-katrina-lessons-community_x.htm Accessed March 27, 2006.
26. U.S. Department of Homeland Security. *Medical Readiness Responsibilities and Capabilities: A Strategy for Realigning and Strengthening the Federal Medical Response. Internal Report.* Washington, DC: U.S. Department of Homeland Security; January 3, 2005.

27. *Hearings before the Subcommittee of Management, Integration and Oversight, House Committee on Homeland Security* (testimony of Jeffrey Lowell), October 27, 2005.
28. U.S. Department of Homeland Security. *What Is a Disaster Medical Assistance Team?* Washington, DC: U.S. Department of Homeland Security, National Disaster Medical System; 2006. Available at: http://www.oep-ndms.dhhs.gov/dmat.html Accessed March 27, 2006.
29. U.S. Department of Homeland Security. *The National Disaster Medical System.* Washington, DC: U.S. Department of Homeland Security; 2006. Available at: http://www.oep-ndms.dhhs.gov/ Accessed on March 27, 2006.
30. U.S. Department of Homeland Security. *FY2007 Budget in Brief.* Washington, DC: U.S. Department of Homeland Security; 2006. Available at: http://www.dhs.gov/dhspublic/interweb/assetlibrary/Budget_BIB-FY2007.pdf Accessed on March 27, 2006.
31. U.S. Department of Homeland Security. *National Disaster Medical System, DMAT Questions and Answers.* Washington, DC: U.S. Department of Homeland Security; 2006. Available at: http://www.oep-ndms.dhhs.gov/dmat_faq.html Accessed on March 27, 2006.
32. Medical Reserve Corps. *About the Medical Reserve Corps.* Rockville, Md: Office of the Surgeon General; undated. Available at: http://www.medicalreservecorps.gov/page.cfm?pageID=5 Accessed on March 27, 2006.
33. U.S. Department of Health and Human Services. *Budgets in Brief FY2006–FY2007.* Washington, DC: U.S. Department of Health and Human Services; 2006. Available at: http://www.hhs.gov/budget/07budget/2007Budget-InBrief.pdf Accessed on March 27, 2006.
34. National Association of County and City Health Officials. NACCHO 2006 Public Health Preparedness Conference. *Sharing Session #6: Getting a Helping Hand (or Hands): Public Health Strategies for Emergency Management,* February 23, 2006.
35. U.S. Health Resources and Services Administration. *Interim Technical and Policy Guidelines, Standards, and Definitions Version 2.* Washington, DC: U.S. Department of Health and Human Services; June 2005. Available at: http://www.hrsa.gov/esarvhp/guidelines/default.htm Accessed on March 27, 2006.
36. Agwunobi J. *Preparedness: Past, Present, and Future.* Testimony before the House Committee on Energy and Commerce Subcommittee on Oversight and Investigations, January 26, 2006. Available at: http://www.hhs.gov/asl/testify/t060126.html Accessed on March 27, 2006.
37. National Emergency Management Association. *Emergency Management Assistance Compact.* Lexington, Kentucky: National Emergency Management Association; 2005. Available at: http://www.emacweb.org/ Accessed on March 27, 2006.
38. National Emergency Management Association. *EMAC Executive Briefing.* Lexington, Kentucky: National Emergency Management Association; December 2005. Available at: http://www.emacweb.org/?323 Accessed on March 27, 2006.
39. U.S. Department of Homeland Security. *About MMRS.* Washington, DC: U.S. Department of Homeland Security; undated. Available at: https://www.mmrs.fema.gov/Main/About.aspx Accessed on March 27, 2006.
40. U.S. Department of Homeland Security. *Metropolitan Medical Response System. Overview.* Washington, DC: U.S. Department of Homeland Security; February 1, 2006. Available at: https://www.mmrs.fema.gov/PublicDocs/MMRS_overview_1_Feb_06.pdf Accessed on March 27, 2006.

Crystal Franco is an analyst at the Center for Biosecurity of the University of Pittsburgh Medical Center, Baltimore, Maryland. Mrs. Franco earned her B.A. in molecular, cellular, and developmental biology in 3 years from the University of Colorado at Boulder.

Eric Toner is senior associate with the Center for Biosecurity of the University of Pittsburgh Medical Center. He is a widely cited author on a range of biosecurity issues, including hospital preparedness, pandemic influenza response, and clinical issues related to bioterrorism response, and an associate editor of the journal Biosecurity and Bioterrorism: Biodefense Strategy, Science and Practice.

Richard Waldhorn is a distinguished scholar at the Center for Biosecurity of the University of Pittsburgh Medical Center, Baltimore, Maryland. He is also a clinical professor of medicine, Georgetown University School of Medicine. Dr. Waldhorn received his undergraduate degree from Columbia University in 1972 and his M.D. from Boston University School of Medicine in 1976.

Beth Maldin is an associate at the Center for Biosecurity of the University of Pittsburgh Medical Center. Prior to joining the Center, Ms. Maldin served as the director of the Emergency Information Technology Unit (EITU) at the New York City Department of Health and Mental Hygiene. She is an associate editor of the journal Biosecurity and Bioterrorism: Biodefense Strategy, Science and Practice.

Tara O'Toole is the CEO and director, Center for Biosecurity of the University of Pittsburgh Medical Center (UPMC) and professor of medicine, University of Pittsburgh. She received her bachelors degree from Vassar College, her M.D. from the George Washington University, and a master of public health degree from Johns Hopkins University. She completed a residency in internal medicine at Yale, and a fellowship in occupational and environmental medicine at Johns Hopkins University.

Thomas V. Inglesby is chief operating officer and deputy director, Center for Biosecurity of the University of Pittsburgh Medical Center (UPMC) and associate professor of medicine and public health, University of Pittsburgh Schools of Medicine and Public Health. He received his undergraduate degree from Georgetown University in 1988 and his M.D. from the Columbia University College of Physicians and Surgeons in 1992. He completed his internal medicine residency and infectious diseases fellowship training at the Johns Hopkins School of Medicine, and served as assistant chief of service in the Johns Hopkins department of medicine in 1996–97.

Robyn Pangi

Consequence Management in the 1995 Sarin Attacks on the Japanese Subway System

In the early to mid-1990s, a group known as Aum Shinrikyo amassed, and used against innocent civilians in Japan, an arsenal of chemical and biological weapons. Two examples are the use of sarin gas in Matsumoto in 1994 and in Tokyo in 1995. The attacks claimed a total of 19 lives and caused thousands of injuries. A review of the scenario, starting in 1994 and early 1995 with the sarin attacks, reveals potential opportunities to preempt such an attack or to mitigate its effects. The Aum Shinrikyo case study is a good learning tool for policymakers and emergency response professionals seeking to form a coherent domestic preparedness strategy.

In the early to mid-1990s, a group known as Aum Shinrikyo amassed, and used against innocent civilians, an arsenal of chemical and biological weapons. A large body of literature details the evolution of Aum Shinrikyo, its shocking attacks on a housing complex in Matsumoto and on five subway lines in Tokyo using a chemical weapon, and Japanese society's reaction to the attacks. Not much analysis, however, has been done on the lessons learned about consequence management from the first significant terrorist attacks with weapons of mass destruction (WMD) to occur in modern times.[1] Recent events in the United States including the dispersal of anthrax spores through the mail and scores of hoaxes alleging use of anthrax have brought the issue of terrorism using WMDs closer to home. The handling of the Aum Shinrikyo attacks offers the opportunity for policymakers, emergency response personnel, and other relevant professionals to learn about WMD consequence management.

An attack with a chemical weapon (as in Tokyo) or with a biological weapon (as in the United States) is different from a conventional attack because the potentially catastrophic effects of the attack can be substantially reduced with prompt intervention. In a large explosion, such as the aircraft bombing of the World Trade Center in New York City and the Pentagon in Washington, D.C., in September 2001, the actual impact of the explosion cannot be mitigated. The only hope is to save lives by rescuing people from the rubble and keeping potential victims away from the unstable structures. However, in a chemical or biological weapon attack, proper decontamination and rapid prophylaxis can often save lives and prevent the spread of disease or chemical exposure to the larger population.[2]

The Aum Shinrikyo case study is a good learning tool for policymakers and emergency response professionals seeking to form a coherent domestic preparedness strategy.[3] A review of the scenario, starting in 1994 and early 1995 with the sarin attacks, reveals potential opportunities to preempt such an attack or to mitigate its effects.[4] This article begins with a brief introduction to Aum Shinrikyo. It then reviews the sarin attacks in the town of Matsumoto in 1994 and in Tokyo in 1995. Following the case studies, the article details the municipal and national governments' rescue and recovery operations. It then summarizes many of the policies that Japan has implemented since 1995 to strengthen response plans and preparedness. Finally, the article analyzes several lessons that emerged from the experience and examines implications for the United States.

Case Studies

Background

Aum Shinrikyo, or Aum Supreme Truth,[5] based its teachings on the belief of impending armageddon. Led by Shoko Asahara, a partially blind man whose given name was Chizuo Matsumoto, cult members believed that only devout followers of Asahara ("the guru") would be saved at the end of the world. The cult was well financed and diverse: by 1995 it had a worldwide membership of 40,000 people and assets estimated at one billion dollars.[6] Cult members represented many different segments of society, but a characteristic that set Aum apart from other groups was that many members had a relatively high level of education and wealth. In fact, Aum recruited at universities, focusing particularly on physics, engineering, and computer departments.[7]

Most Japanese initially dismissed the cult as an oddity. Peculiar rituals such as drinking Asahara's blood to achieve enlightenment or wearing headgear referred to as the Perfect Salvation Initiative clearly set followers apart from mainstream society.[8] Aum was subjected to further ridicule in the 1990 elections when 25 Aum members, including Asahara, ran for parliament seats and suffered an overwhelming defeat, earning fewer votes than the number of cult members who were eligible voters.[9]

The elections brought Aum and the cult leadership into the public eye. Thereafter, Asahara and his followers turned down a more antisocial path.[10] A series of events led to a greater isolation of cult members and radicalization of cult ideals. Part of this trend included increasingly aggressive and ultimately violent responses to internal and external critics. Members were threatened and punished for transgression against Asahara's teachings, outsiders who interfered with cult activities were abducted, and cult members experimented with biological and chemical weapons. Eventually some of those dangerous agents were put to use.

Prior to the 1995 attacks, Aum was able to escape police scrutiny largely because of institutional barriers against religious persecution in Japan. In 1951, the Japanese government passed the Religious Corporation Law, which strengthened constitutionally guaranteed religious freedoms by relieving any organization that could be identified as "religious" of tax obligations and by providing these groups with unusually strong protection from government intrusion.[11] "The Japanese police, like the governmental bureaucracy, exercised extreme caution in handling complaints made against official religious groups.

Partly as a reaction to the harsh suppression of religious freedom by Japan's prewar military government, the postwar constitution and police policy nationwide called for scrupulously avoiding even the appearance of religious persecution."[12] Aum Shinrikyo exploited the laws guaranteeing religious freedom, and under the protective umbrella of these laws was left virtually untouched by authorities.[13]

Aum also benefited from a second type of restraint practiced by the government post–World War II: loosely organized and relatively weak intelligence gathering. To some extent, this resulted from limitations in the Japanese Constitution. For instance there were legal bans on police use of preventive surveillance techniques. In addition to legal restrictions, the rivalries among prefectural police forces hindered information sharing.

Shielded by this combination of civil liberties and limited governmental powers, Aum Shinrikyo was able to accumulate extensive stockpiles of cash and dangerous chemical and biological materials without raising police suspicion and Aum was able to execute not one, but two lethal attacks on civilian populations.[14]

Cultural Context

Prior to the sarin attack in 1995, many Japanese took comfort in their perceived isolation from the high crime rates and corruption of other highly developed countries.[15] Japan is a strikingly homogenous and relatively peaceful society.[16] "Peace (*heiwa*) and fundamental human rights (*jinken*) are twin cultural concepts that have been enshrined in national and international security policy."[17] The Constitution "denounces any type of war" and the Self Defense Force "technically are not interpreted as a military force."[18]

Until recently, terrorism was a phenomenon rarely discussed by government officials or Japanese citizens. This reticence is partially cultural: Naofumi Miyasaka, professor at the National Defense Academy, points out that, "the Manichaean belief of peace and war hinders one from considering an in-between [such as terrorism]."[19] The ethos of peace and human rights gives rise to three national ideas on terrorism. First, terrorism is believed to have root causes such as poverty or prejudice, or to be a response to an oppressive government.[20] Second, Japan's antiterrorism policy is extremely risk-averse: sparing lives is paramount to the Japanese when dealing with a terrorist situation.[21] Third, terrorism remains a taboo subject that is rarely discussed; incidents such as the hijacking of 1999 ANA flight 61 or the 1994 and 1995 sarin gas attacks are seen as unique cases and are not widely labeled "terrorist" acts.[22]

Partly as a result of this sympathetic attitude shared by the Japanese people and government, and partly owing to the overwhelming nationwide support for a free society, "terrorism is not seen as a threat to the nation's core values: democracy, prosperity, and national unity. Rather, antiterrorism is seen as a grave danger to peace and fundamental human rights."[23] Only recently has broad public opinion favored harsh punishment for convicted terrorists. Thus, prior to 1995, counterterrorism policies, where they existed at all, consisted of loosely organized measures that did not give government officials much power. By and large, the only terrorism situations with which the government was prepared to deal were hostage crises.

Matsumoto Attack

On 27 June 1994, a group of cult members drove a converted refrigerator truck to Matsumoto, a village of approximately 300,000 residents located 322 kilometers northwest of Tokyo. The target was a dormitory inhabited by three judges, who were about to decide a civil case over land rights to which Aum was a party.[24] In an effort to stop the verdict from being issued, Aum intended to incapacitate the judges.[25] The Aum members released sarin into the evening air. Poor dispersal technique and contrary wind patterns prevented the attack from being a complete success. However, the devastation was great: 7 people were killed and 500 hospitalized as the result of the attack. Moreover, the judges were injured, resulting in the delay of the decision.[26]

> At first the local police in Matsumoto appeared incapable of understanding what had happened: a chemical weapons attack in a relatively small and quiet Japanese town . . . seemed beyond the bounds of comprehension. The police appeared incapable of even conceptualizing the event as a deliberate act of terrorism or mass murder, and their first step was to blame a local man. . . . According to the police, [main suspect] Kono [Yoshiyuki] had accidentally created the poisonous gases while mixing fertilizers in his garden.[27]

The media were more persistent than the investigators. They emphasized the improbability of making sarin by accident and raised the possibility of a link between Aum Shinrikyo and the Matsumoto attack.[28] This link was substantiated in 1994 when soil taken from outside an Aum compound revealed traces of sarin. Yet the police still refused to adopt a more aggressive stance and actively investigate Aum Shinrikyo. As a result, no arrests were made in connection with this attack until *after* the 1995 subway attack.

The sarin attack on Matsumoto had surprisingly little impact on the community, the nation, or the world. "The sarin attack on Matsumoto was a precedent-shattering episode in the history of modern terrorism, but no one, either inside Japan or out, seemed to attach much significance to the fact that a highly deadly World War Two–era nerve gas, an agent all but unknown in Asia, had been unleashed with deadly results in a remote mountain town in central Japan."[29] Matsumoto, it turns out, served as a practice session for the cult's future exploits in WMD terrorism.

Tokyo Subway Attack

Between 7:30 and 7:45 a.m. on 20 March 1995, five cult members boarded an inbound subway on one of three different subway lines—Hibiya, Chiyoda, and Maronouchi—at different stations, bound in a total of five different directions.[30] Beginning at 7:48 a.m., each cult member pierced one or more bags of sarin and then fled the subway. Shortly before 8:00 a.m., the five trains converged on the Kasumegaseki station of the Tokyo subway system.[31] Kasumegaseki is home to most of Tokyo's government offices and is considered to be the power center of the city. The attack left 12 dead, hundreds injured, and thousands terrorized.

Fortunately, the enormous potential for catastrophic damage was not actually achieved. The more than 30 train lines of the public and private transit system in Tokyo sprawl through 400 miles of underground tunnels and above-ground tracks. Over nine million passengers ride the subway daily. A rush-hour attack could thus have caused chaos and massive numbers of casualties and fatalities.[32] However, the sarin used in the subway attack—like that used in the Matsumoto attack—was only 30 percent pure, sparing most of the subway ridership the disaster of a successful attack. In its pure form, as little as one drop of sarin on the skin is colorless, odorless, and lethal. Impure sarin is less lethal, and when diluted (as in this case) it took on an odor, which alerted subway passengers and responders to the presence of a foreign chemical.[33]

The rudimentary method of delivery also prevented greater devastation. Aum's scientists were unable to master the construction of an aerosol delivery vehicle. The sarin was instead poured into plastic bags that were then wrapped in paper, placed on the ground, and punctured with sharpened umbrellas. Most of the sarin was not released into the air in respirable droplets, which would have effectively entered the lungs and landed on the skin of passengers and caused mass casualties. By merely puncturing the bags, only those in immediate proximity to the release or to severely poisoned individuals suffered severe physical injuries or death.

Even with impure sarin and remedial delivery techniques, thousands of passengers were affected. Subway stations were forced to evacuate passengers en masse, many choking, vomiting, and blinded by the chemicals. They fled up the stairways and collapsed in the streets while fire, police, and emergency medical responders, most unprotected, ran down the stairs to assist the victims. The scene was immediately broadcast over television and radio. Images of confusion and chaos dominated the nine o'clock news and provided Tokyo and the world with its first glimpse of an act of terrorism with a weapon of mass destruction.

Consequence Management

The historical and cultural reluctance among Japanese officials to prepare for or even discuss terrorism was reflected in underdeveloped consequence management capabilities, which hindered the response effort in both sarin attacks.[34] Consequence management comprises those essential services that mitigate or ameliorate the effects of a disaster—in this case, catastrophic terrorism. Management of the consequences of natural or unintentional manmade disasters includes firefighting, rescue and recovery operations, medical treatment, emergency transportation, law enforcement, psychological assistance by medical professionals, securing of buildings and infrastructure, and the provision of clean water and food. After a WMD terrorism attack, additional capabilities are required, including specialized mass-casualty medical operations including triage and prophylaxis, decontamination, possible quarantine or evacuation, environmental analysis, dissemination of public information, and specialized psychological assistance.

Consequence Management in Japan: Basic Principles

In any large-scale disaster, response personnel from multiple agencies and various levels of government must work together. This includes public, private, and volunteer agencies from the local, regional, and national levels.[35] The first trained personnel to arrive on the scene are almost always from local or state emergency services, with state and national resources following. After the sarin attack, for example, the response involved fire, police, emergency medical services, and medical professionals from the municipal, prefectural, and national governments.

Metropolitan Response

The Japanese system is set up so that "in disaster management, most functions are to be borne by local governments."[36] This includes planning and implementing disaster response.[37] In the subway sarin attack, the Tokyo metropolitan government assumed these responsibilities. The metropolitan police have primary jurisdiction over law enforcement, investigation, maintenance of law and order, and prevention of further attacks. Under the Tokyo regional disaster plan, the Tokyo Metropolitan Fire Department (TMFD) is responsible for providing first aid to victims, selecting the hospital(s) to which victims will be transported, and providing transportation to hospitals. To fulfill its mission of providing non-hospital emergency medical care, the TMFD has 182 emergency medical teams and 1,650 emergency medical technicians ready to serve the Tokyo metropolitan area.[38] Each emergency medical team is staffed by one emergency life-saving technician (ELST) who provides basic medical treatment and may provide advanced treatment only with the express permission of a medical doctor. There is no system that provides for doctors to ride along with ELSTs, but the Tokyo Metropolitan Ambulance Control Center (TMACC) has a staff physician on call 24 hours a day who may permit ELSTs to perform advanced medical procedures.

The disaster response plan in place in 1995 recognized that local resources could be overwhelmed in a large-scale disaster. Thus, several provisions for extra assistance were in place. The plan called for staff from surrounding hospitals to be dispatched to the disaster scene to assist local ELSTs. Similarly, mutual aid agreements, in which other localities and prefectures lend assistance to the disaster-stricken site, were in place prior to the sarin attack.[39] Prefectures, which comprise (but do not have legal authority over) several municipalities, provide assistance and support when a disaster overwhelms municipal resources. As 1 of 12 designated "large cities" in Japan, Tokyo functions almost like a prefecture in terms of resource allocation, yet the "wards" that make up the city have less autonomy than municipalities. Moreover, because it is the capital of Japan, Tokyo is home to national government agencies as well as city agencies. Thus Tokyo is more able to coordinate resources and personnel across agencies and levels of government than most prefectures of other large cities.[40]

National Crisis Management Agencies. In Japan, the governor of the affected prefecture is in charge during an emergency. Local government must request assistance from the appropriate national agency in order to secure assistance from that agency.[41] For instance, a request to the Japanese Self Defense Force (part of the Defense Agency) must originate from the local government. Moreover, because the legal head of the SDF is the prime minister, the subsidiary of the Defense Agency cannot act without the prime minister's consent. The SDF possesses a wide knowledge of chemical warfare agents and possesses some decontamination abilities. It also has the ability to rapidly assemble communications systems and medical triage units. There are the two bureaucratic hurdles to overcome before the SDF can enter the disaster area or carry out rescue operations: receipt of a request and approval.[42]

If the disaster is of such magnitude that it requires national emergency measures and is labeled a "major disaster," the national government establishes a Headquarters for Major Disaster Countermeasures. The National Police Agency plays largely a support role, but does have the authority to coordinate and command local law enforcement and to assign police from other prefectures to assist police in the affected municipality.[43]

Major Consequence Management Issues

There are several lessons to be learned from Tokyo's experience regarding actions that can be taken to mitigate the consequences of a WMD terrorist attack. Emergency response has immediate, near-term, and long-term phases. Actions may overlap from one stage to the next, but specific actions may be necessary at particular stages. This section of the article examines the consequence management actions that were taken after the subway sarin attack and outlines the changes made to the Japanese consequence management plans in the years after the attack.

Problem Recognition

Problem recognition, or the ability to gather information, construct a pattern with that information, and disseminate both up the chain of command, is an immediate to near-term response activity. Gathering information is the responsibility of first responders, those best positioned to arrive on the scene to begin rescuing victims after receiving report of a crisis. In the subway attack scenario, transit workers were the first responders because of their proximity to the attack sites.

There was a significant delay in recognizing the nature of the problem during both sarin attacks, as is illustrated by the chronology of the subway attacks. Sarin was released in the subway cars shortly before 8:00 a.m. Immediately after the release, sick passengers staggered from the five affected trains at several stations. By 8:10 a.m., the transit workers operating the Hibiya line recognized that something was amiss. Their announcements to passengers on the trains and in the stations progressed from "sick passenger" to "explosion occurred at Tsukiji" then "Tsukiji next stop" and finally "evacuate, evacuate, evacuate."[44] Despite these alarming announcements and the influx of emergency response personnel into the station, the Hibiya line train departed Tsukiji, headed for Kasumegaseki, only seven minutes late. Not for several more minutes did subway officials direct passengers to leave the station and halt service.[45]

Meanwhile, on the Chiyoda line, passengers pointed out two packages leaking an unknown fluid onto the floor of a train car. Station employees responded by mopping up the mess with newspaper and their bare hands, and sending the train on its way. Two of these employees later died from sarin exposure. When the full impact of the situation was realized, station employees posted handmade signs outside of the stations announcing that they were closed "owing to a terrorist attack."[46]

The Marunouchi line continued to run until 9:27 a.m., long after the others closed down, leaving a trail of sarin up and down the entire line.[47] This potentially contaminated several additional stations, and could have exposed countless passengers and employees to sarin.

It is not surprising that transit workers were unable to identify the nature and scope of the situation. They were not trained to identify or respond to chemical or biological weapons, and they did not have a centralized system to monitor disturbances at the various stations. Thus, in most stations, the employees thought they had isolated sick passengers or chemical spills.

Police and emergency medical technicians are better equipped to identify and respond to a crisis. However, even though the metropolitan police began receiving calls shortly after the attack, it was not until 8:44 a.m. that the National Police Agency (NPA) became convinced that a major problem was at hand and a serious response effort was required.[48] Before 9:00 a.m., the NPA suspected that a chemical agent was the cause of illness. The NPA called upon the Self Defense Force (SDF) to send two chemical warfare experts to assist emergency operations units. Yet, even though police at all levels of government believed there was a major problem, trains continued to run until 9:27 a.m., almost an hour and a half after the metropolitan police began receiving calls, and over 30 minutes after the NPA determined that a major incident had occurred.

Neither the identity of the agent nor the effectiveness of the dispersal methods were known to most victims or emergency response personnel until several hours after the attack. Police and military authorities did not identify the agent as sarin for nearly two hours after the attack.[49] They did not share that information with other emergency response agencies for another hour; according to many sources, hospitals were never officially informed of this assessment.[50]

In Tokyo, the delay in halting service and evacuating passengers had several root causes. First, this type of attack was virtually unprecedented. Thus it presented a completely novel situation for most government employees at all levels.[51] No response plans or training existed to prepare response personnel for a WMD attack.

Second, the coordinated, multisite nature of the attack was initially unknown to train operators and other first responders. Each station thought it had an isolated sick passenger situation. When passengers pointed to the leaking bags that contained the sarin, station employees cleaned them up, assuming they were unrelated incidents. Not for one full hour after the attack were enough calls aggregated at the police emergency switchboard to allow authorities to connect the incidents and formulate an assessment of the situation.

Third, no contingency plans detailing how to respond to a WMD attack existed outside of the military. Thus, even if the inexperienced response personnel had identified the nature of the incident, they would not have had a plan to guide them in how to proceed.

Finally, bureaucratic barriers hindered the immediate recognition and response. *Tatewari,* a term that translates roughly as "compartmentalized bureaucracy," describes the stovepiped agencies that comprise the Japanese government. The agencies do not usually work together, but rather work separate from—or even in competition with—one another.[52] Even when each agency does its job, the lack of cross-agency communication and cooperation hinder effective response and recovery operations. This was particularly acute following the Kobe Hanshin earthquake of 1995 and was also evident in the aftermath of the sarin attack, when the highly independent nature of government agencies contributed to the delay of agent identification.[53] In both of these disasters, agencies did not communicate with one another; thus information and expertise were not readily shared.

Subsequent Revision to Improve Problem Recognition: WMD Training for First Responders. The first responders in the subway attack were transit workers, police officers, emergency medical technicians, firefighters, and physicians. Many of them did not have the requisite training to recognize—and function in—a contaminated environment. One lesson that was acted on by Japanese officials after the attacks was that response personnel need WMD-specific training.

After the sarin attack, the SDF began providing information to the police and the media on dangerous chemical agents. According to a senior military official, "Since the Tokyo sarin attack, nerve agents have become a recognized measure of terrorism. Therefore, information on nerve agents has become open, and a manual for emergency medical services personnel has been published."[54] In addition to education in agent identification, on-the-ground training for police and fire personnel is now being provided by the SDF.[55] The Tokyo municipal fire department is working with Tokyo University on emergency planning. Volunteers are being trained how to respond to chemical and biological weapons. For example, in the sarin attack it was quickly discovered that volunteer and professional responders should not rush in to help without personal protection because of the risk of secondary contamination.[56] This contradicted the working assumption that rescue workers should enter the disaster as soon as possible, in their standard professional attire, to rescue victims.

Training is being reinforced with simulations. A large-scale disaster drill in Tokyo in September 2000 provided multiple agencies at all levels of government with the opportunity to apply their new skills in a simulated catastrophe. This type of large-scale simulation is relatively new to response agencies in Japan.

Despite the progress in training and exercising, however, agencies remain divided in their training and duties. Although one SDF official notes that the SDF has a better working relationship with the police and with other countries now than it did prior to the sarin attack, collaboration has not become a regular part of the relationship between the agencies.[57]

Incident Management

Incident management is an immediate priority in any disaster situation. In Tokyo, within five minutes of determining that the situation merited a serious response, which occurred at 8:44 a.m., the NPA requested the assistance of two SDF chemical warfare experts. The NPA and SDF immediately established a joint police/army investigative unit. A second emergency unit was established to coordinate the police, fire, rescue, and medical responders. There were, nevertheless, significant planning, logistics, and operations difficulties that contributed to the delay in the reaction by transit workers and public safety officials.[58]

Two main issues led to the lack of strong incident management. First, the delay in problem recognition meant that operations began without a properly established incident management system (IMS):

> IMS is a generic term for the design of ad hoc emergency management teams that coordinate the efforts of more than one agency under a unified command. It is a functionally based organizational template that facilitates information flow, decision-making, and operational coordination . . . [that] is designed to manage complex or multisite emergency events.[59]

Because the multisite nature of the incident was initially overlooked, there was no effort to coordinate the provision of resources to each contaminated area. The first emergency call came into the Tokyo Metropolitan Fire Department at 8:09 a.m. For the next hour calls came in from 15 different subway stations. However, the TMFD failed to rapidly establish a link between these events. Approximately one hour after the attack, the TMFD set up emergency response operations headquarters at the affected stations. However, the rapid onset of symptoms meant that the establishment of response centers came after the most severely affected patients had been triaged.[60]

Another example of the problems caused by a lack of coordinated command and control was poor unit assignment. Upon receiving the first call for assistance, the fire department sent all of their personnel to the Tsukiji station, the first station to call in the emergency, leaving minimal resources for other emergency calls. When calls began pouring in from the other affected stations, there were no firefighters left to respond.[61]

A second barrier to efficient incident management was the lack of established inter-agency relationships.[62] Physicians who worked at St. Luke's International Hospital (SLIH) at the time of the subway attack say that, "during this disaster, the concerned organizations acted independently and there was too little communication among them."[63] The police, fire department, and Hygienic Department of the Tokyo Metropolitan government functioned simultaneously but without any central coordination.[64]

This problem was particularly acute between agencies at different levels of government. For months following the Matsumoto attack, for example, the Self Defense Force had been unwilling to cooperate with the police.[65] The police agency had primary responsibility for crisis management, and authority to call in the SDF when support was required. However, "at the early stage of this disaster, the full abilities of the Japanese Self Defense Forces were not used. Complicated formalities delayed the implementation of these forces."[66] This was especially unfortunate given that SDF personnel had far more chemical and biological weapons (CBW) training than did police, as well as de-contamination capability.

The sharp bureaucratic divisions coupled with an organizational culture that did not emphasize cooperation also stymied the subway attack investigation. The lack of cooperation between the NPA and SDF eventually grew so problematic that some specialists quit the SDF so that the police could hire them as trained personnel to investigate the scene.[67]

Subsequent Revisions to Incident Management: Creating Plans. Perhaps the most important change has been in the way officials think about terrorism, and more specifically terrorism as a subset of consequence management for all natural and manmade disaster. The government views the threat of terrorism through a broader lens and no longer focuses solely on left-wing activities and hostage taking in its response plans. Moreover, terrorism with a weapon of mass destruction has moved to the front of the stage to join hijackings on the list of "serious incidents" under the Crisis Classifications for Preparing Response Plans.[68] Japan's government held its first bioterrorism conference in 1999, and in the same year, the SDF secured its first budget for antibioterrorism preparedness.[69]

At the time of the subway attack, "there [were] no concrete articles in the Japanese legal system providing for a single, coordinated headquarters for disaster management."[70] The national government has worked since 1995 to enhance not only its response capabilities, but also its overarching response plan. A formal response plan has been agreed on, as detailed in a graphic supplied by the Cabinet Office for National Security and Crisis Management.

Subsequent Revisions to Improve Incident Management: Bridging Interagency Divides. In an effort to remedy the lack of an agreed-to incident management structure and the lack of interagency cooperation, revisions were made at the national level. The management issues are summarized in Figure 1. Elements of interagency cooperation that have been targeted for improvement include:

- clarifying information liaisons and establishing a chain of communication up to the prime minister,
- providing equipment for information transmission between ministries, agencies, and the prime minister;

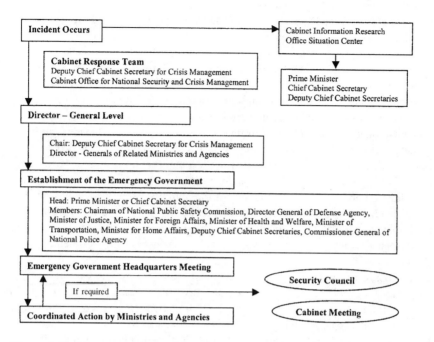

Figure 1 Revisions to management issues. (Graphic supplied by the Cabinet Office for National Security and Crisis Management, October 2000.)

- defining procedures for convening emergency meetings of officials at the prime minister's residence; and
- establishing the position of Deputy Chief Cabinet Secretary for Crisis Management.[71]

The fourth revision enumerated—the post of Deputy Chief Cabinet Secretary—was created in April 1998 to "make primary decisions on initial government response to emergencies and perform overall coordination among measures taken by related ministries and agencies . . . and to prepare various government response plans to different types of emergencies and coordinate those of related ministries and agencies."[72] A second entity, the Office for Crisis Management in the Cabinet Secretariat, was established to support the Deputy Chief Cabinet Secretary. The primary function of the two entities is to assist with preparation and coordination among national agencies. This effort to facilitate interagency cooperation represents a relatively new operating procedure for postwar Japan, and is much needed if agencies are going to break the long-standing tradition of working independent of one another.

More recently, the Council Against NBC Terrorism was created to tackle various issues related to counterterrorism. The council, a meeting of Japanese government officials chaired by the Deputy Chief Cabinet Secretary for Crisis Management, has met twice (August 2000 and April 2001). Other participants include directors-general of ministries and agencies such as Police, Defense, Fire and Disaster Management, Foreign Affairs, Science and Technology, Health, Economy, Trade and Industry, and the Coast Guard. At the 2001 meeting, various agencies described the measures they took in response to the sarin attack, and discussed plans to improve response in the future. Indeed, these meetings are designed to facilitate discussion among the national-level agencies involved in terrorism response, as well as to create a strong national response plan. Thus, several new efforts at bridging interagency divides, at least at the national level, are underway.

The new national response plan will not solve all of the incident management problems that emerged during the response to the subway attack. Deeply entrenched political norms, some of which are embodied in the response plan, remain a hindrance to effective response. First, the Japanese political system is *designed* to be cautious. After World War II, "coordination and integration functions of the administration were carefully constructed to ensure checks-and-balance systems in the inter-rivalry compartmentalization of bureaucratic organizations."[73] The combination of relatively weak authority and massive bureaucracy foster slow and deliberate decision making, which can be problematic in a crisis situation.

Second, the new response plan shown in Figure 1 assumes a "top down" structure in which national-level agencies coordinate the immediate disaster response. However, local and regional governments are almost inevitably the first responders in a terrorist attack or a natural disaster. This is true primarily because of proximity to the disaster site, but also because local and regional response agencies are often better equipped to handle disasters because they routinely respond to natural disasters and because they possess the primary legal authority to respond. Thus national agencies should not presume that circumstances or knowledge will permit them to dictate the terms of the response from the top.

Third, the response plan is designed for national agencies. According to the Cabinet Office for National Security and Crisis Management, comparable response plans for terrorism do not widely exist at the prefecture or local level.[74] Local response plans tend to be generalized to apply to all disasters, although specific contingency plans for earthquakes typically exist. The national cabinet office is encouraging prefectures to emulate the national model establishing specific contingency plans for terrorism as one potential type of disaster.[75] Because local and regional personnel will arrive at the scene before national agencies, response plans must be developed at the local and regional levels, not just at the national level. Moreover, national response plans should be based on—or at least designed to work in concert with—local plans.

Communication

The need for strong communication spans the temporal spectrum, but is particularly important immediately following the attack when a proactive communications strategy can aid rescue and recovery efforts. A good inter-governmental communication strategy facilitates allocation of resources, implementation of response plans, and establishment of a chain of control. Communication between the government and the public can minimize panic, facilitate smooth evacuation or quarantine, and provide instructions and information to victims and others.

In the immediate aftermath of the subway attack, communication across agencies was hindered by a variety of technical and cultural barriers. On the technical front, for example, the Tokyo Metropolitan Ambulance Control Center (TMACC) could not effectively manage the dispatch of emergency medical technicians in part because "information regarding this disaster exceeded their ability to manage communications," which led to a system overload.[76] As a result of communications overload, emergency medical technicians lost radio contact with the TMACC, and were thus unable to secure permission to perform advanced medical treatment such as intubations. This directly affected patient care: all but one victim had to wait until admission to a hospital in order to receive intubation and adequate ventilation.[77]

Another result of communication system overload was that EMTs could not acquire hospital availability information, and were thus forced to find out which hospitals had beds available via public telephone, or simply to take patients to the nearest or largest hospital.[78] This method made tracking the number, location, and medical status of patients all but impossible.

Difficulties were not confined to the medical arena, nor were they all technical: communication infrastructure and information sharing were inadequate across disciplines and levels of government. Channels of communication among local emergency response workers, transit workers, and medical personnel were poor. Although police had information confirming that sarin was the source of the problem by 11:00 a.m., the hospitals and the TMFD were never officially notified that sarin was the agent used in the attack. Some personnel found out by watching the news, some learned it from patients who were watching the news, and others were assisted by tips from physicians who had responded to the Matsumoto attack and recognized the symptoms described by television and radio.[79]

An extended form of cross-agency communication involves working with similarly situated agencies in other countries that have reason to be concerned about the disaster. Communication with the international community about either sarin attack was all but absent. Anxious nations, including those with Aum chapters based within their borders, were not promptly briefed by Japanese officials; most learned of the attack and subsequent investigation via television and radio. Aum had members in Russia and the United States, and some members had visited Australia, where they performed experiments that left livestock dead. The United States, in particular, was worried about a possible attack due to Aum's strident anti-Western teachings. The silence persisted through the near and long-term periods following the attack. FBI officials and other members of the U.S. government were frustrated by the lack of cooperation and information sharing by the Japanese government. One American official complained that he "found out more from the morning paper than from our briefings from the Japanese."[80]

Equally important is communication with the public: victims and concerned citizens alike. A public affairs campaign can provide the public information about evacuation, transportation, and treatment. This did not occur in the subway sarin attack, both because the government did not rapidly identify the nature of the situation or the appropriate response, and because no public affairs strategy had been prepared for a mass-casualty terrorist attack. The first confusing messages were transmitted to the public by the transit department. False announcements on trains added to the confusion among victims and responders. Further messages were transmitted via the media. The images portrayed on the 9:00 a.m. news, which may have exacerbated the nervous frustration of victims and concerned parties, were of confusion and chaos: victims were shown becoming ill, staggering around the city, and searching for answers.

Communication between the government and the Japanese people was no clearer in the early or near-term period after the attack than it was during and immediately following the attack. According to experts, "In contrast to the cult's loud declarations of innocence, Japanese authorities seemed intent on keeping the public in the dark."[81] The silence practiced by most government agencies began immediately after the attack and continued for days. This perpetuated the general fear within the population and among victims, who only knew that the perpetrators were at large and thus could launch a follow-up attack. As a result of the government's silence, "Aum was winning the propaganda war hands down."[82] Cult members even attracted throngs of teenaged groupies who clipped pictures of the charismatic young Aum spokesman and other accused members.

The media, already heavily focused on the sarin attack, became obsessed with Aum Shinrikyo. However, the emphasis was on the nature of Aum and its members, the disintegration of Japanese society and standards, and the loss of safety in society rather than on the phenomenon of terrorism or weapons of mass destruction. The continuing fixation with Aum certainly influenced society's long-term impression of the attack. The constant media coverage and the revelation of new discoveries over several months "heightened the sense of unease [among Japanese] and called into question, [for] many people, the competence of the public authorities."[83]

Subsequent Revisions to Improve Communication: Infrastructure and Strategies.
Under-developed communications systems and strategies resulted in difficulties at all three stages of response: immediate, near term, and long term. Since 1995, the government has under-taken several initiatives designed to repair communications deficiencies. Most of these improvements have focused on infrastructure and on the interagency relationships that need to be in place in order for that infrastructure to be useful in information sharing. There has not been a strong focus on building a public affairs strategy that would enable the government to communicate effectively with the public.

One example of a technical advancement involves "a communication system for disasters, including video and satellite communication systems, [which] has been developed in central and local governments." In tandem with this effort, outdated systems were repaired.[84] In addition, a new disaster reporting system was instituted whereby authorized taxi drivers report details on disasters to a taxi control center via their standard radios.[85] Until the communication infrastructure is widely improved, however, a robust reporting system will exist in plans only, and will be ineffective in practice because telecommunications lines will be overwhelmed and will become disabled as they were after the sarin attack.

Improving communication is not limited to repairing and expanding physical infrastructure. Some of the biggest problems experienced after the sarin attack resulted from organizational and cultural, rather than technical deficiencies. Repairing these deficiencies is difficult, however, because many officials prefer to wait until they can provide full and accurate information before offering any information at all. Communication problems stemmed from two sources: organizational design and culture favoring the withholding of information, and professional reluctance to divulge information that might be incomplete or uncertain. In the first case, many of the organizations and individuals involved in the recovery operation in Tokyo had not often worked together previously and therefore lacked established relationships. For instance, police, fire, medical, and transportation personnel had not necessarily established a trust that could facilitate information sharing. In the second case, communication between agencies, with the public, and with the international community was limited where information was unconfirmed or incomplete. The lesson learned in Tokyo, and in many other disasters around the world, is that officials must share the information they do know in a timely manner. If the media do not have an authorized spokesperson to turn to, they will fill that void with information, correct or otherwise, from whatever sources will step up to the camera.

Personal Protection and Decontamination

Protecting personnel who enter contaminated environments and decontaminating the site are immediate and near-term concerns. In the subway scenario, primary contamination claimed the lives of 10 passengers and 2 transit workers in the subway attack. Secondary contamination—response workers sickened indirectly by exposure to victims who have been in direct contact with the chemical—incapacitated, but did not kill, many response personnel in Tokyo. Natural decomposition of sarin's strength, and the fact that the sarin used was only 30 percent pure were mitigating factors that reduced the casualty count. If Aum had used pure sarin or advanced delivery technology, or if this had been an attack with a biological agent, the lack of rapid decontamination of the subway and the victims could have been fatal to far more people.

The first responders in this incident were, because of their proximity to the attack site, subway workers. Ignorant about the source of the illnesses, many well-meaning transit workers handled sick passengers or touched the sarin while cleaning up the spill-age. Two workers died after they removed the newspaper that had concealed the agent and absorbed some of it.

The second wave of the response included firefighters, police, and emergency medical technicians. At 8:20 a.m. the first call came into the Tokyo emergency switchboard with a complaint of a foul odor in the Kamiyacho station on the Hibiya line. At 8:33 a.m., the fire department emergency squad received a call that six passengers had collapsed at the Nakano Sakaue Station on the Marunouchi line. Emergency workers without appropriate gear took care of severely poisoned victims. Many were overcome by sarin exposure.[86] Emergency medical service personnel at the scene were contaminated by sick victims: of 1,364 EMTs, 135 suffered acute symptoms and required medical treatment.[87] Others were contaminated while transporting victims to the hospital. After witnessing the effects of secondary contamination, police ordered response personnel to wear masks. At 9:00 a.m., police finally began blocking access to subways that transit officials had not yet closed.[88]

Almost simultaneous with the influx of traditional emergency response personnel into the subways and surrounding areas was the involvement of hospital workers. Because no information that the incident was caused by poison gas was available in the first few hours of the attack, patient decontamination was not initially attempted, and 23 percent of the 472 house staff that were exposed to contaminated patients showed signs of sarin poisoning.[89] Table 1 depicts their symptoms.

After St. Luke's Hospital staff learned that the victims were suffering from exposure to a nerve agent, they decontaminated patients "by having them change clothes and shower." This was a time-intensive ordeal because "it took time to determine the cause of the victims' illness . . . and [there was] not enough space for changing clothes and showering."[91] The hospitals lacked adequate decontamination facilities and training, and therefore had to rely on this rudimentary method of decontaminating patients.

Table 1

Secondary exposure symptoms in the hospital workers at St. Luke's Hospital ($n = 472$)

Symptom	#	%
Eye symptoms	66	14
Headache	52	11
Throat pain	39	8.3
Dyspnea	25	5.3
Nausea	14	3
Dizziness	12	2.5
Nose pain	9	1.9

In 1995, the only agency that possessed the ability to decontaminate an area exposed to a chemical or biological agent was a specialized task force of the Self Defense Force.[92] Between 4:50 p.m. and 9:20 p.m.[93]—over eight hours after the attack—the task force decontaminated the subway cars with a bleach and water mixture.[94] The subway was back in service later on the day of the attack. The SDF did not assist hospitals that were attempting to decontaminate patients.

Subsequent Revisions to Protection and Decontamination: Equipment and Infrastructure. Since 1995, the Japanese national government has invested in protective gear and de-contamination equipment. One concrete example is the introduction—purchased with a one-time expenditure of one billion Yen from the national government—of protective gear, decontamination kits, and detectors into police training and response. Forty-seven local police forces benefited from this investment.[95] Another is that a special U.S. Marine Corps unit for CBW management was deployed to Japan to assist with training.

Despite these investments, decontamination capabilities remain underdeveloped.[96] According to an official in the Cabinet for Crisis Management, the NPA decontamination capability is intended for use on police officers, not civilians or buildings. The SDF has more extensive capacity to decontaminate roads, buildings, and members of the public. However, as in both sarin attacks, the bureaucratic barriers to rapid response by the SDF may render this resource ineffective. The Fire Disaster Management Agency has some decontamination equipment that is available for both personnel and the public. Although at least three national agencies and several local police departments possess at least some decontamination equipment, the official notes that the national plan has not yet "determined the specific role or responsibility of [each] agency at the scene."[97] Therefore, what decontamination capability exists may not be rapidly or effectively deployed.

Finally, hospitals' decontamination capability requires further attention. The Japanese government distributed decontamination equipment and personal protection equipment to hospitals beginning in 2000. By 2002 nearly 80 hospitals will have some decontamination capability. However, the budget only allows for four personal protection suits for each hospital, and additional units must be purchased at the expense of the hospital.[98] Because of budget constraints and competing priorities, hospitals may choose not to expand on the government-initiated capacity to operate in a contaminated environment, or to create decontamination facilities.

Medical Surge Capacity

Medical surge capacity is the ability of the healthcare system to handle an influx of patients that exceeds the normal patient load. Surge capacity includes physicians, nurses, hospital staff, medication, physical space, beds, equipment, and communication infrastructure.

One component of medical surge capacity is the system's ability to attend to patients' vital needs at the disaster site: that is, to allocate immediate care capabilities by determining which patients need immediate care, which can safely wait, and which are beyond help. A complementary component is the ability of the medical community to "flex" so that it can accommodate patients' needs within secure health care facilities. Approximately one hour after the subway attack, the TMFD set up emergency response operations headquarters at the affected stations. The TMFD requested assistance from the regional medical association, and 47 doctors, 23 nurses, and 3 clerks responded. In addition, St. Luke's hospital, the nearest medical facility, sent 8 doctors and 3 nurses. However, the rapid onset of symptoms meant that the establishment of response centers came after the most severe patients had been attended to,[99] and by the time supplemental personnel arrived, the patients in most serious need of attention had been transported to the hospital. The hospitals, ironically, had been depleted of key personnel as they had sent them out into the field. In essence, the system "flexed" at the wrong time, and therefore in the wrong direction.

A second aspect of surge capacity is the ability to transport patients to functioning medical facilities. By the end of the day on 20 March 1995, 1,364 emergency medical technicians and 131 ambulances had responded to patients at 15 subway stations.[100] The emergency medical system and medical transportation were overtaxed: 688 patients of the sarin attack were transported by ambulances during the course of the day.[101] Hospitals outside the center of the disaster offered to help the overcrowded hospitals such as St. Luke's, but they could not be fully used due to lack of available transportation.

In several local hospitals, capacity was also put to the test. Approximately 5,500 people went to 280 medical facilities on the days on and following the attack. In all, 1,046 patients were admitted to 98 hospitals.[102] The best data comes from St. Luke's International Hospital, which saw the most patients from the attack. At 8:40 a.m., patients began flooding into St. Luke's; within an hour the hospital had received 150 patients. In total, St. Luke's saw 641 patients that day, and over 1,400 patients the following week.[103] Like other hospitals in the metropolitan area and beyond, it was overwhelmed. Exhausted physicians who had sarin victims added to their existing caseloads treated patients in hallways. At 9:20 a.m., St. Luke's Hospital administrators declared an emergency, canceling routine operations and outpatient services. All hospital facilities, including chapels and halls, were used to treat sarin victims.[104]

Hospital communication systems were also overwhelmed. St. Luke's reported that jammed systems made it impossible to communicate from one department to the next. As a result, "hospital staff resorted to shouting down the halls or personally hunting down a particular colleague."[105]

Part of what overwhelmed the medical system was a category of affected people called the "worried well." The worried well included exposed and unexposed individuals that sought—but did not really require—medical care. Some may have been exposed to the attack but not physically affected. Others may have heard about the attack and were concerned for their welfare even though they had not been exposed to the chemical. Still others exhibited psychosomatic symptoms that led them to believe they were in danger. Some people associated preexisting conditions with symptoms described by sarin victims, such as eye pain or nausea.

Of the more than 5,000 patients whose hospital visits were directly related to the attack, less than 20 patients were admitted and treated in intensive care units.[106] At St. Luke's, only 5 patients were deemed in critical condition, whereas 43 men and 63 women were admitted in "moderate" condition: a small proportion of the 641 victims seen by medical practitioners on the day of the disaster. People who did not exhibit symptoms of exposure—easily over one half of the patients seen at St. Luke's alone—represent the worried well that clogged the system and postponed treatment of affected individuals.[107] Because the source of the attack and the symptoms of patients were unknown, physicians were unable to distinguish exposed patients in need of medical intervention from the thousands of worried well that flooded hospitals all around Tokyo.

Subsequent Revisions to Medical Capacity: Expanded Surge Capacity. There is a concern on behalf of hospital administrators and staff that if hospitals must tend to large numbers of casualties following a disaster, quality of care will suffer because the facilities are unprepared to handle the unexpected influx of patients who flood the system as a result of the disaster.[108] Yet this issue of building adequate medical surge capacity—the resources to handle excess casualties—is difficult to solve. According to Tetsu Okumura, MD, "because of tight medical economics, almost all hospitals in Japan do not have sufficient surge capacity."[109] This is unlikely to change, particularly given the fact that, "directors of Japanese hospitals think that expenses against disasters and terrorism are unprofitable."[110]

As part of an attempt to remedy the lack of adequate medical capacity, the Tokyo National Disaster Center was founded in July 1995. This hospital represents the first disaster-oriented hospital in Japan. In non-disaster times, the hospital serves as an educational facility. In times of crisis, the hospital provides hundreds of extra beds.

Although this facility is a thoughtful step forward in creating medical surge capacity, this approach ignores the fact that surge capacity requires more than hospital beds. Medical capacity in general must be strengthened: transportation, communication, pharmaceutical supplies and delivery channels, and medical professionals all factor into this equation. Thus, Japan has yet to solve the question of how to provide adequate medical surge capacity.

Subsequent Revisions to Medical Capacity: Hospital Plans. In Tokyo at the time of the sarin attack, most hospitals did not have extra capacity or specific plans to deal with mass-casualty disasters. Even where emergency response plans were in place, resources were inadequate to handle the demand. A physician at St. Luke's observed that, "to aid the house staff in achieving and maintaining a proper level of disaster preparedness, SLIH conducts routine disaster drills. The nerve gas attack was so unprecedented in nature and site, however, that management guidelines were inadequate; we had no means of handling such an extraordinarily large number of simultaneously affected patients."[111]

After the attacks, hospitals began developing plans to manage mass casualties. The planning is still in a formative stage, and varies from one facility to the next.[112] The Kawasaki Medical School Hospital, a teaching facility, developed a manual for managing WMD disasters. Dissemination of these standards to other Japanese hospitals will advance preparedness.

Law Enforcement

Much of the near-term and long-term response to the sarin attack consisted of law enforcement. Two different aspects of law enforcement were present: investigation, detention of suspects, and trial; and the passage of legislation intended to facilitate trial and punishment of the perpetrators of the crime, and to prevent future crimes.

In the days after the attack, more than 2,000 police officers mobilized for a nationwide investigation into the sarin attack and Aum Shinrikyo members and facilities. On 22 March 1995, only two days after the subway attack, authorities raided the Aum commune at Kamikuishiki. Preparing for the worst, police wore gas masks and carried canaries into the residence. That same day police raided the 25 offices, compounds, and complexes throughout Japan belonging to the cult. However, even though police raided Aum centers equipped with full protective gear, they refused to publicly acknowledge any link between the sarin attack and the cult.[113]

It was not until days later that the government revealed that Aum had a cache of weapons and weapons-grade chemicals. By the end of the first week in April, the police had gathered enough evidence to begin arresting members of Aum Shinrikyo. More than 150 cult members had been arrested by late April, but none of the arrests were based on a connection with the sarin attack. By mid-1996 over 400 cult members had been arrested on charges ranging from kidnapping to drug production to participation in the sarin attack.[114]

On 30 October 1995, the Tokyo District Court ordered the dissolution of the cult's status as a religious organization. Aum appealed, but lost the case, and on 19 December 1995, its religious status was officially revoked. Legally, this did not prevent Aum members from practicing their faith or running affiliated business ventures. Rather, the cult lost the legal protections guaranteed to religious groups, including its tax-exempt status.[115]

Subsequent Revisions in Law Enforcement: A Narrow Legal Framework. The sarin attack spurred the passage of several pieces of legislation. Some, such as the legislation increasing undercover police powers, had broad impact on police powers.[116] Most, however, were narrowly tailored to apply to Aum Shinrikyo and the sarin attack.

Less than one month after the subway attack, the Japanese Parliament passed the Law Related to the Prevention of Bodily Harm Caused by Sarin and Similar Substances. The law prohibits the manufacture, possession, and use of sarin and similar substances.[117] The laws guaranteeing religious freedom were also modified after the sarin attack. On 8 December 1995, the Diet passed revisions to the Religious Corporations Law that granted authorities "greater leeway in monitoring potentially dangerous religious organizations."[118] The government also began reevaluating laws restricting police actions, antiterrorism policies, and consequence management plans. In June 1996, the Police Law was revised "to enable prefectural police to extend their authority out of their border by their own judgment and responsibility in dealing with transprefectural organized crimes."[119] Finally, The Group

Regulation Act of 1999 was passed to regulate groups that have committed indiscriminate mass murder. The law does not directly refer to Aum Shinrikyo, but it did allow police to put Aum under surveillance for a maximum of three years.

Although several pieces of legislation were passed in direct response to the sarin attack, the government chose moderate language and limited the measures that restricted civil liberties. Some government officials suggested invoking the Anti-Subversive Activities Law of 1952 with regard to Aum Shinrikyo. The law would have prohibited Aum from recruiting and fundraising; training followers; and publishing materials promoting its beliefs. In addition, the law would have permitted ongoing surveillance of the group by the police. To invoke the law, the National Police Agency first had to exhaust all other legal remedies, and then prove that the violence committed by the group "was politically motivated and that there is a strong possibility that future acts of violence will be committed."[120] In this case, however, officials decided not to apply the law both because other remedies were available, and because they determined that Aum did not pose a credible future threat. Moreover, although there was significant political and public support for the measures that were invoked, the majority of the population did not support invoking the Anti-Subversive Activities Law, which many saw as compromising freedom of speech and other civil liberties.

One expert noted that the laws that were passed, "can be located between the Anti-Subversive Activities Law, which the government failed to apply to Aum in 1997, and 'doing nothing.'"[121] The narrow focus of the measures passed after the Aum attack means that they may not be useful should another chemical attack, or even a biological attack, take place in Japan. Although it may be difficult to secure the focus of lawmakers in the absence of an emergency situation, laws pertaining to the possession, transfer, and use of biological and chemical agents should be on the books before another disaster occurs.

Compensation for Damages

The government has not taken significant steps to correct all of the shortcomings revealed in the aftermath of the sarin attacks. One shortfall has to do with financial compensation. Victims are still responsible for much of the cost of their long-term recovery.

Compensation for damages is both a near-term and a long-term concern. The families of 18 individuals who were killed or severely injured by the Matsumoto and Tokyo attacks received a total of $424,000, which averages out to just over $23,000 each.[122] Many other injured Japanese were able to submit worker's compensation claims for damages resulting from the attack. In Japan, an injury received while in transit to or from a place of employment qualifies as a work-related injury. As of September 1995 over 4,000 individuals had filed worker's compensation claims relating to the sarin attack.[123] Of those claims, almost all were recognized as "involved in the accident resulting from commutation and over 300 as having been involved in the accident in the course of duty."[124] The Labor Ministry has incurred $2.6 million in expenses associated with these victims.[125] However, many of the victims' claims remain unpaid.

Aum Shinrikyo, not the national or local government, is actually responsible for paying most of the compensation. Under Japan's worker's compensation laws, the state can claim damages for insurance benefits it pays to a third party in a case where the damage is caused by another entity.[126] In this case, the government has refused to pay for medical or other damages suffered by the victims because Aum, the culpable third party, is considered liable for these expenses. The Health and Welfare Ministry, relying on this legal distinction, has not offered any payment for comprehensive follow-up care or other support, nor has it offered to provide these services.[127] Unfortunately, the cult's assets at the time of dissolution were approximately one billion Yen, not even close to the five billion Yen in claims filed by victims.[128] Furthermore, Aum declared bankruptcy on 14 December 1995.[129] In the end, an estimated 80 percent of the claims against Aum will go unpaid.[130] Not until 1999 did Aum formally acknowledge that two of its members were involved in the attack and offer to pay some compensation to victims.[131]

Subsequent Revisions to Compensatory Services: Government Forfeiture. In early 1998, the state and some local governments announced that they would forfeit their claims against Aum, which total 520 million Yen. This move is an effort to allow more individual victims to recover greater shares of the cult's assets.[132] This government action, although thoughtful and appropriate, does not address the systemic shortcomings of the remediation system. In many instances, victims had to pay their own medical bills and were not reimbursed by the worker's compensation system. This led to some degree of financial suffering for all involved.

Psychological Recovery

Most individuals affected by the attack—both directly and indirectly—have successfully managed the trauma associated with the event. "The first anniversary of the world's largest ultraterrorist attack came and went with only modest observance and emotion. Prime Minister Ryutaro Hashimoto visited the station, transit officials and families held a brief ceremony, families laid small tributes, such as flowers."[133] Subsequent anniversaries have received incrementally less attention. Most of the victims of the sarin attack have recovered physically from the sarin exposure. However, psychological effects linger for many victims and their families.

One study of victims of the sarin attack questioned 35 inpatients in a metropolitan hospital six months after the event. The results showed that 26 percent of the patients were at high risk for posttraumatic stress disorder (PTSD). The overall conclusion drawn from the study was that 20–25 percent of at least moderately poisoned victims suffered from PTSD or subthreshold PTSD symptoms.[134] The same hospital surveyed 20 patients who visited for a checkup 2 years after the event: 10 percent were identified as suffering from PTSD; 10 percent were identified as recovered from PTSD. Although a few victims have suffered permanent or long-term debilitating physical effects, the more common issue has been the psychological trauma associated with the attack.

Subsequent Revisions to Improve Mental Health Care: Awareness and Training. After the sarin attack there was no concerted effort to address the unique psychological challenges of WMD terrorism. Those patients who were admitted to hospitals that had psychological services were offered assistance. Patients at smaller hospitals had to seek out private treatment on their own. All care was the financial responsibility of the patient.

No official government response has occurred in the ensuing years. Five years after the attack, a group of mental health specialists offered psychiatric intervention for victims. Considering the delay in service, a surprisingly high number—84 victims—attended the clinic on the first day of operation.[135] Psychiatrists involved in the effort acknowledge that early intervention would have been much more useful in facilitating rapid and more complete recovery for victims.

In light of this understanding, Japan is making an effort to train physicians and other emergency responders to recognize and treat symptoms of posttraumatic stress disorder. Until 2000, the Ministry of Health provided a day-long lecture on PTSD. Beginning in 2001, the training will last for three days. Thus far over 2,000 people have been trained to deal with PTSD among victims.

Lessons and Implications for the United States

The islands of Japan face myriad natural disasters, including typhoons, earthquakes, and volcanoes, on a regular basis. As a response to one such disaster—the Hanshin Kobe earthquake of January 1995—Japan had already begun revising its disaster management plans before the sarin attack occurred.[136]

After Aum Shinrikyo attacked civilians with sarin on two separate occasions, thereby introducing terrorism with a chemical agent in an urban setting as a new disaster threat, the Japanese government and civil organizations became much more concerned with incorporating antiterrorism efforts and WMD response planning into general disaster plans.[137]

Japan has now made concrete improvements to many consequence management capabilities. This section analyzes some of the lessons of the attack and provides suggestions for further enhancements to consequence management plans that can also be implemented in the United States.

Many of the lessons learned in Japan also offer insights for the United States: relationships between various players need to be built; telecommunications infrastructure strengthened; medical surge capacity enhanced; laws passed to enable appropriate surveillance and prosecution methods; and psychological care capabilities improved. The United States has confronted several of these challenges, some with greater vigor and success than others. By and large the approach has been to enhance the "all-hazards" approach to disaster management, rather than to "specialize," and in this way prepare to handle the aftermath of a WMD terrorist attack.

There are, however, considerations that distinguish a WMD terrorist attack from a natural or other manmade disaster. They have been evident in the response to the anthrax attacks on members of Congress and journalists in the United States since September 2001, which taxed the public health and medical systems, revealed shortfalls in the ability of government officials to communicate effectively with one another and the public, and created a sense of fear across the country. Some of the considerations that are unique to WMD terrorism represent relatively new issues for the public safety community, whereas others reinforce the importance of issues that are already acknowledged, yet remain unsolved.

One issue that is specific to a hazardous materials or public health emergency is that primary and secondary contamination may cripple response efforts.[138] Decontamination is an issue not only for the disaster scene, but also for emergency transportation, hospital workers, and others. Numerous agencies and facilities must be able to recognize contamination, provide decontamination, and function in a "dirty" environment. In Tokyo, for instance, even though the SDF was the only organization with decontamination expertise, the SDF role was largely limited by protocol to the decontamination units that cleaned the trains after the recovery operations were over.

Second, a mass-casualty attack will require medical surge capacity, including sufficient medical personnel to attend to increased casualty loads. At the time of the Tokyo subway attack, mutual aid agreements intended to improve response—had an unexpected adverse effect on patient care. In all fifty-five doctors and 26 nurses were dispatched from area hospitals to affected stations. However, by the time the doctors and nurses arrived at the scene, severe cases had been transported to the hospital. Doctors and nurses in the field treated noncritical patients, a job that could have been done by the EMTs. Meanwhile, the hospitals were suffering a shortage of staff. For example, 11 personnel had been dispatched from St. Luke's, the hospital that saw the most patients that day. The lesson from Tokyo is that, in a disaster that consumes resources from throughout the region, localized mutual aid agreements may simply pull resources from one area that needs them, to another that needs them as much, or less than, the home location. Governments must think creatively about contingency plans to provide and allocate medical surge capacity after an attack.[139]

Third, well-established working relationships and a willingness to prioritize cooperation over inter-agency or inter-government competition is essential to planning for and responding to a WMD attack. As evidenced by the various initiatives described, the Japanese government is trying to build relationships that bridge inter-agency divides. As with many post-sarin attack intiatives, however, these efforts focus on the national government. Although the Response Plan encourages cooperation between the ministries and between local agencies, there is no avenue or mechanism to implement this suggestion.[140] This is an important aspect of preparedness, but it is too narrow of a focus. Local and prefectural governments must be included in planning, training, and even routine meetings. The same is true in the United States. Federal law enforcement and other federal agencies must work closely with state and local law enforcement, public health, fire and EMS, and recovery services. Although agencies such as the Federal Bureau of Investigation and the Federal Emergency Management Agency play lead federal roles, state and local agencies will be "on the ground" at the beginning and conclusion of any disaster. Communication between levels of government will facilitate the building of relationships, and alert the national government to the needs of local response agencies. Additionally, in Japan and in the United States, relationships must be established between military personnel and civilian first responders before a disaster occurs. These two groups need to plan and practice interacting with one another through drills. This is the best way to ensure that, in a mass casualty attack, the military has a clear role commensurate with the constitution and the society's expectations.

Fourth, legal preparation is a vital but often overlooked aspect of domestic preparedness. Japan was forced to pass a variety of laws after the sarin attack that were retroactively applied to Aum Shinrikyo. The legal system in the United States would not permit retroactive application of the law. Therefore it is even more essential that laws be in place before an attack occurs. This enables the nation to determine, with appropriate rational debate, the limitations of investigation and other law enforcement powers. Additionally, robust legal preparedness affords law enforcement the necessary powers to investigate and prosecute those who possess or attempt to use dangerous but not yet illegal chemical, biological, or nuclear components or weapons.[141]

Fifth, although evidence shows that people behave rationally in the face of disaster, including the sarin attacks, there is a heightened risk of immediate panic, short-term trauma, and long-term posttraumatic stress disorder following a WMD attack. Therefore, it is important to tailor psychological intervention to the demands of the occasion. The

United States has successfully set up hotlines and trauma centers following terrorist attacks. Contingency plans for WMD terrorism should be put in place so that counselors are prepared to deal with the particular traumas associated with an intentional use of weapons of mass destruction.

As the attack on the Tokyo subway system showed, most of the emergency response efforts, especially in the immediate aftermath of an attack, will be carried out by local transit police, fire, and medical personnel. Assistance from the federal level is necessary, but the federal government cannot and will not be the dominant player in the first minutes or hours after an attack. Therefore, it is essential that emergency responders in state and local government be prepared to deal with an unannounced attack with a weapon of mass destruction. At the same time, national-level coordination is vital to ensure that training and equipment are provided to localities in accordance with their needs, and exercises are carried out that involve personnel from multiple agencies and levels of government.

In addition, responders from all relevant agencies and all levels of government must practice skills in simulations that involve all aspects of response. Only in this way can these agencies, which may not be accustomed to working together, converge on the scene of a disaster and effectively carry out rescue and recovery operations.

Notes

1. For the purposes of this article, weapons of mass destruction (WMD) include biological, chemical, nuclear, and radiological weapons. Attacks resulting in mass casualties have also occurred through other means, most notably the use of fuel-laden commercial aircraft to destroy the World Trade Center towers in New York City in September 2001. However, this article focuses on the ways in which consequence management after a biological, chemical, nuclear, or radiological attack differs from an attack with a conventional weapon like a high-yield explosive. The Aum Shinrikyo attacks represent the first significant WMD attacks in modern times.
2. This is even more evident after a biological weapon attack, when rapid agent identification and appropriate medical treatment can significantly reduce the spread of the disease and the number of casualties.
3. After the sarin attack on the subway in 1995, the United States revised its assessment of the threat of terrorism to include the new threat of terrorism with a WMD. Since then, U.S. government spending on counterterrorism programs has risen exponentially. The various initiatives, known collectively as the domestic preparedness program, represent a major effort to improve the nation's ability to respond to an act of catastrophic terrorism.
4. Sarin is isopropyl methylphosphonoflouridate.
5. The cult lost its status as a religious organization under Japanese law in 1995. However, it retained a following and officially regrouped in 2000 under the name "Aleph."
6. The members were located around the world: 30,000 in Russia, 10,000 in Japan, and the remainder in the United States, Germany, and elsewhere. David A. Kaplan, "Aum Shinrikyo," in Jonathan B. Tucker, ed., *Toxic Terror* (Cambridge, MA: MIT Press, 2000), pp. 207–226.
7. David E. Kaplan and Andrew Marshall, *The Cult at the End of the World: The Incredible Story of Aum* (London: Hutchinson Press, 1996).
8. The Perfect Salvation Initiative headgear delivered a shock of six volts to adults and three volts to children. Each treatment cost members $7,000 per month.
9. During the campaign, the cult members wore white suits and giant paper mâché masks that looked like Asahara.
10. "The humiliations resulting from this public rejection intensified Aum's own gradual estrangement from the world: one is tempted to speculate that this rejection, when in Aum's eyes Japanese society spurned the chance to be saved . . . might well have pushed Aum's leadership into feeling that society was damned and should be abandoned. It also meant, once

its hopes of influencing society through legal, democratic means such as political campaigns were wrecked, that if "sahara's contention that spiritual action was no longer enough to fulfil its mission were correct, it had to look elsewhere for the means by which to influence or control Japanese society." Ian Reader, *Poisonous Cocktail* (Denmark: Nordic Institute of Asian Studies Special Report, 1996), p. 45.

11. An emphasis on religious freedom is pervasive in post-war Japan. The Japanese Constitution, which was drafted and imposed by the United States during its military occupation of Japan following World War II, emphasizes the individual's right from government intrusion.

12. D. W. Brackett, *Holy Terror: Armageddon in Tokyo* (New York: Weatherhill, Inc., 1996), p. 13.

13. "Aum seemed to enjoy a curious immunity from public complaints. The police investigated each charge made against the sect promptly, yet it never went any farther and there were never any arrests." Brackett, *Holy Terror*, p. 49.

14. "[A] contributing factor to Aum's behavior was the degree of impunity that the cult enjoyed. Despite an extraordinary six-year crime spree, the sect met with surprisingly little resistance from Japanese officials, who were hampered by jurisdictional problems, a reluctance to probe religious organizations, and a lack of investigative initiative. Only after the Tokyo subway attack did authorities move quickly against the cult." Ian Reader, *Religious Violence in Contemporary Japan: The Case of Aum Shinrikyo* (Great Britain: Curzon Press, Nordic Institute of Asian Studies Monograph Series No. 82, 2000), p. 223.

15. Japan is widely considered to be a safe society. Anthony Head explores this perception and concludes that although Japan is safer than the United States, it is not the nonviolent utopia people often describe. For example, Japan is not "gun-free"; there are many illegal handguns, and Japan has more handgun deaths each year than Great Britain. Moreover, there is significant under-reporting of crime in Japan, especially of rape and domestic violence, much of which results from the stigma of being a victim of crimes. Anthony Head, "Japan and the Safe Society," *Japan Quarterly* (April–June 1995).

16. 99.4% of Japanese citizens are ethnic Japanese; 0.6% are classified as "other" and are mostly of Korean heritage. "Ethnicity and Race by Country" available at (http://www.infoplease.com/ipa/A0855617.html).

17. Naofumi Miyasaka, "Terrorism and Antiterrorism in Japan: Aum Shinrikyo and After," prepared for the Japan Society Roundtable on Terrorism: Prevention and Preparedness, October 2000, p. 3, on file with the author.

18. Shun'ichi Furukawa, "An Institutional Framework for Japanese Crisis Management," *Journal of Contingencies and Crisis Management* 8(1) (March 2000), pp. 3–15 at p. 4.

19. Miyasaka, "Terrorism and Antiterrorism in Japan," p. 4.

20. Ibid., p. 5.

21. Ibid., p. 6. "Risk-averse policy is intuitively viewed as the best choice." One component of a risk-averse policy is a fear of casualties: either hostages or terrorists. The operational norm for police is to not to kill terrorists. A second component is to remain neutral regarding international terrorism. Japan does not specify enemies in international society and applies the label of "terrorist" only to domestic organizations. Japan does not have a legal or officially agreed-on definition of terrorism, and it judges terrorist acts only in criminal or civil law.

22. Ibid., pp. 6–7. "The perception of terrorists is so limited that the media did not label, for example, the maniac who hijacked ANA 061 and killed the pilot in July 1999, or the high school math teacher who bombed a neighboring school in February and March 1999, as terrorists. Furthermore, there is no consensus among people in general whether Aum is a terrorist organization or not." Additionally, the spate of attacks in Japan in the 1970s and 1980s, including aircraft hijackings and hostage takings, were widely perceived not as terrorist attacks, but rather as actions taken by marginalized individuals and groups to draw attention to social inequalities.

23. Ibid., p. 6.

24. Aum believed that the judges were likely to rule against them.

25. The Matsumoto attack may have been a trial run for the subway attack. A secondary effect was "to punish the judges and citizens of Matsumoto for having opposed Aum." Reader, *Religious Violence in Contemporary Japan*, p. 209.

26. Kyle Olson, "Aum Shinrikyo: Once and Future Threat?" *Emerging Infectious Diseases* 5(4) (July–August 1999), available at (http://www.cdc.gov/ncidod/EID/vol5no4/olson.htm).

27. Reader, *Religious Violence*, 2000, p. 221. Kono remained a suspect until Aum members confessed to the crime in the summer of 1995.

28. Ibid., p. 211.

29. Brackett, *Holy Terror*, p. 53.

30. The five cult members had left their hideout around 6:00 a.m. in separate vehicles, each with its own driver. Each had two plastic bags filled with sarin (one member had three bags) and an umbrella with a sharpened tip. On the way to their respective subway entry points, each purchased a newspaper or bag with which to conceal the sarin.

31. All of the trains involved in the attack converged at one point: Kasumigaseki. There is speculation that this attack was intended to cripple the National Police Agency: the station serves the NPA and the attack was timed to coincide with the 8:30 a.m. shift change.

32. Reader, *Religious Violence,* p. 23.

33. Early calls to emergency assistance switchboards complained of "strange smells" and "powerful odors" in the subway system. Brackett, *Holy Terror*, p. 1.

34. This assertion is supported by the general consensus expressed by participants at a conference sponsored by the Japan Society in Tokyo (2000).

35. As with most disasters the earliest first responders were victims and bystanders, who were not trained to deal with the aftermath of a disaster, especially a chemical weapon attack.

36. Furukawa, "An Institutional Framework," p. 5. In Japan, "the fundamental law of disaster management" assigns responsibility for managing disasters to the emergency management offices in the wards in metropolitan areas like Tokyo, and in cities, towns, and villages.

37. Tetsu Okumura, Kouichiro Suzuki, Atsuhiro Fukuda, Akitsugu Kohama, Nobukatsu Takasu, Shinichi Ishimatsu, and Shigeaki Hinohara, "The Tokyo Subway Sarin Attack: Disaster Management, Part 1: National and International Response," *Academic Emergency Medicine* 5(6) (1998), pp. 613–617, at p. 625.

38. Ibid., p. 614.

39. Ibid.

40. Furukawa, "An Institutional Framework," p. 4.

41. However, a governor may not have the best information, as was the case following the great Hanshin earthquake of 1995. In other cases, the governor may be reluctant to request help for a variety of political reasons. Interview with Shun'ichi Furukawa, Institute of Policy and Planning Sciences, University of Tskuba, 1 November 2000.

42. Okumura et al., "The Tokyo Subway Sarin Attack," p. 614.

43. Interview with Yoshihide Kuroki, Chief Superintendent, Special Advisor for Counterterrorism, National Police Agency, 31 October 2000.

44. Kaplan and Marshall, *The Cult at the End of the World*, pp. 248–249.

45. Ibid.

46. Ibid.

47. Ibid., p. 250.

48. It is unclear whether there was a lack of reporting or a lack of recognition.

49. Although accounts vary, most assert that police identified the agent prior to 11 a.m. All agree that the diagnostic tool was chromatograph–mass spectrometer analysis.

50. Physicians at St. Luke's Hospital asserted that, "The police did not inform us directly." According to several reports, a physician who treated victims of the Matsumoto attack contacted St. Luke's hospital after seeing news coverage of the subway situation and suggested the possibility that the causative agent was sarin. The physician, from Shinshu University Medical Department, personally phoned all Tokyo regional hospitals and faxed them information on sarin. See Okumura, et al., "The Tokyo Subway Sarin Attack," p. 621. See also Haruki Murakami, *Underground* (New York: Vintage Books, 2000), pp. 217–219.

51. At the time of the Tokyo attack, the Matsumoto attack was still officially labeled an accident. A link between Aum Shinrikyo and the use of sarin in Matsumoto had been established with soil samples from an Aum compound in November 1994, but police did not investigate this connection after the subway attack. The newspaper *Yomiuri Shimbun* had run a story in January

1995 outlining the link and pushing for an investigation. However, Kono Yoshiyuki remained a suspect until Aum confessed to the crime in the summer of 1995. See Reader, *Religious Violence,* p. 221.

52. Interview with Nozomu Asukai, M.D., PhD, Department of Psychiatry, Tokyo Institute of Psychiatry, 1 November 2000.
53. See also Furukawa, "An Institutional Framework."
54. Okumura et al., "The Tokyo Subway Sarin Attack," p. 626.
55. Interview with Colonel Masaaki Iwaki, Chief, Operations Research Office, Japan Defense Agency, 31 October 2000.
56. Interview with Makato Tsuruki, Professor, University of Tokyo, and President of the Antiterrorism Section of the Police Policy Studies Association, 31 October 2000.
57. Inteview with Iwaki, 31 October 2000.
58. In a WMD attack, time is crucial. For example, prophylaxis for victims of a biological attack must often be initiated in the first hours or days after exposure in order to be effective.
59. Hank Christen, Paul Maniscalco, Alan Vickery, and Frances Winslow, "An Overview of Incident Management Systems," *Perspectives on Preparedness*, No. 4, Executive Session on Domestic Preparedness, John F. Kennedy School of Government, Harvard University (September 2001), available at (http://www.esdp.org.).
60. Okumura et al., "The Tokyo Subway Sarin Attack," p. 615.
61. Interview with Asukai, 1 November 2000.
62. "The Aum affair teaches us that . . . coordination among concerned governmental agencies are absolute necessities in preventing and responding to future terrorism." Miyasaka, "Terrorism and Antiterrorism in Japan," p. 8.
63. Okumura et al., "The Tokyo Subway Sarin Attack," p. 616.
64. The Hygienic Department of the Tokyo metropolitan government is directly responsible for metropolitan disaster planning. See Okumura, et al., "The Tokyo Subway Sarin Attack," p. 626.
65. Interview with Tsuruki, 31 October 2000.
66. Okumura et al., "The Tokyo Subway Sarin Attack," p. 626.
67. Interview with Tsuruki, 31 October 2000.
68. The two other categories are natural disasters and serious accidents. See Cabinet Office for National Security Affairs and Crisis Management handout on file with the author.
69. Mike Green, Conference Report, "New Approaches to U.S.–Japan Security Cooperation," proceedings from Japan Society Conference, 30–31 October 2000, p. 11, on file with the author.
70. Okumura et al., "The Tokyo Subway Sarin Attack," p. 626.
71. Furukawa, "An Institutional Framework," p. 6.
72. Kazuharu Hirano, Cabinet Councilor, Cabinet Office for National Security and Crisis Management, notes presented on 30 October 2000, at the Japan Society Conference.
73. Furukawa, "An Institutional Framework," p. 5.
74. Correspondence from government official (who requested anonymity) from the Cabinet Office for National Security and Crisis Management, 7 September 2001, on file with the author.
75. Correspondence from government official, Cabinet Office for National Security and Crisis Management, 7 September 2001.
76. Okumura et al., "The Tokyo Subway Sarin Attack," p. 614.
77. Ibid.
78. Ibid., p. 615.
79. It was not until three hours after the incident that the Tokyo Metropolitan Police communicated the positive identification of sarin to the public at a press conference. Once the medical staff receiving patients were convinced sarin was involved, they were able to tailor patient treatment accordingly. Nozomu Asukai, MD, PhD, "Health Effects Following the Sarin Attack in the Tokyo Subway System," unpublished manuscript on file with the author. See also Okumura et al., p. 615; Amy Smithson and Leslie-Anne Levy, "Ataxia: The Chemical and Biological Terrorism Threat and U.S. Response," Stimson Center Report No. 35 (October 2000), p. 97.
80. Kaplan and Marshall, *The Cult at the End of the World,* p. 265.

81. Ibid., p. 259.
82. Ibid., p. 273.
83. Reader, *Poisonous Cocktail*, p. 108.
84. Furukawa, "An Institutional Framework," p. 6.
85. Okumura et al., "The Tokyo Subway Sarin Attack," p. 617.
86. See Asukai, "Health Effects Following the Sarin Attack," p. 3.
87. Okumura et al., "The Tokyo Subway Sarin Attack," p. 615.
88. Smithson, *Ataxia,* p. 93.
89. None were seriously affected. See Sadayoshi Ohbu, MD, Akira Yamashina, MD, Nobukatsu Takasu, MD, Tatsuo Yamaguchi, MD, Tetsuo Murai, MD, Kanzoh Nakano, MD, Yukio Matsui, MD, Ryuzo Mikami, MD, Kenji Sakurai, MD, and Shigeaki Hinohara, MD, "Sarin Poisoning on Tokyo Subway" (Tokyo, Japan), available at (http://www.sma.org/smj/97june3.htm).
90. Okumura et al., "The Tokyo Subway Sarin Attack," p. 620.
91. Ibid.
92. According to a high-ranking official in the National Police Agency, the police had no decontamination capabilities.
93. Smithson, *Ataxia*, p. 94.
94. This process was shown on the evening news. Interview with senior Cabinet Officer for National Security and Crisis Management.
95. Correspondence from Yoshihide Kuroki, Special Advisor for Counterterrorism, National Police Agency, 1 November 2000.
96. Correspondence from Tetsu Okumura, MD, Department of Acute Medicine, Kawasaki Medical School, 19 September 2001.
97. Correspondence from government official, Cabinet Office for National Security and Crisis Management, 7 September 2001.
98. Correspondence from Tetsu Okumura, 19 September 2001.
99. Okumura et al., "The Tokyo Subway Sarin Attack," p. 615.
100. Ibid., p. 614.
101. Smithson, *Ataxia*, p. 95.
102. Asukai, "Health Effects Following the Sarin Attack," p. 2.
103. Okumura et al., "The Tokyo Subway Sarin Attack," p. 619.
104. Ibid., p. 621.
105. Smithson, *Ataxia*, p. 96.
106. Asukai, "Health Effects Following the Sarin Attack," p. 3.
107. Headache and malaise were the most common persistent, generalized symptoms noted after discharge from the hospital.
108. Correspondence from Tetsu Okumura, MD, 1 December 2001.
109. Correspondence from Tetsu Okumura, MD, 19 September 2001.
110. Ibid.
111. Ohbu et al., "Sarin Poisoning on Tokyo Subway."
112. Correspondence from Tetsu Okumura, 1 December 2001.
113. Kaplan and Marshall, *The Cult at the End of the World*, p. 255.
114. Mark Mullins, "The Political and Legal Response to Aum-related Violence in Japan: A Review Article," *The Japan Christian Review (Tokyo)* 63 (1997).
115. Ibid.
116. Abigail Haaworth, "The Naked City," *Tokyo Journal*, July 1995, pp. 32–37, p. 37.
117. Brackett, *Holy Terror*, p. 155.
118. Mullins, "The Political and Legal Response," p. 63.
119. Available at (http://www.npa.go.jp/keibi2/it8.htm).
120. Mullins, "The Political and Legal Response."
121. Miyasaka, "Terrorism and Antiterrorism in Japan," p. 7.
122. These figures are in 1998 dollars. Mari Yamaguchi, "For Victims of the Subway Nerve Gas Attack, the Nightmare Goes On," Associated Press, 18 March 1998.
123. In addition to the worker's compensation claims, the restitution was made to the families of those killed in the attack in the amount of $23,000 USD each.

124. The government estimates that these claims will total over Y3 million. "Victims of Sarin Incident on Tokyo's Subway System Recognized as Eligible for Workmen's Compensation," *Public Policy*, 34(12) (December 1995).
125. Yamaguchi, "The Nightmare Goes On."
126. Ibid.
127. Ibid.
128. Tetsushi Kajimoto, "Aum Three Years Later: Victims Struggle for Redress," *Japan Times*, March 18, 1998.
129. Mullins, "The Political and Legal Response."
130. Kajimoto, "Aum Three Years Later."
131. Miyasaka, "Terrorism and Antiterrorism in Japan," p. 2.
132. Ibid.
133. Brackett, *Holy Terror*, p. 181.
134. Asukai, "Health Effects Following the Sarin Attack," p. 5.
135. "Sarin Victims Say More Must be Done," *Asahi Shimbun*, 20 March 2000.
136. Furukawa, "An Institutional Framework," p. 3. Over 6,000 people lost their lives in the Hanshin Kobe earthquake.
137. Interview with Tsuruki, 31 October 2000.
138. This is especially true for biological agents that cause contagious diseases.
139. For more on the lack of surge capacity and the consequences for the United States, see Joe Barbera, Anthony G. Macintyre, and Craig A. DeAtley, "Ambulances to Nowhere: America's Critical Shortfall in Medical Preparedness for Catastrophic Terrorism." BCSIA Discussion Paper 2001-15, ESDP Discussion paper ESDP-2001-07, John F. Kennedy School of Government, Harvard University, October 2001.
140. Correspondence from government official, Cabinet Office for National Security and Crisis Management, 7 September 2001.
141. For more information on the status of the law and recommendations for legal preparedness, see Juliette Kayyem, "U.S. Preparations for Biological Terrorism: Legal Limitations and the Need for Planning." BCSIA Discussion Paper 2001-4, ESDP Discussion Paper ESDP-2001-02, John F. Kennedy School of Government, Harvard University, March 2001.

Robyn Pangi is a researcher at the Harvard University's Belfer Center for Science & International Affairs, and was until recently a research associate at the John F. Kennedy School's Executive Session on Domestic Preparedness. She is co-editor of First to Arrive: State and Local Responses to Terrorism (2003) and co-editor of Countering Terrorism: Dimensions of Preparedness (2003).

Unit IV

Lessons Learned and Future Threats

In the final section of this volume, authors predict future WMD threats and seek to draw on past events and mistakes in order to identify lessons and strategies for the future. In the first of these, Jason Ellis, a research professor at the National Defense University's Center for Counterproliferation Research, describes the need for a comprehensive and multinational counterproliferation strategy. He begins by noting that nonproliferation efforts have failed to prevent WMD proliferation effectively in the past, and there is no convincing reason to believe that similar efforts will be able to address future threats. Instead, he argues, the best defense against proliferation and terrorism is a good offense, backed up by effective deterrent, as well as operational and mitigative plans and capabilities. Thus, a comprehensive national counterproliferation strategy is needed, and will require the United States to pursue ambitious diplomatic offensives against recalcitrant proliferants, to improve deterrent and defensive capabilities, and to develop appropriate consequence management and homeland security plans, tools, and organizational structures. This approach will also require the United States to prepare for plausible situations where nonproliferation fails (or has already failed) and WMD capabilities spread, where deterrent measures prove insufficient and WMD use occurs, and where protective and mitigative measures diminish the consequences of such an attack.

Similarly, Ash Carter—a former assistant secretary of defense in the Clinton administration and now co-director of the Preventive Defense Project at Harvard University's Kennedy School of Government—argues that the Bush administration has done little to contain the spread of weapons of mass destruction, even as undeterrable non-state actors grow more intent on obtaining and using them. From his perspective, U.S. counterproliferation policy needs an overhaul, focused on removing nuclear material from circulation, reinforcing nonproliferation agreements, and using new technologies and invasive monitoring to obtain better and more actionable intelligence. He concludes that a comprehensive and aggressive effort to improve counterproliferation intelligence can significantly improve our preparation for—and response to—a potential WMD terror attack, and thus the president should make this a top priority.

In the next chapter, Chen Zak Kane of the Belfer Center for Science and International Affairs at Harvard University's John F. Kennedy School of Government explores gaps in the international framework for combating WMD terrorism. She begins by reviewing the threats and challenges WMD terrorism poses to international efforts and arrangements at combating WMD. Three key trends highlight the new threats and reveal the limits of existing international arrangements: outdated assumptions in the non-proliferation regime, emergence of non-state actors, and the increasing availability of proliferation-related technology and knowledge. The second section of this chapter identifies three trends of the new international measures implemented to address the WMD terrorism threat. These include the assembly of "like-minded" coalitions of the willing, the emergence of non-states actors as problem-solvers, and the adoptions of new measures aimed at fixing existing international arrangements. And finally, this chapter concludes by reviewing five aspects of counterproliferation (intelligence and warning, prevention, crisis management, consequence management and response) in which additional measures need to be incorporated in the international framework to better prepare us for the threat of WMD terrorism.

Next, Forrest Waller and Michael George of Science Applications International Corporation provide an analysis of four technological revolutions with high potential to produce effective, affordable weapons of mass destruction of entirely new kinds. First, while a computer network attack has the potential to undermine social stability, the public's sense of security, national prosperity, and confidence in government, they suggest that one form of information technology—artificial intelligence—could become the basis for a new kind of weapon of mass destruction if integrated with other weapon technologies to replace human decision making. Specifically, a distributed "swarming" attack using robotic weapons with enough intelligence to distinguish between friend and foe, or to navigate precisely with external help, could become a basis for new kinds of WMD. Second, as described in greater detail earlier in this volume, developments in biotechnology have serious implications for new kinds of WMD. Third, nanotechnology also might produce discrete new kinds of weapons of mass destruction. Ongoing research in nanotechnology weaponry includes ultra-high explosive/ultra-incendiary devices, while others have demonstrated that nano-sized carbon particles can introduce respiratory distress and death, depending on the concentration of particles in the atmosphere and the duration of exposure. And fourth, research on new energy sources, driven by the desire to reduce reliance on fossil fuels, could lead to new forms of energy-related WMD. For example, nuclear isomer weapons—which do not use nuclear fission or fusion as the source of energy—could fill a large volume of space with lethal effects (kinetic energy, thermal energy, and gamma radiation). They conclude that we must expand our definition of the term *weapon of mass destruction* to account for new developments in these and other areas of technological research.

The final chapter draws together themes and issues raised throughout the volume, identifying common areas of research, policy, and education. According to James Forest, director of Terrorism at West Point, and Aaron Danis, a career terrorism threat analyst currently working with the Nuclear Regulatory Commission, a review of these chapters reveals a common theme, one that many of us have known since childhood: Knowledge, in its many forms, can empower both states and non-state actors in the global security environment. Terrorists are actively seeking knowledge that would lead to the development of WMD capabilities. Meanwhile, by reflecting upon past experiences and forecasting technological developments of the future, a growing number of government and academic experts have dedicated themselves to the construction of a knowledge base to expand our understanding of the WMD threat, and how to respond with increasing sophistication and success. Overall, the discussions and analyses provided in this volume paint a complex portrait of terrorists' motivations and capabilities for acquiring and using weapons of mass destruction, and our ability to stop them. We wait for the next catastrophic terrorist attack, hoping that it will not come, and preparing ourselves if it does.

Chapter 4.1

The Need for a Comprehensive Multidimensional Strategy

Jason D. Ellis

The Best Defense: Counterproliferation and U.S. National Security

Neither terrorism nor the proliferation of weapons of mass destruction (WMD) are new phenomena; states in key regions of U.S. security concern have for several years aggressively pursued nuclear, biological, or chemical weapons and missile capabilities or have engaged in or sponsored terrorism. What is new is the prospective conjuncture of these twin scourges that constitutes a combined threat greater than the sum of its parts. The Bush administration's new national security strategy, aimed at refocusing U.S. efforts to deal with proliferant states and nonstate actors, essentially replaces the traditional state-centered U.S. nonproliferation approach with one that—for the first time—privileges counterproliferation and explicitly acknowledges prospective requirements for preemption.

Rather than a recipe for further proliferation or a license to hunt those who would harm the United States, the national security strategy is the product of the existing post-proliferated and terror-prone security environment. It is precisely because nonproliferation efforts have failed to prevent WMD proliferation effectively in the past—and there is no convincing reason to believe that nonproliferation will exclusively be able to address these increasingly linked threats in the future—that a comprehensive national counterproliferation strategy is needed. In this context, the best defense against proliferation and terrorism is a good offense—backed up by effective deterrent, operational, and mitigative plans and capabilities.

Why All the Hype about Counterproliferation?

Traditional diplomatic and economic measures, such as sanctions, export controls, international arms control, and technology denial regimes, and their more recently developed nonproliferation counterparts, such as cooperative threat reduction, clearly retain a place in the emergent strategy. But counterproliferation—defined by the secretary of defense as the "full range of military preparations and activities to reduce, and protect against, the threat posed by nuclear, biological, and chemical weapons and their associated delivery means"—is of central importance.[1] Counterproliferation is not the Bush administration's creation. The concept was developed during the last two years of the first Bush administration and officially articulated under Clinton administration secretary of defense Les Aspin.[2] Indeed, in the view of Gilles Andreani, "one finds convincing signs of a gradual shift" toward counterproliferation through the 1990s.[3]

Although that general sense is undoubtedly accurate, the rise of counterproliferation to national stature really begins with the current administration. Relevant counterproliferation capabilities, plans, and programs clearly were developed in Clinton's Department of Defense, but they remained subordinate to a larger national strategy predicated primarily on traditional and more recent nonproliferation measures. Although there were occasions where preemptive or preventive measures were actively contemplated against proliferant states, such as North Korea in 1993–1994, the administration's sustained approach revolved more around diplomatic dissuasion than military operations. (Preemption and prevention are often conflated, but for purposes of this discussion, a preventive attack would be one undertaken to preclude a given actor from obtaining a particular weapons capability, while a preemptive attack would aim to degrade or destroy an existing capability.)

In comparison, for instance, Clinton's national security strategy recognized prospective future requirements for "countering potential regional aggressors" and "confronting new threats," just as Bush's does.[4] But the two documents differ fundamentally in their central policy approaches and specific prescriptions. The Clinton administration defined, in a highly detailed, lengthy section, "Arms Control and Nonproliferation" as the axis around which the U.S. response to WMD and missile proliferation centered, while measures relating to the "Department of Defense's Counterproliferation Initiative" drew just one short paragraph, supplemented with one dedicated paragraph each on deterrence, combating terrorism, and the role of nuclear weapons in the U.S. security posture.[5] The Bush version gives continued importance to "strengthened" nonproliferation efforts but downgrades the prior treaties-and-regimes approach, elevating the status of proactive counterproliferation efforts to deter and defend against WMD and missile threats as well as effective consequence management should such weapons be used.[6] It also issued the first-ever companion *National Strategy to Combat Weapons of Mass Destruction,* an unclassified synopsis of National Security Presidential Directive 17.

Perhaps the most striking distinction between the two strategies—and certainly the one that has drawn the most expert debate—is the Bush administration's avowed determination not to let enemies of the United States strike first, underscoring that the risks of inaction in particular cases may outweigh the risks of action. The new security strategy states that, in the face of a looming threat, the United States "will, if necessary, act preemptively" to "forestall or prevent hostile acts by our adversaries."[7] Even though discussion a decade ago of preemption's potential future requirements, its prospective utility and potential liabilities, the requisite strategic and operational framework, and the military capabilities needed to enact such an approach nearly derailed the Defense Counterproliferation Initiative, issues relating to preemption have once again risen to the forefront of national strategy.[8]

The urgency motivating the current national security team stems from two underlying assumptions: WMD and missile capabilities have and will continue to proliferate; and use of these weapons against U.S. forward-deployed forces, U.S. friends and allies, or even U.S. or allied homelands is increasingly likely. In response, the United States seeks to advance its security along two parallel and mutually reinforcing lines: pursuing a proactive, full-court press against security challenges emerging from the proliferation-terrorism nexus; and strengthening homeland and transforming military capabilities to deter, protect against, and mitigate the effects of an attack. Thus, the administration seeks both to devalue the attractiveness of WMD and missiles and to diminish the adverse consequences to U.S. interests should adversaries execute such attacks.

A Manifest Threat

WMD capabilities continue to deepen and to spread; particular terror organizations and state actors actively threaten U.S. security interests; and the prospective nexus of proliferation and terrorism is an ascendant security concern. The gravity and urgency of the threats we face today, as well as the inadequacy of both U.S. and international efforts to prevent them, necessitate the new national counterproliferation strategy.

Clear and Present Danger

The 1991 Persian Gulf War clearly demonstrated the importance of being prepared to fight WMD-armed adversaries. Although Iraq did not ultimately use chemical or biological weapons in the war, postwar revelations of the scope of Iraqi WMD activities shocked the national security community, surprising even informed observers and highlighting serious potential vulnerabilities in U.S. regional security strategies and war-fighting plans. Had Iraqi chemical and biological weapons (CBW) been employed, U.S. and allied forces would have been inadequately equipped to confront them, and most U.S. coalition partners were even worse off. This Iraqi capacity, coupled with its evident (and largely undetected) technical progress, underscored the emergence of a major post—Cold War defense planning challenge. This development inspired former secretary of defense Les Aspin to declare, while chartering the Defense Counterproliferation Initiative in 1993, that "we are making the essential change demanded by this increased threat . . . adding the task of protection to the task of prevention."[9] In his view, although prevention remained our primary goal, the Defense Department had adopted a new mission: developing military capabilities to cope with WMD-armed regional adversaries.

The spread of WMD and their delivery systems poses major strategic and operational challenges to the United States and a crucial political challenge to the international community. In the hands of hostile states, these weapons threaten stability in key regions, put U.S. forces at risk, and undermine the U.S. ability to project power and reassure friends and allies. The possibility of asymmetric warfare—confrontations with actors unable to challenge U.S. conventional military dominance—must now be a central focus for defense planning. WMD not only afford such nations the ability to attack U.S. interests directly but also may afford adversaries a tool of coercion—an opportunity, as the 1997 *Quadrennial Defense Review* concluded, "to *circumvent* or *undermine* our strengths while *exploiting* our vulnerabilities."[10]

Arguably, even a limited WMD capability may afford regional adversaries a significant strategic advantage: the ability to hold friendly cities and other important strategic assets at unacceptable risk. Conceivably, the mere possession of nuclear weapons could embolden a rogue state and encourage risk-taking behavior. Nations with nuclear capacity may be more likely to employ chemical or biological weapons while reserving a nuclear trump card to deter regime change or to use as leverage during war-termination negotiations. Indeed, states such as North Korea or Iraq are likely to integrate developing capabilities fully into their war-fighting plans and may view nuclear or highly lethal biological weapons as part of an escalation-dominance framework. WMD proliferation also fundamentally changes the very theater of operations, making it possible for states with nascent WMD capabilities to at least threaten, if not attack, the United States and/or allied homelands in response to U.S. or allied military engagement in a regional conflict overseas.[11] Indeed, one clear lesson of September 11, 2001, was that geographic locations traditionally defined as "rear area," such as the U.S. homeland, are increasingly at risk.

Nor is the threat of WMD attack confined to state actors. Although states should remain a principal focus, terrorists and other nonstate actors have never before ranked as high among U.S. national security concerns. If Aum Shinrikyo did not sound the clarion call, then Al Qaeda certainly has. According to Director of Central Intelligence George Tenet, intelligence collected in Afghanistan revealed that Al Qaeda was "working to acquire some of the most dangerous chemical agents and toxins, . . . pursuing a sophisticated biological weapons research program, . . . seeking to acquire or develop a nuclear device, . . . and may be pursuing a radioactive dispersal device."[12] The continuing diffusion of technology, the ongoing risk of diversion of weapons-related expertise, and the clear potential for particular actors—whether at the national or subnational level—to contemplate mass destruction collectively foreshadow an ominous future. WMD-equipped states may also share their capacities with terrorist or other subnational organizations that seek to inflict mass casualties. The product: a distinctly dangerous intersection of threats to U.S. security.

It's a Post-Proliferated World

The Bush administration's national security strategy starts with the reality of a post-proliferated international security environment. The intricate network of nonproliferation treaties and regimes established over the past several decades share one key feature: failure to prevent determined states from developing nuclear, chemical, or biological weapons as well as increasingly capable missile and related delivery systems.

South Africa, for instance, successfully developed and produced six nuclear devices despite its purported adherence to the Nuclear Non-Proliferation Treaty (NPT). Similarly, Iraq was well on its way when the Gulf War interrupted its progress, and North Korea also sought clandestinely to develop nuclear weapons in contravention of its international obligations. At the same time, the voluntary and unenforceable gentleman's agreement among supplier states to refrain from exporting ballistic-missile development technologies to aspirant states has hardly kept key states—whether Iran, North Korea, Pakistan, India, or others—from making steady, incremental progress toward such developments. Several additional states also will develop the ability to produce land-attack cruise missiles indigenously over the next several years.[13]

All told, nuclear- and missile-related treaties and regimes have not prevented the acquisition or development of weapon capabilities, although they have arguably served to slow the pace of development in the past. In the years ahead, foreign assistance—the transfer or sale of technologies, material, or expertise with possible weapons-related applications by key suppliers—and the growing phenomenon of secondary supply—exports or cooperative development of WMD or missile delivery systems, their constituent enabling or production technologies, or the requisite expertise necessary to their development or production by nontraditional suppliers—pose severe challenges to the nonproliferation regime. At the same time, the continued insecurity (and large quantity) of fissile material in the former Soviet Union and other regions, evident advancements in indigenous weapons-related technology among less-developed states, and the potential availability of germane technical expertise together suggest that existing multilateral constraining mechanisms are bound to prove even less effective in the years ahead. In this context, traditional supply-side constraints have and will continue to erode.

The challenge becomes even more acute in combating chemical- and biological-weapon development. The U.S. government has assessed that "many [chemical warfare] agents . . . are simple to produce. They are often based on technology that is at least 80 years old and sometimes older, putting them well within reach of virtually any Third World country that wants them." Although newer agents, such as the reputed, Russian-developed *Novichok*-class of next-generation nerve agents, may not yet be as readily accessible, the "technology for these agents is widely available in the public domain."[14]

A majority of nations are states-parties to the Chemical Weapons Convention (CWC), which prohibits the development, production, acquisition, retention, stockpiling, transfer, and use of chemical weapons; but it is unlikely that this treaty has ended potential chemical weapons threats to U.S. or allied equities. In 1999 the intelligence community assessed that, despite the CWC and related supplier-restraint regimes such as the Australia Group, at least 16 states maintained active, clandestine chemical weapons programs.[15] The twin realities of technology diffusion over time and growing interest among particular states and subnational actors suggest that chemical weapons, as well as the infrastructure needed to develop and produce them, will remain permanent features of the international security landscape.

Supply-side controls face even more daunting prospects in the realm of biological weapons. According to the Office of the Secretary of Defense, "[Virtually] all the equipment, technology, and materials needed for biological-warfare-agent research, development, and production are dual use." This makes offensive programs "relatively easy to disguise within the larger body of legitimate commercial activity, as no specialized facilities are required," and "any country with the political will and a competent scientific base can produce" toxins or infectious agents.[16]

Although only three or four nations were thought to have offensive biological weapons programs when the Biological Weapons Convention (BWC) entered into force in 1975, the intelligence community currently assesses that perhaps a dozen states maintain offensive programs and warns that "credible biological warfare capabilities are becoming more advanced," a trend that may enhance the prospect of biological weapons use in the years ahead.[17] The lasting demand for biological weapons, the relative ease of concealing any offensive effort, the growing availability of weapons-related technologies and expertise, and an ongoing revolution in biotechnology that could significantly alter the threat environment all suggest that determined states—as well as particular subnational actors, especially those supported by states—face few real constraints in establishing, developing, or improving offensive programs with a national decision to do so.

Although some might argue that the threats presented by the greater availability of WMD materials can be addressed by inspections, they will not likely be effective or satisfactory long-term solutions. Even after a series of post—Gulf War "full, final, and complete disclosures" by the Iraqi government and despite more than seven years of intrusive inspections, the United Nations Special Commission (UNSCOM) was ultimately unable to account for critical elements of the Iraqi biological weapons program. Its self-described "select and incomplete" history of the program contained key gaps, including "considerable uncertainty" regarding weaponization; "consistently understated" agent production; an "incomplete" declaration of equipment and raw material imports; "omitted" planning references; "thoroughly planned" research and development, despite Iraqi claims that they were "unplanned"; and, finally, an absence of Iraqi evidence "concerning the termination of its offensive program."[18]

In light of UNSCOM's past experience, there is little reason to believe that its successor—the United Nations Monitoring, Verification, and Inspection Commission (UNMOVIC)—will fare any better with a truncated time line and fewer dedicated personnel and other supporting resources. Meanwhile, the Iraqi government has had years to improve its deception and denial practices based on several years of experience with UNSCOM—sanitizing key sites, migrating program elements to nontraditional locations (e.g., mobile or civilian facilities), and continuing clandestine program-related activities.

U.S. Intelligence Won't Cut It

The states of most egregious proliferation concern and the terror cells probably most willing to strike U.S. equities are what the intelligence community would reference as hard targets. Their restrictive nature, closed processes, and highly stratified leadership structures make timely and accurate threat assessment a difficult prospect.

With respect to the spread of WMD-related technologies, the intelligence community's intrinsic assessment challenges are rooted in at least four principal causes:

- improved deception and denial efforts by would-be proliferants;
- increasing access to dual-use technologies that effectively mask proliferants' intentions;
- the availability of expertise from which proliferants can advance WMD and missile programs; and
- an accelerating pace of technological progress as information and advanced technologies become increasingly available worldwide.[19]

As a result, there are clear reasons to believe that the United States and, by extension, allied nations and the international community as a whole will find it increasingly difficult to track the development of WMD and missile capabilities by key states and within the shadowy networks of subnational actors. Combined with these alarming trends, the research, development, and acquisition community has also warned that improved defenses will lag behind adversarial advances in offensive chemical- and biological-weapon capabilities.[20]

At the same time, getting a handle on adversary capabilities is likely to be considerably easier than obtaining accurate data on their plans and intentions. Although some indicators of an actor's intentions can be revealed through technical means (e.g., movement of forces, unique signatures for particular types of facilities), uncovering planning documents, developing informed and current perspectives on WMD-related issues, or learning the intentions of key-program or senior leaders is a daunting task that will ultimately be only as credible as the human intelligence upon which such judgments are predicated. This is an acute challenge in combating the distinct threats posed by both terrorism and proliferation and the new, greater threat they pose in conjunction. Improving intelligence collection and analysis is critical to a more effective warning capability that hopefully will help prevent specific attacks against the U.S. homeland, allies, and interests abroad. Still, even if U.S. intelligence does improve its net performance, strategic and tactical warning of both WMD proliferation and terrorism are clearly prone to failure.

Chances Are, Once They've Got them, They'll Use Them

For this reason, and because the consequences of particular WMD attacks may be severe, White House officials have argued that the United States must plan as if such weapons will be used. Indeed, not only does the continuing proliferation of WMD capabilities appear inevitable, the potential for adversarial use of WMD against U.S. forces, U.S. friends and allies, or the U.S. homeland is increasingly likely. This reality is hardly news to the Defense Department, which as early as 1997 concluded that the use of chemical and biological weapons would be a "likely condition" of future warfare.[21] In an extended battlefield, however—one that transcends traditionally defined overseas areas of operation, joins civilian with military targets, and relocates the forward edge of the battle area to rear-area targets including the U.S. homeland—this is no longer a judgment for the military alone.

The national security strategy's call for proactive counterproliferation stems directly from the premise that the security landscape has undergone a profound transformation. In this new era, key regional states and terror organizations "are determined to acquire weapons of mass destruction, along with other advanced military technology, to be used as threats or offensively to achieve the aggressive designs of these regimes." As a result, there is a "greater likelihood" that rogue states and terrorists "will use weapons of mass destruction against us."[22] For the U.S. homeland, this judgment differs fundamentally from previously widespread conceptions of the threat. The first Bush and Clinton administrations clearly recognized U.S. vulnerabilities to WMD and other asymmetric attack modes and sought to develop and implement particular defensive measures as well as operational capabilities, but it took the hijacked commercial airliners of September 11 to effect more sweeping change. At the time of the Gulf War, WMD were generally viewed as a last resort to be used principally in overseas theaters and in wartime. Now, however, the possibility of their employment in peacetime, against population centers or on the U.S. homeland, cannot be discounted.

Advancing U.S. National Security

Critics of the shift toward counterproliferation and preemption often promote enhancing existing multilateral nonproliferation agreements while diminishing reliance on the more proactive approach.[23] But it is unclear what a substantially improved nonproliferation regime would look like or whether, in fact, such a regime would ultimately be capable of preventing further proliferation of WMD or weapons-related technologies or expertise, let alone rolling back existing capabilities in key states of proliferation concern. Nor is it necessarily plausible that an inherently reactive, diplomacy-oriented, or multilateral approach would diminish the possibility of a rogue state or terror cell attacking or threatening U.S. interests more than a proactive, military-operational, or unilateral approach. Pandora's box has been cracked open: mass-destructive capabilities continue to spread; there are plausible reasons to believe U.S. adversaries may elect to employ them; U.S. vulnerabilities from the front lines to the homeland remain acute; and warning is failure prone.

To advance U.S. national security in an era when nuclear, biological, and chemical weapons serve to strengthen traditionally weak actors, existing counterproliferation policies, programs, and plans systematically built since the Gulf War must be significantly but carefully extended. To meet the current security threat presented by the proliferation-terrorism nexus, policy officials must address at least four core challenges.

Confronting Strategic Actors

Potential requirements for preemptive or preventive action are not new to U.S. policy debates. The last time U.S. officials contemplated preventive war, however, was almost a decade ago on the Korean peninsula, when Pyongyang threatened to withdraw from the NPT and intelligence assessments indicated that North Korea had produced fissile material sufficient for at least one and possibly two nuclear devices.[24] Policymakers ultimately pursued diplomacy over military action to prevent the North from succeeding in its nuclear quest. Nevertheless, eight years later, the measure negotiated has proven a temporary fix as the issue has reappeared with new revelations of a continued nuclear weapons development program.[25]

In determining how best to respond to either Iraq or the North Korean nuclear issue, it is possible that a diplomatic approach, whether cooperative or coercive, will again carry the day. It is also possible that policy officials, in concert with regional allies, will ultimately opt to explore available military options further. In both cases, it is likely that some mixture of diplomatic, economic, and military options will be brought to bear. Yet, it is unlikely that a one-size-fits-all approach will—or should—be developed and applied equally in these or other cases because regional political-military contexts, operational environments, and available options will vary. Certainly, discussion of options for preventive war, preemption, or other responses to Iraq, North Korea, and other tough proliferation cases will continue for as long as terrorism and WMD proliferation jeopardize U.S. security interests.

At the same time, policy officials will have to continue to balance contending foreign policy priorities. Rediscovering an old truth, single-issue policies tend over time to be difficult to pursue in the face of the more complex mosaic of a state's aggregate foreign policy. For example, in the proliferation context there is a clear tension between potential legal requirements to impose sanctions against such strategic allies as Pakistan for their WMD or missile development (and export) activities, on one hand, and identified strategic requirements and tactical imperatives to bolster a key regional ally, on the other.[26] Similarly, with states such as Yemen, policy officials will have to find the appropriate balance between objectives that sometimes appear to conflict. Although Yemeni antiterrorism cooperation appears generally positive, counterproliferation cooperation is evidently weak—as that state's importation of ballistic missile technology from North Korea would suggest.[27]

Nor are these difficult policy trade-offs limited to decisionmakers in the United States: to avoid military action in Iraq, it appears that the United Nations must demonstrate its ability to implement the relevant Security Council resolutions satisfactorily and that the Iraqi government must unambiguously comply. Similar questions regarding the North Korean nuclear weapons development program confront both the International Atomic Energy Agency and key regional allies. The effectiveness of the strategies pursued by international organizations in these cases will go a long way toward determining their continued relevance—or lack thereof—in managing today's capabilities-proliferated world. Clearly, it is critical to develop more effective options to confront states that do not abide by nonproliferation norms and to counter subnational actors with mass-destructive intent.

Surprise, Surprise, Surprise

Although tactical warning of a specific attack timing, mode, location, or even perpetrator is difficult to come by, the intelligence community has provided credible strategic warning of the attempted development and probable intent to employ WMD against U.S. interests by a range of potential actors at the state and subnational levels. Because adversaries have improved their ability to deceive U.S. threat assessments, the United States must prepare to protect against surprise developments and attacks by expanding its intelligence and law enforcement capabilities and bolstering operations and technologies that seek both to prevent the use of WMD and, if they are used, to defend the homeland against such attacks.

Historically, proliferation surprise has resulted primarily from mistaken estimates of the nature or maturity of specific national indigenous programs, but the potential for strategic surprise also exists if, for example, actors acquire unforeseen capabilities covertly from external sources. At the same time, the states of greatest proliferation concern are also among the hardest intelligence targets, often with closed or restrictive political processes that can make obtaining sensitive information difficult. Crucial information may be unavailable, fragmentary, or misleading, or may change quickly; U.S. security policy, therefore, must hedge its bets by seeking to develop effective capabilities to defend against and mitigate undetected attacks. Employing diplomatic and active operational measures to dissuade adversaries from employing and, where possible, even developing WMD- and missile-delivery vehicles is now and should remain a principal task of national efforts to combat proliferation.

Preparing for and mitigating the effects of surprise, however, also means maintaining a robust counterproliferation science and technology base capable of hedging against emerging—and to some degree unpredictable—threat developments. Similarly, to prove resilient against potential WMD surprise on the battlefield, U.S. military forces must prepare for a range of unforeseen operating conditions and regional circumstances, not just those rigidly validated by intelligence. This capabilities-based approach is central to the Defense Department's 2001 *Quadrennial Defense Review:* an effort to "anticipate the capabilities that an adversary might employ to coerce its neighbors, deter the United States from acting in defense of its allies and friends, or directly attack the United States or its deployed forces."[28]

Focus on Offense as Well as Defense

The United States cannot afford to model future military engagements against WMD-armed regional adversaries after the 1998 and 1999 air-only campaigns against Iraq and Serbia, respectively, or even after the post—September 11 operation in Afghanistan, where the substantial use of special operations forces and precision-guided munitions proved sufficient to defeat battlefield opponents. Indeed, more than a decade ago, the Gulf War demonstrated that an adversary equipped with significant WMD capabilities has the potential to alter the equation fundamentally.

In that conflict, even conventionally armed ballistic missiles arguably had an impact, both strategically, by altering the political dynamics of a coalition, and operationally, by diverting military assets from their assigned wartime missions. Serious deficiencies in the U.S. and coalition ability to locate and target WMD and mobile targets were exposed. Coalition forces expended considerable resources in a largely unsuccessful effort to find and destroy Iraqi mobile missiles, while allied planners significantly underestimated the number, location, and type of Iraqi WMD assets. This left numerous important sites, and a substantial portion of Iraq's WMD capabilities, untouched and undiscovered until postwar UN inspections.[29] Even when nuclear-, chemical-, or biological-weapon sites were detected, their targeting carried with it the potential for collateral release of toxic materials.

Post-Gulf War counterproliferation programs have attempted to come to terms with these vexing challenges. For several years, the Defense Department has undertaken research and development activities to develop strike capabilities that can achieve operational objectives, including the destruction of an adversary's assets located in hardened and/or buried targets with attention to minimizing collateral effects. Developing nonnuclear capabilities that rapidly allow U.S. forces to identify, target, and destroy both fixed and mobile targets is critical to effective counterproliferation planning; some have suggested that development of low-yield nuclear weapons may further enhance U.S. capabilities to hold at risk hardened or deeply buried targets. As the U.S. ability to credibly target such facilities improves, some of the leverage adversaries may have gained by possessing WMD will begin to erode. Although the 1990s witnessed evident progress on this technical front, policy concerns over the potential for collateral effects remained critical seven years after the Gulf War, when the risk of inadvertently releasing chemical or biological materials led the United States and the United Kingdom to proscribe certain targets during Operation Desert Fox.[30] In future military engagements against WMD-armed regional adversaries, policy officials will again have to weigh the prospect of collateral release against the imperative to ensure adversarial nonuse of such weapons.

Finally, the new National Security Strategy specifically calls for adapting "the concept of imminent threat to the capabilities and objectives of today's adversaries," which rely on "acts of terror and, potentially, the use of weapons of mass destruction."[31] In this strategic calculus, effectively defending U.S. national security against certain threats emanating from hostile WMD-armed nations and terrorist organizations calls for the United States, together with committed international partners, to act offensively today to preclude the development and delivery of graver threats down the line. The administration persuasively argues that, under particular strategic or operational circumstances, the best defense against proliferants and terrorists is a good offense. Yet, translating this strategic guidance into credible operational capabilities and plans will present a clear challenge to technicians and operators alike. This challenge is no less acute for the intelligence community, which will have to improve its ability to provide high-fidelity actionable intelligence, or for the policy community, which will need to develop appropriate criteria and standards for the pre-emptive use of force.

Improving Deterrent and Defensive Capabilities

Still, a good offense is insufficient to meet the threats emerging from the proliferation-terror nexus. Rather, it is just one of a long continuum of needed responses—from cooperative and coercive efforts to prevent or roll back WMD acquisition; to measures to defend against WMD if they are obtained or developed; to capabilities and plans designed to mitigate their effects should WMD be used.

Traditional nonproliferation measures including export controls, sanctions, and nonproliferation accords have long been considered the first line of defense against WMD and missile proliferation. More recently, substantial emphasis has been placed on cooperative threat reduction programs with key former Soviet states. Nonproliferation and cooperative threat reduction clearly remain essential parts of the national security strategy. The current national security strategy calls for the continuation of such activities but seeks to bolster them with emphasis on greater—and a different kind of—deterrence and defense. The move toward a national counterproliferation strategy presupposes that, although nonproliferation remains a laudible objective, the United States must come to terms with already proliferated capabilities in the hands of unfriendly or irresponsible actors.

The United States should move, and is moving, beyond traditional deterrent conceptions of retaliatory punishment to implement deterrence by denial—the ability to defeat, defend against, and operate in the context of WMD and, if needed, overcome the effects of WMD use. Although the United States seeks to preserve its ability to deter by threatening overwhelming destruction (whether through nuclear or nonnuclear means) as during the Cold War, the national security strategy is grounded in the conclusion that yesterday's strategies are insufficient for today's threats.

In this context, the June 2002 U.S. withdrawal from the 1972 Anti-Ballistic Missile Treaty and commensurate efforts to field capable missile defense systems more rapidly are part of a new and necessary approach to deterrence. Further, missile defense is just one manifestation of improved denial capabilities; for instance, anthrax and smallpox vaccinations for forces deployed to high-threat areas have also resumed. Nor have defensive measures been limited to the U.S. military. Following the September 11 and subsequent anthrax-by-mail attacks, the administration, together with key members of Congress, moved to improve homeland security. This has translated into activities designed to improve national responses to bioterrorism significantly, for example, in part by increasing the budget to almost $ 6 billion for fiscal year 2003 alone.[32] Although homeland security and force-protection measures have improved over the past few years, much more remains to be done.

Only a cogent and well-implemented response across the spectrum—preventive, offensive, defensive, mitigative, and restorative capabilities—can enhance U.S. security in this new era. The key challenge for the years ahead will be to sustain the momentum, build on the interest of senior leaders on both ends of Pennsylvania Avenue, allocate scarce resources judiciously, and continue developing improved capabilities throughout this layered strategy to combat the security challenges inherent in the WMD proliferation-terrorism nexus.

The Proliferation Endgame

U.S. and international success in this fundamentally transformed security landscape is likely to be measured more by an actor's ability to cope effectively with the persistent threat posed by potential adversaries in a post-proliferated world than its ability to defeat these adversaries unambiguously or even to roll back extant capabilities. This means that smart policy planning is every bit as crucial as improved counterproliferation or counterterrorism operational capabilities.

This new environment yields a number of key questions, including:

- How will the international community respond to the next significant use of nuclear, biological, or chemical weapons? The answer will be precedent setting. When Iran and Iraq exchanged chemical weapons—fire in the 1980s, the international community was virtually silent. To prevent further use, key states and international organizations will have to take appropriate punitive measures or risk an eradicated norm of nonuse in the years ahead.

- How relevant are prominent international organizations in combating WMD proliferation? Clearly, the Iraqi and North Korean challenges to UN affiliates are clear test cases and will provide important data points about the continued viability of concerted multilateral responses to proliferation. If the ultimate penalty for noncompliance with international accords and underlying norms is a round of ineffectively applied or quickly lifted sanctions, why should states not continue to acquire, develop, and export WMD? For many national governments, security competition, rather than trust in unenforceable and unverifiable international restraint mechanisms, may become the preferred alternative.

- Finally, can the United States, along with its friends and allies, effectively reevaluate policy responses to intractable regional proliferants and determine what additional or modified options are needed? These should include solutions that neither reward nor ignore those that seek WMD capabilities but, rather, seek to fundamentally alter the existing perceived incentives for potential adversaries to develop or employ unconventional capabilities.

The reality is that the world has moved completely beyond the time of just five nuclear (and few chemical and biological) weapons states. The United States must similarly move beyond traditional nonproliferation approaches toward a comprehensive counterproliferation strategy. Such a strategy requires the United States to pursue ambitious diplomatic offensives against recalcitrant proliferants, to improve deterrent and defensive capabilities, and to develop appropriate consequence management and homeland security plans, tools, and organizational structures. It requires the United States to prepare for plausible situations where nonproliferation fails (or has already failed) and WMD capabilities spread, where deterrent measures prove insufficient and WMD use occurs, and where protective and mitigative measures diminish the consequences of such an attack. There is no greater strategic imperative for the United States and its friends and allies—indeed, for the international community as a whole—than to pursue a multipronged approach to preclude the development of future threats and to protect against those threats that very much exist today.

Notes

1. Office of the Secretary of Defense, *Proliferation: Threat and Response* (Washington, D.C.: Department of Defense, January 2001), p. 78.
2. On the origins and evolution of counterproliferation, see Jason D. Ellis and Geoffrey D. Kiefer, *Combating Proliferation: Strategic Intelligence and National Policy* (forthcoming, 2003), chap. 1; Harald Muller and Mitchell Reiss, "Counterproliferation: Putting New Wine in Old Bottles," *The Washington Quarterly* 18, no. 2 (spring 1996): 145–149; Thomas G. Mahnken, "A Critical Appraisal of the Defense Counterproliferation Initiative," *National Security Studies Quarterly* 5, no. 3 (summer 1999): 91–102.
3. Gilles Andreani, "The Disarray of U.S. Non-Proliferation Policy," *Survival* 41, no. 4 (winter 1999–2000): 43. See also Brad Roberts, "Proliferation and Nonproliferation in the 1990s: Looking for the Right Lessons," *Nonproliferation Review* 6, no. 4 (fall 1999): 70–82.
4. *A National Security Strategy for a Global Age* (Washington, D.C.: U.S. Government Printing Office, December 2000), pp. 2–3.
5. Ibid., pp. 16–18.
6. *The National Security Strategy of the United States of America* (Washington, D.C.: U.S. Government Printing Office, September 2002), p. 14 (hereinafter *National Security Strategy*). See also *National Strategy to Combat Weapons of Mass Destruction* (Washington, D.C.: U.S. Government Printing Office, December 2002).

7. *National Security Strategy*, pp. 13–15.

8. Robert S. Litwak, "The New Calculus of Preemption," *Survival* 44, no. 4 (winter 2002–2003): 54–60; Jason D. Ellis, "The Gravest Danger: Proliferation, Terrorism, and the Bush Doctrine," *Monitor* 9, no. 1 (winter 2003).

9. Les Aspin, address to National Academy of Sciences on the Defense Counterproliferation Initiative, Washington, D.C., December 7, 1993.

10. Office of the Secretary of Defense, *Report of the Quadrennial Defense Review* (Washington, D.C.: Department of Defense, May 1997), p. 4 (emphasis in original). See also Paul R. S. Gebhard, "Not by Diplomacy or Defense Alone: The Role of Regional Security Strategies in U.S. Proliferation Policy," *The Washington Quarterly* 18, no. 1 (winter 1995): 167–179.

11. Center for Counterproliferation Research, *The Counterproliferation Imperative: Meeting Tomorrow's Challenges* (Washington, D.C.: National Defense University, November 2001), pp. 2, 4–6.

12. George Tenet, testimony before the Senate Select Committee on Intelligence, February 6, 2002, p. 3.

13. National Intelligence Council, "Foreign Missile Developments and the Ballistic Missile Threat 2015," unclassified summary, Washington, D.C., December 2001.

14. U.S. Government Printing Office, *The Biological & Chemical Warfare Threat*, rev. ed. (Washington, D.C.: 1999), p. 32; Office of the Secretary of Defense, *Proliferation: Threat and Response,* p. 4.

15. John A. Lauder, "Unclassified Statement for the Record by Special Assistant to the Director of Central Intelligence for Nonproliferation John A. Lauder to the Commission to Assess the Organization of the Federal Government to Combat the Proliferation of Weapons of Mass Destruction," April 29, 1999, pp. 1, 3 (hereinafter Lauder statement).

16. Office of the Secretary of Defense, *Proliferation: Threat and Response,* p. 4.

17. Lauder statement, pp. 1, 3; U.S. Government Printing Office, *The Worldwide Biological Warfare Weapons Threat* (Washington, D.C.: 2001), p. 1.

18. United Nations Special Commission, *Report to the Security Council on the Status of Disarmament and Monitoring,* S/1999/94, January 29, 1999, app. III.

19. George J. Tenet, testimony before the Senate Foreign Relations Committee, March 21, 2000. See also Director of Central Intelligence, "Unclassified Report to Congress on the Acquisition of Technology Related to Weapons of Mass Destruction and Advanced Conventional Munitions, 1 July Through 31 December 2001," Washington, D.C., January 2003.

20. Center for Counterproliferation Research, *The Counterproliferation Imperative*, p. 27.

21. *Report of the Quadrennial Defense Review,* p. 13. See also John F. Reichart, "Adversary Use of WMD: A Neglected Challenge," *Strategic Forum* 187 (December 2001); Peter R. Lavoy, Scott D. Sagan, and James J. Wirtz, eds., *Planning the Unthinkable: How New Powers Will Use Nuclear, Biological, and Chemical Weapons* (Ithaca, N.Y.: Cornell University Press, 2000).

22. *National Security Strategy*, pp. 13–14. See also Office of Homeland Security, *National Strategy for Homeland Security* (Washington, D.C.: White House, July 2002), pp. vii, ix, 9.

23. See, for example, G. John Ikenberry, "America's Imperial Ambition," *Foreign Affairs* 81, no. 5 (September/October 2002): 56–60.

24. Stephen Engelberg and Michael R. Gordon, "Intelligence Study Says North Korea Has Nuclear Bomb," *New York Times*, December 26, 1993, p. A1.

25. David E. Sanger, "In North Korea and Pakistan, Deep Roots of Nuclear Barter," *New York Times,* November 24, 2002.

26. See Ellis and Kiefer, *Combating Proliferation,* chap. 2. See also Joseph Cirincione with Jon B. Wolfsthal and Miriam Rajkumar, *Deadly Arsenals: Tracking Weapons of Mass Destruction* (Washington, D.C.: Carnegie Endowment for International Peace, 2002), pp. 207–220.

27. Thom Shanker with Terence Neilan, "Yemen Protests Seizure of North Korean Ship; Says Scuds Were Bound for Its Army," *New York Times*, December 11, 2002; Thomas E. Ricks and Peter Slevin, "Intercepted Missile Shipment Released to Yemen," *Washington Post*, December 11, 2002.

28. Office of the Secretary of Defense, *Report of the Quadrennial Defense Review* (Washington, D.C.: Department of Defense, September 30, 2001), p. 14.

29. Center for Counterproliferation Research, *The Counterproliferation Imperative,* pp. 28–31. See also *Gulf War Air Power Survey, Volume I, Part I: Planning and Command and Control* (Washington, D.C.: U.S. Government Printing Office, 1993); Department of Defense, *Final Report to Congress on the Conduct of the Persian Gulf War Pursuant to Title V of the Persian Gulf Conflict Supplemental Authorization and Personnel Benefits Act of 1991, Public Law 102-25* (Washington, D.C.: U.S. Government Printing Office, April 1992).

30. See Ellis and Kiefer, *Combating Proliferation,* chap. 7.

31. *National Security Strategy,* p. 15.

32. See Center for Counterproliferation Research, *Anthrax in America: A Chronology and Analysis of the Fall 2001 Attacks* (Washington, D.C.: National Defense University, November 2002), pp. 1–13. See also George W. Bush, *Securing the Homeland, Strengthening the Nation* (Washington, D.C.: White House, February 2002); *Public Health Security and Bioterrorism Preparedness Act of 2002,* Public Law 188, 107th Cong., 2d sess.

Jason D. Ellis is a research professor at the National Defense University's Center for Counterproliferation Research. He has published widely in journals such as *Survival, Arms Control Today, Orbis,* and *European Security.* He is also the coauthor of *Send Guns and Money: Security Assistance and U.S. Foreign Policy* (Praeger, 1997).

Ashton B. Carter

How to Counter WMD

Worst People vs. Worst Weapons

President George W. Bush has rightly proclaimed that keeping the worst weapons out of the hands of the worst people is Washington's highest national security priority. But so far, the United States has attacked the people much more vigorously than the weapons.

The war on terrorism that Washington is fighting and the war on weapons of mass destruction (WMD) that it needs to fight are related but not identical. The attacks of September 11, 2001, stimulated a comprehensive overhaul of U.S. counterterrorism practices and agencies. The United States went on the offensive in Afghanistan and around the world; border and immigration controls were tightened; emergency response was fortified; and a new Department of Homeland Security was created.

But counterproliferation policies have not been overhauled. The most significant action taken by the United States to counter WMD since September 11 has been the invasion of Iraq. Although at the time intelligence suggesting a recrudescence of Saddam Hussein's WMD programs appeared to justify the war, it now seems that the intelligence was incorrect. Meanwhile, North Korea has quadrupled its stock of plutonium, a far graver setback to counterproliferation than anything Saddam might have been pursuing. A distracted administration has left the initiative for curbing Iran's evident nuclear ambitions to two groups that failed to support the Iraq invasion: the Europeans and the UN. And it has made no new efforts to prevent nonstate actors such as terrorists from getting their hands on WMD.

The term WMD generally applies to nuclear, biological, and chemical weapons; ballistic missiles; and, more recently, "dirty bombs," ordinary explosives containing some radioactive material. But this definition is too broad. Chemical weapons are not much more lethal than conventional explosives and hardly deserve the WMD label. Similarly, long-range ballistic missiles are especially destructive only if they have a nuclear or biological warhead, and so should not be considered a separate category. Dirty bombs cause local contamination and costly cleanup but not true mass destruction; they too should be given lower priority. The primary focus of counterproliferation policy, therefore, should be nuclear and biological weapons.

In February, President Bush laid out his proposal for dealing with the spread of WMD. Some of his ideas are useful, but by and large they represent piecemeal extensions of long-standing policies. In contrast, a true overhaul of counterproliferation policy would recognize that, like the defense against terrorism, the defense against WMD must be multilayered and comprehensive. Such reforms would aim to eliminate the threat of nuclear terrorism entirely by denying fissile materials to nonstate actors and would prepare to contain the scale of the most likely forms of bioterrorism to minor outbreaks. It would revamp outdated arms control agreements, expand counterproliferation programs in the Pentagon and the Department of Homeland Security, and improve the way intelligence on WMD is collected and analyzed. It would favor countering WMD with non-nuclear rather than nuclear measures. And it would at last develop coherent strategies for heading off the two most pressing nuclear proliferation threats: those emanating from Iran and North Korea.

Seeing in 8-D

The counterproliferation toolbox contains what the Department of Defense (DOD) began calling the "8 D's" during the Clinton administration: dissuasion, disarmament, diplomacy, denial, defusing, deterrence, defenses, and destruction. Because the dynamics driving proliferation in different countries vary, no single tool is appropriate or sufficient for every case. The stakes are so high that doctrines relying on one tool to the exclusion of others are foolhardy. A sensible policy must use them all.

A crucial but underappreciated element of a successful policy is getting as many countries as possible not to develop WMD in the first place. The United States has dissuaded Germany, Japan, South Korea, Taiwan, and Turkey from going nuclear by forging stable alliances that offer these countries better security than they could achieve through unconventional weapons programs of their own. A peaceful and just world order led by the United States is the reason why only a few of the world's nearly 200 nations are proliferation "rogues." Providing security in exchange for nonproliferation is something the United States has been doing right and should keep doing right.

The benefits of these long-term bargains are also a reason to avoid so-called "coalitions of the willing." Short-term coalitions do not serve U.S. interests as well as stable partnerships. Alliance partners train to operate with U.S. forces for years, so when they go to war they are not only willing but able to contribute to combined operations. Their militaries routinely exchange threat assessments, making them more likely to share U.S. views on when the use of force is necessary. And because they can rely on the United States for their security, such countries are unlikely to adopt drastic, unilateral defensive measures such as the acquisition of WMD. For all these reasons, in the future, the United States should regard coalitions of the willing as a desperate fallback, not a preferred vehicle for U.S. leadership.

Other states have forgone WMD under disarmament agreements such as the Nonproliferation Treaty (NPT). Under these arrangements, countries agree to renounce acquiring weapons if other signatories do so as well. If existing disarmament regimes could be strengthened so as to offer credible protection for the countries that comply with them, they too could continue to play a vital role in counterproliferation.

When dissuasion and disarmament fail, American diplomacy can sometimes keep a nation from heading down the road to acquiring WMD. Recent decades offer many examples of successful counterproliferation diplomacy under a variety of circumstances: Belarus, Kazakhstan, and Ukraine after the collapse of the Soviet Union; Argentina, Brazil, and South Africa in the 1990s; and perhaps Libya this year (although the depth of Muammar al-Qaddafi's conversion remains to be seen). The Bush administration professes to be engaged in such diplomacy now with Iran and North Korea, but it has not yet presented either country with strong incentives to comply. Predictably, in the absence of significant benefits for stopping their programs or significant costs for continuing them, both countries have chosen to proceed.

Of course, some potential proliferators simply cannot be persuaded to turn back, making them candidates for denial of the necessary means. Measures such as the enforcement of stricter universal controls on the export of sensitive technology, covert action to disrupt proliferators' programs, the Bush administration's new and useful Proliferation Security Initiative (designed to intercept illicit shipments of WMD technology), and an expanded version of the highly successful Nunn-Lugar program to secure the remnants of the Soviet Union's WMD arsenal can help block some countries' WMD ambitions.

If proliferation occurs despite all the efforts to prevent it, a new set of tools comes into play. The dangers of accidental or unauthorized use of WMD in times of crisis can be defused by eliminating hair-trigger alert postures and putting special locks on nuclear weapons. Deliberate attack can be deterred by the threat of overwhelming retaliation, at least where rational, self-interested opponents are involved. Defenses ranging from chemical suits, inhalation masks, and vaccines to ballistic missile defenses, such as those being deployed today in Alaska and California, offer some protection when deterrence fails. Finally, in cases in which the use of WMD appears imminent, the precautionary destruction of weapons—what the Bush administration has popularized as "preemption"—can be a necessary last resort.

No single one of these tools holds the key to protection against WMD, nor do they represent alternative and competing "doctrines" for dealing with the problem. In fact, they complement and reinforce each other, and true counterproliferation hawks should be interested in strengthening each of the 8 D's and deploying all of them as necessary.

Eradicating WMD Terrorism

The worst potential WMD problem is nuclear terrorism, because it combines the unparalleled destructive power of nuclear weapons with the apocalyptic motivations of terrorists against which deterrence, let alone dissuasion or diplomacy, is likely to be ineffective. Luckily, however, eliminating this danger is a realistic goal. To make a nuclear weapon, terrorists must get fissile materials, either plutonium or enriched uranium. But these materials do not occur in nature, and because they require building and operating uranium enrichment facilities or plutonium production reactors and reprocessing facilities, making them will remain beyond the reach of even large and well-organized terrorist groups for the foreseeable future. Therefore, terrorists must obtain fissile materials from governments, and relatively few governments have made such materials thus far.

If terrorists could somehow get fissile materials, however, there would be little hope of relieving civilization from the prospect that any city, anywhere, could suddenly disappear in a poisonous radioactive cloud. There is no "secret" to the atomic bomb anymore; scientists have little doubt that even a moderately organized terrorist group could fashion a crude bomb if it had the material to do so. Because nuclear devices are small and hard to detect with radiation monitors, moreover, they would be exceedingly difficult to find were terrorists to try smuggling them into the United States. And unlike biological weapons, nuclear weapons have a deadly finality: one cannot get vaccinated against a nuclear fireball or take antibiotics against fallout.

Nuclear terrorism, accordingly, must be stopped at the source, and the formula for doing so is simple and clear. As John Kerry recently put it, "No material. No bomb. No nuclear terrorism." That means taking three steps. First, ensure that all governments that have plutonium and highly enriched uranium lock them up securely so they cannot be sold to, seized by, or diverted to terrorists. Second, ensure that no more bomb materials are made. And third, destroy excess stocks of these materials whenever and wherever possible. These are worthy tasks for U.S. global leadership.

The first step would be to lock up every existing lump of fissile material anywhere in the world and treat it as if it were already a bomb. The United States should take the lead in devising and promulgating universal standards for the safe custody of nuclear materials, applicable to all governments whether they are parties to the NPT or not, and establish appropriate measures for monitoring and enforcement. Every government that has nuclear weapons or reprocesses plutonium as part of its long-term energy policy should be expected to give the world reasonable assurances that its materials are safe from both seizure by outsiders and diversion by wayward insiders.

The United States should assist all governments to meet those standards through a dramatic expansion of the Nunn-Lugar programs of the Departments of Defense, State, and Energy. The United States missed a major opportunity to transform Nunn-Lugar after the September 11 attacks, while it had the attention and sympathies of the world. But it is not too late.

A reinvigorated Nunn-Lugar program should begin in Russia, where efforts to secure the staggering quantities of fissile material accumulated by the Soviet Union have been proceeding in desultory fashion for more than a decade. It is technically feasible to secure all these materials within the term of the next U.S. president, and he should make doing so a top priority. But that will require devoting greater funding to the effort and overcoming congressional restrictions and Russian hypersensitivity.

An expanded Nunn-Lugar effort should also aim to sequester all significant caches of highly enriched uranium used in research reactors worldwide, which sometimes double as "sleeper cells" of nuclear terrorism. It should offer Pakistan the same kind of assistance as Russia and draw up plans for the complete and verifiable elimination of WMD programs in Iraq and Libya now and in Iran and North Korea as soon as circumstances permit.

The second step should be to stop adding to the world's stock of fissile materials, by preventing additional governments, especially those hostile to the United States, from making plutonium or enriching uranium. This will require establishing a clear U.S. strategy—diplomatic at first, but coercive if necessary—for the complete and verifiable elimination of Iran's and North Korea's nuclear programs. The United States should also seek agreement that no more fissile material for weapons purposes will be produced anywhere, including in India, Pakistan, and Israel. Addressing the inherent risks associated with nuclear power reactors, U.S. policy should oppose new entrants into the uranium-enrichment and plutonium-reprocessing markets. Research or isotope-production reactors should cease the practice of using weapons-grade uranium fuel.

The third and final step would be to reduce, wherever possible, existing stocks of weapons materials. The long-stalled "blending down" of Russian bomb-grade uranium to reactor fuel and the disposition of excess plutonium, for example, should be accelerated.

Bioterrorism presents a completely different challenge. It cannot be eradicated, but it can be contained. Unlike nuclear weapons, biological weapons contain no single critical ingredient that can be sequestered, and the technology to breed pathogens and turn them into weapons is widespread in both the scientific community and in industry. The underlying science of biological weapons is progressing rapidly, multiplying opportunities to manipulate organisms for good or ill. Tomorrow's biological weapons may well feature engineered pathogens not found in nature.

Still, the president could take steps to contain the danger of bioterrorism so any attempt would end in the would-be mass terrorist's utter failure. Since it would take days for victims of a biological attack to sicken, a quick and effective public health response, together with advance stockpiling of medications and selective immunization, would dramatically reduce the impact of a bioattack. A reasonable goal for the president would be to ensure that professionals in the Department of Health and Human Services could certify that the nation is immune to mass destruction by today's common bioagents.

Anciens Regimes

Much can also be done to strengthen the multilateral regimes intended to curb the use or production of WMD. The NPT has been disparaged in the United States in recent years because, it is said, the "bad guys" can ignore it with impunity (since it has inadequate verification and enforcement provisions) and the "good guys" would be good even without the agreement. This critique is wrong for two reasons.

First, with regard to proliferation, the world does not divide neatly into good guys and bad guys. There is a substantial "in between" category of countries that could be tempted to acquire WMD but might be coaxed out of it. Belarus, Kazakhstan, and Ukraine chose to forsake the nuclear weapons they inherited from the Soviet Union, for example; Argentina and Brazil mutually agreed to give up their nuclear programs; South Korea and Taiwan preferred U.S. protection over developing their own arsenals; and South Africa, after it changed regimes, lost its sense of external threat and its need to protect itself with WMD. Gaining greater international acceptance by signing the NPT and abandoning their nuclear ambitions was a key factor in all of these countries' decisions.

Second, even if bad guys disregard the NPT, such agreements are useful, albeit indirectly. If it became necessary for Washington to lead action against a rogue, the international consensus embodied by the NPT would help the United States marshal the support of other nations.

Even though the NPT has considerable value in its current form, its provisions can and should be strengthened. One of its vexing weaknesses, which dates to the era when the treaty was negotiated, is the concept of the "peaceful atom," which allows states to produce certain nuclear materials for peaceful ends. The NPT permits all signatories to enrich uranium (in order to make fuel for power reactors) and reprocess plutonium (an inevitable byproduct in "spent" fuel removed from the reactor after it is used up), provided they declare what they are doing and submit to periodic inspections.

This is problematic, however, because under the guise of a peaceful power reactor program a nation can come very close to having a bomb. All the owner of a complete fuel cycle needs to do to make weapons in short order is withdraw from the NPT, kick out inspectors, and turn enriched uranium or plutonium into bombs. Both Iran and North Korea have sought to exploit this situation. In an age of terrorism, the creation of new fissile material, in any guise, poses a lasting danger.

To plug this loophole, the United States should champion a revision of the peaceful atom concept, encouraging nuclear power where it is needed but opposing any new nations from operating enrichment or reprocessing facilities. In return, the nations where such facilities exist would offer reliable fuel services (provision of enriched fuel and disposition of spent fuel) at reasonable prices to all nations that wish to use nuclear reactors for electrical power generation and that forgo their own complete fuel cycle. Other steps to strengthen the NPT could include stiffening inspection and enforcement provisions and making withdrawal from the treaty an automatic trigger for international action.

The Pentagon's Role

In the 1990s, the term "counterproliferation" was used in the Pentagon to signify that contending with WMD was an important mission in the post–Cold War world. Nuclear retaliation for use of WMD against U.S. troops was always understood to be an option, but not an attractive one, since it was not clear that all potential opponents could be deterred. If they proved not to be, presidents deserved a better menu of responses. Various programs were thus created to develop non-nuclear counters to WMD on the battlefield, including chemical and biological warning sensors, improved vaccines against bioattack, individual and collective protective coverings, decontamination systems, special munitions for attacking and neutralizing enemy WMD, radiochemical forensics, and active defenses such as ballistic missile defense.

Over time, these programs were expanded to include the protection of rear areas, such as ports and airfields in the theater of war, against chemical and biological attack. Subsequently, these technologies were recognized as useful to the protection of the U.S. homeland from WMD attack. Thus, by September 11, DOD was recognized as the lead agency in the federal government for developing and fielding technology for countering WMD.

Today, the Pentagon is quite rightly devoting a portion of its growing budget to "transforming" the military to anticipate future threats and develop dramatically new technologies. But the core of the effort remains long-range precision strike, close integration of intelligence information with operations, and closer collaboration among Army, Navy, and Air Force units. These are worthy goals for conventional warfare, but they have not been matched by any comparable counter-WMD effort, with the sole exception of missile defense. Counterproliferation programs at DOD remain small and scattered throughout the department. Missile defense spending now reaches about $10 billion per year, but the other counterproliferation programs amount to only a few billion dollars out of the $420 billion defense budget—far too small a fraction given the importance of the mission. (Likewise, WMD-related projects get only a fraction of the new homeland security agencies' $40 billion budget, even though WMD are the homeland's greatest threat.)

Another important question for counterproliferation is whether Washington's own nuclear policy influences the spread of WMD elsewhere in the world. On the one hand, it is entirely unlikely that Pyongyang's or Tehran's calculations, let alone al Qaeda's, hinge on whether the United States has 6,000, 3,500, or 2,200 deployed strategic weapons (the numbers permitted under the last three rounds of U.S.–Russian nuclear arms agreements), retains tactical nuclear weapons deployed in Europe, forswears nuclear retaliation for chemical or biological weapons use, or develops new types of nuclear weapons.

On the other hand, it would be easier to counter the WMD ambitions of Iran and North Korea with international support, and defeating al Qaeda absolutely depends on foreign governments' cooperation in intelligence and law enforcement. To the extent that international support for these U.S.–led efforts is influenced by U.S. nuclear policy, therefore, a growing reliance by Washington on nuclear weapons for its security would complicate its efforts to marshal international cooperation against WMD terrorism and overhaul nuclear arms control regimes. Moreover, the decisions of in-between states are probably strongly shaped by their perception of the nuclear "order" that the United States represents and leads, partly by example.

U.S. nuclear weapons are a deterrent against the use of WMD by others, of course, and a means of destroying WMD preemptively. But the United States has another effective tool of deterrence and destruction: its unmatched conventional military power. (Terrorists, for their part, are unlikely to be deterred by any threats of punishment at all.) So Washington should carefully weigh the marginal benefits of new nuclear capabilities for deterrence and destruction against their diplomatic cost to the overall counterproliferation effort.

Washington's recent efforts to explore a new type of earth-penetrating nuclear warhead, ostensibly to destroy deeply buried WMD facilities, for example, are ill advised. The military rationale for this move is weak, since locating such targets would be very difficult in the first place, the United States already has earth-penetrating nuclear weapons, and the costs of crossing the nuclear threshold would be high.

Instead, DOD should seek to widen the already huge gap between its conventional military capabilities and those of other nations, develop better non-nuclear counters to WMD, and use transformational technology to narrow the range of circumstances in which the United States would resort to nuclear weapons. With such an approach, nuclear weapons would play an enduring but background role as a deterrent of last resort.

Overhauling Intelligence

In the course of his work on ballistic missile proliferation in the 1990s, Donald Rumsfeld became convinced that in most cases intelligence on WMD programs is likely to be inadequate. Given the stakes, he concluded, the United States must assume the worst in formulating its counterproliferation policies. This logic, encapsulated in the maxim that the "absence of evidence is not evidence of absence," drove the Rumsfeld Commission report that paved the way for the Bush administration's national missile defense program. Intelligence about when an intercontinental ballistic missile threat might originate in Iran or North Korea was uncertain enough, the thinking ran, that the United States would be imprudent to rely on a missile defense that would not be ready for deployment for a few years (the Clinton administration policy). Rather, it needed one immediately. The need to act urgently against WMD, even on the basis of scanty evidence, lay behind the case for preemptive war in Iraq.

It would obviously be preferable to avoid such worst-case calculations again. But they cannot be dismissed out of hand, since WMD activities are inherently difficult to monitor. It is comparatively easy to keep tabs on the size and disposition of armies, the numbers and types of conventional weaponry such as tanks and aircraft, and even the operational doctrines and plans of military establishments (since these generally need to be rehearsed to be effective). By their nature, in contrast, WMD concentrate destructive power in small packages and tight groups. Chemical and especially biological weapons can be manufactured in small-scale facilities. And although plutonium-based nuclear weapons require large and relatively conspicuous reactors and reprocessing facilities, uranium-based weapons can be produced in modest facilities that lack distinctive external features.

A crucial question, therefore, is whether adequate intelligence is likely to be available to make counterproliferation efforts effective. If the spread of WMD is by nature simply too difficult to monitor, then the world is doomed to a perpetual state of panic. But it bears remembering that the uncertainties of the 1950s, an era with comparable fears of a "missile gap," were largely dispelled by the invention of satellite reconnaissance. Emerging intelligence technologies might help improve the current situation as well.

Cutting-edge forensics, for example, can analyze material samples for traces of suspicious chemicals, biological material, or radionuclides. The samples can be obtained from air-sniffing planes or by plucking a leaf from a bush or wiping a handkerchief across a countertop. From a distance, a laser light shined on the plume of a smokestack might even reveal something about the plume's composition and thus the activities underway within the building. Tiny unattended ground sensors can be placed by hand or dropped covertly from unmanned aerial vehicles into suspicious locales; they can be networked with cell-phone technology and even made mobile by attaching them to robots, animals, or birds. "Tagging," the covert placement of identifying features, transmitters, or chemical markers on objects destined for WMD facilities, can also help monitor suspect programs. And a revolution is underway in close-in signals intelligence, which may help penetrate and exploit a WMD program's cell phones, laptop computers, local area networks, and other information infrastructure. Information from these specialized WMD-specific techniques can be combined with the usual types of intelligence from intercepted communications, defectors, and the occasional spy.

Nevertheless, no technology in the offing holds the promise of lifting the veil of WMD activities as completely as satellite photography did for the Soviet Union's nuclear missile and bomber programs. Accurate intelligence on WMD thus needs to be enhanced by three additional ingredients, one a matter of international policy and two matters of intelligence community management.

The first, paradoxically, is active cooperation by the parties under surveillance. Just as the Soviet Union eventually accepted satellite overflight of its territory, so too will potential proliferators have to allow greater access to their territory, facilities, and scientists. At a minimum, governments that wish to avoid suspicion—and thus coercion or even preemptive attack—will need to allow the kind of access promised to UN inspectors in Iraq in the winter of 2002–3, including the right to inspect facilities by surprise, take material samples for forensic analysis, and install monitoring equipment. This must be complemented by data declarations, document searches, and interviews of scientists. These are tall orders, of course, since they involve compromises of sovereignty and legitimate military secrecy for the nations inspected and rely on these governments' cooperation. But they are the only way North Korea's WMD ambitions will be verifiably eliminated, for example, or Iran's nuclear power activities fully safeguarded.

At the same time, moreover, there must be a shift of the burden of proof from the international community to the party under suspicion. For a cooperative inspection system to succeed, it must be the responsibility of the inspected party to dispel—not the responsibility of the United States or the international community to prove—concerns that dangerous WMD activities are underway.

The other two ingredients of better WMD intelligence require changes in Washington. Since proliferation is essentially a scientific activity, the intelligence community needs to increase the size and technical training of its workforce. Because intelligence agencies have difficulty recruiting and retaining top talent with more lucrative prospects in private industry, they need to forge better links with the outside scientific community so that advice and insight are "on call." This availability would have the additional benefit of aiding collection, since an essential "open" source of proliferation intelligence comes from monitoring scientific literature, the training and movement of foreign scientists, and commerce in scientific equipment.

Finally, a closer link between intelligence and action always spurs improvements in both collection and analysis. Since September 11, the counterterrorism intelligence effort has moved from producing papers characterizing terrorist groups to supporting operations to interdict terrorists. By all accounts, the intelligence community has risen to the challenge of producing "actionable" intelligence on terrorists. Similarly, an overhauled U.S. counterproliferation program based on the 8 D's will stimulate the intelligence community to focus on the problem of producing solid intelligence on WMD.

A comprehensive and aggressive effort to improve counterproliferation intelligence can start to make headway, but only if the president decides to make it a top priority. Americans regret that their government did not overhaul its counterterrorism capabilities years before the September 11 attacks, neglecting reforms that seemed tragically obvious after the World Trade Center was destroyed. Now, U.S. counterproliferation programs need an overhaul. It will be unforgivable if that too has to wait until after another catastrophe.

Ashton (Ash) B. Carter served as assistant secretary of defense in the Clinton administration and is co-director of the Preventive Defense Project at Harvard's Kennedy School of Government. Dr. Carter received bachelor degrees in physics and medieval history from Yale University, summa cum laude, Phi Beta Kappa. He received his Ph.D. in theoretical physics from Oxford University, where he was a Rhodes scholar. He is a member of the Aspen Strategy Group.

Chapter 4.2

Gaps in Framework

Chen Kane

Gaps in the International Framework for Combating WMD Terrorism

The September 11, 2001 terrorist attacks on the United States coupled with attacks such as the ones in Bali, Madrid and London caused the international community to focus on the issue of terrorism threats with renewed intensity. In this context, the threat of potential weapons of mass destruction (WMD) terrorism gained revived attention.

The long-standing and traditional international arrangements for fighting the threat of WMD were crafted and negotiated in the years since 1925.[1] Over time, the international community developed agreed "rules of the game" enshrined in treaties and norms, as well as recognized signaling of states' intentions. In some cases, dedicated channels for communication were established, such as United States–Soviet Union (Russia, today) and India–Pakistan "hot-lines," to prevent unintended nuclear war. However, the international community has been caught completely off guard since 2001 by mounting evidence that WMD is no longer exclusively in the hands of nation states.

The New WMD Threats

The appearance of new actors and threats in the proliferation theater such as terrorist groups, black-market proliferation networks, the spread of enrichment technology and "rogue" individuals revealed a much more complex world. Traditional measures developed to address the old threats are widely now acknowledged to be important but insufficient.

Existing international arrangements addressing WMD have been negotiated and implemented mostly as part of arms control treaties. The parties have intended the agreements to deter the use of WMD by states; constrain the deployment and testing of WMD; and promote disarmament. Formal arrangements, however, apply only to states and even so, just to those states who are signatories to such treaties.

Three challenges sharply bring into focus the new threats and reveal the limits of existing arrangements to address the threat of WMD terrorism: (1) outdated assumptions on non-proliferation; (2) the emergence of non-state actors; and (3) the increasing availability of WMD-related technology and knowledge.

Outdated Assumptions on Non-Proliferation

Non-proliferation regimes have served as the basis for cooperation in many parts of our daily life such as in the peaceful use of nuclear energy, biotechnology and academic collaboration.[2] Since 1925, non-proliferation regimes have provided the basis for preventing WMD proliferation, reducing the WMD dangers and preventing international anarchy.

However, the convergence of several developments has challenged the integrity of these regimes. Some of these challenges are old—such as the international community's failure to agree on measures to verify and enforce the Biological Weapons Convention, or the decade-long deadlock in the Conference on Disarmament, the single forum for disarmament-negotiating of the international community. Others are new.

The nuclear non-proliferation regime, which has been considered to be the most effective among the WMD regimes, has seen repeated challenges and suffered significant weakening. These challenges include, but are not limited to, North Korea's withdrawal from the Non-Proliferation Treaty (NPT) and its recent nuclear test, as well as Iran's 20-year defiance of its treaty obligations.

Soaring oil prices and the threat of global warming have revived interest in nuclear power as an energy alternative in industrialized and developing states. Australia, Indonesia, Malaysia, Algeria, Saudi Arabia and Egypt, to name only a few, are currently re-examining their past decisions not to acquire nuclear energy technology. In some cases, this economic motivation has encouraged countries to consider acquiring uranium enrichment capabilities. The renewed interest in enrichment technology challenges the nuclear non-proliferation regime for at least two reasons.

First, the technology for enriching uranium fuel for use in nuclear reactors, with few modifications, can be rapidly converted to develop nuclear weapons. Second, highly-enriched uranium reactor fuel in a larger number of countries, some of which are unstable and have active terrorist groups, raise the prospect of it being stolen or targeted for attack by terrorists.

These developments are symptoms of a growing international weariness with the current non-proliferation system. Many countries believe the regimes no longer address modern geopolitical realities.

The Emergence of Non-State Actors

The fact that groups or even individuals today can create or gain access to WMD materials remains unaddressed by the traditional international arrangements. Aum Shinrikyo, the Japanese religious cult that killed twelve people in a 1995 nerve gas attack on the Tokyo subway system, is an example of a terrorist group interested in WMD. Another example is the Chechen group that created disorder and panic in 1995 by placing a radioactive source (cesium-137) in Moscow's Izmailovsky Park and inviting a television news crew to the location.

Under the category of local threats also falls the potential for theft or diversion of WMD materials by workers (or with their cooperation) in facilities owned by states or private companies. Such facilities are also prime targets for terrorist attacks.

On the global scale of WMD threats by non-state actors, we now know that al Qaeda has been interested in acquiring WMD. A laboratory under construction found near Kandahar, Afghanistan appears to have been intended for developing biological weapons such as anthrax. Evidence recovered elsewhere in Afghanistan suggested that al Qaeda was conducting crude chemical warfare experiments on dogs.

We also know that al Qaeda tried during the mid-1990s to acquire nuclear materials and know-how from Africa, Europe and Russia. A 25-page document with information about nuclear weapons, including a design for a nuclear bomb, was found at a former al Qaeda facility in Kabul, Afghanistan. In August 2001, several Pakistani nuclear scientists met with bin Laden in Afghanistan to discuss WMD; they were subsequently indicted and later convicted by the Pakistani government.

More recently, a call was made in an audio released by the al Qaeda leader in Iraq, Abu Hamza al-Muhajir, for scientists (particularly, nuclear scientists and ordinance engineers) to join his group's efforts against United States and Coalition forces, advising them that the large United States bases in Iraq are the "best experimental fields for your knowledge."[3]

Another dimension to the emergence of a new WMD threat by non-state actors is A.Q. Khan's black-market network. A.Q. Khan, known as the father of the Pakistani nuclear program, sold centrifuge parts and other nuclear technology to several countries, including North Korea, Libya and Iran, through a covert commercial network he headed for 20 years.[4] The network was spread over three continents, and involved middle-men in at least 20 countries.

The traditional non-proliferation tools—treaties, sanctions by international bodies, or even military actions authorized by the U.N. Security Council are all irrelevant when dealing with non-state actors. Existing international measures have limited capability to prevent WMD and no enforcement powers. Today, terrorist groups are organized as cells of loose networks with very little centralization or connection between them and defined geographic territory (a "home address") upon which to retaliate. Groups like al Qaeda have no reasons to be too impressed by resolutions adopted by international organizations condemning their activities or to worry that these organizations can realistically act against them.

Increasing Availability of WMD-Related Technology and Knowledge

The third feature of the current proliferation environment is the growing availability of WMD-related information and technology. The technology for developing nuclear, chemical, biological and radiological weapons is available from open sources. The Internet, declassified old documents and "how-to" WMD books allow individuals, organizations and states to gather information needed to fashion crude but lethal weapons.

The fact that individuals can master the technology of WMD is not a new fact. This was first proved in the 1960s during an experiment by the United States nuclear national laboratory at Lawrence Livermore. Two freshly-minted Ph.D. physic graduates with no nuclear weapons background were asked to produce a credible atomic bomb design from scratch, without access to classified information. After a year and a half, they managed to do so. The nuclear laboratory that administered the experiment concluded that the design, if constructed and tested, would have as much explosive force as the weapon that had devastated Hiroshima in August 1945.[5]

The availability of WMD technology has spread much further since the 1960s because of the Internet and the development of digital and mobile communications. The Internet—with its e-mails, blogs and chat room technologies—provides an inexpensive, anonymous, geographically unbounded, and largely unregulated virtual haven for terrorist groups. Terrorists can easily exploit these technologies to anonymously disseminate propaganda, recruit new members, raise funds and provide instruction on weapons and tactics and coordinate operations. These tools also enable terrorist groups to acquire or quickly locate necessary knowledge, experts and track vulnerable targets.

What Has Been Done

The inadequacy of traditional non-proliferation arrangements in addressing the political, technological, and preparedness challenges that countries now confront in the form of a WMD terrorist threat, has brought the international community to seriously reassess its approach. Most of the new measures are still in the formative phase of being implemented, thus their effectiveness is hard to gauge. Nevertheless, it is useful to trace the trends in these new measures, which include the assembly of "like-minded" coalitions of the willing, the emergence of non-state actors as problem-solvers, and the adoption of new measures aimed at fixing existing international arrangements.

"Like-Minded" Coalitions of the Willing

The most high-profile example of a like-minded coalition is the Proliferation Security Initiative (PSI). In 2003, the initiative was launched to promote international cooperation, interdict WMD-related shipments, and stop proliferation finance. The PSI consists of 15 core countries, including the United States, Russia, Japan, France, Germany and the United Kingdom. An additional 60 countries have agreed to cooperate on an ad hoc basis.

Assessing the success of the PSI is problematic because participating countries have not released details of interdiction operations. It is claimed that such secrecy is necessary to protect sensitive operational intelligence. United States officials cite successful joint interdiction missions in Europe, the Middle East and Asia to stop the transfer of WMD and missile technology. In one instance, cooperation is said to have prevented the export to Iran of dangerous equipment and dual-use materials for its missile program. On another occasion, a PSI partner country stopped the export of heavy water-related nuclear equipment to Iran.[6]

Another example of like-minded parties' initiative is the creation of The Global Partnership against the Spread of Weapons of Mass Destruction by the G-8 during the Kananaskis Summit in 2002. The initiative was created to seek additional resources and partners for nonproliferation, disarmament, counter-proliferation and nuclear safety projects in Russia and former Soviet states. Its current projects concentrate on assisting Russia in destroying its chemical weapons, decommissioning its nuclear submarines, safeguarding its fissile materials, and employing its former weapons scientists.

Presidents Bush and Putin announced a new program on July 15, 2006 at the G-8 Summit in St. Petersburg; the *Global Initiative to Combat Nuclear Terrorism.* The two leaders urged like-minded countries to expand collaborative efforts to "combat nuclear terrorism on a determined and systematic basis."[7] The parties to the initiative include the world's five leading nuclear powers (United States, Russia, China, Britain and France), plus Italy, Japan, Canada, China, Turkey, Kazakhstan, Australia and Morocco. They met for the first time in October 2006 in Rabat, Morocco, and signed two agreements asserting common principles and "terms of reference."[8] The initiative is aimed at providing guidelines for tracking radioactive materials, ensuring the safety of nuclear facilities, and combating illicit trafficking that could deliver nuclear materials into the hands of terrorists. The parties to the initiative hope to achieve these objectives by curtailing terrorist financing and improving safeguards for storing and transporting radioactive materials.

The Global Threat Reduction Initiative (GTRI) was launched in 2004 to foster cooperation between the United States, Russia and the International Atomic Energy Agency

(IAEA). This initiative represents an important contribution to the reduction of the WMD terrorist threat. The initiative aims to accelerate efforts to repatriate or secure nuclear fuel around the world and to convert nuclear reactors to use low-enriched uranium (LEU) instead of highly enriched uranium (HEU), the latter being a key component for making nuclear weapons and an attractive target for a potential terrorist attack.

Under the GTRI, from 2004 to 2006, six research reactors around the world were converted to operate with LEU instead of HEU; ten shipments took place to return to Russia more than 132 kilograms of Russian-origin HEU and more than 81 kilograms of United States-originated HEU was returned to the United States. Further, physical protection upgrades have been completed in over 40 countries, along with the securing of over 420 potentially vulnerable radiological sites containing over 6 million curies (enough to produce approximately 6,000 dirty bombs).[9]

Other programs, primarily led by the United States, are the Container Security Initiative and Megaports. Under the Container Security Initiative, the United States works with 26 host nations' customs authorities to establish security criteria used in identifying and screening high-risk containers before they ship to United States ports. A complementary program is the Megaports initiative, which is aimed at enhancing ports' ability to screen cargo using radiation detection equipment. Host country personnel are trained to use the equipment to screen for nuclear or radioactive materials and share data with the United States on detentions and seizures they may make. The program currently operates in six countries and is being implemented in nearly 30 other countries.

The Emergence of Non-State Actors as Problem-Solvers

Just as non-state actors have emerged as offenders, they have also shown themselves to be assets as problem-solvers. Individuals, non-governmental organizations (NGOs) and groups take an active part in addressing the WMD threat. One of the most prominent examples is the billionaire businessman Ted Turner and former U.S. Senator Sam Nunn's Nuclear Threat Initiative (NTI). The NTI is a non-profit organization that directly contributes to reducing the WMD terrorism threats; its activities and achievements prove that private citizens, NGOs and partnerships can make a difference and complement or supplement governments, when the latter failed, unable or unwilling to act. Some of NTI's most noted achievements in addressing the WMD threat include the removal of nuclear fuel from Kazakhstan (two dozen nuclear bombs' worth of material which had been abandoned after the closing of a nuclear reactor); a commitment of $5 million that sealed a deal between Yugoslavia, the United States, Russia and the IAEA to move out of the reach of terrorists half-a-bomb's worth of enriched uranium that sat poorly guarded outside Belgrade; and the sponsorship of a National Academy of Sciences study that outlined ways to manage the practice of "safe science"—under which the global bio-science community ensures that appropriate norms and practices are established to minimize the potential for misuse of biotechnology. The study prompted the creation of a new United States government advisory board to develop guidelines for the bio-security of life sciences research and a code of conduct for scientists and lab workers.[10]

Another example is the billionaire investor and philanthropist Warren Buffett who pledged $50 million to start a global nuclear fuel bank. His offer is contingent on receipt of a matching pledge of $100 million coming from the 141 members of the IAEA. The objective of the program is to enable the IAEA to provide nuclear fuel to any country that wants to use it for peaceful purposes in nuclear power plants. Such a fuel bank would discourage countries from developing their own individual nuclear programs and industries. The bank would also ensure supplies of LEU for nuclear power plants rather than HEU, which can be used by a state that decides to "go nuclear," and represents a desirable target for terrorists. By concentrating global supplies of nuclear fuel in fewer places, the possibility and probability it would reach the hands of terrorists will be reduced.

Another initiative that falls into this category is a proposal by the Harvard/Sussex Program on CBW Disarmament and Arms Limitation to make the development, retention, acquisition, and transfer of biological and chemical weapons a crime under international law. The group formulated a draft treaty that augments the Biological Weapons Convention of 1972 and the Chemical Weapons Convention of 1993. It builds on national court's jurisdiction over individuals on their national territory, regardless of their nationality or official capacity, who order, direct, or knowingly render substantial assistance to the use of biological or chemical weapons anywhere.[11]

New Measures Aimed at Fixing Existing International Arrangements

The last five years have seen new international efforts and proposals aimed at strengthening existing measures against WMD being obtained by terrorists. An important measure was adopted in April 2004 by the U.N. Security Council Resolution 1540. The resolution requires member states to establish, enact and enforce national legal and regulatory measures to prevent proliferation of WMD, their delivery systems and related materials, as well as establish financial controls to prevent the financing of such transactions.

The resolution established a committee charged with monitoring and reporting on the progress of implementing the resolution. As of October 2006, over 130 states submitted their first report, most of which were reviewed by the Committee and requests for clarifications were sent to the reporting states.

Other measures aimed at strengthening states' laws and enforcement mechanisms include the criminalizing of WMD terrorism under treaty law in the *U.N. Convention on the Suppression of Terrorist Bombings,*[12] and the *International Convention for the Suppression of Acts of Nuclear Terrorism.* The latter was adopted in 2005 by the U.N. General Assembly. It provides a legal basis for international cooperation in investigating, prosecuting, and extraditing those who commit terror acts involving radioactive materials or a nuclear device.

In September 2006, the United Nations General Assembly adopted the *United Nations Global Counter-Terrorism Strategy.* The strategy, a resolution and an annexed plan of action—is a global instrument aimed at enhancing national, regional and international counter-terrorism efforts. This is the first time that all U.N. members have agreed to a common strategic approach in fighting terrorism. It sends a clear message to all that terrorism is unacceptable in all its shapes, forms and manifestations, and commits all UN members to take practical steps individually and collectively to prevent and combat it.[13]

The World Health Organization's (WHO) four-layer strategy to respond to deliberate use of biological and chemical agents or radioactive material is an example of measures that aim to address crisis management and prevention. The strategy covers areas such as international and national preparedness, global alert and response, and treatment for selected diseases and toxins.

Under these programs, the WHO has seen an increased number of requests by states for technical assistance on national chemical and biological weapons preparedness. The WHO has published updated guidelines about health aspects, preparedness for, and response to the use of biological and chemical weapons. The WHO also established the "Global Outbreak Alert and Response Network" that provides an operational framework to link the expertise and skills needed to keep the international community constantly on alert for outbreaks and ready to respond.

International cooperation and legal activity has also begun to address the ease of assembling technological components for WMD. International activity intended to improve national control and regulation of, access to, and transfer of WMD materials began within the Australia Group[14] and through the Biological Weapons Convention. Multilateral initiatives like these contribute to those international efforts designed to protect WMD materials from malevolent appropriation.

New measures have also been undertaken under the auspices of the IAEA. In 2002, the IAEA established the Nuclear Security Program to assist member states in improving the safety and security of nuclear and radiological materials residing in their territories. Under this program, the IAEA helps states to strengthen their border monitoring and to search for and dispose of radioactive sources. Another measure adopted by the IAEA member states is the 2005 amendment to the *Convention on the Physical Protection of Nuclear Material*. The convention was amended to create a legal obligation for nations to secure nuclear materials during transport or storage, and criminalize acts of sabotage against nuclear facilities. The IAEA has also worked on strengthening its Emergency Response Center capabilities for reacting to radiological emergencies following a terrorist attack.

What Remains to Be Done

The common thread to all these new measures to forestall the new WMD threats is the need for coordinated action. No country can address the magnitude, complexity and severity of WMD terrorism on its own. However, coordinated action is very hard to achieve as it requires countries, more than ever before, to part with more of their sovereignty, tendency towards secrecy, and compartmentalization on the dearest of subjects—a state's national security.

The steps that need to be taken must cover two fronts, the WMD perpetrator and those who seek to defend against WMD, with counter-proliferation measures such as intelligence and early warning, crisis prevention, crisis management, consequence management and response.

Intelligence and Early Warning

In combating non-state actors, the key to success is good, actionable intelligence on individuals and groups. One significant area is identifying who are the most likely proliferators and perpetrators, their objectives, and whether the threat they pose can be met or deflected. Although it is a challenging task, there is a "work flow" to acquiring WMD, which if properly understood, can serve as a map for how to gather necessary intelligence on the source, origin and avenues to weapon materials and devices.[15] With proper inter- and intra-intelligence cooperation, an intelligence database can be created which would, when the need arises for pinpointing the origin of stolen or transferred material, identify individuals who had access to it and facilitate the materials recovery.

In addition to the creation of such an intelligence database, more and better systems technologies should be developed for tracking materials and covert activities indicative of WMD development, production or transport. There also needs to be a better understanding of what forensic science can and cannot do. Although forensic identification and attribution of nuclear, biological, chemical and radiological materials has recently been considered the new panacea for orchestrating an effective response to a WMD attack, or deterring such a threat, it has many limitations which should be fully understood. Two examples serve to point its limitations.

First, most chemical, biological or radiological materials would be impossible to trace back to their origin. Second, many of today's nuclear states are quite reluctant to share and supply forensic information on their nuclear material's isotopic ratios, chemical compositions and physical structures. Without such information, the database would lack essential information needed to trace the material used in a WMD terror attack back to the state that supposedly transferred it. Nevertheless, even a partial database has merit, as it could enable us to short-list the suspects.

Crisis Prevention

Nuclear fissile material has traditionally been subjected to strenuous protective measures by countries. However, when the Cold War ended, thousands of highly skilled scientists and engineers previously involved in the Soviet Union's weapons programs were laid-off or found their incomes drastically reduced. Another legacy of the Cold War is the disturbing reports, albeit unsubstantiated, of missing Soviet nuclear weapons. Pledges to assist Russia and the former Soviet states in their efforts to disarm existing WMD stockpiles, secure materials and provide alternative employment opportunities for their scientists need to be expedite and acted upon now. But above and beyond these existing efforts, we must fully exploit diplomatic means, foreign policy and treaties to promote WMD nonproliferation, strengthen international law enforcement, and counter the conditions that foster terrorism.

Experts are also concerned that terrorists could develop a crude device to disperse radiological material from commonly available sources used in every day life (a "dirty bomb"). The number of such radioactive sources around the world is vast. Such materials are used to identify cracks in buildings, pipelines and structures; deliver medical treatments in hospitals and for cold-store food preservation. There are a large number of unwanted radioactive materials sources, many of them abandoned, others simply unregistered and "orphaned" of any regulatory control. In many countries, the regulatory oversight of radiation sources is weak. Better material control programs worldwide are needed to prevent weapons materials from reaching terrorists, along with expanded border protection programs to intercept WMD materials.

Further, on the prevention side, issues related to better understanding WMD and preventing terrorism should be more widely taught and incorporated into undergraduate and graduate level classes. Awareness and education are key first steps to prevention today and toward ensuring the next generation of qualified professionals is adequately trained to address WMD challenges.

Crisis Management

More resources and focus should be put on specialized training for national security policy-makers, practitioners and first-responders (fire, law enforcement, medical and emergency management personnel). Although much effort has been invested on the local level, most of this new experience has not been shared on the national, regional or global levels. As past experiences with large-scale natural disasters like Katrina or the Indian Ocean tsunami of 2004 or conventional terrorist attacks that have became a daily phenomenon have shown, rarely can a state manage such a major catastrophe by itself. Even in the U.S., which is considered one of the most advanced states in terms of WMD terrorism preparedness, a recent survey of emergency room doctors in Chicago illustrates the urgent need for better education and awareness of likely WMD terror attack. The survey was taken during 2005 with 36 physicians and 37 doctors in residency at Resurrection Medical Center. The respondents gave incorrect answers on 66% of the chemical weapons-related questions and on over half the biological agents-related questions.[16]

The development of detection technologies should be expedited in a coordinated fashion, capitalizing on existing technologies, agreed standards and identified real needs. The first crucial step after any WMD attack or incident would be to identify the material correctly and quickly. Research efforts should therefore be accelerated for developing new sensor systems and improving existing systems for detecting, identifying and locating WMD materials, and bringing online devices and technologies for disabling and disarming weapons of mass destruction.

Consequences Management

Consequence management is composed of those essential services that mitigate or ameliorate the effects of a WMD terror attack. Many lessons can and should be learned and shared from United States experiences dealing with 9/11, Hurricanes Katrina and Rita, international efforts after the 2004 tsunami, Japanese experience with the Aum Shinrikyo's sarin attack and Israel's experience preparing for WMD scud attacks during the 1991 Gulf War.

These combined experiences with conventional terrorist attacks and natural disasters all called upon coordinated efforts between firefighting, rescue and recovery operations, medical treatment, emergency transportation, law enforcement, securing buildings and infrastructure, and providing clean water and food. After a WMD terror attack, additional capabilities would suddenly be required: specialized mass-casualty medical triage, treatment and prophylaxis, decontamination, quarantine or evacuation, environmental analysis, dissemination of public information, and specialized psychological care.

Sharing past experience and current ongoing preparation will also allow for early identification of real decontamination capabilities, the location of national antidote reserves, and how they would be streamed into a crisis zone, thereby requiring effective lines of communication to gather information, construct a system using that information, and disseminate it up and down among and across organizations. Preparing for proper communication between the government and the public could help minimize panic, facilitate smooth evacuation or quarantine, provide instructions and information to victims and the likely large numbers of "worried well," and enable a more rapid restoration of confidence, order and civic well-being of an affected area.[17]

Crisis management requires intensified planning and preparation. "Gaming" and simulation exercises over time create well-established working relationships and a willingness to place priority on cooperation instead of on interagency, intergovernmental and national turf battles. Cooperation is therefore essential element to planning for and properly responding to a WMD attack.

Response

On the response level, international efforts should further explore the concept and possibilities for "deterrence" with regard to a WMD terror attack. The idea of using or threatening preventive war, or the ability to trace material back to its original state represent creative first steps for preventing WMD use. Both, however, have many moral and practical limitations.

Another measure that should be taken to strengthen the international community response capabilities is the adoption by the U.N. Security Council of a "positive security assurance" resolution, similar to Resolution 255 adopted in 1968.[18] Under such a resolution each U.N. member state would commit to act immediately to provide assistance to a state falling victim to an act of WMD terror or to prevent any threat of such aggression. Lastly, additional efforts should be invested on the still open issue of enforcement. There are two recent examples of enforcement gaps: the fact that A. Q. Khan can still today be sheltered by the Pakistani government from interrogation so we might better understand what he transferred and to whom over the past 20 years; and the extradition problems encountered today with A. Q. Khan's network middle-men who are now held in custody, but cannot be extradited for prosecution.

Conclusions

It is clear that the threat of WMD terrorism will stay with us for many more decades. It is up to us collectively to decide what as individuals, states and the international community will be done about it. The traditional tendency of states to prepare for such a threat unilaterally is no longer sufficient. Much has been done on the local, national and international levels, but these efforts and hard-earned experiences have not been connected and shared. We are in dire need of more coordinated efforts. Given all that we now know, do we not already possess the wisdom to act on the imperative for collective action? After the next episode of WMD terror, will we look back at the signs clearly pointing the way for us that were consciously ignored?

Notes

1. The first multilateral agreement addressed WMD is "The Protocol for the Prohibition of the Use in War of Asphyxiating, Poisonous or other Gases, and of Bacteriological Methods of Warfare," usually called the Geneva Protocol. The protocol, signed in Geneva on June 17, 1925 prohibits the use of chemical and biological weapons.
2. For more on nonproliferation regimes, please see the chapter in this volume by Natasha Bajema.
3. A Speech by Abu Hamza al-Muhajir on the Occasion of Ramadan 1427, "Come to a Word that is Just Between Us and You," September 28, 2006.
4. For more on the A.Q. Khan network, please see the chapter in this volume by David Albright and Cory Hinderstein.

5. Lawrence Radiation Laboratory, "Summary Report of the Nth Country Experiment," W. J. Frank, ed., University of California, Livermore, March 1967.

6. Robert G. Joseph, U.S. Under Secretary for Arms Control and International Security, "Broadening and Deepening Our Proliferation Security Initiative Cooperation," Warsaw, Poland, June 23, 2006.

7. "Announcing the Global Initiative to Combat Nuclear Terrorism," Joint Statement by U.S. President George Bush and Russian Federation President V.V. Putin, St. Petersburg, Russia, July 15, 2006. See also, U.S. State Department, "U.S.-Russia Joint Fact Sheet on the Global Initiative To Combat Nuclear Terrorism," online at: http://www.state.gov/r/pa/prs/ps/2006/69016.htm

8. See U.S. Department of State, "Statement of Principles by Participants in the Global Initiative to Combat Nuclear Terrorism," October 31, 2006. Online at: http://www.state.gov/r/pa/prs/ps/2006/75405.htm

9. "GTRI: Two Successful Years of Reducing Nuclear Threats," National Nuclear Security Administration, U.S. Department of Energy, available online at http://www.nnsa.doe.gov/docs/factsheets/2006/NA-06-FS04.pdf

10. Nuclear Threat Initiative, 2005 Annual Report, available at http://www.nti.org/b_aboutnti/annual_report_2005.pdf

11. Harvard/Sussex Program on CBW Disarmament and Arms Limitation, "Draft Convention on the Prevention and Punishment of the Crime of Developing, Producing, Acquiring, Stockpiling, Retaining, Transferring, or Using Biological or Chemical Weapons," http://fas-www.harvard.edu/~hsp/crim01.pdf.

12. "U.N. Convention on the Suppression of Terrorist Bombings," Jan. 12, 1998, available at http://untreaty.un.org/English/Terrorism/Conv11.pdf.

13. "United Nations General Assembly Global Counter-Terrorism Strategy," Sept. 8, 2006, available at http://www.un.org/terrorism/strategy.

14. The Australia Group is an informal-voluntarily group of countries established in 1985 to help reduce the spread of chemical and biological weapons by monitoring and controlling the spread of technologies required to produce them. The group maintains a common list of technologies that could be used in chemical and biological weapons programs which have export restrictions placed upon them. Delegations representing member nations meet annually in Paris.

15. See for example, a summary of an unclassified work done by Rand Corporation for the U.S. Air force. Michael V. Hynes, John E. Peters, and Joel Kvitky "Denying Armageddon: Preventing Terrorist Use of Nuclear Weapons," in Confronting the Specter of Nuclear Terrorism, *The Annals of the American Academy of Political and Social Science*, Vol. 607, Sept. 2006, pp. 150–61.

16. "Chicago ER Docs Unfamiliar with WMD Symptoms," *Global Security Newswire*, October 16, 2006, available online at http://www.nti.org/d%5Fnewswire/issues/2006/10/16/669d1461%2Dfb85%2D458f%2D8616%2D6d6a2c0cc74a.html.

17. See for example, "Consequence Management in the 1995 Sarin Attacks on the Japanese Subway System," BCSIA Discussion Paper 2002-4, ESDP Discussion Paper ESDP-2002-01, John F. Kennedy School of Government, Harvard University, February 2002.

18. UN Security Council Resolution 255, "Questions Relating to Measures to Safeguard Non-Nuclear-Weapon States Parties to the Treaty on the Non-Proliferation of Nuclear Weapons," S/RES/255, 19 June 1968.

Chen Zak Kane is a post-doctoral fellow at the Belfer Center for Science and International Affairs at Harvard's John F. Kennedy School of Government. She has published extensively on nuclear non-proliferation safeguards, Iran's nuclear program, and nuclear decision making. Dr. Kane worked for 6 years at the Israel Atomic Energy Commission (IAEC) in the External Relations Division, eventually becoming its director. Prior to joining the IAEC, Dr. Kane served as an officer in the Israel Defense Forces.

Chapter 4.3

Future Threats

Forrest E. Waller, Jr., and Michael A. George

Emerging WMD Technologies

Technological advance has contributed significantly to the lives of nearly every human being on earth over the last two decades. Advances in information technology have changed how we work, learn, and play; those in biotechnology have improved the health and life expectancy of hundreds of millions; others in microminiaturization and advanced energy systems promise to produce new materials with unprecedented properties and new, clean sources of energy. Scientific and technological advances have the potential to transform the modern world, both for good and ill. Will advances in modern technology proliferate devastating new weapons, create new forms of warfare, and present new threats to U.S. national security as the technologies of the industrial age and nuclear era did? If so, what could these weapons be, how might they be used, and what challenges do they present to the United States?

This chapter's focus is on technological advances with the potential to result in "new kinds" of weapons of mass destruction. This focal point contains an important assumption—that the definition of "weapon of mass destruction" is incomplete. The United States defines *weapon of mass destruction* in policy and in law as nuclear, radiological, biological and chemical weapons. The Department of Justice definition includes large chemical explosive bombs. The Federal Bureau of Investigation classifies as a weapon of mass destruction any weapon that overwhelms the ability of local responders to deal with the consequences of attack. Thus, the U.S. definition of *weapon of mass destruction* is political and qualitative in nature. An alternative approach, and the one used here, is to define *weapon of mass destruction* in terms of effects. Nuclear, biological, and chemical weapons are based on different sciences and technologies. Their effects are very different. However, they share one attribute important to their natures as weapons of mass destruction: they fill a large volume of space with lethal effect. This chapter seeks to identify technology areas that have the potential to fill large volumes with lethal effect, do not fall under the current definition of weapon of mass destruction, and could affect the character of conflict in the future.

The Technology Revolutions: Four Areas of Particular Concern and their Enablers

Forecasting technology futures is an uncertain business. Some technologies that appear to have great potential today may never be developed for institutional or political reasons. Or, there may be unforeseen limitations in physics or chemistry that make impossible the technology achievements some now think possible. Technology experts have different opinions on discrete technologies and their potential to be weaponized, but there is a consensus that some technologies that emerge from the following four technology revolutions have high potential to produce effective, affordable weapons of mass destruction of entirely new kinds.

Information Technology

Over the next two decades, information technology is likely to complete the information-communication revolution that began with general public acceptance of personal computers, Internet access, and wireless communication. It appears almost inevitable that global connectivity, information abundance, and integrated sensor-communications networks will be an important part of our future. Over the next ten years, computer operating speeds could increase by a factor of one million.[1] Broadband and wireless connections are likely to spread globally. In short, those with access to modern information technology will have near-instantaneous connectivity with more information, sources of knowledge, people, products and services, and institutions than was ever available before. The sensor-data-communications networks forming the backbone of the information technology revolution will support the information and connectivity requirements for conflict between individuals, non-state groups, and states. Already the United States is at the forefront of a military transformation initiative based on networked combat units.[2] The Department of Defense believes the initiative will create unprecedented military effectiveness. In the future, this type of transformation will be available to many states and non-state actors.

Information technology is already an enabler of existing weapons of mass destruction. Information technology is critical to every supporting and operating system associated with United States nuclear forces. However, information technology alone is unlikely to be a discrete new kind of weapon of mass destruction. Computer network attack, corruption of the information sphere, and impairment of critical infrastructures is disruptive, but it is unlikely to fill large volumes of space with lethal effects. Experts on information operations warn that a computer network attack has the potential to undermine social stability, the public's sense of security, national prosperity, and confidence in government.[3] These values are intangible compared to lost lives and physical destruction, but intangible values are still real. Although we do not believe that cyber weapons deserve to be ranked alongside nuclear, biological or chemical weapons, we are persuaded that information technology is one of a handful of technologies with the potential to be disruptive on a massive scale.

One form of information technology, artificial intelligence, could become the basis for a new kind of weapon of mass destruction if integrated with other weapon technologies to replace human decision-making. The weapons would be small, smart, autonomous, lethal robots. The technology to produce a weapon system of this kind is already available in the United States. At least one entry-level system has been developed for an advanced concept technology demonstration. Small, smart, autonomous, lethal robots would be *distributed* weapons of mass destruction. That is, large numbers would be required to be massively destructive. However, advances in nanotechnology and micro-electromechanical systems potentially could reduce the overall mass of distributed robotic weapons to a level roughly comparable to existing unitary weapons of mass destruction. Distributed, swarming robotic weapons with enough intelligence to distinguish between friend and foe, or to navigate precisely with external help, could become a basis for new kinds of WMD.[4]

Biotechnology

Human intervention has been a factor in the evolution of plant and animal species for millennia. Technological advances in genetic research promise to vastly accelerate the pace of human-directed evolution in animal and plant biology. Advances in biotechnology, for example, may provide environment-friendly sources of energy (renewable biomass), yield more abundant food crops, generate pharmaceuticals more cheaply, promote greater human longevity, and improve overall human health.[5] However, the science and technology underlying these achievements also could produce harmful biological pollution, genetic accidents, deadly genomic weapons and new forms of warfare based on destruction of the environment. Biological warfare pathogens and toxins are already defined as weapons of mass destruction. However, a new generation of biological weapons based on genomic research has the potential to create new tools and approaches to biological warfare. Some of these will not fall within the current definitions of biological weapons used in treaties outlawing biological warfare. Many advances with the greatest potential for biological warfare are likely to tax our ability to detect attacks, diagnose disease sources, and develop remedies.[6] Interviews with experts in the field indicate that most genomic research takes place with the objective of expanding the frontiers of science and producing life-saving, life-enhancing medicines. Nonetheless, this research already produced disquieting accidents that have expanded the frontiers of biological warfare.[7]

Specific areas of research that appear to hold great potential for new approaches to biological warfare include:

- *Aptamers*—single strands of ribonucleic acid (RNA) that act in a manner similar to antibodies. Aptamers bind and block cell receptors responsible for a variety of biological functions. They bond irreversibly, so antidotes may be of limited or no use. Aptamers may be able to confuse the human immune system, making it believe a pathogen is present when it is not or suppressing the immune system making ordinary infections life threatening. Research to date leads many to conclude that aptamers are highly tailorable and able to achieve wide-ranging biological effects.[8]

- *Molecular poisons*—nano-particles capable of working at the subcellular level. Molecular poisons are toxic molecules designed to create specialized biological effects. Due to the size of the molecule, the body's immune response is not triggered, and normal biological barriers will not control nano-particle passage to sites normally protected, such as the brain.[9]

- *Genetic difference*—using biological markers, such as respiration, as a genetic assessment tool for targeting biological weapons. Research in several countries is underway to develop technologies for assessing human health by reading metabolic signatures in a patient's breath. Although the results are controversial, early research indicates this approach can differentiate groups by age, race and ethnicity.[10] As this technology advances, and large population samples are collected, researchers may be able to develop a baseline of metabolic signatures to identify, profile, and target individuals based on race or ethnicity.[11]

- *Binary biological weapons*—as presently used, the term includes biological agents that are a) chimera (combined genetic attributes of different pathogens), b) genetically modified pathogens (greater virulence, heartiness, or resistance to therapy), or c) require two exposures of different kinds to trigger disease effects. Binary biological weapons would challenge present ability to detect, diagnose, and treat victims of attack.[12]

Nanotechnology

Nanotechnology[13] has the potential to be both an enabler of other forms of WMD and a discrete weapon of mass destruction. As an enabler, nanotechnology already plays a role in chemistry, biology, and advanced energy systems. Some experts believe that nanotechnology can help chemists produce compounds that are much more energetic than current high explosives. Experts disagree on just how much greater that energy will be, but optimists believe nanotechnology will provide tools for producing new energy-dense molecules tens of times more energetic than today's high explosives. Some believe that it is unrealistic to expect more than doubling, or perhaps tripling, current energy densities. Some experts believe nanotechnology will give biologists new tools for manipulating genetic material[14] or will permit organic and inorganic materials to be used in new products and devices. Nanoscale engineering is already a critical element of modern nuclear weapon design. In sum, nanotechnology already plays a supporting role in the other three technology revolutions.[15]

Nanotechnology also might produce discrete new kinds of weapons of mass destruction. Ongoing research in nanotechnology weaponry includes ultra-high explosive/ultra-incendiary devices.[16] The U.S. Department of Defense and other ministries of defense have conducted research into micro-metallic particle-air explosives that have the potential to deliver greatly improved blast and combustion effects compared to standard military high explosives. The United States is ready to prototype its first explosive device based on "micro-dust." Visionaries predict the eventual appearance of destructive nanites or "nano-bots" capable of carrying out anti-materiel or anti-personnel missions.[17] Such devices face formidable development hurdles before they face the cost-effectiveness/performance calculations that defense organizations apply to weapon acquisition. Regardless, there is a growing body of scientific evidence that nano-particles themselves may be capable of massively destructive effects.

Experiments at Rice University have demonstrated that nano-sized carbon particles can introduce respiratory distress and death in laboratory animals depending on the concentration of particles in the atmosphere and the duration of exposure. Respected scientific bodies outside the United States have begun to warn about the potential health consequences of releasing nano-sized particles into the environment. The British Royal Society and Royal Academy of Engineering published a report warning of the potential risks to human health of the increasing use of nano-particles in consumer products.[18] In short, nanotechnology appears to be able to produce effects comparable to large high-explosive/incendiary devices, chemical weapons and biological weapons.

Advanced Energy Sources

Research on new energy sources is driven by the desire to reduce reliance on fossil fuels, reduce associated pollution, and find cheaper and more reliable sources of renewable energy. The economic benefits of advanced energy sources are clear—the global economy runs well when supplied with abundant, inexpensive energy and falters when energy is scarce and expensive. However, advanced energy sources also produce devastating weapons of mass destruction. One potential advanced energy source is metastable nuclear isomers.[19] Research into metastable nuclear isomers is underway in half a dozen advanced industrialized states. Much has been written of the scientific controversy surrounding an isomer of the element Hafnium and unsupported claims made about its potential as an ultra-high explosive.[20] If proven feasible, ultra-high explosive/ultra-incendiary devices based on nuclear isomers appear to fall into a definitional void.[21] Although a form of nuclear energy involving a radioactive element, nuclear isomer weapons do not use nuclear fission or fusion as the source of energy and may not qualify as a weapon of mass destruction under United States law. Although theoretically only 1/100th of the yield of fissile materials, the energy release from an isomer weapon could be 10,000 times that of existing chemical high explosives. Thus, the ability of an isomer bomb to fill a large volume of space with lethal effects (kinetic energy, thermal energy, and gamma radiation) would argue for its inclusion in a broadened definition.[22]

Similarly, a weapon based on anti-matter annihilation also falls into a definitional void. Neither fission nor fusion, anti-matter annihilation produces more energy per unit of mass than any other known material or process. Anti-matter produces 100 times the amount of energy produced by thermonuclear reactions and, thus, holds great potential for energy production.[23] The Air Force Research Laboratory reportedly is pursuing research programs in anti-matter production and storage, hoping to advance basic science in the field and to examine future military applications for anti-matter energy sources.[24]

The United States is also ready to prototype high-power microwave weapons. The Department of Defense is interested in high-power microwaves as a non-lethal weapon against electronic systems. The Air Force is also developing land-based microwave weapons as a non-lethal anti-personnel weapon for the Army and Marine Corps.[25] Anti-personnel microwave weapons effects are scalable. That is, predictable physiological outcomes occur as power levels and frequencies change. Current weapons are being developed for the purpose of area denial and crowd control. These weapons inflict intense pain without permanent injury. At higher intensities of power, longer exposure times, or different frequencies, microwave energy can disable or kill. As a general rule, directed energy weapons do not have great potential as weapons of mass destruction. However, microwave weapons may be the exception to the rule. They can operate at standoff distances (several kilometers from the target) and fill large volumes of space with disabling, near-lethal or lethal effects.

Disruptive Technologies

Several technologies have the potential to disrupt basic operational assumptions the United States makes as it goes to war. New weapon delivery platforms characterized by small mass, long range, and great precision will make it possible to deliver potent payloads against fixed targets—particularly if breakthroughs occur in ultra-high explosive/ultra-incendiary weapons. Advances in artificial intelligence, the adoption of network-centric warfare, and new delivery platforms will make it possible to field small, smart, autonomous lethal systems capable of creating mass effects on land, sea or air.[26] Some potential disruptive technologies include:

- Ultra-light unmanned aerial vehicles (UUAVs).[27] Programmable UUAVs with a mass of only 15 kilograms, a range of 1900 kilometers, and GPS accuracy are commercially available today. UUAVs with a mass of only 10 kilograms have crossed the Atlantic Ocean. The present mass limit for a transatlantic crossing appears to be 5 kilograms. Made of composite materials and supported by microelectronic navigation-flight control systems, these aircraft are virtually invisible to present detection systems. The cost of UUAVs ranges from a few thousand dollars to $25,000 per unit—far less than the cost of United States weapon systems designed against traditional aerodynamic threats. The level of technical expertise required to build and produce UUAVs, while high, is not insurmountable to any state with an aircraft industry or a non-state actor with engineering talent. The biggest problem for those wishing to turn UUAVs into a weapon system is the small payload.[28]

- Novel intercontinental projectile systems. United States engineers have designed two novel approaches to placing small satellites in near-earth orbit. One is a blast wave accelerator in which sequential explosive charges propel a small satellite to escape velocity.[29] The second is a spiral mass accelerator using mechanical energy to hurl small satellites into near-earth orbit.[30] The latter appears capable of lofting tens-to-hundreds of 10–20 kilogram projectiles every minute to intercontinental distances. Significant technical hurdles must be overcome, but alternatives to traditional intercontinental rocketry exist.

At the present time, neither UUAVs nor intercontinental projectile systems would interest the Department of Defense, because the mass of the payloads is too small. However, in an age of nanotechnology and energy dense materials, payload masses in the 2–20 kilogram range eventually will be able to perform many useful missions, including delivering significant kinetic energies.

Concerns Over Emerging WMD Technologies

Based on a study of these areas, including interviews with nearly 40 experts in the four areas of scientific and technological revolution, several themes can be identified in terms of technological feasibility, political control of new technologies, technology leadership, and the definition of *weapons of mass destruction*. In general, experts interviewed for this study expressed concern with the application of a highly charged political term, *weapon of mass destruction,* to areas of research whose potential for good or ill cannot be known with certainty. While some avenues of research might have the potential to create new kinds of weapons of mass destruction, many interviewees believed that most would prove infeasible as weapons or would produce no useful advance over existing weapons. Nearly all interviewees were anxious that examining the new technologies through the prism of WMD might encourage attempts to impose political controls over basic research, particularly in advanced energy systems, nanoscience, and genetic engineering. They unanimously believed that constraints on scientific research would be counterproductive, causing the United States to lag other advanced technology societies. All interviewees expressed frustration and disappointment with the current definition of *weapon of mass destruction* in United States policy and law.

Feasibility of "New Kinds"

Many claims associated with the lines of research mentioned about the four revolutions are controversial among scientists. For example, operating under the principle "extraordinary claims demand extraordinary proofs," many experts have lost patience with, and confidence in, experimental results alleged to show the potential of metastable Hafnium 178 to release enormous amounts of energy rapidly and efficiently. Critics believe the experimental results disprove the claims of great energy release. Advocates of the claims believe that it is only a matter of time until someone discovers how to do it. Advocates of research into new chemical explosives often operate in the realm of theoretical chemistry, not empirical science, when making claims about the potential of new, energy-dense compounds to multiply the yields of high explosives by factors of more than ten. More conservative chemists believe that it is unreasonable to expect yields to increase more than two or three times.

In each of the four areas of rapid scientific and technological advance, unknowns affect the potential to create new kinds of weapons of mass destruction. These unknowns include research priorities, funding, and the natural properties of materials. The decision to pursue one line of research means that other lines of research will close or never open. In addition, the lines of research having potential to create new kinds of weapons of mass destruction will require expensive, multiyear efforts in major research laboratories. This is particularly true for destructive nanotechnology and advanced energy sources. In short, the feasibility of creating new kinds of weapons of mass destruction is far from certain. Nonetheless, experts believe that the likelihood is great that one or more new kinds of weapons of mass destruction will emerge from the four revolutionary technology sectors.

Political Controls

Experts believe that political controls over scientific research and technology development should be avoided and, if they are imposed, they are destined to fail. Political control over emerging science and technology is undesirable, it is argued, because it stigmatizes avenues of research that are immature. Even the most problematic technologies are too immature to be turned into weapons in the near future. Controls over science and technology almost certainly will be ineffective and unacceptable to the advanced technology states, because the commercial value of the research exceeds its military value by many times. Stated another way, the benefits of unfettered R&D may outweigh the potential risks of developing a new kind of weapon of mass destruction. Some believe political control may already be too late. Advances in the sciences and technologies of greatest concern are taking place globally in private research institutions, universities, multinational industries, and government laboratories. While specific research results may be confidential or proprietary, the global accessibility of research tools, materials, and theory will make effective political control impossible.[31]

Technology Leadership

One of the potential perils of slowing or halting the advance of the emerging technology sectors is the hazard of technological inferiority. While the United States is a leader in all of the emerging technology sectors, it is not—and never has been—dominant in all of them. Competition is keen in each sector. Even in genetic research, a field the United States has led for decades, it has begun to lose ground, partly due to the increasingly unfriendly political environment in which genetic research takes place in the United States, and partly due to foreign governments' earnest efforts to overtake the United States. Less developed states have focused on particular niches, like nanoscience and nanotechnology, because they believe these areas are destined to become the basis of a new world economy and they want to share in the redistributed social, economic, and political benefits accompanying that new world.

The United States is responsible for 40 percent of global R&D expenditures. Given that the United States accounts for only 4.7 percent of the global population, the American commitment to basic research and technology development is an astonishing accomplishment. However, 60 percent of global research and development occurs abroad. Seventy thousand students take university degrees in science and technology in the United States every year. The vast majority are foreign students. The United States cannot employ all of these graduates, and many return to their homelands to work. Therefore, the United States is training its future competition. It is unrealistic to expect every emerging technology breakthrough to occur in the United States. On the contrary, the United States should expect foreign technological surprise, including military surprise.

The Definition of Weapon of Mass Destruction

There is strong consensus among experts that the United States definition of *weapon of mass destruction* is inadequate or unhelpful. The chief complaint is that the definition includes weapons that are not massively destructive—like chemical weapons—and excludes others that have a dark history of mass death and destruction. The definitional issue is complicated by the fact that the threshold of destruction that qualifies as "massive" is falling. A weapon no longer needs to kill millions to be categorized a weapon of mass destruction. As the threshold for massive destruction falls, the list of tools capable of causing mass destruction necessarily lengthens.

Mass destruction is an interaction between a weapon and target producing effects over a period of time. The political definition ignores these parameters. In so doing, the definition used in the United States admits severe internal inconsistencies. For example, chemical weapons are distributed weapons of mass destruction. Huge quantities of chemical agent are required to cause massive casualties. Common high explosives (another kind of chemical weapon) are also distributed weapons of mass destruction, they cause massive casualties when used on a large scale, and they also inflict massive infrastructure damage that poison gas does not. The political definition does not classify chemical high explosives as a weapon of mass destruction. Perhaps, poison gas should not be classified as one either.

For example, the systematic use of incendiary munitions in Japan between late 1944 and early 1945 killed roughly 1 million people, caused 1 million others to become homeless, burned 2.5 million buildings to the ground, and destroyed almost one quarter of the total urban area of Japan's 20 largest cities. The nuclear attacks of 1945 reduced the incendiary air raids to an historical footnote. Over the next decade or so, emerging technologies may produce ultra-high explosive, ultra-incendiary devices which, when combined with new long-range means of delivery, will change our perceptions of non-nuclear incendiary attack as a tool of mass destruction. Incendiary munitions, like contagious biological weapons, use their targets as their medium of propagation. Although the probability is low, a small incendiary device can potentially destroy an entire city, just as a small amount of contagious, lethal pathogen has a small chance of infecting and killing an entire population. The political definition of *weapon of mass destruction* includes lethal pathogens, but it ignores incendiary munitions.

Over the next ten years, perhaps earlier, scientific and technological advance will make our current definition of *weapon of mass destruction* obsolete. Inevitably, many will wish to change the definition—some will wish to broaden it, others to narrow it. Any effort to re-define *weapon of mass destruction* will be a policy issue of the greatest importance to the Department of Defense and the Armed Services. Broadening the definition may have unintended consequences. Current ordnance and military systems under development may be re-categorized as weapons of mass destruction. Preferred approaches to military operations may be prohibited due to their potential for massive destruction. Narrowing the definition may subject United States military installations and personnel to greater levels of destruction than they have known in recent decades.

Conclusion

Few in the United States defense circles are thinking about new kinds of weapons of mass destruction. New military technologies are evaluated against validated mission requirements. And the United States has no validated requirement for new kinds of weapons of mass destruction. Many American technologists object to their field of research having the term *weapon of mass destruction* applied to any of its product, even theoretically. They are concerned that speculation about future weapon technology developments will taint their ongoing research. For example, U.S. developers of high-power microwave weapons emphasize that their research is for non-lethal applications. However, the Department of Defense's program objectives do not alter the fact that microwave energy can disable and kill. Somewhere, sometime, someone eventually will experiment with lethal microwave energy and may create a deadly high-power microwave weapon. Powerful new kinds of weapons of mass destruction almost certainly will emerge from one or more of the four technological revolutions described in this chapter.

Many potential "new kinds" of weapons of mass destruction appear to escape the constraints of existing non-proliferation and export control agreements. Developments in biology that produce neither pathogens nor toxins, but confuse or suppress the immune system, may not fall within the terms of the Biological Weapons Convention. They would also not fall under the Chemical Weapons Convention, with its reliance on agreed schedules of controlled compounds. Chemical ultra-high explosives and ultra-incendiary devices do not fall under any treaty. Nuclear isomers would probably not qualify as nuclear weapons under the Nuclear Non-Proliferation Treaty, because they do not involve nuclear fission or fusion. However, they may qualify as radiological weapons under United States policy and law.

The United States is a leader in the four technology revolutions we have reviewed here. However, it is not, and has never been, the leader in all technology areas. In the biological sciences, United States leadership is usually taken for granted. Most of the G-8 states and several advancing industrialized states are making important breakthroughs in genomic research. The United States is a leader in advanced energy sources and systems, but Japan, Russia, and France are keen competitors and niche technology leaders. The United States has a national initiative in nanotechnology, but other G-8 states and China are also leaders in this area of research with national initiatives of their own. Many experts are concerned that the United States is falling behind in key areas of the four technology revolutions.

Finally, the current United States definition of *weapon of mass destruction* is inadequate in many ways, and the problem can only grow worse as revolutionary military technologies appear. Efforts to find a new definition may take a quantitative approach (i.e., number of casualties), but this is insufficient because the direct casualties of an attack are not necessarily the primary objective of terrorism—rather, these acts are largely meant to spread terror among a populace, as a means for achieving certain political objectives. Further, current and future military capabilities and operations could be constrained by a new, erroneously conceived definition. Thus, although imperfect, a political, qualitative approach to defining *weapon of mass destruction* is best.

Notes

1. In other words, computer operating speeds could increase to tens of petaflops—one petaflop equates to one million billion arithmetic operations per second involving two numbers containing decimal points.
2. The transformation efforts of the Department of Defense have the objective of creating "network centric" combat units organized to accept and act on operational intelligence with unprecedented speed and effect. Other nations, primarily allies, are aware of U.S. transformation objectives and some are attempting to adopt them.
3. Interview with Mr James Gosler, Senior Fellow, Sandia National Laboratory
4. An entry-level technology having many of the characteristics of a distributed robotic weapon system is Lockheed Martin's Low Cost Autonomous Attack System (LOCAAS). LOCAAS is a miniature, powered, smart submunition designed to search for, identify, and destroy mobile ground targets. The submunition has a small turbojet engine and enough fuel to fly for roughly 30 minutes. A laser detection and ranging system senses ground objects and an on-board computer has algorithms allowing it to recognize enemy targets. Destruction is accomplished using a multimode warhead (penetrating rod for hard armor, aerostable slug for increased stand-off, and fragmentation for soft targets). The objective is to have LOCAAS weigh 90–100 pounds, have a length of 30 inches and have a wingspan of 40 inches. The Air Force has contracted with Lockheed Martin to provide a prototype for an advanced technology demonstration. If the demonstration is a success, the Air Force intends to buy several thousand LOCAAS units configured for deployment from current and future Air Force fighter, attack, and bomber aircraft.
5. Dennis Bushnell, "Future Strategic Issues/Future Warfare [Circa 2025]," PowerPoint presentation, July 2001.
6. For more on this topic, please see the chapter by Dave Franz in this volume.
7. In 2001, genetic researchers at the Australian National University inadvertently created a lethal biological agent using the mousepox virus. Although mousepox is related to smallpox, it normally causes only mild symptoms among the variety of mice used in the experiment (and does not affect humans at all). The researchers were experimenting ways to suppress mouse fertility as a means of pest control. They inserted into mousepox virus a gene that stimulates the production of a compound, Interleukin-4, known to suppress the fertility of female mice. Mousepox virus was simply a delivery vehicle for the foreign gene. The genetically altered mousepox virus had the desired effect. It stimulated the production of Interleukin-4 in the mice; however, it also unexpectedly suppressed the test animals' immune defenses against viral infection. The normally harmless mousepox virus killed every test animal in less than ten days. The modified virus also proved highly deadly to mice vaccinated against mousepox. When a mousepox vaccine was administered to infected animals, half died anyway. In subsequent research in the United States and Australia, the mousepox virus was modified again. Now, it is 100 percent lethal even against inoculated laboratory mice. The research conducted in the United States after the Australian accident has generated much discussion among genetic researchers and laypersons, many of whom question its ethical propriety and fear its consequences for biological warfare.

8. See Osborne, M Matsumura, and Ellington. "Aptamers as therapeutic and diagnostic agents: problems and prospects." *Current Opinion in Medical Biology* 1997, 1:5–9 (http://biomednet. com/elecref/1367593100100005). Also of note is White, Sullenger, and Rusconi, "Developing aptamers into therapeutics," *J Clin Invest*, October 2000, Volume 106, Number 8, 929–934.

9. Specifically, Molecules that act as subcellular poisons might be engineered to prevent deoxyribonucleic acid from being read in cells, thereby interfering with the manufacture of messenger RNA and subsequent protein synthesis. This projection is based on Interviews with Michael Callahan, Director of Biological Weapons Defense at Massachusetts General Hospital; John Parker, MD, Vice-President at SAIC; David Franz, PhD and DVM; and Dr. Barbara Johnson (SAIC).

10. Ethnicity and race are partly social constructs. As a matter of biology, broad groups of humanity share distinct genetic markers, and some of the markers are medically significant. However, it is also true that the four major genetic groups—European (including North Africa and the Middle East), Sub-Saharan African, East Asian (including Melanesia), and Native American— share many genetic markers. See Michael J. Bamshad and Steve E. Olson, "Does Race Exist," *Scientific American,* December 2003, pp. 80–85.

11. Jurgen Altmann and Mark A. Gubrud, "Risks from Military Uses of Nanotechnology—The Need for Technology Assessment and Preventive Control" in *Nanotechnology–Revolutionary Opportunities and Societal Implications*, M. Roco, R. Tomellini (eds.) 3[[rd]] JOINT EC-NSF Workshop on Nanotechnology, Leece (Italy), 31 Jan–1 Febr. 2002, Luxembourg: European Communities, 2002.

12. Interview with Dennis Bushnell, Chief Scientist, NASA Langley Research Center. Also see David Hearst, "Smart bio-weapons are now possible." *The Guardian*, Tuesday 20 May 2003, and CIA Directorate of Intelligence, "The Darker Bioweapons Future." 3 November 2003.

13. Nanoscience is the study of phenomena and manipulation of materials at atomic, molecular and macromolecular scales, where the properties differ significantly from those at larger scale. Nanotechnologies are the design, characterisation, production and application of structures, devices and systems by controlling shape and size at nanometre scale. (Nanoscience and nanotechnologies, The Royal Society & Royal Academy of Engineering, July 2004, chapter 2, page 5.

14. Rick Weiss, "Nanoparticles Toxic in Aquatic Habitat, Study Finds." *Washington Post*, 29 March 2004.

15. The prefix "nano" is Greek and means dwarf. One nanometer is one billionth of a meter— 1/80,000[th] of the thickness of a human hair. The conceptual basis for nanotechnology was the work of Nobel Laureate Richard Feynman of the California Institute of Technology. In a now famous lecture, Feynman imagined the possibility of manipulating matter at the molecular and atomic scales. The term "nanotechnology" was used for the first time in 1974 when Norio Taniguchi of Tokyo University used it to describe precision engineering at nanometer levels of measurement. The size range of most interest in nanotechnology is typically from 100 nanometers to 0.2 nanometers. In this range, materials behave differently for two reasons: they have increased exposed surface area per unit of mass, and, thus, they are more reactive chemically than when in larger amounts; and in this size range, quantum effects dominate matter, and, thus, matter has different optical, electrical and magnetic properties compared to larger amounts. Size-dependent properties have been known about for centuries. Nanoparticles of gold and silver have been used to color pigments in stained glass and ceramics since the 10th Century AD.

16. Interview with a senior scientist and head of nuclear isomer research, Sandia National Laboratory.

17. Jurgen Altmann, and Mark A. Gubrud, "Risks from Military Uses of Nanotechnology—The Need for Technology Assessment and Preventive Control" in *Nanotechnology—Revolutionary Opportunities and Societal Implications*, M. Roco, R. Tomellini (eds.) 3[[rd]] JOINT EC-NSF Workshop on Nanotechnology, Leece (Italy), 31 Jan–1 Febr. 2002, Luxembourg: European Communities, 2002. See also David Hearst, "Sci-fi war put under the microscope." *The Guardian*, 20 May 2003.

18. *Nanoscience and nanotechnologies: opportunities and uncertainties.* London, The Royal Society & Royal Academy of Engineering (2004). Nano-sized particles of titanium are used in

some sunscreens to achieve high sun protection factor ratings. The human immune system did not evolve to protect against chemical elements in such small sizes. The British societies warn that the effects of routine exposure to nano-sized chemical particles cannot be predicted. They worry that genetic damage may result.

19. Metastable nuclear isomers are elements with highly charged nuclei that emit gamma radiation to reach their normal energy state. Most isomers release this energy over the period of no more than a day. One isomer, hafnium-178, has a high-energy state and longer half-life. For the purposes of weapons or other applications, the goal is to have the energy released in a very short period of time, instead of slowly over time. Controversy exists over the ability to release this energy. Bertram Schwarzschild, "Conflicting Results on a Long-Lived Nuclear Isomer of Hafnium Have Wider Implications." *Physics Today,* May 2004. http://www.physicstoday. org/vol-57/iss-5/p21.html

20. Laura Durnford, "Isomer Wars." *Radio Nederland* online edition. http://www.rnw.nl/science/ html/031027isomer.html. Also of note is David Hambling, "Gamma-ray weapons could trigger next arms race." *New Scientist* online edition, 19:00 13 August 2003. http://www.newscientist. com/news/news.jsp?id5ns99994049

21. Hans de Vrejj, "New nukes in the making." *Radio Nederland* online edition. http://www.rnw. nl/hotspots/html/iso031024.html

22. Laura Durnford, "Tapping the power of isomers." *Radio Nederland* online edition. http://www. rnw.nl/science/html/031020isomer.html

23. One gram of antimatter contains the same amount of energy as 23 space shuttles. One millionth of a gram of antimatter contains as much energy as 80 pounds of TNT.

24. "Air Force pursuing antimatter weapons," *San Francisco Chronicle*, 4 October 2004.

25. Eileen M. Walling, "High-Power Microwaves: Strategic and Operational Implications for Warfare." Occasional Paper No.11, *Center for Science and Technology*, Air War College: May 2000.

26. Arnall, Alexander Huw. *"Future Technologies, Today's Choices: Nanotechnology, Artificial Intelligence and Robotics; A technical, political, and institutional map of emerging technologies."* Department of Environmental Science and Technology et al., University of London. Greenpeace Environmental Trust, Canonbury Villas, London: July 2003.

27. Air superiority is a vital factor in United States military power. In recent conflicts, airpower has contributed to rapid military success and reduced American, allied, and adversary casualties. Few potential opponents can match the technology, force structure, or training of American air forces. However, new technologies involving robotic aircraft could begin to challenge some planning assumptions about air superiority. Ultra-light Unmanned Aerial Vehicles (UUAVs) have been commercially available for years. The Aerosonde Company (Australia) manufactures a UUAV used around the world to conduct atmospheric measurements. The aircraft is small (15 kilograms), rugged (used to monitor cyclones and sea storms), high endurance (1900 nautical mile range on two gallons of fuel), precise (GPS navigation), easy to operate (flight path programmed with a laptop, launched from a detachable carriage on a car roof), and inexpensive ($25,000 per aircraft). The Acrosonde UUAV has a payload capacity of 2 kilograms, enough for a scientific payload, but not large enough to interest the Defense Department. If an Aerosonde-like UUAV were married with a biological warfare agent, high-incendiary device, or ultra-high explosive, numbers of these aircraft launched from ships one thousand miles at sea have the potential to inflict massive destruction on targets hundreds of miles inside an enemy coastline, provided that the aircraft operated as a distributed weapon system. The Aerosonde vehicle is small and made of composite materials. In large numbers, Aerosonde-like aircraft would present formidable challenges to detection, interception and destruction. In short, they could disrupt operational expectations pertaining to air superiority, supremacy, and long-range precision strike that the United States Air Force routinely carries into armed conflict.

28. See Tom Clarke, "Pilotless research aircraft: Flying free," *Nature News Service*, 7 June 2002 and *BBC Online*, "Aviation first for robotic spy plane," Tuesday 24 April 2001.

29. Dennis Bushnell, "Future Strategic Issues/Future Warfare," PowerPoint presentation, July 2001.

30. Mark L. Bundy, Gene R. Cooper, and Stephen A. Wilkerson, "Optimizing a Slingatron Launcher Using MATLAB." Army Research Lab, Aberdeen Proving Ground, MD. January 2001. See also Andrew Higgins, Posting to *sci.space.science newsgroup*, 9 December 1998. See Usenet archives: http://yarchive.net/space/exotic/sling_launcher.html
31. The United States Government walked out of the international negotiations to strengthen the Biological Weapons Convention in part, because it concluded that stronger controls were doomed to failure.

Forrest Waller is a senior scientist and corporate officer in Science Applications International Corporation's System, Strategy, and Policy Operation.

Michael A. George is a senior analyst with Science Applications International Corporation in the System, Strategy, and Policy Operation.

Chapter 4.4

Conclusion

James J.F. Forest and Aaron Danis

Terrorism and WMD:
The Road Ahead

The discussions and analyses provided in this volume paint a complex portrait of terrorists' motivations and capabilities for acquiring and using weapons of mass destruction (WMD). From a macro-strategic perspective, several implications can be drawn from these chapters to inform our understanding of the WMD threat, including four which highlight the centrality of knowledge in terrorism and counterterrorism:

1. Terrorist groups have a capacity for organizational learning. The most dangerous terrorists are capable of adapting, learning from each other in their search for ways to expand their lethal capabilities. Given the organic and dynamic nature of terrorist organizations, which several chapters in this volume have described, we must come to understand the evolving nature of the threat and its long-term trajectory, particularly when it comes to chemical, biological, radiological and nuclear (CBRN) weapons. There is a burgeoning field of research in the study of organizational behavior which some might call "knowledge traffic analysis." Our understanding of knowledge traffic in the terrorist world must encompass a truly global, multi-organizational dimension.[1] Further, once we have developed an understanding of the characteristics that affect a particular terrorist group's learning abilities, the next step in a comprehensive counterterrorism strategy involves trying to reduce these abilities. A recent study conducted by the RAND Corporation offered a set of "learning-focused strategies for combating terrorism" which inform such efforts.[2] First, the report suggests we must target a terrorist group's learning activities directly, in order to reduce their ability to adapt over time. This could involve actions such as restricting access to the kinds of knowledge they require to successfully achieve their lethal objectives; identifying and breaking the interconnections among a group's members that facilitate learning; and denying groups the safe havens they require for experimentation, innovation and training.[3] Of particular importance here is the fact that developing WMD capabilities requires a safe haven for testing. It is thus disquieting to note that on September 28, 2006, Abu Ayyub al-Masri—the leader of al Qaeda in Iraq—encouraged his fellow terrorists to consider testing these weapons in Iraq: "The field of jihad (holy war) can satisfy your scientific ambitions, and the large American bases (in Iraq) are good places to test your unconventional weapons, whether biological or dirty, as they call them."[4] Obviously, preventing this (or any other) theater of conflict from becoming a WMD testing ground for terrorists must be a high priority for the U.S. and its allies.

2. Our counterterrorism strategies must distinguish a group's intentions from its capabilities. Disrupting an organization's ability to acquire WMD capabilities is paramount for our national security strategy. However, there are many different armed groups which pose a potential threat to our security, and thus it is necessary to focus our efforts where the combination of motivations, knowledge and intentions behind the WMD terrorism threat are the greatest.[5] As Jonathan Tucker observed in his groundbreaking book, *Toxic Terror*, "only a tiny minority of terrorists will seek to inflict indiscriminate casualties" with WMD, and few of them are likely to succeed, predominately because of the enormous difficulties in developing effective delivery systems. Further, he notes, groups that will try to deploy WMD tend to have certain traits, including apocalyptic ideology, innovation in weapons and tactics, paranoia and grandiosity, charismatic leadership, defensive aggression, and other characteristics.[6] According to Gavin Cameron, extremist religious groups are of particular concern because they lack the moderating influence of an external "audience" or "constituency," and to them "violence is perceived to be part of an all-encompassing struggle between good and evil."[7] David Kaplan's study of Aum Shinrikyo supports this view by demonstrating how the group's particular worldview rationalized its plans for mass murder.[8] Overall, we must evaluate the WMD threat posed by various groups by asking an important question: since most forms of terrorism are fueled by a vision of the future that its adherent believe can only be achieved through violence, what sort of future is envisioned by a group willing to use a CBRN weapon? In particular, the worst case scenarios of nuclear and biological attacks indicate that whole areas of the planet would be uninhabitable, so how can any terrorist group convince its members that the use of a weapon of mass destruction will help them secure a better future? In combating the threat of WMD terrorism, we must develop an understanding of the underlying ideology and vision behind the threat, and then work to discredit this vision and deter its adherents. Differentiating the threat according to both motivations and capabilities helps us focus our resources most appropriately.

3. Thwarting a terrorist WMD attack is everyone's responsibility. In July 2005, the U.S. government requested that the National Academy of Sciences delay publication of a research paper that offered potentially lethal information for terrorists to exploit. The paper assessed the vulnerability of the dairy industry to a bioterrorism attack, and recommended steps to prevent that from happening. However, in a letter to the Academy, Stewart Simonson, assistant secretary of the Department of Health and Human Services, stated that the paper was a "road map for terrorists." He contended that the paper provided too much detail on potentially vulnerable areas of the milk supply, processing and distribution systems and argued that its publication "could have very serious health and national security consequences."[9] This event exemplifies the centrality of knowledge in the terrorist world and suggests implications for the academic community, U.S. institutions of higher learning, and the media more broadly in terms of self-monitoring. We have already witnessed the role of flight schools in contributing to an individual's capacity to carry out a terrorist attack. One only hopes that heightened vigilance is now common at all institutions of higher learning, from truck schools and large ship or tanker pilot programs to postgraduate biotechnology research institutes. Further, as Cindy Combs recently noted, the media has become a tool of modern terrorists—offering a "showcase" through which those carrying out terrorist acts can impress and threaten an audience, recruit and train new members, and support and coordinate an emerging network of followers—and thus there is a need for better media self-regulation.[10] Overall, we must develop a clear sense of what kinds of knowledge are needed by an ideologically motivated individual seeking to operationalize his or her terrorist intentions, and explore how the most dangerous knowledge can be protected from those who would use it to cause mass casualties.

4. We must be—and we are—getting smarter about the WMD terror threat and our response. In addition to multinational cooperation and private sector involvement, countering the threat of terrorism requires a highly educated cadre of security specialists as well as a properly informed and resilient public. Just as knowledge plays a critical role in a terrorist group's capability for WMD attacks, it is also central to our counterterrorism response to such a threat. Thus, developing and sharing this knowledge has rapidly become a focal point for many colleges and universities nationwide. A growing cadre of knowledge workers in academe and government are collaborating with national security practitioners to develop educational programs that will support the mandate for smarter responses to the WMD terror threat. Before the attacks of 9/11, the study of terrorism was largely seen as a marginally important sub-field of political science or history disciplines. However, within the last several years the number and diversity of new educational programs on terrorism, counterterrorism and homeland security throughout the United States has skyrocketed. Courses and seminars on these subjects are now taught to undergraduates and graduate students, new security professionals, emergency responders and the general public. The study and teaching of WMD terrorism is becoming an increasingly prominent component of these courses, and therein lies the impetus for producing this volume. This concluding chapter of the volume will draw on several themes reflected in the previous chapters to highlight critical areas for counterterrorism knowledge advancement and sharing.

Security Education for a New Era

Naturally, considerable attention must be given to educating a new generation of policy-makers and practitioners to respond to the threat of WMD terrorism with greater sophistication and success. This volume is meant to support such efforts. Individual chapters can be used to frame a variety of important discussions and learning objectives in courses of a national security or international affairs curriculum, or political science programs more generally. Further, within a course on terrorism and WMD, there are many approaches beyond assigned readings and lectures which can enhance learning about this complicated and difficult subject. For example, students in the introductory terrorism studies class at West Point view films like the Nuclear Threat Initiative's *Last Best Chance*,[11] followed by a class discussion about the terrorist motivations and capabilities demonstrated in the film. Exemplary Hollywood films like *Twelve Monkeys* and *Outbreak* offer students a sense of the threat posed by misuse of biotechnology. Other multimedia instructional aids include interactive websites and maps.[12]

Case studies offer another important avenue for learning about WMD terrorism. Savvy educators will incorporate case studies from several different countries, because a comparative perspective helps us identify phenomena that, while framed by different political and social arrangements, leads to a better understanding of a complex world and our place within it. In the study of counterterrorism and counterinsurgency, we are so often bound by the constraints of national thinking that a comparative perspective become especially valuable, because the security challenges facing the global community of responsible nations have many common characteristics.

In terms of course content, there are any number of themes which can generate classroom debate, themes around which educators can organize their courses. At a minimum, we recommend that courses on the intersection of WMD and terrorism should develop an understanding of core definitional issues, the trajectory of the growing threat, and the ways in which the U.S. and its allies are responding to the threat.

Definitional Issues

As the chapters in this volume illustrate, a single, unifying definition of the term "weapons of mass destruction" eludes policymakers, public/private researchers, law enforcement officials, and intelligence analysts alike. Once the American Dialect Society's 2002 word or phrase of the year, it more recently has been lampooned, overused and rendered almost worthless as a descriptor.[13] In July 2005, the Carnegie Endowment for International Peace took the unusual step of declaring that it will no longer use the phrase weapons of mass destruction, because it "confuses officials, befuddles the public, and justifies policies that more precise language and more accurate assessments would not support." In its place, Carnegie will "disaggregate" the threats, listing them individually as they actually appear (e.g., nuclear weapons, chemical weapons, etc.).[14]

Carnegie's efforts, however, do not appear to include highly destructive conventional means of terrorist attack, such as using aircraft as missiles. This has become a new category of WMD in and of itself which exceeds the destructive power of large vehicle-bomb attacks, even ones as destructive as the 1983 Marine Barracks bombing in Beirut, Lebanon or the 1996 Khobar Towers attack in Saudi Arabia. In Andrew O'Neill's chapter on the severity of the WMD threat, he states:

> The 1993 attacks on the World Trade Center, the 1995 Oklahoma City bombing, and the 11 September 2001 attacks each had the effect of dramatically illustrating America's vulnerability to terrorism. *While none of these attacks involved the use of WMD*, they nevertheless raised fears about the possibility of such an attack on American territory. (author's emphasis)

This viewpoint is not necessarily incorrect, but the U.S. has chosen to include conventional explosives in its legal definition, and convicted Oklahoma City bomber Timothy McVeigh on the charge of using a Weapon of Mass Destruction.[15]

This does not mean the U.S. government has not tried to define the more unconventional WMD threats. There are now a dozen different laws on the books, found mostly in the Title 18 U.S. Code (USC),[16] which deal with various aspects of WMD terrorism. Some of these may be more appropriately considered "weapons of mass *disruption*"—for example, William Potter notes that radiological dispersal devices (RDDs) will not kill many people or cause massive damage, but potentially could have economic and psychological effects.[17] In 18 USC Section 2332h, which focuses specifically on RDDs, it states:

> [I]t shall be unlawful for any person to knowingly produce, construct, otherwise acquire, transfer directly or indirectly, receive, possess, import, export, or use, or possess and threaten to use (A) any weapon that is designed or intended to release radiation or radioactivity *at a level dangerous to human life*; or (B) any device or other object that is capable of and designed or intended *to endanger human life* through the release of radiation or radioactivity. (author's emphasis)

In other words, this part of the statute is focused on a RDD being dangerous to human life, as opposed to its more likely non-lethal consequences. Such a statute could present loopholes to potential prosecution. However, Section 831 of Title 18, "Prohibited transactions involving nuclear materials," generally covers the illicit acquisition of radioactive material to be used in a RDD, and Section 832, "Participation in nuclear and weapons of mass destruction threats to the United States," states that:

> Whoever without lawful authority *develops, possesses, or attempts or conspires to develop or possess a radiological weapon, or threatens to use or uses a radiological weapon* against any person within the United States, or a national of the United States while such national is outside of the United States or against any property that is owned, leased, funded, or used by the United States, whether that property is within or outside of the United States, shall be imprisoned for any term of years or for life. (author's emphasis)

By using three overlapping sections of 18 USC, the U.S. government has most legal bases covered in relation to the radiological weapon threat, although one can see the difficulty in this patchwork approach, which has been developed over time and in response to our expanding knowledge of terrorist intent and potential capabilities.

Many scholars and practitioners prefer the more tactically-oriented and all-inclusive phrase "chemical, biological, radiological, nuclear, and explosives terrorism," or CBRNE, because it covers the full spectrum of unconventional and conventional explosive weapons that can cause either mass damage and casualties ("mass" also has still not been adequately defined, but presumably it means more than what a typical community's first responders could handle), and more small scale uses, such as assassination. Such a definition is more useful in the terrorism milieu, where even a failed small-scale attack will command media attention. However, given the prevalence of the acronym WMD in scholarly literature, mainstream media and policy debates, it is unlikely to be replaced anytime soon by the more fine-grained CBRNE. We will use both acronyms interchangeably throughout the remainder of this chapter.

The Ballooning Threat: Perception and Reality

Students of WMD and terrorism courses should come to understand how the lack of a generally agreed definition has led to a hyping of the threat. With no defined boundaries, literally everything and anything toxic in our society is touted as an equally threatening unconventional mode of attack: chemical plants, nuclear power plants, toxic industrial chemicals in all forms and shipped in all modes of transportation, any radioactive source, and every natural and man-made disease affecting man and his food supply allegedly are fair game for the terrorist, with worst case consequences for all who don't spend a king's ransom to protect against it. As Brian Jenkins points out in his chapter, "Scenarios that seemed far-fetched in the 1970s are now plausible; in fact, 9/11 redefined plausibility. In present attempts to anticipate and prepare for what terrorists might do next, virtually no scenario is dismissed."[18]

However, the reality is more sobering. There are real constraints and hurdles—psychological, technical, operational, and organizational—that terrorists must overcome before using many (if not most) of these much touted threats.[19] Only two terrorist groups are known to have ever semi-seriously considered (or are considering) acquiring a nuclear weapon: Aum Shinrikyo and al Qaeda. Yet since the late 1960s, analysts and scholars have talked about the increasing potential for nuclear terrorism and loosening constraints against its use, so we must now ask ourselves nearly 40 years later if the recent (but already ubiquitous) "not if, but when" mentality which permeates the CBRNE terrorism debate is still applicable in all cases of the threat. Otherwise, we should be awash in terrorist attacks using improvised chemical, biological, radiological or nuclear weapons by now. The reality is that despite all the ink dedicated to the topic, there have only been a handful of CBRNE terrorist incidents, few of which have been effective in killing anyone. If one expands the field to include criminal cases, the numbers go into the tens or dozens.[20]

Furthermore, as illustrated in several chapters of this volume, not all types of CBRNE weapons can be treated the same. Terrorists must determine which of these threats— chemical, biological, radiological, nuclear or conventional explosives—strike the right balance of effectiveness (both real and psychological), cost effectiveness and ease of acquisition, and operational deployability. Aum Shinrikyo's expensive program to develop and deploy weapons using sarin, anthrax, and botulinum toxin presents a stark contrast to the crude chemical and toxin recipes found in mujahedin training manuals and al Qaeda videos of senseless cyanide chemical tests on tethered animals recovered in Afghanistan by the U.S. media. Only after we invaded Afghanistan did we find out the true nature of the al Qaeda WMD threat at the time.[21] As described earlier in this chapter, knowledge plays a central role in a group's WMD capabilities.

U.S. Policy Response

A third important area of study and classroom discussion examines the myriad policy responses to the WMD threat. In June 1995, only three months after the Tokyo subway sarin gas attack, President Clinton signed *Presidential Decision Directive 39* which clearly stated that:

> The United States shall give the highest priority to developing effective capabilities to detect, prevent, defeat and manage the consequences of nuclear, biological or chemical (NBC) materials or weapons use by terrorists. The acquisition of weapons of mass destruction by a terrorist group, through theft or manufacture, is unacceptable. *There is no higher priority* than preventing the acquisition of this capability or removing this capability from terrorist groups potentially opposed to the U.S.[22] (author emphasis).

More recently, the post-9/11 flurry of policies has included the release of several new strategic documents which outline how the U.S. will confront the threat of CBRNE terrorism. To begin with, the Bush administration released its first *National Security Strategy of the United States* (NSS) in 2002, followed by a *National Strategy for Combating Terrorism* (NSCT) in 2003, and then issued an updated version of both strategy documents in 2006. The most recent NSS describes how the U.S. must "prevent our enemies from threatening us, our allies, and our friends with weapons of mass destruction (WMD)"[23] and states that we must:

> Deny WMD to rogue states and to terrorist allies who would use them without hesitation. Terrorists have a perverse moral code that glorifies deliberately targeting innocent civilians. Terrorists try to inflict as many casualties as possible and seek WMD to this end. Denying terrorists WMD will require new tools and new international approaches. We are working with partner nations to improve security at vulnerable nuclear sites

worldwide and bolster the ability of states to detect, disrupt, and respond to terrorist activity involving WMD.[24]

Similarly, the 2006 NSCT notes that "Our greatest and gravest concern is WMD in the hands of terrorists. Preventing their acquisition and the dire consequences of their use is a key priority of this strategy."[25]

As illustrated in Figure 1, there are six specific areas in which the U.S. seeks to counter the WMD threat. First, knowledge and intelligence about a particular terrorist group (and particularly its capabilities and intentions) is vital, as described earlier in this chapter. Second, denying terrorists access to materials and expertise is a critical component of any counterterrorism strategy. Third, reflecting a debate articulated in several chapters of this volume, we must find ways to deter terrorists from using WMD if they do acquire the capability to do so. Fourth, our strategy must include better intelligence on the trafficking of WMD-related materials, weapons and experts. Fifth, if our efforts produce actionable intelligence of a potential WMD attack, we must be prepared to act quickly to prevent and respond to this. And lastly, our strategy requires us to develop the capacity for determining the true source of a WMD terror attack, in order to respond accordingly. These six elements of the NSCT reflect the absolute necessity of bilateral and multilateral cooperation, as well as interagency coordination, in combating the threat of WMD terrorism.

Global cooperation is also emphasized in the *National Strategy to Combat Weapons of Mass Destruction (NSPD-17/HSPD-4),* formally issued in December 2002, which states that: "The United States, our friends and allies, and the broader international community

Figure 1 National Strategy for Combating Terrorism, 2006 (excerpt on WMD terrorism)

Our comprehensive approach for addressing WMD terrorism hinges on six objectives, and we will work across all objectives simultaneously to maximize our ability to eliminate the threat.

– *Determine terrorists' intentions, capabilities, and plans to develop or acquire WMD.* We need to understand and assess the credibility of threat reporting and provide technical assessments of terrorists' WMD capabilities.

– *Deny terrorists access to the materials, expertise, and other enabling capabilities required to develop WMD.* We have an aggressive, global approach to deny our enemies access to WMD-related materials (with a particular focus on weapons-usable fissile materials), fabrication expertise, methods of transport, sources of funds, and other capabilities that facilitate the execution of a WMD attack. In addition to building upon existing initiatives to secure materials, we are developing innovative approaches that blend classic counterproliferation, nonproliferation, and counterterrorism efforts.

– *Deter terrorists from employing WMD.* A new deterrence calculus combines the need to deter terrorists and supporters from contemplating a WMD attack and, failing that, to dissuade them from actually conducting an attack. Traditional threats may not work because terrorists show a wanton disregard for the lives of innocents and in some cases for their own lives. We require a range of deterrence strategies that are tailored to the situation and the adversary. We will make clear that terrorists and those who aid or sponsor a WMD attack would face the prospect of an overwhelming response to any use of such weapons. We will seek to dissuade attacks by improving our ability to mitigate the effects of a terrorist attack involving WMD — to limit or prevent large-scale casualties, economic disruption, or panic. Finally, we will ensure that our capacity to determine the source of any attack is well-known, and that our determination to respond overwhelmingly to any attack is never in doubt.

– *Detect and disrupt terrorists' attempted movement of WMD-related materials, weapons, and personnel.* We will expand our global capability for detecting illicit materials, weapons, and personnel transiting abroad or heading for the United States or U.S. interests overseas. We will use our global partnerships, international agreements, and ongoing border security and interdiction efforts. We also will continue to work with countries to enact and enforce strict penalties for WMD trafficking and other suspect WMD-related activities.

– *Prevent and respond to a WMD-related terrorist attack.* Once the possibility of a WMD attack against the United States has been detected, we will seek to contain, interdict, and eliminate the threat. We will continue to develop requisite capabilities to eliminate the possibility of a WMD operation and to prevent a possible follow-on attack. We will prepare ourselves for possible WMD incidents by developing capabilities to manage the range of consequences that may result from such an attack against the United States or our interests around the world.

– *Define the nature and source of a terrorist-employed WMD device*. Should a WMD terrorist attack occur, the rapid identification of the source and perpetrator of an attack will enable our response efforts and may be critical in disrupting follow-on attacks. We will develop the capability to assign responsibility for the intended or actual use of WMD via accurate attribution — the rapid fusion of technical forensic data with intelligence and law enforcement information.

must undertake every effort to prevent states and terrorists from acquiring WMD and missiles."[26] While international cooperation is called for in these national-level strategic documents, the practical implementation involves a more focused, agency-level approach, and thus we have seen numerous individual organizations within the U.S. government releasing their own strategies for combating terrorism and WMD, particularly the Department of Defense.[27] At all levels, strategic documents like these help set the stage for the public debate on defining the priorities of the War on Terrorism. They also demonstrate that under the Bush Administration, countering both state-sponsored WMD programs and terrorist CBRN threats remains a national priority. As Vice President Richard Cheney observed during a November 2001 intelligence briefing, "If there's a one percent chance that Pakistani scientists are helping al Qaeda build or develop a nuclear weapon, we have to treat it as a certainty in terms of our response."[28]

There are three general policy approaches to dealing with both government-sponsored WMD programs and CBRNE terrorism: preemption, deterrence, and nonproliferation regimes. Preemption, the subject of so much debate since it was first articulated by President Bush during his commencement address in May 2002 at West Point, was subsequently enshrined in a few short passages in his administration's first *National Security Strategy* later that September. The 2006 NSS articulates this policy as follows: "To forestall or prevent such hostile acts by our adversaries, the United States will, if necessary, act preemptively in exercising our inherent right of self-defense."[29] In practice, there have been few opportunities to preempt terrorist acquisition or use of CBRNE weapons, although the Bush administration has claimed state acquisition of WMD by Iraq—and its potential for passage to terrorist groups—as part of its rationale for the war in Iraq.

The concept of deterrence—long a principle of Cold War foreign policy—is receiving increasing attention for its potential use against terrorist CBRNE. In this volume,

Daniel Whiteneck's chapter on terrorist deterrence and Lew Dunn's case study on deterring possible al Qaeda nuclear weapons acquisition and use are just the most recent and thoughtful contributions of a burgeoning literature in this area.[30] Both eschew the long-held idea that terrorists willing to die for their cause are undeterrable. In addition to trying to determine conclusively whether al Qaeda is trying to acquire a nuclear weapon (and thus what action(s) it is The U.S. is trying to deter), Dunn proposes several courses of action, highlighting three potential deterrence leverage points: "technical assistance from black marketeers as well as from individuals with insider access; funding and logistics support from al Qaeda fellow-travelers; and official or governmental direct or indirect support for al Qaeda's acquisition of NBC/R weaponry."[31] Perhaps there *are* actionable pressure points that policymakers can target to help keep terrorists in the conventional weapons box. If al Qaeda in Iraq leader Abu Ayyub al-Masri is looking for scientific expertise to come to Iraq to create biological or "dirty" weapons (as implied by his quote provided earlier this chapter), then maybe expertise is harder for terrorists to acquire than we currently think. It is clearly an avenue for further research.

In addition, confidence in the nation's ability to respond to a successful CBRNE incident is also a potentially useful deterrent, as well as a boost to citizen morale. The disastrous U.S. consequence management response to Hurricane Katrina in 2005, outlined in part in Crystal Franco's chapter on the collapse of the medical system[32]—coming close on the heels of the much ballyhooed and lengthy re-write of the bloated 426-page *National Response Plan* published in December 2004—does not inspire such confidence. While a terrorist CBRNE attack, short of a nuclear weapon, is unlikely to cause the widespread damage that results from a major hurricane, it can still demonstrate the U.S.' impotence if the response is disjointed and ineffective. An excellent performance by the Department of Homeland Security (DHS) and special CBRNE units such as the FBI Hazardous Materials Response Unit (HMRU), the U.S. Marine Corps Chemical Biological Incident Response Force (CBIRF) and the National Guard's WMD Civil Support Teams (not to mention local and state first responders and hazmat teams) might make a terrorist group think twice about wasting its scarce resources carrying out an embarrassingly ineffective CBRN attack. While the historical record is not good, as shown in the 2001 Anthrax and 1995 Tokyo Subway case studies in this compendium, more recent cases such as the intercepted ricin letters mailed to Senate office buildings and the White House in late 2003 provided such units with valuable operational experience and demonstrated an effective response. We can also learn from the experience of our allies, as shown in Bruce Hoffman's timely case study of the 2003 ricin threats in the United Kingdom.[33]

In the area of non-proliferation regimes, the fundamental question is this: can agreements designed by and for nation states have an effect on the acquisition of CBRNE weapons by terrorists? Certainly, they can be somewhat effective against state sponsors of terrorism and national-level WMD programs. Those more optimistic about non-proliferation agreements believe they can retard the ability of a terrorist group to receive such technology, or a complete weapon, from a state sponsor.

The logic is that if the nation state is prevented, then it cannot hand unconventional weapons over to terrorists. Meanwhile, others—such as Andrew O'Neil in his chapter of this volume—argue that it is doubtful that any nation state would give up its valuable CBRN weapons to terrorist groups anyway, and would risk a U.S. and international military response if the link were uncovered. If so, such non-proliferation agreements are superfluous to how a terrorist group acquires CBRNE capabilities, as they will be forced to do it indigenously. Still others would point to the case of the Aum Shinrikyo and how the group was able to acquire much of its CBRN technology despite the existence of international agreements. Thus, there are seams that both proliferators and terrorists can exploit—as described in the chapters by Ellis, Carter and Kane[34]—and the vulnerabilities created by these seams must be addressed through a mix of strategies and international agreements that involve both the public and private sectors.

Beyond preemption, deterrence and nonproliferation, a fourth area of activity has recently emerged as a critical component of any WMD strategy: combating the visions that seek to rationalize mass destruction. For most terrorist groups, the rationalization for violence is framed by an ideology which articulates a particular vision of the future, a vision that its adherents believe cannot be achieved without resorting to terrorism. This vision can take any number of forms, including political change—like an insurgency movement's objective to overthrow an established government—as well as religious devotion. Most terrorist groups engage in their own form of strategic influence, seeking to connect with individuals on an intellectual and emotional level in order to provide a rationale for the use of violence in pursuit of their vision. Understanding the ideological nature of modern terrorism thus becomes an important component of any counterterrorism strategy. Historically, ideas and visions have rarely (if ever) been defeated purely by kinetic force. In fact, the use of hard power in many cases may actually strengthen the appeal and perceived validity of a group's ideology. The ideology of a particular group may also help determine their likelihood for acquiring and using weapons of mass destruction. Indeed, as described earlier in this chapter, a number of scholars have suggested that groups fueled by a religious ideology—and particularly an apocalyptic ideology—are more likely than non-religious oriented groups to pursue WMD.[35] Clearly, according to the April 2006 *National Intelligence Estimate,* "CBRN capabilities will continue to be sought by jihadist groups."[36]

As British terror expert JP Larsson has observed, there are several reasons why religious ideologies provide a uniquely powerful challenge for counterterrorists. First, these ideologies are often theologically supremacist—meaning that all believers assume superiority over non-believers, who are not privy to the truth of the religion. Second, most are exclusivist—believers are a chosen people, or their territory is a holy land. Third, many are absolutist; in other words, it is not possible to be a half-hearted believer, and you are either totally within the system, or totally without it. Further, only the true believers are guaranteed salvation and victory, whereas the enemies and the unbelievers—as well as those who have taken no stance whatsoever—are condemned to some sort of eternal punishment or damnation, as well as death. Overall, religious ideologies help foster polarizing values in terms of right and wrong, good and evil, light and dark—values which can be co-opted by terrorist organizations to convert a "seeker" into a lethal killer.[37]

According to Steve Simon, religious ideology and devotion provides the lens through which a group's members see their purpose in life, and thus traditional strategies of deterrence are unlikely to work, given the group's willingness to die in the process of fighting, and given the messianic beliefs associated with the members of these groups.[38] Combating terrorism that is driven by an extreme religious or apocalyptic vision thus requires sophisticated skills in public diplomacy and strategic communication, in order to influence the communities which might find these kinds of vision appealing. Furthermore, the communication of compelling ideas and visions to various audiences around the world in the hopes of impacting their behavior—often called strategic influence, "winning hearts and minds," or "winning the war of ideas"—must involve credible voices from within the target audience. For example, we must engage credible Islamic leaders in our global efforts to combat Islamic extremist groups who attempt to rationalize a WMD attack as God's will.

Today, a central battleground in this war of ideas (or ideologies) is the Internet. The struggle for influence taking place online between liberal democracies and extremists involves various forms of strategic communication. Members of the global salafi jihadist network use the Internet to provide motivational/ideological and operational information to potential recruits and supporters. They offer a simple, clear message to all kinds of "seekers"—join the global jihad. Further, there are multiple ways in which an individual can participate, such as providing funds, safe havens, or encouragement. The spectrum of participants can thus range from website designers to financiers to weapons experts and combat veterans. Meanwhile, the U.S. and its allies have launched a public diplomacy effort to dissuade these same individuals from supporting the terrorists' agenda. Our success in this strategic communications battleground—particularly as it pertains to religiously based arguments that support or refute the use of WMD terrorism—will have a long-lasting impact on our future national security.

The Long and Winding Road

What unconventional threats lie in wait for us in the future? Terrorism analysts (both private and government) have at times been notoriously bad at predicting the next trend in terrorism. While waiting for the last eleven years for the "next Aum" to emerge and conduct a true mass-casualty WMD attack, the U.S. has suffered the anthrax letters attack (not an inconsequential psychological or economic event, but one that was arguably lost in the noise of its conventional "big brother," the 9/11 attacks, which caused significantly more casualties), and a number of low-level ricin cases, mostly involving loners and right-wing extremists. The balance between CBRN and E (conventional explosives) must be addressed in our threat analysis. Recent revelations that U.S. government officials knew about the threat of liquid explosives on airliners since the time of Ramzi Yousef's "Bojinka" plot in 1994 have not necessarily been met with action, or even higher prioritization.[39] Yet as the thwarted United Kingdom-United States airline plot of August 2006 demonstrated, the use of novel explosives that can defeat current detection technology are very much in the minds of terrorists.[40]

How can we develop an accurate portrait of the future WMD terror threat? This is a critical question that should drive future research. One of the top issues for the DHS today is how to conduct accurate and realistic CBRNE threat and risk assessments, and how to translate these assessments into resource allocation formulas for CBRNE prevention and consequence management. In their chapter "Emerging WMD Technologies," Forrest Waller and Michael George recommend that we consistently monitor the evolving technical aspects of CBRN technology in order to avoid surprise.[41] The recent development of the *al-Mubtakker* toxic chemical dispersion device is but one example of this.[42] However, while a focus on technological developments is certainly a useful endeavor, the traditional "soft" factors such as intent, group dynamics, and operational capability are also important, and yet still defy easy solutions.

Gary Ackerman, the former Director of the Weapons of Mass Destruction Terrorism Research Program at the Monterey Institute for International Studies, has suggested several new lines of research in CBRN terrorism which would incorporate a range of dynamics and "soft factors" into our threat assessment equations. He also recommends a focus on the collaborative nexus between extremist groups and what this implies for the prospects of WMD terrorism; and a proposed mechanism for deterring state assistance to terrorists in the realm of WMD.[43] According to Ackerman, there is often a gap between purely academic and practical research in the terrorism arena, and this must be replaced by a more operational-friendly approach, such as producing a realistic threat assessment models that government analysts and policymakers can use on a daily basis. We would add the adjective "intuitive;" in other words, does it pass a common-sense test? Further, he writes that "Less quantifiable aspects such as the strength of the terrorist's motivation to use such weapons and the psychological vulnerability of American society to WMD are just as important, but are rarely included in current threat assessment models (at least in open sources)."[44]

The future of WMD terrorism research should also include what Ackerman calls "second order questions:" will any transition to terrorist CBRN use will be incremental and perceptible, with WMD incidents gradually increasing in frequency and severity, or can technological or motivational developments cause a sudden shift towards WMD use?[45] In addition, as discussed earlier in this chapter, we must examine how terrorists learn from each other, and how they might cooperate with other terror groups, states, or particularly dangerous individuals in developing their WMD capabilities. Within the global Sunni Islamic extremist network of which al Qaeda is but one part, there are many opportunities for collaboration and information transfer, as we have already seen with conventional weapons and tactics. Clearly, terrorists can glean knowledge from scientific open sources (a topic subject to a separate debate in academia), but there are also key scientific or technically competent individuals who—if properly motivated—could further a clandestine CBRN program. Understanding the centrality of knowledge (and critical knowledge workers) in the global WMD threat has implications for intelligence and counterterrorism policy.

There are several notable examples of this, including—as Adam Dolnik and Rohan Gunaratna describe in their chapter of this volume—how the Indonesian terror group Jemaah Islamiyah (JI) relied heavily on the bomb-making expertise of key members like Dr. Azahari bin Husin and Noordin Mohammed Top, and has sought to develop some expertise in CBRN weapons.[46] In 2001, al Qaeda operative Mohammed Atef approached JI leader Hambali with a request to find a scientist that would help them develop chemical and biological weapons. Hambali introduced Yazid Sufaat, a U.S. trained bio-chemist and former Malaysia military officer, who subsequently spent several months attempting to cultivate anthrax in a laboratory near the Kandahar airport. These and other examples reflect centrality of particularly knowledgeable individuals in the terrorist world.

Aum Shinrikyo's biological weapons program was founded in 1990 under the direction of Dr. Seichi Endo, a molecular biologist with a degree in genetic engineering, genetics, and medicine from the prestigious Kyoto University.[47] According to a 2001 report issued by the White House, Bashir-ud-Din Mahmood—a former Director for Nuclear Power at the Pakistani Atomic Energy Commission (PAEC)—founded a non-governmental organization Umma Tameer-E-Nau(UTN) which reportedly advocated equipping other Islamic nations with enriched uranium and weapons-grade plutonium.[48] During 2001, Mahmood allegedly met with Mullah Omar and with Osama bin Laden, and in a follow-up meeting, an associate of Osama bin Laden indicated he had nuclear material and wanted to know how to use it to make a weapon. Mahmood provided information about the infrastructure needed for a nuclear weapons program and the effects of nuclear weapons. In November 2001, the Taliban left Kabul and the workers at UTN's Kabul offices fled the area with them. Searches of UTN locations in Kabul reportedly yielded documents setting out a plan to kidnap a U.S. attaché and outlining basic nuclear physics related to nuclear weapons. Because of this, the U.S. government blocked the assets of UTN and three of its members, and according to press reports, Mahmood was placed under house arrest.[49]

Responding to the issue of knowledge proliferation, the U.S. government has begun providing millions of dollars in grants to Boston-area universities, medical centers, and high-tech companies to help employ idle scientists in the former Soviet Union, including weapons specialists who might otherwise be enticed to sell their deadly expertise on the black market.[50] The concern over scientists who might be tempted by bribes or coerced by terrorists is very real. In the first poll of its kind, a recent U.S. Department of Energy survey of more than 600 Russian physicists, chemists, and biologists found that about 20 percent say they would consider working for terrorist groups or so-called rogue states accused of sponsoring terrorism if they became desperate enough for work. Since the mid- to late 1990s, the U.S. government has granted more than 14,000 former Soviet scientists direct payments—sometimes called "welfare science"—simply to keep them from working for countries that support terrorism. But this more recent grant program is offering scientists meaningful work with some of the top American research institutions in hopes that they can bring some of their ideas to the commercial market.

Clearly, as this example illustrates, there are many future opportunities for practical, applicable research in the CBRN terrorism arena which can improve our nation's security. The dynamic complexities of the threat demands fresh approaches and perhaps closer cooperation with local, state and federal government agencies to find out what is required to support policy.[51]

Concluding Thoughts: Reasons for Optimism?

For many, the specter of WMD terrorism brings a dark cloud of impending doom. However, there are at least three reasons for optimism about the future. First, every indication suggests that we are becoming smarter about the threat and how to respond in creative and successful ways. A flurry of new research, policy statements, strategic doctrines, documentaries, and media reports reflect a rapidly increasing attention towards the issues addressed in this volume. Through new education programs, courses, and seminars, many countries are working to educate new generations of security professionals to think critically and creatively about the WMD threat and our response. As a result, an increasing amount of intellectual energy throughout the world is being directed toward finding ways to counter the threat with greater sophistication and success.

Second, we are constantly developing new technologies to help us mitigate the threat of WMD terrorist attacks. For example, Los Alamos National Laboratory scientists have developed a detector that can see through lead or other heavy shielding in truck trailers or cargo containers to detect uranium, plutonium or other dense materials that smugglers are trying to bring into the United States. Their technique—muon radiography—is far more sensitive than x-rays, with none of the radiation hazards of x-ray or gamma-ray detectors now in use at U.S. borders.[52] The U.S. has also invested in radiation detection devices at its ports to thwart attempts to smuggle a nuclear device or dirty bomb into the country.[53] The Department of Homeland Security is working to expand the Bio Watch system—a nation-wide array of sensors sniffing the air in select cities for signs of a bioterror attack—to a far more integrated network of potentially thousands of linked detectors, each monitoring areas as small as the section of a single building. The system was hurriedly put into place in the months before the war in Iraq in 2003 by piggybacking on a pollution-sensor system already built by the Environmental Protection Agency.[54]

And finally, a third reason for optimism is that the international community is showing new resolve in combating the proliferation of CBRN weapons and materials as well as other terrorism-related capabilities, such as financial networks and safe havens. In 2005, Libya renounced its weapons of mass destruction program and indicated it would convert its notorious Rabta chemical weapons factory into a pharmaceuticals plant to combat infectious diseases. Assistant Secretary of State Paula DeSutter called this "a real nonproliferation success story of the new millennium."[55] In May 2005, India's parliament passed a bill banning the transfer of weapons of mass destruction and related technology to states and terrorist groups. The Weapons of Mass Destruction and their Delivery Systems (Prohibition of Unlawful Activities) Bill seeks to prevent the leakage of missile technology to terrorist groups or states that are seeking to build nuclear weapons.[56] And the UN Security Council's October 2006 response to North Korea's nuclear weapons test—a unanimous condemnation and imposition of sanctions against a regime that had so clearly violated the will of the international community—is equally encouraging.

Amid these and other promising developments, the U.S. is providing technical assistance and educational support for other countries in order to develop their capacity to stem the proliferation of WMD materials and knowledge. Clearly, there is a widespread recognition in the U.S. that we cannot effectively counter the WMD terror threat on our own. From biological pathogens to clouds of deadly chemicals or radioactive material, CBRN weapons produce an impact which does not adhere to political or geographic borders. Thus, fueled by a growing understanding of shared risk, we are encouraged by the evolution of a worldwide collaborative effort to come to terms with the WMD threat and respond with increasing sophistication and success. For the sake of our children's future, we can do no less.

Acknowledgments

The views expressed are those of the authors and not of the Department of the Army, the U.S. Military Academy, or any other agency of the U.S. Government, nor do they constitute an endorsement of the publications cited.

Notes

All websites cited accessed and checked for functionality on October 1, 2006.
1. For more on this, please James J.F. Forest (ed.), *Teaching Terror: Strategic and Tactical Learning in the Terrorist World* (Lanham, MD: Rowman & Littlefield, 2006).
2. Brian A. Jackson, *Aptitude for Destruction, Volume 1: Organizational Learning in Terrorist Groups and its Implications for Combating Terrorism* (Santa Monica, CA: Rand Corporation, 2005), 51–59.
3. Ibid, 52.
4. Patrick Quinn, "Iraq terror leader recruits scientists," Associated Press, September 28, 2006.

5. For example, see Steve Bowman and Helit Barel. *Weapons of Mass Destruction—The Terrorist Threat* (CRS Report for Congress, RS20412). Washington, DC: Congressional Research Service (8 December 1999). Available online at: http://www.fas.org/irp/crs/RS20412.pdf.

6. Jonathan B. Tucker (ed.), *Toxic Terror: Assessing Terrorist Use of Chemical and Biological Weapons* (Cambridge, MA: MIT Press, 2000).

7. Gavin Cameron, *Nuclear Terrorism: A Threat Assessment for the 21st Century* (New York: St. Martin's, 1999).

8. Kaplan, David. "Aum Shinrikyo," in *Toxic Terror: Terror: Assessing Terrorist Use of Chemical and Biological Weapons,* edited by Jonathan Tucker (Cambridge, MA: MIT Press, 2000), 207–226. See also Manabu Watanabe, "Religion and Violence in Japan Today: A Chronological and Doctrinal Analysis of Aum Shinrikyo," *Terrorism and Political Violence* 10, no. 4 (Winter 1998), 80–100.

9. See "Scientific Paper on Milk Supply Delayed for Security Reasons," *The Associated Press,* 7 June 2005.

10. Cindy C. Combs, "The Media as a Showcase for Terrorism" in *Teaching Terror: Strategic and Tactical Learning in the Terrorist World*, edited by James J.F. Forest (Lanham, MD: Rowman & Littlefield, 2006).

11. For a free DVD of this movie, see the Nuclear Threat Initiative's website, at: http://www.lastbestchance.org.

12. For maps and reports on CBRN proliferation, see the Carnegie Endowment for International Peace website, at: http://www.carnegieendowment.org/npp.

13. American Dialect Society, "2002 Words of the Year," January 13, 2003, http://www.americandialect.org/index.php/amerdial/2002_words_of_the_y/; one of the most popular lampoons is the 2004 Trey Parker and Matt Stone film, "Team America: World Police," by Paramount Pictures, which spares no one and nothing in its portrayal of the war on terror and WMD. However, it's not for the easily offended.

14. Joseph Cirincione, "The End of 'WMD,' " July 07, 2005, http://www.carnegieendowment.org/npp/publications/index.cfm?fa=view&id=17166.

15. The main definition is in 18 USC Section 2332a and the referenced 18 USC Section 921 (which includes firearms and explosive devices). Even a small explosive device with less than a pound of explosive material, which can take down a commercial jet such as in the Pan Am 103 case if properly placed, is included. In the McVeigh case, there were 11 counts filed against him in the Federal case. Count 1 was "conspiracy to detonate a weapon of mass destruction" in violation of 18 USC § 2332a, culminating in the deaths of 168 people and destruction of the Alfred P. Murrah Federal Building in Oklahoma City, Oklahoma. Count 2 was "use of a weapon of mass destruction" in violation of 18 USC § 2332a (2)(a) & (b). Count 3 was "destruction by explosives resulting in death", in violation of 18 USC § 844(f)(2)(a) & (b). Counts 4 through 11 were first degree murder in violation of 18 USC § 1111, 1114, & 2 and 28 CFR § 64.2(h), each count in connection to one of the 8 law enforcement officers who were killed during the attack.

16. These are found in 18 USC Chapter 10—Biological Weapons, Chapter 11b—Chemical Weapons, and other sections of Chapter 113b—Terrorism, where Section 2332a is found. The amended Atomic Energy Act (42 USC) also contains several pertinent provisions relative to nuclear and radioactive materials and facilities.

17. William Potter, et al "Dispersing Radiation," in this volume.

18. Brian Jenkins, "The New Age of Terrorism," in this volume.

19. For more on this, see William Rosenau's chapter in this volume, "Aum Shinrikyo's Biological Weapons Program: Why Did It Fail?" which is an excellent case study of the many hurdles that must be overcome.

20. By criminal we mean those done for purposes of a purely criminal enterprise such as murder, revenge, extortion, etc. there have been a notable number of "lone criminal" cases in the U.S. in that past several years involving the manufacture of ricin toxin from castor beans.

21. Nic Robertson, "Disturbing scenes of death show capability with chemical gas," CNN, August 19, 2002, http://archives.cnn.com/2002/US/08/19/terror.tape.chemical/index.html. While some "terrorism experts" at the time jumped on the sarin bandwagon while viewing the video tests, more reasoned analysis later suggested a process consistent with creating hydrogen

cyanide gas by mixing cyanide crystals and acid. This is also consistent with the testimony of captured al Qaeda operatives like Ahmed Ressam, the so-called "Millennium Bomber," about tests he allegedly witnessed while in Afghanistan prior to 9/11. The state of affairs of the al Qaeda CBRN program at the time of the U.S. invasion in December 2001, and the accuracy of U.S. intelligence analyst efforts prior to then are contained in *The Commission on the Intelligence Capabilities of the United States Regarding Weapons of Mass Destruction,* "Chapter Three Case Study: Al-Qa'ida in Afghanistan," March 31, 2005; http://www.wmd. gov/rcport/chaptcr3_fm.pdf.

22. The White House, "U.S. Policy on Counterterrorism," *Presidential Decision Directive–39,* June 21, 1995, partially redacted version found at http://www.gwu.edu/~nsarchiv/NSAEBB/ NSAEBB55/pdd39.pdf; descriptions of the development of PDD-39 can be found in Richard A. Clarke, *Against All Enemies* (New York: Free Press, 2004), p. 90–92, and Daniel Benjamin and Steven Simon, *The Age of Sacred Terror* (New York: Random House, 2002), p. 228–231.

23. The White House. *National Security Strategy of the United States* (March 2006), online at: http://www.whitehouse.gov/nsc/nss/2006.

24. The White House. *National Security Strategy of the United States* (March 2006), online at: http://www.whitehouse.gov/nsc/nss/2006.

25. The White House. National Strategy for Combating Terrorism (September 2006). Online at http://www.whitehouse.gov/nsc/nsct/2006.

26. The White House. *National Strategy to Combat Weapons of Mass Destruction* (NSPD-17/ HSPD-4), online at: http://www.fas.org/irp/offdocs/nspd/nspd-17.html.

27. Chairman of the Joint Chiefs of Staff, *National Military Strategic Plan for the War on Terrorism,* 1 February 2006 & *National Military Strategy to Combat Weapons of Mass Destruction,* 16 February 2006.

28. Quoted in Ron Suskind, *The One Percent Doctrine: Deep Inside America's Pursuit of its Enemies Since 9/11* (New York: Simon and Schuster, 2006), p.62.

29. The White House. *National Security Strategy of the United States* (March 2006), online at: http://www.whitehouse.gov/nsc/nss/2006.

30. See Daniel Whiteneck, "Deterring Terrorists: Thoughts on a Framework," and Lewis A. Dunn, "Can al Qaeda Be Deterred from Using Nuclear Weapons?" in this volume. Another analysis of this issue includes the little known "Can We Deter Terrorists From Employing Weapons Of Mass Destruction on the U.S. Homeland?" by Colonel Gordon Drake, United States Army, Group Captain Warrick Paddon, Royal Australian Air Force, and Lieutenant Colonel Daniel Ciechanowski, United States Air Force, written as part of the National Security Program Discussion Paper Series, 2003, at the JFK School of Government, Harvard University.

31. Dunn, "Can al Qaeda Be Deterred from Using Nuclear Weapons?"

32. See Crystal Franco, et al., "Systemic Collapse: Medical Care in the Aftermath of Hurricane Katrina" in this volume.

33. See Elin Gursky, Thomas V. Inglesby and Tara O'Toole, "Anthrax 2001: Observations on the Medical and Public Health Response," and Bruce Hoffman, "London Ricin Plot" in this volume. Also, for more on the U.S. ricin case, see the FBI Press release at http://www.fbi.gov/ pressrel/pressrel04/ricin022304.htm.

34. See Jason D. Ellis, "The Best Defense: Counterproliferation and U.S. National Security," Ashton B. Carter, "How to Counter WMD," and Chen Zak Kane, "Gaps in the Framework" in this volume.

35. See Mark Juergensmeyer, "Holy Orders: Religious Opposition to Modern States." *Harvard International Review* Vol. 25 (Winter 2004), p. 34–38; Jonathan B. Tucker (ed.), *Toxic Terror: Assessing Terrorist Use of Chemical and Biological Weapons* (Cambridge, MA: MIT Press, 2000); Gavin Cameron, *Nuclear Terrorism: A Threat Assessment for the 21st Century* (New York: St. Martin's, 1999); Paul Pillar, "Counterterrorism after Al Qaeda." *The Washington Quarterly,* Volume 27, Number 3 (Summer 2004); and Stephan P. Lambert, *"Y: The Sources of Islamic Revolutionary Conduct."* Washington, DC: Center for Strategic Intelligence Research, 2005.

36. Director of National Intelligence, "Declassified Key Judgments of the National Intelligence Estimate. Trends in Global Terrorism: Implications for the United States," dated April 2006, released September 26, 2006, http://www.dni.gov/press_releases/Declassified_NIE_Key_Judgments.pdf.

37. JP Larsson, "The Role of Religious Ideology in Terrorist Recruitment," in *The Making of a Terrorist (Volume 1: Recruitment)*, edited by James JF Forest (Westport, CT: Praeger Security International, 2005).

38. Steven Simon, "The New Terrorism," *Brookings Review,* Vol. 21, Issue 1 (Winter 2003). Online at: http://www.brookings.edu/press/review/winter2003/simon.htm.

39. For more on this plot, please see Rohan Gunaratna, "Al Qaeda's Lose and Learn Doctrine: The Trajectory from Oplan Bojinka to 9/11," in *Teaching Terror: Strategic and Tactical Learning in the Terrorist World,* edited by James J.F. Forest (Lanham, MD: Rowman & Littlefield, 2006).

40. Matthew L. Wald and Eric Lipton, "Technology: Liquid Threat Is Hard to Detect," *The New York Times*, August 11, 2006, and "Domestic Security: Focused on 9/11, U.S. Is Seen to Lag on New Threats," *The New York Times*, August 12, 2006; also Spencer S. Hsu, "DHS Terror Research Agency Struggling: Science and Technology Unit Crippled by Turnover, Budget Cuts, Priority Shifts," *The Washington Post*, August 20, 2006; A08.

41. Forrest Waller and Michael George, "Emerging WMD Technologies" in this volume.

42. Initially reported in Ron Suskind, "The Untold Story of al Qaeda's Plot to Attack the Subways," *TIME*, June 19, 2006, http://www.time.com/time/magazine/printout/0,8816,1205478,00.html, then in his book cited in footnote 3. A detailed analysis of the *al-Mubtakker* is found in Sammy Salama, "Special Report: Manual For Producing Chemical Weapon To Be Used In New York Subway Plot Available On Al Qaeda Websites Since Late 2005," *WMD Insights,* July/August 2006 Issue, http://wmdinsights.com/I7/I7_ME1_SP_MaunualFor.htm. Salama works with Ackerman at the Monterey Institute Center for Nonproliferation Studies and with the Combating Terrorism Center at West Point.

43. Gary Ackerman, "WMD Terrorism Research: Whereto from Here?" *International Studies Review*, 7:1, p.140–143. A copy of his paper was presented at the Conference on Non-State Actors, Terrorism, and Weapons of Mass Destruction in October 2004, and is posted at posted on the at University of Maryland's Center for International Development and Conflict Management (CIDCM) website: http://www.cidcm.umd.edu/carnegie/papers/ackerman.pdf#search=%22gary%20ackerman%20wmd%20research%22.

44. Ackerman, Ibid,.

45. Ackerman, Ibid, p. 8–9.

46. For more on this, see Adam Dolnik and Rohan Gunaratna, "Jemaah Islamiyah and the Threat of Chemical and Biological Terrorism," in this volume.

47. Miller, Judith, *Germs: Biological Weapons and America's Secret War,* (New York: Touchstone, 2002) p. 160. Cited in *Adam Dolnik and Rohan Gunaratna*, "Jemaah Islamiyah and the Threat of Chemical and Biological Terrorism," in this volume. For more on this, see *William Rosenau,* "Aum Shinrikyo's Biological Weapons Program: Why Did it Fail?" in this volume.

48. The White House, "Fact Sheet—Day 100 of the War on Terrorism: More Steps to Shut Down Terrorist Support Networks," December 20, 2001, http://www.whitehouse.gov/news/releases/2001/12/20011220-8.html. In addition to Mahmood, Abdul Majeed, a former high-ranking official at the PAEC and an expert in nuclear fuels; and S.M. Tufail, an industrialist, also had assets blocked.

49. Ibid., in addition to Mahmood, Abdul Majeed, a former high-ranking official at the PAEC and an expert in nuclear fuels; and S.M. Tufail, an industrialist, also had assets blocked. A lengthier article on Mahmood and UTN was published by David Albright and Holly Higgins, "Pakistani Nuclear Scientists: How Much Nuclear Assistance to Al Qaeda?" August 30, 2002, http://www.exportcontrols.org/pakscientists.html. For the interview with Mahmood's son Asim, see Peter Baker, "Pakistani Scientist Who Met Bin Laden Failed Polygraphs, Renewing Suspicions," *Washington Post Foreign Service*, Sunday, March 3, 2002; Page A01, http://www.washingtonpost.com/ac2/wp-dyn/A29790-2002Mar2.

50. "US Funding Boosts Ex-Soviet Scientists," *Boston Globe* (14 October, 2005). Online at: http://www.boston.com/news/nation/articles/2005/10/14/us_funding_boosts_ex_soviet_scientists?mode=PF.
51. The Department of Homeland Security has started such a program with a number of U.S. universities and affiliated organizations called Homeland Security Centers of Excellence, http://www.dhs.gov/dhspublic/interapp/editorial/editorial_0498.xml.
52. "Muon Detector Could Thwart Nuclear Smugglers," *Science Blog*, (3 March, 2005). Online at: http://www.scienceblog.com/cms/node/7136/print.
53. "U.S. Invests in Radiation Detectors for Ports," *Reuters* (2 March, 2005). Online at: http://www.reuters.com/printerFriendlyPopup.jhtml?type=domesticNews&storyID=7787983.
54. "BioWar: Biowatch Expansion Developing," *The Washington Times* (24 February, 2005). Online at: http://www.washtimes.com/upi-breaking/20050223-050219-2359r.htm.
55. *"Libya Renounces Weapons of Mass Destruction,"* The Daily Nonproliferator, (Department of State E-Journal), 6 April 2005. online at: http://usinfo.state.gov/journals/itps/0305/ijpe/desutter.htm.
56. "India OKs WMD Bill," *World Peace Herald* (5/13/2005). Online at: http://www.wpherald.com/print.php?StoryID=20050513-112809-5137r.

James J.F. Forest is director of terrorism studies and associate professor of political Science at the U.S. Military Academy at West Point, where he teaches courses on terrorism, counterterrorism and information warfare, and directs research initiatives for the Combating Terrorism Center. His recent publications include *Teaching Terror: Strategic and Tactical Learning in the Terrorist World* (2006), *Homeland Security and Terrorism* (2005), and *The Making of a Terrorist: Recruitment, Training and Root Causes* (2005). His research has also appeared in the *Cambridge Review of International Affairs,* the *Journal of Political Science Education,* and *Democracy and Security.*

Aaron Danis is a career terrorism threat analyst with the U.S. government, having worked for five different agencies in that capacity over the past 17 years.

Appendix A.1.1

National Strategy to Combat Weapons of Mass Destruction

The White House, December 2002

"The gravest danger our Nation faces lies at the crossroads of radicalism and technology. Our enemies have openly declared that they are seeking weapons of mass destruction, and evidence indicates that they are doing so with determination. The United States will not allow these efforts to succeed. . . . History will judge harshly those who saw this coming danger but failed to act. In the new world we have entered, the only path to peace and security is the path of action."

—President Bush, The National Security Strategy of the United States of America,
September 17, 2002

Introduction

Weapons of mass destruction (WMD)—nuclear, biological, and chemical—in the possession of hostile states and terrorists represent one of the greatest security challenges facing the United States. We must pursue a comprehensive strategy to counter this threat in all of its dimensions.

An effective strategy for countering WMD, including their use and further proliferation, is an integral component of the National Security Strategy of the United States of America. As with the war on terrorism, our strategy for homeland security, and our new concept of deterrence, the U.S. approach to combat WMD represents a fundamental change from the past. To succeed, we must take full advantage of today's opportunities, including the application of new technologies, increased emphasis on intelligence collection and analysis, the strengthening of alliance relationships, and the establishment of new partnerships with former adversaries.

Weapons of mass destruction could enable adversaries to inflict massive harm on the United States, our military forces at home and abroad, and our friends and allies. Some states, including several that have supported and continue to support terrorism, already possess WMD and are seeking even greater capabilities, as tools of coercion and intimidation. For them, these are not weapons of last resort, but militarily useful weapons of choice intended to overcome our nation's advantages in conventional forces and to deter us from responding to aggression against our friends and allies in regions of vital interest. In addition, terrorist groups are seeking to acquire WMD with the stated purpose of killing large numbers of our people and those of friends and allies—without compunction and without warning.

We will not permit the world's most dangerous regimes and terrorists to threaten us with the world's most destructive weapons. We must accord the highest priority to the protection of the United States, our forces, and our friends and allies from the existing and growing WMD threat.

Pillars of Our National Strategy

Our National Strategy to Combat Weapons of Mass Destruction has three principal pillars:

Counterproliferation to Combat WMD Use

The possession and increased likelihood of use of WMD by hostile states and terrorists are realities of the contemporary security environment. It is therefore critical that the U. S. military and appropriate civilian agencies be prepared to deter and defend against the full range of possible WMD employment scenarios. We will ensure that all needed capabilities to combat WMD are fully integrated into the emerging defense transformation plan and into our homeland security posture. Counterproliferation will also be fully integrated into the basic doctrine, training, and equipping of all forces, in order to ensure that they can sustain operations to decisively defeat WMD-armed adversaries.

Strengthened Nonproliferation to Combat WMD Proliferation

The United States, our friends and allies, and the broader international community must undertake every effort to prevent states and terrorists from acquiring WMD and missiles. We must enhance traditional measures—diplomacy, arms control, multilateral agreements, threat reduction assistance, and export controls—that seek to dissuade or impede proliferant states and terrorist networks, as well as to slow and make more costly their access to sensitive technologies, material, and expertise. We must ensure compliance with relevant international agreements, including the Nuclear Nonproliferation Treaty (NPT), the Chemical Weapons Convention (CWC), and the Biological Weapons Convention (BWC). The United States will continue to work with other states to improve their capability to prevent unauthorized transfers of WMD and missile technology, expertise, and material. We will identify and pursue new methods of prevention, such as national criminalization of proliferation activities and expanded safety and security measures.

Consequence Management to Respond to WMD Use

Finally, the United States must be prepared to respond to the use of WMD against our citizens, our military forces, and those of friends and allies. We will develop and maintain the capability to reduce to the extent possible the potentially horrific consequences of WMD attacks at home and abroad.

The three pillars of the U.S. national strategy to combat WMD are seamless elements of a comprehensive approach. Serving to integrate the pillars are four cross-cutting enabling functions that need to be pursued on a priority basis: intelligence collection and analysis on WMD, delivery systems, and related technologies; research and development to improve our ability to respond to evolving threats; bilateral and multilateral cooperation; and targeted strategies against hostile states and terrorists.

Counterproliferation

We know from experience that we cannot always be successful in preventing and containing the proliferation of WMD to hostile states and terrorists. Therefore, U.S. military and appropriate civilian agencies must possess the full range of operational capabilities to counter the threat and use of WMD by states and terrorists against the United States, our military forces, and friends and allies.

Interdiction

Effective interdiction is a critical part of the U.S. strategy to combat WMD and their delivery means. We must enhance the capabilities of our military, intelligence, technical, and law enforcement communities to prevent the movement of WMD materials, technology, and expertise to hostile states and terrorist organizations.

Deterrence

Today's threats are far more diverse and less predictable than those of the past. States hostile to the United States and to our friends and allies have demonstrated their willingness to take high risks to achieve their goals, and are aggressively pursuing WMD and their means of delivery as critical tools in this effort. As a consequence, we require new methods of deterrence. A strong declaratory policy and effective military forces are essential elements of our contemporary deterrent posture, along with the full range of political tools to persuade potential adversaries not to seek or use WMD. The United States will continue to make clear that it reserves the right to respond with overwhelming force—including through resort to all of our options—to the use of WMD against the United States, our forces abroad, and friends and allies.

In addition to our conventional and nuclear response and defense capabilities, our overall deterrent posture against WMD threats is reinforced by effective intelligence, surveillance, interdiction, and domestic law enforcement capabilities. Such combined capabilities enhance deterrence both by devaluing an adversary's WMD and missiles, and by posing the prospect of an overwhelming response to any use of such weapons.

Defense and Mitigation

Because deterrence may not succeed, and because of the potentially devastating consequences of WMD use against our forces and civilian population, U.S. military forces and appropriate civilian agencies must have the capability to defend against WMD-armed adversaries, including in appropriate cases through preemptive measures. This requires capabilities to detect and destroy an adversary's WMD assets before these weapons are used. In addition, robust active and passive defenses and mitigation measures must be in place to enable U.S. military forces and appropriate civilian agencies to accomplish their missions, and to assist friends and allies when WMD are used.

Active defenses disrupt, disable, or destroy WMD en route to their targets. Active defenses include vigorous air defense and effective missile defenses against today's threats. Passive defenses must be tailored to the unique characteristics of the various forms of WMD. The United States must also have the ability rapidly and effectively to mitigate the effects of a WMD attack against our deployed forces.

Our approach to defend against biological threats has long been based on our approach to chemical threats, despite the fundamental differences between these weapons. The United States is developing a new approach to provide us and our friends and allies with an effective defense against biological weapons.

Finally, U.S. military forces and domestic law enforcement agencies as appropriate must stand ready to respond against the source of any WMD attack. The primary objective of a response is to disrupt an imminent attack or an attack in progress, and eliminate the threat of future attacks. As with deterrence and prevention, an effective response requires rapid attribution and robust strike capability. We must accelerate efforts to field new capabilities to defeat WMD-related assets. The United States needs to be prepared to conduct post-conflict operations to destroy or dismantle any residual WMD capabilities of the hostile state or terrorist network. An effective U.S. response not only will eliminate the source of a WMD attack but will also have a powerful deterrent effect upon other adversaries that possess or seek WMD or missiles.

Nonproliferation

Active Nonproliferation Diplomacy

The United States will actively employ diplomatic approaches in bilateral and multilateral settings in pursuit of our nonproliferation goals. We must dissuade supplier states from cooperating with proliferant states and induce proliferant states to end their WMD and missile programs. We will hold countries responsible for complying with their commitments. In addition, we will continue to build coalitions to support our efforts, as well as to seek their increased support for nonproliferation and threat reduction cooperation programs. However, should our wide-ranging nonproliferation efforts fail, we must have available the full range of operational capabilities necessary to defend against the possible employment of WMD.

Multilateral Regimes

Existing nonproliferation and arms control regimes play an important role in our overall strategy. The United States will support those regimes that are currently in force, and work to improve the effectiveness of, and compliance with, those regimes. Consistent with other policy priorities, we will also promote new agreements and arrangements that serve our nonproliferation goals. Overall, we seek to cultivate an international environment that is more conducive to nonproliferation. Our efforts will include:

- Nuclear
  - Strengthening of the Nuclear Nonproliferation Treaty and International Atomic Energy Agency (IAEA), including through ratification of an IAEA Additional

Protocol by all NPT states parties, assurances that all states put in place full-scope IAEA safeguards agreements, and appropriate increases in funding for the Agency;
- Negotiating a Fissile Material Cut-Off Treaty that advances U.S. security interests; and
- Strengthening the Nuclear Suppliers Group and Zangger Committee.
- Chemical and Biological
  - Effective functioning of the Organization for the Prohibition of Chemical Weapons;
  - Identification and promotion of constructive and realistic measures to strengthen the BWC and thereby to help meet the biological weapons threat; and
  - Strengthening of the Australia Group.
- Missile
  - Strengthening the Missile Technology Control Regime (MTCR), including through support for universal adherence to the International Code of Conduct Against Ballistic Missile Proliferation.

Nonproliferation and Threat Reduction Cooperation

The United States pursues a wide range of programs, including the Nunn-Lugar program, designed to address the proliferation threat stemming from the large quantities of Soviet-legacy WMD and missile-related expertise and materials. Maintaining an extensive and efficient set of nonproliferation and threat reduction assistance programs to Russia and other former Soviet states is a high priority. We will also continue to encourage friends and allies to increase their contributions to these programs, particularly through the G-8 Global Partnership Against the Spread of Weapons and Materials of Mass Destruction. In addition, we will work with other states to improve the security of their WMD-related materials.

Controls on Nuclear Materials

In addition to programs with former Soviet states to reduce fissile material and improve the security of that which remains, the United States will continue to discourage the worldwide accumulation of separated plutonium and to minimize the use of highly-enriched uranium. As outlined in the National Energy Policy, the United States will work in collaboration with international partners to develop recycle and fuel treatment technologies that are cleaner, more efficient, less waste-intensive, and more proliferation-resistant.

U.S. Export Controls

We must ensure that the implementation of U.S. export controls furthers our nonproliferation and other national security goals, while recognizing the realities that American businesses face in the increasingly globalized marketplace.

We will work to update and strengthen export controls using existing authorities. We also seek new legislation to improve the ability of our export control system to give full weight to both nonproliferation objectives and commercial interests. Our overall goal is to focus our resources on truly sensitive exports to hostile states or those that engage in onward proliferation, while removing unnecessary barriers in the global marketplace.

Nonproliferation Sanctions

Sanctions can be a valuable component of our overall strategy against WMD proliferation. At times, however, sanctions have proven inflexible and ineffective. We will develop a comprehensive sanctions policy to better integrate sanctions into our overall strategy and work with Congress to consolidate and modify existing sanctions legislation.

WMD Consequence Management

Defending the American homeland is the most basic responsibility of our government. As part of our defense, the United States must be fully prepared to respond to the consequences of WMD use on our soil, whether by hostile states or by terrorists. We must also be prepared to respond to the effects of WMD use against our forces deployed abroad, and to assist friends and allies.

The National Strategy for Homeland Security discusses U.S. Government programs to deal with the consequences of the use of a chemical, biological, radiological, or nuclear weapon in the United States. A number of these programs offer training, planning, and assistance to state and local governments. To maximize their effectiveness, these efforts need to be integrated and comprehensive. Our first responders must have the full range of protective, medical, and remediation tools to identify, assess, and respond rapidly to a WMD event on our territory.

The White House Office of Homeland Security will coordinate all federal efforts to prepare for and mitigate the consequences of terrorist attacks within the United States, including those involving WMD. The Office of Homeland Security will also work closely with state and local governments to ensure their planning, training, and equipment requirements are addressed. These issues, including the roles of the Department of Homeland Security, are addressed in detail in the National Strategy for Homeland Security.

The National Security Council's Office of Combating Terrorism coordinates and helps improve U.S. efforts to respond to and manage the recovery from terrorist attacks outside the United States. In cooperation with the Office of Combating Terrorism, the Department of State coordinates interagency efforts to work with our friends and allies to develop their own emergency preparedness and consequence management capabilities.

Integrating the Pillars

Several critical enabling functions serve to integrate the three pillars—counterproliferation, nonproliferation, and consequence management—of the U.S. National Strategy to Combat WMD.

Improved Intelligence Collection and Analysis

A more accurate and complete understanding of the full range of WMD threats is, and will remain, among the highest U.S. intelligence priorities, to enable us to prevent proliferation, and to deter or defend against those who would use those capabilities against us. Improving our ability to obtain timely and accurate knowledge of adversaries' offensive and defensive capabilities, plans, and intentions is key to developing effective counter- and nonproliferation policies and capabilities. Particular emphasis must be accorded to improving: intelligence regarding WMD-related facilities and activities; interaction among U.S. intelligence, law enforcement, and military agencies; and intelligence cooperation with friends and allies.

Research and Development

The United States has a critical need for cutting-edge technology that can quickly and effectively detect, analyze, facilitate interdiction of, defend against, defeat, and mitigate the consequences of WMD. Numerous U.S. Government departments and agencies are currently engaged in the essential research and development to support our overall strategy against WMD proliferation.

The new Counterproliferation Technology Coordination Committee, consisting of senior representatives from all concerned agencies, will act to improve interagency coordination of U.S. Government counterproliferation research and development efforts. The Committee will assist in identifying priorities, gaps, and overlaps in existing programs and in examining options for future investment strategies.

Strengthened International Cooperation

WMD represent a threat not just to the United States, but also to our friends and allies and the broader international community. For this reason, it is vital that we work closely with like-minded countries on all elements of our comprehensive proliferation strategy.

Targeted Strategies Against Proliferants

All elements of the overall U.S. strategy to combat WMD must be brought to bear in targeted strategies against supplier and recipient states of WMD proliferation concern, as well as against terrorist groups which seek to acquire WMD.

A few states are dedicated proliferators, whose leaders are determined to develop, maintain, and improve their WMD and delivery capabilities, which directly threaten the United States, U.S. forces overseas, and/or our friends and allies. Because each of these regimes is different, we will pursue country-specific strategies that best enable us and our friends and allies to prevent, deter, and defend against WMD and missile threats from each of them. These strategies must also take into account the growing cooperation among proliferant states—so-called secondary proliferation—which challenges us to think in new ways about specific country strategies.

One of the most difficult challenges we face is to prevent, deter, and defend against the acquisition and use of WMD by terrorist groups. The current and potential future linkages between terrorist groups and state sponsors of terrorism are particularly dangerous and require priority attention. The full range of counterproliferation, nonproliferation, and consequence management measures must be brought to bear against the WMD terrorist threat, just as they are against states of greatest proliferation concern.

End Note

Our National Strategy to Combat WMD requires much of all of us—the Executive Branch, the Congress, state and local governments, the American people, and our friends and allies. The requirements to prevent, deter, defend against, and respond to today's WMD threats are complex and challenging. But they are not daunting. We can and will succeed in the tasks laid out in this strategy; we have no other choice.

Chemical Attack

Warfare Agents, Industrial Chemicals, and Toxins

What Is It?

A **chemical attack** is the spreading of toxic chemicals with the intent to do harm. A wide variety of chemicals could be made, stolen, or otherwise acquired for use in an attack. Industrial chemical plants or the vehicles used to transport chemicals could also be sabotaged. Harmful chemicals that could be used in an attack include:

- Chemical weapons (warfare agents) developed for military use.

- Toxic industrial and commercial chemicals that are produced, transported, and stored in the making of petroleum, textiles, plastics, fertilizers, paper, foods, pesticides, household cleaners, and other products.

- Chemical toxins of biological origin such as ricin.

The toxicity of chemicals varies greatly. Some are acutely toxic (cause immediate symptoms); others are not very toxic at all. Chemicals in liquid or vapor form generally lead to greater exposures than chemicals in solid form.

How Toxic Chemicals Could be Used

The severity of an attack is related to the toxicity of the chemical and its concentration when it reaches people. Many variables affect the concentration of a chemical including wind and the volatility of the chemical. The release of toxic chemicals in closed spaces (e.g., in subways, airports, and financial centers) could deliver doses high enough to injure

---

Facts about Chemical Weapons

- First used in World War I, chemical weapons drew from existing industrial chemicals (chlorine, phosgene).

- The Chemical Weapons Convention was ratified by more than 160 nations in 1997 with the goal of eliminating state production, storage, and use. The United States is actively destroying its stockpile of chemical agents and has successfully eliminated over 25% to date.

- The 1995 sarin attack on the Tokyo subway by the cult Aum Shinrikyo proves that fabrication and use of chemical weapons by non-state groups is possible. Twelve people died and more than 5,000 were injured.

Facts about Industrial Chemicals

- Industrialized countries produce, transport, and store large quantities of chemicals, some of which are toxic.
- In 1984, a release from a tank of methyl isocyanate at the Union Carbide plant in Bhopal, India killed more than 3,800 people and injured 170,000.
- Environmental laws enacted in 1986 and 1990 were aimed at reducing risk of accidental releases.
- The overall safety record of the chemical and transportation industries are very good, and recent engineering and other advances have made them even safer.

Facts about Toxins of Biological Origin

Agents such as botulinum toxin and ricin are toxins produced by plants, animals, and bacteria. Other examples include toxins from dangerous algal blooms and snake venoms. These substances can be gathered in nature, or alternatively created in labs. Unlike biological agents, they do not reproduce or spread from person to person. Unlike other chemical agents, they are not volatile (do not vaporize) and tend to be more toxic on a weight basis.

Botulinum toxin is a nerve toxin produced by bacteria. It causes botulism, a rare but serious paralytic illness that can be fatal. The three naturally-occuring forms of the illness are food-borne, infant, and wound botulism. An antitoxin is available to treat botulism, but must be administered within hours of exposure.

Ricin is a toxin from castor beans that is part of the waste produced when castor oil is made. It is very toxic—a dose the size of the head of a pin could be lethal but only if injected. Ricin is not absorbed by the skin and is not effective when eaten or inhaled except in impractically large amounts. Ricin was reportedly found in Al Qaeda caves in Afghanistan in the 1980s. There is no antidote.

---

or kill a large number of people. In an open area, a toxic chemical cloud (plume) would become less concentrated as it spreads and would have to be released in large quantities to produce a lot of casualties. Potential delivery methods of toxic chemicals include:

- Ventilation systems of a building.
- Misting, aerosolizing devices, or sprayers.
- Passive release (container of chemical left open).
- Bombs, mines, or other explosive devices that contain chemicals other than those used to create the explosion.
- Improvised chemical devices that combine readily available chemicals to produce a dangerous chemical.
- Sabotage of plants or vehicles containing chemicals.
- Introduction of toxins in the food and water supply.

Detection

Many chemicals at high concentrations can be readily detected with hand-held detection equipment carried by many emergency responders.

Symptoms of Exposure

Visual signs of exposure could include people grouped together who have similar symptoms such as choking or eye irritation. Symptoms in the animal population (birds, wildlife, pets) can be important first indicators, often at concentrations much lower than detected by hand-held devices.

What is the Danger?

Immediate Impact to Human Health

Acutely toxic chemicals can cause injury or fatalities if they are inhaled or absorbed by the skin. The harm that chemicals can cause depends on; 1) their degree of toxicity, 2) the concentration of the chemical, 3) the route of exposure, and 4) the duration of the exposure. The symptoms of exposure to most toxic chemicals would appear in minutes to hours. Different chemicals have different effects on the body. Table 1 shows the health effects for some chemical weapons. Some of the most toxic industrial chemicals can produce similar types of health effects at high concentrations. Table 2 shows lethal concentrations for some chemical weapons and industrial chemicals.

The Area Affected

In an open-air environment, the area affected would depend upon such factors as the type and amount of the chemical agent, the means of dispersal, the local topography, and the local weather conditions. For highly toxic chemicals, lethal or immediately life-threatening results could be seen close to where the agent is released where the concentration is highest, while severe to moderate symptoms could be seen at some distance from the event. A toxic cloud would spread roughly with the speed and direction of the wind, but the concentration of the chemical would be greatly diminished at distances far from the source. For a release in a closed space, a volatile chemical will disperse to fill the space. The smaller the space, the greater the concentration of the chemical.

Exposure Through Contaminated Food

Chemical agents can make foods highly toxic, sometimes without changing the appearance or taste of the foods. Butter, oils, fatty meats, and fish absorb nerve agents so readily that removal of the agents is virtually impossible. Foods in bottles, cans, or wrappings are not affected by agent vapor and can be salvaged following decontamination. The food supply is vulnerable to intentional contamination by toxins such as botulinum toxin.

Exposure Through Contaminated Water

Toxic chemicals could be used to contaminate the drinking water distribution system. Surface water sources in the area of a chemical release could become contaminated, but

Table 1

Effects and treatment of some chemical weapons developed for military use

	Nerve Agents		Blister Agents (injure skin, eyes, and airways)		Blood Agents (cause blood changes and heart problems)		Choking Agents	
Examples	Sarin	VX	Mustard	Lewisite	Hydrogen Cyanide	Cyanogen Chloride	Chlorine	Phosgene
Odor	Odorless		Garlic or Mustard	Geraniums	Burnt almonds		Bleach	Mown hay
Persistency*	Non-persistent (min. to hrs.)	Persistent (>12 hrs.)	Persistent		Non-persistent		Non-persistent; vapors may hang in low areas	
Rate of Action	Rapid for vapors; liquid effects may be delayed		Delayed	Rapid	Rapid		Rapid at high concentrations; delayed at lower concentrations	
Signs and Symptoms	Headache, runny nose, salivation, pinpointing of pupils, difficulty in breathing, tight chest, seizures, convulsions, nausea, and vomiting		Red, burning skin, blisters, sore throat, dry cough; pulmonary edema, eye damage, nausea, vomiting, diarrhea. Symptoms may be delayed 2 to 24 hrs		Cherry red skin/lips, rapid breathing, dizziness, nausea, vomiting, convulsions, dilated pupils, excessive salivation, gastrointestinal hemorrhage, pulmonary edema, respiratory arrest		Eye and airway irritation, dizziness, tightness in chest, pulmonary edema, painful cough, nausea, headache	
First Aid	Remove from area, treat symptomatically, Atropine and pralidoxime chloride (2-PAM chloride), diazepam for seizure control		Decontaminate with copious amount of water, remove clothing, support airway, treat symptomatically		Remove from area, assist ventilations, treat symptomatically, administer cyanide kit		Remove from area, remove contaminated clothing, assist ventilations, rest	
Decontamination	Remove from area, remove clothing, flush with soap and water, aerate							

*How long a chemical remains at toxic levels

Table 2

Varying toxicity of chemicals.

The more toxic a chemical, the smaller the amount of chemical required to cause harm. The table compares the lethal concentrations in parts per million (ppm) for acute (all-at-once) exposures to some chemical weapons and some common industrial chemicals.

Chemical agent	Approx. lethal concentration* (in ppm)
Some Chemical Weapons	
Sarin (GB)	36
Hydrogen Cyanide**	120
Some Industrial Chemicals	
Chlorine**	293
Hydrogen chloride	3,000
Carbon monoxide	4,000
Ammonia	16,000
Chloroform	20,000
Vinyl chloride	100,000

*Based on LC_{50} values in laboratory rats: exposure concentration for 60 minutes at which 50% of rats would die. Rats are used for toxicology tests in part because of similarity to humans, but they are likely to be more susceptible because they have higher metabolisms.

**Used both as chemical weapons and as industrial chemicals

Source: NRC, EPA, and ATSDR

---

dying fish or aquatic life might warn of the release before human use. Deep ground water reservoirs and protected water storage tanks are regarded as safe sources of drinking water following a vapor release of chemical agents. There are methods of treating large volumes of potentially contaminated water for emergency drinking.

What Should People do to Protect Themselves?

Practical Steps

If the release is inside a building or a closed space, people should:

1. Do whatever it takes to find clean air quickly: exit the building if they do so without passing through the contaminated area or break a window to access clean air.

2. Remove outer clothing and place it in a sealed plastic bag.

3. Wash with soap (preferably liquid) and water. Flush skin with lots of water; flush eyes with water if they are irritated.

4. Put on clean clothes.

5. Seek medical attention if they have been exposed, even if they have no immediate symptoms.

If they are near an outdoor chemical release, people should:

1. Avoid any obvious plume or vapor cloud.

2. Walk away from the site and into a building in order to shelter-in-place.

3. Bring family and pets inside.

4. Lock doors, close windows, air vents, and fireplace dampers.

5. Turn off fans, air conditioning, and forced air heating systems.

6. Go into a room with as few windows as possible. Seal the room to create a temporary barrier between people and the contaminated air outside.

7. Seal all windows, doors, and air vents with plastic sheeting and duct tape.

8. Improvise with what is on hand to seal gaps to create a barrier from any contamination.

9. Watch TV, listen to the radio, or check the Internet often for official news and instructions as they become available.

Decisions Regarding Evacuation

Evacuation as a toxic cloud is passing could result in greater exposures than staying inside. The best course of action will be provided by emergency officials who may use computations from models to calculate the path and potential health effects of the toxic cloud.

Medical Treatment

Immediate medical treatment is required for those exhibiting signs and symptoms of exposure to toxic chemicals. (See Table 1)

Antidotes

There are reliable antidotes for nerve agent exposure, which may be available from medical professionals. Some antidotes, such as atropine, pralidoxime chloride (2-PAM chloride), and diazepam, are contained in the medical kits of first responders, but larger quantities of these antidotes may be found at hospitals and treatment facilities. A specific antidote kit is available for cyanide, but it may have to be administered in a hospital. Supportive medical care and hospital therapy is required for large exposures to phosgene and chlorine vapor.

What are the Long-Term Consequences?

Late Health Effects of Chemical Agent Exposure

Most health effects from a chemical attack would occur quickly. Some injuries from acute exposure to toxic chemicals, such as eye damage and chemical burns, can persist for a lifetime. Detailed information on the possibility of developing other types of health effects later in life would be made available once a specific exposure is known. Of the military chemical weapons, only mustard gas is a known carcinogen. Although some industrial chemicals are carcinogenic, the risk of developing cancer later in life is not likely to increase significantly following a one-time exposure.

Monitoring and Clean-up of Affected Areas

In the days and weeks following the use of a chemical agent, officials might be expected to:

- Evacuate the limited area near the release site.
- Ensure proper ventilation of the area.
- Establish a plan for careful monitoring and assessment of affected areas.
- Decontaminate areas where liquid agent was present.
- Assure the public that the threat has passed after thorough testing of the affected area.

Economic Impact

Such impacts might involve disruption to lives and livelihoods as the contaminated area is being cleaned up. An attack on a food or agricultural crop could result in long-lasting economic impact for suppliers and their communities as well as consumers.

Additional Information

Department of Homeland Security—http://www.dhs.gov/dhspublic, http://www.ready.gov
Centers for Disease Control and Prevention—http://www.bt.cdc.gov/agent/agentlistchem.asp, http://www.atsdr.cdc.gov, http://www.bt.cdc.gov/agent, http://www.bt.cdc.gov/planning
Department of Defense—http://www.njha.com/ep/pdf/bio-USAMRICDResources.pdf, http://chemdef.apgea.army.mil/TBMED296.aspx
Other Resources—http://www.biomedtraining.org, http://www.chem-bio.com/resource

This report brief was prepared by the National Academy of Engineering and the National Research Council of the National Academies in cooperation with the Department of Homeland Security. For more information, contact Randy Atkins at 202-334-1508, atkins@nae.edu, or visit www.nas.edu/factsheets. *Making the Nation Safer, Tracking the Atmospheric Dispersion of Hazardous Materials Releases,* and other National Academies reports related to this topic are available from the National Academies Press, 500 Fifth Street, NW, Washington, DC 20001; 800-624-6242; www.nap.edu.Appendix A.2.1 Chemical Attack

Radiological Attack
Dirty Bombs and Other Devices

"The ease of recovery from [a radiological] attack would depend to a great extent on how the attack was handled by first responders, political leaders, and the news media, all of which would help to shape public opinion and reactions."

—Making the Nation Safer
National Research Council (2002)

What is it?

A **radiological attack** is the spreading of radioactive material with the intent to do harm. Radioactive materials are used every day in laboratories, medical centers, food irradiation plants, and for industrial uses. If stolen or otherwise acquired, many of these materials could be used in a "radiological dispersal device" (RDD).

Radiological Dispersal Devices, a.k.a. Dirty Bombs

A **"dirty bomb"** is one type of RDD that uses a conventional explosion to disperse radioactive material over a targeted area. The term dirty bomb and RDD are often used

---

What is Ionizing Radiation?

When radioactive elements decay, they produce energetic emissions (alpha particles, beta particles, or gamma rays) that can cause chemical changes in tissues. The average person in the United States receives a "background" dose of about one-third of a rem* per year— about 80% from natural sources including earth materials and cosmic radiation, and the remaining 20% from man-made radiation sources, such as medical x-rays. There are different types of radioactive materials that emit different kinds of radiation:

Gamma and X-rays can travel long distances in air and can pass through the body exposing internal organs; it is also a concern if gamma emitting material is ingested or inhaled.

Beta radiation can travel a few yards in the air and in sufficient quantities might cause skin damage; beta-emitting material is an internal hazard if ingested or inhaled.

Alpha radiation travels only an inch or two in the air and cannot even penetrate skin; alpha-emitting material is a hazard if it is ingested or inhaled.

*A rem is a measure of radiation dose, based on the amount of energy absorbed in a mass of tissue. Dose can also be measured in Sieverts (1 Sievert = 100 rem).

What are Some Common Radioactive Materials Used in our Society?

Gamma Emitters

> **Cobalt-60 (Co-60)**—cancer therapy, industrial radiography, industrial gauges, food irradiation.
> **Cesium-137 (Cs-137)**—same uses as Cobalt-60 plus well logging.
> **Iridium-192 (Ir-192)**—industrial radiography and medical implants for cancer therapy.

Beta Emitter

> **Strontium-90 (Sr-90)**—radioisotope thermo-electric generators (RTGs), which are used to make electricity in remote areas.

Alpha Emitters

> **Plutonium-238 (Pu-238)**—research and well logging and in RTGs for space missions.
> **Americium-241 (Am-241)**—industrial gauges and well logging.

---

interchangeably in technical literature. However, RDDs could also include other means of dispersal such as placing a container of radioactive material in a public place, or using an airplane to disperse powdered or aerosolized forms of radioactive material.

A Dirty Bomb Is Not a Nuclear Bomb

A nuclear bomb creates an explosion that is thousands to millions of times more powerful than any conventional explosive that might be used in a dirty bomb. The resulting mushroom cloud from a nuclear detonation contains fine particles of radioactive dust and other debris that can blanket large areas (tens to hundreds of square miles) with "fallout." By contrast, most of the radioactive particles dispersed by a dirty bomb would likely fall to the ground within a few city blocks or miles of the explosion.

How an RDD Might be Used

It is very difficult to design an RDD that would deliver radiation doses high enough to cause immediate health effects or fatalities in a large number of people. Therefore, experts generally agree that an RDD would most likely be used to:

- Contaminate facilities or places where people live and work, disrupting lives and livelihoods.
- Cause anxiety in those who think they are being, or have been, exposed.

Detection and Measurement

Radiation can be readily detected with equipment carried by many emergency responders, such as Geiger counters, which provide a measure of radiation dose rate. Other types of instruments are used to identify the radioactive element(s) present.

What do RDDs do?

The Area Affected

Most dirty bombs and other RDDs would have very localized effects, ranging from less than a city block to several square miles. The area over which radioactive materials would be dispersed depends on factors such as:

- Amount and type of radioactive material dispersed.
- Means of dispersal (e.g. explosion, spraying, fire).
- Physical and chemical form of the radioactive material. For example, if the material is dispersed as fine particles, it might be carried by the wind over a relatively large area.
- Local topography, location of buildings, and other landscape characteristics.
- Local weather conditions.

Spread of a Radioactive Plume

If the radioactive material is released as fine particles, the plume would spread roughly with the speed and direction of the wind. As a radioactive plume spreads over a larger area, the radioactivity becomes less concentrated. Atmospheric models might be used to estimate the location and movement of a radioactive plume.

What is the Danger?

Immediate Impact to Human Health

Most injuries from a dirty bomb would probably occur from the heat, debris, radiological dust, and force of the conventional explosion used to disperse the radioactive material, affecting only individuals close to the site of the explosion. At the low radiation levels expected from an RDD, the immediate health effects from radiation exposure would likely be minimal.

Health Effects of Radiation Exposure

Health effects of radiation exposure are determined by the:

Amount of radiation absorbed by the body.

- Radiation type (see "What is ionizing radiation?" ...).
- Means of exposure—external or internal (absorbed by the skin, inhaled, or ingested).
- Length of time exposed.

The health effects of radiation tend to be directly proportional to radiation dose. If a reasonable estimate can be made of a person's dose, a lot is known about the health effects at that dose.

Acute Radiation Syndrome (ARS)

ARS is not likely to result from a dirty bomb. It is a short-term health effect that begins to appear when individuals are exposed to a highly radioactive material over a relatively

Comparison of Common Radiation Exposures with Doses known to Produce Near-term Health Effects.

	Approx. dose (in rems)
Chest X-ray	0.03
Average annual dose from exposure to natural sources	0.2-0.3
CAT scan (whole body)	1
Recommended annual limit in occupational exposure (exclusive of medical exposures)	1 to 5 max per year
No symptoms of illness	15
No symptoms of illness; minor, temporary decreases in white cells and platelets	50
Possible acute radiation syndrome; 10% will have nausea and vomiting within 48 hours and mildly depressed blood counts;	100
Half of those exposed will die within 30 days without medical care	300-400[1]

[1]Hall, EJ. 2000. *Radiobiology for the Radiologist*. Lippincott Williams & Wilkins.

small amount of time. The chart shows that an estimated 10% of the population may exhibit signs of ARS if they are exposed to large radiation doses of 100 rems or more. Principal signs and symptoms of ARS are nausea, vomiting, diarrhea, and reduced blood cell counts.

Psychological Impacts

Psychological effects from fear of being exposed may be one of the major consequences of a dirty bomb. Unless information about potential exposure is made available from a credible source, people unsure about their exposure might seek advice from medical centers, complicating the centers' ability to deal with acute injuries.

What Should People do to Protect Themselves?

Time, Distance, and Shielding

Following any radiological explosion, people should:

- Minimize the time they are exposed to the radiation materials from the dirty bomb.

- Maximize their distance from the source; walking even a short distance from the scene could provide significant protection since dose rate drops dramatically with distance from the source.

- Shield themselves from external exposure and inhalation of radioactive material.

Practical Steps

If people are near the site of a dirty bomb or release of radioactive material, they should:

1. Stay away from any obvious plume or dust cloud.
2. Cover their mouth and nose with a tissue, filter, or damp cloth to avoid inhaling or ingesting the radioactive material.
3. Walk inside a building with closed doors and windows as quickly as can be done in an orderly manner and listen for information from emergency responders and authorities.
4. Remove contaminated clothes as soon as possible; place them in a sealed container such as a plastic bag. The clothing could be used later to estimate a person's exposure.
5. Gently wash skin to remove possible contamination; people should make sure that no radioactive material enters the mouth or is transferred to areas of the face where it could be easily moved to the mouth and ingested. For example don't eat, drink, or smoke.

Questions such as when it's safe to leave a building or return home, what is safe to eat and drink and when, and how children will be cared for if they are separated from their parents would be answered by authorities who would have to make decisions on a case-by-case basis depending on the many variables of the situation.

Decisions Regarding Evacuation

Evacuation as a plume is passing could result in greater exposures than sheltering in place. The best course of action will be provided by emergency officials who may use computations from models of plume travel and potential radiation health effects.

Reducing Contamination

Contaminated individuals can expose or contaminate other people with whom they come in close contact and should avoid contact with others until they are decontaminated. People who have inhaled or ingested radioactive material require assistance by medical personnel.

Antidotes

There are no reliable antidotes once radioactive material is inhaled or ingested; however, symptoms can be treated. There are some chemicals that help cleanse the body of specific radioactive materials. Prussian blue has been proven effective for cesium-137 ingestion. Potassium iodide (KI) tablets are recommended only for exposure to iodine-131 (I-131), a short-lived radioactive element produced in nuclear power plants. Trained medical professionals will determine how to treat symptoms.

What are the Long-Term Consequences?

Monitoring and Clean-up of Affected Areas

In the days and weeks following the use of an RDD, officials might be expected to:

- Establish a plan for careful monitoring and assessment of affected areas.
- Impose quarantines as necessary to prevent further exposures.
- Remove contamination from areas where persons might continue to be exposed.

Delayed Health Effects of Radiation

One concern of radiation exposure is an elevated risk of developing cancer later in life, although studies have shown that radiation is a relatively weak carcinogen. Exposure at the low radiation doses expected from an RDD would increase the risk of cancer only slightly over naturally occurring rates. Long-term health studies on the survivors of the 1945 nuclear bombings of Hiroshima and Nagasaki indicate that for those who received radiation doses from 0 up to 10 rems, less than 1% of cancers in that population were attributable to radiation. A long-term medical surveillance program might be established for victims of a significant radiological attack to monitor potential health effects.

Economic Impact

Such impacts might involve disruption to lives and livelihoods as the contaminated area is being cleaned up. This impact could continue even after the site has been cleaned up if people are reluctant to return to the affected area.

Additional Information

General information on radiation and radiological emergencies:
  Centers for Disease Control and Prevention—http://www.bt.cdc.gov/radiation/index.asp
  Department of Homeland Security—http://www.ready.gov
  Nuclear Regulatory Commission—http://www.nrc.gov/what-we-do/radiation/what-is.html
Radiation protection and measurement:
  International Commission on Radiological Protection—http://www.icrp.org
  National Council on Radiation Protection and Measurements—http://www.ncrp.com
Health effects of radiation:
  Health Physics Society—http://hps.org/publicinformation/radfactsheets/
  Radiation Effects Research Foundation—http://www.rerf.or.jp

This report brief was prepared by the National Academy of Engineering and National Research Council of the National Academies in cooperation with the Department of Homeland Security. For more information or referrals to subject-matter experts, contact Randy Atkins at 202-334-1508, atkins@nae.edu, or visit www.nae.edu/factsheets. *Making the Nation Safer, Tracking the Atmospheric Dispersion of Hazardous Materials Releases* and other National Research Council reports related to this topic are available from the National Academies Press, 500 Fifth Street, NW, Washington, DC 20001; 800-624-6242; www.nap.edu.

Nuclear Attack

What is it?

Unlike a "dirty bomb" which disperses radioactive material using conventional explosives,[1] a **nuclear attack** is the use of a device that produces a nuclear explosion. A nuclear explosion is caused by an uncontrolled chain reaction that splits atomic nuclei (fission) to produce an intense wave of heat, light, air pressure, and radiation, followed by the production and release of radioactive particles. For ground blasts, these radioactive particles are drawn up into a "mushroom cloud" with dust and debris, producing fallout that can expose people at great distances to radiation.

Nuclear Devices

Traditional cold-war concerns were focused on the possible use of military nuclear weapons. A nuclear terrorist attack might be carried out with an improvised nuclear device (IND), which is a crude nuclear device built from the components of a stolen weapon or from scratch using nuclear material (plutonium or highly enriched uranium).

Access and Use of Nuclear Materials or Weapons

The primary obstacle to a nuclear attack is limited access to weapon-grade nuclear materials. Highly enriched uranium, plutonium, and stockpiled weapons are carefully inventoried and guarded. Nuclear attack is also impeded because:

- Building nuclear weapons is difficult—general principles are available in open literature, but constructing a workable device requires advanced technical knowledge in areas such as nuclear physics and materials science.
- Crude nuclear weapons are typically very heavy, ranging from a few hundred pounds to several tons, and are difficult to transport, especially by air. Specially designed small nuclear weapons, including the so-called "suitcase nuclear weapons" are much lighter, but they are difficult to acquire and to construct.

What is the Impact of a Nuclear Attack?

A nuclear attack could cause substantial fatalities, injuries, and infrastructure damage from the heat and blast of the explosion, and significant radiological consequences from both the initial nuclear radiation and the radioactive fallout that settles after the initial event. An electromagnetic pulse from the explosion could also disrupt telecommunications and power distribution. The energy released by a nuclear explosion is distributed roughly as 50% shockwave; 35% heat; 5% initial nuclear radiation; and 10% fallout radiation. This

---

Box 1. Characteristics of a Nuclear Explosion

- A **fireball**, roughly spherical in shape, is created from the energy of the initial explosion. It can reach tens of millions of degrees.

- A **shockwave** races away from the explosion and can cause great damage to structures and injuries to humans.

- A **mushroom cloud** typically forms as everything inside of the fireball vaporizes and is carried upwards. Radioactive material from the nuclear device mixes with the vaporized material in the mushroom cloud.

- **Fallout** results when the vaporized radioactive material in the mushroom cloud cools, condenses to form solid particles, and falls back to the earth. Fallout can be carried long distances on wind currents as a plume and contaminate surfaces miles from the explosion, including food and water supplies.

- The ionization of the atmosphere around the blast can result in an **electromagnetic pulse (EMP)** that, for ground detonations, can drive an electric current through underground wires causing local damage. For high-altitude nuclear detonations, EMP can cause widespread disruption to electronic equipment and networks.

---

distribution varies depending on the design of the weapon and the altitude of the explosion. Box 1 describes the characteristics of a nuclear explosion.

Size of Nuclear Explosions

Nuclear explosions are classified based on the amount of energy they produce, or "yield." A nuclear attack by terrorists would be expected to have a yield of less than one to several kilotons. A kiloton is not the weight of the bomb but rather the equivalent energy of an amount of the explosive TNT (1kT = 1,000 tons of TNT). Large military nuclear weapons are in the megaton (MT) range (1MT = 1,000kT).

The Area Affected

The area affected depends on the yield of the nuclear device, the topography at the explosion site (buildings and geological structures), the altitude of the explosion, and weather conditions. The range of significant effects is shown in Table 1 for 1-kT and 10-kT bombs. The general pattern of damage, shown in Figure 1 for a 10-kT bomb, is as follows:

- Initial effects (or prompt effects) of the nuclear explosion—the shockwave, thermal (heat) energy, and initial radiation—cover an approximately circular area of devastation. Effects decrease with distance from ground zero. For nuclear devices with a higher yield, heat damage becomes the primary initial effect of concern, eclipsing both the damage from the shockwave and the initial radiation.

- Radioactive fallout spreads in an irregular elliptical pattern in the direction the wind blows. The most dangerous fallout would occur near the explosion site

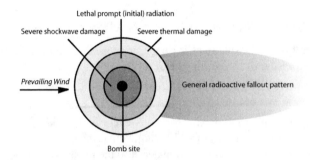

Figure 1 Representation from above of the general patterns of damage from a 10-kT nuclear explosion on the ground. The destruction from the initial effects— shockwave, thermal (heat) energy, and initial radiation—expands in a circular pattern. Severe shockwave damage could extend to about a half a mile. Severe thermal damage would extend out about a mile. Flying debris could extend up to a few miles. Initial (prompt) nuclear radiation for a 10-kT blast could expose unprotected people within about ¾ mile of the explosion site to a lethal radiation dose. Radioactive fallout occurs in an irregular elliptical pattern in the direction the wind is blowing; lethal radiation could extend up to 6 miles.

within minutes of the explosion, but fallout carrying lethal radiation doses could be deposited several miles away. Fallout could potentially travel hundreds of miles, but its concentration and radiation dose decrease as it spreads and as time passes.

Secondary Hazards

The intense heat of the nuclear explosion will produce fires throughout the immediate blast zone. Damaged buildings, downed power and phone lines, leaking gas lines, broken water mains, and damaged roads, bridges, and tunnels are among the hazardous conditions that could exist. The detonation can also produce an electromagnetic pulse (EMP, see Box 1) that interferes with electronic equipment.

Persistence of Radioactivity Levels

The mixture of radioactive elements formed in a nuclear explosion is so complex, with both short- and long-lasting isotopes, that radioactive decay can only be estimated. During the first hour after a nuclear explosion, radioactivity levels drop precipitously. Radioactivity levels are further reduced by about 90% after another 7 hours and by about 99% after 2 days.

What is the Danger?

The number and type of fatalities and injuries depend on many factors including the yield of the nuclear device, the population near the site of the explosion and in the fallout path, and weather conditions. Even a partial nuclear detonation could produce many casualties in a densely populated area. An extensive weapons effects testing program and studies of the 1945 bombings of Hiroshima and Nagasaki provide what we know about the effects of nuclear explosions (see Box 2).

Box 2. The Nuclear Bombs at Hiroshima and Nagasaki, Japan

The August 1945 bombings of Hiroshima and Nagasaki have been the only use or detonation of nuclear weapons except for testing purposes. The Hiroshima bomb was approximately a 16-kiloton uranium bomb; the Nagasaki bomb was approximately a 21-kiloton plutonium bomb. Both were detonated in the air at an altitude of approximately 1,600 feet. The bomb at Hiroshima destroyed buildings over roughly 4 square miles of the city, and about 60,000 people died immediately from the blast, thermal effects, and fire. Within 2–4 months of the bombings, a total estimated 90,000 to 140,000 deaths occurred in Hiroshima and about 60,000 to 80,000 deaths occurred in Nagasaki, mostly as a result of the immediate effects of the bomb and not to fallout.

In a group of 87,000 survivors exposed to radiation who were followed in health studies over the past 60 years,*there were about 430 more cancer deaths than would be expected in a similar but unexposed population (there were 8,000 cancers from all causes compared to an expected 7,600). The additional cancer deaths are attributable to radiation. Nearly half of the people in those studies are still alive.

*The mean dose of those survivors was 16 rad.

Health Effects from the Shockwave and Thermal Energy

Fatalities and injuries will result from the pressure of the shockwave, bodies being thrown, falling buildings, and flying debris. Thermal (heat) energy including the fireball can cause fatalities and severe burns to the skin and eyes.

Health Effects from Radiation

People who survive the physical shockwave and heat may suffer health effects from radiation. The health effects of radiation depend on the:

- Amount of radiation absorbed by the body (the dose, measured in unit called rads),
- Type of radiation,
- Route of exposure (absorbed by the body, inhaled, or ingested),
- Length of time exposed.

If a reasonable estimate can be made of a person's dose, health effects at that dose can be predicted with good accuracy. There are both short- and long-term effects of radiation.

Short-term Effects

Acute Radiation Syndrome (ARS) may develop in those who are exposed to radiation levels of 50-100 rad, depending on the type of radiation and the individual. Symptoms of ARS include nausea, vomiting, diarrhea, and reduced blood cell counts. Radiation, especially beta radiation, can also cause skin burns and localized injury. Fatalities begin to appear at exposures of 125 rad, and at doses between 300-400 rad, about half of those exposed will die without supportive treatment.[2] At very high doses, greater than 1000 rad, people can die within hours or days due to effects on the central nervous system. Radiation

Table 1

Range in miles for significant effects.[3]

Significant effects are 50% mortality from shockwave and heat, and a radiation dose of 400 rads.

Yield (KT)	Shockwave	Heat	Initial radiation	Fallout radiation (downwind)
1	0.2	0.4	0.5	up to 3.4
10	0.4	1.1	0.8	up to 6.0

exposure inhibits stem-cell growth; for those who die within weeks to months, death is usually caused by damage to the gastrointestinal lining and to bone marrow where stem cell growth is crucial. Fetuses are more sensitive to radiation; effects may include growth retardation, malformations, or impaired brain function.

Long-term Effects

Radiation exposure increases the risk of developing cancer, including leukemia, later in life. The increased cancer risk is proportional to radiation dose. The survivors of the Hiroshima and Nagasaki atomic bombs have about a 10% increased risk of developing cancers over normal age-specific rates, some occurring more than 50 years following the exposure. A long-term medical surveillance program would likely be established to monitor potential health effects of survivors of a nuclear attack. There is no evidence of genetic changes in survivors' children who were conceived and born after the bombings in Hiroshima and Nagasaki.

What Should People do to Protect Themselves?

The three basic ways people can reduce exposure to radiation are through time, distance, and shielding:

Time: Decrease the amount of time spent in areas where there is radiation.

Distance: Increase your distance from a radiation source. Doubling your distance from a point source divides the dose by four. If sheltered in a contaminated area, keep your distance from exterior walls and roofs.

Shielding: Create a barrier between yourself and the radiation source with a building or vehicle. Buildings—especially those made of brick or concrete—provide considerable shielding from radiation. Exposure is reduced by about 50% inside a one-story building and by about 90% a level below ground.

Practical Steps

If there is advanced warning of an impending nuclear attack, people should listen to authorities about whether to evacuate the area or to seek shelter underground as soon as possible.

People outside when a blast occurs should:

1. Lie face down on the ground and protect exposed skin (i.e., place hands under the body), and remain flat until the heat and shock waves have passed.
2. Cover the mouth and nose with a cloth to filter particulates from the inhaled air.
3. Evacuate or find shelter:

   a. Evacuation: If a cloud of debris is moving toward them, leave the area by a route perpendicular to the path of the fallout.
   b. If a cloud is not visible or the direction of the fallout is unknown, seek shelter. A basement or center of a high-rise building away from windows or doors would be best.
4. If possibly exposed to contaminated dust and debris, remove outer clothing as soon as is reasonable; if possible, shower, wash hair, and change clothes before entering a shelter. Do not scrub harshly or scratch skin.
5. Listen for information from emergency responders and authorities.

People sheltering-in-place should:

1. Go as far below ground as possible. Shut off ventilation systems and seal doors or windows until the fallout cloud has passed, generally a matter of hours.
2. Stay inside until authorities say it is safe to come out.
3. Use stored food and drinking water.
4. Listen to the local radio or television for official information. Broadcasts may be disrupted for some time as a result of power outages.

For those in the path of the fallout who have survived the initial effects of the explosion, protection from fallout radiation is the most important life-saving measure. Because the material can travel high into the atmosphere, the fallout dispersal pattern cannot be accurately predicted using surface winds. Authorities will advise people to either shelter-in-place or to evacuate.

People advised to evacuate should:

1. Listen for information about evacuation routes, temporary shelters, and procedures to follow.
2. If there is time before leaving, close and lock windows and doors and turn off air conditioning, vents, fans, and furnace in order to keep radioactive material from being sucked inside.

Medical Treatment

Medical treatment would be provided to people with burns and injuries and to those suffering from radiation sickness. Treatment for acute radiation syndrome would include the prevention and treatment of infections, stem cell and platelet transfusions, psychological support, and careful observation of skin injury, weight loss, and fever. Exposed and contaminated people can be safely handled by trained responders and medical personnel. If people ingest or inhale fallout, treatment could include the use of various diluting or mobilizing agents that help rid the body of radioactive elements. Potassium iodide or KI pills are not a general cure-all; they are only effective in blocking the uptake of inhaled or ingested radioactive iodine into the thyroid gland if taken before or just after inhalation or ingestion. (Radioactive iodine can cause thyroid cancer and disease.)

What Are the Long-Term Consequences?

Monitoring and Clean-up of Affected Areas

Most of the fallout will dissipate after a few weeks to months. Clean-up activities would focus on areas near ground zero contaminated with long-lasting radioactive isotopes, such as certain plutonium and uranium isotopes. There are temporary measures that can be taken to "fix" radioactive materials in place and stop the spread of contamination. These include "fixative" sprays such as flour and water mixtures, road oil, or water that can be used to wet ground surfaces. In the days and weeks following the attack, officials might be expected to:

- Establish a plan for careful monitoring and assessment of affected areas.
- Impose quarantines on contaminated areas as necessary to prevent further exposures.
- Remove contamination from areas where people might continue to be exposed.
- Keep citizens informed about the situation.

Control of Contaminated Food Supplies

Public health officials should be able to identify contaminated water and food, such as milk and produce, and replace them with clean food from outside the area.

Economic Impact

Economic impacts would result from deaths, illnesses, loss of jobs, and destruction of workplaces and homes. Increased government spending and stock market swings could significantly impact the national economy. Cleanup, rebuilding, and replacement of lost property and goods could cost many billions of dollars. Local economic impacts could continue even after the site has been cleaned up if people are reluctant to return to the affected area.

Psychological Impact

The psychological impacts of a nuclear attack will vary. Most individuals will prove resilient. Some will experience post-traumatic chronic distress and fear. Many of those who were or believe they were exposed will likely worry about delayed radiation health effects. Depending on how the attack evolves and its aftermath is handled, there may be loss of confidence in societal institutions. If severe damage to the communications network disrupts communication from authorities, public anxiety and fear could be heightened.

Additional Information

Centers for Disease Control and Prevention—http://www.bt.cdc.gov/radiation
See fact sheets: "Radioactive Contamination and Radiation Exposure" and
"Radiation Measurement"

Radiation Emergency Assistance Center—http://www.orau.gov/reacts/

U.S. Department of Energy, National Nuclear Security Administration—http://www.
nnsa.doe.gov

U.S. Department of Homeland Security—http://www.dhs.gov/dhspublic/ • http://www.
ready.gov

U.S. Nuclear Regulatory Commission—http://www.nrc.gov/what-we-do/safeguards.
html

Armed Forces Radiobiology Research Institute (AFRRI)—http://www.afrri.usuhs.mil

Health Physics Society—http://hps.org/publicinformation/radterms

Radiation Effects Research Foundation—www.rerf.jp

This report brief was prepared by the National Academy of Engineering and the National
Research Council of the National Academies in cooperation with the U.S. Department
of Homeland Security. For more information, contact Randy Atkins at 202-334-1508, at-
kins@nae.edu, or visit www.nae.edu/factsheets.

Notes

1. The effects of RDDs (radiological dispersal devices, including "dirty bombs") are discussed in
   another brief in this series entitled, Radiological Attack: Dirty Bombs and Other Devices.
2. Hall, E.J., 2001
3. National Council on Radiation Protection and Measurements, Report No. 138, 2001.

Biological Attack
Human Pathogens, Biotoxins, and Agricultural Threats

"Communication before, during and after a biological attack will be a critical element in effectively responding to the crisis and helping people to protect themselves and recover."

—*A Journalist's Guide to Covering Bioterrorism* (Radio and Television News
Director's Foundation, 2004)

What Is It?

A **biological attack** is the intentional release of a pathogen (disease-causing agent) or biotoxin (poisonous substance produced by a living organism) against humans, plants, or animals. An attack against people could be used to cause illness, death, fear, societal disruption, and economic damage. An attack on agricultural plants and animals would primarily cause economic damage, loss of confidence in the food supply, and possible loss of life. It is useful to distinguish between two kinds of biological agents:

- Transmissible agents that spread from person to person (e.g., smallpox, Ebola) or animal to animal (e.g., foot and mouth disease).

- Agents that may cause adverse effects in exposed individuals but that do not make those individuals contagious to others (e.g., anthrax, botulinum toxin).

Availability of Agents

The Centers for Disease Control and Prevention (CDC) lists the bio-threat agents considered to pose the highest threat (see Table 1). Once obtained, agents must be cultured or grown in quantity and then processed for use in an attack ("weaponized"). Agents can be:

- **Isolated from sources in nature.** The threat agents in Table 1 are either biotoxins or agents that cause zoonotic diseases (that occur in wildlife and are transmissible to humans)—except for smallpox, which is solely a human disease and has been eradicated from nature.

- **Acquired from laboratories or bioweapons stockpile.** Smallpox virus is officially studied in only two laboratories in the world. Anthrax is widely studied in labs. Hemorrhagic fever viruses are studied only in limited high-security locations. Most high threat agents had been studied and stockpiled in bioweapons programs outside the United States until as recently as the 1990s.

Table 1

Diseases/Agents Listed by the CDC as Potential Bioterror Threats (as of March 2005). The U.S. Department of Agriculture maintains lists of animal and plant agents of concern.

CATEGORY A: Easily disseminated and/or contagious; high mortality rates; might disrupt society; requires special action for public health preparedness.

Bacteria (single-celled organisms):

  Anthrax (*Bacillus anthracis*)

  Plague (*Yersinia pestis*)

  Tularemia (*Francisella tularensis*)

Viruses (DNA or RNA requiring other host cells to replicate):

  Smallpox (Variola major virus)

  Viral Hemorrhagic Fevers: Ebola, Marburg, Lassa, Machupo (*various families of viruses*)

Biotoxins (poisonous substances produced by living organisms):

  Botulism (*Clostridium botulinum toxin*)

CATEGORY B: Moderately easy to disseminate; moderate illness rates, low mortality; requires enhanced diagnostic capacity, surveillance.

Bacteria:

  Brucellosis (*Brucella species*)

  Glanders (*Burkholderia mallei*)

  Melioidosis (*Burkholderia pseudomallei*)

  Psittacosis (*Chlamydia psittaci*)

  Food safety threats (*e.g., Salmonella species, Escherichia coli O157:H7, Shigella*)

  Water safety threats (*e.g., Vibrio cholerae, Cryptosporidium parvum*)

Viruses:

  Viral encephalitis (Alphaviruses)

Rickettsia (micro-organisms that live in cells):

  Q fever (*Coxiella burnetii*)

  Typhus fever (*Rickettsia prowazekii*)

Biotoxins:

  Epsilon toxin of Clostridium perfringens

  Ricin toxin from castor beans

  Staphylococcal enterotoxin B

CATEGORY C: Emerging infectious diseases that could be a future threat. (not all-inclusive)

Viruses:

  Examples are Nipah virus and Hantavirus

- **Synthesized or genetically manipulated in a laboratory.** This would require expertise and access to advanced technology.

How Biological Agents Could Be Disseminated

For an attack on people, biological agents could be disseminated in one or more of the following ways:

- **Aerosol dissemination** is the dispersal of an agent in air from sprayers or other devices. The agent must be cultured and processed to the proper size to maximize human infections, while maintaining the agent's stability and pathogenicity (ability to produce illness). An aerosol attack might take place outdoors in a populated

---

Historical Perspective on Biological Attack

- In 2001, the anthrax attacks through the U.S. mail infected 11 people with inhalational anthrax, of which five died. An additional 11 people were infected with cutaneous (skin) anthrax, of which there were no fatalities.
- In the 1990s, the cult Aum Shinrikyo failed in attempts to release anthrax and botulinum toxin in Tokyo but did succeed in a chemical attack with Sarin nerve agent.
- In 1984, the cult followers of Baghwan Shree Rajneesh sickened 751 people in Oregon by placing salmonella bacteria in salad bars in 10 restaurants to keep people from voting in an election.
- In World War II, Unit 731 in Japanese-occupied Manchuria dropped plague-infected fleas in China, allegedly resulting in more than 50,000 deaths.
- In World War I, German agents successfully infected Allied livestock with anthrax and glanders.
- In the 1340s, Europeans threw plague-infected cadavers over city walls to infect those within.

Laws and Treaties Governing Biological Weapons

- The Geneva Convention of 1925 was the first international agreement to address chemical and biological weapons. It prohibits "bacteriological methods of warfare," but did not outlaw the development of such weapons.
- The Biological and Toxins Weapons Convention (BWC) of 1972 is the first arms control treaty to outlaw an entire class of weapons and forbids States from developing, producing, stockpiling, or retaining biological weapons or assisting other States in developing these weapons systems.
- The Australia Group is a loose association of nations that agrees not to export tools and technologies, including pathogens, that have "dual uses"— that is, they can be used for both legitimate and nefarious purposes.

area or indoors, e.g., in the ventilation system of a building, in the subway, on planes. It takes expertise to process biological agents to *maximize* the effect of aerosol dissemination, but even relatively crude devices could have an impact.

- **Food or water,** especially ready-to-eat food (vegetables, salad bars) could be intentionally contaminated with pathogens or toxins. The water supply is less vulnerable because dilution, filtration, and the addition of chlorine can kill most disease-causing organisms.
- **Human carriers** could spread transmissible agents by coughing, through body fluids, or by contaminating surfaces. Most agents would make people ill or incapacitated before they become highly contagious, thereby reducing transmission of the disease.
- **Infected animals** can cause people to become ill through contact with the animals or contaminated animal products.
- **Insects** naturally spread some agents such as plague bacteria (vector borne illnesses) and potentially could be used in an attack.
- **Physically distributed** through the U.S. mail or other means.

For an agricultural attack:

- **A point introduction** of an infected plant or animal or its fluids could spread disease through the rest of the crop or livestock. Agricultural biothreat agents (e.g., foot and mouth disease, avian influenza, soy bean rust, and karnal bunt of wheat) do not have to be aerosolized to be effectively disseminated.

Impact Following the Release of a Pathogen

Detection of a Biological Attack

Unlike a chemical or nuclear attack, a biological attack may go undetected for hours, days, or potentially weeks (depending on the agent) until people, animals, or plants show symptoms of disease. If there are no immediate signs of the attack as with the anthrax letters, a biological attack will probably first be detected by local health care workers observing a pattern of unusual illness or by early warning monitoring systems that detect airborne pathogens. Evidence of an attack may appear in animals before humans.

The Area Affected

For an aerosol release, the area affected would depend on the quantity of agent released, whether the release is indoors or outdoors, and weather conditions. Agents released outdoors would disperse roughly in the direction of the prevailing wind and could degrade with sunlight and by drying out from environmental exposure. Agents released indoors could initially have a higher concentration. Sometimes agents can be re-aerosolized by machinery, foot traffic, or other means.

Finding the Cause and Source of Illness

There may be uncertainties about crucial facts such as the exact location or extent of the initial release, the type of biological agent used, and likelihood of additional releases. Laboratory scientists will work quickly to identify the specific agent. Epidemiologists will attempt to trace the path of infections back toward a single person, vector (insect or animal), vehicle (food or water), or other point of origin. Attribution of a biological attack is typically much more difficult than attribution of a conventional terrorist attack.

What Is The Danger?

Impact on Human Health

Biothreat agents have the potiential to produce a life-threatening illness. Biotoxins are essentially poisons that can be fatal at high enough doses. Table 2 lists health impacts and medical treatments for the Category A and some Category B agents. Even a small amount of some biothreat agents released in air could result in significant loss of life, depending on a number of factors that include the:

- Infectivity of the agent (how many particles are needed to cause illness).
- Lethality of the agent.
- Length of time it takes to detect and treat those who are exposed or have become ill.

Dose Response in Humans

The exact infectious dose (the number or organisms needed to make one sick) of most biological agents is unknown; approximate doses are extrapolated from animal studies. Whether a person becomes ill after exposure to a biological agent depends on a number of factors including:

- Type and amount of agent taken into the body.
- Duration of exposure.
- Route of exposure (inhalation, ingestion, insect bite).
- "Host" factors (e.g., age, immune status, other illnesses of the person exposed).

Differences in Intentional vs. Natural Outbreaks of Disease

Naturally occurring outbreaks of category A agents have become rare because of improved living standards, hygiene, and health services in developed nations. For example, human bubonic plague, which was transmitted by rats and fleas to humans in past centuries resulting in large losses of life, has virtually been wiped out. However, agents used in an aerosol attack may act differently than naturally occurring outbreaks and could produce a form of the disease with a shorter time of onset of illness, making timely diagnosis, treatment, and containment more difficult.

Spread of Diseases

Some transmissible (contagious) diseases can spread through respiratory droplets from coughing and sneezing or when a person comes in contact with a surface harboring a virus or bacteria and then touches their mouth or nose. The viral hemorrhagic fevers and cholera are spread by direct contact with body fluids or feces. People infected with contagious diseases may widely disseminate the disease by travel.

Psychological Impact

Psychological responses following a bioterrorism event may include anger, fear, and social isolation. Following the 2001 anthrax attacks, thousands of people who thought they were infected sought treatment. Trying to distinguish those who haven't been infected could complicate medical centers' ability to treat those who have been exposed and infected, especially when diagnoses are unclear.

What Should People do to Protect Themselves?

Practical Steps

During a declared biological emergency:

1. People in the group or area that authorities have linked to exposure who have symptoms that match those described should seek emergency medical attention.
2. Use common sense, practice good hygiene and cleanliness to avoid spreading germs.

People who are potentially exposed should:

1. Follow instructions of health care providers and other public health officials.
2. Expect to receive medical evaluation and treatment. Be prepared for long lines. If the disease is contagious, persons exposed may be quarantined.

If people become aware of a suspicious substance nearby, they should:

1. Quickly get away.
2. Cover their mouths and noses with layers of fabric that can filter the air but still allow breathing.
3. Wash with soap and water.
4. Contact authorities.
5. Watch TV, listen to the radio, or check the Internet for official news and information including the signs and symptoms of the disease, if medications or vaccinations are being distributed, and where to seek medical attention if they become sick.
6. Seek emergency medical attention if they become sick.

Infectious Is Different From Contagious

The terms "infectious" and "contagious" are often confused. Infectious refers to the number of particles (spores or organisms) needed to infect an individual. The fewer number of particles needed, the more infectious the agent. Agents are contagious if they spread from person to person. Some agents that are highly infectious, such as Tularemia and Q fever, are not contagious.

Table 2

Onset, Health Impacts, and Treatments for Some Agents of Concern

Disease (agent)	Incubation period*	Symptoms
HIGH THREAT AGENTS (CATEGORY A)		
Anthrax (*Bacillus anthracis*) (inhalational)	typically 1–6 days, but up to 42	Fever, cough, profound sweats, malaise, fatigue, myalgiaus
Plague (*Yersinia pestis*)	1–7 days (usually 2–3 days)	Fever, cough, shortness of breath, sore lymph nodes
Tularemia (*Francisella tularensis*)	1–21 days (avg 3–6)	Fever, cough, pneumonia, headache
Marburg (Viral hemorrhagic fever)	4–21 days	Sudden onset, fever, headache, followed by vomiting and diarrhea, rash, generalized bleeding in severe cases
Ebola (Viral hemorrhagic fever)	4–21 days	Sudden onset, fever, headache, followed by vomiting and diarrhea, rash, generalized bleeding in severe cases
Smallpox (Variola major virus)	7–17 days (avg 12)	Fever, aches, after 2–4 days rash appears
Botulism (*Clostridium botulinum* toxin)	12 hours–5 days	Muscle paralyzing illness
LOWER THREAT AGENTS (SELECTED CATEGORY B AGENTS)		
Cholera (*Vibrio cholerae*)	4 hours–5 days (usually 2–3 days)	Sudden onset of voluminous watery diarrhea, vomiting, cramps, dehydration
Glanders (*Burkholderia mallel*)	1–14 days via aerosol	Pneumonia with or without blood poisoning, ulcers in nose, mouth, throat and lungs
Q fever (*Coxiella burnetii*)	7–41 days	Flu-like illness that can lead to pneumonia and hepatitis
Encephalitis (Alphaviruses)	2–6 days	Fever, aches, pain behind the eye, nausea, vomiting
Ricin (*Ricinus communis*)	18–24 hours	Can shut down organ function

*Incubation periods listed are for naturally occurring outbreaks, which could differ for agents used as weapons. Diseases Blue Book, August 2004.

Spread (person to person)	Lethality if untreated	Persistence of Organism	Vaccine Status (as of March 2005)	Medical Treatment
No (only skin form spreads)	High (if inhaled) viable in soil >40 yrs	Very stable spores	Licensed	Antibiotics
Moderate	High unless treated within 12–24 hours (pneumonic)	For up to 1 year in soil; 270 days in live tissue	Not current	Antibiotics
No	Moderate	For months in moist soil or other media	Not current	Antibiotics
Via fluids	>25% lethal	Relatively unstable	None	Supportive treatment only
Via fluids	50–80% lethal	Relatively unstable	Investigational	Supportive treatment only
Moderate	High to moderate ≥30% lethal	Very stable	Licensed	Supportive
No	High without respiratory support	Stable for weeks in nonmoving food/water	Licensed (availability uncertain)	Antitoxin if administered quickly
Rare, although spreads rapidly via untreated water	Low with treatment, high without	Unstable in aerosols & fresh water, stable in salt water	Investigational	Antibiotics
No	Death in 7–10 days in blood poisoning form	Very stable	None	Antibiotics
No	Very low	For months on wood and sand	Not licensed in U.S.	Antibiotics
Low	Low	Relatively unstable	None	Supportive treatment
No	High (injected)	Stable supportive treatment	Investigational	No antidote

Data for incubation period, lethality, and persistency from U.S. Army Medical Research Institute of Infectious

Medical Treatment

Table 2 lists general medical treatments for several biothreat agents. In general, bacterial illnesses are treated with antibiotics, and viral illnesses are treated with supportive care, although there are a few specific medications to treat viral infections. Biotoxins are treated with antidotes or antitoxins, if available. Vaccines can prevent or mitigate the effects of a disease. The smallpox vaccine may provide protection even if given 1–4 days after exposure, and the anthrax vaccine can be given after inhalation exposure if accompanied by treatment with antibiotics for a number of weeks.

Controlling the Spread of Contagious Diseases

Methods to control contagious disease include isolation, quarantine, barrier methods (gloves, filter masks, eye protection), and hand washing. Rapid identification of potentially infected persons increases the effectiveness of these methods.

What are the Long-Term Consequences?

Monitoring and Clean-up

After a biological agent has been identified, officials will take steps to characterize how long the agent will persist. Clean-up within buildings may entail the use of gas or liquid decontaminants to kill the agent. For example, chlorine dioxide gas was released through ventilation systems of buildings contaminated with anthrax. In some cases, multiple rounds of decontamination may be necessary. Decisions regarding how much clean-up is necessary will depend on:

- The amount of agent released.
- How far the agent has spread.
- How the space will be used following clean-up.

Long-term Health Consequences Following Exposure

The long-term health consequences for those who survive exposure to biological attack agents are unknown. A long-term medical surveillance program would likely be established to monitor potential health effects of those exposed.

Economic Impact of an Agricultural Attack

Once detected, an act of agricultural bioterrorism may quickly halt the movement and export of livestock or the affected crop, resulting in potentially severe economic consequences for producers, shippers, and consumers. It may also disrupt normal travel and commerce.

Additional Information

Centers for Disease Control and Prevention—http://www.bt.cdc.gov
Infectious Disease Society of America—http://www.idsociety.org

National Institute of Allergy and Infectious Disease—http://www.niaid.nih.gov/biode-fense/

U.S. Army Medical Research Institute of Infectious Diseases—http://www.usamriid.army.mil

U.S. Department of Health and Human Services—http://www.hhs.gov/emergency

U.S. Department of Homeland Security—http://dhs.gov/dhspublic • http://www.ready.gov

This report brief was prepared by the National Academy of Engineering and National Research Council of the National Academies in cooperation with the Department of Homeland Security. For more information or referrals to subject-matter experts, contact Randy Atkins at 202-334-1508, atkins@nae.edu, or visit www.nae.edu/factsheets. *Making the Nation Safer, Tracking the Atmospheric Dispersion of Hazardous Materials Releases* and other National Research Council reports related to this topic are available from the National Academies Press, 500 Fifth Street, NW, Washington, DC 20001; 800-624-6242; www.nap.edu.

Integrating the AGENTS OF BIOTERRORISM into the General Biology Curriculum
I. A Primer on Bioterrorism

Jeffrey Pommerville

T he anthrax attacks that occurred on the east coast in October 2001 confirm what many health and governmental experts have been saying for more than 10 years—it is not *if* bioterrorism will occur, but *when* and *where* (Osterholm & Schwartz 2000). Bioterrorism has struck and the potential for future attacks undoubtedly will remain with us as a serious threat for some time to come (Atlas, 1999; Henderson, 1999; Block, 2001).

As awful and horrific as bioterrorism could be, the recent events and discussions of potential threats have generated both public anxiety and curiosity about bioterrorism. More specifically, our students clearly see these events and future bioterrorist threats as significant to their lives. Therefore, as biology educators, we can take this opportunity to use the mechanisms of action of bioterrorism agents—that is, how they cause illness and sometimes death—to infuse new examples into our general biology classes/courses that should engage and interest today's students.

To effectively use the information about these biological agents in the classroom, biology educators need to have a general understanding and comprehension of bioterrorism and know the types of agents that have or could be used. We discovered from the anthrax attacks of October 2001 that although we were adequately equipped to deal with the attacks, the public at times was exposed to contradictory information, or misinformation, that caused heightened anxiety and confusion. Therefore, this paper serves as a primer on the topic of bioterrorism—in other words, what every biology educator should know. The material discussed in this paper can be used to communicate more effectively with students and the community, and to prepare a classroom discussion on the topic. In addition, the information can be used as background material when applying the interesting features of these bioterror agents to the general themes and concepts taught in high school biology classes and general biology courses in colleges and universities. Part II of this series will be published in the January 2003 issue of *ABT* and will specifically detail the modes of action for the top bioterror agents and give examples of how their biology can be exploited in the classroom to reinforce basic biological principles and concepts (Pommerville, 2003).

How Biological Weapons Could Be Used

There are several ways that biological weapons have and could be used. *Biological* (germ) *warfare* involves the deliberate or threatened use of viruses, bacteria, fungi, or toxins from living organisms to cause disease in or kill an enemy's military forces, population, or food supplies. *Biocrimes* are the intentional introduction of biological agents into food or water, or by injection, with the aim to harm or kill a number of individuals. The first known deliberate biocrime in this country occurred in Oregon in 1984 when the Rajneeshee religious cult, in an effort to influence local elections, intentionally contaminated salad bars with the bacterium *Salmonella typhimurium*. The unsuccessful plan sickened over 750 citizens and hospitalized 40. Other examples include the deliberate contamination of donuts and muffins in a hospital workroom with *Shigella dysenteriae* and the threat to poison two Colorado judges with ricin toxin.

Bioterrorism represents the intentional or threatened use of biological agents to cause fear in or actually inflict death or disease upon a large population for political, religious, or ideological reasons. Although bioterrorism against humans is the focus of this article, specific threats to agriculture, called agroterrorism or economic warfare, also are of concern and have been addressed (Rogers et al., 1999; Frist, 2002; Sobel et al., 2002). In all cases, one of the most appealing features of bioweapons is the tremendous psychological impact that their use, or threatened use, produces on individuals and populations.

Bioterrorism Is Not New

One of the earliest known cases of bioterrorism occurred in 1346 when the Tartars (Monguls) were besieging Kaffa, a grain port on the Black Sea (present day Feodosia in Ukraine). When plague broke out within the ranks of the Tartar army, the bodies of dead plague victims were catapulted over the walls and into the city. This action was quite effective psychologically as it caused defenders of Kaffa to surrender or flee the city. Many who fled sailed to Italy, bringing infected rats and fleas with them, which may have initiated, or at least accelerated, the wave of plague that would soon spread across Europe.

In the 18th century, in the aftermath of the French and Indian Wars (1754–63), British forces, under the guise of good will, gave smallpox-laden blankets to rebellious tribes sympathetic to the French. The disease decimated the Native Americans, who had never been exposed to the disease before and had no immunity.

Following the use of chlorine and mustard gases in World War I, the Geneva Protocol of 1925 also included the prohibition of bacteriological methods in warfare. Since the treaty did not ban the research or production of these agents, biological weapons research continued. Between 1937 and 1945, the Japanese established Unit 731 in Japanese-occupied Manchuria. Unit 731 carried out experiments to test the lethality of several biological weapons on Chinese soldiers and civilians. In all, some 10,000 "subjects" died of bubonic plague, cholera, anthrax, and other diseases (Harris, 2002).

The U.S. and the Soviet Union expanded their offensive biological weapons programs after WWII. The American program culminated in 1969 with a series of successful offensive biological weapons tests in the Pacific using aerosolized agents released onto ships loaded with caged animals. Then, in late 1969, President Nixon announced that the U.S. would terminate the program and destroy all stockpiled bioweapons.

In 1973, the U.S., the Soviet Union, and more than 100 other nations signed the Biological and Toxin Weapons Convention, which prohibited nations from developing, deploying, or stockpiling biological weapons. Defensive research purposes were still permitted. Unfortunately, the treaty provided no way to distinguish between offensive and defensive work (dual-use facilities) or monitor compliance. As a result, Ken Alibek, former first deputy director of Biopreparat (the civilian arm of the Soviet Union's biological warfare program), described to U.S. officials how the Biopreparat was involved in offensive research and stockpiled many biological agents, including smallpox, anthrax, and plague, while using genetic engineering to produce enhanced "doomsday" biological weapons (Alibek, 1999).

After the 1991 Gulf War, the United Nations Special Commission (UNSCOM) was able to clarify Iraq's biological warfare potential. UNSCOM analysts reported that Iraq had produced 8,000 liters of concentrated anthrax solution, more than 20,000 liters of botulinum toxin solution, and 10 liters of concentrated ricin toxin solution (Zilinskas, 1997). Several biological weapons, including anthrax and botulinum toxin, also had been loaded onto SCUD missiles.

Table 1 outlines some of the more noteworthy bioterrorism events throughout history. A brief account of biological weapons development over the past half-century can be found

Table 1.

Some key historical events of bioterrorism.

1346	During the siege of Kaffa, the Tartar army hurls plague-ridden dead over the walls of the city. The defenders flee or surrender.
1422	At the battle of Carolstein, bodies of plague-stricken soldiers plus 2000 cart-loads of excrement are hurled into the ranks of enemy troops.
1710	During Russia's war with Sweden, Russian troops hurl plague corpses over the city walls of Reval to provoke an epidemic.
1767	During the French and Indian War, British forces give blankets laced with smallpox to Native Americans loyal to the French. The epidemic decimates the tribes.
1797	Napoleon attempts to force the surrender of Mantua by infecting the citizens with swamp fever.
1860–1865	Sherman's memoirs contain an account of Confederate soldiers poisoning ponds with the carcasses of dead animals.
1914–1918	During World War I, Germany is accused of trying to spread cholera in Italy, plague in St. Petersburg, and biological bombs over Britain.
1925	The Geneva Protocol bans chemical and biological weapons. The multilateral agreement does not ban research on or the production of such weapons.
1932–41	During Japan's invasion of Manchuria, experiments begin on biological warfare. Unit 731 tests biological agents on Chinese soldiers and civilians. Thousands die.
1942	On Gruinard Island, off the Scottish coast, the British conduct anthrax experiments with sheep.
1941–1949	The United States begins studies on the use of and defense from biological agents. The program emphasizes research capabilities.
1969	President Nixon announces that the United States will stop all offensive biological warfare research.
1972	The Biological Weapons Convention is established and is eventually signed by 144 nations.
1979	An unusual outbreak of anthrax in Sverdlovsk, USSR, results in the death of at least 64 people. The U.S. suspects bioweapons are being developed by the Soviets.
1991	The Iraqi government announces that it has conducted research into a number of biowarfare agents.
1995	Members of the Aum Shinrikyo release Sarin gas in the Tokyo subway, killing 12 and injuring more than 5,000.
1995	Iraq acknowledges they had 100 botulinum toxin, 50 anthrax, and 16 aflatoxin bombs, 13 botulinum toxin, 10 anthrax, and 2 aflatoxin in Scud missile warheads, and 122-mm rockets filled with anthrax, botulinum toxin, and aflatoxin.
1998	Larry Wayne Harris is arrested after he, allegedly, threatened to release anthrax in Las Vegas. The strain in his possession was a harmless veterinary vaccine strain.
10/5/2001– 11/21/2001	Anthrax-by-mail attacks occur in the United States. There are 22 confirmed cases (11 inhalational, 11 cutaneous). Five deaths occur from the inhalational form.

in Daniels (2001). A fascinating account that chronicles the U.S. and Soviet bioweapons programs and the attempts by UN investigators to determine the extent of the Iraqi program and its status after the Gulf War can be found in Miller et al. (2001).

Why Use Biological Weapons?

It is believed that at least 17 nations have the capability of bioweapons production. Such biological weapons offer certain advantages to these nations and terrorist organizations in general. Perhaps most important, biological weapons represent "The Poor Nation's Equalizer." Biological weapons are cheap when compared to chemical and nuclear weapons and thus pose a great threat. For example, to "affect" one square kilometer, it costs about $2,000 using conventional weapons, $600 to $800 using chemical or nuclear weapons, but only $1 for biological weapons. This is because most of the development process to grow the microorganisms as biological weapons can be accomplished with $10,000 in fermentation equipment and can be concealed easily in a 16′ × 16′ room. With biological weapons, you get high impact and the most "bang for the buck."

Several other common features that make biological weapons excellent bioterror agents are outlined in Table 2.

Developing a Bioterror Agent

All known bioterrorism agents represent natural agents found in the environment. Therefore, an agent like the anthrax-causing bacterium would be easy to obtain because the bacterium is found in soils around the world. Since other agents could be obtained

Table 2

Characteristics of bioterror agents.

CHARACTERISTIC	DESCRIPTION
Deadly in minute amounts to a defenseless population	• Most agents require a low infective dose and are hundreds of times more lethal than chemical weapons.
	• The majority of the civilian population lacks immunity, so an attack could result in high morbidity and mortality.
Nonvolatile, odorless, colorless, tasteless	• Inhaling an aerosolized agent in minute amounts would go undetected until symptoms appear days or weeks later.
Kills/incapacitates people, not infrastructure	• As dry agents, most biological agents are environmentally stable.
	• Unlike conventional and nuclear weapons, bioweapons do not damage buildings or roads, yet can contaminate such areas for extended periods.
Difficult to diagnose, treat, manage	• Most medical personnel are unfamiliar with symptoms of these rare diseases, making diagnosis difficult.
	• For most bioterror agents, casualties will be high without rapid medical treatment.
	• Widespread attack would overwhelm medical services.
Creates panic/anxiety	• Represents the very nature of terrorism.
	• Prior to October 2001, there were more than 700 anthrax threats and hoaxes that heightened public anxiety and stimulated greater health care preparedness.

from biological supply houses or culture collections, the U.S. government has established guidelines that make it almost impossible to obtain these agents today. Assuming one has the agents, they would be relatively easy to grow (culture). Simple procedures will induce the bacterium that causes anthrax to produce spores in large quantities, which can be maintained in a viable state.

Some bioterror agents must be "weaponized"; that is, they must be modified into a form that will be deliverable, stable, and have increased infectivity and/or lethality. Since many of the biological agents are most infective as inhaled aerosols, the agents must be "milled" to a size that is less than five μm so that when inhaled they will effectively reach deep into the respiratory system. As an aerosol, the bioagents must be prepared so that the particles do not stick together or form clumps that would not stay suspended in the air. The anthrax letters of October 2001 involved such weaponized spores.

The final step is to design a way to disseminate (transmit) the bioweapon. Aerosol transmission, the most likely form for dissemination, can occur in one of two ways. In a point source attack, the agent is disseminated from a focused site. In the anthrax mail cases, a spore-filled envelope represented the point source. The source remains relatively confined, although spores did contaminate a number of postal facilities and government offices. However, under ideal weather conditions, an Iraqi SCUD warhead (a point source) filled with a biological agent could contaminate a substantial area.

In a line source attack, casulaties could be much higher because the bioagent initially is spread over a greater distance. If a crop duster, for example, were used to disseminate anthrax spores over Washington, DC, it has been estimated that on a calm, clear night the spores could cover 300 square kilometers and the death toll could reach 1 to 3 million (U.S. Congress, Office of Technology Assessment, 1993). According to UNSCOM investigators, Iraq may have a modified aircraft that can spray up to 500 gallons of biological agents.

Dissemination of biological agents by conventional means has technical difficulties because most bioweapons are sensitive to environmental conditions. Excessive heat, ultraviolet light, and oxidation decrease bioagent potency and persistence. Although anthrax spores are relatively resistant to typical environmental conditions, the bacterial cells causing tularemia (see below) become ineffective after just a few minutes in sunlight. Additionally, wind patterns and humidity can reduce the lethality of a terrorist line source attack.

The Diseases of Bioterror Agents

Various governmental and health agencies, including the Centers for Disease Control and Prevention (CDC), have published lists of approximately 36 agents that could be used as biological weapons (Khan & Sage, 2000). When separated by type of biological agent, three significant groups result—bacteria, viruses, and toxins—that could have devastating effects on human populations (Table 3).

Seven of the more potentially lethal microbiological agents, and the plant toxin ricin, are briefly described below. Disease symptoms and mode of action of the agents are included in Pommerville (2003). First (2002) and Tierno (2002) describe these and additional biological agents, provide history, background, clinical features, and suggest a protective (home) response strategy for these agents.

Table 3

Types of bioterror agents and perceived risk of use.

Type	Description	Examples (species name)	Perceived Risk
Bacteria	Disease is caused by invasion of human tissue, producing poisons (toxins), or both.	• Anthrax (*Bacillus anthracis*) • Plague (*Yersinia pestis*) • Tularemia (*Francisella tularensis*)	High Moderate Moderate
Viruses	As intracellular parasites, viruses infect host cells during which time illness and disease might occur.	• Smallpox (variola major) • Hemorrhagic fevers (Ebola, Marburg, Lassa)	Moderate Low
Toxins	Many toxins at sub-lethal doses incapacitate individuals or populations and generally are the most lethal and quickest acting.	• Botulinum toxin (*Clostridium botulinum*) • Ricin toxin (*Ricinus communis*)	Moderate Moderate

Anthrax

Anthrax is caused by the spore-forming bacterium *Bacillus anthracis*. It can be found in soil samples from around the world. Natural anthrax cases usually are occupational, being acquired by contact with infected animals (cattle, sheep, goats) or animal products (*cutaneous anthrax*), by ingestion (*gastrointestinal anthrax*), or by inhalation of spores (*inhalational anthrax*). Between 1955 and 1999, 236 cases (mostly cutaneous) of occupational anthrax were reported in the U.S.

Inhalational anthrax is the most dangerous form for bioterrorism and accounted for the five deaths via letter-disseminated spores in October 2001. However, treatment outcomes are promising if antibiotics are started early. Anthrax vaccine is available to high-risk groups, including military personnel. Recent references for anthrax as a bioweapon include articles by Inglesby et al. (2002), Simon (2002), and Young & Collier (2002).

Plague

Yersinia pestis, the causative agent of plague, is transmitted by fleas from infected rodents to humans. It swept through Europe in the 14th century, killing an estimated 25 million people. Nearly 19,000 cases were reported worldwide between 1980 and 1994. In the U.S., there are about a dozen cases each year, usually resulting from its endemic nature in small rodents in the Southwest and Pacific States. Lethal cases in the U.S. are extremely rare.

Although human plague has three clinical forms—bubonic (lymph node swelling), septicemic (blood-stream infection), and pneumonic—as a bioterror agent, pneumonic plague is of most concern. Bacteria could be disseminated in an aerosol form and, after infection, transmitted person-to-person by sneezing and coughing. Early administration of antibiotics is critical because pneumonic plague is almost 100 percent fatal if antibiotic therapy is delayed more than one day after the onset of symptoms. No vaccine is currently available. References for plague include the article by Inglesby et al. (2000) and a recent historical perspective by Cantor (2001).

Tularemia

The causative agent of tularemia is the non-spore forming bacterium *Francisella tularensis*. It is one of the most infectious pathogenic bacteria known because as few as 10 to 25 cells can initiate disease. Humans can acquire the disease incidentally by contact with diseased rodents and rabbits (thus the common disease name "rabbit fever") or through bites from infected ticks, mosquitoes, or deerflies. Found worldwide, *F. tularensis* causes about 200 disease cases per year in the U.S., primarily in the south-central states, where it is endemic. Person-to-person transmission has not been reported.

An aerosol form of the bacterium most likely would be used by terrorists because infection can lead to pulmonary or septicemic tularemia, which has a kill rate of greater than 30 percent. Antibiotics are very effective with early treatment and an investigational vaccine is available for high-risk groups. A recent review by Dennis et al. (2001) summarizes medical and health management aspects.

Smallpox

This highly contagious disease killed more than 500 million people in the 20th century before world-wide vaccinations eradicated the virus in 1977. Most severe cases of smallpox are caused by the variola major variant of the virus. Since vaccinations against smallpox stopped in the U.S. in 1972, most of our students lack immunity to the disease. In fact, even those of us who were vaccinated probably have minimal immunity remaining.

In a purposeful attack, the virus most likely would be released in an aerosol form, where lack of surveillance could lead to a major outbreak. Sufficient smallpox vaccine should be available for all Americans by the end of 2002.

In another scenario, could a suicide disease bomber (terrorist) deliberately be infected with smallpox and fly to a U.S. airport, infecting unknowing numbers of travelers who then spread it nationwide? It is unlikely that this scenario could occur because smallpox is not communicable until the pox or pustules appear on the skin. At that time, the infected person would be so ill that it is highly unlikely the terrorist could get out of bed, yet fly on an airplane or roam the streets of a U.S. city spreading the disease.

There are many excellent reviews and books on smallpox. The articles by Henderson et al. (1999) and Preston (1999), and the book by Tucker (2001), make for interesting reading.

Hemorrhagic Fevers

Viral hemorrhagic fevers (VHFs) are clinically characterized as febrile (fever-causing) illnesses causing bleeding, edema, and shock. VHFs are caused by several distinct families of viruses, some of the most serious being the Ebola, Marburg, and Lassa fever viruses. Ebola and Marburg viruses are transmitted to humans through direct contact with infected animal carcasses. Although outbreaks in Africa have been sporadic and unanticipated, once humans are infected, the viruses can spread to nearby individuals through direct contact with blood or secretions. Mortality rates run from 50 to 90% for Ebola to 15 to 20% for Lassa fever.

Even though the hemorrhagic fever viruses are much more difficult to obtain and maintain than the other agents, their potential for aerosol dissemination, high mortality rates, and widespread panic make them potential bioweapons. There is no standard treatment for infected individuals beyond intensive supportive therapy although ribavirin, an antiviral drug, has shown some success against Lassa fever virus. There are no vaccines available for the three VHFs described above. The article by Borio et al. (2002) presents the most up-to-date information on the VHFs as bioterror agents.

Botulinum Toxins

Botulism is a muscle-paralyzing disease caused by the bacterium *Clostridium botulinum*. The seven toxins produced by different strains of *C. botulinum* are among the most powerful toxins produced by living organisms. In the U.S., fewer than 200 cases of botulism are reported each year, 90% of cases being food-borne.

Food-borne botulism does not represent a practical bioterror threat. However, weaponized and aerosolized botulinum toxin could be inhaled or used to contaminate food. Unique to the agents described here, botulism toxin can be absorbed through the skin. Antitoxin treatment given before the onset of symptoms is very effective, at least in animal studies. An investigational vaccine is available for high-risk exposures. Arnon et al. (2001) covers the topic of botulism terrorism in good depth.

Ricin Toxin

Ricin toxin, found in the bean of the castor plant *Ricinus communis*, is a toxic and easily produced plant toxin. Waste from the commercial production of castor oil typically contains 5% ricin, making it relatively easy for bioterrorists to obtain and prepare the agent.

Ricin has been used as a bioweapon for assassination (see Pommerville, 2003). Although ricin is approximately 1,000-fold less toxic than botulinum toxin, it could be used as an agent of bioterrorism because castor bean plants grow worldwide. Reports have suggested that terrorist organizations and Iraq have stockpiled ricin (Zilinskas, 1997). The toxin is most lethal when injected via ricin-laced projectiles or by a liquid or freeze-dried aerosol. Patient management is supportive and no vaccine or antitoxin is available.

Conclusions

This review is intended to familiarize biology educators with the history of bioterrorism and the specter and potential of biological agents as weapons for bioterrorism. In addition, this primer gives sufficient detail to form a classroom presentation/discussion on bioterrorism or to use the material as a foundation for describing the biological nature of these agents through new application examples in the classroom (Pommerville, 2003).

Before September 11, 2001, the general opinion of governmental and health agencies was that terrorism was a growing threat to America. The possibility of bioterrorism became reality with the letter-disseminated anthrax events. In May 2000, Ken Alibek testified before the House Armed Services Committee. He said that the best bio-defense is to concentrate on developing appropriate medical defenses that will minimize the impact of bioterrorism agents. If these agents are ineffective, they will cease to be a threat. To that end, vaccination perhaps offers the best defense. However, the absence of a vaccination program for the public leaves most of us vulnerable to a bioterrorist attack.

The possibility also exists that some nations have developed or are developing more lethal bioweapons though genetic engineering and biotechnology (Alibek, 1999). Recently, Jackson et al. (2001) reported that they had accidentally created a deadly strain of mouse-pox to which vaccines were almost completely ineffective. The authors point out that their work shows how commonly used techniques in biotechnology could create new, never-before-seen bioweapons, making the resulting "designer diseases" true doomsday weapons. On the other hand, mouse antibodies have been engineered that target and eliminate anthrax toxins from the body, making the genetically-engineered "antitoxin" a potential treatment for late stage anthrax infections (Maynard et al., 2002). Therefore, we can only hope that biotechnology will not be used to design weapons against humanity and that the Biological and Toxin Weapons Convention can establish verification procedures to guard against such a dangerous potential.

References

1. Alibek, K. with Handelman, S. (1999). *Biohazard*. New York: Random House.
2. Arnon, S.S., Schechter, R., Inglesby, T.V., Henderson, D.A., et al., for the Working Group on Civilian Biodefense. (2001). Botulinum toxin as a biological weapon. *Journal of the American Medical Association, 285*(8), 1059–1070. Available online at http://jama.ama-assn.org/issues/v285n8/ffull/jst00017.html.
3. Atlas, R.M. (1999). Combating the threat of biowarfare and bioterrorism. *Bioscience, 49*(6), 465–477.
4. Block, S.M. (2001). The growing threat of biological weapons. *American Scientist, 89*(1), 28–37. Available online at http://www.sigmaxi.org/amsci/articles/01articles/Block.html.
5. Borio, L., Inglesby, T., Peters, C.J., Schmaljohn, A.L., et al., for the Working Group on Civilian Biodefense. (2002). Hemorrhagic fever viruses as biological weapons. *Journal of the American Medical Association, 287*(18), 2391–2405. Available online at http://jama.ama-assn.org/issues/v287n18/ffull/jst20006.html.
6. Cantor, N.F. (2001). *In the Wake of the Plague*. New York: The Free Press.
7. Daniels, A. (2001). Germs against man: bioterror: a brief history. *National Review*, (Dec. 3), 42–44.
8. Dennis, D.T., Inglesby, T.V., Henderson, D.A., Bartlett, J.G., et al., for the Working Group on Civilian Biodefense. (2001). Tularemia as a biological weapon. *Journal of the American Medical Association, 285*(21), 2763–2773. Available online at http://jama.ama-assn.org/issues/v285n21/ffull/jst10001.html.
9. Frist, B. (2002). *Why Every Moment Counts*. Lanham, MD: Rowman & Littlefield.
10. Harris, S.H. (2002). *Factories of Death: Japanese Biological Warfare, 1932–1945, and the American Cover-Up*. New York: Taylor & Francis.
11. Henderson, D.A. (1999). The looming threat of bioterrorism. *Science, 283*(5406), 1279–1282.
12. Henderson, D.A., Inglesby, T.V., Bartlett, J.G., Ascher, M.S., et al., for the Working Group on Civilian Biodefense. (1999). Smallpox as a biological weapon. *Journal of the American Medical Association, 281*(22), 2127–2137. Available online at http://jama.ama-assn.org/issues/v281n22/ffull/jst90000.html.
13. Inglesby, T.V., Dennis, D.T., Henderson, D.A., Bartlett, J.G., et al., for the Working Group on Civilian Biodefense. (2000). Plague as a biological weapon. *Journal of the American Medical Association, 283*(17), 2281–2290. Available online at http://jama.ama-assn.org/issues/v283n17/ffull/jst90013.html.

14. Inglesby, T.V., O'Toole, T. Henderson, D.A., Bartlett, J.G., et al., for the Working Group on Civilian Biodefense. (2002). Anthrax as a biological weapon. *Journal of the American Medical Association, 287*(17), 2236–2252. Available online at http://jama.ama-assn.org/issues/y287n17/ffull/jst20007.html.

15. Jackson, R.J., Ramsay, A.J., Christensen, C.D. Beaton, S., et al. (2001). Expression of mouse interleukin-4 by a recombinant ectromelia virus suppresses cytolytic lymphocyte responses and overcomes genetic resistance to mousepox. *Journal of Virology, 75*(3), 1205–1210.

16. Khan, A.S. & Sage, M.J. (2000). Biological and chemical terrorism: strategic plan for preparedness and response. *Morbidity and Mortality Weekly Report, 49*(RR04), 1–14. Available online at http://www.cdc.gov/mmwr/preview/mmwrhtml/rr4904a1.htm

17. Maynard, J.A., Maassen, C.B.M., Leppla, S.H., Brasky, K., et al. (2002). Protection against anthrax toxin by recombinant antibody fragments correlates with antigen affinity. *Nature Biotechnology, 20*(6), 597–601.

18. Miller, J., Engelberg, S. & Broad, W. (2001). *Germs: Biological Weapons and America's Secret War.* New York: Simon & Schuster.

19. Osterholm, M.T. & Schwartz, J. (2000). *Living Terrors: What America Needs to Know to Survive the Coming Bioterrorist Catastrophe.* New York: Delacorte Press.

20. Pommerville, J.C. (2003). Integrating the agents of bioterrorism into the general biology curriculum. II. Mode of action of the biological agents. *The American Biology Teacher* (in press).

21. Preston, R. (1999). The demon in the freezer. *The New Yorker* (July 12), 44–61. Available online May 30, 2002 at http://cryptome.org/smallpox-wmd.htm

22. Rogers, P., Whitby, S. & Dando, M. (1999). Biological warfare against crops. *Scientific American, 182*(6), 70–75.

23. Simon, E.J. (2002). Anthrax: A guide for biology teachers. *The American Biology Teacher, 64*(1), 11–19.

24. Sobel, J., Khan, A.S. & Swerdlow, D.L. (2002). Threat of a biological terrorist attack on the U.S. food supply: the CDC perspective. *The Lancet, 359*(9309), 874–880.

25. Tierno, P.M. Jr. (2002). *Protect Yourself Against Bioterrorism.* New York: Pocket Books.

26. Tucker, J.B. (2001). *Scourge: The Once and Future Threat of Smallpox.* New York: Atlantic Monthly Press.

27. U.S. Congress, Office of Technology Assessment. (1993). *Proliferation of Weapons of Mass Destruction: Assessing the Risks* (OTA-ISC-559). Washington, DC: U.S. Government Printing Office. Available online at http://www.anthrax.osd.mil/Site_Files/articles/INDEXeducational/proliferation.pdf

28. Young, J.A.T. & Collier, R.J. (2002). Attacking anthrax. *Scientific American, 185*(3), 48–59.

29. Zilinskas, R.A. (1997). Iraq's biological weapons: the past as future? *Journal of the American Medical Association, 278*(5), 418–424. Available online at http://jama.ama-assn.org/issues/v278n5/ffull/jsc7087.html

Jeffrey Pommerville, Ph.D., is Professor of Biology at Glendale Community College, Glendale, AZ 85302; e-mail: jeffrey.pommerville@domailmaricopa.edu.

Near Term Threats of Chemical Weapons Terrorism

Margaret E. Kosal

Introduction

The use of box cutters and small blades by terrorists during the September 11th attacks has been reported widely, whereas, the use of a chemical agent—"mace, pepper spray, or some other irritant"—in the airplane hijackings is much less well known.[1] Rather than setting up the proposition that such agents are the "latest-greatest" threat, this work aims to consider the potential threat of improvised chemical agents for terrorist use.

Traditional state-based chemical weapons (CW) programs share three technical characteristics that differ from terrorist use of chemical agents. States invest in substantial infrastructure for CW production and storage. This may be dedicated facilities, as was the case of the former U.S. and Soviet offensive programs, or dual-use facilities as seen in the covert Iraqi and Libyan state programs. States will also invest significantly in physical protection of their own troops and medical intervention in the event of exposure. Finally, traditional CW programs invest in research and development of munitions for open-air battlefield dispersal.

In comparison, non-state actors have shown a propensity to improvise the dissemination method and the agents. The use of improvised distribution methods was observed, most notably, in the 1990s by Japan's quasi-religious doomsday cult, the Aum Shinrikyo, who employed syringes, garbage bags, and condoms to deliver classical chemical warfare agents. But, in more recent incidents, plots, and seizures, both the distribution methods and the agents themselves have been improvised.

Improvised chemical terrorism is critically different from an improvised nuclear or mass effect bioterrorism attack that would likely result in more than one thousand fatalities or 10,000 casualties. To execute an improvised chemical terrorism attack, a group or individual does not need sophisticated knowledge, elaborate engineering or growth requirements, nor complicated dissemination methods.

Improvised explosive devices (IEDs) are currently a tremendous problem for U.S. troops in Iraq, Afghanistan and around the globe. Over half of the U.S. fatalities in Iraq have been due to IEDs, typically roadside bombs. This strongly suggests that there is a significant tacit knowledge base for constructing these types of weapons—one guy in a Mosul garage has not been making them all. Incorporating chemicals into roadside bombs would not substantially change the military casualties; the scenario would be significantly different, however, for devices used in enclosed spaces like dining tents or civilian facilities.

The path from the street chemistry of high explosives and detonators for IEDs to improvised chemical devices (ICDs) that incorporate commercial chemicals is very short. Conversely, the path from IEDs to effectively weaponized, transgenic biological agents effectively weaponized is a substantial leap for states and, even more so, for terrorists. While U.S. policy is focused on defending against a mass-effect bioterrorism attack, we may be missing a lower-tech threat of much higher probability. Rather than leaping from making bombs to producing mass quantities of aerosolized, genetically engineered, hyper-virulent *Yersinia pestis* (the bacteria responsible for the plague and used as part of the national terrorism preparedness exercise scenarios, TOP OFF 2 and 3), this article examines trends toward improvising both the delivery method (munitions) and the agent for chemical terrorism.

Is there substantive evidence of a shift, an "upping" of the sophistication level, to incorporate chemical agents into such devices? What policy responses can reduce the threat of improvised chemical devices? Is this shift part of a larger escalation to the use of unconventional weapons—that is, weapons of mass destruction (WMD)—by non-state actors? If such a large-scale escalation from IEDs to ICDs were to occur, the number of agents of concern would expand from approximately 50 traditional chemical warfare agents to thousands of known industrial and research chemicals. This analysis should be the basis for policy development regarding threat anticipation, threat reduction, and countermeasures to limit harm to U.S. troops deployed around the world and U.S. civilians at home.

Prior Work

A number of prominent authors have addressed the questions of terrorist desire and capability to pursue chemical or biological weapons.[2] Extensive analysis of terrorist incidents involving chemical and biological agents has been done on well-known incidents, such as the Aum Shinrikyo sarin "gas" attack on the Tokyo subway in March 1995 and the Rajneeshees salad bar dispersal of *Salmonellatyphimurium* bacteria.[3] A far smaller number of researchers have gone the other direction and challenged the precept that biological agents are within the technical capability of most terrorists.[4] At least one renowned terrorism expert has asked why terrorists have not escalated to fulfill the "lurid hypotheses of worst-case scenarios, almost exclusively involving chemical, biological, radiological or nuclear (CBRN) weapons" and "America's intense preoccupation with the threat of bioterrorism."[5] None of the authors have considered an escalation to chemical weapons as an outgrowth of "street chemistry," the chemistry involved in manufacturing IEDs.

Traditional Chemical Warfare Agents with Improvised Dispersal Methods

One type of chemical terrorism—using traditional chemical warfare agents associated with state-based programs, but employing improvised distribution means—has received a great deal of attention.[6] This type of chemical terrorism may have been most infamously utilized by the Aum Shinrikyo cult in the mid-1990's. Transfer of chemical weapons by those states suspected of operating clandestine offensive chemical weapons programs, such as North Korea—to non-state actors is another example.

Aum Shinrikyo

Aum Shinrikyo was a highly organized and well-financed group, having members with significant technical expertise. While the group succeeded in synthesizing sophisticated traditional nerve agents, they employed rudimentary delivery methods.

In the infamous March 1995 attack on the Tokyo subway system, sarin nerve agent was dispersed via garbage bags punctured by sharpened umbrellas. The nerve agent was manufactured from precursor chemicals the day before and diluted with acetonitrile. Approximately 600 mgs (1.3 lbs) were transferred to 11 polyethylene bags and distributed among five Aum Shinrikyo members. While there were only 12 fatalities associated with the subway attack, more than 5,000 individuals sought medical attention. More than 500 were seriously affected, including a few individuals whose corneas were so damaged that they had to be removed, resulting in permanent blindness. One small, but remarkable, lingering effect of the terrorist incident on the Tokyo population is the lack of garbage cans in public areas; even 10 years later, they are still associated with the sarin attack. This incident vividly illustrates the large-scale panic and disruption that chemical terrorism can produce in major urban areas.

The subway incident was [not] the Aum cult's only foray into chemical terrorism. In the five years leading up to the most renowned sarin attack, Aum Shinrikyo executed at least ten separate attacks. Four months earlier, in December 1994, Aum Shinrikyo released 20 kgs of sarin—from a truck using an industrial sprayer connected to a commercial heater—in the Matsumoto prefecture. The late night attack killed seven people and injured an additional 144 civilians. At least two deaths are associated with Aum Shinrikyo's production of limited quantities of VX nerve agent. Synthesized for dispersal via hypodermic syringes, the attacks specifically targeted enemies of the cult. VX was dribbled on the back of one former cult member's neck in a fatal December 1994 assault in Osaka.[7] Aum also employed an improvised apparatus at train and subway stations in May and July 1995 to generate the classic choking agent, hydrogen cyanide, from commercial sodium cyanide.

Homegrown Terrorists

Radical Islamists are not today's only potential terrorists of concern, particularly with respect to chemical terrorism. Domestically, use of improvised chemical devices was part of the case against William J. Krar of Tyler, Texas.[8] An outspoken anti-government white supremacist, Krar was a traveling arms salesman. In January 2003, he was arrested in Tennessee during a routine traffic stop for handgun and drug possession. Along with conventional weapons, such as knives, stun guns, smoke grenades, over 250 rounds of ammunition, fuses, and hand combat items, Krar's rental car contained a "syringe of an unknown substance, one white bottle with an unknown white substance, forty wine like bottles of unknown liquid . . . (and) three military style packaged atropine injections."[9] A year later, after a package from Krar containing fake Department of Defense (DOD), Defense Intelligence Agency (DIA) and United Nations (UN) badges was delivered to the wrong address, federal investigators uncovered a disturbing array of weapons in an east Texas storage space rented by Krar and his female companion, Judith Bruey. Krar had amassed a sizable weapons cache, including half a million rounds of ammunition, hundreds of explosives, illegal firearms and stockpiles of cyanide salts and strong acids.

In his weapons armory were a number of improvised devices in varying stages of construction. The most complete device combined solid sodium cyanide with a strong acid to generate 440 grams of hydrogen cyanide (HCN). This would be, hypothetically, enough to kill almost 6,500 people based on percutaneous exposure. It could also kill half the people in a $9 \times 40 \times 40$ foot enclosure in one minute.

What did Krar's hydrogen cyanide device look like? He had placed just under two pounds of sodium cyanide powder—that Krar indicated he obtained from an electroplating company[10]—in an old ammo box . It was to be combined with less than a half-liter of hydrochloric acid (HCl), or just over 0.7 liters of nitric acid (HNO_3), to produce the hydrogen cyanide vapor. One four-liter bottle of acid of a standard research size used at university and research facilities—would provide excess acid. Alternatively, excess acid could readily be obtained from eight bottles of a popular commercial toilet cleaner.[11] This was a readily concealable and easily transportable contraption, one that could easily fit in a small suitcase or be carried in a backpack.

Al Qaeda

Al Qaeda's exploits in Afghanistan, testing unspecified lethal vapors on dogs and rabbits, have been well-covered in the commercial media.[12] Additional evidence of and analysis on al Qaeda's extensive interest in chemical warfare agents was noted in a 2005 Intelligence Commission report.[13] U.S. troops are reported to have recovered "trace amounts of two common chemicals that can be used to produce a blister agent," most likely sulfur monochloride (S 2Cl 2) or thiodiglycol (S(C 2H 4OH) 2). It was also reported that al Qaeda "almost certainly" had obtained or produced a number of traditional choking agents, such as chlorine, hydrogen cyanide, and phosgene. Those chemical warfare agents represent products commercially available or readily synthesized with basic skills, equipment and minimal infrastructure. These are not complex reactions requiring sophisticated laboratory equipment, controlled power sources for sensitive heating or cooling, or controlled environmental conditions.

In September 2003, the Department of Homeland Security issued an "Information Bulletin" alerting law enforcement and allied professionals regarding suspicions that al Qaeda intended to utilize an improvised method to generate hydrogen cyanide or cyanogen chloride from cyanide salts.[14] A primitive binary weapon for generating a choking agent, the device uses dual-purpose commercial chemicals, requires little or no training for assembly and operation, but does require some basic chemistry knowledge for initial design.

Improvised Chemical Agents

There is another type of potential chemical terrorism that has received almost no attention. Legitimate industrial or research chemicals, not traditionally associated with state-based chemical weapons programs, may be co-opted in order to generate improvised choking, blister, or nerve agents. In this case, both the agents themselves and the dispersal method are improvised.

Using reports available in the open-source literature, there appears to be an increasing interest among radical Islamists in exploiting fairly sophisticated chemistry for terrorist purposes. One case will be examined in detail.

Osmium Tetroxide

March 2004 Osmium Tetroxide Plot. A March 2004 plot disrupted in Britain was intended to combine an industrial chemical with an improvised explosive device to generate a choking and blistering agent. Osmium tetroxide (OsO 4) serves legitimate functions in biological research and in specialized chemical industry, but its suitability as a terrorist agent—a dual-use compound—is limited, despite the characterizations of it generating "chemical fallout."[15]

GCHQ, the British electronic eavesdropping intelligence agency, learned that a group of terrorists were discussing the use of OsO 4 during phone calls among themselves, both within Britain and to Pakistan.[16] Hundreds of British anti-terrorism police tracked the group over the course of several months.[17] On March 30, 2004, raids were conducted at 24 locations throughout the London area. Authorities arrested eight British citizens—some of Pakistani origin, a Canadian, and a British-Algerian—who were allegedly involved in the planning stages of a terrorist attack. In the following week, reports emerged that these suspects, allegedly sympathetic to al Qaeda, were researching the potential of detonating a chemical bomb in a crowded, civilian location within London[18]—targeting Gatwick airport, the London subway, or other enclosed high-traffic areas. Fortunately, the suspects reportedly were not able to acquire the osmium tetroxide before being intercepted by authorities.

Although al Qaeda has previously produced training manuals containing plans for use of choking agents, this is the first time osmium tetroxide has been included among the list of possible chemical agents. This is the first incident in the open literature in which the chemical has been connected with terrorism. Although this plot did not progress beyond the planning stages, the potential use of osmium tetroxide has raised new fears about al Qaeda's pursuit of dual-use chemicals as terrorist weapons. It has also encouraged discussion about the potential lethality of such a substance when combined with a conventional explosive.

Scientists were already familiar with the use and effects of OsO_4 even though those reports introduced the general public to the compound for the first time. OsO_4, occasionally called osmic acid, is a colorless to pale yellow solid at room temperature. An open canister of OsO_4 left in an enclosed area would be readily noticeable based on the characteristic pungent, ozone- or chlorine-like smell. The solid has a high vapor pressure, meaning it readily evaporates at room temperature. The vapor pressure of a chemical is important in determining the inhalation hazard. Liquids with very low vapor pressures, like VX nerve agent, do not evaporate readily and, therefore, are considered a much more significant threat for exposure via direct skin contact. Solids and liquids with no vapor pressure do not evaporate and therefore do not pose an inhalation hazard unless they are mechanically aerosolized.

Physiological Effects of OsO_4 Exposure. Osmium tetroxide is highly toxic and a rapid oxidizer. Severe reactions may result through all routes of exposure: inhalation, ingestion, contact with the eyes and other mucous membranes, and contact with skin. Because of its volatility, the vapor hazard is usually emphasized. Very short-term contact with the vapor may generate a lachrymation (tear-causing) response, accompanied by coughing, headaches, and dizziness.[19] Lengthier exposure can cause severe chemical burns to the eyes, skin, and respiratory tract. Symptoms may not be noticed until several hours following exposure. This delayed-effect feature may make this compound attractive to terrorists as a chemical weapon. People may not realize the extent of the toxic effects of a compound to which they have been exposed immediately; rather the damage will be occurring as they continue their day. Another delayed effect as a result of substantial inhalation exposure is an accumulation of fluid in the lungs (edema)—eventually leading to "dryland-drowning." Exposure to osmium tetroxide dissolved in water will turn the skin black. Painful burns or dermatitis may result depending on the concentration. It is not known, however, to be cancer-causing. Among the most insidious effects of osmium tetroxide is its capacity to cause irreversible blindness—literally turning the corneas black.[20]

Table 1

Toxicity Comparison of Osmium Tetroxide with Traditional Chemical Warfare Agents

	Threshold effects (mg / m 3)	LCt 50* (mg-min / m 3)	LD 50** (mg / kg)
Osmium Tetroxide (OsO 4)[24]	0.1–0.6	1316	162
Phosgene (PG)[25]	2	3200	n/a***
Sulfur Mustard (HD)[26]	12–500	1500	100
Sarin (GB)[27]	2	70	24.3

* LCt 50 is the vapor concentration that will cause death by inhalation in fifty percent of a population.

** LD 50 is the liquid concentration that will cause death via exposure through the skin (percutaneous), in this comparison, in fifty percent of a population. Values are given in mg per kg of total body weight; a 150 lb human weighs approximately 68 kg.

*** n/a = not applicable. Phosgene is a gas at ambient conditions.

OsO 4 can be compared to traditional chemical warfare agents (see Table 1). The first appearance of a physiological response, also known as a threshold effect, is observed at a lower concentration for osmium tetroxide vapor exposure than for phosgene (CG), sulfur mustard (HD), or sarin nerve agent (GB). At first glance, the inhalation hazard associated with OsO 4 is comparable to that of the traditional asphyxiant phosgene and blister agent sulfur mustard based on lethal inhalation concentrations. Phosgene is a gas at ambient conditions, so all of the material will be available as an inhalation hazard. On the other hand, sulfur mustard is a liquid with a fairly low vapor pressure,[21] making it less volatile than OsO 4. This means that, in an enclosed area, there will be over 150 times more vapor available with OsO 4 than with sulfur mustard vapor.

While the lethal inhalation concentration of OsO 4 is substantially larger than that for sarin, again the decreased volatility of the traditional warfare agent should be considered in evaluating the relative threat. Under similar conditions, there will be six times more OsO 4 vapor in an enclosed area compared to sarin vapor. The overall inhalation risk for osmium tetroxide is estimated to be closer to sarin nerve agent than sulfur mustard or phosgene gas.

Legitimate Uses of OsO 4. This substance is used primarily in the preparation of biological samples—a technique called fixation or fixing—to help maintain cellular and subcellular structures that would otherwise be damaged during further processing. Fixing is an important step in most biological applications of electron microscopy—looking at very small structures with electrons rather than light. OsO 4 reacts with the olefins in fatty acids and other tissues. Fixing has some similarities to staining used in traditional microbiology. The osmium atomic nucleus helps make the biological structures more easily seen under an electron microscope.

Osmium tetroxide is also used in specialized organic chemistry reactions[22]—such as the synthesis of the synthetic human hormone norestradiol[23]—and industrially significant glycol compounds. These reactions using solid osmium tetroxide are most commonly done on a laboratory scale.

Commercial Availability. Osmium tetroxide is commercially available as either a solid or as an aqueous solution (less than 6% OsO_4 by weight, due to limited solubility in water). Commercial quantities are typically very small and prices are high. Cost for the largest, commercially available units from a leading U.S. chemical supplier range from $118 for 1 gram of the solid compound to $195 for a 25 mL ampoule containing 2.5% OsO_4 by weight, dissolved in water (0.625 grams OsO_4 per vial). A terrorist attempting to use OsO_4 in the creation of a chemical terrorist weapon would most likely be hindered by its high cost. There would also be a danger to the terrorist in attempting to prepare an improvised explosive device containing large quantities of the chemical compound.

In packages of five grams or more, larger quantities are commercially available in which osmium tetroxide is bound to a polymer backbone. The polymer backbone, or support, eliminates the vapor hazards associated with solid OsO_4. Since immobilized OsO_4 was designed specifically to protect industrial workers, its utility as a weapon, even in large quantities, would be extremely low.

A leading U.S. chemical supplier of OsO_4 does not take any special precautions regarding sale of the chemical. But because of the potential dual-use nature of many chemicals with legitimate industrial and research purposes, all orders are screened prior to shipment.

Decontamination. If an OsO_4-containing solution were to be used as a chemical terrorist weapon, it could be decontaminated with copious amounts of any unsaturated cooking oil or dry milk.[28] Once a solution is black, the risk of rampant oxidation (burning) is abated.

Viability as a Chemical Terrorism Weapon. The feasibility of using a bomb to disperse OsO_4 is highly suspect. When heated, OsO_4 rapidly decomposes to OsO_2, which is effectively a rock. OsO_2 is used as a ceramic resistor in specialty electronic applications. Rather than generating chemical fallout, as in a dirty bomb scenario, the inhalation hazard would be destroyed with the bomb explosion. In addition to the difficulties and hazards faced by anyone seeking to use OsO_4 as a dirty bomb, the effect of the compound would be minimal in an open space and it would not leave lasting contamination in the same manner as a radioactive bomb. Because it is such a rapid oxidizer, it would most likely first enhance the combustion of the materials used for the bomb. As an oxidizer for an improvised explosive device, OsO_4 is very expensive choice and very risky for the bomb assembler. Thus, its utility in the creation of a dirty bomb, when combined with conventional explosives, is questionable.

Chemical terrorism incidents are not limited to those events involving explosives or incendiary materials. The danger and harm from OsO_4 as a chemical agent alone is substantially greater than as part of a dirty bomb. As a solid, the major danger comes from its inhalation. Therefore, OsO_4 presents the greatest hazard in an enclosed space with poor ventilation, whereas it would not be effective in a large, open air venue. In solution form, the major danger is via the skin (percutaneous) or ingestion.

As a terrorist weapon, however, the biggest problem with osmium tetroxide is its nature as a rapid, indiscriminate oxidizer. OsO_4 doesn't distinguish between membranes in the human eye and lungs, plants, rubber, or cooking oil. While it has the potential to inflict horrifying damage to the body in the form of chemical burns and blindness, it does not specifically target a critical physiological function as nerve agents do. A second limitation as a terrorist weapon is its volatility. The persistency of both sarin and VX substantially exceeds that of OsO 4.

OsO 4, although unquestionably a lethal compound, is not estimated to be a viable dirty bomb hazard as it will readily decompose if utilized with explosives. In comparison to traditional chemical warfare agents, OsO 4 has similarities to the choking agents: high volatility and targeting of the respiratory system. It resembles the blister agents, like sulfur mustard, in that it attacks the eyes, burns the skin (by a different molecular mechanism than sulfur mustard), and has some delayed effects. Unlike sulfur mustard, however, the blindness from OsO 4 vapor exposure is permanent. Because of its high volatility in combination with its high toxicity, the inhalation risk of OsO 4 vapor verges that of sarin nerve agent; but it does not target critical nerve connections that control the cardiovascular and respiratory systems as the nerve agents do. Additionally, the persistency of osmium tetroxide vapor is low in comparison with the nerve agents and sulfur mustard.

The incorporation of osmium tetroxide, a fairly obscure inorganic compound, into terrorist training manuals, suggests some familiarization with advanced undergraduate level chemistry. The British terrorist suspects recognized the deleterious health effects, but their plan to incorporate OsO 4 into a conventional explosives bomb showed a lack of sophisticated and detailed understanding of inorganic chemistry. Their level of knowledge might be indicative of a member who is a graduate-level individual or a technician. Either one could be in a research lab or industrial biochemistry, molecular biology, or biomedical engineering laboratory and have access to OsO 4. The plot does not point to people with graduate-level experience in synthetic chemistry or significant experience in an industrial setting. This incident may also hint at an escalating terrorist interest in pursuing non-traditional chemicals as improvised weapons. Put concisely, in a chemical weapon incident, one cannot assume just chemists are involved; similarly in a biological weapon incident, one cannot assume just biologists are involved. One is more likely to obtain skills for dissemination of biological agents from experience and expertise in polymer science, materials engineering, or chemical engineering rather than from modern molecular biology.

Hydrazoic Acid

Another example of an improvised chemical weapon is the reported interest in hydrazoic acid (HN 3)—a toxic gas generated when from solid sodium azide (NaN 3) is combined with an aqueous oxidizer. Large amounts of the chemical compound were recovered from two Islamist terrorist groups with ties to al Qaeda—the Jemaah Islamiah in Malaysia and Indonesia[29] and part of the April 2004 plot discovered in Jordan linked to Mus'ab al-Zarqawi.[30] Malaysian police confiscated an unspecified amount of sodium azide as part of a cache of explosive chemicals outside of Kuala Lumpur that they linked to Jemaah Islamiah, the terrorists responsible for the October 2002 Bali bombing. There is some dispute as to whether the cache of material seized in April was intended for a chemical bomb or a conventional explosion.

Sodium azide (NaN 3) is a thermodynamically unstable, but kinetically inert, chemical that generates nitrogen gas (N 2) when heated. It is used commercially in automotive airbags and has legitimate use as a fungicide and pesticide. The compound has also long been used to generate shock-sensitive detonators. The addition of an acid yields hydrazoic acid, a poisonous gas more lethal than the traditional blood agent, hydrogen cyanide. It is also a lethal chemical when ingested and has previously been used in criminal homicides and suicide, particularly in Japan.[31]

Iraqi Insurgents

Reportedly the Al-Abud network in Iraq has shown interest in chemical weapons.[32] The Jaysh Muhammed (JM) formed the Al-Abud network in late 2003 in response to Operation Iraqi Freedom. Initial attempts to produce traditional agents were unsuccessful, so the terrorists shifted to improvised agents. They recruited an "inexperienced Baghdad chemist" to attempt to produce two traditional chemical warfare agents—the nerve agent tabun and the vesicant nitrogen mustard. Precursors were obtained from "chemical suk district" and "farmers" who looted state companies. After initial, unsuccessful attempts, the terrorist network shifted emphasis to the production of "napalm" and sodium fluoride acetate with which to fill conventional mortars obtained from JM contacts. The specific composition of the "napalm" is not provided.

Related Potential Terrorist Threats

There are two additional types of improvised chemical terrorism that have not been addressed directly in this study. The first is deliberate attack on an industrial chemical facility as a means to cause either mass effect terrorism—release of toxic vapor—or the destruction of a nation's critical infrastructure.[33] The Union Carbide disaster in Bhopal, India in December 1984 is illustrative of the catastrophic scale that is possible from mass-effect terrorism. There were more than 3,800 fatalities from the initial release of methyl isocyanate in that accident, and it is estimated that 200,000+ were affected during the ensuing 20 years. Attacks may also involve targeting commercial infrastructure as a means of economic terrorism or to disrupt the critical infrastructure of the nation.[34]

According to the U.S. Army Surgeon General's Office, the worst-case scenario for a terrorist attack on a domestic, industrial chemical facility is "up to 2.4 million people killed or injured—close to the number estimated by chemical companies themselves," as calculated by the U.S. Army Surgeon General's Office.[35] More than 15,000 facilities throughout the U.S. produce, store, and transport industrial chemicals in substantial quantities.[36] In 1996, the U.S. Environmental Protection Agency (EPA) determined "a worst-case release" could endanger more than one million people located near any one of its 123 identified facilities.[37] More recent assessments assert that, "at present, about 600 facilities could potentially threaten between 100,000 and a million people . . . [Another] 2,000 facilities could potentially threaten between 10,000 and 100,000 people."[38] The numbers are staggering.

A speaker at an industry-sponsored Chemical Security Summit surmised, "You've heard about sarin and other chemical weapons in the news. But it's far easier to attack a rail car full of toxic industrial chemicals than it is to compromise the security of a military base and obtain these materials."[39] Attacks on industrial chemical facilities may be seen as one element of the greater shift in chemical warfare from the state-based chemical weapons programs toward improvised agents, munitions, and methods for terrorism.

The second additional type of improvised chemical terrorism involves unsecured or under-secured traditional chemical warfare agents and munitions. The principal hazards of this sort are the stockpiles of former Soviet Union,[40] although there are several others. Alleged chemical proliferator states, such as Pakistan and North Korea, are suspected of a willingness to sell to terrorists. Insurgents have reportedly threatened use of looted Iraqi chemical munitions against U.S. troops.[41] Recovery of abandoned or sea-dumped chemical munitions may pose an extreme threat. And, even while highly secure, the destruction of the remaining U.S. chemical weapons stockpiles is being accelerated since these sites are considered potential terrorist targets following the September 2001 terrorist attacks.

Conclusions and Recommendations

The path from street chemistry IEDs to improvised chemical devices is very short. There are two divergent concerns: 1) traditional CW agents dispersed via improvised methods, and 2) improvised agents and delivery methods. Although Japan's Aum Shinrikyo mimicked a small-scale version of state-based programs, it is not the only model—and may not be the best model—for urban chemical terrorism. Lone individuals or small groups may improvise more. Large quantities and extensive facilities are not required for urban chemical terrorism. Within the global Salafist jihad, there is evidence to suggest an increasing interest in exploiting fairly sophisticated chemistry for terrorist purposes.

Chemical terrorism is likely to be a crime of opportunity for those familiar with chemistry and having access to chemicals. Controlling the materials for use as improvised chemical agents is not a trivial issue, requiring the list of agents of concern to be expanded from the approximately 50 associated with traditional CW to thousands of known commercial chemicals. Former Secretary of the Navy, Richard Danzig, has written on what he calls the "reload" phenomenon: "Our national power to manage the consequences of repeated biological attacks could be exhausted while the terrorist ability to reload remains intact."[42] With ICDs, the "reload" factor—the potential to repeat an attack, multiple times—is equivalent to or higher than that for biological terrorism given the ubiquitous dispersion of chemical compounds throughout the industrialized world.

Perhaps basic knowledge and materials are too globally widespread to justify efforts to control the capability of terrorists to co-opt them for malfeasant uses. Unlike the stocks of fissile material from the Cold War that can be secured, materials for bioterrorism—with some exceptions—are widespread and unsecured.

Leaping from this threat assessment directly to recommendations for governmental or individual action is not something I want to advocate. Rather this threat assessment needs to be considered as part of a broader, comprehensive assessment of terrorist weapons and terrorist targets, which should contribute to policy decisions about funding for research, countermeasures and emergency response. It is a piece of a much wider puzzle, not a 'turf war.' While the probability of attack employing ICDs is high, the potential consequence of an improvised nuclear or mass-effect bioterrorism event is much higher. This type of threat assessment needs to be integrated with robust technical evaluations of the risks of bioterrorism, nuclear terrorism and radiological terrorism. Threat assessments also should be integrated into the dialogue of those involved in emergency response, as well as those involved in the experimental laboratory research that may have implications for homeland defense and international security.

Dr. Margaret Kosal is a Science Fellow at Stanford University's Center for International Security and Cooperation (CISAC). Her research has explored a range of issues relating to biological and chemical terrorism and nonproliferation. Specific interests include the entanglement of emerging and dual-use technologies, such as nano- and biotechnology, that impact security concerns. Most recently, she has published research on proliferation and terrorist risks of nanotechnology and on an unaddressed issue of agricultural terrorism. She is currently leading a study of chemical and biological weapons detectors and the integration of policy and technical issues for civilian use, including attribution and verification. She has also investigated the unanticipated role of the public in chemical weapons destruction and their impact on an international arms control treaty.

She received her B.A. in Chemistry from the University of Southern California in Los Angeles and did her doctoral work at the University of Illinois at Urbana-Chicago, investigating the synthesis and behavior of solid-state porphyrinic nanoporous networks, resulting in the publication of seven papers and a book chapter. She continued at the University of Illinois as a post-doctoral researcher exploring thin-film molecular recognition materials that mimic human proteins. She has also held positions at Northwestern University's Feinburg School of Medicine and at the Monterey Institute of International Studies' Center for Nonproliferation Studies (CNS). In early 2001, Kosal and three colleagues founded a sensor company, ChemSensing, leading research on the detection of explosives, chemical agents, neuroactive poisons and bacterial biological warfare agents.

References

1. Based on transcripts of phone calls from flight attendant Betty Ong on American Airlines Flight 11, which struck the North Tower, quoted from *The 9/11 Commission Report, Final Report of the National Commission on Terrorist Attacks Upon the United States*, (July 2004), 5. Transcript of Ong's call (from Mike M. Ahlers), *"9/11 Commission Hears Flight Attendant's Phone Call,"* CNN Washington Bureau, January 27, 2004: "Somebody's stabbed in business class, and, um, I think there's Mace that we can't breathe. I don't know; I think we are getting hijacked;" See also William Langewiesche, *American Ground: Unbuilding the World Trade Center*, (New York: North Point Press, 2003), 79–80.
2. Neither an exclusive, nor exhaustive, selection of references includes the following: John F. Sopko, "The Changing Proliferation Threat," *Foreign Policy* 105 (1996–1997), pp. 3–20; Richard K. Betts, *"The New Threat of Mass Destruction,"* *Foreign Affairs* 77 (1998), 26–41; Ehud Sprinzak, "The Great Superterrorism Scare," *Foreign Policy* (1998), 110–125; D.A. Henderson, *"The Looming Threat of Bioterrorism,"* *Science* 283 (1999), 1279–82; Jessica Stern, *The Ultimate Terrorists* (Cambridge, MA: Harvard University Press, 1999); Jean Pascal Zanders, *"Assessing the Risk of Chemical and Biological Weapons Proliferation to Terrorists,"* *The Nonproliferation Review* (Fall 1999), 17–34; Nadine Gurr and Benjamin Cole, *The New Face of Terrorism: Threats From Weapons of Mass Destruction* (New York: I.B. Tauris, 2000); Christopher F. Chyba, "Biological Terrorism and Public Health," *Survival* 43 (2001), 126–50; Brian M. Jenkins, "Terrorism and Beyond: A 21st Century Perspective," *Studies in Conflict and Terrorism* 24 (2001), 321–7; Jonathan Tucker, "Chemical Terrorism: Assessing Threats and Responses," in *High Impact Terrorism: Proceedings of a Russian-American Workshop*, (Washington, D.C.: National Academy Press, 2002), 117–33; and Audrey Kurth Cronin, "Terrorist Motivations for Chemical and Biological Weapons Use: Placing the Threat in Context," *Defense & Security Analysis,* vol. 20 (2004), 313–20.
3. T. J. Torok, et al., "A Large Community Outbreak of Salmonellosis Caused by Intentional Contamination of Restaurant Salad Bars," *JAMA* 278 (1997), 389–95; see also Kyle B. Olson, "Aum Shinrikyo: Once and Future Threat?" *Emerging Infectious. Diseases* 5 (1999), 513–6; Jonathan B. Tucker, *Toxic Terror: Assessing Terrorist Use of Chemical and Biological Weapons,*

(Cambridge, MA: MIT Press, 2000); Amy E. Smithson and Leslie-Anne Levy, *Ataxia: The Chemical and Biological Terrorism Threat and the US Response*, Report No. 35 (Washington, D.C.: Stimson Center, October 2000); Neal A. Clinehens, "Aum Shinrikyo and Weapons of Mass Destruction: A Case Study," Maxwell Air University, April 2000.

4. Milton Leitenberg, "Biosecurity and Bioterrorism," in M. Martellini, ed., *An Assessment of the Threat of the Use of Biological Weapons or Biological Agents* (Landau Network Centro Volta, 2000); see also Jonathan B. Tucker and Amy Sands, "An Unlikely Threat," *Bulletin of the Atomic Scientists* 55 (1999), 46–52; Dean A. Wilkening, "BCW Attack Scenarios," in Sidney D. Drell, Abraham D. Sofaer and George D. Wilson, eds. *The New Terror: Facing the Threat of Biological and Chemical Weapons* (Stanford, CA: Hoover Institution Press, 1999), 76–114; Rebecca L. Ferichs, Reynolds M. Salerno, Kathleen M. Vogel, Natalie B. Barnett, Jennifer Gaudioso, Loren T. Hickok, Daniel Estes, and Danielle F. Jung, *Historical Precedence and Technical Requirements of Biological Weapons Use: A Threat Assessment*, International Security Initiatives (Albuquerque, NM: Sandia National Laboratory, May 2004).

5. Bruce Hoffman, "Rethinking Terrorism and Counterterrorism Since 9/11," *Studies in Conflict & Terrorism* 25 (2002), 303–16.

6. See, for example, the leaked draft of the *U.S. Homeland Security National Planning Scenarios*, which include the use of nerve or blister agents as 2 of 15 potential man-made and natural emergency disasters.

7. Hitoshi Tsuchihashi, Munehiro Katagi, Mayumi Nishikawa, and Michiaki Tatsuno, "Identification of Metabolites of Nerve Agent VX in Serum Collected from a Victim," *Journal of Analytical Toxicology* 22 (1998), 383–8.

8. Michael Reynolds, "Homegrown Terror," *Bulletin of the Atomic Scientists* 60 (2004), 48–57; see also Julian Borger, "U.S. Extremists to be Sentenced Over Bomb Plot: Texas Couple Had Arsenal Capable of Killing Thousands," *The Guardian* (London, UK), January 8, 2004, 13; and Tyler Thomas Korosec, "Gun Dealer Sentenced, but Motive Still Mystery; Weapons Case Called Win Over Terror," *The Houston Chronicle*, May 5, 2004, A23.

9. *USA v. William J. Krar*, Criminal Complaint filed April 3, 2004, United States District Court Eastern Texas District, 7–8. Later in the complaint, reference is made to a "gas mask," documents "which contained directions for exerting a covert type plans/operations to avoid law enforcement," and a "syringe of brown liquid and the unknown white powder, all taken from his (Krar's) rental car," during his January 2003 arrest in Tennessee (24).

10. Michael Reynolds, private communication with the author, March 21, 2005.

11. Note: not all commercially available products contain hydrochloric acid.

12. Judith Miller, "Qaeda Videos Seem to Show Chemical Tests," *The New York Times*, August 19, 2002, 1A; see also Dana Priest, "Archive of Al Qaeda Videotapes Broadcast; Dogs Shown Dying from Toxic Vapor," *The Washington Post*, August 21, 2002, A13; and Jack Kelley and Bill Keveney, "Tapes of al-Qaeda Supply Evidence of Terror Plans," *USA Today*, August 20, 2002, 4A.

13. "Report to The President of the Commission on the Intelligence Capabilities of the United States Regarding Weapons of Mass Destruction," (Unclassified), March 31, 2005.

14. "Terrorist Chemical Device," DHS Information Bulletin, (Unclassified), September 16, 2003.

15. Ben Taylor and Stephen Wright, "Britain Foils Chemical Bomb Plot," *The Advertiser* (Sydney), April 8, 2004, 1A.

16. Brian Ross and Chris Isham, C., "Very Nasty: Potential Bomb Plot Involved Deadly Chemical," *ABCNEWS.com,* April 5, 2004.

17. *Ibid.*

18. Richard Norton-Taylor and Rosie Cowan, "Chemical Bomb Plot Uncovered," *The Guardian*, April 7, 2004, A1.

19. National Academy of Sciences, *Prudent Practices in the Laboratory: Handling and Disposal of Chemicals*, (Washington, D.C.: National Academies Press, 1995), 364.

20. Unlike the painful but temporary blindness associated with sulfur and nitrogen mustard vesicant agents.

21. *Army Field Manual 3–9*, 94.

22. F. A. Cotton and Geoffrey Wilkinson, *Advanced Inorganic Chemistry* (New York: John Wiley & Sons, Inc., 1998), 880–881.

23. Alexander Kuhl, Heiko Karels, and Wolfgang Kreiser, "New Synthesis of 18-norestradiol," *Helvetica Chimica Acta* 82 (1999), 30–31.

24. A. McLaughlin, R. Milton, and K. Perry, "Toxic Manifestations of Osmium Tetroxide," *British Journal of Industrial Medicine* 3 (1946), 183–6.

25. *Army Field Manual 3–9, Op. Cit.,* 94.

26. Frederick R. Sidell, John S. Urbanetti, William J. Smith, and Charles G. Hurst, "Vesicants," in *Textbook of Military Medicine: Medical Aspects of Chemical and Biological Warfare* (Washington, D.C.: Office of the Surgeon General, Department of the Army, 1997).

27. Frederick R. Sidell, "Nerve Agents," in R. Zajtchuk, and B. F. Bellamy, eds., *Medical Aspects of Biological and Chemical Warfare* (Washington, D.C.: Office of the Surgeon General, Department of the Army, 1997); 129–79.

28. National Academy of Sciences, *Prudent Practices,* 364.

29. Simon Elegant, "Poisonous Minds," *Time* (Asia) 161, June 30, 2003; see also Darren Goodsir, "Chemical Find Raises JI Strike Alarm," *The Sydney Morning Herald,* July 14, 2003; see also Zachary Abuza, "Reasons Why Jakarta Should Worry Us," *The Sydney Morning Herald,* August 7, 2003.

30. David Blair, "Al-Qa'eda Plot Would Have Killed 20,000," *The Daily Telegraph* (London), April 19, 2004, 11; see also "Chemical Attack Said Thwarted on Jordan Security HQ, US Embassy," *BBC Monitoring International Reports,* April 16, 2004; "Jordan 'Was Chemical Bomb Target,'" *BBC News World Edition,* April 17, 2004; FBIS documents; also Author's private communication with ABC News correspondent, July 2004.

31. "5 Sickened by Poison at Mie University," *The Daily Yomiuri* (Tokyo), October 17, 1998, 1; see also "Poison Tea Fells Four in Aichi Lab," *Asahi News Service* (Tokyo), October 28, 1998; "Long Jail Time Sought for Nigata Poisoner," *Mainichi Daily News* (Japan), July 31, 1999, 12; "Coffee Spiked With Deadly Poison, *Mainichi Daily News* (Japan), January 17, 2001, 12; "Doctor Faces 18 Months Jail for Poisoning Staff," *Mainichi Daily News* (Japan), November 14, 2002, 1; "Chemical Researcher Held in Poisoning Case," *Asahi Shimbun* (Tokyo), August 30, 2002; and "High Court Returns Hospital Poisoning Case to Lower Court," *The Daily Yomiuri* (Tokyo), August 6, 2004, 2.

32. Central Intelligence Agency, "Comprehensive Report by the Special Advisor to the DCI on Iraq's WMD: Iraq's Chemical Warfare Program," September 30, 2004.

33. Margaret E. Kosal, "Terrorism Targeting Industrial Chemical Facilities: Strategic Motivations and International Repercussions," manuscript submitted to International Security.

34. Office of the White House, "The National Strategy for the Physical Protection of Critical Infrastructures and Key Assets," February 2003, xii, 6, 65–66; see also United States General Accounting Office (GAO), "Homeland Security: Voluntary Initiatives are Under Way at Chemical Facilities, but the Extent of Security Preparedness is Unknown," GAO-03-439, March 2003.

35. U.S. Army, "Draft Medical NBC Hazard Analysis of Chemical-Biological-Radiological-Nuclear-High Explosive Threat, Possible Scenarios & Planning Requirements," (Army Office of the Surgeon General, October 2001), cited in United States General Accounting Office (GAO), "Homeland Security: Voluntary Initiatives are Under Way at Chemical Facilities, but the Extent of Security Preparedness is Unknown," Report to Congressional Requesters, GAO-03-439, (Washington, D.C.: United States General Accounting Office, March 2003) 11, and in Eric Pianin, "Study Assesses Risk of Attack on Chemical Plant," *Washington Post,* March 12, 2002, A8.

36. R. Nicholas Palarino and Robert Briggs, Briefing Memorandum for the hearing "Combating Terrorism: Chemical Plant Security," U.S. House of Representatives, Subcommittee on National Security, Emerging Threats and International Relations, February 19, 2004; see also Lois Ember, "Worst-Case Scenario for Chemical Plant Attack," *Chemical & Engineering News* 80 (2002), 8; and "Homeland Unsecured: The Bush Administration's Hostility to Regulation and Ties to Industry Leave America Vulnerable" (Washington, D.C.: Public Citizen, October 2004), 19–40, 63–5.

37. U.S. Senate, "Chemical Security Act of 2002: Report to Accompany S. 1602," Report 107–342, November 15, 2002, contains internal reference to data submitted in accordance with EPA-required Risk Management Plans (40 CFR 68).

38. U.S. Department of Homeland Security, "Characteristics and Common Vulnerabilities Report for Chemical Facilities," version 1, revision 1, (July 17, 2003).

39. FBI Special Agent Troy Morgan quoted in Carl Prine, "Chemical Industry Slowly Boosts Security," *Pittsburgh Tribune-Review*, June 22, 2003.

40. See, for example, Joby Warrick, "An Easier, but Less Deadly, Recipe for Terror," *Washington Post,* December 2004, A1.

41. Hala Jaber, "Falluja's Defenders Says They Will Use Chemical Weapons," *Sunday Times* (London), October 31, 2004; see also Charles J. Hanley, "Looters Said to Overrun Iraq Weapons Site," *The Washington Post,* October 31, 2004.

42. Richard Danzig, "Catastrophic Bioterrorism—What Is To Be Done? Center for Technology and National Security Policy," (National Defense University: Washington, D.C., August 2003), 8, 9, 15.

Credits

Chapter 1

From *Foreign Policy*, January/February 2002, pp. 52–62. Copyright © 2002 by the Carnegie Endowment for International Peace. Reprinted with permission. www.foreignpolicy.com

From THE MCGRAW-HILL HOMELAND SECURITY HANDBOOK, by Brian Michael Jenkins (2006), pp. 117–130. Copyright © 2006 by McGraw-Hill Companies. Reprinted by permission.

From *The Washington Quarterly*, vol. 29, no. 2, Spring 2006, pp. 27–53. Copyright © 2006 by the Center for Strategic and International Studies (CSIS) and the Massachusetts Institute of Technology. Reprinted by permission.

From *Australian Journal of International Affairs*, vol. 57, no. 1, April 2003, pp. 99–112. Copyright © 2003 by Taylor & Francis Journals. Reprinted by permission

From *Foreign Affairs*, vol. 77, issue 1, January/February 1998. Copyright © 1998 by Foreign Affairs. Reprinted by permission.

From THE MCGRAW-HILL HOMELAND SECURITY HANDBOOK, David G. Kamien, editor, 2006, pp. 157–174. Copyright © 2006 by McGraw-Hill Companies. Reprinted by permission.

Chapter 2

From *American Behavioral Scientist*, vol. 46, no. 6, February 2003, pp. 727–743. Copyright © 2003 by Sage Publications. Reprinted by permission.

Reprinted from *Current History*, April 2005, pp. 153–161. Copyright © 2005 by Current History, Inc. Reprinted with permission.

From THE FOUR FACES OF NUCLEAR TERRORISM, 2004, pp. pages 259–317. Copyright © 2004 by Routledge. Reprinted by permission.

From *Issues in Science and Technology*, Fall 2003, pp. 67–73. Copyright © 2003 by Issues in Science and Technology. Reprinted by permission.

From *American Behavioral Scientist*, vol. 46, no. 6, February 2003, pp. 712–726. Copyright © 2003 by Sage Publications. Reprinted by permission.

Chapter 3

From *Politics & Policy*, vol. 34, no. 2, 2006, pp. 400–424. Copyright © 2006 by Blackwell Publishing, Ltd. Reprinted by permission.

From HOMELAND SECURITY: PROTECTING AMERICA'S TARGETS, James J.F. Forest, ed., 2006, pp. 222–253. Copyright © 2006 by Greenwood Publishing Group. Reprinted by permission.

From Biosecurity and Bioterrorism: Biodefense Strategy, Practice, and Science, vol. 1, no. 2, 2003, pp. 97–110. Copyright © 2003 by Mary Ann Liebert, Inc. Reprinted by permission.

From Biosecurity and Bioterrorism: Biodefense Strategy, Practice, and Science, vol. 4, no. 2, 2006, pp. 135–146. Copyright © 2006 by Mary Ann Liebert, Inc. Reprinted by permission.

From *Studies in Conflict & Terrorism*, Volume 25, Number 6 / November-December 2002, pp. 421–448. Copyright © 2002 by of Taylor & Francis Group, LLC. Reprinted by permission. www.taylorandfrancis.com

Chapter 4

From *The Washington Quarterly*, vol. 26, no. 2, Spring 2003, pp. 115. Copyright © 2003 by the Center for Strategic and International Studies (CSIS) and the Massachusetts Institute of Technology. Reprinted by permission.

Reprinted by permission of *Foreign Affairs*, Vol. 83, No. 5, September/October 2004, pp. 72–85. Copyright © 2004 by the Council on Foreign Relations, Inc.

Appendixes

From Chemical Attack: Warfare Agents, Industrial Chemicals, and Toxins, National Academy of Sciences, 2004.

U.S. Department of Homeland Security, *National Academy of Sciences*, 2005.

From U.S. Department of Homeland Security, *National Academy of Sciences*, 2004.

From *The American Biology Teacher*, by Jeffrey Pommerville (November/December 2002), pp. 649-657. Copyright © 2002 by Jeffrey Pommerville. Reprinted by permission.

From *Strategic Insights*, July 2006. Copyright © 2006 by Dr. Margaret E. Kosal. Reprinted by permission.